DATABASE SYSTEMS:
PRINCIPLES, DESIGN, AND IMPLEMENTATION

DATABASE SYSTEMS: PRINCIPLES, DESIGN, AND IMPLEMENTATION

CATHERINE M. RICARDO
Iona College
New Rochelle, New York

MACMILLAN PUBLISHING COMPANY
New York

DEDICATION

To my husband, Henry,
and my children,
Henry, Jr., Cathy, and Christine

Printed in the Republic of Singapore

Macmillan Publishing Company
866 Third Avenue, New York, New York 10022

Collier Macmillan Canada, Inc.

Library of Congress Cataloging in Publication Data

Ricardo, Catherine M.
Database systems: principles, design and implementation /
Catherine M. Ricardo.
p. cm.
Includes bibliographical references.
1. Data base design. 2. Data base management. I. Title.
QA76.9.D26R53 1990 89-12645
005.74—dc20 CIP
ISBN 0-02-399665-X (Hardcover Edition)
ISBN 0-02-946194-4 (International Edition)

IE Printing: 1 2 3 4 5 Year: 0 1 2 3 4

ISBN 0-02-946194-4

Preface

Purpose of this book

The study of database theory, design, and management is an important component in the education of computer science students. A database course should provide these students with both a strong theoretical background and knowledge about current database systems. Having taught several different database courses, I have learned from my students, many of whom have worked in the database field, that a balance of theory and practice is needed. I have used several different textbooks, and reviewed many others, but have never found one that strikes the proper balance between theory and practice. There are some texts that concentrate on database principles, theory, and concepts, some that use database design as their focus, and others that present a wealth of detail about physical implementation and applications. This book is designed to provide that elusive integration of theoretical material and its application. My objective was to balance all of these approaches in a single readable text, because database professionals are expected to know about all facets of database systems.

Structure of the book

Theoretical foundations are presented early and the concepts are used repeatedly throughout the book. Part I presents the background and motivation for the study of databases. Part II covers the logical design process. Logical database design is given full consideration, with the entity-relationship model chosen as a vehicle for logical design. A continuing example of a university database is introduced here and used throughout the text, to illustrate concepts and techniques and to provide both continuity and contrast. Other examples are introduced as needed. Normalization is studied in detail, and many examples of the normalization process are presented. Part III covers the physical model. Details of several important database management systems are described, so that readers can learn the specifics of these current systems, including the physical implementation level. Alternative semantic models are also presented. Chapters in Part IV deal with the implementation issues of concurrency control, recovery, security, integrity, and query optimization. Special topics, including distributed databases, database machines, and knowledge-based systems, are covered in Part V.

Purpose of the projects

The various approaches are integrated in a sample project which is a unique feature of this book. Starting at the end of the first chapter, there is a sample project section which is developed as the book progresses. The design stage begins with a description of the application, a database needed by an agency that provides temporary clerical workers. When readers study planning techniques, they see how to create a complete data flow diagram and user-oriented data dictionary for the sample project. When they learn about logical models, they see the development of a complete E-R diagram worked out for the sample project. They see the steps involved in mapping the diagram to the relational model and normalizing the model. Details for creating and manipulating a DB2 database are presented for the relational model and applied to the sample project. When the hierarchical model is presented, the E-R diagram is transformed into a tree structure, and the actual code needed to create and manipulate an IMS database is presented. For the network model, the implementation and management of an IDMS database are explained in detail. The sample project is extended to show a distributed design after the chapter on distributed databases. Thus, important techniques of planning, design, and physical implementation are illustrated using actual systems. The sample project section is always followed by a student project section, which provides an opportunity for the reader to apply the techniques just studied in the chapter and illustrated in the sample project. Student projects are also presented in detail, with explicit instructions for each step. Students are expected to choose one project to develop as they progress through the text. I have assigned similar projects while teaching my database courses and have found that students really profit by developing a project and creating a working database. Such realistic experiences provide insights that no amount of lecturing or reading can produce. Using the sample project as a model, the student projects are self-explanatory and almost self-correcting. The continuity of the sample project and the student projects also illustrate how early choices and assumptions affect later options.

Features

Balanced coverage of theory, design, implementation, and applications: This book integrates these various facets of database systems in a single readable text. Theory and concepts are presented early, so that students have a firm grasp of the foundations before examining the various implementations. Design techniques are explained and illustrated in the text, and applied in the sample project and student projects. The problems of implementation are presented, and various solutions are discussed. Current representative database management systems are described, so that readers can see how the theory is applied.

Motivation: New topics are motivated to provide a framework for learning. Each chapter begins with an informal statement of objectives. When appropriate, historical material is included. The introductory section of each chapter explains how the material to be presented relates to previous topics and why it is important.

Continuity of examples: Examples and applications are presented throughout the text. The university database provides a familiar example to illustrate new material and shows how the same application appears using different models.

Unique sample project: The sample project at the end of chapters is a unique feature that provides an immediate application of the material presented in the chapter and serves as a model for student projects. The example of a temporary clerical help agency is sufficiently meaty to illustrate real-world problems, without an overwhelming amount of detail. Unlike the university example in the text, which is presented as a finished, working design and used to illustrate concepts, the clerical agency project allows readers to watch the database evolve and see how the concepts and techniques are applied.

Realistic student projects: Six projects, dealing with database design for an art gallery, a pharmacy, a car rental agency, a hotel, a credit card agency, and an insurance agency, are described for readers to develop. Each step is explained and illustrated by the sample project. The examples provide real problems, but the amount of detail is manageable.

Balanced coverage of data models: While the E-R model is used as the vehicle for logical design, other semantic models are described as well. The relational model is emphasized, but the hierarchical and network models are also covered in depth.

Instructional support: An Instructor's Manual is available. It contains masters for overheads of figures, full statements of objectives for each chapter, teaching hints, quizzes, chapter tests, comprehensive examinations for each of the five parts of the text, and solutions to exercises.

Additional learning features: Illustrations clarify the material and vary the presentation. Exercises appearing at the end of each chapter reinforce the material presented. Chapter summaries are included to provide a rapid review or preview of the material and to help readers understand the relative importance of the concepts presented. The chapter bibliographies point to additional readings and provide a basis for independent research.

Conversational style: Throughout the book, the writing style is informal and conversational, resembling a classroom presentation.

Audience

This book is intended for junior or senior courses in Database Principles, Design, or Systems. It is also suitable for introductory database courses on the graduate level, and for independent self-teachers. As a prerequisite, a knowledge of data structures is helpful, but the book contains a quick review of the necessary material.

Acknowledgements

I wish to thank the many people who assisted in the writing of this text. My chairman, John Mallozzi, offered his encouragement and advice from the beginning of this project. My students in introductory and advanced database courses at both the undergraduate and graduate level provided feedback that directly influenced the design, style, and scope of the manuscript.

I am especially grateful to Nancy Osman, former Computer Science editor at Macmillan, for her encouragement, her enthusiasm for the project, her understanding of my vision of the book I wanted to produce, her guidance, and her unfailing good humor. I would also like to thank the production staff at Macmillan, in particular Edward Neve, Production Supervisor. I am grateful to my editor, Ed Moura, for his guidance and support.

I wish to thank Keith Marzullo, Z. M. Ozsoyoglu, John Forsyth, James Ames, Sharon Salveter, Michael Carey, and Yannis Ioannidis, who reviewed the work and made helpful suggestions that improved the final manuscript. I am grateful, too, to several anonymous reviewers who saw early sample chapters and whose suggestions were also incorporated.

Finally, I would like to thank my children for their patience during this project and, above all, my husband, Henry, for his encouragement, support, and active assistance in proofreading and critiquing the manuscript throughout all of its stages.

C. M. R.

Brief Table of Contents

Contents

PART I

BACKGROUND

CHAPTER

1

Introductory Database Concepts

1 Chapter Objectives

In this chapter you will learn

- how databases are used in everyday life
- characteristics and defects of the traditional file processing environment
- how the integrated database environment differs from file processing
- some of the functions of the Database Management System
- who designs and manages the database
- several advantages of integrated databases
- several disadvantages of integrated databases
- roles in the integrated database environment
- how microcomputers fit in the database environment

1.1 *Examples of Databases*

Databases are so widely used today that they can be found in organizations of all sizes, ranging from large government agencies such as the Internal Revenue Service to small businesses and homes. Everyday activities often bring you into contact with databases.

- When you use a **credit card**, the salesperson usually waits for computer approval of your purchase before you sign your receipt. The approval process involves consulting a database to verify that your card has not been lost or stolen and to find your credit limit, current balance, and amount of purchases already approved. The database is automatically updated to reflect the new approved amount.
- As you purchase goods, scanners may be used to read **universal product codes** or other identifiers of merchandise. Using the scanned code, the system consults a database to identify the exact item and produce a receipt with the name and price of the item, taking into account any special sale price. The system may also provide input for an **inventory control system**, so that the inventory record for each item may be updated to reflect the sale. If the inventory falls below a level called the **reorder point**, the computer may automatically place an order to replenish the stock.
- When you make travel plans, your travel agent may consult several databases. One may be an **airline reservations system** that uses a database to store fare information and passenger reservations for scheduled flights. Since several travelers may request reservations simultaneously, the system must be able to handle requests quickly, accepting reservations until the maximum number of seats is reached. Airlines must also provide information about connecting flights on other carriers, so there must be a link or **gateway** to reservations systems of other airlines. Your travel agent may also make a reservation for a rental car, using the database of a car rental agency. The agent may use a **centralized hotel reservation system** belonging to a hotel chain to make reservations for rooms at any of the chain's locations. Some of these systems may be linked. For example, the American Airlines' **SABRE** reservation system provides compact disc images of destinations and hotel rooms along with flight information.
- If you visit a doctor, you may find that your **medical records** and billing data have been entered into a database. If you have a prescription filled, your pharmacist may use a database to record data about the prescription, check for interactions with drugs you are currently using, and print the label and receipt. Both the doctor and the pharmacist may use their databases to do third-party billing for you, automatically generating insurance claims for covered expenditures.
- If you work, your **employment records** may be kept in a database that stores basic information such as your name, address, employee ID, social security number, job assignments, and performance evaluations. Your payroll is probably produced using a database that stores information about each pay period and data about the year's gross pay, tax deductions, and taxes withheld, among other things. Your pay stub reflects this data each payday.

- If you attend school, your records are probably kept in a database that is updated each semester to record your registration in, completion of, and grade for each course.
- When you do library research for a paper, you may use a **computerized card catalog**, which is actually a database that keeps information about the library's holdings. For additional listings, you may search a **bibliographic database**. You enter keywords that describe your topic, using connectives such as "AND", "OR", and "NOT" to narrow your search. For example, you may ask for all listings using the words "COGNITION" AND "CHILD" BUT NOT "ADOLESCENT". You may request journal articles only, newspaper articles only, conference papers, or other sources or combinations of sources. You may specify only listings prior to a certain date, after a certain date, or between two given dates. Bibliographic databases usually return references only, but some systems return abstracts or entire articles.
- Another tool that has the potential to revolutionize both education and industry is a **knowledge-based management system**, which combines a database with an **expert system**. An expert system is designed to allow the user to ask questions about a very specific area of knowledge, often using natural language, and to have the computer respond as if it were capable of intelligent human thought. It consists of a **knowledge base** containing knowledge or abstractions about the subject area and a **reasoner** or **inference engine** capable of drawing conclusions about the subject. Expert systems have been developed for medical diagnosis, planning computer configurations, diagnosing automobile engine flaws, performing process control in manufacturing, diagnosing disk drive problems, and student advisement. Several thousand expert systems are currently in use, and the number is increasing rapidly. The combination of database technology with expert system technology in a knowledge-based management system holds great promise and is the focus of much current research.

As this short survey of applications demonstrates, databases are used to satisfy the information needs of many organizations and individuals in a variety of areas. However, a poorly designed database may fail to provide the required information, or may provide outdated, flawed, or contradictory information. To maximize their potential benefits, it is important to understand the theoretical foundations, internal structure, design, and management of databases.

1.2 *The Traditional File Processing Environment*

Before the advent of database systems, computer-readable data was usually kept in files stored on magnetic tape or disk. In a typical file processing system, each department has its own set of applications and its own files, designed specifically for those applications. The department itself, working with the data processing staff, sets policies or standards for the format and maintenance of its files. For example, in a college environment, the admissions office may have programs to track potential students and to generate letters and reports concerning their applications. The admissions office decides what information will be stored, what data may be left blank in a record, what abbreviations will be used, how long records will be retained, and when and by whom the file will be updated. Since it "owns" the file, this office also controls access to the information. A department chairperson who wants a list of names and addresses of potential students must obtain permission from the admissions office for such a list to be generated. Eventually, the admissions office forwards information about enrolled students to the dean and the registrar, both of whom have files on current students. If the information comes in the form of a printed report, all the data about each new student must be reentered. The registrar's office "owns" not only its file of current students, but also files concerning course offerings, schedules, and so on. The dean's office may have its own student and course files, as well as faculty files. Faculty information is also kept by the personnel department, for use in payroll and other applications. In each case, the file is owned by a particular department, and others who need some of the same information must either store it in their own files or obtain a printout by permission of the owner. Having multiple copies of the same data (redundancy) leads to inconsistency, since different departments may have different data standards and update policies. As a student, you may have had the experience of registering for a course with a particular professor, only to find that the actual instructor was not the one listed. The registrar's file may have had the old instructor still listed, while the dean's file had the new one.

Figure 1.1 depicts such a traditional file processing system. In this diagram, the **Accepted Student Data file**, owned by the admissions office, is used in a matriculation program to generate a list of matriculated students. The **Matriculated Student Data file** contains information about all active matriculated students. The **Course Data file** has information about courses. These two files, owned by the registrar's office, along with a temporary file showing students' course enrollment requests, are used by a scheduling program to produce individual student schedules and class lists. The dean's office may have its own files for student and course data, as well as a **Dean's Faculty Data file** used to assign a final teaching schedule to each professor. The **Faculty Payroll Data file** has information needed for calculating pay and producing checks, paystubs, and other payroll reports. Each program contains details of the physical structure and storage of the files it accesses.

Consider the amount of duplication of labor and storage that these separate files represent. We noted that the records of accepted students may have to be reentered when they matriculate. In the process, new errors may be introduced. The Course Data file includes some faculty information, which is repeated in the Dean's Faculty Data file. The Faculty Payroll Data file contains much of the same information as the Dean's Faculty Data file. In addition to wasting data entry time and storage space, this duplication leads to data inconsistency, since an update such as a change of address may be performed on one file and not another.

When data is isolated in separate files, it is difficult to access information that should be available. For example, if we want a list of high schools attended by all students in a particular class, we need to create a temporary file of those students in the Matriculated Student Data file who have the class listed in their records, and then consult the Accepted Student Data file for the high schools of students whose social security numbers

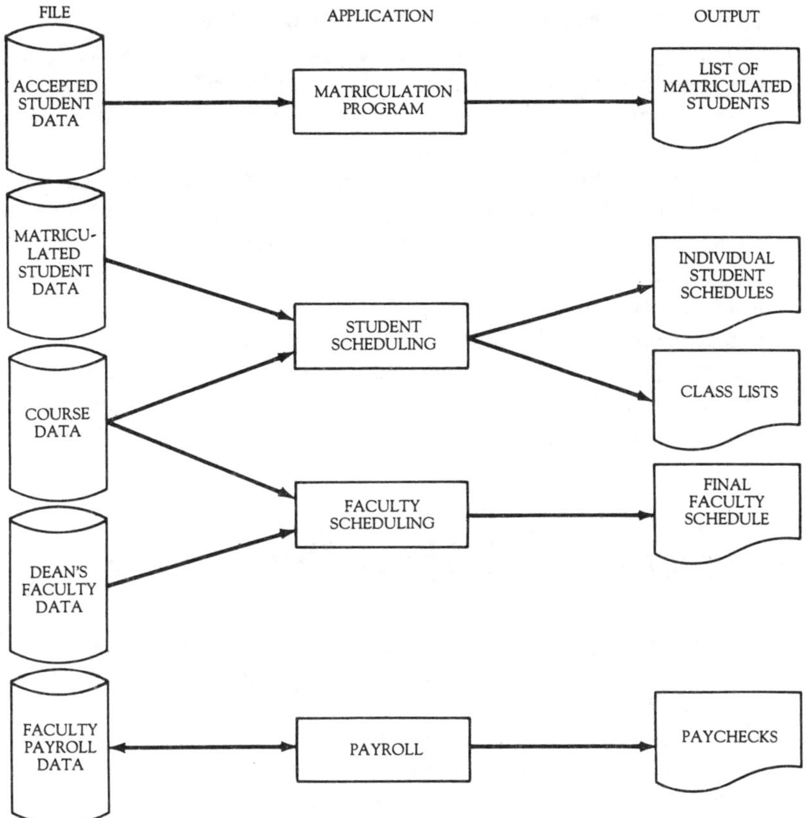

ACCEPTED STUDENT DATA FILE: name, address, social security number, telephone, intended major, date of birth, high school attended

MATRICULATED STUDENT DATA FILE: student ID, permanent address, social security number, local address, major, date of birth, advisor, (course title, grade) for all courses

COURSE DATA FILE: course number, course title, schedule, room, faculty ID, faculty name, number enrolled, max enrollment

DEAN'S FACULTY DATA FILE: faculty ID, name, department, rank, date hired

FACULTY PAYROLL DATA FILE: faculty ID, name, social security number, date of birth, date hired, annual salary, exemptions, deductions, other tax data

Figure 1.1

match those in the temporary file. (Note that we match social security numbers because we assume here that names are not unique, meaning that two different students may have the same name.) The situation is even worse if we ask a question requiring data from three files. For example, suppose that we ask for the names and majors of all students taught by any associate professor in the English Department. We examine the Dean's Faculty Data file, choosing records of faculty members whose rank is "Associate Professor" and whose department is "English" and put their faculty IDs in a temporary file. We then sort the file and compare it with the Course Data file, making a new temporary file containing the course number of all courses taught by those faculty members. We sort this temporary file and compare it with the Matriculated Student Data file. For those records with matching course numbers, we print the student name and major. This sounds troublesome enough, but actually the situation may be worse. Since different programming languages require different record formats, the files themselves may be incompatible. If the matriculation program is written in Pascal, the student scheduling program in PL/1, the faculty scheduling program in C, and the payroll program in COBOL, the corresponding files are stored in formats peculiar to those languages, and it is a time-consuming task to write the conversion routines to change the data from one format to another. Therefore, even though the data is stored in the computer, it may be almost impossible to access. In a traditional file processing system, these "one of a kind" requests normally go unanswered, because there is usually a large backlog of applications to be developed, and it is not worth a programmer's time to write the required programs.

1.3 *The Integrated Database Environment*

In contrast to the file processing environment, the integrated database environment has a single large repository of data, called the **database**, which is used simultaneously by many departments and users. Instead of disconnected files with redundant data, all data is stored together, with a minimum of repetition. Several different types of records may appear in the database, along with the logical connections among the data items and records. The database is not owned by a single department, but is a shared resource. It is managed by an individual (or group) called the **database administrator (DBA)**, who is responsible for designing, creating, and maintaining the database to satisfy the needs of users. The DBA interviews users to determine their data needs, examines the current system, analyzes the organization and its information needs, and develops an initial model for the database. The model is refined and improved as the DBA, in consultation with users, becomes more aware of their data needs and learns more about the functioning of the organization. When a mutually satisfactory design is developed, the DBA implements it. Users are again consulted to determine whether the operational system is adequate. The design, redesign, and refinement of the system are all team efforts, with DBA staff and users working together to develop the best information system for the entire organization.

All access to the database is controlled by a sophisticated software package called the **database management system (DBMS)**. It has programs to set up the storage structures, load the data, accept data requests from programs and users, format retrieved data so that it appears in the form the program or user expects, hide data that a particular user should not have access to, accept and perform updates, allow concurrent use of the data without having users interfere with each other, and perform backup and recovery procedures automatically. These are just some of the many functions of a database management system.

Figure 1.2 demonstrates how the file processing environment of Figure 1.1 would be modified in an integrated database environment. Here, all of the data about applicants, students, courses, and faculty is stored in a single large file called the **database**. The data is **integrated**, meaning that the data items are stored in compatible formats and logical connections among them are also stored. The database contains a **description of its own structure** so that the DBMS "knows" what data items exist and how they are structured or grouped. It is **shared** by many users, usually **concurrently**. All access is through the DBMS. The applications programs that formerly accessed files directly now go through the DBMS, which can present data in the form each program expects. Thus it is possible to keep the programs in their original languages, although they must be modified to remove storage details. In addition to providing support for applications, the DBMS provides a **user interface** for **on-line queries**. Authorized users can question the database directly from terminals, using the **query language** of the particular DBMS to ask one-of-a-kind questions of the type discussed earlier.

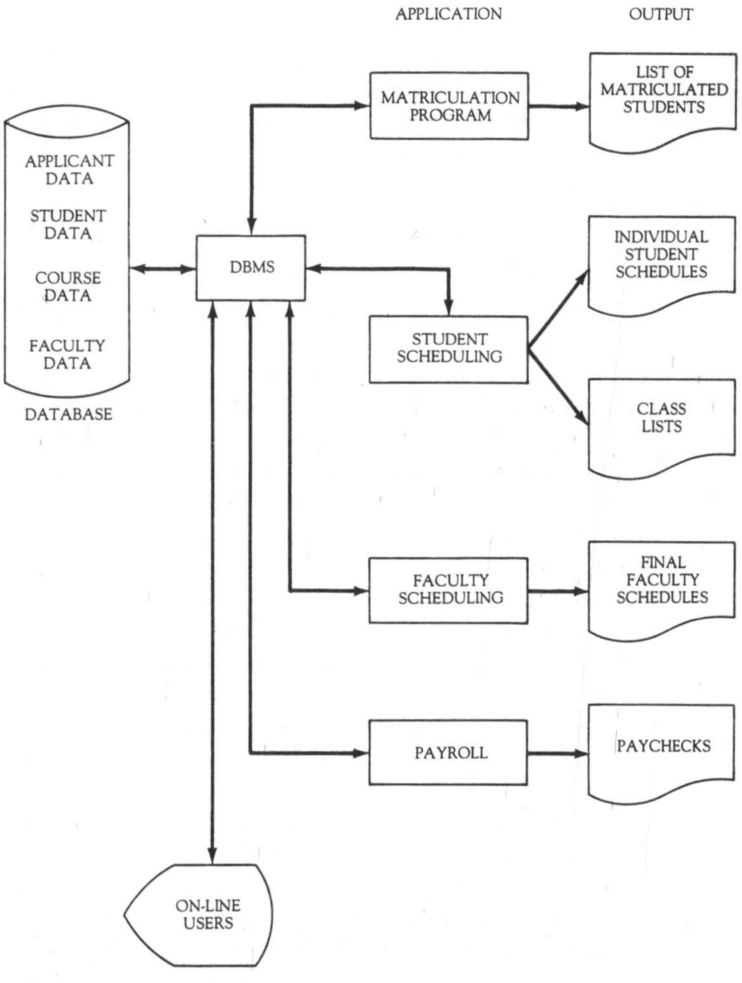

Figure 1.2

1.4 *Advantages and Disadvantages of the Integrated Database Approach*

Compared with the traditional file processing approach, the integrated database approach has several advantages:

1. **Sharing of data** Unlike files, which are "owned" by the departments whose applications they serve, the database belongs to the entire organization. The DBA manages the data, but it does not belong to any individual or department. Many users can be authorized to access the same piece of information. Thus the organization now has control over the data it needs to conduct its business.
2. **Control of redundancy** The file processing system of Figure 1.1 wasted space by storing some information in two or more files. For example, the dean's faculty file and the faculty payroll file contained several items that were identical. When converted to an integrated database, information is integrated so that several copies of the same data are not stored. Some limited redundancy is permitted to keep logical connections among data items or to improve performance, but the system is usually aware of which items are stored twice.
3. **Data consistency** One effect of eliminating or controlling redundancy is that the data is **consistent.** If a data item appears only once, any update to its value needs to be performed only once, and all users have immediate access to the new value. If the system has some controlled redundancy, when it receives an update to an item that appears more than once it can often do **cascading updates**, automatically updating every occurrence of that item, keeping the database consistent.
4. **Improved data standards** The DBA, who is responsible for designing and maintaining the database to serve the needs of all users, must define and enforce organization-wide standards for representation of data in the database. This includes such concerns as the format of all data items, conventions on data names, documentation standards, frequency of update, update procedures, and permitted usage of the database.
5. **Better data security** Data security is the protection of the database from unauthorized access. All authorized access to the database is through the DBMS, which can require that users go through **security procedures** or use **additional passwords** to gain access to data. To preclude the possibility of having a user bypass the DBMS to gain illegal access, the DBMS can **encrypt** the data before storing it. Then when an authorized user wishes to retrieve data, it will be decrypted automatically, but data retrieved in any other way will appear in its encrypted form. Authorized users may be unaware of data encryption. Each user is provided with a **view,** or predefined portion of the database. For example, the registrar's office may have access to some faculty information, but not to such items as salary. Included in the view are descriptions of the data items the user is permitted to access, and the type of access allowed, whether retrieval only, update or deletion of existing records, or insertion of new records. If a user attempts to access an item that is not included in his or her view or attempts an unauthorized operation, the DBMS may automatically record the user ID in a **security log** that is available to the DBA.

6. **Improved data integrity** Some database management systems allow the DBA to define **integrity constraints**, or consistency rules that the database must obey. These constraints may apply to items within a record (**intra-record constraints**), or to the relationship between records (**inter-record constraints**), or may be **general constraints**. For example, in course records, there may be a rule that the number of students enrolled in a course may never exceed the maximum enrollment. Another rule may be that the faculty ID in a course record must correspond to an actual faculty ID in a faculty record. The DBMS is responsible for never allowing a record insertion or update that violates an integrity constraint.
7. **Balancing of conflicting requirements** Each department or individual user has data needs that may be in conflict with those of other users. The DBA is aware of the needs of all users and can make decisions about the design, use, and maintenance of the database that provide the best solutions for the organization as a whole. These decisions should favor the most important applications, possibly at the expense of the less vital ones.
8. **Faster development of new applications** A well-designed database provides an accurate model of the operations of the organization. When a new application is proposed, it is likely that the data required is already stored in the database. Development time is reduced because no file creation phase is needed for the new application.
9. **Better data accessibility** In addition to providing data for programs, most database management systems allow **on-line access by users**. They provide **query languages** that permit users to ask one-of-a-kind questions and obtain the required information at interactive terminals, rather than by waiting for a programmer.
10. **Economy of scale** When all of the organization's data requirements are satisfied by one database instead of many separate files, the size of the combined operation provides several advantages. The portion of the budget that would ordinarily be allocated to various departments for their data design, storage, and maintenance costs can be pooled, possibly resulting in a lower total cost. The pooled resources may be used to purchase a more sophisticated and powerful system than any department could afford individually. Programmer time that would ordinarily be devoted to designing files can be spent on improving the database. Any improvement to the database benefits many users.
11. **More control over concurrency** In a file system, if two users are permitted to access data simultaneously, it is possible that they will interfere with each other. For example, if both attempt to perform updates, one update may be lost, because one may overwrite the value recorded by the other. Most database management systems have subsystems to control concurrency so that transactions are not lost or performed incorrectly.
12. **Better backup and recovery procedures** In a file processing system, the recovery system may consist of making a tape of all files each night. In the event of a failure during the day, recovery is performed by taking the data from the previous night's tape and informing users that none of that day's changes have been performed, so that they can reenter any updates. In a database environment, the tape is usually supplemented by a **log of changes**. Whenever the database is modified, a log entry is made. If the system fails, the tape and log are used to bring the database to the state it was in just prior to the failure. The system is therefore **self-recovering**.

There are also some disadvantages to an integrated database environment:

1. **High cost of DBMS** Because a complete database management system is a very large and sophisticated piece of software, it is expensive to purchase or lease.
2. **Higher hardware costs** Additional memory and processing power may be required to run the DBMS, resulting in the need to upgrade hardware.
3. **Higher programming costs** Because a DBMS is a complex tool with many features, the organization's programmers need a thorough knowledge of the system to use it to best advantage. Whether the organization hires experienced database programmers or retrains its own programming personnel, it is paying extra for this expertise.
4. **High conversion costs** When an organization converts to a database system, data has to be removed from files and loaded into the database. Because of the different formats used in files, this may be a difficult and time-consuming process. In addition, the applications programs, which contain details about the storage and structure of the old files, must be modified to work with the DBMS.
5. **Slower processing of some applications** Although an integrated database is designed to provide better information more quickly than a file processing system, certain applications will be slower. For example, the faculty payroll file is set up in a sequence that matches the payroll program and contains only the data needed for this application. In the database, the faculty records may not be stored consecutively and the normal retrieval may not be in the sequence needed by the payroll program. Therefore, this program might take longer to execute. In general, batch processing may be less efficient with a database system than with file processing.
6. **Increased vulnerability** Whenever resources are centralized, there is an increased security risk. The integration of files also makes a failure more serious. Since all applications depend on the database system, the failure of any component can bring operations to a standstill.
7. **More difficult recovery** The recovery process after a system failure is more complicated because the system must determine which transactions were completed and which were in progress at the time of failure. Transactions involving several database changes that were in progress at the time of failure may have updated some values and not others. These have to be **rolled back** (i.e., completely undone), and then **restarted**. Transactions that were completed and written to the I/O buffer but not yet to disk may also have to be rolled back, but completed transactions whose results were written to the database need not be rolled back. If the database is damaged, it can be recovered by using the backup tape and the log. The fact that a database allows users to make updates concurrently further complicates the recovery process.

1.5 *Roles in the Integrated Database Environment*

Many individuals or groups are involved in the operations of a database system. They play different roles, depending on the way they interact with the database, as depicted in Figure 1.3.

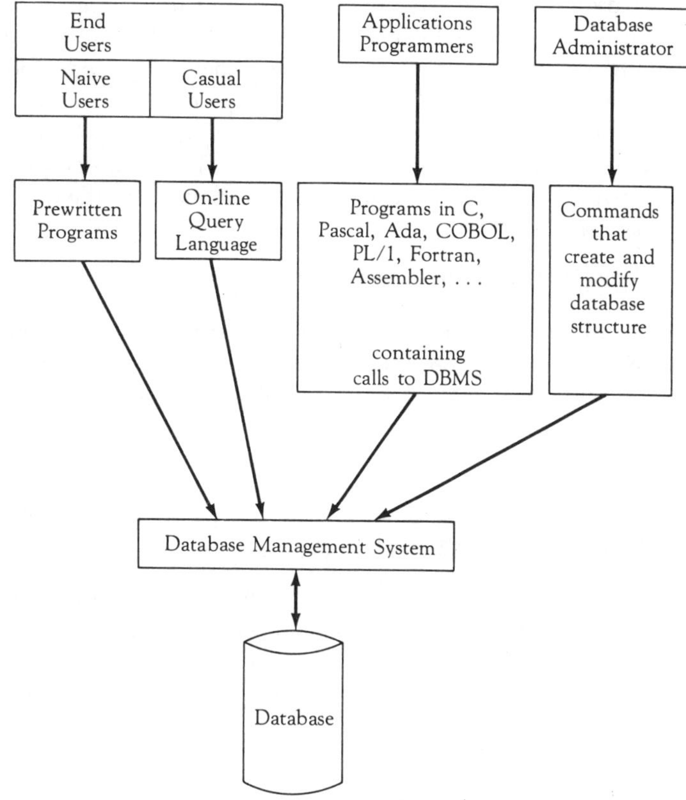

Figure 1.3

End Users

The database is designed, created, and maintained to serve the information needs of **end users**, who use the data to perform their jobs. Regardless of the elegance of the database design or the sophistication of the hardware and software used, if the database does not provide adequate information to users, it is a failure. Users can be categorized according to the way they access data. **Sophisticated users** (also called **casual users**) are trained in the use of the on-line query language, and access data by entering queries at terminals. The flexibility of the query language allows them to perform many different operations on the database, limited only by the views they have been assigned and their authorizations. **Naive users** access data through application programs that have been written for them. They invoke the programs by entering simple commands or choosing options from a menu. They do not need to know any details of the structure or language of the database system. They interact with the system in a less sophisticated way, restricting their access to operations performed by the programs. The programs themselves may perform update or retrieval operations.

For example, in the registrar's office, clerks may be naive users, while the registrar may be a casual user. The clerks perform simple, repetitive tasks such as printing out student transcripts. They may enter the name of the transaction, TRANSCRIPT, or choose an option such as PRINT OUT TRANSCRIPT from a menu. The TRANSCRIPT program prompts the clerk for the student ID or other identifying information, and completes its task without further instructions from the clerk. The registrar may use the query language to ask one-of-a-kind questions such as "How many students are registered for six or more courses this semester?" There is no prewritten program to answer this question, so the registrar must write statements in the query language of the particular database used.

Applications Programmers

This group includes programmers who write batch or on-line applications for other users. Their application programs may be written in a variety of host programming languages such as C, Pascal, COBOL, PL/1, Fortran, or Assembler. Each program that accesses the database contains statements that call the database management system to perform update or retrieval operations on the database. Some sophisticated end users may write applications programs for their own use.

Database Administrator

The database administrator was described in Section 1.3 as the person or group responsible for designing, creating, and maintaining the database. The DBA interacts with the database as a "superuser" who not only accesses data but who controls and accesses information about the database itself. Chapter 2 contains a more detailed description of the functions of the database administrator.

1.6 The Microcomputer Environment

The widespread availability of microcomputers has shifted the pattern of computer use in many organizations. Formerly, a central data processing facility supported the computing needs of the entire organization. End users wishing to use the information resource had to work with the central data processing staff, especially with the DBA, who controlled access to the data. Those end users who had the sophistication and training to master the query language and who could demonstrate their need to know were granted authorization to use the database system directly. However, the majority of users remained dependent on the central staff for support, often because the database lacked a user-friendly interface. In most organizations, there is a large backlog of applications to be developed, resulting in frustration as user requests are postponed indefinitely.

End users recognize that the microcomputer provides a solution to their immediate computing needs. Microcomputer systems are relatively inexpensive and require less technical expertise than do mainframe systems, so that system start-up is easy. Often, microcomputer software is more user-friendly than mainframe software, and even novice users can become productive very quickly. Using microcomputer-based database management systems, end users are quite capable of creating their own database systems without the support of the central staff. The development of independent microcomputer-based databases offers both advantages and limitations.

Some advantages of microcomputer-based databases are:

1. When users assume more responsibility for some of their own computing needs, the central staff is free to concentrate on other problems. The applications backlog can be addressed, and technical issues that affect the entire organization can be studied.
2. As the organization shifts from the mainframe to microcomputers, the central system processing load is reduced. Without the shift, the processing load would inevitably increase, making upgrading of the central system necessary.
3. The data models used by microcomputer database management systems are simple, allowing users to design a database that matches their information needs exactly.
4. Microcomputer data manipulation languages tend to be simple, so that users are able to perform the operations needed without extensive training.
5. Hardware and software advances in the microcomputer field are so rapid that these systems are now capable of performing many of the functions of the mainframe database systems.

Some limitations of microcomputer-based databases are:

1. The development of many independent microcomputer-based database systems within an organization leads to problems of redundancy and inconsistency of data. The same problems that plagued traditional file systems can arise in the organization. The advantages of an integrated database that were identified and discussed in Section 1.4 will not be realized with multiple independent databases.
2. Hardware storage limitations may restrict the size of files severely, so that microcomputers cannot support very large databases using current storage media. Processing speed also limits the size of the database that can be supported.
3. The database management software may be less sophisticated, since the code may be designed to fit in smaller main memory. Some microcomputer operating systems are not designed to provide all the functions of mainframe operating systems, resulting in less efficient use of the resources.
4. Many of the current microcomputer database systems are designed for single users. In single-user environments, security and authorization systems are minimal. Problems arise when there are sequential users or when an unauthorized person gains access to the system. Some microcomputer systems do provide support for multiple users and include a DBA function to define authorizations.
5. Backup and recovery systems are often minimal and are under user control. Unsophisticated users may not understand the need for backup, resulting in data loss.
6. Independent, user-selected systems may be incompatible. If users decide that they want to share data, linkage of the separate systems presents a major technical challenge.
7. Organization-wide data standards may be nonexistent or ignored by users.
8. The end user generally is not capable of designing a database as well as an expert trained in design techniques would be. The resulting database may not be efficient or flexible enough to handle changing information needs.

Each of these limitations can be minimized or eliminated if the organization has a corporate-wide computing strategy for integrating computer and information resources.

End users who choose to use microcomputers for their information needs should be required to select systems that are compatible and that can be supported by the central data processing staff. There should be an efficient file transfer system between microcomputers and the mainframe, so that data can be shared easily. Large files can be uploaded to the mainframe, and subsets downloaded to microcomputers when users need them. Newer microcomputer operating systems provide most of the functions of mainframe operating systems, allowing very efficient use of resources. Some database management systems for microcomputers offer the same functions, including enhanced security and recovery procedures, as mainframe systems. Database design can be carried out as a joint effort between end users and central staff. Integration of new systems with existing ones should be planned from the start, and corporation-wide data standards should be defined and enforced. Whether a database is targeted for a mainframe or a microcomputer, the theory, structure, design, and database management issues remain the same.

1.7 Chapter Summary

Databases are used in thousands of organizations, ranging from large government agencies to small businesses. The study of the theory, design, and management of databases enables us to maximize their potential benefits.

Databases often replace earlier **file processing systems**, in which departments have control over their own data. The resulting **data redundancy** leads to **inconsistency** from data entry errors or inconsistent updates. In an integrated database environment, all data is kept in a single large repository called the **database** and is managed by a **database administrator (DBA)**. All access to the database is through the **database management system (DBMS)**, a software package that sets up storage structures, loads data, provides access for programs and on-line users, formats retrieved data, hides certain data, does updates, controls concurrency, and does backup and recovery for the database. Data in a database is **integrated, self-describing,** and **shared concurrently** by many users. The DBMS provides a **program interface** and a **user interface** for **on-line queries** that are expressed in the **query language** of the particular DBMS.

Some of the advantages of the integrated database approach are sharing of data, control of redundancy, data consistency, improved data standards, better data security, improved data integrity, balancing of conflicting requirements, faster development of new applications, better data accessibility, economy of scale, more control over concurrency, and better backup and recovery procedures.

Some of the disadvantages of the integrated database approach are the high cost of the DBMS, higher hardware costs, higher programming costs, high conversion costs, slower processing of some applications, increased vulnerability, and more difficult recovery.

Microcomputer-based database systems offer another alternative to organizations. Some of the advantages of these systems are that the central staff may be freed to concentrate on other problems, the central system processing load is reduced, simple data models are used, simple data manipulation languages are available, and system functions are comparable to mainframes.

Possible limitations of microcomputer-based systems are redundant and inconsistent data, restricted file size, less sophisticated database and operating systems, minimal security and authorization systems, minimal backup and recovery systems, incompatible systems that make integration difficult, nonexistent or widely ignored data standards, and poorly designed databases. These limitations can be overcome if there is a corporate-wide computer strategy that emphasizes integration. Other technical issues remain the same whether the environment involves a mainframe or microcomputers.

1.8 *Exercises*

1. Give four examples of database systems other than those listed in Section 1.1.
2. List the components of a knowledge-based management system.
3. List five disadvantages of a file processing system and give an example of each.
4. List three responsibilities of the DBA.
5. Name five tasks performed by the DBMS.
6. Distinguish between a database and a database management system.
7. List five advantages of a database system and give an example of each.
8. List five disadvantages of a database system and explain each.
9. Briefly define each of the following terms used in database systems:
   a) data integration
   b) concurrency
   c) query language
   d) data consistency
   e) cascading updates
   f) data encryption
   g) transaction rollback
   h) economy of scale
   i) recovery log
   j) user view
   k) integrity constraint
   l) security log

1.9 *Bibliography*

Atre, S. *Data Base: Structured Techniques for Design, Performance, and Management*. New York: John Wiley & Sons, 1980.

Bonczek, R., C. Holsapple, and A. Whinston. *Micro Database Management*. Orlando, FL: Academic Press, 1984.

Cardenas, A. *Data Base Management Systems*. Boston: Allyn & Bacon, 1985.

Date, C. *An Introduction to Database Systems*. Reading, MA: Addison-Wesley, 1986.

Elmasri, R., and S. Navathe. *Fundamentals of Database Systems*. Redwood City, CA: Benjamin/Cummings, 1989.

Harrington, J. *Relational Database Management for Microcomputers: Design and Implementation*. New York: Holt Rinehart & Winston, 1987.

Howe, D. *Data Analysis for Data Base Design*. London: Edward Arnold, 1983.

Korth H., and A. Silberschatz. *Database System Concepts*. New York: McGraw-Hill, 1986.

Litton, G. *Introduction to Database Management: A Practical Approach*. Dubuque, IA: Wm. C. Brown, 1987.

McFadden, F., and J. Hoffer. *Data Base Management*. Menlo Park, CA: Benjamin/Cummings, 1988.

Pratt, P., and J. Adamski. *Database Systems: Management and Design*. Boston: Boyd & Fraser, 1987.

Ullman, J. *Principles of Database and Knowledge-Base Systems Volume I*. Rockville, MD: Computer Science Press, 1988.

Vasta, J. *Understanding Data Base Management Systems*. Belmont, CA: Wadsworth, 1985.

Wiederhold, G. *Database Design*. New York: McGraw-Hill, 1983.

SAMPLE PROJECT: INTRODUCTION TO THE PROBLEM: *ClericalTemps*

Purpose of the Sample Project

The sample project sections at the end of many of the chapters of this book are intended to provide the student with models for applying the concepts covered in the chapters. The project is a continuing example that illustrates a practical application of database design and implementation techniques. Following the sample project are several student projects. Students should choose at least one of the projects and work on its development as they progress through the book. The sample project shows how each step can be done. The student should read the sample and apply the steps to the chosen project.

General Description

ClericalTemps is an agency that provides temporary clerical help to its clients. It currently has about 1000 workers and about 250 clients, but it is growing rapidly. At present, many of its activities are performed using a simple file processing system or by hand, but the continuing expansion of the market for its services has made the present system obsolete. The company is considering developing a database system to control its operations.

Basic Operations

The agency is managed by Ann King, who is also the owner. She is assisted by a personnel director, an accounting manager, and a client representative. Ann oversees all operations of the agency. The personnel director recruits and hires new workers, does periodic performance evaluations and performance interviews of all workers, promotes good workers, suspends and/or fires unsatisfactory workers, and matches workers to job requests. The accounting manager is responsible for accounts receivable and payroll. The client representative solicits new clients, communicates with all clients, and accepts job requests, which are then forwarded to the personnel director.

Information Needs

The database will be used to keep track of payroll, accounts receivable, personnel records of active workers, client records, job requests, and job assignments. The system should be capable of producing a variety of periodic reports and performing several on-line transactions. The most crucial and time-sensitive transaction is matching workers to job requests. That process is currently performed by the personnel director, who goes through records by hand to seek a match. The personnel director identifies several potential workers and telephones each until one is found who is willing to take the job assignment. The director attempts to rotate workers. Although job requests are usually submitted several days in advance, they are sometimes telephoned in on the same day, and it is imperative that potential workers be identified quickly.

Project Steps:

Step 1.1:

Write out the format of every input document and every report, and the input and output screens for every routine transaction to be performed against the database. (Note: In real life, this step should be preceded by meetings and interviews with users of the present system and of the proposed system to determine their data needs and preferences. We will assume that these meetings have taken place and the information that follows has been developed from them.)

The following forms are used to provide information:

1. **Worker Application Form** Most of this form, shown in Figure 1.4, is filled in by a prospective worker applying for a job. The personnel director interviews the applicant and fills in the skill level and the result, giving the date hired or the reason not hired.

```
Date of Application______________
Name___________________________________________________
Address________________________________________________
_______________________________________________________
Telephone______________________________________________
Social Security Number_________________________________
*Date of Birth____________________ *Sex________________
Skills
Applicant:  Check each of the following skills you have.   Do
not enter the level of skill.    You will be tested on each of
the skills you check and the interviewer will fill in the
level, based on your test performance.

(To be completed by interviewer)
                        Low         Average       High
___Bookkeeping          ___           ___          ___
___Filing               ___           ___          ___
___Stenography          ___           ___          ___
___Typing               ___           ___          ___
___Word Processing      ___           ___          ___
Date Available to Work:________________________________
Restrictions on Work Dates:____________________________
_______________________________________________________
To be filled in by interviewer:
Date Hired_______________   Reason not hired____________
* ClericalTemps does not discriminate on the basis of age or sex
of applicant.
```

Figure 1.4 Worker Application Form

2. **Client Registration Form** This form is filled in by clients and/or the client representative. It is shown in Figure 1.5. The Client ID is issued sequentially by the system.

```
Client Name___________________________________________
Client Address________________________________________
______________________________________________________
Client Telephone______________________________________
Contact Person________________________________________
Client ID_____________________________________________
```

Figure 1.5 Client Registration Form

3. **Job Request Form** This form is filled in by the client or the client representative,

and is shown in Figure 1.6. The Job No. is issued sequentially by the system. The Daily Rate is the amount the worker will be paid by ClericalTemps. The client will pay more than the daily rate.

```
Client ID______________________________________________
Client Name____________________________________________
Client Address_________________________________________
_______________________________________________________
Client Telephone_______________________________________
Contact Person_________________________________________
Job Title______________________________________________
Start Date____________ Expected End Date_______________
Daily Hours________________
Report to:  (Name)_______________________________________
(Address)_____________________________________
______________________________________________
(Telephone)___________________________________
To be filled in by ClericalTemps:
Job #_____________________Daily Rate____________________
```

Figure 1.6 Job Request Form

4. **Worker Evaluation Form** This form, shown in Figure 1.7, is filled in by the client when a job is completed. ClericalTemps fills in the top portion and mails the form to the client, who fills in the rating and provides the rater's signature with date and title.

```
Client ID______________________________________________
Client Name____________________________________________
Client Address_________________________________________
_______________________________________________________
Client Telephone_______________________________________
Employee ID____________________________________________
Employee Name__________________________________________
Job # __________ Job Title _____________________________
Starting Date __________________________________________
Employee Rating:  Please evaluate the performance of the Cleri-
calTemps worker named above on the job indicated above:
___  Excellent - 5
___  Good - 4
___  Average - 3
___  Fair - 2
___  Unsatisfactory - 1
Signature of Rater______________________________________
Name of Rater (Please print or type)____________________
Title of Rater__________________________________________
Date of Rating__________________________________________
```

Figure 1.7 Worker Evaluation Form

The following reports are needed periodically:

5. **Client Report** This report, shown in Figure 1.8, lists all clients and the income from each for any period specified.

```
Client Report for Period from mmddyy to mmddyy
Client ID   Client Name   Client Add   Billings YTD  Payments YTD
_________________________________________________________________
XXXXXX      XXXXXXXXXXX   XXXXXXXXXX      999999        999999
                          XXXXXXXXXX
XXXXXX      XXXXXXXXXXX   XXXXXXXXXX      999999        999999
                          XXXXXXXXXX
XXXXXX      XXXXXXXXXXX   XXXXXXXXXX      999999        999999
                          XXXXXXXXXX
_________________________________________________________________
                              TOTALS: 99999999      99999999
```

Figure 1.8 Client Report

6. **Worker Report** Shown in Figure 1.9, this report displays data about an individual worker, including jobs held during the period covered by the report.

```
Worker Report for Period from mmddyy to mmddyy
Employee ID__________________
Name_____________________________________________________
Address__________________________________________________
_________________________________________________________
Phone____________________________________________________
Date of Birth____________Sex__________________
Availability Code ________________________________
Date Hired______ Last Date Worked______ Average Rating______
Skill Levels:
____Bookkeeping     ____Filing      ____Steno
____Typing          ____Word Processing
Jobs Held During Period:
Job Number   Job Title  Client ID   Client Name   Rating
XXXXXX       XXXXXXX    XXXXXX      XXXXXXX       9
XXXXXX       XXXXXXX    XXXXXX      XXXXXXX       9
XXXXXX       XXXXXXX    XXXXXX      XXXXXXX       9
```

Figure 1.9 Worker Report

7. **Report of Current Assignments** This report, shown in Figure 1.10, can be generated for any day and shows the assignments in progress that day. For each job, it shows the corresponding client and the employee assigned to it.
8. **Accounts Receivable Report** This report is shown in Figure 1.11. It lists all clients who owe money to ClericalTemps. For each, it provides a summary of current billing data and year-to-date billing data.
9. **Weekly Client Bill** This form, shown in Figure 1.12, is sent to clients who have employed ClericalTemps workers during the previous week. Each worker is listed, along with the job data, rate, and total for that worker. The Total Due is the amount for all workers employed by the client. The client returns the statement with payment, and fills in the Amount Paid.

```
Current Assignments - mmddyy
Client  Client  Client    Job   Job     Daily    Daily
ID      Name    Address   #     Title   Hours    Rate
----------------------------------------------------------
XXXXXX  XXXXXX  XXXXXXX   XXXX  XXXXX   XXX-XXX  999.99
                XXXXXXX
XXXXXX  XXXXXX  XXXXXXX   XXXX  XXXXX   XXX-XXX  999.99
                XXXXXXX
XXXXXX  XXXXXX  XXXXXXX   XXXX  XXXXX   XXX-XXX  999.99
                XXXXXXX
EmpID       EmpName       Start Date    Expected End Date
------------------------------------------------------------
XXXXX       XXXXXXXXX     99/99/99      99/99/99
XXXXX       XXXXXXXXX     99/99/99      99/99/99
XXXXX       XXXXXXXXX     99/99/99      99/99/99
```

Figure 1.10 Report of Current Assignments

```
Accounts Receivable - mm/dd/yy
Client  Client  Client   Amt     Bill  Amt   Billings   Payments
ID      Name    Address  Billed  Date  Paid  YTD        YTD
-------------------------------------------------------------------
XXXXX   XXXXXX  XXXXXXX  9999    99/99 9999  99999999   99999999
                XXXXXXX
XXXXX   XXXXXX  XXXXXXX  9999    99/99 9999  99999999   99999999
                XXXXXXX
XXXXX   XXXXXX  XXXXXXX  9999    99/99 9999  99999999   99999999
                XXXXXXX
```

Figure 1.11 Accounts Receivable Report

```
Client Invoice for Week Ending mm/dd/yy
Invoice # 999999
Client  Client  Client   Job  Job   Emp  Emp  Daily  Days
ID      Name    Address  #    Title ID   Name Rate   Worked
-------------------------------------------------------------
XXXXXXX XXXXXXX XXXXXX  XXXX  XXXXX XXXX XXXX 999.99  9
                XXXXXX  XXXX  XXXXX XXXX XXXX 999.99  9
                        XXXX  XXXXX XXXX XXXX 999.99  9
Total New Charges:  999999
Old Balance:  999999
Total Due:  999999
Amount Paid:  999999
```

Figure 1.12 Weekly Client Bill

10. **Verification of Days Worked** This form, shown in Figure 1.13, is given to the client by the temporary worker at the end of each week to verify the number of days worked that week.
11. **Weekly Payroll Report** Shown in Figure 1.14, this weekly report lists each employee's salary data and totals for the week and year-to-date, as well as total payments for all workers.

```
Week of mm/dd/yy
Client ID______________________________________
Job#____________________
Employee ID_________________________
Employee Name__________________________________
Number of days worked this week________________
Client Signature_________________________________
Date__________________
```

Figure 1.13 Verification of Days Worked

```
Payroll Report - Week Ending mm/dd/yy
Emp  Emp  Emp  Emp   Num  Gross    Fed     FICA  State   Local
ID   SSN  Name Add   Days Pay      With    With  With    With
_____________________________________________________________
XXXX XXXX XXXX XXXX  9     9999.99  999.99 99.99 99.99   99.99
               XXXX
XXXX XXXX XXXX XXXX  9     9999.99  999.99 99.99 99.99   99.99
               XXXX
XXXX XXXX XXXX XXXX  9     9999.99  999.99 99.99 99.99   99.99
               XXXX
Net      Gross    Fed  FICA  State  Local  Net
Pay      YTD      YTD  YTD   YTD    YTD    YTD
_____________________________________________
9999.99  999999  99999 9999  9999   9999   99999
9999.99  999999  99999 9999  9999   9999   99999
9999.99  999999  99999 9999  9999   9999   99999
Totals for All Employees:
Gross  Net  Fed  FICA State  Local  Fed  FICA  State  Local
Pay    Pay  With With With   With   YTD  YTD   YTD    YTD
_____________________________________________________________
99999  9999 9999 9999 9999   9999   9999 9999  9999   9999
```

Figure 1.14 Weekly Payroll Report

12. **Worker Pay Stub** The pay stub, shown in Figure 1.15, is mailed to each worker along with a weekly paycheck.

```
Check #:  9999999                 Week Ending mm/dd/yy
Emp  Emp  Emp  Emp   Num  Gross    Fed     FICA  State   Local
ID   SSN  Name Add   Days Pay      With    With  With    With
_____________________________________________________________
XXXX XXXX XXXX XXXX  9     9999.99  999.99 99.99 99.99   99.99
               XXXX
Net      Gross    Fed  FICA  State  Local  Net
Pay      YTD      YTD  YTD   YTD    YTD    YTD
_____________________________________________
9999.99  999999  99999 9999  9999   9999   99999
```

Figure 1.15 Worker Pay Stub

13. **End-of-Year Wage and Tax Statement (W2 form)** This form, shown in Figure 1.16,

is mailed to each worker and to the Internal Revenue Service after the end of each year. The worker uses it for income tax preparation.

```
Emp   Emp          Emp                      Emp
ID    SSN          Name                     Add
_______________________________________________________________________
XXXX XXXXXXXXX     XXXXXXXXXXXXXXXXXXXXXXX XXXXXXXXXXXXXXXXXXXXXX
Total    Total    Total    Total    Total    Total
Gross    Net      Fed      FICA     State    Local
Pay      Pay      With     With     With     With
_______________________________________________
99999    99999    99999    99999    99999    9999
```

Figure 1.16 End-of-Year Wage and Tax Statement - W2 form

For all transactions, the user is prompted to choose from a menu of possible transactions and is provided with a variety of instructions, including how to exit from the transaction. The following screens are needed for transactions:

14. **Worker Entry and Edit: Input Screen** Shown in Figure 1.17, this screen allows the user to enter a new worker record or to correct the data in an old one. If it is a new record, the user sees the headings but the data areas are blank. If the record is an existing one, the old data values are displayed, and the user can type over to correct data.

```
_______________________________________________________________
1.     To add a new worker, enter the data in the blank spaces.
2.     To correct data for a worker, enter the new data by typing
over the old values.
_______________________________________________________________
Employee ID___________     Social Security Number____________
Name ________________________________
Address ______________________________
_________________________________________
Telephone________________________________
Date of Birth________________     Sex _____     Date Hired__________
Availability Code_____________________________________________
Average Rating_____________
Skill Levels:  ___Bookkeeping    ___Filing   ___Stenography
___Typing     ___Word Processing
```

Figure 1.17 Worker Entry and Edit

15. **Client Entry and Edit: Input Screen** This screen, shown in Figure 1.18, allows a user to enter new client data or to correct data about an existing client.
16. **Job Entry and Worker Search Transaction** The purpose of this transaction, illustrated in Figure 1.19, is to allow the user to enter a job request and receive a list of workers who are qualified for the job.
    Input screen: Job Entry and Edit. Shown in Figure 1.19(a), this screen displays the job data.

```
1.    To add a new client, enter data in the blank spaces.
2.    To correct the data for a client, enter the new data by
typing over the old values.

Client ID_______
Client Name__________________________
Client Address____________________________________
_____________________________________________________
Client Phone______________________________________
Contact___________________________________________
```

Figure 1.18 Client Entry and Edit

```
1.    For a new job, enter the data in the blank spaces.
2.    To edit data for an old job, type the new information over
the old.

Job#____________ Job Title___________________ Job Status______
Daily Hours________ Daily Rate__________________
Starting Date________ Expected Ending Date____________
ClientID___________ Client Name________________________
Client Address________________________________________
_______________________________________________________
Client Phone______________Contact Person_________________
Report to Name_______________________________________
Report to Address____________________________________
Report to Phone______________________________________
Employee ID of Requested Employee (if any)_____________
```

Figure 1.19 (a) Input Screen: Job Entry and Edit

```
1.    The following worker is eligible for the job.
2.    To see other eligible workers, press enter until the
message ''No others are eligible" is displayed.

Employee ID___________________Social Security Number_________
Name______________________________________
Address___________________________________________
__________________________________________________
Telephone_________________________________________
Average Rating____________________________________________
Last Date Worked__________________________________
Skill Levels:    ___Bookkeeping   ___Filing    ___Steno
___Typing   ___Word Processing
```

Figure 1.19 (b) Output Screen: Potential Workers for Job

Output screen: Potential Workers for Job. Shown in Figure 1.19(b), the screen displays data about each worker eligible for the job. If a specified worker is requested in the input screen, that worker's record will appear first.

17. **Worker Evaluation Entry and Edit** This screen, shown in Figure 1.20, allows a user to enter a new job rating or to correct an old rating for a worker.

```
1.    To enter a new rating, type the data in the blank spaces.
2.    To correct an old rating, type the new values over the old.

Client ID___________________Job #_________________________
Employee ID___________
Employee Name______________________________________
Rating_________________
Rater Name___________________________
Rating Date_____________
Starting Date of Job_________________
```

Figure 1.20 Worker Evaluation Entry and Edit

Step 1.2:

Study the environment and write out a list of assumptions for it. (In real life, these assumptions would be based on interviews with key personnel in the organization and potential users of the database.) You may add to this list as the project progresses.

List of Assumptions:

1. Prospective workers fill out an application form, are tested to verify their skills and to determine their skill level, and are interviewed by the personnel director before they can be added to the list of active workers.
2. Clients normally submit job requests at least one week in advance to guarantee a worker. Late requests are accepted, but there is no guarantee that a suitable worker will be found. The job request always includes a starting date and expected ending date.
3. Clients may request a specific worker for a job. The worker is automatically offered the job, but if he or she rejects the offer, another worker may be assigned.
4. Each job lasts at least one day. A day is eight working hours. Same-day assignments are considered a full day. There is no maximum length for a job.
5. Clients are charged a daily rate and are billed weekly.
6. Workers are paid weekly, after their jobs and days worked have been verified.
7. There are currently five skill types: word processing, typing, filing, bookkeeping, and stenography. There are three skill levels for each: low, average, and high.
8. The ClericalTemps personnel director and client representative have a list of job titles with the skill types and skill levels required for each one. When clients submit job requests, the appropriate ClericalTemps job title is associated with the job.
9. The rate charged to clients and the salary paid to workers depend on the job title, which is determined by the required skill types and levels.
10. At the end of each job, the client is asked to submit an evaluation of the worker. Ratings range from 1 (unsatisfactory) to 5 (excellent). Individual ratings are entered

into the computer, and the paper ratings are kept for six months. A weighted average of all ratings received by each worker is calculated every six months. The weights are based on the number of days worked, so that a rating for a job lasting 10 days counts 10 times as much as a rating for a single day's work. Since individual ratings are stored, an up-to-date average rating can always be calculated, if needed, using a worker's latest ratings or using all ratings within a specific time period.

11. An outstanding average rating results in a letter of commendation and possible raise in skill level. A consistent above-average rating over a period of six months results in a possible raise in skill level. An unfavorable average rating results in an interview with a warning and possible drop in skill level. Two consecutive unfavorable average ratings result in dismissal. ClericalTemps does not offer training programs.
12. ClericalTemps takes care of all federally required wage and tax reporting, since clients do not pay workers directly. There are no medical or other benefits.

Student Projects: Introduction to Student Projects

Several projects are described on the next few pages. You should study the project you will work on, read the sample project above, and use it as a model in carrying out the steps for your project:

Step 1.1

If you can do so, interview people who are familiar with the environment described in the project. Based on your interviews, the written description, or your own analysis of the project you have chosen, write out the format of all input documents and output reports, and the input and output screens for all routine transactions against the database.

Step 1.2

Write out a list of assumptions for your project. Remember to add to this list as you progress through the project.

Project 1: The Art Gallery

General Description

The Art Gallery accepts works by living contemporary artists to be sold on a commission basis. It currently offers work from about 100 artists and sells approximately 1000 pieces each year. The average selling price is several thousand dollars. There are about 5000 customers who have purchased pieces from the gallery. The sales staff consists of the gallery owner, Alan Hughes, and four sales associates. Their activities are supported by an office staff of two people.

Basic Operations

When an artist wishes to sell one or more works, he or she contacts the gallery. Alan Hughes, the owner, visits the artist's studio and selects the works to be sold through the gallery, working with the artist to set an asking price for each piece. The sales staff attempt to sell the work at that price, but customers may negotiate with salespeople, so that the actual selling price may be below the asking price. In that case, the final selling price must be approved by the artist. The commission charged by the gallery is 10 percent of the selling price. The gallery splits the commission with the salesperson who makes the sale. Any salesperson can sell any work in the gallery. However, customers work with a single salesperson when they buy each piece, so that the salesperson's portion of the commission for a single piece goes to only one employee.

The gallery promotes the works by holding showings featuring various pieces. The showings are advertised in newspapers and other media, and past customers are sent personal invitations. A showing provides an opportunity for the public to see the pieces and to meet the artist or artists whose works are featured. Works of art that have been featured at a showing remain on display until they are sold or returned to the artist. A piece may be purchased at the showing or any time afterward. Occasionally, a work may be purchased from the gallery prior to the show and included in the exhibit to provide the public with a better view of the artist's work.

Information Needs

At present, all data relating to artists, unsold works, sales, and customers are kept in separate files. The files have the following data:

- **Unsold_Work:** Title, Artist, Type, Medium, Style, Size, Asking_Price, Date_Of_Show
- **Artist:** Name, Address, Phone, SocSecNo, UsualType, UsualMedium, UsualStyle, Sales_Last_Year, Sales_Year_To_Date
- **Sale:** Title, Artist, Cust_Name, Cust_Add, Date_Sold, Salesperson, Selling_Price
- **Customer:** Cust_Name, Cust_Add, Cust_Phone, Amt_Bought_Last_Year, Amt_Bought_Year_To_Date

The Unsold_Work file keeps track of the works currently on exhibit, and is used by salespeople. Each work must have a title, which is unique to the artist but may not be totally unique to the gallery. For example, many artists may have works such as "Composition Number 5," but no artist has two works with that title. Each work is by a single artist. The type refers to the type of work, which may be painting, sculpture, collage, and so on. The medium refers to the materials used in the work, such as oil, watercolor, marble, mixed, and so on. A piece using more than one medium is categorized as mixed. The style means the style of the work, which may be contemporary, impressionist, folk, and so on. The size is expressed in units appropriate for the work; for example, for a painting, the size would be the number of inches in height and width. The Artist file is used to keep track of artists and to report to the Internal Revenue Service the amount of sales for each artist. Sales_Last_Year is a dollar figure giving the total amount of sales for that artist last year, and Sales_Year_To_Date gives the total amount of sales so far this year. Information is kept about the usual type, medium, and style of each artist, where these words have the same meanings as in the Unsold_Work file. The Customer file keeps track of customers who have made purchases, and includes information about the dollar amount of their purchases last year and so far this year. When a purchase is made, a receipt is made out for the customer, a payment check and stub are made out for the artist, the commission is allocated between the gallery and the salesperson, and all files are updated individually.

Alan realizes that a database would provide more information from the stored data than is available now. He also wants to capture data not presently stored. In addition, he foresees that the gallery may begin to accept works owned by collectors as well as works directly from artists. Your database design should include the possibility that the owner is not the artist, storing both artist data and owner data. He would like to hire you as a consultant to design and implement a database that the office staff can maintain. The database should be capable of producing the following reports:

1. **Active Artists:** Lists data about each artist, including Artist's Name, Address, Telephone, Usual Type, Usual Medium, Usual Style, Last Year's Sales, This Year's Sales
2. **Collector Owners:** Lists data about each owner, including Owner's Name, Address, Telephone, Last Year's Sales, This Year's Sales
3. **Works for Sale:** Lists data about each work, including Title, Artist, Type, Medium, Style, Owner's Name, Asking Price, Date of Showing
4. **Sales This Week:** Lists data about all sales of works during the current week. Divided by salesperson, it shows Salesperson Name. For each work sold by that person, it shows Selling Price, Title, Artist, Owner, Customer Name, Customer Address, Date of Sale
5. **Customers:** In alphabetical order by name, shows Customer Name, Address, Telephone, Dollar Amount of Last Year's Purchases, Dollar Amount of This Year's Purchases

It should print receipts such as the following:

6. **Customer Receipt:** Date of Sale, Name, Address, Title, Artist, Type, Medium, Style, Size, Selling Price, Salesperson

A payment stub for the artist or owner should be printed:

7. **Payment:** Owner Name, Owner Address, Artist Name, Owner Social Security Number, Title, Type, Medium, Style, Size, Salesperson, Selling Price, Amount Remitted

Alan would like to target potential customers as well as present ones, by making lists of all those who attend showings or whose names are gathered in other ways. For each present and potential customer, he would like to keep the identifying data now in the customer file, and add information about the customer's preferences, such as the name of a preferred artist, type, medium, and style. He hopes to increase sales and hold down costs by using this information to make up targeted invitation lists for showings of works that match customer preferences. For example, he would like to be able to get a report such as the following:

8. **Preferred Customer Report:** Artist, Title, Type, Medium, Style. For each person who might be interested in the work, it lists Customer Name, Customer Address, Preferred Artist, Preferred Type, Preferred Media, Preferred Style

Here, the values for artist, type, medium, and style of the piece may match some of the values of the customer preferences, and the gallery can send private invitations to those customers.

Alan would also like to be able to combine artist and works data, making lists of all the works, whether sold or unsold, of a particular artist, in a report such as the following:

9. **Artist Report:** Lists Artist Name, Artist Address. For each work by that artist, it shows Title, Type, Medium, Style, Asking Price, Selling Price, Date Sold

If a work has been sold, there will be values for Selling Price and Date Sold. Unsold works will have blanks in these areas.

He would like a similar report for owners and their works, as follows:

10. **Owner's Report:** Shows Owner Name, Owner Address. For each work owned, it lists Artist Name, Title, Type, Medium, Style, Asking Price, Selling Price, Date Sold

Alan might also like reports on the sales of individual salespeople for the current quarter or the past year:

11. **Salesperson Performance Report:** Lists Report Starting Date, Report Ending Date, Salesperson, Total Sales This Period. For each work sold by that person, it shows Title, Artist, Asking Price, Selling Price

This report would be generated for a period starting with whatever date is selected (e.g., January first of the current year) and ending with another selected date (e.g., today's date). It provides an individual listing of each of the works sold by that person during the period, as well as his or her total sales for the period chosen.

There are several other reports that could be helpful, and several routine transactions that are needed. You should show these, and give layouts of the ones listed above, in Step 1.1. In Step 1.2 you should write assumptions that summarize the operations of the gallery as described here or as described by someone you interviewed.

Project Two: The Prescription Database

General Description

A local independent pharmacy now keeps manual records of prescriptions. The pharmacy serves about 1000 patients, filling approximately 4000 prescriptions per year. There are four pharmacists: the owner and three associates. They alternate shifts, with two working weekdays, one during the evening hours, and one during the weekend.

Basic Operations

Patients normally come to the pharmacy in person with prescriptions from their physicians, dentists, or other health practitioners. Most prescriptions can be refilled a specified number of times, as determined by the physician, who writes the number on the original prescription. Any prescription marked "NO REFILLS" cannot be refilled, while one marked "UNLIMITED REFILLS" can be refilled any number of times. Refill requests are often telephoned in by the patient, to be delivered or picked up later. At present, the patient must provide the prescription number, but your design should require only the patient's name and a general description such as date or drug name. The pharmacy has to take special care when filling prescriptions for controlled substances such as tranquilizers. To prevent abuse, periodic reports about the number of such prescriptions are required by various government agencies. Prescriptions for controlled substances can never be refilled.

When a prescription is filled, a label and a receipt are printed. The label is attached to the bottle or other container, and the receipt is given to the patient for insurance or tax reporting purposes. To permit third-party billing, the pharmacist must keep track of all prescriptions filled for patients who have health plans or coverage for prescription drugs, so that the insurance company can be billed directly. Some plans require that the patient pay the pharmacy a flat fee for each prescription (typically, $1), others require that the patient pay 20 percent of the cost, while others require no payment. The pharmacy must obtain the customer's signature at the time the drug is issued, so that it can provide proof, if needed, that the drug was actually issued. However, the signature is kept in a manual ledger, outside the proposed database.

Information Needs

The burden of maintaining the manual system is increasing, because the number of prescriptions is growing, and because customers expect more services than in the past. For example, customers expect the pharmacist to be able to find a prescription record and refill a prescription without providing the prescription number, to do third-party billing, and to check for possible drug interactions with medications they are now taking before filling a prescription. Families and individuals expect to be able to obtain a detailed annual or on-demand report of prescription charges for tax or insurance reporting. To compete with large chains that offer these services, the owner has decided to hire you to design and create a database system that replaces the manual one and provides support for these new services.

The database must print several routine reports:

1. **Label:** Rx Number, Doctor Name, Patient Name, Patient Address, Directions, Drug Name, Form, Strength, Quantity, Pharmacist's Initials, Date Filled, Original Date, Previous Date, Number of Refills Remaining

The Rx Number is issued sequentially by the system. If the prescription is a refill, the Rx Number for the original prescription is used. There are several standard directions, such as "Four times a day" or "Every six hours." If the directions are not one of the standard phrases, the label reads "As directed by physician." Drug Name is the name of the medication. It may be a brand name or a generic name, depending on which is used in filling the prescription. Medications come in several forms, including tablets, capsules, creams, elixirs, and others. The label tells the quantity of medication, which varies with the form (e.g., for capsules or tablets it is the number, but for elixirs it may be the number of fluid ounces). The strength of the medication is also given, usually in milligrams. The initials of the pharmacist who actually fills the prescription are included. Date Filled refers to the actual date issued. Original Date is the date of the original prescription, and the Previous Date, if any, is the date of the refill prior to the present one. Number of Refills Remaining is decreased by one every time a refill is made, except when unlimited refills are permitted.

2. **Receipt:** All of the information on the label, plus Price, Amount Due

Here, Price is the entire cost of the prescription, while Amount Due is what the patient should pay the drugstore. For patients who do not use third-party billing, these are identical. For those using third-party billing, Amount Due is Price minus the anticipated insurance payment.

3. **Insurance Claim:** A universal claim form is used for third-party billing. It contains the following information: Patient Name, Patient Address, Insurance Company, Policy Number, Insured Name, Relationship to Insured, Patient Date of Birth, Rx Number, Drug, Form, Strength, Quantity, Date Filled, Price, Amount Paid.

Amount Paid here is the same as the Amount Due on the receipt. Note that Insured Name may be different from Patient Name. For example, a child might have coverage under a parent's policy. A claim could be filed for each covered prescription individually, or the pharmacist could submit the claims in batches, at the end of each week or other time period.

4. **Family Report:** This report, generated as needed, contains the following information: Report Date, Starting Date. For each member of the family, it shows Last

Name, First Name, Patient Address, Date of Birth. For each prescription for that family member, it lists Rx Number, Date, Drug, Form, Strength, Quantity, Date Filled, Price, Amount Paid.

The report lists each family member who had prescriptions filled during the period from the Starting Date to the Report Date. For each member, it lists the information about every prescription filled during the period.

5. **Controlled Substance Report:** This report is filed monthly or quarterly with agencies that supervise distribution of controlled substances. It contains: Report Date, Starting Date. For each physician who has written prescriptions for controlled substances, it shows Physician Name, Physician Address. For each prescription from that physician, it lists Rx Number, Patient Name, Patient Address, Drug, Form, Strength, Quantity, Date Filled.

The report is in order by Physician Name and lists information about every prescription for controlled substances written by that physician and filled by the pharmacy.

6. **Drug Inventory Report:** Drug Name, Generic Name, Form, Strength, Controlled Substance, Quantity on Hand, Quantity on Order, Reorder Point, Supplier Name, Supplier Address, Unit Cost.

We assume that there is only one supplier for each drug. Controlled Substance is a flag that displays a value of "true" for drugs that are controlled substances.

In addition to the reports listed, there are several others that would be useful. In Step 1.1 you should show the layouts of all reports, and the input and output screens for all transactions. Step 1.2 should list assumptions about the operations of the pharmacy. Use the sample project to guide you.

Project Three: The Rental Car Agency, Auto-Rent

General Description

Auto-Rent is a car rental agency that operates within one state. It has 50 locations where cars may be picked up or dropped off. There is a central office where the main computer is located, and each location has terminals linked to the central site. Your project is to design the database for the central computing facility. The agency has a fleet of 750 cars, all registered in the state. It handles almost 40,000 reservations per year. There are 500 corporate accounts, which account for about half of the reservations. The remaining reservations are made by individual customers.

Basic Operations

Customers or their travel agents usually make reservations about a week in advance by dialing a toll-free number. If there are sufficient available cars, some last-minute rentals are arranged. Reservations can also be made in person at any location. All reservations are sent to the central computer. Each location can generate lists of reservations for that site as needed. A car can be picked up at one location and returned to another. It is the responsibility of the central office to ensure that cars are dispatched to the sites where they will be needed to fill reservations. The sites are responsible for notifying the central location as soon as cars are returned.

All rentals require a credit card number or corporate account number. Customers can choose from a variety of car models, mileage plans, and insurance coverage options. There are daily, weekly, or monthly rates. Corporate accounts receive a negotiated reduction of up to 15 percent of the normal rates. Every car is rented out with a full tank of gasoline. When a car is returned, the mileage and the amount of gasoline are checked. If the tank is not full, the customer is charged for the missing gasoline. If the customer has chosen a plan other than unlimited mileage, the mileage is used to calculate mileage charges. The car is also checked for damage, and the customer may be liable for repairs unless the damage occurred and was reported before the rental began.

Auto-Rent contracts with garages to perform routine maintenance and do repairs on its cars. Maintenance jobs such as oil changes and tune-ups are scheduled at regular intervals for all cars in the fleet. Repairs are performed as needed, using authorized garages. If a car needs repairs during a rental, the customer normally calls Auto-Rent to report the problem, and representatives bring a replacement car to the customer, arrange to bring the defective car to an authorized garage, and obtain an estimate of repairs. If a problem is spotted while the car is not rented, the car is brought to an authorized garage, and an estimate is obtained. A garage must have written authorization from Auto-Rent before it performs a repair job. Cars are normally kept active for about two years. After that time, they are sold as used cars and new cars are purchased to replace them.

Information Needs

All data relating to cars, rentals, maintenance, and repair are stored at the central site. Local sites are responsible for sending updates of the information they generate. They make up tentative bills for clients who return cars to their sites, based on the customer's report of mileage and gasoline level. The final bill is generated from the central site, once mileage, gasoline level, and damage checks have been made locally. Local sites can download information they need. For example, each site requests data about reservations made for that location, and each can request records of cars rented elsewhere and returned to their site, so that they can generate tentative bills. The following reports are needed:

1. **Reservations for Location A for Date mm/dd/yy:** Date, Customer Name, Customer Address, Customer Phone, Credit Card Type, Credit Card Number, Corporation Name, Corporation Account Number, Make, Model, Mileage Plan, Insurance Plan, Rate Period, Rate, Discount, Estimated Length of Rental

If the customer is renting under a corporate account, the Corporation Name, Account Number, and Discount are given. Mileage Plan and Insurance Plan are codes indicating the choices the customer has made. Rate Period is day, week, or month, and Rate is the actual amount per day, week, or month, before any discount is taken. The Estimated Length is included to help Auto-Rent in its planning. However, any rental can be extended beyond the estimated length if the customer notifies the agency and provides a new estimate.

2. **Individual Customer Bill:** Customer Name, Customer Address, Customer Phone, Corporation Name, Corporation Address, Corporate Account Number, Contract#, Bill Date, Credit Card Type, Credit Card Number, Lic#, Make, Model, Mileage Plan, Insurance Plan, Rate Period, Rate, Date Rented, Time Rented, Date Returned, Time Returned, Starting Miles, Ending Miles, Gasoline Level, Basic Charge, Mileage Charge, Insurance Charge, Gasoline Charge, Tax, Final Charge

The individual customer bill is prepared for customers. If they are corporate clients, the Corporation Name, Corporation Address, and Corporate Account Number appear. If they are individual customers, the Credit Card Type and Credit Card Number appear. Both the tentative bill and the final bill have the same format.

3. **Corporate Customer Bill:** Corporation Name, Corporation Address, Account Number, Bill Date, Contract Number, Customer Name, Customer Address, Date Rented, Time Rented, Date Returned, Time Returned, Rate Period, Rate, Discount, Lic#, Make, Model, Mileage Plan, Insurance Plan, Starting Miles, Ending Miles, Gasoline Level, Basic Charge, Mileage Charge, Insurance Charge, Discount, Tax, Final Charge

The first four items appear only once on the bill, while the rest of the data is repeated for each rental made by anyone from the corporation during the billing period. In addition, each of the corporate customers receives an individual statement that contains all the data on the individual bill described above.

4. **Available Cars Report:** Today's Date, Make, Model, Color, License Number, Vehicle Identification Number, Mileage, Condition, Location

This report lists every car not currently rented and identifies the location of the car. It can be used to plan reservations and to provide cars for last-minute requests. The condition is described by a code; for example, 1 = new, 2 = excellent, 3 = good, and so on. The cars are all licensed in a single state, so the License Number is sufficient to identify each car uniquely. The Vehicle Identification Number is a unique number stamped on the engine of a car at the time it is manufactured.

5. **Maintenance Report:** License Number, Vehicle Identification Number, Make, Model, Color, Date of Procedure, Procedure Name, Cost, Garage Name, Garage Address, Mileage, Condition

This report lists a single car and gives details of maintenance procedures performed on it. The first four items appear only once and the remaining items are repeated for each date on which maintenance was performed on the car.

6. **Repairs Report:** License Number, Vehicle Identification Number, Make, Model, Color, Date of Repair, Repair Name, Garage Name, Garage Address, Authorization Number, Estimate, Final Cost, Mileage, Condition

This report details all the repairs done on a single car. The condition is the state of the car after the repair is performed. The estimate and final cost are stored to allow the agency to spot garages that routinely underestimate costs.

7. **Activity by Location:** Location, Manager Name, Starting Date, Ending Date, Number of Daily Rentals, Number of Weekly Rentals, Number of Monthly Rentals, Total Income

This report provides information about the activity of any location during any period desired.

8. **Activity by Corporation:** Corporation Name, Corporation Address, Representative Name, Representative Phone, Account Number, Corporate Discount, Starting Date, Ending Date, Number of Daily Rentals, Number of Weekly Rentals, Number of Monthly Rentals, Total Income

This report allows us to obtain information about rental income from corporate clients during any period desired.

Several other reports and transactions are needed. You should show the formats of the reports above, plus any new reports or transactions in Step 1.1. Step 1.2 should list assumptions about the information described above.

Project Four: Metropolitan Hotel Reservation System

General Description

The Metropolitan Hotel is an independent hotel located in a midsized city. It has 300 guest rooms, 10 meeting rooms, and 5 banquet rooms. The rooms are normally 80 percent occupied, with an average length of stay of three days. Meeting rooms are reserved at least a week in advance. The banquet rooms are used for various social functions such as dances and wedding receptions. They are usually booked several months in advance. The hotel also has two restaurants and a coffee shop. In the lobby there are several small shops, including a jeweler, a beauty shop, and a clothing boutique. The lobby shops are operated by concessionaires who pay a flat rental fee.

Basic Operations

Guest room reservations are usually made by individuals or their travel agents several days in advance, using a credit card number to guarantee the reservation. At that time they specify the type of accommodations desired, the number of people who will occupy the room, the date and estimated time of arrival, and the length of stay. The hotel makes the reservation and returns a confirmation number. Customers who have confirmed reservations are guaranteed a room. If they do not show up and do not cancel, they are charged for one day. Guests may extend their stay beyond the stated length provided that there are rooms available. Customers without reservations are also accepted if there are rooms available.

Hotel guests may charge meals at the restaurants or coffee shop to their rooms, and the charge will appear on their room bill. Room service charges for items delivered to a guest's room or a meeting room are also added to the bill. Telephone calls from a room are automatically charged to the room. Telephone charges include the actual charge determined by the telephone company and a service fee of 50 cents per call. There is no charge for incoming calls.

Meeting rooms are usually booked about a month in advance. A deposit is required at the booking time. They are ordinarily reserved by business people for meetings. Each meeting room is furnished with a large table and chairs for approximately 25 people. Room dividers can be rolled back to combine two or more rooms and provide a larger meeting space. There is a flat rate for use of each room for a four-hour period. At the customer's request, audiovisual equipment owned by the hotel can be set up in the room at no additional charge. If special equipment that must be rented is needed, the hotel charges the rental and a setup fee. There are additional charges for food or beverage service, if any. Bills for the use of meeting rooms are prepared immediately after the meeting and customers must pay the bill within 30 days.

The five banquet rooms are designed to hold 100, 150, 200, 300, and 500 people, respectively. Customers, who may be individuals or corporations, book the rooms for various events, such as political fundraisers, dances, or wedding receptions. The customer must guarantee a minimum of 75 percent of the occupancy in order to reserve a banquet room. Reservations are accepted up to two years in advance. Each room can be rented for two banquets per day, one in the afternoon and one in the evening. Each banquet is scheduled to last five hours, unless special arrangements are made. There is a one-hour room preparation time between banquets. Customers who reserve banquet rooms are required to provide a deposit which they forfeit if they cancel.

When a customer reserves a banquet room, he or she specifies the date, the time, the number of guests expected, the room desired, and the menu. The hotel estimates the cost per person, assigns the room, and draws up a contract which is then signed by both parties. The customer pays a deposit of 10 percent. As the event nears, the final menu is selected and the final guest count is provided, usually resulting in a modification of the contract. The customer will be charged according to the final guest count, even if fewer guests attend. If additional guests attend, there is a charge for each extra person at the per-person rate. The hotel provides the room and related facilities, the table settings, floral arrangements, waiters and waitresses, and food and beverage service, all of which are specified in the contract. Musicians, entertainers, photographers, or other nonhotel employees are provided by the customer, but the hotel management must be told in advance who will be providing any of these services, and can refuse to admit anyone it deems unsuitable. The final bill is prepared immediately after the event, and the customer must pay it within 30 days.

Information Needs

The hotel needs a database to handle guest room reservations, check-in with guest room assignment, guest room billing, meeting room reservations and billing, concession rental, and banquet room reservations, contracts, and billing. Your assignment is to design this database. Some of the reports or transactions required are the following:

1. **Room Reservation Transaction:** A reservations clerk provides the following information: Guest Name, Address, Telephone, Credit Card Type, Credit Card Number, Number of Guests, Arrival Date, Arrival Time, Expected Departure Date, Room Type Desired. The system returns: Confirmation Number. Normally, the reservation is entered and a confirmation is generated by the system. However, if the hotel is already fully booked for the date specified, the reservation will not be entered and the message "No available rooms" will be returned. The clerk can reattempt the transaction with a different room type, provided the guest agrees.
2. **Check-in Transaction:** The check-in transaction requires the Confirmation Number, if any, or data similar to the room reservation transaction. The output is the Room Number of the room assigned.
3. **Guest Room Bill:** The bill heading has the following data: Invoice Number, Guest Name, Address, Telephone, Room Number, Number of Persons. For each day, the following data appears: Date, Room Charge, Room Tax, Room Service Charges, Restaurant Charges (for each, Restaurant Name, Amount), Telephone Charges. The following data appears at the end of the bill: Total Charges, Discount, Net Charges, Amount Paid, Amount Due, Method of Payment, Credit Card Type, Credit Card Number.

The hotel may offer discounts as promotional devices, or give corporate discounts. The amount of the discount, if any, appears on the bill, and the Net Charges entry represents the Total Charges less any discount. The guest may pay by cash, check, traveler's check, or credit card. If a credit card is used, the type and account number appear on the bill. Normally, the guest pays the bill in full, and the Amount Due is zero. Otherwise, the Amount Due is Net Charges less Amount Paid.

4. **Banquet Room Contract:** The banquet room contract contains the following data: Contract Number, Contract Date, Customer Name, Address, Telephone, Date of Event, Time of Event, Room, Number of Persons, Type of Event, Menu, Table Decor, Floral Arrangements, Per-Person Cost, Total Cost, Deposit, Balance.

The customer chooses the menu from several possible ones, and the code for the menu appears on the contract. Table Decor includes color of linen and other details, and Floral Arrangements indicates the number and size of centerpieces. The Total Cost is found by taking the product of the Per-Person Cost and the Number of Persons, and adding any charges for special decor or floral arrangements.

5. **Concession Rent Bill:** This bill is produced monthly and includes the following data: Bill Date, Location, Renter Name, Address, Telephone, Type of Business, Monthly Rent, Amount Past Due, Date of Last Payment, Amount of Last Payment, Total Amount Due.
6. **Banquets Scheduled for Date mm/dd/yy:** This report shows all the events planned for the banquet rooms on any given date. It may be generated routinely each day for that day's events, or may be produced on request for any date desired. It lists the date in the heading, and the following items: Room, Time, Type of Event, Customer Name, Menu, Table Decor, Floral Arrangements, Number of Persons.
7. **Guest Room Utilization for Month of <Month,Year>:** This monthly report summarizes the utilization of guest rooms for the month indicated. It is normally generated at the end of the month. It includes a line for each day of the month, showing Date, Number Available, Number Unavailable, Number Occupied, Number Unoccupied, Number of Reservations, Number of NoShows, Number of WalkIns. There is a summary for the month, showing Total Occupied, Total Unoccupied, Total Reservations, Total NoShows, Total WalkIns. The Number Available indicates how many guest rooms could have been rented on a particular day. The Number Unavailable shows how many could not have been rented, because they were undergoing repairs, were held for hotel employees or other nonpaying guests, or other reasons. The total of these two columns should always be 300, the number of guest rooms in the hotel. The Number Occupied means the number of rooms rented to paying guests who actually checked in, while the Number Unoccupied is the number of available rooms for which no guest checked in. The total of these two columns should be the number of rooms available. NoShows are people who made reservations but did not check in, while WalkIns are guests who checked in without reservations. The report contains the figures for each day and the totals for the month in each category indicated.

There are several other transactions and reports in addition to the ones described here. You should show the formats of all reports and transactions in Step 1.1. In Step 1.2, write assumptions describing the hotel's operations.

Project Five: Passport Credit Card Processing

General Description

Passport is a credit card company with customers throughout the United States. At present, the card is distributed by major banks in all 50 states. There are approximately 500,000 customers holding Passport cards, and the card is accepted by merchants throughout the country in payment for goods and services of all types. Customers average five purchases per month and receive a monthly bill reflecting new purchases posted during the last month, as well as any amount carried over from the previous month. They must pay at least 10 percent of the balance each month. Any unpaid amount is carried over to the following month, with an interest charge of 1.5 percent of the unpaid balance. Payment is due within 20 days of receipt of the bill.

Basic Operations

Customers apply for the card through local banks. The application lists the terms and conditions of the charge agreement and requires the customer's signature. The bank runs a credit check and if the result is satisfactory, it forwards information about the new customer to the Passport central office, keeping a microfilm copy of the application. The Passport agency sets an initial credit limit for the account, issues the card, and mails it to the customer, along with a letter specifying the terms and conditions, advising the customer to sign the card immediately, and stating that using the credit card constitutes legal acceptance of the terms and conditions. A week later, the agency sends a follow-up letter reminding the customer that a card has been mailed and asking him or her to call the agency immediately if the card was not received. Fewer than 1 percent of cards are lost during the initial mailing, and almost all of these cases are reported to the agency by customers receiving the follow-up letter. When such a report is received, the card is canceled immediately and a new one is issued. Any charges on the lost card are covered by Passport, and law enforcement agencies are alerted to try to recover any losses.

The customer uses the card at any of the shops, hotels, restaurants, department stores, travel agencies, or other locations that accept it. When a purchase is made, the salesclerk fills out a sales slip, filling in the total amount of the sale and taking an impression of the card showing the account number, expiration date, and cardholder name and an impression of a plate showing the merchant number, name, and location. Merchants set their own policies regarding authorizations. For example, they may require that all purchases over $50 be authorized by calling the Passport authorization service. Authorization involves checking the customer's credit limit, current unpaid balance, and previously approved authorizations not reflected in the current balance. If the customer still has credit available, an authorization code is returned to the clerk, who writes it on the sales slip. Otherwise, the sale is rejected. Merchants are reminded to check the signature and those who accept unauthorized sales for credit cards that turn out to be stolen are responsible for their losses. The on-line authorization process is supplemented by a monthly listing of card numbers of lost or stolen cards, which the merchant can check manually. The customer signs the sales slip, which is in triplicate. The original is the Passport copy, the first carbon is the merchant's copy, and the third copy is the customer's.

The merchant returns the original, called the Receipt of Charge, or ROC, to the Passport processing office. There the ROC is microfilmed and the image is stored in a filing cabinet, from which it can be retrieved if there is a problem with the transaction. However, retrieval of the ROC image can take several days. After microfilming, the actual receipt is scanned by an optical character reader for the account numbers of the customer and the merchant. A data entry clerk checks the receipt and enters the total. A transaction number is generated by the system. These items, together with the date of sale and the date posted, are also stored on disk, and the ROC is discarded.

Credit for returned merchandise is handled in much the same way as purchases, except that authorization is not required. The clerk fills out a credit voucher, taking an impression of the credit card and one showing the merchant data, and writes in the amount of the credit. The customer signs the voucher and keeps the third copy. The original is sent to Passport, and the first carbon is kept by the merchant.

Each month, bills are generated for each customer. Billing involves retrieving the balance from the previous month's bill, data about any payments made or credits received since that bill was created, any corrections of earlier errors, and transaction records for any sales posted during the current month. During the first month the card is used in any year, there is a $50 annual fee added to the bill. The bill-generating program consolidates this data and adds any interest charges to produce the new bill. The bill shows the customer data, the transaction number, posting date, merchant name, location, and amount of each transaction, and the balance forward, interest charges, current amount due, minimum payment, and due date. In the past, the paper receipts were sorted by customer account number and sent as a packet along with the bill to the customer. This method, called "country club billing," was dropped by Passport because it was too expensive, and the paper receipts are now simply discarded after the microfilming and data entry.

Merchants' accounts are also processed monthly. Merchants agree to pay Passport a percentage of the amount of each sale as a transaction fee. Merchant accounts are processed by adding the totals of all transactions for each merchant during the previous month, deducting transaction fees, and printing a check for the merchant.

All accounts are reviewed annually to determine whether the customer's credit limit should be adjusted. In addition, customers may initiate such a review if they want their credit limit raised.

The agency provides a hotline for reporting lost or stolen credit cards. Customers are responsible for the first $50 charged on a stolen card, but not for any losses after they have reported the card lost or stolen. When a report is received, Passport immediately cancels the card, issues a new card with a different account number to the customer, and flags the card as stolen so that no further authorizations will be granted on the old card.

Information Needs

The Passport agency wishes to devise a new system that will take advantage of technological advances. It would like to reinstate "country club billing." A major competitor that retained this more expensive type of billing has recently switched to image processing of receipts and is able to send its customers laser-printed sheets with reduced images of the receipts. Customers appreciate the service because it allows them to keep records of expenses for tax and reimbursement purposes and is more convenient than the traditional packet of ROC receipts.

In the competitor's new system, the ROCs are scanned by an image processing camera that produces a digital image of the contents and they are then discarded. To create a transaction record, an optical character reader takes the date of sale, account number, and merchant number from the digital image and a data entry clerk reads the handwritten amount from the image, since the optical character reader is not able to recognize handwritten characters at its present stage of development. The transaction record is then stored on disk, and the digital image is stored on an optical disk, from which it can be retrieved within seconds. The billing processing consists of consolidating data from the previous month's bill, credit and payment records, and disk records of new transactions and adding interest charges, if any. In addition, ROC images for the transactions are retrieved and printed by laser in reduced form. A sheet of images is produced along with each bill, and both are mailed to the cardholder.

The method is slightly more expensive than Passport's present billing system, but it provides the customer with more information. When customers receive the laser-printed images of receipts, there are fewer questions about items on bills, resulting in lower costs for customer inquiries and greater customer satisfaction. At present, Passport receives customer billing questions at the central processing facility, where clerks can retrieve the billing and transaction records saved on disk. If the customer still challenges a transaction, the microfilmed ROC must be retrieved and a copy mailed, a process that is expensive and time consuming. This step would be eliminated with the new system.

Another change the agency would like to make with a new system is to provide for electronic funds transfer both for receiving payments from customers and making payments to merchants' banks instead of mailing checks.

The following documents and transactions are used:

1. **Receipt of Charge:** This document is the original of the sales slip completed by the salesclerk and signed by the customer. It contains the following items: Customer Account Number, Expiration Date, Cardholder Name, Merchant Number, Merchant Name, Merchant Address, Amount of Sale, Date of Sale, Authorization Number, Customer Signature.
2. **Customer Monthly Bill:** This monthly bill sent to the customer has the following preprinted information: Passport name and address, finance charge rates, hotline number for lost or stolen cards, and customer service number for questions about the bill. The system prints the following items: Customer Name, Customer Address, Passport Card Number, Bill Date, Due Date, Previous Balance, Payments, Credits, Total New Charges, Finance Charge, New Balance, Minimum Payment

Due. For each transaction, the following items appear: Transaction Date, Posting Date, Transaction Number, Transaction Details, Amount.

The Transaction Number is actually a reference number used to retrieve the disk record of the transaction and the microfilmed ROC, if needed. It could be used to identify the digital image of the ROC in the future. The Posting Date is the date on which the transaction data reached Passport's office. The Transaction Details for a sale lists the merchant's name and location. For a credit, they include the same information.

3. **Merchant Report:** This monthly report is sent to each merchant along with a check. It contains: Merchant Name, Merchant Address, Merchant Number, Date of Report, Total Sales, Total Credits, Total Transaction Fees, Amount of Check. For each sale, it contains: Customer Account Number, Date of Sale, Authorization Number, Amount of Sale, Posting Date. For each customer credit, it contains: Customer Account Number, Date of Credit, Amount of Credit, Posting Date.
4. **Customer Payment Transaction:** The input screen contains: Passport Card Number, Date, Amount Paid. The output screen shows: Customer Name, Customer Address, Old Balance, New Balance.

There are several other reports and several transactions that could be used. In Step 1.1, write the complete formats of all reports and transactions. In Step 1.2, write a list of assumptions summarizing the operations of the organization.

Project Six: The Global Insurance Agency

General Description

Global is an independent insurance agency that sells policies from several different companies. It has only one location and five agents, one of whom is the owner. They each have about 300 customers. The agency sells only individual homeowner's, automobile, and life insurance policies.

A basic homeowner's policy covers a client's home and its contents against fire, theft, lightning, and similar dangers. The policy lists the specific dangers included and those excluded, and the client pays more for policies that are more inclusive. There is usually a deductible, a fixed amount that the client must pay before the insurance company pays.

Automobile insurance is designed to provide coverage for damage caused by use of a car. Policies provide varying limits for liability, which is damage a driver causes, medical payments, personal injury protection, protection from uninsured motorists, collision, and comprehensive coverage. Collision covers damage to the insured's own car from colliding with an object or another car, while comprehensive covers damage to the insured's car by fire, theft, or other causes not including collision. Both collision and comprehensive have associated deductibles.

There are several types of life insurance, including term, whole life, limited-payment life, endowment, and combination plans.

Basic Operations

Names, addresses, and telephone numbers of prospective customers are obtained from various sources. Agents contact potential clients by mail or phone and try to set up appointments. At these meetings, the agent reviews the client's present insurance coverage and tries to identify the policy or policies that will best meet the client's insurance needs. To buy insurance, the client fills out an application for coverage and the agent draws up a tentative contract furnished by the appropriate insurance company. The application is signed by both the client and the agent, and forwarded to the insurance company. The insurance company may conduct an investigation, the nature and scope of which are determined by the type of insurance, the characteristics of the policy, and the identity of the client. If the outcome of the investigation is positive, the company sends a policy to the agent, who signs it and meets with the client for his or her signature. Both the agent and the client keep copies of the contract. If the outcome is negative, the agent is informed of the problem and he or she meets with the client to discuss alternatives. The policy is in effect once the client signs it and makes the first insurance premium payment.

Every policy carries with it a schedule of premiums, which varies with the type and coverage. Each policy also provides a commission for the agency. The commission varies with the insurance company, policy type, and coverage. However, a given insurance company will always pay the same commission for the same policy, regardless of the agency or seniority of the agent. The Global agency works on a strict commission system and does not pay a salary to any of its agents. It splits the commission received for each policy with the agent who sold it.

Once a policy has been sold, the agency submits premium bills to the client, collects payment, and sends the payment, minus its commission, to the insurance company. If a client fails to pay premiums, the agent who sold the policy is informed so that he or she can contact the client. There is a short "grace period" once a payment is missed, during which coverage continues and the agent attempts to resolve the problem. If the grace period expires without payment, the policy is dropped by the insurance company. Some life insurance policies pay dividends at the end of the year. The client may choose to receive dividends in cash or to use them as credit toward premium payments.

Claims can be made on insurance policies as specified in the policy itself. Clients or their beneficiaries contact the agent to file such claims. For an automobile insurance policy, claims are made when the car is involved in an accident, damaged, or stolen. Homeowner's policy claims are made when property is damaged or lost. Life insurance claims may be made by the beneficiaries on the death of the insured, or by the insured, if the policy has a cash value. Once the insurance company receives a claim, it assigns an adjustor who investigates the legitimacy of the claim and handles payment, if any. The agency is not involved in following up on the claim.

Information Needs

The agency now handles all records manually, using an office staff of two clerical workers. The owner wishes to computerize all data relating to insurance policies and has hired you to design a database for this purpose. You are to design a system that can be maintained by the clerical staff and accessed by the agents. The following reports, documents, and transactions will be used:

1. **Application for Life Insurance:** This form is filled out by the client and the agent during the initial visit. It contains: Agent Name, Client Name, Address, Years Living There, Phone, Date of Birth, Sex, Previous Address, Years at Previous Address, Employer Name, Employer Address, Years There, Previous Employer, Previous Employer Address, Years at Previous Employment, Marital Status, No. of Children, Height, Weight, Smoker, High Risk Employment, High Risk Hobby, History of Mental Illness, History of Heart Disease, History of Cancer, Date of Most Recent Physical, Physician Name, Physician Address, Physician Telephone, General Condition.

The client provides information on previous address only if he or she has been at the present address less than five years. The same rule applies to previous employment. The application contains a few questions designed to help the insurance company assess the health of the applicant. Some of these, such as Smoker, are flags that contain only true or false values. The form contains a printed statement verifying that all answers are complete and truthful, and agreeing that the company has a right to contact the client's physician for additional health information. The company also reserves the right to request a physical examination. The client's signature signifies agreement to these conditions.

2. **Application for Automobile Insurance:** This form contains: Agent Name, Client Name, Address, Phone, Liability, Medical Payments, Personal Injury, Uninsured Motorist. For each driver, it lists: Lic State, Lic No, Date of Birth, Sex, Number of Points. For each car, it lists: Make, Model, Style, Year, Mileage, Primary Driver, Used for Work, Collision, Comprehensive, Collision Deductible, Comprehensive Deductible.

The application lists up to four drivers to be covered by the policy, and up to three cars. The coverage for Liability, Medical Payments, Personal Injury, and Uninsured Motorist is the same for all drivers and all cars covered by the policy, but the Collision and Comprehensive deductibles may be different for each of the three cars covered. The amount of collision and comprehensive coverage is always the actual cash value less any deductible.

3. **Premium Invoice:** This form contains: Insured Name, Address, Insurance Company Name, Policy Number, Policy Type, Policy Coverage, Amount Due, Date Due, Agent Name.

The invoice is generated by the agency, which receives the payment and sends the appropriate portion to the insurance company.

4. **Monthly Activity by Agent:** This report is generated each month to track the sales activity of each of the agents. It contains: Agent Name, Number of First Appointments, Number of Auto Policies Sold, Annual Total New Auto Premiums, Number of Homeowner's Policies Sold, Annual Total New Homeowner's Premiums, Number of Life Policies Sold, Annual Total New Life Premiums.
5. **Automobile Insurance Policy:** Most of this document is preprinted, with the insurance company's name and address, and the terms and conditions of the insurance. The following items are individually printed on the policy: Policy Number, Insured Name, Insured Address, Liability Coverage, Medical Payments Coverage, Personal Injury Coverage, Uninsured Motorist Coverage, Premiums, Valid Until. For each driver, it lists: Lic State, Lic Number. For each car, it lists: Make, Model, Style, Year, Collision, Collision Deductible, Comprehensive, Comprehensive Deductible.
6. **Policies by Agent <name>:** This report lists all the policies, new or old, that the named agent has sold or is responsible for. It appears in order by Customer Name. The items are: Customer Name, Address, Telephone. For each policy belonging to the customer, the following data appears: Insurance Company, Policy Number, Insurance Type, Type of Policy, Coverage, Annual Premiums, Annual Commission. At the bottom of the report, the following summary appears: Number of Customers, Number of Policies, Total Annual Premiums, Total Annual Commission.

There are similar applications and policies for other types of insurance, transactions to calculate agents' commissions, to record payments, and other reports that would be useful. You should show the formats of all reports and transactions in Step 1.1. In Step 1.2, write assumptions to summarize the agency's operations. Use the sample project as a guide.

PART II

DESIGNING THE LOGICAL MODEL

C H A P T E R

2

Database Planning

2 Chapter Objectives

In this chapter you will learn

- why data is viewed as a corporate resource
- the distinction between data and information
- the three levels of discussion about data
- the meaning of the following terms: **entity, entity set, attribute, relationship**
- the meaning of the terms **metadata, record type, data item type, data item, data aggregate, record, data dictionary, data instance**, and **file**
- the steps in staged database design
- how to construct and use a data flow diagram
- how a data dictionary is constructed and used
- what skills are needed for the Database Administrator position
- the functions and organizational placement of the DBA
- the responsibilities of the DBA's staff
- the distinction between a Data Administrator and a Database Administrator

2.1 Data as a Resource

If you were asked to identify the resources of a typical business organization, you would probably include capital equipment, financial assets, and personnel, but you might not think of data as a resource. In the traditional file processing environment, data was linked to applications and appeared to be the property of the managers of the departments that owned the applications. It was not uncommon for department managers to keep data tapes locked in their desks or to "protect" their data by bringing the tapes home. With the development of databases, this private ownership gradually yielded to corporate ownership of data and led to the recognition that **data is a genuine corporate resource**. Since the database contains data about the organization's operations (called **operational data**) that is used by many departments, and since it is professionally managed by a DBA, there is an increased appreciation of the value of the data itself, independent of the applications. We could define a **resource** as **any asset that is of value to an organization and that incurs costs**. An organization's operational data clearly fits this definition. You can appreciate the value of an organization's data more fully if you think about what would happen if the data were lost or fell into the hands of a competitor. Many organizations, such as banks and brokerage houses, are heavily dependent on data and would fail very quickly if their data were lost. Most businesses would suffer heavy losses if their operational data were unavailable. In fact, an organization depends on the availability of operational data in managing its other resources. For example, decisions about the purchase, lease, or use of equipment, financial investments and financial returns, and staffing needs should be made on the basis of information about the organization's operations. The recognition of data as a corporate resource is an important objective in developing a database environment. The database protects the data resource by providing data security, integrity, and reliability controls through the DBMS.

2.2 Characteristics of Data

To appreciate the importance of data as a corporate resource, we need to examine its characteristics more closely.

2.2.1 Data and Information

We often think of data as information, but these two terms have slightly different meanings. The term **data** refers to the bare facts recorded in the database. They may be items about people, places, events, or concepts. **Information** is processed data that is in a form that is useful for making decisions. Information is derived from the stored data by rearranging, selecting, combining, summarizing, or performing other operations on the data. For example, if we simply print out all the stored items in the database, we have data. However, if we print a formatted report showing the data in some order that helps us make a decision, we have information. In practice, most people use the two terms interchangeably.

2.2.2 *Levels of Data*

When we discuss data, it is important to distinguish between objects in the real world, the structure of the database, and the data stored in the database. There are actually three levels of discussion or abstraction to be considered when we talk about data.

The first is the **real world** or **reality.** On this level, we talk about the **enterprise**, the organization for which the database is designed. The enterprise might be a corporation, government agency, university, bank, brokerage house, school, hospital, or other organization that actually exists in the real world. In the realm of reality, we identify **entities**, which are persons, places, events, objects, or concepts about which we collect data. For the organizations mentioned above, examples of entities are a customer, an employee, a student, a bank account, an investment, a class, and a patient. We group similar entities into **entity sets**. For example, the set of all customers forms the entity set we might call Customers. Similarly, we might have entity sets Employees, Students, Accounts, Investments, Classes, and Patients, each consisting of all entities of the corresponding type. An organization may have dozens or hundreds of entity sets. Each entity has certain **attributes**, which are characteristics or properties that describe the entity and that the organization considers important. Each entity set may have several attributes that describe its members. For the Student entity set, attributes may include Student ID, Name, Address, Telephone Number, Major, Credits Passed, Grade Point Average, and Advisor. For the Bank Account entity set, attributes may include Account Number, Owner Name, Co-Owner Name, and Balance. Some entities may have **relationships** or **associations** between them. For example, in a university, students are related to classes by being enrolled in those classes and faculty members are related to classes by teaching them. Students and faculty members may be related to one another by the teacher-student relationship or by the advisor-student relationship. Students may be related to one another by being roommates. The concepts of entity, attribute, and relationship are discussed in more detail in Chapter 4.

As the organization functions in the real world, it is impossible to obtain information needed for decision making by direct observation of reality. There is just too much detail involved for us to keep track of all the facts we need. Instead, we develop a model of the organization. The database should be designed to be a faithful model or representation of the organization and its operations. Every entity should be represented, along with its attributes and the relationships in which it participates. In the real world, changes are made to the entities, attributes, or relationships. For example, employees leave the organization, customers change their addresses, and students enroll in different classes. To keep track of the facts about entities and such changes, we need to develop a model that allows not only the representation of the basic entities, attributes, and relationships, but also allows us to make changes that mirror the changes in reality.

The structure of the database, called the **logical model of the database**, is the second level of discussion. On this level, we talk about **metadata**, or data about data. For each entity set in the real world, we have a **record type** in the logical model of the database. For example, for the student entity set in the university, we have a STUDENT record type. A record type contains several **data item types**, each of which represents an attribute of an entity. For the STUDENT record type, the data item types may be STUID, STUNAME, ADDRESS, PHONE, MAJOR, CREDITS, GPA, and ADVISOR. A **data item** is the **smallest named unit of stored data**. Other words sometimes used for data item are **data element, field, or attribute**. Generally, a **field** means a set of adjacent bytes identified as the physical location for a data item, so it has a more physical meaning than the term *data item*. **Attribute** usually refers to a characteristic of an entity in the real world, but since there is a correspondence between attributes and data items, the two words are often interchanged. Data items are sometimes grouped together to form **data aggregates**, which are **named groups of data items** within a record. For an EMPLOYEE record, there may be a data aggregate called EMPADD, which consists of the data items STREET, CITY, STATE, and ZIP. Data aggregates allow us to refer to the group of data items as a whole or to the individual items in the group. A **record** is a **named collection of related data items and/or data aggregates.** As mentioned above, there is usually a record type for each entity set and a data item type for each attribute. Relationships may also be represented by record types, but there are other ways to represent relationships.

Information about the logical structure of the database is stored in a **data dictionary** or **data directory**. This repository of information contains the **database schema**, a written description of the logical structure of the database. It contains descriptions of the record types, data item types, and data aggregates in the database, as well as other information. For example, the data dictionary/directory might contain an entry for the EMPLOYEE record type, stating that it consists of the data items EMPID, EMPNAME, JOBTITLE, SALARY, DEPT, and MGR and the data aggregate EMPADD. For each of the data items, there is a descriptive entry showing the data item name (e.g., EMPID), its data type [e.g., CHAR(5)], and any **synonyms**, which are other names used for the data item (e.g., EMP#). For data aggregates, the dictionary/directory would list the components. For example, for EMPADD it would state that its components are the data items STREET, CITY, STATE, and ZIP, each of which is listed as a data item. The data dictionary/directory is actually a database about the database. However, data dictionaries usually do much more than simply store the schema. They often control database documentation, and for some systems, are actively involved in all database accesses.

The third level of discussion is concerned with **actual data in the database itself**. It consists of **data instances** or **occurrences**. For each entity in the real world, there is an occurrence of a corresponding record in the database. For each student in the university, there is an occurrence of a student record. So while there is only one STUDENT record type, which is described in the data dictionary and corresponds to the student entity set, there may be thousands of student record occurrences, corresponding to individual student entities, in the database itself. Similarly, there are many instances of each of the data item types that correspond to attributes. A **file** (sometimes called a **data set)** is a **named collection of record occurrences**. Usually a file contains all occurrences of one record type. For example, the Student file may contain 5000 student records. Finally, the **database** may be thought of as a named collection of related files. Figure 2.1 summarizes the three levels of data.

REALM	OBJECTS	EXAMPLES
REAL WORLD	Entity	A student, a class
	Attribute	Name, schedule
	Entity set	All students, all classes
	Relationship	Student relates to class by being enrolled in it
METADATA data definitions, stored in Data Dictionary	Record type	STUDENT record type, CLASS record type
	Data item type	STUID, COURSE#
	Data aggregate	STUADD, consisting of STREET, CITY, STATE, ZIP
DATA OCCURRENCES stored in the database	Student record occurrence	Record of student Tom Smith
	Data item occurrence	'S1001','Tom Smith','CS101'
	File	Student file with 5000 Student record occurrences
	Database	University database-containing Student file, Class file, Faculty file, etc.

Figure 2.1 Three Levels of Discussing Data

2.3 *Design Stages*

The process of analyzing the organization and its environment, developing a database model that accurately reflects the organization's functioning in the real world, and implementing that model by creating a database requires an appropriate methodology. Traditional systems analysis provides a possible approach, but a staged database approach offers a better solution.

2.3.1 *Traditional Systems Analysis Approach*

A database design and implementation project could be viewed as a specific example of a systems development project. Traditionally, software systems are developed using a systems analysis approach which identifies the steps in designing and implementing a system. There is an assumption that every system has a **life cycle**, a period of time during which the system is designed, is created, is used, and is then replaced by a new system. A typical life cycle extends over several years and consists of the stages shown

STAGE	ACTIVITIES
Preliminary Investigation	Interview users, study reports, transactions, procedures, software, documentation to identify problems in present system and goals of new system
Feasibility	Study alternatives, estimate costs, Study schedules, benefits. Make recommendation.
Preliminary Design	Work with users to develop general system design. Choose best design. Develop system flowchart. Identify hardware, software, and personnel needs. Revise estimates.
Detailed Design	Do technical design. Plan program modules, algorithms, files, databases, I/O forms. Revise estimates.
System Implementation	Program modules, convert files, test system, write documentation, develop operational procedures, train personnel, do parallel operations, cut over to new system
System Operation	Evaluate system. Monitor and modify system as needed.

Figure 2.2 Stages in Systems Analysis Life Cycle

in Figure 2.2. Using the traditional life cycle approach, the system will eventually fail to meet users' needs, problems will be identified, and the cycle will begin again.

2.3.2 *Staged Database Design Approach*

A basic assumption behind the systems analysis life cycle approach is that systems will eventually become obsolete and have to be replaced. In the database environment, there is reason to question this assumption. The database can be designed in such a way that it can evolve, changing to meet future information needs of the organization. This evolution is possible when the designer develops a true logical model of the organization with the following characteristics:

- The model faithfully mirrors the operations of the organization.
- It is flexible enough to allow changes as new information needs arise.
- It supports many different user views.

- It is independent of physical implementation.
- It does not depend on the model used by a particular database management system.

A well-designed database model protects the data resource by allowing it to evolve so that it serves both today's and tomorrow's information needs. If the system is truly independent of its physical implementation, it can be moved to new hardware to take advantage of technical developments. Even if the database management system chosen for implementation is replaced, the logical model of the enterprise survives.

The staged database design approach is a top-down method that begins with general statements of needs and progresses to more and more detailed consideration of problems. Different problems are considered at different phases of the project. Each stage uses design tools that are appropriate to the problem at that level. Figure 2.3 shows the major design stages. They are

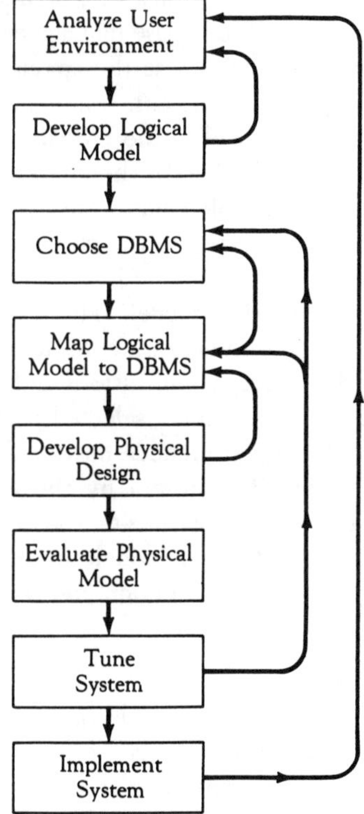

Figure 2.3

1. **Analyze the user environment.** The first step in designing a database is to determine the current user environment. The designer should study all present applications, determine their input and output, examine all reports generated by the present system, and interview users to determine how they use the system. After the present

system is thoroughly understood, the designer should work closely with present and potential users of the new system to identify their needs. The designer should consider not only present needs but possible new applications or future uses of the database. The result of this analysis is a model of the user environment and requirements.

2. **Develop a logical data model.** Using the model of the user environment, the designer develops a detailed logical model of the database, identifying the entities, attributes, and relationships that will be represented. In addition to the logical model, the designer has to consider how the database is to be used. The types of applications and transactions, the kinds of access, the volume of transactions, the volume of data, the frequency of access, and other quantitative data must be specified. Other constraints, such as budgetary restrictions and performance requirements, must also be identified. The result of this phase is a set of database specifications.
3. **Choose a DBMS.** The designer uses the specifications and his or her knowledge of available hardware and software resources to evaluate alternative database management systems. Each database management system imposes its own restrictions. The designer attempts to choose the system that best satisfies the specifications for the environment, within the constraints given.
4. **Map the logical model to the DBMS.** The designer maps the logical model to the data structures available for the chosen DBMS.
5. **Develop the physical model.** The designer plans the layout of data considering the structures supported by the chosen DBMS and hardware and software resources available.
6. **Evaluate the physical model.** The designer then estimates the performance of all applications and transactions, considering the quantitative data previously identified and priorities given to applications and transactions. It may be helpful to develop a **prototype**, implementing a selected portion of the database so that user views can be validated and performance measured more accurately.
7. **Perform tuning if indicated by the evaluation.** Adjustments such as modifying physical structures or optimizing software can be done to improve performance.
8. **Implement the physical model.** If the evaluation is positive, the designer then implements the physical design and the database becomes operational.

The loops in Figure 2.3 provide opportunities for feedback and changes at various stages in the design process. For example, after developing the logical model, the designer communicates with user groups to make sure that their data requirements are represented properly. If they are not, the logical model must be adjusted. If the logical model does not map well to a particular DBMS, another should be considered. If the physical model is not acceptable, a different mapping or a different DBMS can be considered. If the results of the performance evaluation are not satisfactory, additional tuning and evaluation may be performed. If tuning and optimization are not sufficient, it may be necessary to change the way the logical model is mapped to the DBMS or to consider a different database management system. Even after the system is implemented, changes may be needed to respond to changing user needs or a changing environment.

2.4 Design Tools

Many methodologies exist that can make the database design process easier for both designers and users. They vary from general design techniques described in the literature to commercial products whose aim is to automate the design process. For example, **CASE** (computer-aided software engineering) packages that include various tools for system analysis and programming are available from over 100 vendors. Two useful tools that can be developed with or without CASE packages are **data flow diagrams** and **data dictionaries.**

2.4.1 Data Flow Diagrams

As the designer collects information about the present system, he or she can determine where data originates, where it is captured, where it is processed, and where it is directed after processing. **Data flow diagrams** (**DFD**s) show the flow of data through the organization. They provide a useful model for communicating with users, other designers, and managers about the present system and the proposed system. Figure 2.4 shows the symbols used in constructing data flow diagrams, along with their meanings. Note that in this context the word "entity" means any person, other system, or organization that supplies data to or receives data from the system. It is not the same as an entity to be represented in the database. Data flow diagrams can be constructed at several levels, to show different amounts of detail about the system. There are few rules to be followed in constructing a data flow diagram, so the designer has great freedom to decide what should be represented, how much detail should be included, and whether the diagram will be primarily **logical**, showing only data and processes, or **physical**, showing the sequence of processing, changes to data and files, and reports or other output. Often the designer produces several such diagrams, showing various aspects of the system or various levels of detail. If a CASE package or similar design product is used, the diagrams may be produced automatically, after the analyst has provided sufficient information about the system.

Three types of diagrams we will examine are **context**, **Diagram 0** (diagram zero), and **detailed data flow diagrams**.

1. **Context DFD.** Here, the emphasis is on the relationship between the system and its environment. The system as a whole is represented by a bubble, and the external entities are shown as squares from which input flows and to which output is directed. Figure 2.5 shows a context DFD for an on-line registration system for a university. Note that this example concentrates exclusively on the registration system, ignoring other applications, such as payroll. No information about the structure of the system itself is pictured in a context DFD.
2. **Diagram 0.** A Diagram 0 is a diagram showing the system itself. It pictures the major processes along with the external entities, data stores, and data flow. Figure 2.6 shows a Diagram 0 for the on-line registration system. It is a single, top-level diagram of the system, and does not describe each process in detail. Parts of the diagram can be expanded or "exploded" using more detailed subdiagrams.

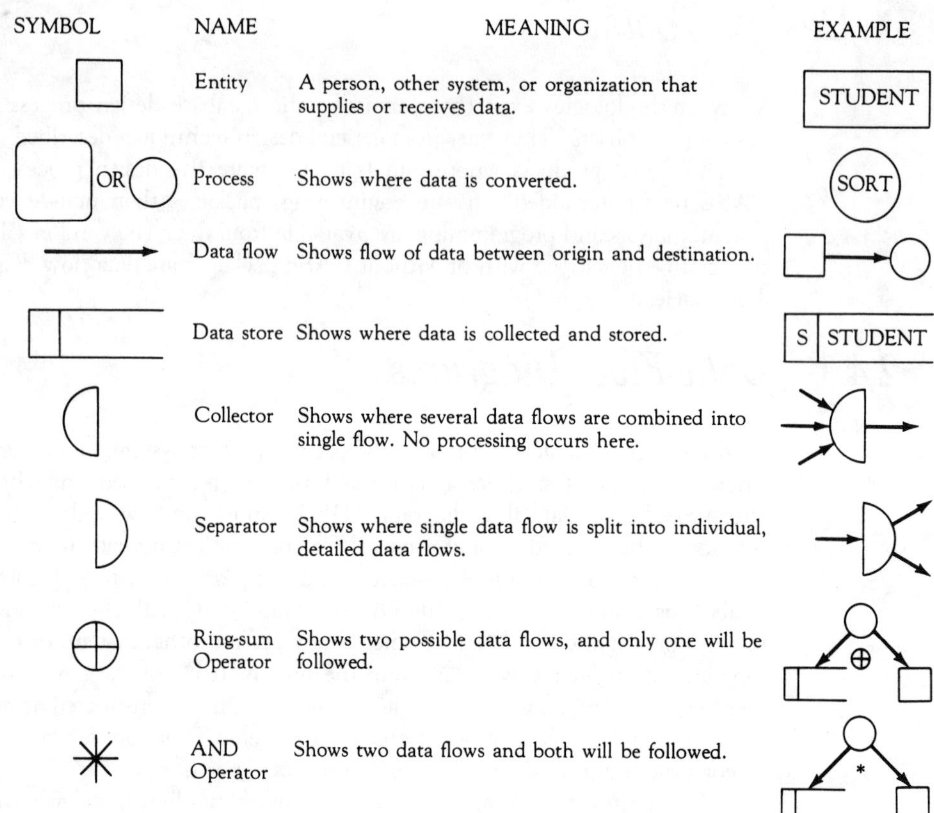

Figure 2.4

3. **Detailed DFD.** Detailed DFDs are "explosions" of higher-level representations and are detailed pictures of major processes or subsystems. They are likely to be used by designers in their own work rather than for presentations to users or managers. Figure 2.7 shows a detailed DFD for the on-line registration system that expands the "Process Requests" bubble of the Diagram 0. Since that process was assigned the identifying number 1.0 in the Diagram 0, the detailed diagram is called Diagram 1.0. The processing bubbles in the detailed diagram have identifying numbers 1.1, 1.2, and so on. If more detail is needed, each of the processes shown on this diagram can be further exploded using a still more detailed diagram. For example, if we wish to expand the "Check Class Counts" process, we would construct a diagram called Diagram 1.2, which would have subprocesses 1.2.1, 1.2.2, and so on. This numbering system helps the designer keep track of the relationships between diagrams.

To construct a data flow diagram, you should decide what level of detail you need, work on one part or segment of the diagram at a time, and then combine the segments to form a single DFD. General guidelines are:

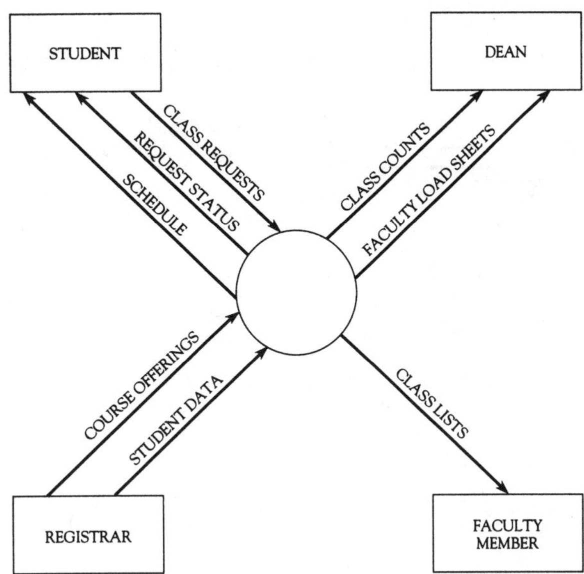

Figure 2.5

- Keep the diagram simple. It should fit on a single page and should not contain so many elements that readers are unable to absorb all of it.
- Label each element.
- Do not include processing logic of the type shown in program flowcharts. Do not indicate decision making or repetition of processes.
- Picture the operational system, not the start-up of the system. Unlike a flowchart, a data flow diagram does not show the timing of operations.
- Show only the flow of data. Do not show how material other than data flows through the organization. Omit error routines and controls except in detailed DFDs.
- Use processing bubbles to show when data is collected or changed.
- Make sure that each data flow begins and/or ends at a processing bubble.
- If a symbol is to be repeated in the diagram, put a slash (/) in the lower right corner of the symbol. Designers repeat symbols to avoid drawing too many long or intersecting lines.

To construct a context data flow diagram, follow these steps:

1. Use a large processing bubble in the center of the diagram to represent the system. Label it with the system's name.
2. Identify an entity, which is any person, other system, or organization that supplies data to or receives data from the system, and represent it by a square.
3. For each data flow between the entity and the system, draw an arrow to show the direction of the data flow and label it to show the content of the data being transferred.

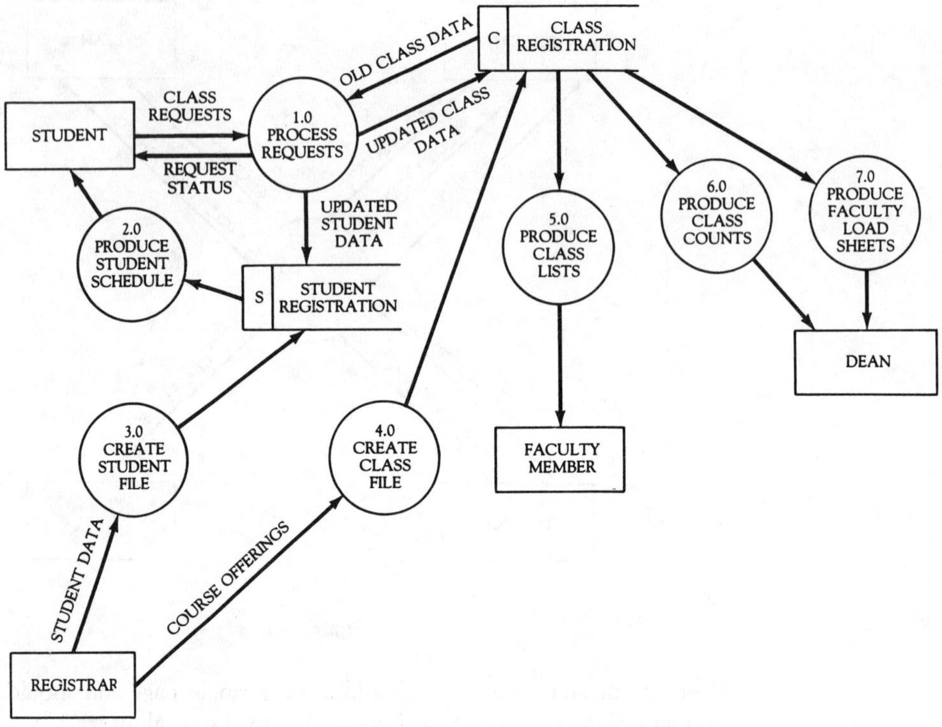

Figure 2.6

4. Repeat steps 2 and 3 until all entities have been represented on the diagram.

Note that the context DFD does not show data stores or procedures and uses a single processing bubble to show all system processing. More detail is shown on the next type of DFD, a Diagram 0.

To construct a Diagram 0, follow these steps:

1. Identify the data stores that are used. They may be **master files**, that store relatively permanent data, or **transaction files**, that contain temporary data used for processing.
2. Identify a major event within the system. This might be one that generates input, produces output, or represents regular functions of the system.
3. For that event, draw a segment showing the associated processing bubble(s), data store(s), and data flow(s). Name the process and assign positive whole numbers 1.0, 2.0, 3.0, and so on to identify each processing bubble.
4. Repeat steps 2 and 3 until all major processes or subsystems are represented, connecting the segments into a complete data flow diagram. Data stores and entities usually serve as connecting points for the subsystems.

A Diagram 0 shows only input, entities involved, and output produced for major processes or subsystems. It does not show details such as error routines, editing, or

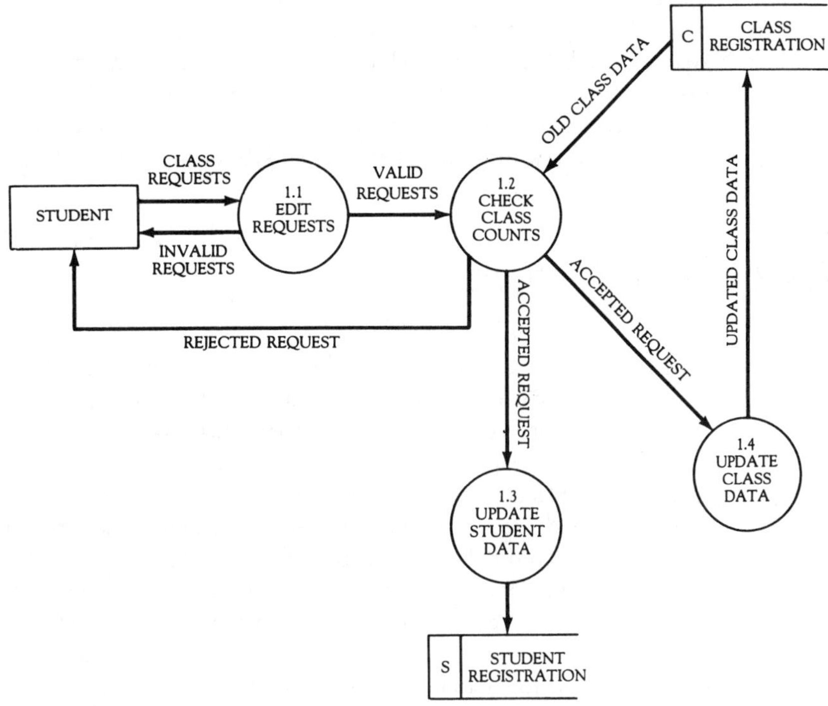

Figure 2.7

controls. These items, along with more information about subsystems, can appear on detailed DFDs.

To construct a detailed data flow diagram from a context data flow diagram, follow these steps:

1. Identify the major process you wish to detail and examine its representation in the Diagram 0. The number of the process becomes the number of the diagram.
2. Identify the data stores for the subsystem.
3. Identify a major event for the subsystem.
4. Draw a segment showing the data store(s), processing bubble(s), and data flow(s) for this event, whether or not they are represented on the higher-level diagram. Number the processing bubbles using the number of the diagram, followed by a decimal point and a positive integer, such as 2.1, 2.2, and so on.
5. Repeat steps 3 and 4 until all major events are represented, connecting the segments into a complete data flow diagram.

If necessary, the diagrams can be carried to another level of detail. For example, if process 2.1 is to be expanded using Diagram 2.1, its subprocesses will be 2.1.1, 2.1.2, and so on.

Data flow diagrams can be used early in the database design process to represent the flow of information in the present system. A Diagram 0 can often point out flaws, redundancies, or gaps in the existing system. Later in the design process, DFDs can be used to represent the proposed system. A Diagram 0 representation of the proposed system may be useful for making presentations to management, communicating with users, and guiding the work of a design team. A detailed DFD of each subsystem can be used as a reference by those working on a portion of the project. At the end of the project, data flow diagrams of the actual system should be kept as documentation.

2.4.2 *Data Dictionary*

A data dictionary, as discussed in Section 2.2.2, is a repository of information that describes the logical structure of the database. It has entries for record types, data item types, and data aggregates, along with other information. The amount of information and the way the information is used vary with the system. Most vendors of DBMSs offer data dictionaries or data directories that not only store the database schema but can be used in creating and processing the database. The data dictionary contains **metadata**, data about the data in the database. If the data dictionary is part of the DBMS, we refer to it as an **integrated** data dictionary. An integrated data dictionary may be **active,** meaning that the DBMS checks it every time the database is accessed, or **passive**, meaning that it is not involved in day-to-day database processing. An active data dictionary is always consistent with the actual database structure, because it is maintained automatically by the system. Integrated data dictionaries perform many functions throughout the life of the database, not only in the design phase. If the data dictionary is available without a particular DBMS, we refer to it as a **freestanding** data dictionary. A freestanding data dictionary can be a commercial product or a simple file developed and maintained by the designer. For example, CASE packages often include a data dictionary tool, and freestanding data dictionaries are available even for nondatabase environments. Both integrated and freestanding data dictionaries have advantages and disadvantages, but a freestanding dictionary may be preferable in the initial design stages, before the designer has chosen a particular DBMS. Since it is not tied to a DBMS, it allows the designer to enjoy the advantages of having this tool without committing to a particular implementation. A major disadvantage is that once the database is created, adjustments to its structure may not be entered into the freestanding data dictionary and, over time, the dictionary will not be an accurate reflection of the database structure.

Regardless of whether the data dictionary is integrated or freestanding, it is useful in the early design stages for collecting and organizing information about data. Each data item, its source(s), its name(s), its uses, its meaning, its relationship to other items, its format, and the identity of the person or group responsible for entering it, updating it, and maintaining its correctness must be determined. The data dictionary provides an effective tool for accomplishing these tasks. The database administrator can begin development of the data dictionary by identifying data items, securing agreement from users on a definition of each item, and entering the item in the dictionary. Since users should not be aware of other users' data, the DBA should control access to the dictionary.

A data dictionary is useful for

- Collecting and storing information about data in a central location. This helps management to gain control over data as a resource.
- Securing agreement from users and designers about the meanings of data items. An exact, agreed-upon definition of each item must be developed for storage in the data dictionary.
- Communicating with users. The data dictionary greatly facilitates communication, since exact meanings are stored. The dictionary also identifies the persons, departments, or groups having access to or interest in each item.
- Identifying redundancy and inconsistency in data item names. In the process of identifying and defining data items, the DBA may discover **synonyms**, which are different names for the same item. The database can accept synonyms, but the system must be aware of them. The DBA may also discover **homonyms,** which are identical names for different data items. These are never permitted in a database.
- Keeping track of changes to the database structure. Changes such as creation of new data item and record types or alterations to data item descriptions should be recorded in the data dictionary.
- Determining the impact of changes to the database structure. Since the data dictionary records each item, all its relationships, and all its users, the DBA can see what effects a change would have.
- Identifying the sources of and responsibility for the correctness of each item. A general rule for data entry is that data should be captured as near to its source as possible. The persons or departments that generate or capture values for each data item and those responsible for updating each item should be listed in the data dictionary.
- Recording the external, logical, and physical models and the mappings between models. This aspect is discussed in Chapter 3.
- Recording access control information. An active integrated data dictionary can record the identities of all those who are permitted to access each item, along with the type of access—retrieval, insertion, update, or deletion.
- Providing audit information. The data dictionary may record each access, allowing usage statistics to be collected for auditing the system and spotting attempted security violations.

Note that not all data dictionaries provide support for all of these functions, and some provide additional functions. Some just store the schema, some control documentation, and some are "metasystems" that control access to the database, generate system code, and keep statistics on database usage as well.

2.5 *Role of the Database Administrator*

The database administrator (DBA) is responsible for the design, operation, and management of the database. He or she must be technically competent, a good manager, a skilled diplomat, and possess excellent communication skills. Management skills are required to plan, coordinate and carry out a multitude of tasks during all phases of the database project and to supervise a staff. Technical skills are needed because the DBA has to be able to understand the complex hardware and software issues involved and to work with system and application experts in solving problems. Diplomatic skills are used to communicate with users and determine their needs, to negotiate agreements on data definitions and database access rights, to secure agreements on changes to the database structure or operations that affect users, and to mediate between users with conflicting requirements. Excellent communications skills are required for all of these activities.

2.5.1 *Functions of the DBA*

The DBA has many functions that vary according to the stage of the database project. Since there are so many tasks to be performed, especially during the design and creation phases, the DBA must be able to delegate some of these responsibilities. Major functions include the following:

Planning the Database

- Preliminary database planning

If the DBA is chosen early enough in the project, he or she should participate in the preliminary investigation and feasibility study.

- Identifying user requirements

The DBA examines all reports generated by the present system and consults with users to determine whether the reports satisfy their information needs. He or she may work with present and potential users to design new reports they would like the proposed system to produce. Users are also asked what on-line transactions they would like to perform. The DBA studies all present applications, especially their input and output. The frequency of reports and transactions and the time frame within which they must be produced are also recorded. The DBA uses his or her knowledge of the long-term and short-term objectives of the organization to prioritize user requirements.

- Developing and maintaining the data dictionary

As he or she determines the data needs of users, the DBA stores data item names, sources, meanings, usage, and synonyms in the data dictionary. The DBA revises the data dictionary to include more information about the database as the project progresses.

- Designing the logical model

The DBA identifies all entities, attributes, and relationships that are to be represented in the database, and develops a logical model that is an accurate reflection of the operations of the organization in the real world.

- Choosing a DBMS

The DBA considers the logical model and other database specifications and the computer hardware and software available for the database, and chooses the DBMS that best fits the environment and meets the specifications.

- Developing the physical model

Once the DBMS is chosen, there may be several ways that the logical model could be mapped to the physical devices. The DBA evaluates each mapping by estimating performance of applications and transactions. The best mapping becomes the physical model.

Developing the Operating Database

- Creating and loading the database

Once the physical model is developed, the DBA creates the structure of the database using the data definition language for the chosen DBMS. He or she establishes physical data sets, defines libraries, and loads the data into the database, usually using a DBMS utility program that accepts linear files, places the data in the appropriate locations, and builds indexes and/or sets pointer values as records are loaded.

- Developing user views

The DBA attempts to satisfy the data needs of all users. A user's view may be identical to the one requested in the initial design stages. Often, however, users' requests change as they begin to understand the system better. If the view does not coincide with the user's request, the DBA should present cogent reasons why the request has not been met and secure agreement on the actual view. Since user support is vital to the success of the database project, it is essential that users feel that the database serves them well.

- Writing and maintaining documentation

Ideally, the database documentation is written automatically by the data dictionary system as the project progresses. When the database is created, the DBA makes sure that the documentation accurately reflects the structure of the database.

- Developing and enforcing data standards

Since the database is shared by many users, it is important that standards be defined and enforced for the benefit of all. Users who are responsible for inserting and updating data must follow a standard format for entering data. The user interface should be designed to make it easy for users to follow the standards. For example, input screens should display default values, show acceptable ranges for items, and so on. Typical data standards include specifications for null values, abbreviations, codes, punctuation, and capitalization. The system can automatically check for errors and range restrictions.

Other restrictions that may be checked by the DBMS before updates are accepted involve uniqueness of key values and relationships between data values in a single record, between records in the same file, and between records in different files.

- Developing and enforcing application program standards

The DBA must develop standards for applications programs so that they obey database security and privacy restrictions, are subject to the auditability mechanism, make proper use of the high-level data manipulation language, and fit the application development facilities provided by the DBMS. These standards apply to both old applications that are converted for use with the database and to new applications.

- Developing operating procedures

The DBA is responsible for establishing procedures for daily startup of the DBMS (if necessary), smooth running of database operations, logging of transactions, periodic dumps, security and authorization procedures, recording hardware and software failures, taking performance measurements, shutting down the database in an orderly fashion in case of failure, restarting and recovering after failure, and shutting down at the end of each day (if necessary). Since these procedures are performed by operators, the DBA must consult with the operations manager to ensure that operators are trained in all aspects of database operations.

- Doing user training

End users, application programmers, and systems programmers who access the database should participate in training programs so that they can learn to use it most effectively. Sessions may be conducted by the DBA, the vendor of the DBMS, or other technical trainers, either on-site or in a training center.

Ensuring Best Database Performance

- Monitoring performance

The DBA is responsible for collecting and analyzing statistics on database performance and responding to user complaints and suggestions regarding performance. The running time for applications and the response time for on-line queries should be measured, so that the DBA can spot problems in database use. Usually, the DBMS provides facilities for recording this information. The DBA continually compares performance to requirements and makes adjustments when necessary.

- Tuning and reorganizing

If performance begins to degrade as changes are made to the stored data, the DBA may respond by adding or changing indexes, reorganizing files, using faster storage devices, or optimizing software. For serious performance problems, he or she may have to change the physical model and reload the entire database.

- Keeping current on database improvements

The DBA should be aware of new features and new versions of the current DBMS that become available. He or she should evaluate these new products and other hardware and software developments to determine whether they would provide substantial benefits to the organization.

2.5.2 *DBA Staff*

Because of the many tasks involved, database administration may be assigned to an office of database administration rather than to a single person. Figure 2.8 shows possible staff positions in an office of database administration. The size of the staff depends on the phase of the database project, the size of the organization, the importance of the database within the organization, the sophistication of its data processing operations, the sophistication of users, and the number and complexity of applications using the database. In large organizations with sophisticated data processing needs, several people may be assigned to each function. In a small organization, a single DBA may be responsible for all of these tasks.

2.5.3 *Placement of the DBA*

Because the DBA must impose restrictions on users, and standards on programmers, operations staff, and systems designers, he or she must have an organizational placement that facilitates these tasks. An organization's choice for DBA placement may depend on the type of operations it performs, the management style within the organization, the importance of the database and the applications, the sophistication of data processing functions, and the personality of the DBA. The DBA should be at least on the level of the managers of the departments with which he or she works, and preferably on a staff level, reporting directly to the director of data processing or director of information systems. It is not desirable to have the DBA placed too high in the organization, because that would make it difficult for him or her to be involved in daily activities and problems related to database operations. Figure 2.9 shows some typical organizational placements for the DBA. Figure 2.9(a) is the preferred one, showing the DBA as a staff function reporting directly to the DP director, independent of the systems, operations, and applications development functions, which report to the same director. Figure 2.9(b) shows the DBA in line with the systems, operations, and applications development managers. This is the lowest acceptable level for the DBA function. Figure 2.9(c) shows a lower but undesirable position, with the DBA serving as a support function for applications development. In this position, the DBA designs and manages a database

POSITION	RESPONSIBILITIES
Operations Expert	. Communicate with operations staff . oversee creation and loading of database . arrange operator training program for database operations . establish and enforce standard operating procedures for the database . establish, enforce, and evaluate security, privacy, backup and recovery procedures . investigate performance problems
User Representative	. interview users to determine requirements . communicate user requirements to DBA . arrange for user training . determine impact of changes on users . help users adjust to changes
Documentation Manager	. develop and maintain data dictionary . record changes to data dictionary . maintain other database design documents . develop and publish data standards
Applications Expert	. identify entities, attributes, relations . work with users to develop logical design . estimate usage frequency . implement applications . develop and enforce application program standards . assist in development of new applications . assess impact of changes to applications
DBMS Expert	. know the DBMS and all its features . serve as consultant to users & programmers in use of data manipulation language . estimate performance of queries . assist users in designing queries . evaluate new DBMS features & new versions . assist in tuning system . provide feedback to DBMS vendor
Auditor	. obtain usage statistics . identify security defects . track attempted security violations
Systems Expert	. estimate performance of physical models . choose hardware and software configuration for database . install the database . tune the system when necessary . consult with operations expert to set up security, privacy, backup and recovery procedures . consult with applications expert to implement applications and identify causes of problems in program execution

Figure 2.8 DBA Staff and Functions

for the support of a particular project and does not have an organization-wide view of data. In Figure 2.9(d) the DBA is parallel to the DP director, a position that is too high in the organization for the DBA to be involved with day-to-day database operations.

2.6 *The Data Administrator*

In large organizations where several databases may coexist, a distinction should be made between the data administration function and the database administration function. A **data administrator (DA)** is responsible for the entire information resource of an organization. The DA develops the functional requirements for databases. He or she performs the nontechnical tasks and develops the logical design for each database project. The DA should control and manage all of the organization's databases, establish organization-wide data standards, communicate with users, do logical database design, develop a data dictionary system for the organization, plan for development of databases and applications, conduct user training, and develop documentation. The DA serves as a liaison between users and the data processing staff. A database administrator is responsible for one or more databases within the organization, and concentrates on the more technical issues. The DBA does the physical design of the database, monitors performance, tunes the database, and performs other technical tasks related to a specific DBMS.

2.7 *Chapter Summary*

An organization's operational data is a **corporate resource**, an asset that is of value to the organization and incurs cost. A database, which is shared by many users, protects operational data by providing data security, integrity and reliability controls, and professional management by a DBA.

Data means facts, while **information** is processed data in a form useful for making decisions. There are three levels of discussion about data: **reality** (the real world), **metadata** (data about data), and **database data** (data instances). In the real world we identify **entities, entity sets, attributes**, and **relationships**. The structure of the database is called the **logical model of the database**. The database **schema**, a description of the structure, is recorded in the data dictionary. The data dictionary contains **metadata**, or data about data, and it tells us what **record types**, **data item types**, and **data aggregates** exist in the database. The database itself contains **data instances** or occurrences. There is a record in the database for each entity in the real world. A **file** is a named collection of record occurrences.

A staged approach to database design is a top-down approach that allows the designer to develop a logical model that mirrors the operations of the organization, allows changes, supports many user views, is independent of physical implementation, and does not depend on the model of a particular DBMS. This approach, unlike the traditional

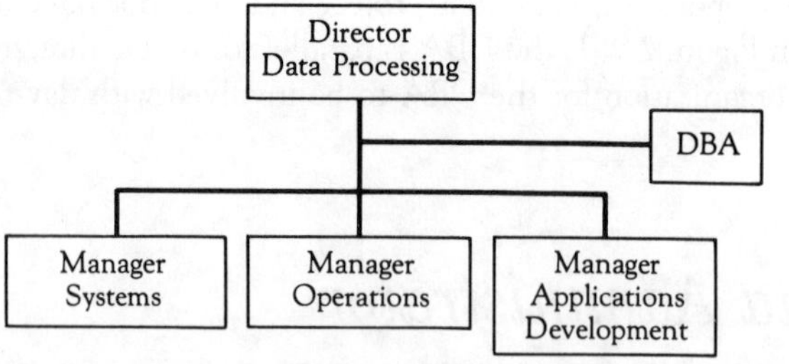

(a) DBA as Staff Function Reporting Directly to DP Director

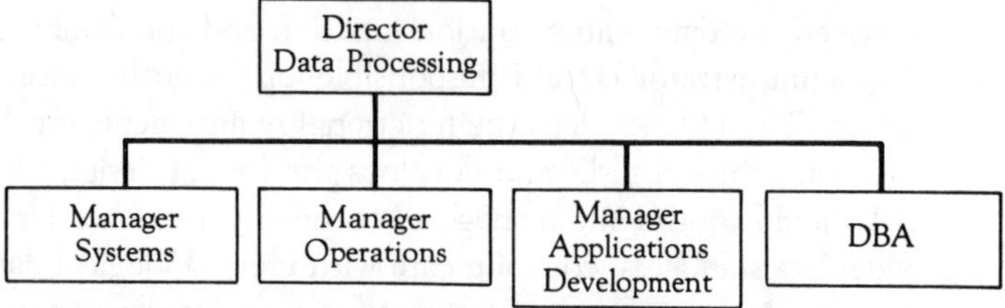

(b) DBA as Line Manager Parallel to Other line Organizations

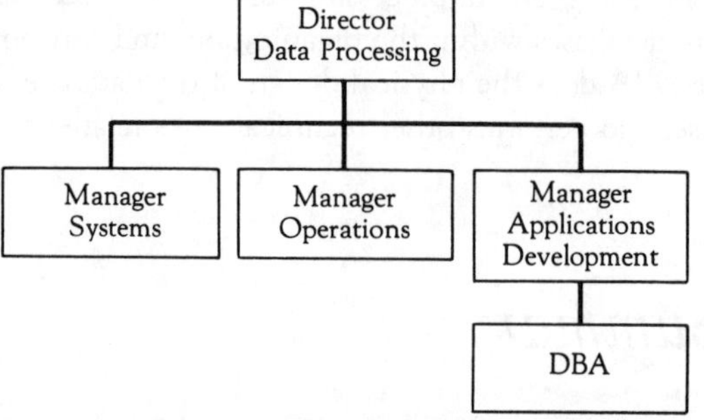

(c) DBA as Applications Support Reporting to Applications Development Manager

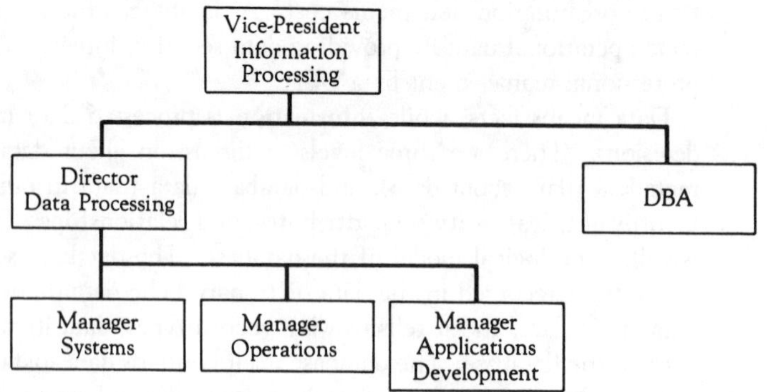

(d) DBA Parallel to DP Director, Reporting to Vice-President of Information Processing

Figure 2.9

systems analysis life cycle approach, allows the database to evolve as needs change. In staged database design the designer must analyze the user environment, develop a logical data model, choose the DBMS, map the logical model to the DBMS, develop the physical model, evaluate the physical model, perform tuning if needed, and implement the physical model. Steps may be repeated until the design is satisfactory. **Data flow diagrams** and **data dictionaries** are useful design tools. A data flow diagram is a graphical depiction of the flow of data through an organization. Different levels of detail are shown in the three types of data flow diagrams: **context, Diagram 0,** and **detailed DFDs**. A data dictionary may be **integrated** (part of the DBMS) or **freestanding** (independent of a DBMS). An integrated data dictionary may be **active** or **passive**. A data dictionary is useful for collecting information about data in a central location, securing agreement about data item meanings, communicating with users, identifying redundancy and inconsistency, recording changes to database structure, determining the impact of such changes, identifying sources of and responsibility for the correctness of items, recording external, logical, and physical models and their mappings, recording access control information, and providing audit information.

The **Database Administrator** must be technically competent, a good manager, a skilled diplomat, and have excellent communication skills. He or she has primary responsibility for planning the database, developing the operating database, and ensuring best database performance. The size of the DBA staff varies with time and the needs of the organization. The placement of the DBA also varies but is often a staff position reporting directly to the director of data processing. Large organizations with many databases may have a **Data Administrator,** who is responsible for the entire information resource, as well as one or more database administrators.

2.8 *Exercises*

1. Name four resources of a typical business organization.

2. Identify the three levels of abstraction in discussing data. For each, give an example of an object that appears on that level.

3. Distinguish between an entity set and an entity instance, giving an example of each.

4. Distinguish between a record type and a record occurrence, giving an example of each.

5. What level of data abstraction is represented in the data dictionary? Give examples of the types of entries that would be stored there.

6. Name and describe the six stages in a typical system life cycle, along with the activities and possible outcomes of each.

7. Name the eight major design stages in staged database design, along with the activities and possible outcomes of each.

8. Explain what is meant by saying that staged database design is a "top-down" method.

9. Explain how a CASE package can be used in database design.

10. Distinguish between logical and physical data flow diagrams, giving an example of an entry on each.

11. Name two advantages and two disadvantages of
a) integrated data dictionaries
b) freestanding data dictionaries

12. Explain why users should not have access to the data dictionary.

13. Give five examples of data dictionary entries.

14. What types of skills must a database administrator possess? For what tasks are they needed?

15. Identify five possible positions in a DBA's office along with the major responsibilities of each.

16. Describe a typical placement of the DBA position in an organization, explain the advantages of that placement, and describe the disadvantages of higher or lower placement.

17. Distinguish between a data administrator and a database administrator.

18. Define each of the following terms.
(a) operational data
(b) corporate resource
(c) metadata
(d) entity
(e) attribute
(f) data item
(g) data aggregate
(h) data record
(i) data file
(j) system life cycle
(k) prototype
(l) system tuning
(m) CASE
(n) DFD
(o) integrated data dictionary
(p) active data dictionary
(q) data dictionary synonyms
(r) data dictionary homonyms
(s) data standards
(t) DA
(u) DBA

2.9 Bibliography

Albano, A., V. DeAntonellis and A. diLeva (Ed.). *Computer-Aided Database Design: The DATAID Project*. North-Holland, 1985.

Atre, S. *Data Base: Structured Techniques for Design, Performance, and Management*. New York: John Wiley & Sons, 1980.

Brackett, M. *Developing Data Structured Databases*. Englewood Cliffs, NJ: Prentice-Hall, 1987.

Brathwaite, K. *Data Administration*. New York: John Wiley & Sons, 1985.

Brodie, M., J. Mylopoulos, and J. Schmidt (Ed.). *On Conceptual Modeling*. New York: Springer-Verlag, 1984.

Ceri, S. (Ed.). *Methodology and Tools for Database Design*. North-Holland, 1983.

DeMarco, T. *Structured Analysis and System Specifications*. New York: Yourdan, 1979.

Gane, C., and T. Sarson. *Structured Systems Analysis: Tools and Techniques*. New York: Improved System Technologies, 1977.

Gillenson, M. *Database Step-by-Step*. New York: John Wiley & Sons, 1985.

Hawryszkiewycz, I. *Database Analysis and Design*. Chicago: Science Research Associates, 1984.

Howe, D. *Data Analysis for Data Base Design*. London: Edward Arnold, 1983.

Inmon, W. *Effective Data Base Design*. Englewood Cliffs, NJ: Prentice-Hall, 1980.

Leeson, M. *Systems Analysis and Design*. Chicago: Science Research Associates, 1985.

Litton, G. *Introduction to Database Management: A Practical Approach*. Dubuque, IA: Wm. C. Brown, 1987.

McFadden, F. and J. Hoffer. *Data Base Management*. Menlo Park, CA: Benjamin/Cummings, 1988.

Pratt, P., and J. Adamski. *Database Systems: Management and Design*. Boston: Boyd & Fraser, 1987.

Teague, L. Jr., and C. Pidgeon. *Structured Analysis Methods for Computer Information Systems*. Chicago: Science Research Associates, 1985.

Teorey T., and J. Fry. *Design of Database Structures*. Englewood Cliffs, NJ: Prentice-Hall, 1982.

Tsichritzis, D., and F. Lochovsky. *Data Models*. Englewood Cliffs, NJ: Prentice-Hall, 1982.

Uhrowczik, P. "Data Dictionary/Directories," IBM Systems Journal 12:4 (December, 1973) pp. 332-350.

Weldon, J. *Data Base Administration*. New York: Plenum, 1981.

Wiederhold, G. *Database Design*. New York: McGraw-Hill, 1983.

SAMPLE PROJECT: DESIGNING THE DATA FLOW DIAGRAM AND CREATING THE DATA DICTIONARY FOR CLERICALTEMPS

Step 2.1:

Draw a data flow diagram for the organization.

Figure 2.10 shows a context DFD for ClericalTemps, and Figure 2.11 is a Diagram 0 representation of the system.

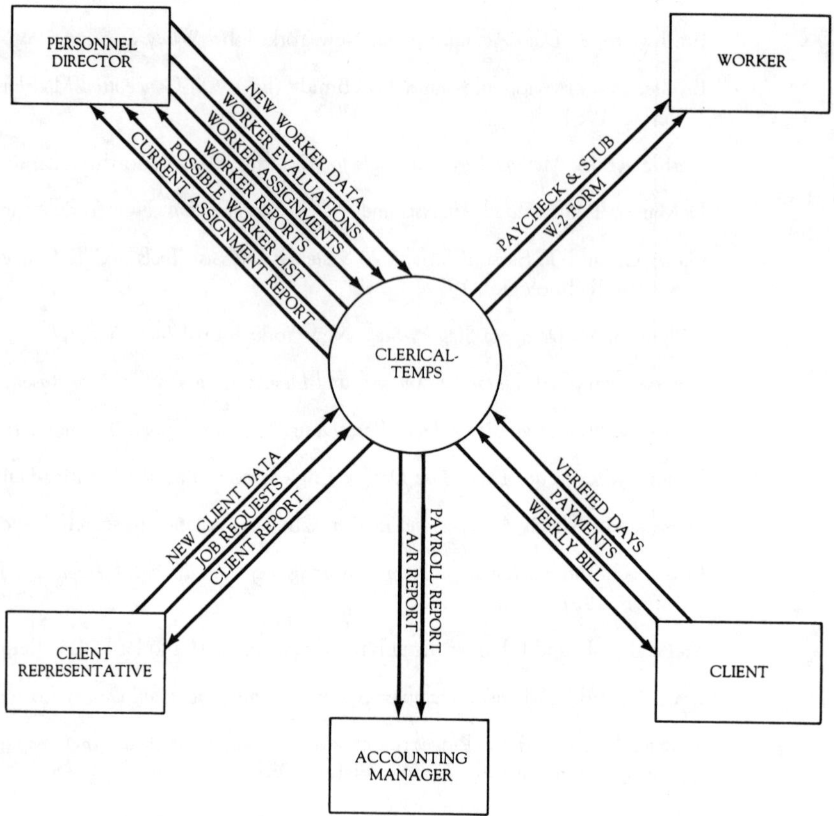

Figure 2.10

Step 2.2:

Write out a user-oriented data dictionary, consisting of an alphabetical list of every data item referenced in any report or routine transaction and an informal definition for each item.

The ClericalTemps user-oriented data dictionary is as follows:

AVAILCODE: A code that tells what days a worker is available to work during the current month.

AVERRATING: The weighted average of the individual job ratings the worker has received during the six-month period evaluated.

BILLDATE: The date of the weekly bill sent to a client.

BILLINGYTD: The total amount of all weekly billings sent to a client for the current year.

BOOKKPING: The skill level of worker in bookkeeping.

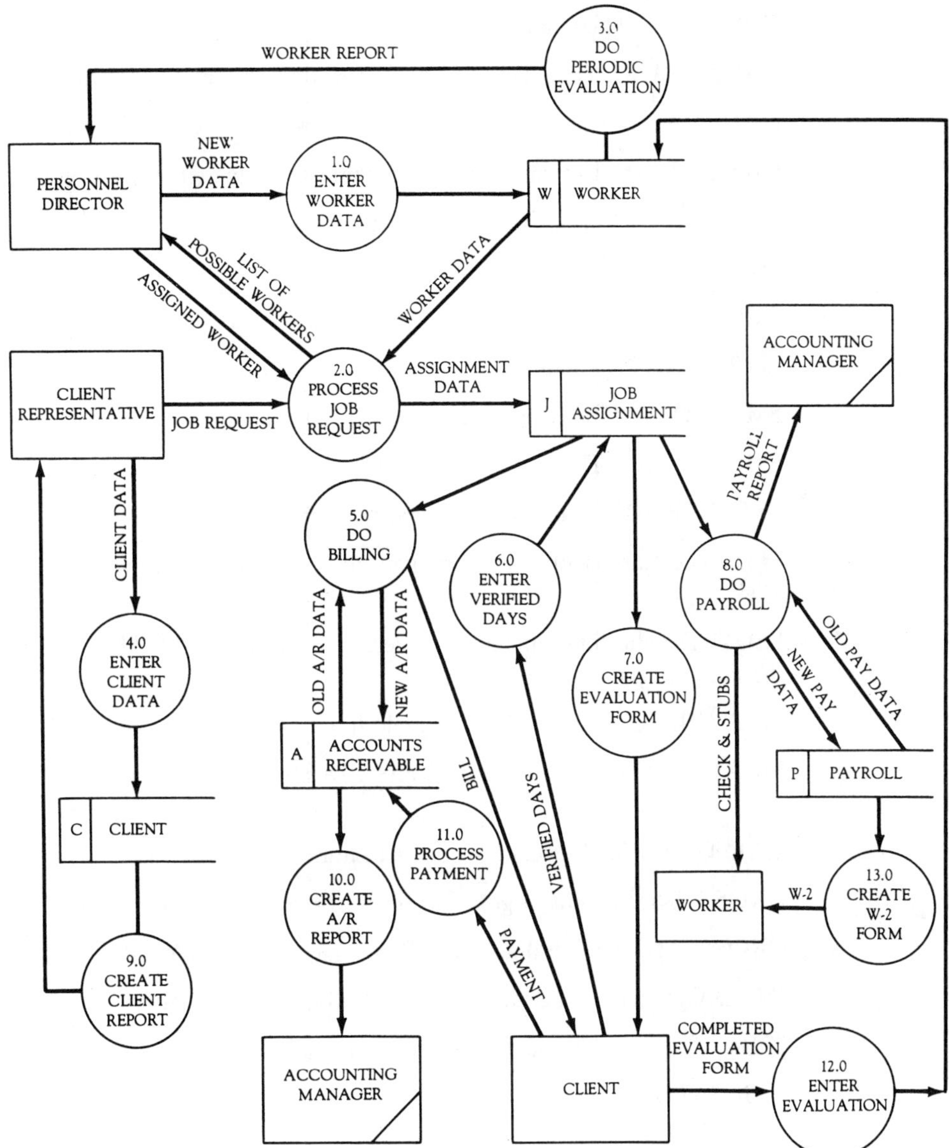

Figure 2.11

CHECK#: The unique number on the weekly payroll check sent to a worker.

CLADD: The address of the client.

CLID: The unique identifier assigned to each client.

CLNAME: The name of the client.

CLPHONE: The telephone number of the client.

CONTACT: The name of the contact person for a client.

DAILYHOURS: The daily schedule of working hours for a particular job.

DAILYRATE: The amount of money a worker will be paid for a particular job.

DATEHIRED: The date a worker became an active employee of ClericalTemps.

DOB: The date of birth of the worker.

EMPADD: The worker's address.

EMPID: The unique identifier assigned to a worker.

EMPNAME: The name of the worker.

EMPPHONE: The telephone number of the worker.

EMPRATING: The rating given by a client to a worker after completing a specific job.

EXPECTENDDATE: The expected termination date for a specific job.

FED: The amount of federal income tax withheld from a worker's pay for a specific week.

FEDYTD: The total amount of federal income tax withheld from a worker's pay for the current year.

FICA: The amount of FICA withheld from a worker's pay for a specific week.

FICAYTD: The total amount of FICA withheld from a worker's pay for the current year.

FILING: The skill level of a worker in filing.

GROSS: The amount of gross pay for a worker for a specific week.

GROSSYTD: The total amount of gross pay for a worker for the current year.

INVOICE#: A unique identifier for each bill sent to a client.

JOB#: A unique identifier assigned to each job request.

JOBSTATUS: The current status of the job request: open, assigned, unfilled, in progress, or completed.

JOBTITLE: The job title associated with a specific job request.

LASTDATEWORKED: The last date of the most recent job assignment for a worker.

LOCAL: The amount of local income taxes withheld from a worker's pay for a specific week.

LOCALYTD: The total amount of local income taxes withheld from a worker's pay for the current year.

NET: The amount of net pay for a worker for a specific week.

NETYTD: The total amount of net pay for a worker for the current year.

NEWBAL: The new balance the client owes ClericalTemps, calculated by adding TOTCHARGES to OLDBAL.

NUM-DAYS-WORKED: The number of days a worker has spent on a specific job assignment during a specific week.

OLDBAL: The amount a client owes ClericalTemps from a previous invoice.

PAYDATE: The closing date for a weekly payroll and for a weekly report of days worked.

PAYMENTSYTD: The total amount a client has paid ClericalTemps for the current year.

RATERNAME: The name of the person filling out a rating form for a worker for a particular job.

RATINGDATE: The date a client filled out a rating form for a particular worker's performance on a single job.

REPORTTOADD: The address to which a worker should report for a specific job.

REPORTTONAME: The name of the person to whom a worker should report for a specific job.

REPORTTOPHONE: The telephone number of the person to whom a worker should report for a specific job.

SEX: The sex of the worker.

SSN: The social security number of the worker.

STARTDATE: The date a particular job starts.

STATE: The amount of state income tax withheld from a worker's pay for a specific week.

STATEYTD: The total amount of state income tax withheld from a worker's pay for the current year.

STENO: The skill level of a worker in stenography.

TOTCHARGES: The amount of money a client is billed for a particular invoice.

TOTPAID: The amount of money a client has paid for a particular invoice.

TYPING: The skill level of a worker in typing.

WKTOTALFED: The total federal tax deducted from all workers' pay for a single week's payroll.

WKTOTALFEDYTD: The year-to-date total federal tax deducted from all workers' pay as of a particular week.

WKTOTALFICA: The total FICA tax deducted from all workers' pay for a single week's payroll.

WKTOTALFICAYTD: The year-to-date total FICA deducted from all workers' pay as of a particular week.

WKTOTALGROSS: The total gross pay of all workers for a single week's payroll.

WKTOTALGROSSYTD: The year-to-date total gross pay of all workers as of a particular week.

WKTOTALLOCAL: The total local tax deducted from all workers' pay for a single week's payroll.

WKTOTALLOCALYTD: The year-to-date total local tax deducted from all workers' pay as of a particular week.

WKTOTALNET: The total net pay of all workers for a single week's payroll.

WKTOTALNETYTD: The year-to-date total net pay of all workers as of a particular week.

WKTOTALSTATE: The total state tax deducted from all workers' pay for a single week's payroll.

WKTOTALSTATEYTD: The year-to-date total state tax deducted from all workers' pay as of a particular week.

WORDPROC: The skill level of a worker in word processing.

Step 2.3:

Draw a cross-reference table showing which data items appear on which documents, reports, or transactions.

Figure 2.12 shows the cross-reference table for ClericalTemps. It is constructed by listing all the documents, reports, and transactions for the system along the top of the table, and all the data items from the data dictionary along the side. A check mark in the item row indicates that the item appears on the document named at the top of the column.

Student Project: Applying Planning Techniques

For the project you have chosen from those described at the end of Chapter 1, carry out the following steps, using the Sample Project as a guide:

Step 2.1:

Draw a data flow diagram (Diagram 0) for the new system.

Step 2.2:

Write out a user-oriented data dictionary, consisting of an alphabetical list of every data item referenced in any document, report, or routine transaction and an informal definition for each item.

	APPLICATION FORM	CLIENT REGISTRATION	JOB REQUEST	EVALUATION	CLIENT REPORT	WORKER REPORT	CURRENT ASSIGNMENTS	A/R	CLIENT BILL	VERIFICATION OF DAYS	PAYROLL	PAY STUB	W-2	WORKER ENTRY/EDIT	CLIENT ENTRY/EDIT	JOB ENTRY/ WORKER SEARCH	EVALUATION ENTRY/EDIT
AVAILCODE	✓					✓								✓			
AVERRATING						✓								✓		✓	
BILLDATE								✓	✓								
BILLINGYTD					✓			✓									
BOOKKPING	✓					✓								✓		✓	
CHECK#												✓					
CLADD		✓	✓	✓	✓		✓	✓	✓						✓	✓	
CLID		✓	✓	✓	✓	✓	✓	✓	✓	✓					✓	✓	✓
CLNAME		✓	✓	✓	✓	✓	✓	✓	✓						✓	✓	
CLPHONE		✓	✓	✓											✓	✓	
CONTACT		✓	✓												✓	✓	
DAILYHOURS			✓				✓										
DAILYRATE			✓				✓		✓							✓	
DATEHIRED	✓					✓								✓			
DOB	✓					✓								✓			
EMPADD	✓					✓					✓	✓		✓		✓	
EMPID				✓		✓	✓		✓	✓	✓	✓	✓	✓		✓	✓
EMPNAME	✓			✓		✓	✓		✓	✓	✓	✓	✓	✓		✓	✓
EMPPHONE	✓					✓								✓		✓	
EMPRATING				✓		✓											✓
EXPECT-ENDDATE			✓				✓									✓	
FED											✓	✓					
FEDYTD											✓	✓	✓				
FICA											✓	✓					
FICAYTD											✓	✓	✓				
FILING	✓					✓								✓		✓	
GROSS											✓	✓					
GROSSYTD											✓	✓	✓				
INVOICE#										✓							
JOB#			✓	✓		✓	✓		✓	✓						✓	✓
JOBSTATUS																✓	
JOBTITLE		✓	✓	✓		✓	✓		✓							✓	
LASTDATEWORKED						✓										✓	
LOCAL												✓					
LOCALYTD											✓	✓	✓				
	1	2	3	4	5	6	7	8	9	10	11	12	13	14	15	16	17

Document, Report, or Transaction

Figure 2.12(a)

	APPLICATION FORM	CLIENT REGISTRATION	JOB REQUEST	EVALUATION	CLIENT REPORT	WORKER REPORT	CURRENT ASSIGNMENTS	A/R	CLIENT BILL	VERIFICATION OF DAYS	PAYROLL	PAY STUB	W-2	WORKER ENTRY/EDIT	CLIENT ENTRY/EDIT	JOB ENTRY/ WORKER SEARCH	EVALUATION ENTRY/EDIT
NET											✓	✓					
NETYTD											✓	✓					
NEWBAL									✓								
NUM-DAYS-WORKED										✓	✓	✓					
OLDBAL									✓								
PAYDATE											✓	✓					
PAYMENTSYTD					✓			✓									
RATERNAME				✓													✓
RATING DATE				✓													✓
REPORT-TO-ADD		✓														✓	
REPORT-TO-NAME		✓														✓	
REPORT-TO-PHONE		✓														✓	
SEX	✓					✓								✓			
SSN	✓										✓	✓	✓	✓		✓	
STARTDATE		✓		✓			✓									✓	✓
STATE											✓	✓					
STATEYTD											✓	✓	✓				
STENO	✓					✓								✓		✓	
TOTCHARGES								✓	✓								
TOTPAID								✓	✓								
TYPING	✓					✓								✓		✓	
WKTOTALFED											✓						
WKTOTALFICA											✓						
WKTOTALGROSS											✓						
WKTOTALLOCAL											✓						
WKTOTALNET											✓						
WKTOTALSTATE											✓						
WKTOTALFEDYTD											✓						
WKTOTALFICAYTD											✓						
WKTOTALGROSSYTD											✓						
WKTOTALLOCALYTD											✓						
WKTOTALNETYTD											✓						
WKTOTALSTATEYTD											✓						
WORDPROC	✓					✓								✓		✓	
	1	2	3	4	5	6	7	8	9	10	11	12	13	14	15	16	17

Document, Report, or Transaction

Figure 2.12(b)

Step 2.3:

Draw a cross-reference table showing which items appear on which documents, reports, or transactions.

CHAPTER

3

Physical Data Organization

3 Chapter Objectives

In this chapter you will learn

- the types of storage devices used for databases
- the characteristics of various storage devices
- some techniques for improving efficiency in disk storage
- why and how records are blocked
- record formats for fixed-length and variable-length records
- basic file organizations and access methods: sequential, indexed sequential, direct, virtual sequential
- data structures for databases: inverted files, linked lists, trees, B+ trees, B trees

3.1 *File Organization*

The tasks of storing and retrieving records in a database are handled by the database management system and the operating system access methods. Normally, the user is unaware of the methods used to locate and store data. However, the designer of the database management system, the database administrator and, in some systems, applications programmers need to be familiar with the physical organization of the database. The DBA designs the layout of data and may need to choose other physical options that affect database performance. Some database management systems require that users or programmers "navigate the database," or specify how a desired record is to be found. The purpose of this section is to summarize the file organization and processing techniques used in database management.

3.1.1 *Storage Media*

Database systems use several types of memory, but the three that are most common are disk storage, magnetic tape, and main memory. Optical disks and other devices also play a role in the database environment.

Magnetic Disk Storage

The entire database is usually stored on disk. Unlike main memory, disk storage is **nonvolatile**, not erased when the system is shut off. Disk is a **direct access storage device (DASD)**, meaning that portions of data can be accessed in any order. Magnetic disks are circular metal or plastic platters coated with a film of some easily magnetized material. Common sizes include 3 1/2, 5 1/4, 8, or 14 inches. To be used, all must be mounted on **disk drives**, which are devices that allow data to be stored and read from disk. The disks may be permanently mounted on the drives, or they may be portable. **Winchester cartridges** consist of high-capacity rigid disks in sealed housing, and **Winchester disk drives** are high-capacity units that hold portable or permanently-mounted sealed disks.

Figure 3.1(a) shows a single disk surface. Data is stored by magnetically encoding positions on concentric circles or **tracks** on the surface of the disk. Encoding and reading are performed by a **read/write head**, a small electromagnetic device that floats just above the surface and can write by magnetizing spots on the disk and read by detecting the magnetization. In movable-head disk units, the read/write head is attached to an **access arm**, a rod that can be moved across the surface. Once the head is positioned over a track, the disk is rotated so that the entire track passes under the read/write head. The combination of arm movement and disk rotation allows data to be placed or read at any position on the disk. In fixed-head units, there is a read/write head for every track.

The storage capacity of a disk is determined by its composition, its size, and its **data density**, the number of bits stored per inch of track and the number of tracks per inch of surface. The closer the read/write head can be to the surface, the higher the data density, since the magnetized spots can be smaller and still be read. In the past, dust

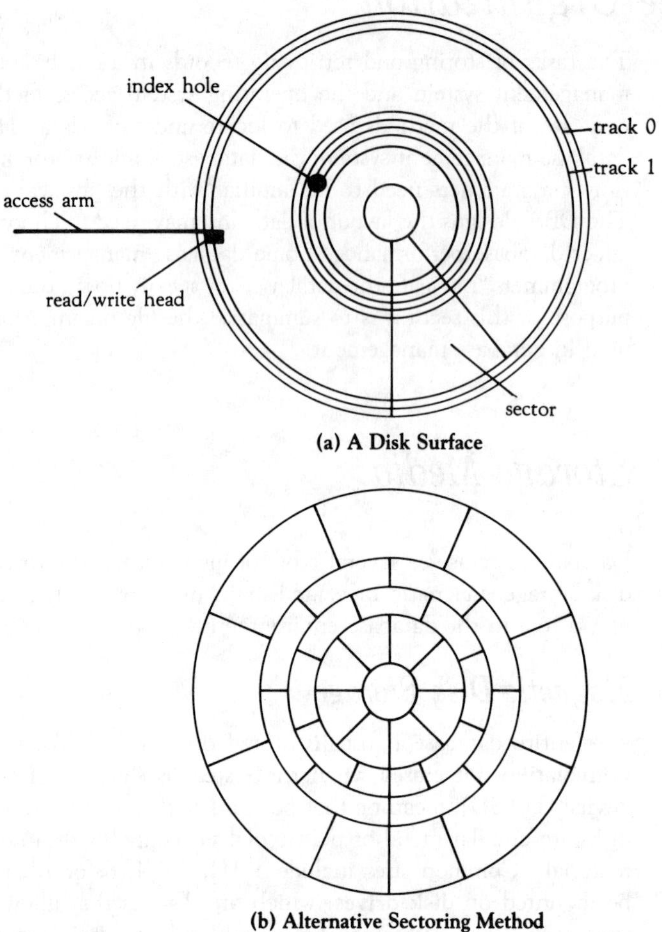

(a) A Disk Surface

(b) Alternative Sectoring Method

Figure 3.1

or smoke particles on disk surfaces posed a major problem when the read/write heads were moved closer to tracks, since a read/write head skimming within millionths of an inch of the surface could "trip" over such a comparatively large particle, bounce, and crash down on the surface, damaging the hardware and the data. Winchester technology reduces dust and smoke contamination by sealing the disk and the read/write heads in a dustproof housing.

Traditionally, a **sector** is a wedge-shaped portion of the disk surface, as shown in Figure 3.1(a). A hole in the disk called the **index hole** or **index point** marks the beginning of the track, and the system marks off sectors from that position. Disks rotate at a constant rate, with rigid disks rotating significantly faster than floppy disks, and Winchester technology allowing even greater speed. Floppy disks usually rotate in the range of 300 to 600 revolutions per minute, while hard disks range up to about 4700 rpm. The inside track of each sector is shorter than the outside track, but the amount of data recorded must be the same, since it takes the same amount of time for each track of the sector to pass under the read/write head. Therefore, the magnetized spots on the inside track are closer together than those on the outside, wasting space on the outside tracks. Some microcomputers use a slightly different sectoring method that makes all sectors have approximately the same length, as shown in Figure 3.1(b). These systems use a variable rotation rate, from 390 to 600 rpm depending on the track being accessed, and have approximately the same data density for all tracks.

In a multidisk pack, the disks are mounted on a single central spindle so that there is some space between them. When the disk pack is placed in a disk drive, the read/write heads slip between the disks. If Winchester technology is used, the heads are contained in the sealed housing with the disks. Figure 3.2 shows a disk pack with seven disks and the access arms that fit between them. Each access arm has two read/write heads, one for the surface above it and one for the surface below. The double heads allow recording on both surfaces of each disk, but normally the very top and the very bottom surfaces are not used. Therefore, although the 7-disk pack pictured actually has 14 surfaces, only 12 of them are used. The access arms are all connected to a common mechanism, the **actuator**, that causes them to move across the disk surfaces. However, they all move together. For example, if we wanted to read a record stored on track 10 of the second recording surface, the read/write heads would all move together, so that all of them would be positioned above (or below) track 10 of their respective surfaces. The set of tracks that are in the corresponding positions on their surfaces (e.g., all the track 10s) is called a **cylinder**. The number of cylinders in a disk pack is obviously the same as the number of tracks on each surface. One typical disk pack for a large system has 16 disks, with 30 recording surfaces, each having 555 tracks. In this case, the disk pack has 555 cylinders, each having 30 tracks for recording.

The time it takes to transfer data from disk to main memory is determined by the following:

- **Seek time**. The time it takes to move the read/write head to the correct track or cylinder. The closer the current position of the head is to the desired position, the shorter this will be.
- **Rotational delay time**, also called **latency time**. The time it takes to rotate the disk so that the desired data is under the read/write head.
- **Head switching time**. The time it takes to choose the correct read/write head for the surface needed. This is a factor only when there is more than one recording surface.
- **Transfer time**. The time it takes for actual movement of data from the disk to main memory.

Of these, the longest is seek time. In the worst case, the read/write heads have to move all the way across the disk. Seek time can be minimized by placing data so that the read/write head moves as little as possible. For example, suppose that a file is to be placed on a disk pack so that it can be read sequentially in the order in which it is stored. Assume that 10 records can be stored per track. Seek time would be minimized if each cylinder is filled in order, as shown in Figure 3.3(a). Note that there are blank spaces called **interrecord gaps** between records. The gaps signal the end of a record and allow time for the system to transfer data from one record before reading the next. When

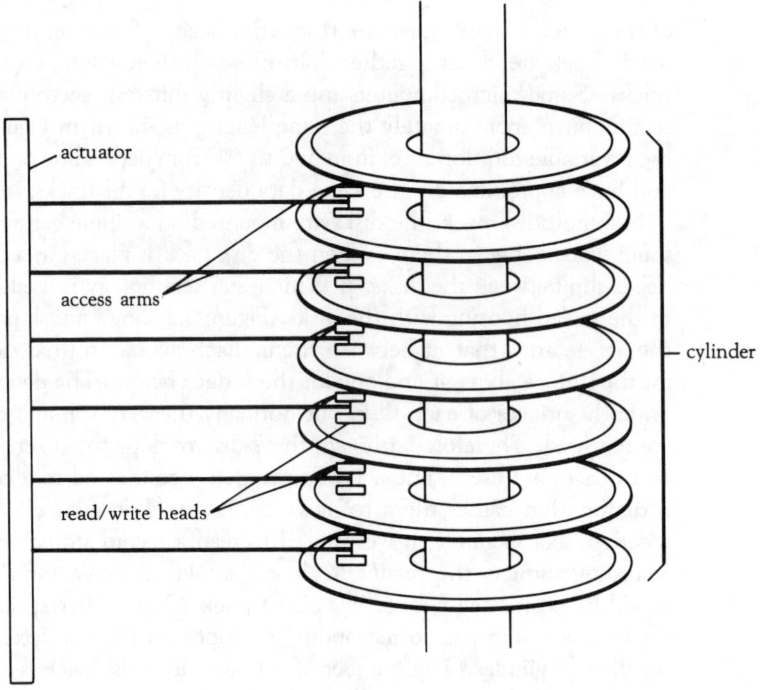

Figure 3.2

the data is read sequentially, all the records on cylinder 1 can be read without moving the access arms, followed by all the records on cylinder 2 by moving the arms just one track width, and so on. By contrast, if the data had been placed by filling up the first surface, then the second, and so on, as shown in Figure 3.3(b), reading all the records on surface 1 would require moving the access arm one track width after every 10 records, and moving all the way across the surface after finishing the previous surface. From this example it is clear that we can reduce seek time by **clustering**, placing records that are usually accessed together on the same cylinder or on adjacent cylinders whenever possible. If it is impossible to predict which records will be accessed together, we may be able to minimize seek time by placing the records most frequently accessed near the middle cylinder, as shown in Figure 3.4. This placement would guarantee that the arms would need to move at most halfway across the surface when one of these frequently used records is accessed. If read/write heads are always retracted after every operation, the data most frequently accessed should be on the outside cylinder.

Maximum rotational delay occurs when the data needed has just passed the read/write head, as shown in Figure 3.5(a). In that case, a complete rotation must be performed before the target record passes under the read/write head again. We can ensure that no more than a half-turn is required by **double-writing**, or recording each piece of data twice, diametrically opposite itself, as shown in Figure 3.5(b). With this technique, a copy of the target record will pass under the read/write head within a half rotation. This practice also improves reliability, since an error in one copy of the record is unlikely to appear in the second copy, but it doubles storage requirements. Another technique to

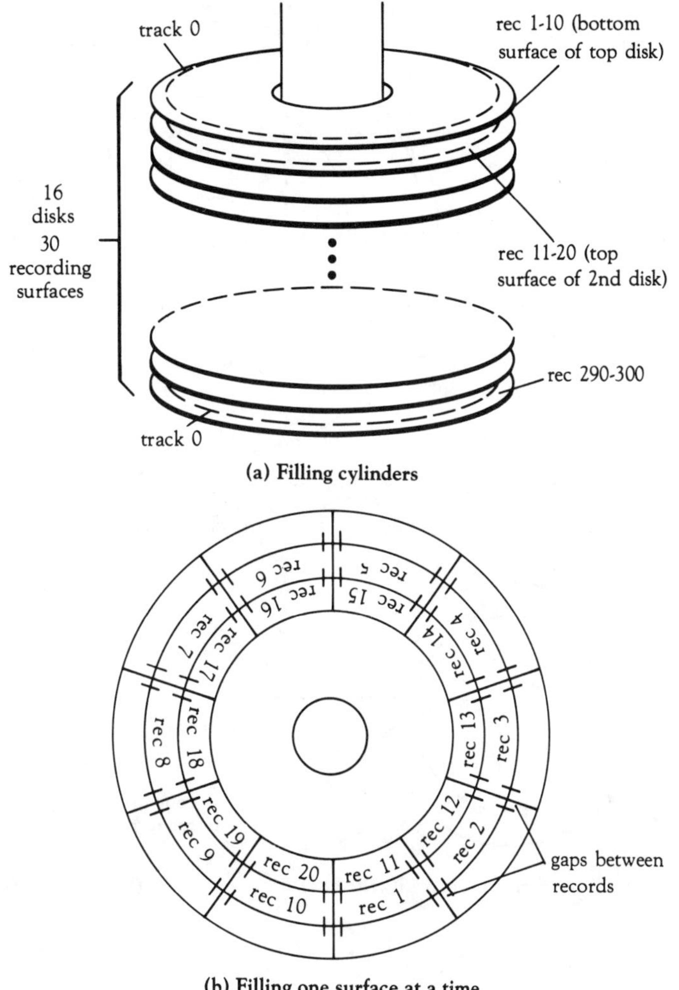

(a) Filling cylinders

(b) Filling one surface at a time

Figure 3.3

minimize rotational delay is to store records on a track in the order in which they are usually accessed, so that they pass under the read/write head in the desired sequence. Figure 3.5(c) shows the order in which records 1, 2, and 3 should be stored if they are normally accessed in that order. If we stored them as shown in Figure 3.5(d), two rotations would be needed to access them in the desired order. Time saved by double writing or ordering records within a track is much less significant than potential savings in seek time, since head movement takes much longer than rotation.

Head switching time, if needed, is minimal, requiring only an electrical switch. Transfer time depends on the device, and except for selecting faster devices, the DBA has no control over it. The storage aspects that can be controlled, such as placement of related records on the same cylinder or adjacent cylinders, double-writing, and sequencing of records on a track, allow the DBA to place records so that some applications obtain

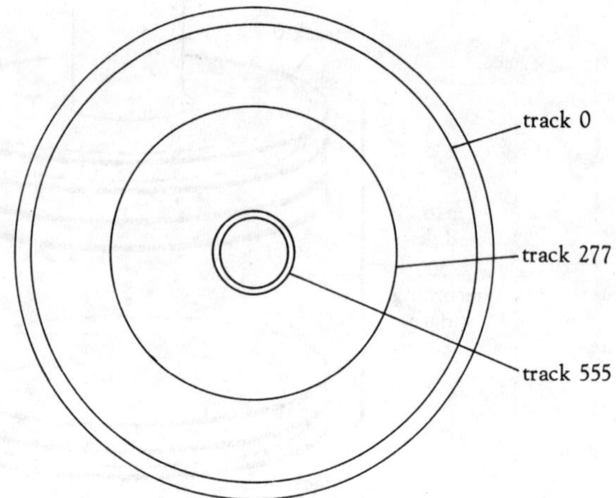

Figure 3.4

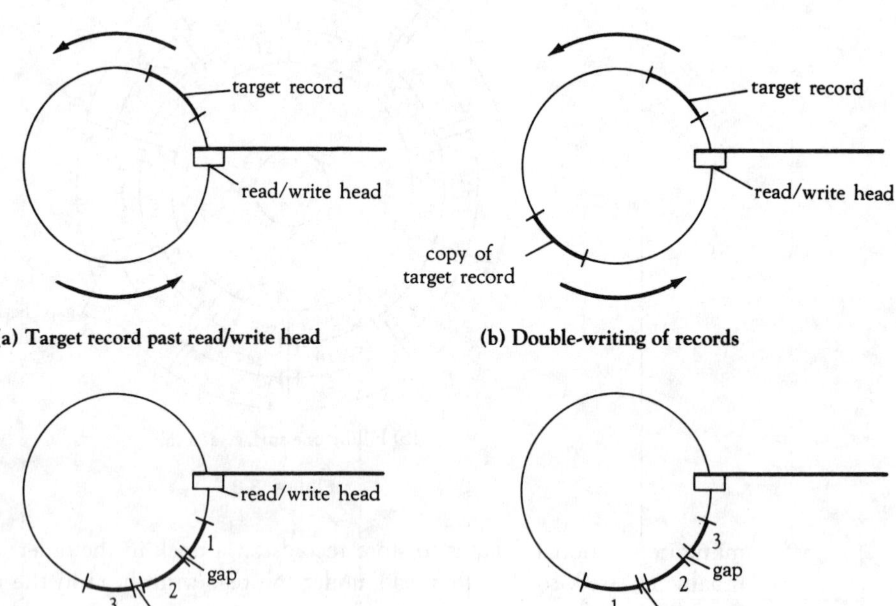

Figure 3.5

data quickly. However, applications that require records in a different sequence will be processed more slowly. The DBA has to be familiar with the needs of all users in order to choose the layout that will give the best overall performance. The sequencing or relationships most frequently used should be favored in the physical layout.

Disk is the most common type of storage for databases, but it has disadvantages caused by the technology. Although data on disk is not affected by a system failure, a major problem occurs when disk units fail and destroy data. Problems such as head crashes occur because of the mechanical movement involved in using disks. In addition, as we have seen, there are delays in accessing data caused by the movement of access arms and spinning of the disks. For situations in which time is crucial, fixed-head disk units may be used.

Magnetic Tape

Magnetic tape is a nonvolatile storage medium that provides **sequential access**, meaning that to reach a piece of data it is necessary to go through all the data before it. Tape is not used for ordinary database processing, which usually requires direct access. However, it is used extensively for storing archival data and for backups. In the event that the disk copy of the database is destroyed, the latest backup tape is used to reconstruct the database. Tape is also the medium most widely used for transferring data from one organization to another.

Magnetic tape is a plastic ribbon with an easily magnetized coating on one side. Many systems use 1/2 or 1/4-inch-wide reels of tape on which data is recorded by magnetizing spots on an iron oxide or chromium dioxide coating. The tape is vertically partitioned into columns called **frames**, and horizontally partitioned into rows called **tracks** or **channels**. Figure 3.6 illustrates a nine-track tape. To be used, a tape must be loaded on a **tape drive**, a device that has a read/write head for each track, so that an entire frame is read simultaneously as the tape passes under the heads. Different tape drives allow different **data density**, which is measured by the number of bits per inch of tape. The first few feet are blank to allow threading of the tape on a tape drive. The start of recording is indicated by a marker called the **load point**. Similarly, the last few feet at the end of the tape are left blank, and the last recorded symbol on the tape is a special **end-of-reel** marker. The recorded data itself starts with a **header control label**, giving information about the tape. Just before the end-of-reel marker is a similar **trailer control label** and a special tape mark or **end-of-file** symbol. Data records on the same tape may be the same length (**fixed-length records**) or can have different lengths (**variable-length records**). Records are separated by blank spaces called **interrecord gaps**. In a file with many short records, the interrecord gaps occupy a lot of space and can slow the reading of a file considerably. Therefore, short records are usually combined into **blocks**. Figure 3.7 shows the composition of a tape file. Tapes provide a cheap, reliable medium for storing large volumes of data. The most common reel holds 2400 feet of tape and allows hundreds of millions of characters to be stored at a very low cost. Many computer installations have vast tape libraries holding thousands of reels of tape.

Main Memory

Main memory is **volatile**, which means that it is lost when the system is shut off. It provides direct access to data stored in it. The database does not usually fit in main memory, which is limited in size and must hold not only data but systems programs and applications programs. However, any data that is to be processed must first be brought into a portion of main memory called the **buffer**. When a record is requested, the system

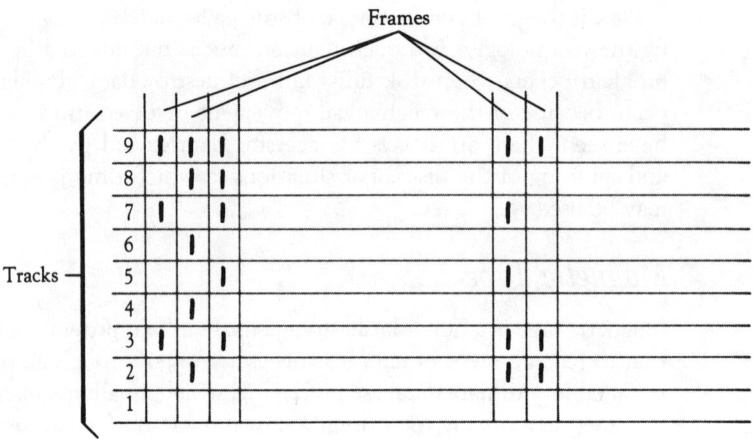

Figure 3.6

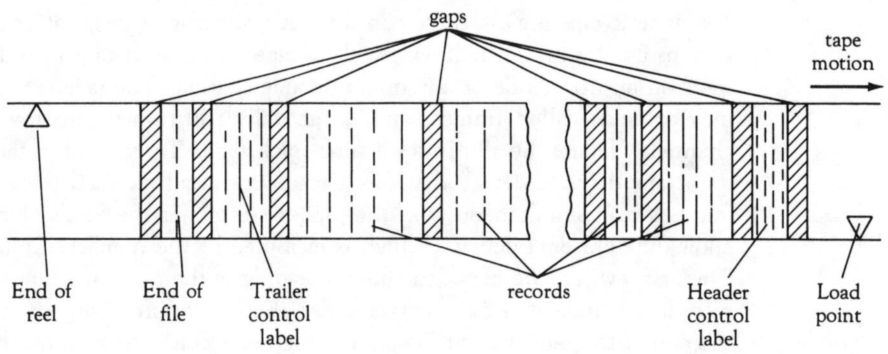

Figure 3.7

checks to see if it is already in the buffer. If so, the system simply passes the address in the buffer to the requesting process. If not, the system finds the location on disk where the record is stored and directs the reading of the record into the buffer. Actually, as we shall see in Section 3.1.2, it usually reads more than one record at a time. The system then passes the address in the buffer to the requesting process. Note that the record still exists on disk; the buffer contains a copy of it. Since accessing records in the buffer is many times faster than accessing those on disk, records that are used most frequently are sometimes kept in the buffer whenever the database is in use.

Optical Disks

Optical disks or **videodisks** can store data as well as images and sound. Laser systems can be used both to record data on the disk and to read it back. The volume of data that can be stored is enormous. Videodisk versions of reference materials such as unabridged dictionaries and encyclopedias are available on rigid 5 1/4-inch **compact disk read-only memory (CDROM)**. Optical disk is also available in 12-inch **write-once-read-many**

(**WORM**) form, which allows the user to record data that will be permanently stored. This form is useful for archival data that should never be erased, such as documents for government, legal, banking, and financial industries. Another form is 5 1/4-inch **erasable optical disk**, which allows the user to record, erase, and rewrite on the same disk repeatedly. Rigid optical disks may replace both microfilm and magnetic tape as a medium for storing archival data. Because they are still relatively slow and expensive compared with magnetic disk, they are not used for ordinary database processing at the present time. However, some manufacturers have developed an inexpensive medium called **digital paper**, which is actually a film that allows high-density digital recording. The "paper" is manufactured as flexible 5 1/4-inch diskettes that can store 1 GB (one gigabyte, a billion bytes) of data and as 12-inch optical tape reels that store 1 TB (one terabyte, a trillion bytes) of data. The storage capacity of the tape is equivalent to that of 5000 magnetic tapes. The digital paper devices have a longer storage life than magnetic media and promise access times and data transfer rates that compare with magnetic devices.

Cache Memory

A **cache** is a small portion of main memory with very-high-speed memory chips. In newer microcomputers, most of the main memory consists of **DRAM** (dynamic random-access memory) chips which have an access time of 80 to 120 nanoseconds. A small portion of the memory (32 or 64 bytes) uses much more expensive **SRAM** (static random-access memory) chips, which have an access time of 25 to 35 nanoseconds. SRAM is by nature faster than DRAM and, unlike DRAM, does not need to be "refreshed" or regenerated before being read. The result is almost instantaneous access, so that the processor is not kept waiting for data. To use cache successfully, the system has to anticipate which data will be needed next, and try to ensure that it is in cache when needed. When data is needed, the system looks in cache first and then in the slower DRAM. The higher the number of "hits," when the data needed is actually in the cache when requested, the faster the system will be. There are statistical procedures used by cache controllers to decide which items to hold in cache. For a database using hierarchical indexes (as described in Section 3.2.4), the higher levels of the index might be kept in cache whenever the database is in use.

Other Devices

Other direct-access storage devices used by database systems are **mass storage devices** and **magnetic bubble memory**. Mass storage devices use cartridges containing small rolls of magnetic tape, which are stored in cells in a honeycomb-like storage wall, as shown in Figure 3.8. When data is needed, an arm retrieves the cartridge and its data is **staged** or moved to disk. Magnetic bubble storage uses semiconductor chips which store large amounts of data by moving bubbles captured within a layer of a material such as garnet. The position of the bubbles indicates the data values stored. Once positioned, the bubbles remain in place until they are moved by the system, so that bubble memory is nonvolatile.

The range of storage devices from the fastest and most expensive primary storage components to the slowest and cheapest secondary storage devices forms a **memory hi-**

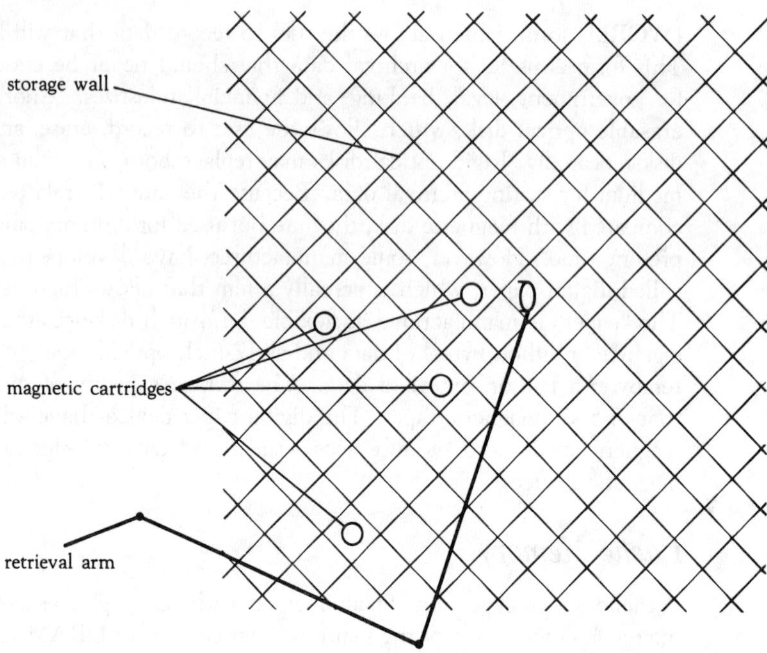

Figure 3.8

erarchy, as shown in Figure 3.9. In a very sophisticated storage management system, a database could be spread across several devices in the hierarchy, with the most active records kept in cache storage or regular main memory whenever the database is operational, slightly less active records arranged on disk according to their relative activity and relationships, still less active records in a mass storage device, and the least active on tape. This type of planning requires a careful analysis of record activity and is rarely done.

3.1.2 *Blocking*

In the section on main memory, we mentioned that the system normally reads more than one record into the buffer. This is because all data is stored and transferred in fixed-size units called **blocks** that can usually hold more than one record. A block appears to the programmer to be a contiguous set of bytes on a single track of a single disk surface. Block size is usually set by systems programmers or, for some devices (called **fixed-block architecture** devices), preset by the manufacturer. A typical block size is a multiple of 512 bytes, but a block may be as large as several thousand bytes. Figure 3.10(a) illustrates a disk in which each track contains four blocks. In this case, each disk access would bring the entire contents of approximately a quarter of a track into the buffer. A block is sometimes called a **page** or a **physical record**. If we use the term *physical record* to refer to a block, we refer to the data records we want (e.g., student records, employee records,

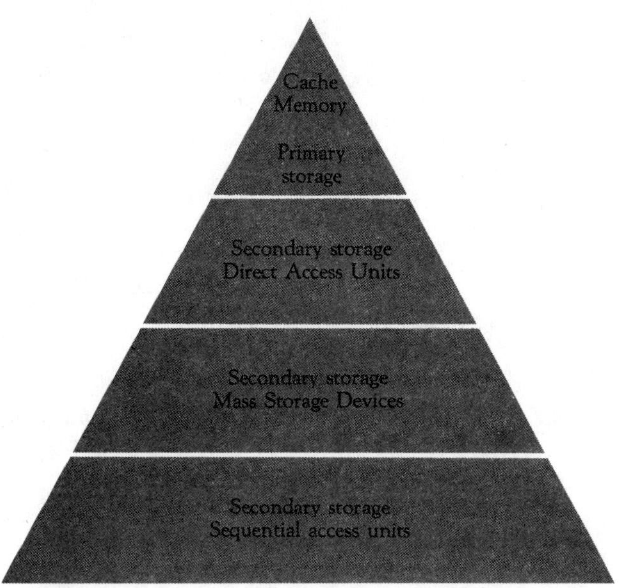

Figure 3.9

order records) as **logical records**. In general, then, one physical record will contain several logical records. The number of logical records in a block is called the **blocking factor** for a file. Figure 3.10(b) shows a block from the track in Figure 3.10(a) with a blocking factor of 3 (i.e., three records per block). The entire track would contain 12 logical records, but only four physical ones.

Blocking is done to save space. For each physical record on a track, there is a certain amount of overhead information required. At the beginning of each physical record there is a **header** containing several fields with such information as the address of the physical record (either **relative address**, which is the block number relative to the start of the file or **physical address**, which is the cylinder, head, and record number of the block), whether the track is defective, the length of the record key, the length of the data in the record, and where the record begins. These fields are separated by gaps, further increasing the number of bytes needed before usable data is found. If each physical record held just one logical record, there would be a header for each logical record. When records are blocked, there is a single header for each block. Figure 3.11(a) shows 10 unblocked records on a track, while Figure 3.11(b) shows 12 records blocked three per block on a track holding four blocks. Since the first arrangement requires 10 headers and interrecord gaps for the 10 logical (and physical) records, while the second requires only 4 headers and gaps for the 12 logical records, there is a saving in storage space. The amount of space saved depends on the size of records, the size of blocks, and the amount of overhead information required. There is a trade-off for this saving in storage. The operating system always brings an entire block into the buffer. To pass the buffer location of the desired logical record to the requesting process, the system must **deblock** or break up the block into separate logical records in the buffer. Similarly, when

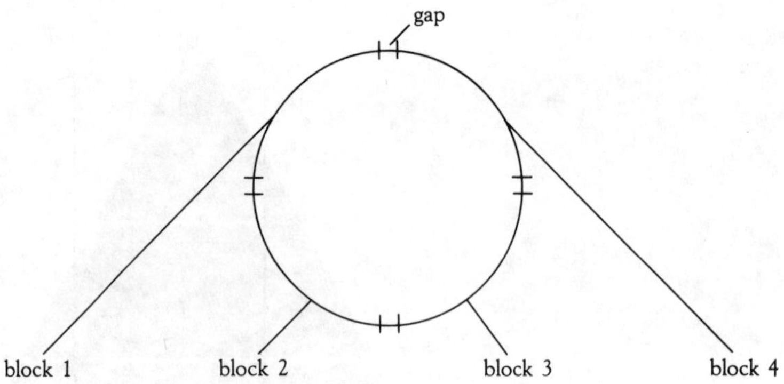

(a) Track containing 4 blocks

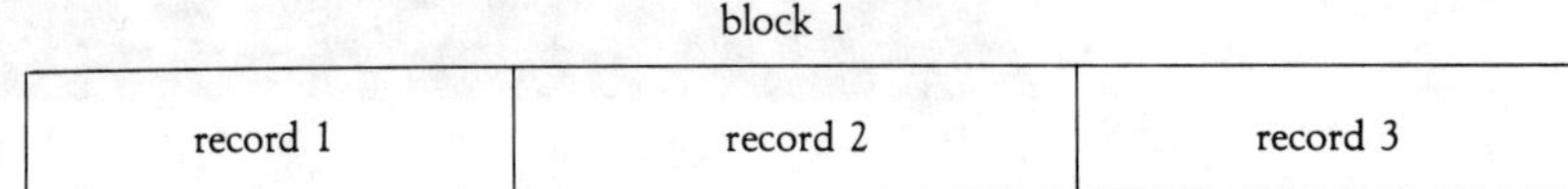

(b) A block containing 3 logical records

Figure 3.10

writing records, the system must place them in blocks in the buffer before writing them out to disk. The blocking and deblocking is additional processing that is the tradeoff for more efficient use of storage. The DBA, working with the systems programmers, may be able to choose the optimal block size(s) and blocking factor(s) for the database. If fixed-block architecture is used, block size is already determined, but the DBA may be able to tailor record sizes to block size. If there is a poor fit between record size and block size, there will be a lot of wasted space in the database.

3.1.3 *Record Formats*

In our discussion, we have assumed that all logical records have the same length. Since working with such **fixed-length records** makes it easier to create and manage files, the DBA may choose to create the database by using several files, each with one type of fixed-length record. However, the records still may not fit neatly into the block size. If there is space left over at the end of blocks, the DBA may decide to place part of a record at the end of one block and the remainder at the beginning of the next

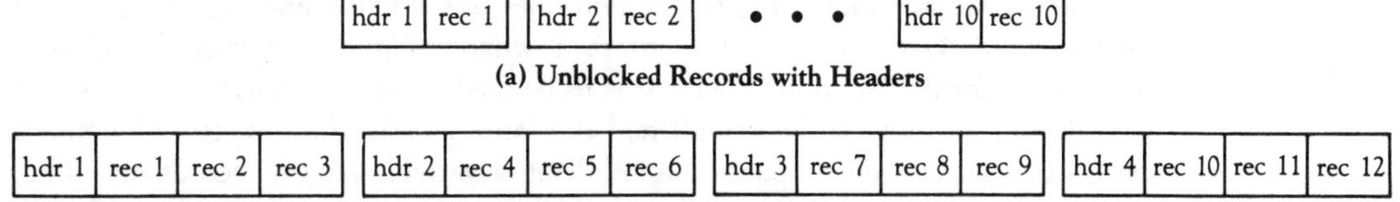

(a) Unblocked Records with Headers

(b) Blocked Records-Blocking Factor of 3

Figure 3.11

one. This technique is called **spanning** records and is illustrated in Figure 3.12(a). For simplicity, we are ignoring headers in this illustration. The problem with spanning records is that retrieving a record may require two disk accesses. A simpler solution is to leave unoccupied space at the end of the block, as shown in Figure 3.12(b). This solution, of course, wastes space.

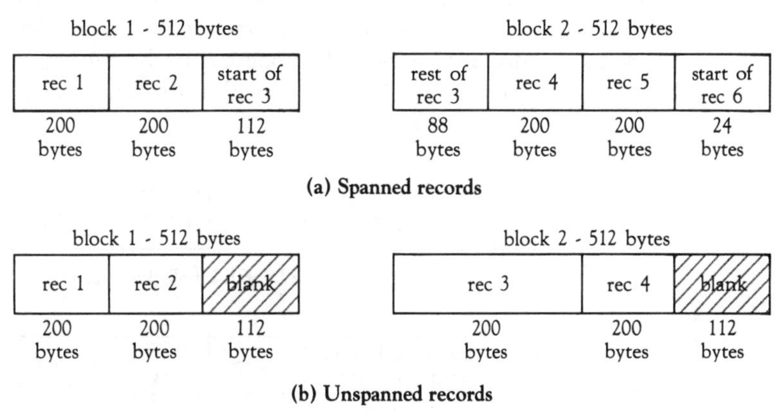

(a) Spanned records

(b) Unspanned records

Figure 3.12

Some database files may have records with different lengths, called **variable-length records**. Different record lengths result when different record types are stored in the same file (because of clustering of related records) or when records of the same type have variable-length fields or repeating fields that may occur a different number of times in different records. When the database is first loaded, variable-length records are easy to accommodate. For unblocked format, we simply add a header field showing the total length of the record, as seen in Figure 3.13(a). For blocked records, each logical record in the block is preceded by its length, as shown in Figure 3.13(b). In both cases the record header tells the system where to stop reading. One problem with this choice is that it is impossible to add additional data to a variable-length record without relocating it. For example, if we needed to add 20 more bytes to the first record in Figure 3.13(b), we would have to relocate the record to a larger space. Another problem arises when we delete a record. Normally, the system does not actually erase a record from a slot, but instead marks it as deleted and ignores it when reading. The space should, however, be available for use when an insertion is to be made, so the system keeps track of spaces from deleted records. If records all had the same length, the new record would fit the space exactly. However, spaces left by deleted variable-length records are difficult to reuse, since new records may not fit exactly in the empty slot. Generally, only a shorter record can be stored in the space left after a deletion, resulting in many empty spaces being left. A possible solution to the problem of reusing empty spaces is to identify the maximum length for records and use that fixed length for all records, leaving empty space at the end of those that are shorter than the maximum. This technique is shown in Figure 3.14(a). However, if many records are shorter than the maximum, this leads to a lot of wasted space. A better solution is to set up a **prime area** with a fixed-length record space of the most common record length and have an **overflow area** for parts of records that do not fit into the usual space. To access the overflow data, we use a **pointer**, a field that contains the address of the overflow, inserted in the prime area portion. When a record is inserted, we begin storing it in the prime area. If it is too long for the space, we put the remainder in the overflow area and use a pointer to connect the beginning of the record with its overflow. Figure 3.14(b) illustrates this choice. This method also allows a record to grow, since additional overflow space can be used as needed and connected by pointers to the existing fields of a record. It is also easy to reuse space, since every record within the same area has the same length.

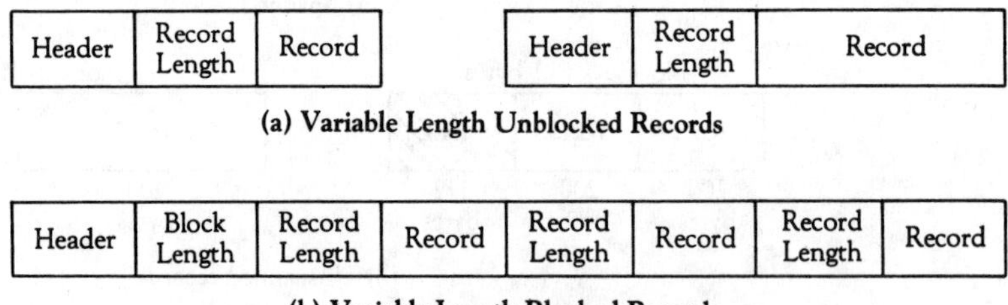

Figure 3.13

3.1.4 *File Organizations*

File organization means the way we store data so that it can be retrieved when needed. It includes the physical order and layout of records on storage devices. The techniques used to find and retrieve stored records are called **access methods**. Since the retrieval methods depend to a large extent on the way the records are stored, the terms *access method* and *file organization* are used interchangeably. The operating system provides the basic access methods and performs the actual I/O, but the DBMS is responsible for requesting this service of the operating system. Although there are many operating system access

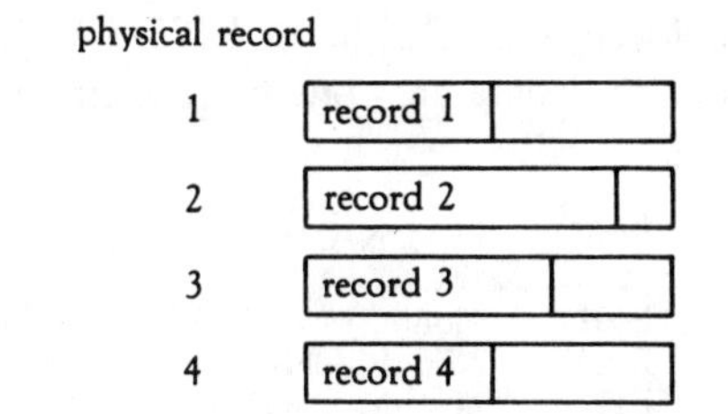

(a) Using Fixed Maximum Length for all Records

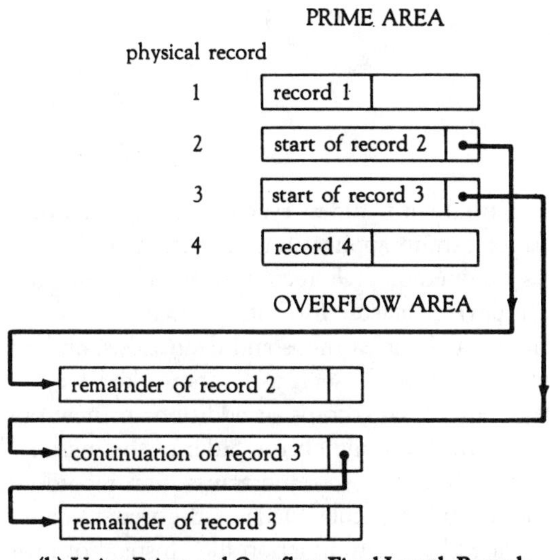

(b) Using Prime and Overflow Fixed Length Records

Figure 3.14

methods available, database processing uses three basic methods: sequential, indexed sequential, and direct.

Sequential File Organization

In **sequential file organization** records are arranged in physical sequence by the value of some field, called the **sequence field.** Often the field chosen is a **key field,** one with unique values that are used to identify records. The records are simply laid out on the storage device, often magnetic tape, in increasing or decreasing order by the value of the sequence field. For example, IBM's **Sequential Access Method (SAM),** among others, uses this organization. Figure 3.15 illustrates an employee file in sequence by EMPID, the key. This organization is simple, easy to understand, and easy to manage, but is best for providing **sequential access,** retrieving records one after another in the same order in which they are stored. It is not good for **direct** or **random access,** which means picking out a particular record, because it generally requires that we pass over prior records in order to find the target record. It is also not possible to insert a new record in the middle of the file. In Figure 3.15 we would not have room to insert a new employee with EMPID of E103. With sequential organization, record insertion, deletion, and update are done by rewriting the entire file.

EMPID	EMPNAME	JOBTITLE	DEPT	SALARY
E101	Jones, Jack	Sales Rep	Marketing	35000
E104	Smith, John	Research Asst	Research	30000
E110	Lyons, Mary	Sr Researcher	Research	50000
E115	Chin, Greg	Planner	Development	45000
E120	...	...	...	...
E125	...	...	...	...
E130	...	...	...	...
...				
...				
...				

Figure 3.15

Sequential is the oldest type of file organization and, despite its shortcomings, is well suited for certain applications. For example, a payroll program usually requires that we access every employee's record in order by EMPID. In a typical payroll application, we have a **payroll master file** with permanent information about the employee and year-to-date data about earnings and deductions, and a **payroll transaction file** holding data about the past week, such as hours worked for each employee, and any changes, such as deletions of old records or additions of new ones. The transaction file is sorted in order by EMPID to match the order of the master file. When the payroll program runs, it matches IDs of master and transaction records, computes pay and deductions, prints paychecks and pay stubs, updates the year-to-date totals, and inserts or deletes records as indicated by the transaction file. Instead of rewriting the records on the master file, it produces a new master file each week. Figure 3.16 summarizes this system, which is typical for sequential file processing.

Since much of database processing requires direct access and immediate update, insertion, or deletion of records, sequential organization is not appropriate for ordinary processing. However, it is widely used by database management systems for producing **dumps** or **backups**, copies of the database kept on tape as archival data, or in case the database must be reconstructed after a disk failure.

Indexed Sequential File Organization

We can enjoy the advantages of sequential files and still have direct access by creating an **index**, a table that tells where particular records are stored. IBM's **Indexed Sequential Access Method (ISAM)** uses this organization, and most vendors have a similar method available. Suppose that we want to keep employee records in order by EMPID because we have several applications that access them in that order, but we want to be able to locate a particular employee's record when needed. If we store the records on disk and can fit five per track, we might set up our file as shown in Figure 3.17(a). Since the file is in order by EMPID, it is easy to access the records sequentially. To provide direct access, we could create a **track index** listing every EMPID and giving the address (track number, in this case) of the record with that EMPID value. Figure 3.17(b) shows such an index. This is an example of a **dense** index, one that has an entry for every record

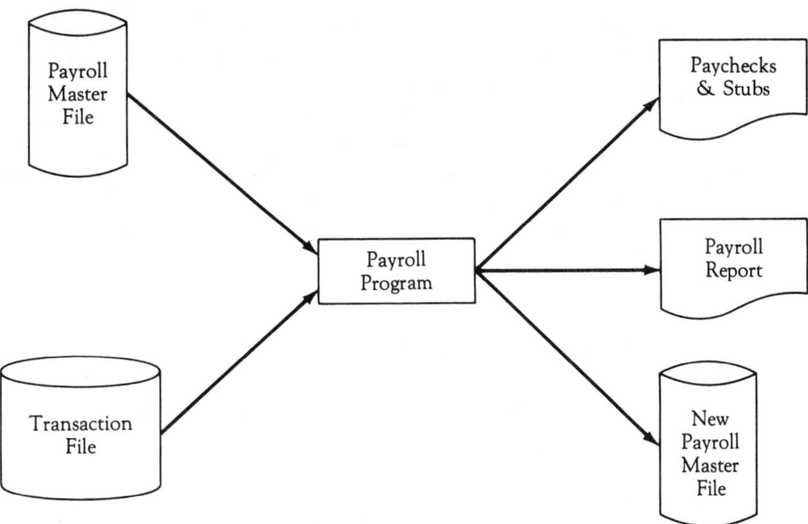

Figure 3.16

in the file. However, we can see that many of the index entries are unnecessary because we can get the same information if we list just the highest key on each track, as shown in Figure 3.17(c). This **nondense** or **sparse** index does not have an entry for every record, but it is sufficient to give the location of each one. For example, to find the record of employee E121, we notice that it cannot be on track 1 because the employee ID is higher than the highest ID on that track, E112. Since it is lower than the highest ID on track 2, E128, the record, if it exists, must be somewhere on track 2. Now we read track 2 sequentially until we either find the record or reach a record with a higher EMPID without finding it. Since a typical file occupies many tracks, the track index will be very long and searching the index may be too time consuming. Therefore we can set up another level of index, the **cylinder index.** If our employee file has 1500 records and each cylinder has 30 tracks, each holding five records, we need 10 cylinders for our file. We could set up a cylinder index that gives the highest key on each cylinder. This leads to the correct track index that lists the highest key on each track of the cylinder. Figure 3.18 illustrates the use of a cylinder index to locate a record. We could carry this process further by grouping cylinders into **volumes**, sets of cylinders on the same or different disk packs, and setting up a **volume index** or **master index** that leads to a cylinder index that leads to a track index.

The difficulties we had with insertion, deletion, or update of records in sequential file organization can be corrected with indexed sequential organization because we can limit the amount of reorganizing we need to perform. Records can be **updated in place**, simply by writing over the old record within the same track. When we delete a record, we locate the track and put a deletion flag at the beginning of the record to indicate that it should not be read. Insertion, however, requires more planning. We want to be able to insert records in sequential order, but we do not want to rewrite the entire file whenever we insert a record. For example, suppose that the file appears exactly as shown in Figure 3.17(a) and we want to insert a new employee with EMPID E103. The record belongs

```
          --------------------------------------------------------
track 1 |   E101    |   E104    |   E110    |   E115    |   E120    |
          --------------------------------------------------------
          --------------------------------------------------------
track 2 |   E125    |   E130    |   E131    |   E134    |   E138    |
          --------------------------------------------------------
          --------------------------------------------------------
track 3 |   E140    |   E143    |   E145    |   E150    |   E153    |
          --------------------------------------------------------
...
...
...
```

3.17(a) Indexed Sequential Organization

```
EMPID  |  TRACK              HIGHEST KEY    |
--------------               ON TRACK       |   TRACK
E101   |  1                  ----------------------
E104   |  1                  E120            |    1
E110   |  1                  E138            |    2
E115   |  1                  E153            |    3
E120   |  1                  ...             |    .
E125   |  2                  ...             |    .
E130   |  2                  ...             |    .
...    |  .
...    |  .
...    |  .
```

3.17(b) Dense Index **3.17(c) Nondense Track Index**

Figure 3.17 Indexed Sequential File Processing

on the first track, but we have no room for it there. If we insert it and move the other records, all remaining tracks will have to be rewritten and the index recreated. We could anticipate insertions by leaving some room, or **distributed free space**, on each track for additional records. For example, if we placed only four records on each track when the file was first created, we would have room for one additional record on each track, as shown in Figure 3.19(a). Then we could insert E103 by placing it in its correct position and shifting the other records on track 1 as shown in Figure 3.19(b). However, this is a short-term solution, since we would now have a problem if another new employee record, this time with ID E108, had to be added. To allow for an unknown number of such additions, we create an **overflow area** for records that do not fit on their correct tracks. To ensure that we can find an overflow record, we extend the track index by adding an **overflow pointer**, which gives the address of the first overflow record for each track. Records in the overflow area contain pointer fields, so that if a track has more than one overflow record the first will point to the second, the second to the third, and so on. Figure 3.19(c) shows an extended track index. The area into which the original records are written is now called the **prime area** and the overflow records occupy the **overflow area**. Note that records in the prime area are kept in strict sequential order, even if that means moving a record previously stored in the prime area into the overflow area. Records in the overflow area are written in the order in which they enter the overflow,

```
HIGHEST KEY
ON CYLINDER      CYLINDER
-------------------------
E820                1
E1236               2
E2121               3
...                 .
...                 .
...                 .
```

3.18(a) Cylinder Index

```
For Cylinder 1:        For Cylinder 2:       For Cylinder 3:      ...
HIGHEST                HIGHEST               HIGHEST
KEY       TRACK        KEY          TRACK    KEY          TRACK   ...
--------------         --------------        --------------
E120      1            E890         1        E1259        1
E138      2            E908         2        E1278        2
E153      3            E923         3        E1297        3
...       .            ...          .        ...          .
...       .            ...          .        ...          .
...       .            ...          .        ...          .
E820      30           E1236        30       E2121        30      ...
```

3.18(b) Track Indexes

```
Example:    To find E915:
▪ Consulting cylinder index, we see record belongs on cylinder
2, since E915 > E820 and E915 < E1236.
▪ Consulting track index for Cylinder 2, we see record belongs
on track 3, since E915 > E908 and E915 < E923.
▪ Search track 3 sequentially until we reach E915 or reach a
record with higher key value without finding E915.
```

Figure 3.18 Cylinder and Track Indexes

and sequence is preserved there by means of pointers. When records enter the overflow area, the extended track index is updated by changing entries for "Highest Key on Track" and "Address of First Overflow Record" as needed. Figure 3.19(d) illustrates the prime and overflow areas for the index in Figure 3.19(c). Whenever possible, the overflow should be on the same cylinder as the prime area. When setting up the file on a device with 30 tracks per cylinder, we might designate 25 tracks of a cylinder as prime area and 5 as overflow. This minimizes access arm movement (seek time) when we need to retrieve from an overflow area. There should also be a general overflow area for records that do not fit in the correct cylinder overflow area. As the overflow area is filled, long pointer chains may develop, resulting in long searches for records and a decrease in performance. At this point, the file should be reorganized with all deleted spaces reclaimed, all records once again placed in sequence in the prime area, and the index recreated.

Indexed sequential file organization is used by operating systems to manage some nondatabase files, but database files are not managed by the operating system's indexed sequential access method. However, the techniques are used by the DBMS to set up its own indexed file organization.

```
         ------------------------------------------
track 1  |  E101  |  E104  |  E110  |  E115  |  blank |
         ------------------------------------------
         ------------------------------------------
track 2  |  E120  |  E125  |  E130  |  E131  |  blank |
         ------------------------------------------
         ------------------------------------------
track 3  |  E134  |  E138  |  E140  |  E143  |  blank |
         ------------------------------------------
...
...
...
```

3.19(a) Distributed Free Space on Each Track

```
         ------------------------------------------
track 1  |  E101  |  E103  |  E104  |  E110  |  E115  |
         ------------------------------------------
         ------------------------------------------
track 2  |  E120  |  E125  |  E130  |  E131  |  blank |
         ------------------------------------------
         ------------------------------------------
track 3  |  E134  |  E138  |  E140  |  E143  |  blank |
         ------------------------------------------
```

3.19(b) Shifting Records on Track 1 to Insert E103

TRACK	HIGHEST KEY ON TRACK	HIGHEST KEY IN OVERFLOW	POINTER TO FIRST OVERFLOW
1	E110	E115	add of E112
2	E128	E131	add of E129
3	E140	E143	add of E143
...	.	.	.
...	.	.	.
...	.	.	.

3.19(c) Extended Track Index

```
                     PRIME AREA
TRACK      RECORDS
           --------------------------------------
1          | E101 | E103 | E104 | E109 | E110 |
           --------------------------------------
           --------------------------------------
2          | E118 | E120 | E125 | E127 | E128 |
           --------------------------------------
           --------------------------------------
3          | E132 | E134 | E135 | E138 | E140 |
           --------------------------------------
...
...
...
                       OVERFLOW AREA
--------  --------  --------  --------  --------  --------  --------
|0|E115|  |6|E129|  |5|E112|  |0|E143|  |1|E113|  |7|E130|  |0|E131|
--------  --------  --------  --------  --------  --------  --------
```

3.19(d) Prime and Overflow Areas With Track Index of 3.19 (c)

Figure 3.19 Handling Overflow Records

Direct File Organization

Database management systems use **direct file organization** to help manage the database. This is also one of the basic organizations used by the operating system. For example, IBM's **Basic Direct Access Method (BDAM)** uses the techniques described in this section. Other vendors provide direct access methods as well. This organization is designed to provide **random access,** rapid direct nonsequential access to records. Using this organization, records are inserted in what appears to be a random order, not in sequence by key field value. When a record is to be stored, the system takes the value of a specified field and usually performs some type of calculation to derive a target address for the record. Normally, the record is then stored at the target address. To retrieve a record, the system uses the key value supplied to figure out where the record should be stored and goes to that address to find it.

If the values of the chosen field are simply consecutive integers, the field value becomes the relative address. For example, suppose that we are creating a database to keep track of customer orders for a vendor. If all orders are assigned consecutive order numbers, then the order records might have a field called ORDER NUMBER which can be used as the relative address. If the field uses nonconsecutive numbers or is nonnumeric, it is necessary to convert its value in some way. The conversion scheme for numeric values is called a **hashing scheme** and the field on which it is performed is the **hashing field**. Nonnumeric values are easily converted into numeric ones by using some type of code—for example, alphabetical position or ASCII values. Once a number is obtained, there are many possible algorithms for deriving a target address. For example, suppose that we are storing employee records and our hashing field is SOCSECNO. A sample social security number, expressed as a numeric field, is 123456789. We are seeking an algorithm that can take a nine-digit number with possible values 0–999,999,999 and convert it into one of the addresses available. It is not appropriate to use the social security number as the address, because that would require a file with 1,000,000,000 positions, most of which would be empty, since there are large gaps between social security numbers of employees. Suppose, for example, that we have 1000 positions for storage. If we only have 800 employees, there should be enough room in a file with 1000 addresses for all their records. However, we must remember that we are trying to map values in the range 0–999,999,999 into the range 0–999, as indicated in Figure 3.20. We do not care if the social security numbers are kept in increasing order, so it is acceptable to have a high social security number map to a low address, or a low one to a high address, as shown in Figure 3.20.

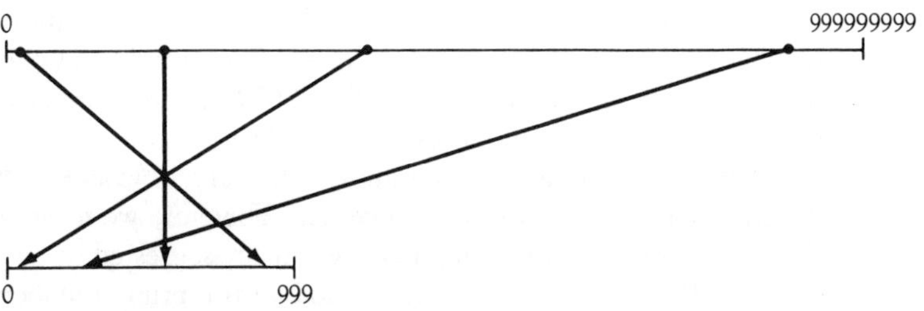

Figure 3.20

One hashing scheme, called the **division/remainder** method, is to divide by some fixed divisor and take the remainder as the address. For our example, if we use 1000 as the divisor, the remainder will be in the range 0–999 and will simply be the last three digits of the social security number. The values are guaranteed to be in the correct range for addresses, 0–999. For example, the social security number 085439598 gives a remainder of 598 on division by 1000, so its target address is 598. Figure 3.21(a) illustrates this scheme. Our choice of 1000 as the divisor was arbitrary and was designed to make our calculations easy. In fact, it is customary to choose divisors that are prime numbers slightly less than the number of addresses available. Many other hashing algorithms exist. Another simple one is **folding,** in which the field value is split into parts which are then added. Suppose that we had room for 3000 records in our file. We could split the social security number into three parts, each with three digits, and add the parts, as shown in Figure 3.21(b). The resulting sum will be in the range 0–2997. Since we have 3000 spaces, this means that we will have at least two blank spaces at the end of the file. If we used folding and it were possible to obtain a value that did not fit into the range, we could multiply the result by an appropriate decimal fraction to bring it into the range, or we could use the division/remainder method on the result of folding.

```
Key Value:               085439598
Hashing Method:     DIVISION/REMAINDER
        Do Division          085439598/1000
        Take Remainder         598
TARGET ADDRESS: 598
```

3.21(a) Division/Remainder Method

```
Key Value:             085439598
Hashing Method:  FOLDING
        Split number into 3 3-digit parts       085  439  598
        Add the parts    085 + 439 + 598 = 1122
TARGET ADDRESS:  1122
```

3.21(b) Folding Technique

Figure 3.21 Hashing schemes

A major problem, called a **collision,** occurs when two different key values yield the same target address. The keys are then called **synonyms**. For example, we know that the social security number 085439598 hashes to 598 using division/remainder with a divisor of 1000, but so does 998876598, so these two social security numbers are synonyms. If we had previously inserted the record of the employee with social security number 085439598 in the target address 598, we would be unable to store the employee record with social security number 998876598 in the correct address. A good hashing algorithm is one that produces addresses that fit the range, provides a fairly uniform distribution of records, and minimizes collisions. No algorithm, no matter how well designed, eliminates collisions altogether. Therefore we must find ways to handle collisions. One way of minimizing them, as already suggested, is by choosing a good hashing scheme. The division/remainder method with a prime number as the divisor is one of the best. However, there may be some pattern in the key values that causes many collisions when this method is used. Therefore, the DBA should be familiar with several schemes and should study the effect that each would have on the distribution of records. Another way to minimize collisions is to calculate a **block address** (also called a **page** or **bucket number**) rather than an individual record address. As explained in Section 3.1.2, records in a database are usually stored in blocks or pages that may hold several logical records. For our employee file with 800 records, we may choose a page size that will hold four employee records. Although theoretically we would need only 200 pages to hold our 800 records, we cannot expect the records to be perfectly distributed, so we allow a little extra room. We might choose to reserve 250 pages, or room for 1000 records. This would give us a **packing density**, which is the percentage ratio of stored records to the number of spaces, of 80 percent. We now change our hashing algorithm so that it yields addresses in the range 0–249 and plan to place four records in each address or bucket. Recall that a bucket is a space that can hold several records. For example, we can use the division/remainder method with the prime number 241 as our divisor and get addresses in the range 0–240. Now we can store four synonyms in the same bucket. The effect of collisions can be further reduced by increasing the bucket size. For example, we can leave room for five records in each bucket. However, we may be constrained by the system to fixed block sizes. A second method of reducing the effect of collisions is to reduce the packing density by increasing the number of buckets allocated. As the packing density decreases, however, more space will be wasted, so we are trading off storage efficiency for better collision management. Our sample packing density of 80 percent is about the highest practical one. Average packing density is closer to 60 percent.

Regardless of algorithm efficiency or bucket size, we will eventually reach a point where some record does not fit into the correct bucket. There are two ways of handling such an **overflow**. The first is to search forward until we find an empty slot or record space. We may find room in the next bucket or the one after that for the record. Figure 3.22(a) illustrates this method. The record with key value of 5500 is to be inserted in a hashed file with a bucket size of 4, using division/remainder with a divisor of 100. It belongs in bucket 0, but there is no room for it there. Therefore, we look at bucket 1 and find that there is no room, then look at bucket 2 and find there is no room, then look at bucket 3, find an empty slot, and insert the record there. If we search forward some predetermined number of addresses (perhaps five) without finding room for the record, we simply cannot insert the record and have to reorganize the file because it is too full or **dense** in that region. A predetermined number is chosen because we want to avoid long record searches which would delay processing. A second method of dealing with overflows is to set aside an overflow area into which records that do not fit in their correct buckets are inserted, and connect the overflow record with its correct address by placing a **synonym pointer** in the record stored at that address. Records in the overflow area also have "next synonym" pointers that give the address in the overflow area of the next synonym for the same target address, so that all synonyms for a particular address can be retrieved by following a chain of pointers. Figure 3.22(b) illustrates the overflow area method of dealing with synonyms. Again, record 5500 is to be inserted using division/remainder with divisor of 100 as the hashing algorithm. Since there is no room in bucket 0 for the record, we place it in the overflow area and put a pointer in the home bucket that will lead to the record in the overflow area. If another synonym,

```
               ------------------------------------------------   ----------
bucket 0 | rec 2500 | rec 5300 | rec 2200 | rec 3400| |rec 5500|
               ------------------------------------------------   ----------
               ------------------------------------------------       |
bucket 1 | rec 8901 | rec 7901 | rec 3201 | rec 5701|                 |
               ------------------------------------------------       |
               ------------------------------------------------       |
bucket 2 | rec 4502 | rec 2202 | rec 3702 | rec 9802|                 |
               ------------------------------------------------       |
               ------------------------------------------------       |
bucket 3 | rec 3903 | rec 2803 | rec 1103 |  blank | <-------------
               ------------------------------------------------
Note:  Record 5500 belongs in bucket 0, using division/remainder
with divisor of 100 as the hashing algorithm.  Since bucket 0 is
full, we search forward to find an empty space, and insert the
record in bucket 3.
```

3.22(a) Forward-Search Method

```
PRIME AREA                                        OVERFLOW AREA
               ---------------------------------     ---------
bucket 0   | 2500   5300   2200   3400 | -------->|| 5500 |
               ---------------------------------     ---------
               ---------------------------------
bucket 1   | 8901   7901   3201   5701 |  |
               ---------------------------------
               ---------------------------------
bucket 2   | 4502   2202   3702   9802 |  |
               ---------------------------------
               ---------------------------------
bucket 3   | 3903   2803   1103        |  |
               ---------------------------------
Note:  Record 5500 belongs in bucket 0, using division/remainder
with divisor of 100 as the hashing algorithm.  Since bucket 0 is
full, we put record 5500 in the overflow area, and connect it by
a pointer to the bucket.
```

3.22(b) Overflow Area Method

Figure 3.22 Two Methods of Handling Bucket Overflows

record 2800, for example, were to be inserted now, we would place it in the overflow area and put a pointer to it in record 5500.

IBM's **Virtual Storage Access Method (VSAM)** provides all three methods discussed here. One organization, called **Entry Sequenced Data Set (ESDS)**, uses sequential files. A second, called **Relative Record Data Set (RRDS)**, uses hashing. The third, **Key Sequenced Data Set (KSDS)**, uses a multilevel index that is more sophisticated than the ISAM indexes described above. The KSDS index structure is a B tree which is easily reorganized and which is described in Section 3.2. The KSDS storage space is broken up into **control areas**, which correspond roughly to cylinders and are in turn made up of **control intervals**, which correspond roughly to tracks. The control interval is the unit of data transfer between the disk and the buffer. When a control interval gets full and an additional record must be inserted, the control interval **splits**. This means that an empty control interval in the same control area is chosen, and the data from the original interval plus the new record is split so that half ends up in the original control interval and half in the new control interval. The index is also changed to lead to the new control interval in the correct order. If the control area becomes too full, it also splits and the index is adjusted accordingly. This incremental reorganizing is more efficient and easier to manage than the periodic major reorganization needed with ISAM files.

3.2 *Data Structures*

The database management system uses a variety of techniques to allow rapid direct retrieval of records for both on-line and batch applications, retrieval of data on the basis of relationships between records, and retrieval on the basis of the value of a nonkey field. To do so, the DBMS uses **data structures**, which are structured or composite data types made up of simpler data types.

3.2.1 *Inverted Files*

Inverted files are commonly used to allow the database management system to retrieve records on the basis of the value of a nonkey field. Such a field, which may or may not have unique values, is referred to as a **secondary key.** For example, we may have student records physically arranged in order by student ID, as in Figure 3.23(a). This order makes it easy for the operating system to retrieve records by ID, using either sequential or indexed sequential access. However, if we want to retrieve records in alphabetical order by last name, we need another organization. We could sort the records on last name each time, but that wastes processing time. We could store records in two different files, one as shown in Figure 3.23(a) and one in order by last name, but this duplication of data wastes space and eventually causes data to become inconsistent. Instead, we can create an **index** or **inverted list** using STUNAME as the field for ordering. We say that we have **inverted** the file on the field STUNAME. The **secondary index** for the inversion is shown in Figure 3.23(b). Note that we are using relative addresses and ignoring blocking of records. If we want to access the student file on the basis of major, we could create a secondary index on MAJOR, using separate records for each repeated value, as shown in Figure 3.23(c). If we set up indexes for each of the fields in the STUDENT record, we say that the file is **fully inverted**. Since only two of the fields are indexed in Figure 3.23, our example shows a **partially inverted file**. The indexes provide for very efficient direct access to records on the basis of the values of the indexed field. In addition, the indexes themselves are sufficient to give information such as the number of CS majors without accessing the file at all. Note that these indexes are created by the DBMS, not by the access method, although the DBMS needs the access method to tell it the addresses of records in order to build the index. When retrieving a record by using the index, the DBMS looks up the appropriate value of the indexed field, determines the relative address of the record desired, and tells the access method to retrieve the record stored at that address. The access method uses its own technique to find and retrieve the record. The indexes themselves, as well as the files they index, are stored in the areas under the control of the DBMS.

STUID	STUNAME	MAJOR	CREDITS	GPA
S1001	Smith,Tom	History	90	3.50
S1002	Chin,David	Math	36	2.75
S1010	Burns,Edward	Art	63	3.25
S1013	McCarthy,Owen	Math	9	4.00
S1015	Jones,Mary	Math	42	2.50
S1020	Rivera,Jane	CS	15	3.00

3.23(a) Student File in Order by STUID

KEY	RELATIVE ADDRESS
Burns,Edward	3
Chin,David	2
Jones,Mary	5
McCarthy,Owen	4
Rivera,Jane	6
Smith,Tom	1

3.23(b) Index on STUNAME for Student File in 3.23(a)

KEY	RELATIVE ADDRESS
Art	3
CS	6
History	1
Math	2
Math	4
Math	5

3.23(c) Index on MAJOR for Student File in 3.23(a)

Figure 3.23 Partially Inverted File Structure

3.2.2 *Linked Lists*

A second technique for handling secondary keys or setting up any other desired order is the **linked list** or **pointer chain**. A linked list is created by adding an extra **link field** to each data record. The field contains a **pointer**, the address of the next record in the logical sequence being created. Figure 3.24(a) shows student records in a linked list with links arranged in order by STUNAME. Once again, we are using relative addresses and ignoring blocking. Note that we must identify the **head** or first record in the list to start with. When we reach that record, we look at the value of the link to see where the next logical record appears. We follow that link to the next record, and so on, until we reach

STUNAME Head Pointer: 3

Relative Record Number	STUID	STUNAME	MAJOR	CRED	GPA	Pointer
1	S1001	Smith,Tom	History	90	3.50	0
2	S1002	Chin,David	Math	36	2.75	5
3	S1010	Burns,Edward	Art	63	3.25	2
4	S1013	McCarthy,Owen	Math	9	4.00	6
5	S1015	Jones,Mary	Math	42	2.50	4
6	S1020	Rivera,Jane	CS	15	3.00	1

3.24(a) Linked List with Pointers for STUNAME

EMPID Head Pointer: 3

Relative Record Number	EMPID	EMPNAME	DEPT	SALARY	Pointer
1	E125	Jones,Mike	Marketing	38000	7
2	E110	Lyons,Mary	Research	50000	6
3	E101	Jones,Jack	Marketing	35000	4
4	E104	Smith,John	Research	30000	2
5	E120	Miranda,Jane	Sales	48000	1
6	E115	Chin,Greg	Development	45000	5
7	E130	DiNoto,Steve	Research	55000	3

3.24(b) Circular Linked List with Pointers for EMPID

EMPNAME Head Pointer: 6
EMPNAME Tail Pointer: 4

	EMPID	EMPNAME	DEPT	SALARY	Forward Pointer	Backward Pointer
1	E125	Jones,Mike	Marketing	38000	2	3
2	E110	Lyons,Mary	Research	50000	5	1
3	E101	Jones,Jack	Marketing	35000	1	7
4	E104	Smith,John	Research	30000	0	5
5	E120	Miranda,Jane	Sales	48000	4	2
6	E115	Chin,Greg	Development	45000	7	0
7	E130	DiNoto,Steve	Research	55000	3	6

3.24(c) Two-Way Linked List with Pointers for EMPNAME

EMPID Head Pointer: 3
EMPNAME Head Pointer: 6

	EMPID	EMPNAME	DEPT	SALARY	EMPID Pointer	EMPNAME Pointer
1	E125	Jones,Mike	Marketing	38000	7	2
2	E110	Lyons,Mary	Research	50000	6	5
3	E101	Jones,Jack	Marketing	35000	4	1
4	E104	Smith,John	Research	30000	2	0
5	E120	Miranda,Jane	Sales	48000	1	4
6	E115	Chin,Greg	Development	45000	5	7
7	E130	DiNoto,Steve	Research	55000	0	3

3.24(d) Linked List with Pointers for EMPID and EMPNAME

Figure 3.24 Linked Lists

the end of the pointer chain, identified by a null link value, which we are writing as 0. If we wish, we can replace the null pointer at the end of the chain with the address of the head of the list, thereby creating a **circular linked list** or **ring.** A ring allows us to reach any record in the chain from any other. Figure 3.24(b) illustrates a circular linked list of employee records, this time using EMPID as the ordering field. A **two-way** linked list is one in which each record has two pointers—a **forward** or **next** one to indicate the location of the next record and a **backward** or **prior** one to indicate the location of the previous record. Figure 3.24(c) shows the Employee file using a two-way linked list to create alphabetical and reverse alphabetical order on EMPNAME. We can create more than one logical order for the same file by using two or more pointer fields in each record. Figure 3.24(d) shows the Employee file with the EMPID link creating order by EMPID and the EMPNAME link creating order by EMPNAME.

Insertion is easy with a linked list. We simply add the new record at the physical end of the file and include it in the correct order by changing only two links. Figure 3.25(a) shows how to insert a new student record at the end of the file shown in Figure 3.24(a). Deletion is equally easy. We simply readjust the pointer that used to lead us to the deleted record by setting it to the pointer value that appeared in the deleted record. Figure 3.25(b) shows how to delete a record from the Student file of Figure 3.24(a). To keep track of which slots are occupied by deleted records, we do **garbage collection** by means of another linked list. This time we have a header for unused slots, which leads to the first deleted record, which in turn leads to the second deleted record, and so on, as shown in Figure 3.25(c). When we need to insert a record, we can reuse the space by placing the record in the address indicated by the unused space header and using as the new header value the pointer value that used to appear there. This process is shown in Figure 3.25(d).

The DBMS is responsible for creating and maintaining its own linked lists for various logical orders. To do so, it must get addresses from the operating system access method. To permit following of pointers, the operating system must use indexed sequential or direct organization as the access method, with direct being the usual choice.

A combination of inverted and linked lists can be used for secondary keys with nonunique values. The index can list each secondary key value only once, with a pointer to the first record having that value. The first record then becomes the head of a linked list, pointing to the second record with the same secondary key value, which in turn points to the third record, and so on. Figure 3.26 shows student records inverted on MAJOR, with the first student record for each major acting as the head of a linked list that points to all students with the same major.

3.2.3 *Trees*

Many database management systems use a data structure called a **tree** to hold data or indexes. A **tree** is a data structure that consists of a **hierarchy of nodes**. The nodes contain data and are connected by lines or branches. At the highest level there is a single node, called the **root** of the tree. The root may have any number of dependent nodes, called its **children**, directly below it. These child nodes, in turn, may have children dependent on them. A strict rule for tree structures is that each node, with the

STUNAME Head Pointer: 3

Relative Record Number	STUID	STUNAME	MAJOR	CRED	GPA	Pointer
1	S1001	Smith,Tom	History	90	3.50	0
2	S1002	Chin,David	Math	36	2.75	5
3	S1010	Burns,Edward	Art	63	3.25	2
4	S1013	McCarthy,Owen	Math	9	4.00	6
5	S1015	Jones,Mary	Math	42	2.50	7
6	S1020	Rivera,Jane	CS	15	3.00	1
7	S1005	Lee,Perry	History	3	3.50	4

3.25(a) Adding record of S1005 to End of Student File

STUNAME Head Pointer: 3

Relative Record Number	STUID	STUNAME	MAJOR	CRED	GPA	Pointer
1	S1001	Smith,Tom	History	90	3.50	0
2	S1002	Chin,David	Math	36	2.75	5
3	S1010	Burns,Edward	Art	63	3.25	5
4	S1013	McCarthy,Owen	Math	9	4.00	6
5	S1015	Jones,Mary	Math	42	2.50	4
6	S1020	Rivera,Jane	CS	15	3.00	1

3.25(b) Deleting Record of S1002 from Student File

STUNAME Head Pointer: 3
UNUSED Head Pointer: 2

Relative Record Number	STUID	STUNAME	MAJOR	CRED	GPA	Pointer
1	S1001	Smith,Tom	History	90	3.50	0
2	S1002	Chin,David	Math	36	2.75	6
3	S1010	Burns,Edward	Art	63	3.25	5
4	S1013	McCarthy,Owen	Math	9	4.00	1
5	S1015	Jones,Mary	Math	42	2.50	4
6	S1020	Rivera,Jane	CS	15	3.00	0

Note: Both S1002 and S1020 have been deleted.

3.25(c) UNUSED: Linked List of Spaces from Deleted Records

STUNAME Head Pointer: 3
UNUSED Head Pointer: 6

Relative Record Number	STUID	STUNAME	MAJOR	CRED	GPA	Pointer
1	S1001	Smith,Tom	History	90	3.50	0
2	S1012	Dempsey,Joe	CS	3	2.50	5
3	S1010	Burns,Edward	Art	63	3.25	2
4	S1013	McCarthy,Owen	Math	9	4.00	1
5	S1015	Jones,Mary	Math	42	2.50	4
6	S1020	Rivera,Jane	CS	15	3.00	0

3.25(d) S1012 Added to First UNUSED Location

Figure 3.25 Adding and Deleting Records in a Linked List

ADD	STUID	STUNAME	MAJOR	CREDITS	GPA	Ptr
1	S1001	Smith,Tom	History	90	3.50	0
2	S1002	Chin,David	Math	36	2.75	4
3	S1010	Burns,Edward	Art	63	3.25	0
4	S1013	McCarthy,Owen	Math	9	4.00	5
5	S1015	Jones,Mary	Math	42	2.50	0
6	S1020	Rivera,Jane	CS	15	3.00	0

KEY	RELATIVE ADDRESS
Art	3
CS	6
History	1
Math	2

Figure 3.26 Student File Inverted on MAJOR, Using Linked Lists for Each Major

exception of the root, has **exactly one parent**, that is, one node on the level immediately above it to which it is related. Parent-child relationships are shown by drawing a line or an **edge** between the parent and child nodes.

Figure 3.27 represents an example of a tree structure. In that example, node *A* is the root. Nodes *B*, *C*, and *D* are its children. *B* has two children, *E* and *F*. *C* has one child, *G*, while *D* has three children, *H*, *I*, and *J*. *E* has two children, *K* and *L*. *G* has one child, *M*, and *H* has one child, *N*. From the diagram it is clear that a node can have zero, one, or many children, but a node can have only one parent. The root node has no parent. A node that has no children is called a **leaf**, so nodes *K*, *L*, *F*, *M*, *N*, *I*, and *J* are leaves. Note that leaves can occur on different levels. Nodes that are children of the same parent are called **siblings**. For example, from the diagram, you can see that nodes *E* and *F* are siblings, since they have the same parent, *B*. For any node, there is a single path, called the **hierarchical path**, from the root to that node. The nodes along this path are called that node's **ancestors**. For example, the hierarchical path to node *L* begins with *A*, goes through *B*, then *E*, and finally *L*. Therefore, *A*, *B*, and *E* are ancestors of *L*. Similarly, for a given node, any node along a path from that node to a leaf is called its **descendant.** If you visualize a node as if it were a root node in a new tree, the node and all its descendants form a **subtree** of the original tree structure. In the diagram, we see that the descendants of *B* are nodes *E*, *K*, *L*, and *F*. *B* forms the root of the subtree containing itself and all its descendants.

The root of the tree is assigned **level 0**. Its children are on **level 1**. Their children are on **level 2**, and so on. The **height** or **depth** of a tree is the maximum number of levels or, alternatively, the number of nodes on the longest hierarchical path from the root to a leaf. The tree in Figure 3.27 has height of 4. A tree is said to be **balanced** if every path from the root node to a leaf has the same length. The tree in our example is not balanced, since the path from *A* to *F* has length 3, while the path from *A* to *K* has length 4. The **degree** or **order** of a tree is the maximum number of children any node has. The tree in Figure 3.27 has order 3. A **binary tree** is one of order 2, in which each node has no more than two children. Our example is clearly not a binary tree, since both *A* and *D* have three children.

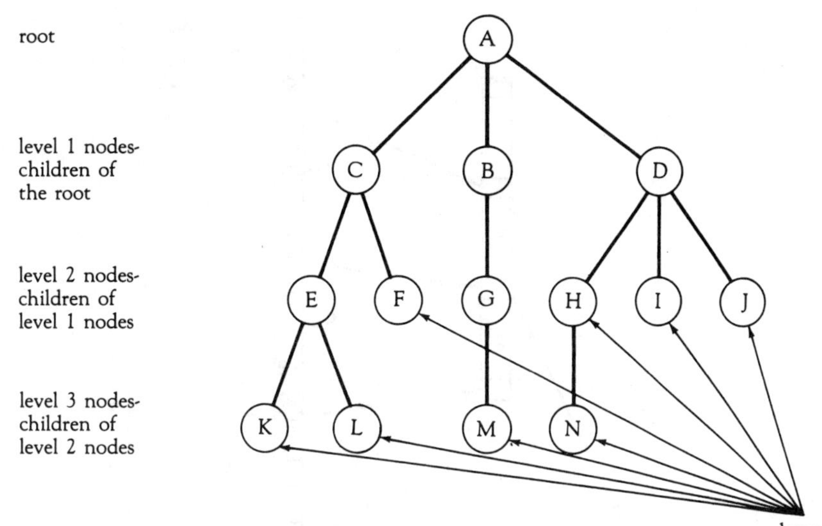

Figure 3.27

3.2.4 *B+ Trees*

Trees are used for holding and processing various database structures, but they are also used for indexing a file. For example, IBM's VSAM index is tree-structured. A structure called a B+ tree can be used to store an efficient and flexible hierarchical index that provides both sequential and direct access to records. The index consists of two parts, called an **index set** and a **sequence set**. The sequence set is at the bottom level of the index (the leaf nodes) and consists of all the key values arranged in sequence with a pointer from each key value to its corresponding record in the data file. Figure 3.28 illustrates a B+ tree index. If you look at the bottom level, you will see the sequence set showing all key values and their corresponding pointers that lead to the appropriate data records. We are not showing the data records, which may be arranged randomly or in any desired physical sequence. We are assuming that data records are unblocked and each pointer leads to a single record. However, the pointers may lead to **buckets**, spaces that can hold several records, if desired. You will also notice that the rightmost pointer of each leaf node, the **horizontal pointer,** is used to link the node with the next one in the sequence set. This allows us to use the sequence set for sequential access to the file. All we need to do is start at the leftmost leaf node and locate each record from that leaf in turn, then follow the horizontal pointers to reach the next sequence set node, and so on.

Direct access to records is accomplished by using the index set, starting at the root node and taking a strict hierarchical path to the appropriate node in the sequence set. The root node in Figure 3.28 has the same structure as all the other nodes of the tree. It has room for three key values and four pointers that could lead to four child nodes, so the tree has order four. Since we are using only two key values and three pointers in the root node, we leave the rightmost key and pointer values blank, and show only three

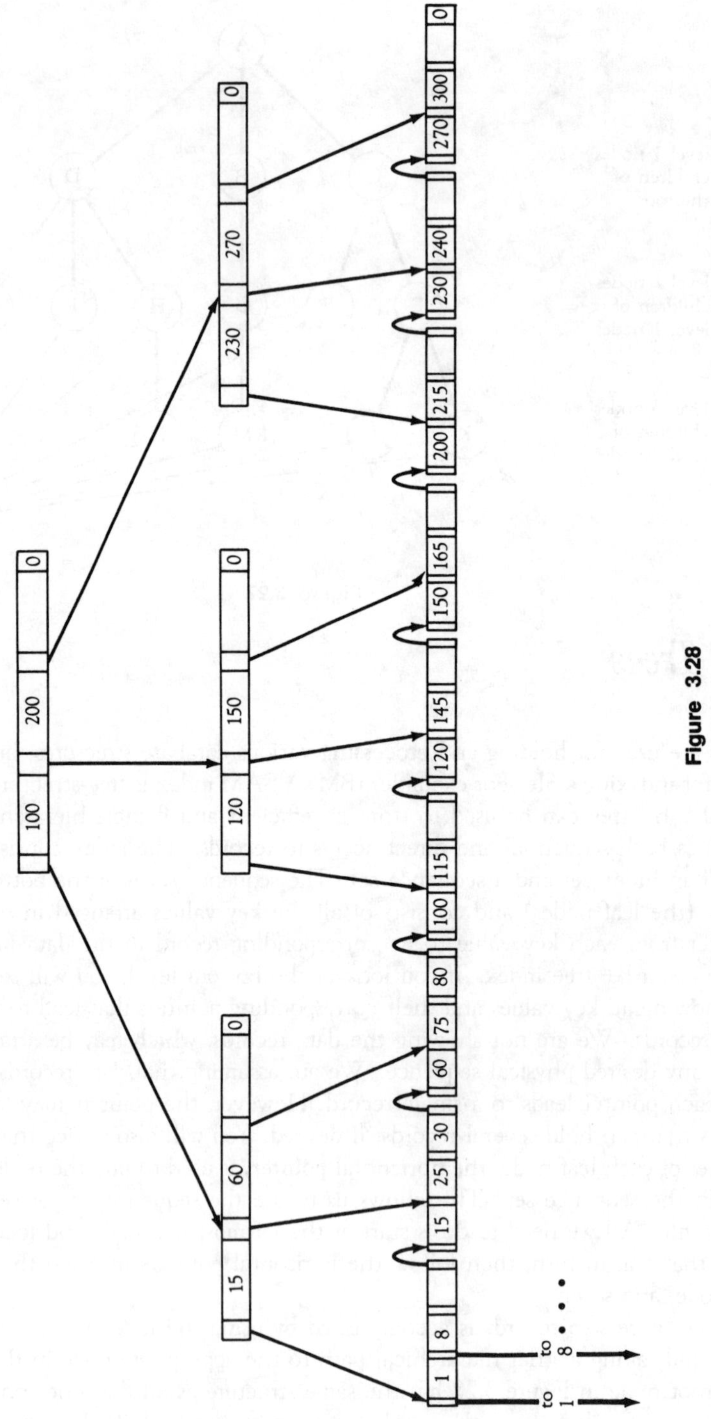
100
200
15
60
120
150
230
270
1
8
15
25
30
60
75
80
100
115
120
145
150
165
200
215
230
240
270
300
to 1
to 8

Figure 3.28

level 1 nodes. The leftmost pointer is used to access all records whose key values are less than 100. The middle pointer leads to all records with key values greater than or equal to 100 but less than 200, while the rightmost nonnull pointer leads to all records with key values greater than or equal to 200. Following the root node's leftmost pointer, we reach a level 1 node with room for three key values and four pointers. We are storing two key values, 15 and 60, and three pointers in this node. The leftmost pointer in this node is used to access all records with key values less than 15, the next pointer for records with keys greater or equal to 15 but less than 60, the next for keys greater than or equal to 60 but less than 100, and the last is empty at the moment. If we follow the leftmost pointer once again, we arrive at the leftmost node of the sequence set. This has key values 1 and 8. The leftmost pointer leads to the data record with key value of 1, the next to the data record with key value of 8, the third is blank, and the fourth leads to the next node of the sequence set. You will recall that this pointer is used to chain together sequence set nodes for sequential processing and is not used for direct access.

Suppose that we wanted to access the record with key value 115. We would begin at the root node and follow the second pointer, since the value we seek is greater than 100 but less than 200. This leads to the middle level 1 node. This time, we would follow the leftmost pointer, since the value we seek is less than 120. This leads to the sequence set, where we find the value 115 in the second position of the appropriate node. The pointer to the left of 115 leads us to the correct data record.

There are strict rules for constructing B+ trees, among them:

- If the root is not a leaf, it must have at least two children.
- If the tree has order n, each node, with the exception of the root and leaf nodes, must have between $n/2$ and n pointers (and children). If $n/2$ is not an integer, round up to determine the minimum number of pointers.
- The number of key values contained in a nonleaf node is 1 less than the number of pointers.
- If the tree has order n, the number of key values in a leaf node must be between $(n - 1)/2$ and $n - 1$. If $(n - 1)/2$ is not an integer, round up to determine the minimum number of key values.
- The tree must be balanced; that is, every path from the root node to a leaf must have the same length.

These requirements account for the efficiency of a B+ tree index. In practice, each node in the tree is actually a block, so we can store many more than three key values and four pointers in a typical node. If we had room for 20 pointers in each node, we could easily access 1000 records using a three-level index. Since the root node is usually kept in main memory during processing, we would need only two disk accesses to reach the sequence set, or only a total of three accesses to reach any one of the 1000 data records.

Insertion and deletion of records in a data file with a B+ tree index can be complicated, particularly if the index nodes become too full or too empty. First we consider the simple case where no problems arise when we insert records into the index shown in Figure 3.28. Suppose that we wish to insert a record with key value of 5. We see that its key belongs in the leftmost leaf node, since it is less than 15. To place it in the correct order, we move the value 8 and its pointer to the right and insert 5 and its pointer in the correct sequential position, so the tree index now appears as in Figure 3.29(a). The record with key value 5 is inserted into the data file, and its address becomes the pointer value stored to the left of the 5 in the sequence set. The leftmost leaf node in now completely filled, and no other insertions can be made into it without some reorganizing. Now suppose that we wish to delete the record with key value of 80. The sequence set node containing 80 is the third from the left. If we simply erase the key value and its pointer, the leaf node would now have only two key values. We must check the requirements to see whether two keys are sufficient for a leaf node. Recall that this tree has order 4. The rule for leaves is that a leaf must have between $(n-1)/2$ and $n - 1$ keys. Calculating $(4-1)/2$ we see that the leaf node has enough key values. Therefore we erase the key value and its pointer and delete the data record. Figure 3.29(b) shows the present state of the index, after inserting 5 and deleting 80.

Now we consider what happens when a leaf node becomes too full. Suppose that we wish to insert a record with key value of 20. The key value belongs in the second leaf node from the left, between 15 and 25. However, this leaf node is already filled, so we must reorganize. The existing node must be **split**, or divided up into two nodes. We add a new leaf node immediately to the right of the existing one, and split up the key values so there are about half in each of the two resulting leaves. Now the old node will contain key values 15 and 20, with their pointers, while the new one will contain the values 25 and 30, with their pointers. However, we must consider what effect this may have on the parent of the leaf node. We see that 25 should appear in the parent node, which is the leftmost level 1 node. Therefore, we rewrite that node so that the key values will appear in proper sequence, which is 15, 25, 60. We also adjust the pointers to lead to the proper leaf nodes, including the new one. We can now insert the data record. Figure 3.29(c) shows the new state of the index. We were fortunate that the parent had enough space for the key value and the pointer to the new leaf. If it did not, we would have had to split the parent as well, and adjust its parent, the root node. If the root node were full, we would have to split the root, which would require creating a level above the present root, resulting in another level being added to the index. This example shows why B+ tree indexes are usually created with some empty spaces to allow for limited insertion without splitting.

Now we consider an example where deletion causes a problem. Starting with the index as it appears in Figure 3.29(c), let us delete the record with key value of 75. The leaf node affected is the fourth from the left. If we were to erase the 75, this leaf would have only one key left, 60. For a tree of order 4, leaves must have a minimum of two keys, so we are not permitted to have such a leaf. Note that if the leaf were now empty, we could simply delete it and adjust the parent node. However, it contains information that we need, namely the key value of 60 and the pointer to the corresponding record. To preserve this information, we look for a sibling node in which we might store it. The node immediately to the left has the same parent and contains only two keys, 25 and 30. Therefore, we **coalesce** or combine the two sibling leaf nodes into one with the three key values, 25, 30, and 60. We must also adjust the parent node by deleting the value of 60 and the pointer from it to the old node.

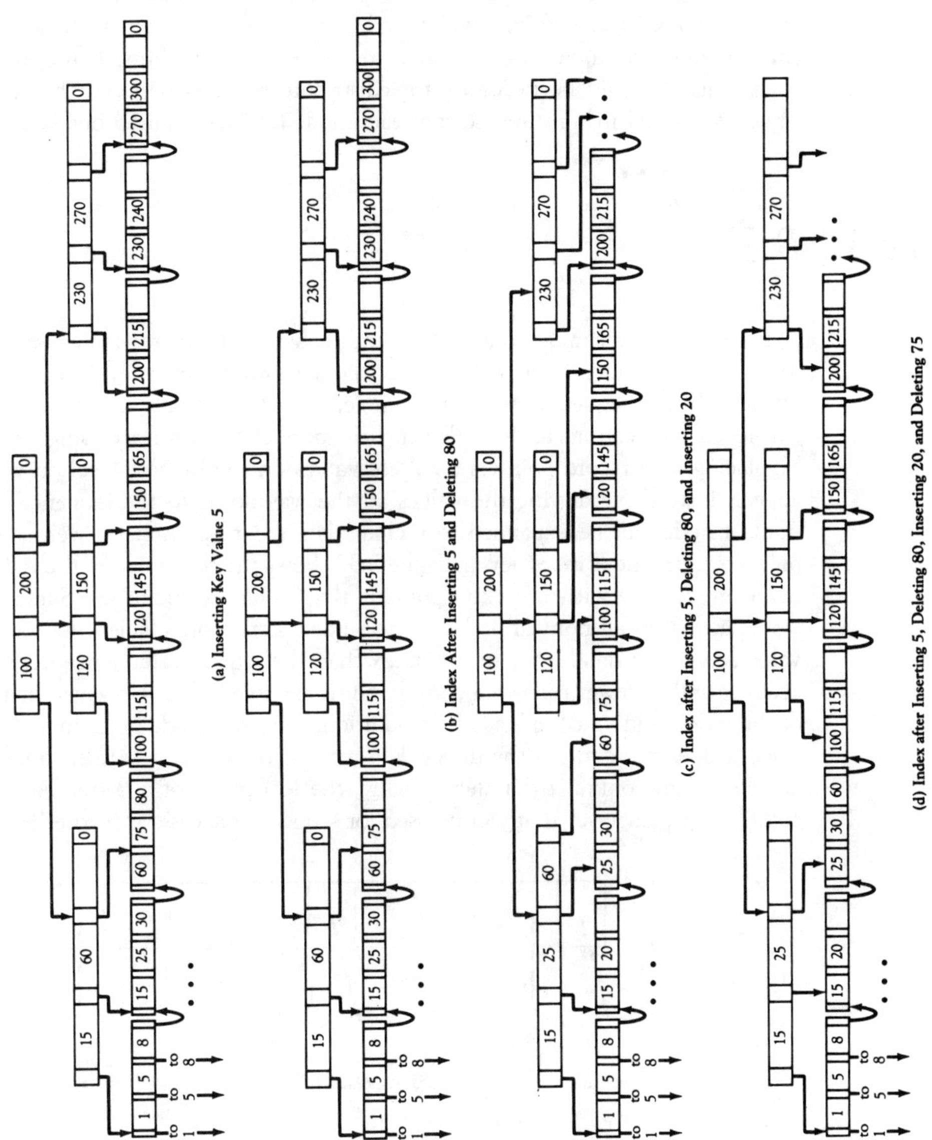

(a) Inserting Key Value 5

(b) Index After Inserting 5 and Deleting 80

(c) Index after Inserting 5, Deleting 80, and Inserting 20

(d) Index after Inserting 5, Deleting 80, Inserting 20, and Deleting 75

Figure 3.29

The result is shown in Figure 3.29(d). Note that if the parent node had become too small (fewer than two pointers, for this index), we would have had to coalesce level 1 nodes. If coalescing level 1 nodes ever causes the root to have fewer than two children, the index loses a level. In a case where a sibling is too full to allow coalescing, it would be necessary to redistribute pointers between the two siblings (much as we did in splitting) so that each node has the required number.

3.2.5 *B Trees*

A B tree index is similar to a B+ tree index, but it eliminates redundant storage of some keys. In Figure 3.29(d) the values that appear on higher levels of the index are repeated in the sequence set. For example, 100, 200, 15, 25, and others appear on two levels. We can make the index slightly more efficient for accessing some records by placing data record pointers for these values on the highest level on which they appear, instead of carrying the values all the way down to the sequence set. Each nonleaf node will be expanded to include data record pointers as well as the usual pointers to the next index level. Figure 3.30 shows the root node of the index shown in Figure 3.29(d) with the extra pointers that would be included. Similar pointers would appear in all nonleaf nodes. B tree indexes are more efficient for lookup if the value sought appears higher in the index than the sequence set, since the number of accesses will be fewer than in a corresponding B+ tree index. However, maintenance of the index is more complicated. In addition, a B+ tree node holds more key values, since it does not contain the direct data record pointers of a B tree, so fewer nodes are needed to contain the index. Finally, the leaf nodes of a B tree do not form a complete sequence set that can be used for sequential access, as in the B+ tree.

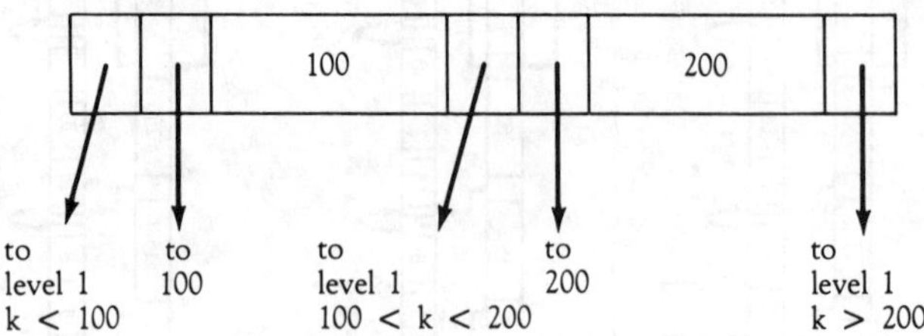

Figure 3.30

3.3 *Chapter Summary*

The most commonly used storage device for the database itself is **magnetic disk**, a **nonvolatile, direct access** device. Some disks units use **Winchester technology** to seal out contaminants. Data is magnetically encoded on circular **tracks** on the recording surfaces, which are also divided into **sectors**. Data is accessed by positioning **read/write heads** on the target track and rotating the disk. Disk capacity depends on the composition of the disk, its size, and its **data density**. The set of tracks in the corresponding positions on all the surfaces of a disk pack is called a **cylinder.** Time required to access data depends on **seek time, rotational delay time, head switching time**, and **transfer time**. Seek time can be minimized by **clustering,** and by placing the most active records near the middle cylinder. Rotational delay can be minimized by **double-writing** and by matching storage order to access order. **Interrecord gaps** separate records.

Magnetic tape is a **nonvolatile sequential access device**, often used for storing archival data and backups. The tape is divided vertically into **frames** and horizontally into **tracks** or **channels**. A **tape drive** is a device for recording and reading tape. **Data density** for tape is measured by the number of bits per inch of tape. The tape contains, in order, a **load point**, a **header control label**, data records that may be **fixed length** or **variable length**, separated by **interrecord gaps**, a **trailer control label**, an **end-of-file** symbol, and an **end-of-reel** marker.

Main or **core memory** is **volatile** and provides **direct access**. A **buffer** is a portion of main memory that holds records for processing. **Optical disks** are available in three forms: **CDROM**, which are read-only, **WORM**, or write-once-read-many, and **erasable optical disk**. Other storage devices include **mass storage devices, magnetic bubble memory**, and **cache memory**. The range of storage devices forms a **memory hierarchy** across which data may be spread according to its relative activity.

Data is stored and transferred in fixed-size units called **blocks, pages**, or **physical records**, whose size may be predefined in **fixed-block architecture devices**, or set by systems programmers. The **blocking factor** is the number of **logical records** in a block. Blocking saves space by reducing the number of **headers** and interrecord gaps. Logical records may be **fixed** or **variable length**. Logical records may be **spanned** or empty spaces may be left at the end of blocks. Variable-length records make deletions and subsequent insertions difficult. Techniques such as allowing a fixed length of the maximum length record or setting up a **prime area** with fixed length of the most common length record and an **overflow area** for portions that do not fit in the prime area are used to handle variable-length records.

File organization means the way data is stored in a file, and **access method** means the way data is found and retrieved, but the two are closely linked. Three basic access methods are **sequential, indexed sequential**, and **direct**. Direct file organization provides **random access** to records and is most often used with databases. A **hashing scheme** such as **division/remainder** or **folding** is used to convert the value of some field into a target address. A **collision** occurs when two keys are **synonyms**, yielding the same target address. Collisions can be minimized by choosing a better hashing scheme, increasing the **bucket size** so that each page holds more records, or reducing **packing density.** Overflow is handled by searching forward a predetermined number of slots or using an overflow area. **Synonym pointers** connect overflow records.

Inverted files, linked lists, and **trees** are data structures used by database management systems. An inverted file is created by **indexing** on a secondary key field. The DBMS uses linked lists to create its own structures. A **B+ tree** can be used to hold a hierarchical index consisting of an **index set** and a **sequence set**, which contains all key values in sequence with pointers to data records. The index must be balanced and obey strict rules about the number of pointers in each node. Insertions or deletions may cause nodes to **split** or **coalesce**. In a **B tree**, nonleaf nodes include data record pointers for search-key values.

3.4 *Exercises*

1. Assume that we have a file consisting of 500 records, each containing 100 bytes. Suppose that a header must contain 10 bytes, a track can hold 1024 bytes, and records are not spanned.

(a) Show the layout of the first track if records are not blocked.
(b) How many tracks will be needed to hold the entire file if records are not blocked?
(c) If there are 10 tracks per cylinder, how many cylinders are needed if records are not blocked?
(d) Show the layout of the first track if records are blocked with block length of 512.
(e) How many tracks will be needed to hold the entire file if records are blocked as in part (d)?
(f) If there are 10 tracks per cylinder, how many cylinders are needed if records are blocked as in part (d)?

2. Let the prime area of an indexed sequential file be organized as follows:

```
track 1     rec 1     rec 3     rec 7     rec 9     empty
track 2     rec 11    rec 21    rec 23    rec 29    empty
track 3     rec 35    rec 37    rec 47    rec 50    empty
track 4     rec 56    rec 57    rec 61    rec 63    empty
```

Assume that the overflow area is empty at present.

(a) Construct a track index using the following headings:

```
TRACK NO   HIGHEST ON TRACK   HIGHEST IN OVERFLOW   OVERFLOW PTR
```

(b) Assume that record 12 is to be inserted. Show the area(s) affected and any changes to the index.
(c) Now assume that record 22 is to be inserted. Show changes to all affected areas and pointers.
(d) Now assume that record 15 is to be inserted. Show changes.
(e) Now assume that record 30 is to be inserted. Show changes.

3. Let a hashing scheme use social security number as the key and the division/remainder method with a divisor of 1000. Target addresses are 1–1000, so 1 is added to the remainder.
   (a) What are the target addresses for the records with the following social security numbers?
      (i) 085349251
      (ii) 983494621
      (iii) 095463612
   (b) Give a synonym for 085349251.
   (c) If the bucket size is 1, explain how the record with social security number 085349251 and the record with its synonym would be stored and retrieved.

4. Assume that a file contains 1000 records with key values in the range 0–999,999. Suppose that the physical file has room for 1500 record addresses.
   (a) What is the packing density for this file?
   (b) Devise a hashing scheme other than division/remainder or folding to yield addresses in the range 0–1499.
   (c) Calculate target addresses for records with the following key values.
      (i) 123456
      (ii) 456789
      (iii) 789012
   (d) Give a synonym for 123456 and explain how you would insert this record.
   (e) Now assume that the bucket size is 5. Target addresses are now in the range 0–299, but five records fit in each bucket. What adjustments must be made to your hashing scheme? How does this affect your overflow handling method?

5. Let a file contain 500 key values in the range 0–9,999. A physical file has room for 800 record addresses.
   (a) What is the packing density for this file?
   (b) Give a hashing scheme other than division/remainder to yield addresses in the range 0–799 for the file.
   (c) Give a synonym for 1234 and explain how you would insert it.
   (d) If the bucket size is changed to 3, what adjustments do you have to make to your hashing scheme?

6. Using any programming language with which you are familiar, write and execute three programs to simulate hashing.
   (a) Your first program should do the following

      1. Generate 100 random key values in the range 0–99,999
      2. For each key value, calculate a target address in the range 0–149, using any hashing scheme you choose.
      3. Keep a count of the number of records targeted for each address and print a report noting the number of overflows resulting from collisions.

   (b) Now modify your program to allow a bucket size of 3 and count the number of overflows.

(c) Modify the program again to allow a bucket size of 5 and count the number of overflows.

(d) Examining your three program runs, determine what effect, if any, changing bucket size had on the number of overflows.

7. Let a file have the following set of key values.
{2,5,8,10,15,18,23,25,28,31,33}

(a) Construct a B+ tree index, assuming 4 key values fit per node.

(b) Show what changes occur to the index when each of the following operations is done in turn.
   (i) insert 24
   (ii) delete 2
   (iii) insert 35

(c) Repeat parts (a) and (b) for a B tree.

8. Define each of the following terms.

(a) DASD
(b) sector
(c) actuator
(d) cylinder
(e) clustering index
(f) sequential access device
(g) volatile storage
(h) buffer
(i) block
(j) fixed-block architecture
(k) blocking factor
(l) spanning records
(m) dense index
(n) hashing
(o) collision
(p) bucket
(q) packing density
(r) partially inverted file
(s) ring
(t) root of a tree
(u) leaf node
(v) sibling nodes
(w) subtree

3.5 *Bibliography*

Bayer, R. and E. McCreight. "Organization and Maintenance of Large Ordered Indices," Acta Informatica **1**:3 (1972) pp. 173–189.

Bayer, R. and M. Schkolnick. "Concurrency of Operating on B-trees," Acta Informatica **9**:1 (1977) pp. 1–21.

Bradley, J. *File and Data Base Techniques*. New York: Holt, Rinehart and Winston, 1982.

Comer, D. "The Ubiquitous B-tree," ACM Computing Surveys **11**:2 (June, 1979) pp. 121–138.

Ellis, C. "Concurrency in Linear Hashing," ACM Transactions on Database Systems **12**:2 (1987) pp. 195–217.

Fagin, R., J. Nievergelt, N. Pippenger, and H. Strong. "Extendible Hashing—a Fast Access Method for Dynamic Files," ACM Transactions on Database Systems **4**:3 (September, 1979) pp. 315–344.

Ghosh, S. *Data Base Organization for Data Management.* Orlando, FL: Academic Press, 1986.

Gillenson, M. *Database Step-by-Step.* New York: John Wiley & Sons, 1985.

Held, G. and M. Stonebraker. "B-trees Reexamined," Communications of the ACM **21**:2 (February, 1978) pp. 139–143.

Knuth, D. *The Art of Computer Programming.* Reading, MA: Addison-Wesley, 1973.

Larson, P. "Performance Analysis of Linear Hashing with Partial Expansions," ACM Transactions on Database Systems **7**:4 (December, 1982) pp. 566–587.

Litwin, W. "Linear Hashing: A New Tool for File and Table Addressing," Proceedings of the International Conference on Very Large Data Bases (1980) pp. 212–223.

Smith, P. and G. Barnes. *Files & Databases: An Introduction.* Reading, MA: Addison-Wesley, 1987.

Teorey, T. and J. Fry. *Design of Database Structures.* Englewood Cliffs, NJ: Prentice-Hall, 1982.

Walter, R. *Introduction to Data Management and File Design.* Englewood Cliffs, NJ: Prentice-Hall, 1986.

Wiederhold, G. *Database Design.* New York: McGraw-Hill, 1983.

Wiederhold, G. *File Organization for Database Design.* New York: McGraw-Hill, 1987.

CHAPTER

4

Database Architecture

4 Chapter Objectives

In this chapter you will learn

- the origin of the three-level database architecture
- the functions of a data sublanguage and a host language
- the distinction between data definition language (DDL) and data manipulation language (DML)
- the rationale for the three-level architecture
- the contents of the external, conceptual, and internal levels
- the purpose of the external/conceptual and the conceptual/internal mappings
- how user requests are passed through the levels
- how data appears at each level
- the meaning of logical and physical data independence
- the importance of the logical data model
- characteristics of semantic data models
- the basics of the entity-relationship model
- characteristics of record-based models
- the basics of the relational, hierarchical, and network models
- how the three record-based models manage a typical query

4.1 *The Three-Level Architecture*

In Chapter 2 we presented a staged database design process which distinguished between a logical database model and a physical model. Now we are ready to examine these and related concepts more closely. When we discuss a database, we need some means of describing different aspects of its structure. An early proposal for a standardized vocabulary and architecture for database systems was developed and published in 1971 by the Database Task Group appointed by the Conference on Data Systems and Languages, **CODASYL DBTG**. A similar vocabulary and architecture were developed and published in 1975 by the Standards Planning and Requirements Committee of the American National Standards Institute Committee on Computers and Information Processing, **ANSI/X3/SPARC**.

As a result of these and later reports, databases can be viewed at **three levels of abstraction**. The levels form a **three-level architecture** and are depicted by **three schemas,** or **three models.** The models refer to the permanent structure of the database, not to the data that is stored at any given moment. This permanent structure is called the **intension of the database**, or the **database scheme**, while the information stored at a given moment is called an **extension of the database**, or a **database instance**. A **database model** is a collection of tools that may include a type of diagram and specialized vocabulary for describing the structure of the database. The model gives a description of the data, the relationships within the data, constraints on the data, and data semantics or meanings.

The purpose of the three-level architecture is to separate the way the database is physically represented from the way the users think about it. There are several reasons why this separation is desirable:

- Different users need different views of the same data.
- The way a particular user needs to see the data may change over time.
- Users should not have to deal with the complexities of the database storage structures.
- The DBA should be able to change the overall logical structure of the database without affecting all users.
- The DBA should be able to change data and file structures without affecting the overall logical structure or users' views.
- Database structure should be unaffected by changes to the physical aspects of storage, such as changes to storage devices.

The way users think about data is called the **external view level**. The way the operating system and the DBMS see the data is the **internal** or **physical level**. The internal level is the way the data is actually stored using the data structures and file organizations described in Chapter 3. However, there are many different users' views and many physical structures, so there must be some method of mapping the external views to the physical structures. A direct mapping is undesirable, since changes made to physical structures or storage devices would require a corresponding change in the external-to-physical mapping. Therefore, there is a middle level that provides both the mapping and the desired independence between the external and physical levels. This is called the **conceptual level**. Figure 4.1 shows the three-level architecture of database systems.

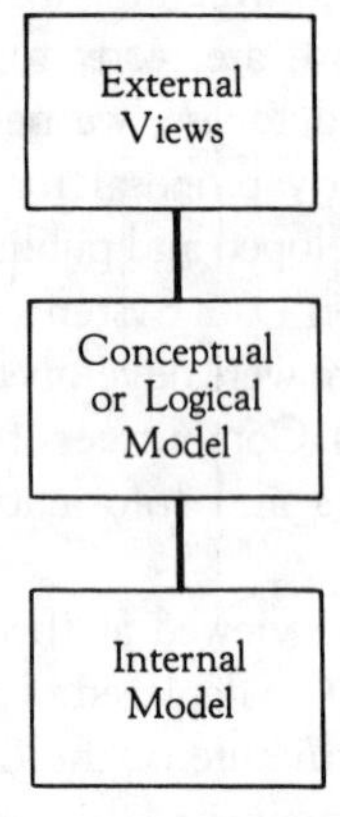

Figure 4.1

The language that is used to describe a database, **data definition language (DDL)**, is part of a **data sublanguage**. A data sublanguage consists of two parts: a DDL and a **data manipulation language (DML)** that is used to process the database. These languages were called data **sub**languages because it was planned that general-purpose programming languages would be extended to provide database operations, so that the commands for definition and manipulation of database objects would be a subset of the programming language itself, which would be called the **host language.** There are standards for C, Pascal, Ada, COBOL, FORTRAN, and other languages as host languages for a standard data sublanguage called SQL. However, many database management systems have their own unique sublanguages that do not conform to any standard, and not all general-purpose languages have database extensions. In many database systems, there is not a close connection between the host language and the data sublanguage, and commands in the data sublanguage are flagged, removed from the host-language program, and replaced by subroutine calls before compilation of the program. They are then compiled by the DBMS, placed in an object module, and the object module is executed at the appropriate time. When data sublanguage commands occur as part of a program in a host language, the sublanguage is said to be **embedded** in the host language. In addition, most data sublanguages allow nonembedded, or **on-line**, commands for access from terminals.

4.1.1 *External Views*

The **external level** consists of many different **external views** or **external models** of the database. Each user has a model of the real world represented in a form that is suitable for that user. A particular user interacts with only certain entities in the real world and is interested in only some of their attributes and relationships. Therefore, that user's view will contain only information about those aspects of the real world. Other entities or other attributes or relationships not of interest may actually be represented in the database, but the user will be unaware of them. Besides including different entities, attributes, and relationships, different views may have different representations of the same data. For example, one user may believe dates are stored in the form (month, day, year), while another may believe they are represented as (year, month, day). Some views might include **virtual** or calculated data, data not actually stored as such, but created when needed. For example, age may not be actually stored, but date of birth may be, and age may be calculated by the system when the user refers to it. Views may even include data combined or calculated from several records. An **external record** is a record as seen by a particular user, a part of his or her external view. An external view is actually a collection of external records. The external views are described in **external schemas** (also called **subschemas**) which are written in the data definition language (DDL). Each user's schema gives a complete description of each type of external record that appears in that user's view. The schemas are compiled by the DBMS and stored in object form for use by the data dictionary in retrieving records if the data dictionary is an active one. They should also be kept in source form as documentation. The DBMS uses the external schema to create a **user interface**, which is both a facility and a barrier. An individual user sees the database through this interface. It defines and creates the working environment for that user, accepting and displaying information in the format the user expects. It also acts as a boundary below which the user is not permitted to see. It hides the conceptual, internal, and physical details from the user.

To develop a user's view, the database designer first interviews the user and examines reports and transactions that he or she creates or receives. After the entire design of the database is planned, the DBA determines what data will be available to that user and what representation the user will see and writes an external schema for that user. Whenever possible, this external schema includes all the information the user has requested. Over time, the user's needs may change and modifications may be made to the view. Often, the new data required is already present in the database, and the user's external schema is rewritten to allow access to it.

4.1.2 *Logical or Conceptual Model*

The middle level in the three-level architecture is the **logical,** or **conceptual,** level. This model includes the entire information structure of the database, as seen by the DBA. It is the "community view" of data and includes a description of all of the data that is available to be shared. It is a complete model or view of the workings of the organization in its environment. All the entities, their attributes, and their relationships are represented in the logical model. The data record types that represent the entities, the data item types that represent their attributes, the relationships that will be stored, the constraints on the data, semantic information about the data meanings, and security and integrity information are all part of the conceptual model. The conceptual model supports the external views, in that any data available to any user must be present in or derivable from the conceptual model. The conceptual model is relatively constant. When the DBA originally designs it, he or she tries to determine present and future information needs and attempts to develop a lasting model of the organization. Therefore, as new data needs arise, the conceptual model may already contain the objects required. If that is not the case, the DBA expands the conceptual model to include the new objects. A good conceptual model will be able to accommodate this change while still supporting the old external views. Only the users who need access to the new data should be affected by the change. The **conceptual schema** is a complete description of the information content of the database, including every record type with all its fields. It is written in DDL, compiled by the DBMS, and stored in object form in the data dictionary and in source form as documentation. The DBMS uses the conceptual schema to create the **logical record interface**, which is a boundary below which everything is invisible to the conceptual level and which defines and creates the working environment for the conceptual level. No internal or physical details such as how records are stored or sequenced cross this boundary. The conceptual level is actually a collection of logical records.

4.1.3 *Internal or Physical Model*

The **internal,** or **physical,** level covers the physical implementation of the database. It includes the data structures and file organizations used to store data on physical storage devices. The DBMS chosen determines, to a large extent, what structures are available. It works with the operating system access methods to lay out the data on the storage devices, build the indexes, and/or set the pointers that will be used for data retrieval. Therefore, there is actually a physical level below the one the DBMS is responsible for, one that is managed by the operating system under the direction of the DBMS. The line between the DBMS responsibilities and the operating system responsibilities are not clear cut and vary from system to system. Some DBMSs take advantage of many of the operating system access method facilities, while others ignore all but the most basic I/O managers and create their own alternative file organizations. The DBA must be aware of the possibilities for mapping the logical model to the physical model and choose a mapping that supports the conceptual view and provides suitable performance. The **internal schema,** written in DDL, is a complete description of the internal model. It includes such items as how data is represented, how records are sequenced, what indexes exist, what pointers exist, and what hashing schemes, if any, are used. An **internal record** is a single stored record. It is the unit that is passed up to the internal level. The **stored record interface** is the boundary between the physical level, for which the operating system may be responsible, and the internal level, for which the DBMS is responsible. This interface is provided to the DBMS by the operating system. In some cases where the DBMS performs some operating system functions, the DBMS itself may create this interface. The physical level below this interface consists of items only the operating system knows, such as exactly how the sequencing is implemented and whether the fields of internal records are actually stored as contiguous bytes on the disk. The operating system creates the **physical record interface**, which is a boundary below which storage details such as exactly what portion of what track contains what data are hidden.

The data dictionary not only stores the complete external, conceptual, and internal schemas, but it also stores the mappings between them. The **external/conceptual mapping** tells the DBMS which objects on the conceptual level correspond to which objects in a particular user's external view. There may be differences in record names, data item names, data item order, data types, and so on. If changes are made to either an external view or the conceptual model, the mappings must be changed. Similarly, the **conceptual/internal mapping** gives the correspondence between conceptual objects and internal ones, in that it tells how the conceptual objects are physically represented. If the stored structure is changed, the mapping must be changed accordingly. Figure 4.2 presents a more detailed picture of the three-level database architecture.

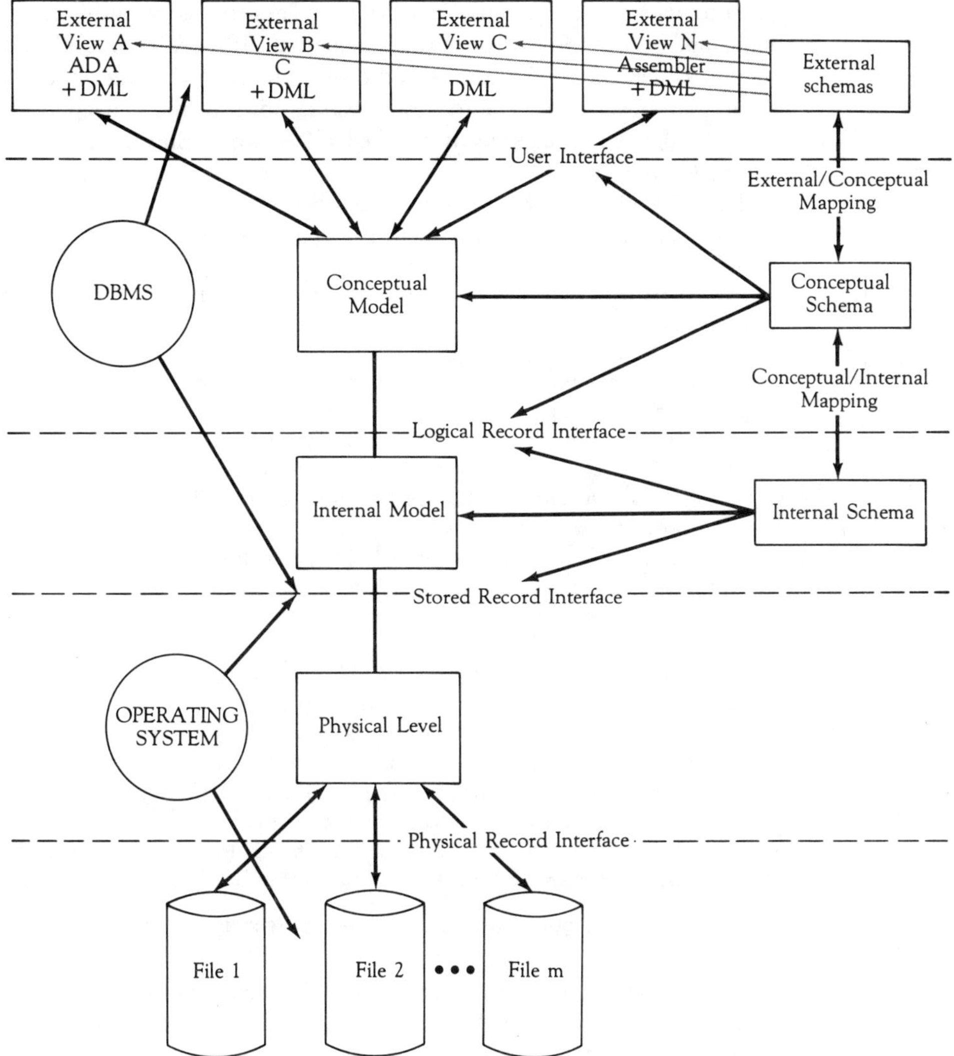

Figure 4.2

To understand the distinctions among the three levels, we consider what happens when we request data. Suppose that we examine what each level receives and passes on when we request the record of a particular employee. Using Figure 4.3, when user A requests such a record, the DBMS intercepts the request. If the request is an on-line one, entered at a terminal using a nonembedded data manipulation language (DML), the DBMS receives the request from the data communications system. If the request is submitted as part of a program, the DBMS takes it out of the program and substitutes a subroutine call for it. In either case, once the DBMS receives the request, it checks the user's external view and the external/conceptual mapping. Both the views and the mapping are stored in object form in the data dictionary, so the checking can be accomplished easily. The DBMS also checks the user's authorization to access the items and to perform the operations requested. If there is no such authorization, the request is denied. If the user is authorized, the DBMS notes which conceptual-level objects are needed, and the request is passed down to the conceptual level. Next, the conceptual/internal mapping is checked to see what internal structures correspond to the conceptual items. Once again, the data dictionary has stored both of the models and the mapping in object form. The DBMS identifies the internal objects that are required, and it passes the request to the operating system.

```
1.  User A requests record of employee E101 through User
Interface.
2.  DBMS receives request.
3.  DBMS checks User A's External Schema, External/Conceptual
Mapping, Conceptual Schema in DD.
4.  DBMS checks User A's Authorization.
5.  a)  If not authorized, User A's request is rejected.
    b)  If authorized, DBMS uses Logical Record Interface to
    request logical record.
6.  DBMS checks Conceptual/Internal Mapping to determine
corresponding internal structures.
7.  DBMS uses Stored Record Interface to request stored record
of Operating System.
8.  Operating System identifies desired physical record and
requests Access Method to retrieve it.
9.  Access Method retrieves block of records, places it in
buffer, and passes address of stored record to DBMS.
10.  DBMS checks Conceptual/Internal Mapping, edits stored
record, and passes logical record to conceptual level.
11.  DBMS checks External/Conceptual Mapping, edits logical
record, and passes external record to User A.
```

Figure 4.3 Steps in Retrieving Record of E101 for User A

On the physical level, a employee record is contained in a physical record, a page or block that may hold several employee records. This is the unit that is brought to the buffer from the disk. The operating system is responsible for performing the basic job of locating the correct block for the requested record and managing its retrieval. When the retrieval is complete, the proper block is in the buffer, and the operating system passes to the DBMS the exact location within the buffer at which the stored record appears. The DBMS receives only the requested employee record, not all the records in the block. However, it receives the complete stored record, exactly as it is coded or encrypted, together with any pointers that may appear in it, but without its header. This is, then, a description of an internal record, which is the unit that passes up through the stored record interface. The DBMS uses the conceptual/internal mapping to decide what items to pass up through the logical record interface to the conceptual level.

At the conceptual level, the record appears as a logical record, with encryption and special coding removed. Pointers that are used for establishing relationships do not appear on the conceptual level, since that level is concerned only with the existence of relationships, not with how they are implemented. Similarly, pointers used for sequencing are not of interest on the conceptual level, nor are indexes. The conceptual-level record therefore contains only the information for that particular employee, but it contains all the fields stored for the employee, in the order in which they are stored. The DBMS checks the external/conceptual mapping to decide what the user's external record should look like. When the record is passed up through the user interface to the external level, certain fields may be hidden, some may have their names changed, some may be rearranged, some may appear in a form different from their stored form, and some may be virtual ones, created from the stored record. Some external records may be combinations of stored records or the result of operations such as calculations on stored records. The user then performs operations on the external record. That is, he or she can manipulate only those items that appear in the external record. These changes, if legal, are eventually made to the stored record. Figure 4.3 summarizes the steps in this process, and Figure 4.4 illustrates the differences in the appearance of the employee record as it is passed up to the external level.

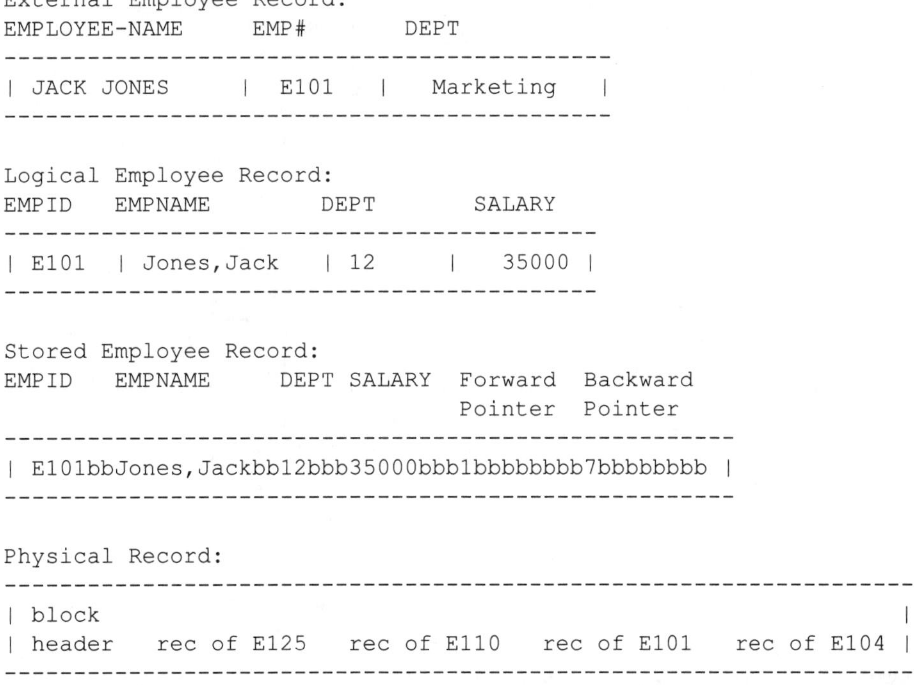

External Employee Record:
EMPLOYEE-NAME EMP# DEPT
| JACK JONES | E101 | Marketing |
Logical Employee Record:
EMPID EMPNAME DEPT SALARY
| E101 | Jones,Jack | 12 | 35000 |
Stored Employee Record:
EMPID EMPNAME DEPT SALARY Forward Pointer Backward Pointer
| E101bbJones,Jackbb12bbb35000bbb1bbbbbbbb7bbbbbbbb |
Physical Record:
| block header rec of E125 rec of E110 rec of E101 rec of E104 |

Figure 4.4 Differences in External, Conceptual, Stored, and Physical Records

4.1.4 *Logical and Physical Data Independence*

A major reason for the three-level architecture is to provide **data independence**, which means that upper levels are unaffected by changes to lower levels. There are two kinds of data independence: **logical** and **physical**. Logical data independence refers to the immunity of external models to changes in the conceptual model. Conceptual model changes such as the addition of new record types, new data items, and new relationships should be possible without affecting existing external views. Of course, the users for whom the changes are made need to be aware of them, but other users should not be. In particular, existing application programs should not have to be rewritten when conceptual-level changes are made.

Physical data independence refers to the immunity of the conceptual model to changes in the internal model. Internal or physical changes such as a different physical sequencing of records, switching from one access method to another, changing the hashing algorithm, using different data structures, and using new storage devices should have no effect on the conceptual model. On the external level, the only effect that may be felt is a change in performance and, in fact, a deterioration in performance is the most common reason for internal model changes. Figure 4.5 shows where each type of data independence occurs.

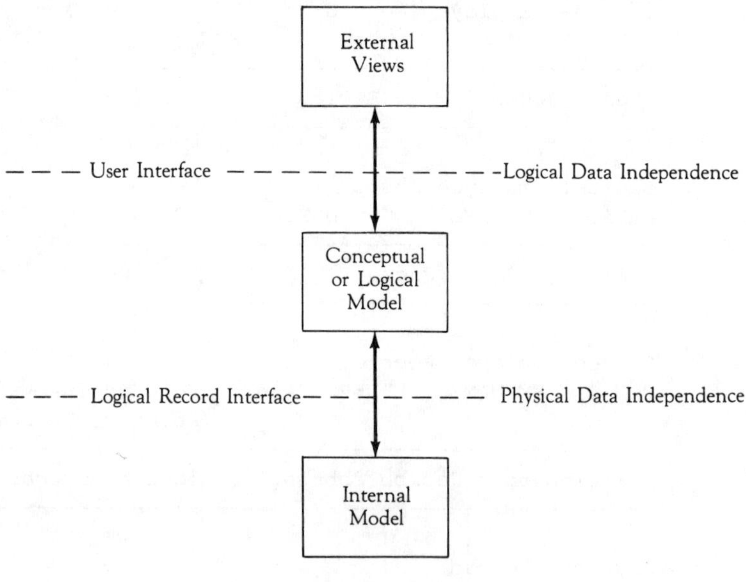

Figure 4.5

4.2 *Logical Data Models*

The conceptual, or logical, model is the heart of the database. It supports all the external views and is, in turn, supported by the internal model. However, the internal model is merely the physical implementation of the conceptual model. The conceptual model should be a complete and accurate representation of the workings of the organization in its environment. If that is not the case, some information about the organization is missing or incorrectly represented, and eventually some external view will be inadequate.

If the conceptual model is correct, it should support any external view needed. The conceptual model should be the most permanent part of the database architecture. External views can and should be changed. The internal model should change when new devices or new techniques for representing data and improving performance are developed. However, the conceptual model represents the permanent structure of the data resource of the organization. It should require changes only when the actual workings of the organization or the environment change.

Developing the logical model is the most challenging, interesting, and rewarding part of database design. During the logical design process, there may be many errors and several false starts. Like many other problem-solving processes, logical database design is a matter of intuition, guided by knowledge. There may be many possible solutions, but some are better than others. The process itself is a learning situation, as the designer gradually comes to understand the workings of the organization and the meanings of its data, and expresses that understanding in the chosen model. If the designer produces a good logical model, it is a relatively easy task to convert it to an internal model and complete the physical design. Often the DBA has the assistance of systems personnel in doing the physical design. If the logical model is a good one, the external views are easy to define as well, since any data that a user might be interested in should be included in the logical model and it is a simple task to put it into the user's external view. On the other hand, a poor logical model may be hard to implement, particularly if data and relationships are not well defined. It will also be inadequate to provide all the needed external models. A poor logical design will continue to cause problems during the lifetime of the database, because it will have to be "patched up" whenever different information needs arise. The ability to adjust to change is one of the hallmarks of good logical design. Therefore, it is worthwhile to spend the time and energy necessary to produce the best possible logical design. The payoff will be felt not only at the internal design stage but in the future.

We have already seen in Chapter 2 that logical design begins with an examination of the organization in its environment. Interviewing users, examining transactions and reports, designing the data flow diagrams, and compiling a data dictionary are the initial steps we have already discussed. Having completed those steps, the DBA is ready to begin the logical design itself. The designer must be able to identify, classify, and structure objects in the design. The process of **abstraction**, which means identifying common properties of a set of objects rather than focusing on details, is used to categorize data. The concept of number is a familiar mathematical abstraction. In computer science, abstraction is used to simplify concepts and hide complexity. For example, abstract data types are considered apart from their implementation; you can describe the behavior of queues and stacks without considering how they are represented. The designer may look at different levels of abstraction, so that an abstract object on one level becomes a component of a higher-level abstraction. The designer must have some method of representing possible structures. The logical models in this section provide such representation methods. It is important to understand that what the models represent is the permanent logical structure of the database, the intension or scheme of the database, rather than an extension or instance of the database. The intension of the database is actually a complex abstract data structure that formally defines all possible extensions. There is much disagreement over what constitutes a logical model, and that debate is reflected in the dozens of proposed models found in the literature. It is also difficult to categorize these models, since each represents an alternative approach and distinguishes itself by how it differs from the others. However, for the sake of simplicity, we will attempt to categorize them and we will discuss two different types which we will call **semantic models** and **record-based models.**

4.2.1 *Semantic Data Models*

These models are used to describe the conceptual and external levels of data and are independent of the internal and physical aspects. In addition to specifying what is to be represented in the database, they attempt to incorporate some meanings or semantic aspects of data, such as explicit representation of objects, attributes, and relationships, categorization of objects, abstraction, and explicit data constraints.

The Entity–Relationship Model

Some of the concepts of the **entity-relationship (E-R)** model were introduced in Chapter 2 when we described the three levels of abstraction in discussion of data. The model was introduced by Chen in the mid-1970s and is widely used for logical design. It is based on identifying real-world objects called **entities** which are described by their **attributes** and which are connected by **relationships.** In Chapter 2 we described entities as persons, places, events, objects, or concepts about which we collect data. A more proper description is that an entity is **any object that exists and is distinguishable from other objects.** The attributes describe the entities and distinguish them from one another. We defined an **entity set** as a collection of entities of the same type. Now we also define a **relationship set** as a set of relationships of the same type, and we add the fact that relationships may themselves have descriptive attributes. The E-R model also allows us to express **constraints,** or restrictions, on the entities or relationships. Chapter 5 contains a more complete description of the E-R model, including details about constraints.

One of the most useful and attractive features of the E-R model is that it provides a graphical method for depicting the logical structure of the database. **E-R diagrams** contain symbols for entities, attributes, and relationships. Figure 4.6 shows some of the symbols, along with their names, meanings, and usages. Figure 4.7 illustrates a simple E-R diagram for students and classes. It shows an entity set called STUDENT, with the attributes STUID, STUNAME, MAJOR, and CREDITS. There is a second entity set, CLASS, with attributes COURSE#, CTITLE, PROF, SCHED, and ROOM. The two entity sets are connected by a relationship set, ENROLL, which has descriptive attribute GRADE. Note that GRADE is not an attribute of STUDENT, since knowing the grade for a student is meaningless unless we know the course as well, and similarly, GRADE is not an attribute of CLASS, since knowing that a particular grade was given for a class is meaningless unless we know to which student the grade was given. Therefore, since GRADE has meaning only for a particular combination of student and class, it belongs to the relationship set.

The E-R model describes only a logical structure for the database. We do not attempt to describe how the model could or should be represented internally. Therefore, the

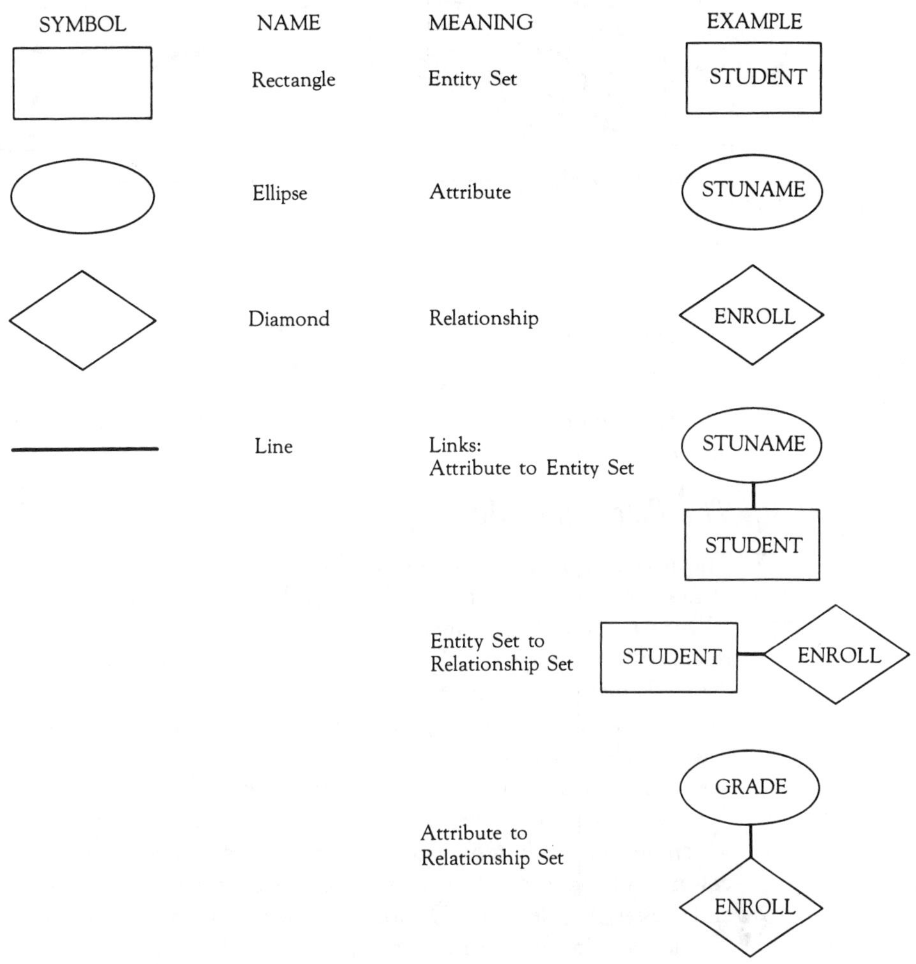

Figure 4.6

material in Section 2.2.2 in which we described data items, records and files is not part of the E-R model itself.

There are many other semantic models that have been proposed in the research literature, some of which have been developed and implemented. We will postpone discussion of other semantic models to Chapter 11.

4.2.2 *Record-Based Models*

These models are used to describe the external, conceptual, and to some extent, the internal levels of the database. They allow the designer to develop and specify the logical structure and provide some options for implementation of the design. They have been implemented using a variety of database systems. However, they do not provide much

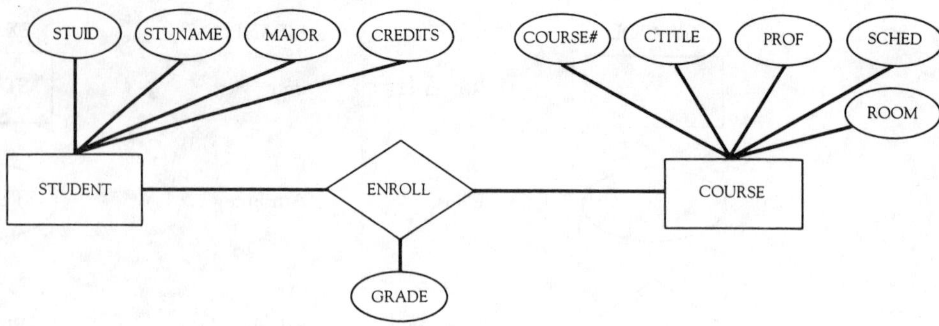

Figure 4.7

semantic information, such as categorization of objects or relationships, abstraction, or data constraints.

The Relational Model

The relational model was proposed by Codd in 1970 and continues to be the subject of much research. It is now widely used by both mainframe and microcomputer-based DBMSs because of its simplicity from the user's point of view and its power. The relational model uses the theory of relations from mathematics and adapts it for use in database theory. The same type of theoretical development of the subject, complete with formal notation, definitions, theorems, and proofs that we usually find in mathematics can be applied to databases using this model. The results of this theoretical development are then applied to practical considerations of implementation.

In the relational model, both entities and relationships are represented by **relations,** which are physically represented as **tables** or two-dimensional arrays, and attributes as **columns** of those tables. For example, if we wish to store information about students and classes, we need a table for the student entity set, another for the class entity set, and a third for the relationship between the student and the class. A student is related to a class by being enrolled in that class. The columns of the STUDENT table have headings for the student attributes: STUID, STUNAME, MAJOR, and CREDITS. The CLASS table has a column for each of its attributes, COURSE#, CTITLE, PROF, SCHED, and ROOM. The ENROLL table is used to show the relationship between the other two tables, by including the columns STUID and COURSE#. It also has the attribute GRADE, which belongs to the relationship. Figure 4.8 shows a sample relational database for this data. Note that the records in the ENROLL table show what students are enrolled in what classes. We study the relational model in detail in later chapters.

The Hierarchical Model

The hierarchical model is the basis of the oldest database management systems, which grew out of early attempts to organize data for the U.S. space program. Since these databases were ad hoc solutions to immediate problems, they were created without the strong theoretical foundations that later systems had. Their designers were familiar with file organizations and data structures, and used these concepts to solve the immediate

STUDENT Table

STUID	STUNAME	MAJOR	CREDITS
S1001	Smith,Tom	History	90
S1002	Chin,Ann	Math	36
S1005	Lee,Perry	History	3
S1010	Burns,Edward	Art	63
S1013	McCarthy,Owen	Math	9
S1015	Jones,Mary	Math	42
S1020	Rivera,Jane	CS	15

CLASS Table

COURSE#	CTITLE	PROF	SCHED	ROOM
ART103A	Intro to Art	Adams	MWF9	H221
CSC201A	Programming I	Tanaka	TuThF10	M110
CSC203A	Programming II	Tanaka	MThF12	M110
HST205A	Western Civil	Smith	MWF11	H221
MTH101B	Calculus I	Byrne	MTuTh9	H225
MTH103C	Calculus II	Byrne	MWF11	H225

ENROLLMENT Table

COURSE#	STUID	GRADE
ART103A	S1001	A
CSC201A	S1020	B
CSC201A	S1002	F
ART103A	S1010	B
ART103A	S1002	A
MTH101B	S1020	A
HST205A	S1001	C
MTH103C	S1010	A
MTH103C	S1002	B

Figure 4.8 A Sample Relational Data Base for STUDENT-CLASS Example

data representation problems of users. Later, study groups used some of their solutions to design a theoretical framework. Ideas such as the three-level database architecture stem from these early systems.

The hierarchical model uses the **tree** as its basic data structure. Unlike the trees used for indexes in Chapter 3, **nodes** of the trees in the hierarchical model represent data **records** or **record segments,** which are portions of data records. **Relationships** are represented as **links** or **pointers** between nodes. Figure 4.9(a) shows the scheme or structure of a sample hierarchical database for the student and class data. In this example, CLASS is the root node and STUDENT is its child. CLASS is a record segment having fields COURSE#, CTITLE, PROF, SCHED, and ROOM, while STUDENT is a dependent segment having fields STUID, STUNAME, MAJOR, CREDITS, and GRADE. In an occurrence of the structure, a CLASS segment may have zero, one, or many STUDENT segments associated with it. Figure 4.9(b) shows an instance or extension of the hierarchical database with six occurrences. Figure 4.9(c) shows this instance represented as a sequential file. All the segments are shown laid out sequentially, as if on tape. Each CLASS segment begins a new occurrence of the tree, and each has zero, one, or many STUDENT segments following it before the next CLASS segment appears. The STUDENT segments appear nested inside CLASS segments. To get to a STUDENT segment, you must go through its parent CLASS segment. If a particular student is enrolled in more than one class, the student's ID, name, major, and credits are repeated. There is no need for a separate ENROLL record because the position of the STUDENT segment, following its parent CLASS segment, tells what class the student is enrolled in.

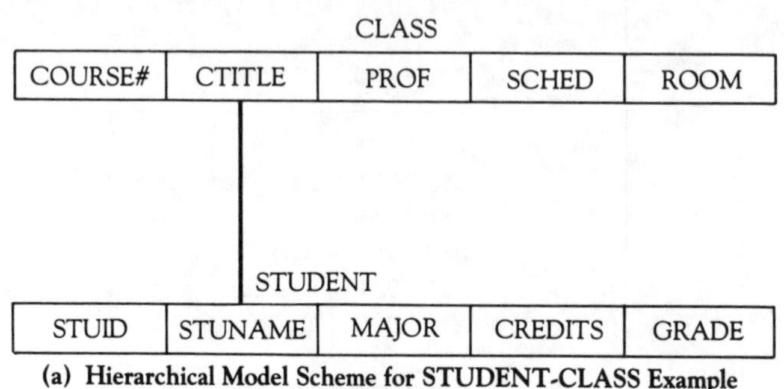

(a) Hierarchical Model Scheme for STUDENT-CLASS Example

Figure 4.9(a)

We discuss the hierarchical model in detail in Chapter 10.

Network Model

The network model uses a network or **plex** structure, which is a data structure consisting of **nodes and branches**. Unlike a tree, a plex structure allows a node to have more than one parent. The nodes of the network represent records of various types. Relationships between records are represented as **links**, which become **pointers** in the implementation. Figure 4.10(a) shows a scheme of a network database for the student and class data. Here, CLASS is a parent or owner record and ENROLL is a child or member record. STUDENT is also an owner record for ENROLL. Each ENROLL record represents the enrollment of one student in one class. In the physical implementation of this scheme, shown in Figure 4.10(b), each CLASS record is the head of a circular linked list that goes through all the ENROLL records for that class. For example, the ART103A record points to the enrollment record having COURSE# of ART103A and STUID of S1001, which has a CLASS pointer to the next enrollment record for the same class, having COURSE# of ART103A and STUID of S1002. This points to the record having COURSE# of ART103A and STUID of S1010. This last enrollment record for ART103A points back to the owner, the CLASS record for ART103A. Similarly, each STUDENT record is the head of a circular linked list that goes through all ENROLL records for that student. For example, the STUDENT record with STUID S1001 points to the first ENROLL record for that student, the one having STUID of S1001 and COURSE# of ART103A. The STUDENT pointer of that ENROLL record points to the next ENROLL record for the same student, the one having STUID of S1001 and COURSE# of HST205A. Since this is the last ENROLL record for S1001, its STUDENT pointer points back to the STUDENT record. The network model is presented in detail in Chapter 9.

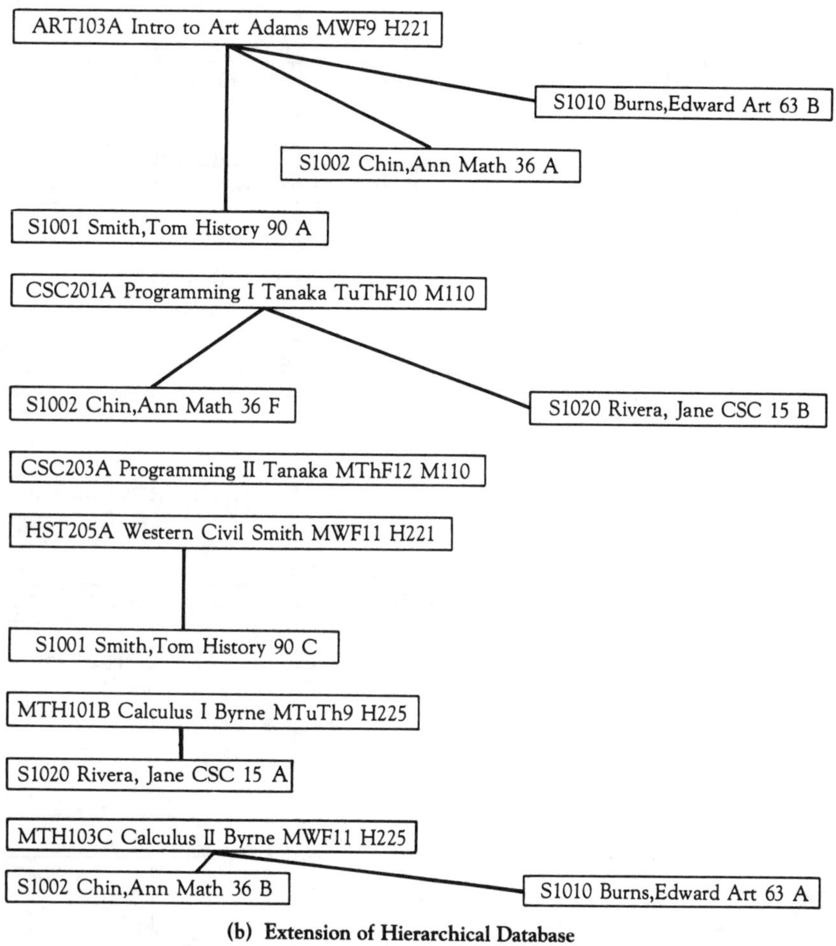

(b) Extension of Hierarchical Database

Figure 4.9(b)

4.2.3 *Query Example in Record-Based Models*

To illustrate some of the differences among the three record-based models, we will consider the following questions:

1. Find the names of all the students enrolled in ART103A.
2. Find the titles of all the courses taken by student S1001.

Looking at the sample relational database pictured in Figure 4.8, we see that the ENROLL table talls us which students are enrolled in ART103A. However, it gives us the STUID of each student, not the name. Student names appear on the STUDENT table. Our plan for answering question 1, then, is to look at the ENROLL table and find all the rows where the value of COURSE# is ART103A and make note of the STUID in those rows, namely, S1001, S1010, and S1002. Then we go to the STUDENT table and find the rows containing those values in the STUID column. We find

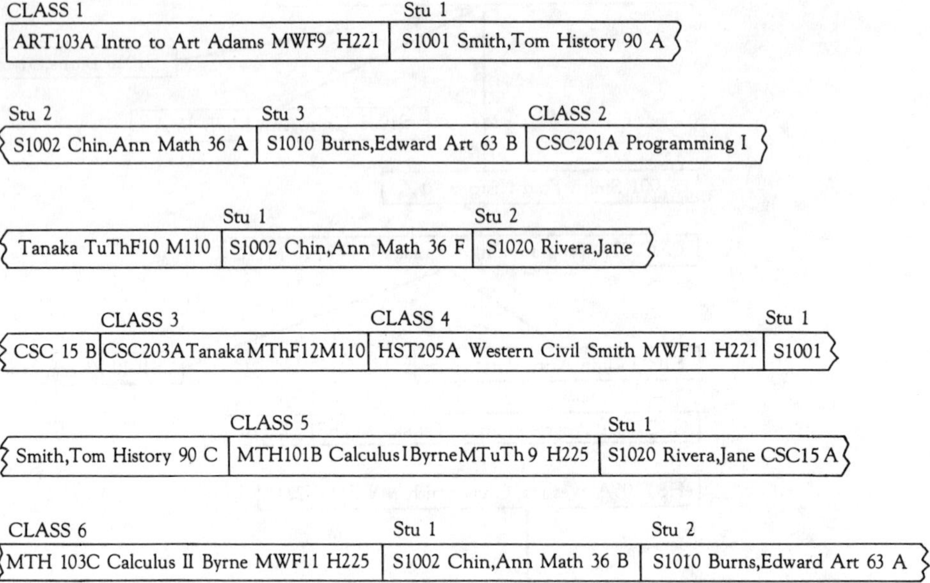

(c) A sample Hierarchical Data Base for STUDENT-CLASS

Figure 4.9(c)

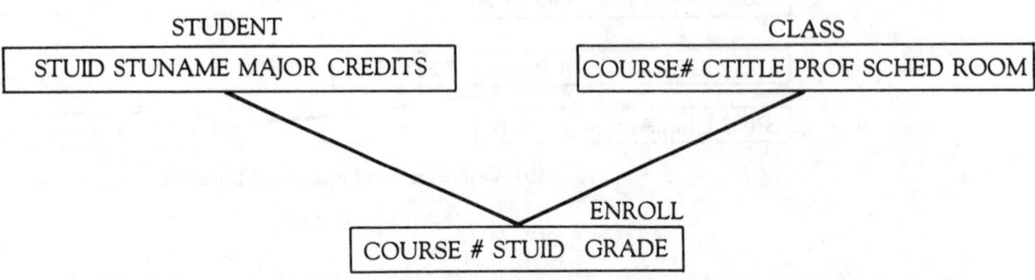

Figure 4.10(a)

the answer to the question by listing the STUNAME values in those rows, giving us "Smith,Tom", "Burns,Edward", and "Chin,Ann". To answer the second question, we note that although the ENROLL table can tell us the COURSE# of all classes taken by S1001, we need to consult the CLASS table to find the course titles. Again, we start with the ENROLL table, looking this time for rows where the STUID is S1001. We find two such rows and note the corresponding COURSE# values, ART103A and HST205A. We now look at the COURSE# column of the CLASS table to see which rows have those values for COURSE#. For those rows, we make a list of the CTITLE values, "Intro to Art" and "Western Civil".

Applying the same two questions to the hierarchical example shown as a sequential file in Figure 4.9(c), we see that the first question is easy to answer. To find the names of all students in ART103A, we simply locate the ART103A record and see what student

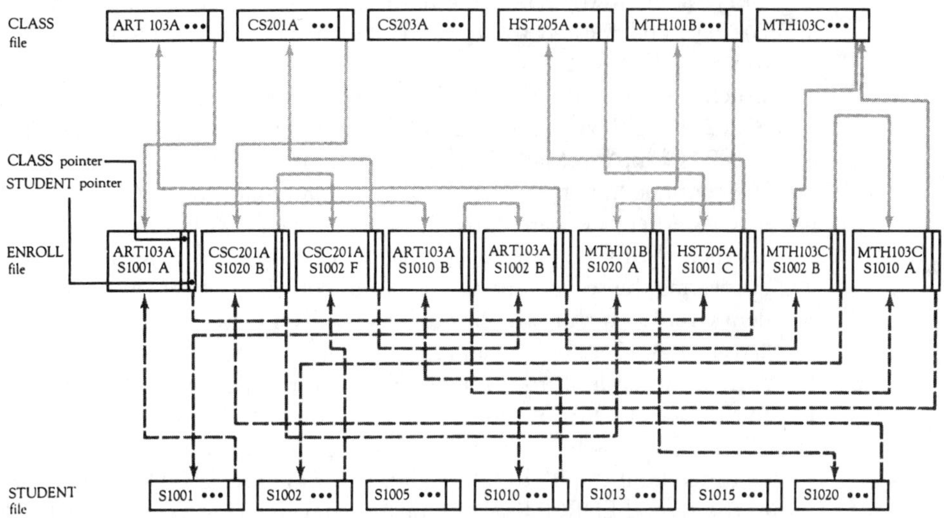

Figure 4.10(b)

segments are dependent on it. We find three such segments, and we read the names "Smith,Tom", "Chin,Ann", and "Burns, Edward". The second question is much more difficult to answer. To see what courses S1001 takes, we must look through the first occurrence, see whether S1001 appears, and if it does, we must "back up" to find what class this STUDENT segment is dependent on. We find that S1001 appears in the first STUDENT segment for the first CLASS record, so we go back to find the title of the course "Intro to Art". Now we search the second occurrence and find that S1001 does not appear there. We continue and find that it does not appear in the third occurrence. It does appear in the fourth occurrence, so we note the CLASS segment before it and find the title of "Western Civil". We continue searching throughout the rest of the database records and see that S1001 does not appear again. Notice that we had to search the entire database to answer this question.

We now consider the first question, using the network model example shown in Figure 4.10(b). We begin with the CLASS file, locating the record for ART103A. We follow its pointer to the first ENROLL record for that class, the one that contains values "ART103A S1001 A". Unfortunately, this gives us only the ID of a student enrolled, not the name. To find the name of the student whose ID is S1001, we follow the STUDENT pointer in the current ENROLL record, which leads to the next ENROLL record for the same student, one that contains "HST205A S1001 C". Following the STUDENT pointer from that record leads us to the STUDENT record with data "S1001 Smith,Tom History 90". Now we know that the first ENROLL record for ART103A is associated with STUNAME of "Smith,Tom". To find the second ENROLL record for ART103A, we need to go back to the first ENROLL record for that class, and this time follow the CLASS pointer, which brings us to the record having entries "ART103A S1010 B". To find the name of the student associated with this record, we follow its STUDENT pointer, which brings us to the ENROLL record with entries "MTH103C S1010 A". We follow its STU-

DENT pointer, which brings us to the STUDENT record with data "S1010 Burns,Edward Art 63", and we find the name of the student, "Burns,Edward". We now go back to the second ENROLL record for this class, and this time we follow its CLASS pointer, which leads us to the third ENROLL record for the class, the one with data "ART103A S1002 A". Following its STUDENT pointer, we go to the STUDENT record with data "S1002 Chin,Ann Math 36", which gives us the value of "Chin,Ann" for STUNAME. We continue from the third ENROLL record, following its CLASS pointer, which leads us back where we started, the CLASS record for ART103C. Now we know there are no more ENROLL records for that class, so we are finished with the first question. Answering the second question is just as complicated. We begin with the record of student S1001, which leads us to the first ENROLL record for that student, having entries "ART103A S1001 A". To find the associated course title, we need to follow the CLASS pointer, which leads to two more ENROLL records for the same class before leading us to the correct CLASS record, which has entries "ART103A Intro to Art Adams MWF9 H221". We now have the title of the first course, "Intro to Art", for this student. We continue from the ENROLL record, following the STUDENT pointer, which leads us to the second ENROLL record for this student. This has values "HST205A S1001 C". To find the course title, we follow the CLASS pointer, which leads us to the CLASS record with entries "HST205A Western Civil Smith MWF11 H221", and we now have the second course title for the student, "Western Civil". We continue from the second ENROLL record for this student, following the STUDENT pointer, which brings us back to the STUDENT record where we started, so we are finished with the search.

Comparing the queries on the three models, we find that the two questions were about equally difficult for the relational model. They both started with one table and required comparison with a second table, but the process was fairly simple. The first question was easy to answer in the hierarchical model, but the second required searching the entire database. We note that if we had chosen to make STUDENT the root node and CLASS the child, the situation would be reversed, with the second question being easy and the first difficult. We observe from this that the choice of the root node has a great effect on the efficiency of queries. For the network model, answering both questions was equally difficult, since both required following strings of pointers. It was very important for us to know which pointer to follow next, and to remember our position in the files. This type of pointer "navigation" in a database is characteristic of the network model.

Of the four models discussed so far, which is the best? There is no simple answer to this question. Each model has its advantages and disadvantages. One is more suitable than another depending on the enterprise data, the applications, and the environment. Many designers find it convenient to begin by using a semantic model to capture the data and interrelationships in the enterprise and then to move on to a record-based model. Since semantic models such as the entity-relationship model capture the meanings of the organization's data but do not yet have widely-used implementations, while record-based models are lacking in semantic information but are easily converted to physical form, it is desirable to try to capitalize on the best aspects of both types. Therefore, the approach we will use is to develop a semantic model first, using the entity-relationship approach, and once we have a good representation of the organization, to convert it to a record-based model such as the relational. This is the plan we will follow in the remaining design chapters.

4.3 Chapter Summary

Standard database architecture uses **three levels of abstraction: external, logical,** and **internal**. An **external view** is the model seen by a particular user, and consists of **external records**, which may be subsets or combinations of actual records. An **external schema** is an external model description written in the **data definition language** which is part of the **data sublanguage** for the particular DBMS being used. The **user interface** creates the user's working environment and hides lower levels from the user. The **logical schema** is a complete DDL description of the logical or conceptual model. It specifies the information content of the database, including all record types and fields, but does not contain details of storage or physical representation. The **logical record interface** is a boundary below which the conceptual level cannot see. The **internal schema** is a DDL description of the internal model. It specifies how data is represented, how records are sequenced, what indexes and pointers exist, and what hashing scheme is used. The **stored record interface** is the boundary below which the DBMS does not see. The operating system should be responsible for all physical details below this interface, including creating a **physical record interface** for itself to handle low-level physical details such as track placement. The **external/conceptual mapping** tells how the external views correspond to the conceptual items. The **conceptual/internal mapping** tells how conceptual items correspond to internal ones. **Data independence** makes each level immune to changes on lower levels. **Logical data independence** means that the conceptual level may be changed without changing external views. **Physical data independence** means internal and physical changes will not affect the logical model.

The logical model is the heart of the database. A good logical design is easy to implement and supports the desired external views. Logical design is a challenging and rewarding task. Two types of logical models are **record-based models**, which include the **relational, hierarchical**, and **network**, and **semantic data models**, which include the **entity-relationship**, among others. The entity–relationship model uses **E-R diagrams** to show entity sets, attributes of entities, relationship sets, and descriptive attributes of relationships. The hierarchical model uses a **tree** structure to hold data in its nodes or **segments**. Each occurrence of the structure begins with a root node. The entire database extension consists of multiple occurrences of the tree, each of which starts with an occurrence of the root node. The **network** model uses a network or **plex** structure, which consists of nodes and branches. Unlike a tree, a network allows a node to have more than one parent or **owner** node on which it is dependent. Pointers are used to represent relationships in the network model.

4.4 Exercises

1. Describe the three-level architecture for databases.

2. Describe the two parts of data sublanguages.

3. Give five reasons why it is desirable to separate the physical representation from the logical structure of a database.

4. Distinguish among the following: user interface, logical record interface, stored record interface, physical record interface.

5. Describe each of the following: external schema, conceptual schema, internal schema.

6. Explain the purpose of the external/conceptual mapping and of the conceptual/internal mapping.

7. Distinguish between logical and physical data independence, giving examples of possible changes they allow.

8. Explain why the conceptual model is called the heart of the database.

9. Describe abstraction and explain how it is used in database design.

10. Distinguish between the intension and extension of a database.

11. Explain how record-based logical models differ from semantic models.

4.5 *Bibliography*

Atre, S. *Data Base: Structured Techniques for Design, Performance, and Management*. New York: John Wiley & Sons, 1980.

Brackett, M. *Developing Data Structured Databases*. Englewood Cliffs, NJ: Prentice-Hall, 1987.

Brodie, M., J. Mylopoulos, and J. Schmidt (Ed.). *On Conceptual Modeling*. New York: Springer-Verlag, 1984.

Date, C. *An Introduction to Database Systems*. Reading, MA: Addison-Wesley, 1986.

Hawryszkiewycz, I. *Database Analysis and Design*. Chicago: Science Research Associates, 1984.

Howe, D. *Data Analysis for Data Base Design*. London: Edward Arnold, 1983.

Kent, W. "Limitations of Record-based Information Models," ACM Transactions on Database Systems 4:1 (March, 1979) pp. 107-131.

Tsichritzis, D., and F. Lochovsky. *Data Models*. Englewood Cliffs, NJ: Prentice-Hall, 1982.

Wiederhold, G. *Database Design*. New York: McGraw-Hill, 1983.

CHAPTER

5

The Entity-Relationship Model

5 Chapter Objectives

In this chapter you will learn

- what an enterprise schema consists of
- the meaning of **entity type**, **entity set**, and **entity instance**
- how to represent entities on the E-R diagram
- how attributes are associated with entities
- the meaning of attribute **domain**
- what a null value is
- the meaning of **superkey**, **candidate key**, **primary key**, **alternate key**, **secondary key**, and **foreign key**
- the meaning of **relationship type**, **relationship set**, and **relationship instance**
- how to represent relationship sets as ordered pairs, triples, or *n*-tuples
- how to represent relationship sets and their attributes on an E-R diagram
- the meaning of the cardinality of a relationship
- examples of one-to-one, one-to-many, many-to-one, and many-to-many relationships
- properties of functional mappings
- how to show mappings on an E-R diagram
- when and how to indicate roles on an E-R diagram
- the meaning and types of existence dependencies
- how to use the aggregation and decomposition abstraction
- how to use the generalization and specialization abstraction
- how aggregation and generalization are related
- how to represent aggregation and generalization on an E-R diagram

5.1 *Purpose of the E-R Model*

The entity-relationship model was developed by Chen to facilitate database design by allowing the designer to express the logical properties of the database in an **enterprise schema**. The word enterprise means the organization for which the database is kept. The enterprise schema is a description that corresponds to the conceptual level in the three-level architecture. E-R diagrams are used to express the logical structure of the model. Some of the diagram symbols and their uses were described in Figures 4.5 and 4.6. The enterprise schema will be valid regardless of the database system chosen, and it can remain correct even if the DBMS is changed. Unlike a schema written in a DDL, the E-R diagrams that we will use are not generally available to be used by the DBMS for creating the logical structure or doing external/conceptual or conceptual/internal mappings. The diagrams are basically design tools and documentation for the system. We note that there is an implementation of the E-R model that actually uses the diagrams to create the database structure. However, we are more interested in using them as design tools and discussing how they could be useful in implementing a variety of systems. We also note that the discussion of the E-R model here differs slightly from Chen's. We have added concepts and used terminology that will be useful in later discussions, even though they differ from Chen's.

The E-R model was classified in Chapter 4 as a semantic model, one that attempts to capture meaning as well as structure. The items in the model represent "things" in the real world, and the relationships between real-world "things" are expressed by relationships in the model. The model describes the environment in terms of **entities, attributes**, and **relationships**.

5.2 *Entities*

The term **entity** is formally undefined, but it was described in previous chapters as any object that exists and can be distinguished from other objects. It is a person, place, event, object, or concept in the real world that we wish to represent in the database. It can be a physical object or an abstraction. Different designers may disagree about what entities exist in the organization's environment. For different enterprises, entity examples or instances may be a particular student, a specific class, an individual customer, a particular employee, an account, a patient, a conference, an invention or a club. Applying abstraction, we can identify the common properties of entity instances and define an **entity type**, which is a representation in the data model of a category of real-world entities. For example, if the enterprise is a university, we can consider all students in the university and identify the common properties of the Student entity type. A collection of entities of the same type is called an **entity set**. For example, all the students in the university would form the Student entity set. The set must be **well-defined**, meaning that it must be possible to determine whether a particular entity instance belongs to it or not. The entity type and the well-defined entity set form the

intension of the entity, the permanent definition part. All the entity instances that fulfill the definition at the moment form the **extension** of the entity. The members of the Student entity set change as students come and go, but the Student entity type and the set definition remain constant. Entity sets can intersect, that is, have common members. For example, in the model of the university we might have a Faculty entity type and an Administrator entity type. A particular person may satisfy the definition of both types, being simultaneously both a faculty member and an administrator in the university, and would therefore be an instance in both of these entity sets. An entity set is represented in E-R diagrams by a rectangle having the name of the entity set inside.

5.3 *Attributes*

The **attributes** of an entity set are the defining properties or qualities of the entity type. For the Student entity type, the defining properties might be student ID, student name, major, and number of credits accumulated. The attributes are the representation in the model of those properties: namely, StuID, StuName, Major, and Credits. An attribute is represented in an E-R diagram by an ellipse with the name of the attribute inside.

5.3.1 *Domains*

The set of values permitted for each attribute is called the **domain** of that attribute. For the Student entity example, the domain of the Credits attribute might be the set of integer values between 0 and 150 inclusive, depending on how the university computes credit hours. The domain of the StuName attribute is somewhat more difficult to define, since it consists of all legal names of students. It is certainly a string, but it might consist of not only letters but apostrophes, blanks, hyphens, or other special characters. Different attributes may have the same domains. For example, a subset of the set of positive integers is often used as a domain for attributes with quite different meanings, such as Credits and Age. Just as with entities, different designers may disagree about the attributes for an entity set. For example, another designer may choose to include StuAddress, StuPhone, and StuStatus, but not Credits. In addition, what appears to be an attribute to one designer may be an entity to another. Major, for example, might be seen as an entity in a different design. An attribute actually maps an entity set to the domain of the attribute. For example, the attribute Credits is a function that takes the set of students and maps each student to a specific value in the domain 0,. . .,150. Figure 5.1 illustrates Credits as a function mapping the Student entity set to the Credits domain. You may notice that the use of the word domain as used here does not fit the mathematical notion of domain as the set on which a function is defined. In fact, the domain of the attribute is actually the range of a mathematical function. A particular entity instance could be described as a set of ordered pairs, with each pair being the name of an attribute and the value of the attribute. For a specific student, such a set might be {(StuID,S1001), (StuName,Tom Smith), (Major,History), (Credits,90)}. Figure 5.2 shows an entity instance with its attributes shown as functions that map the entity to their domains. The named attribute itself and its domain are part of the intension of the model, while the attribute values are part of the extension.

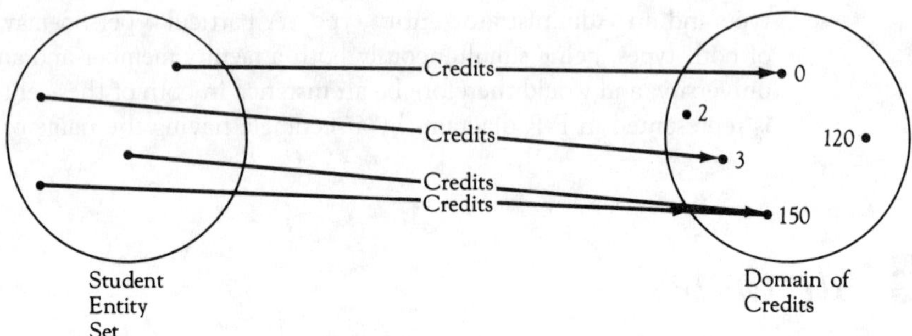

Figure 5.1

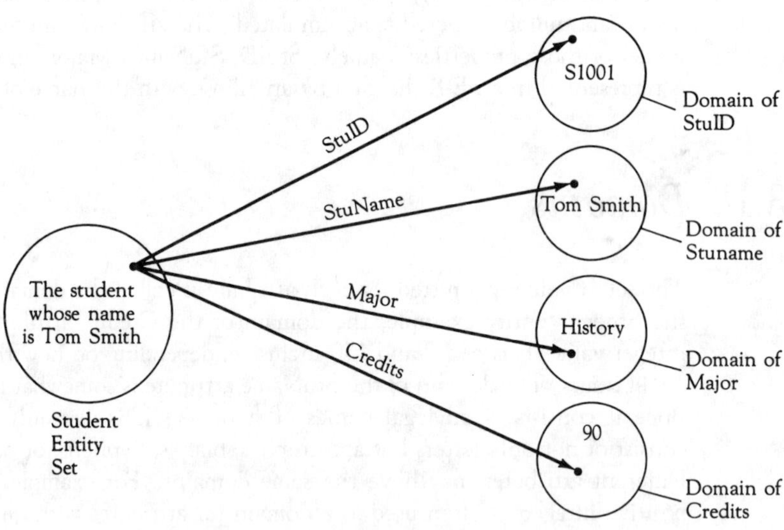

Figure 5.2

5.3.2 *Null Values*

Some attributes are permitted to have **null** values for some entity instances. This simply means that the value of that attribute is unknown at the present time or is undefined for this instance. In that case, the entity instance will not map to the domain of the attribute, although other instances of the same entity set will map to the attribute domain.

5.4 Keys

Intuitively, we think of a key as a data item that allows us to tell records apart. We need a more exact definition of the concept of key. We begin with the notion of superkey.

5.4.1 Superkeys

A superkey is an attribute or a set of attributes that uniquely identifies an entity. This means that it always allows us to tell one entity instance from another. For example, for the Student entity set, the StuID is a superkey because it can be used to identify each student uniquely. If you have a list of all students, with their IDs, names, majors, and credits, and you are told the student ID value, there is only one student on the list with that value. If you were told the student's name, you might not be sure which student to choose, since two or more students might have the same name. Therefore StuName is not a superkey. Any set of attributes containing a superkey is also a superkey. Therefore, the combination of StuID and Major, written {StuID,Major}, is also a superkey. Note that a superkey provides unique identification for all extensions of the database, not just for one or two examples. We may use examples to help us fix our ideas about superkeys, but an example might be misleading. For instance, it might happen that at the moment no two students in the university have the same name and we might incorrectly infer from the particular extension that StuName is a superkey. To identify a superkey we must consider the meaning of the attributes, a semantic notion, before deciding whether we have uniqueness over all extensions.

5.4.2 Candidate Keys

Since a superkey like {StuID,Major} may contain extra attributes that are not necessary for unique identification of entity instances, we are interested in finding superkeys that do not contain these extra attributes. A **candidate** key is a superkey that does not contain such extra attributes. We define a candidate key as a superkey such that no proper subset of its attributes is itself a superkey. There may be several candidate keys for an entity set. In our example, {StuID,Major} is not a candidate key because it contains a subset, StuID, that is a superkey. However, StuID by itself is a candidate key, since it has no proper subset that identifies entities. If we stored social security numbers of students, then the attribute SocSecNo would also be a candidate key. Note that a candidate key may consist of a single attribute, as StuID and SocSecNo both did, or it may be a combination of attributes. For example, the combination {Name, Address}, if it is unique, may be a candidate key for some entity set. When a key consists of more than one attribute, we call it a **composite** key.

5.4.3 *Primary Keys*

An entity set may have several candidate keys. The database designer chooses among them and identifies one as the normal way of identifying entities and accessing records. This becomes the **primary key.** In other words, the primary key is the "successful" candidate key—the one actually chosen. It may be a single attribute or a composite key. Often the other candidate keys become **alternate keys,** whose unique values provide another method of accessing records. The term **secondary key** is sometimes used to mean alternate key, but *secondary key* usually means an attribute or set of attributes whose values, not necessarily unique, are used as a means of accessing records. With this meaning, several records may have the same secondary key value, so we will generally avoid using this term. In our example, StuID might be the primary key for the Student entity set. If SocSecNo is also stored, it might be an alternate key. Course# might be the primary key for the Class entity set, and FacID for the Faculty entity set. An important characteristic of a primary key is that none of its attributes may have null values. If we permitted null values in keys, we would be unable to tell entities apart, since two entities with null values for the same key attribute might be indistinguishable. To ensure data correctness, we should insist that no attribute of a candidate key be permitted to have null values.

5.5 *Relationships*

Entities are often linked by associations or **relationships,** which are connections or interactions between the entity instances. A student may be related to a class by being enrolled in that class. By abstraction, we can identify the common properties of certain relationships and define a **relationship type** and a corresponding well-defined **relationship set** as the collection of relationships of that type. The relationships that satisfy the requirements for membership in the relationship set at any moment are the instances or members of the relationship set. The keys of the related entities are used as attributes of the relationship set. As with entities and attributes, the relationship type and the well-defined relationship set are part of the intension and the instances are part of the extension of the model. For example, we have a Student-Class relationship type that links every student with each of the classes in which he or she is enrolled. We then have a Student-Class relationship set, with attributes StuID and Course#.

5.5.1 *Types of Relationships*

Student-Class is an example of a **binary** relationship set, one that links two entity sets. It is possible to describe this relationship set more formally as a set of ordered pairs, in which the first element represents a student and the second a class. At a given moment, the instances of this relationship set, which we call Enroll, might appear as

$$\text{Enroll} = \{(\text{S1001}, \text{ART103A}), (\text{S1020}, \text{CSC201A}), (\text{S1002}, \text{CSC201A}), (\text{S1010}, \text{ART103A}), (\text{S1002}, \text{ART103A}), (\text{S1020}, \text{MTH101B}), (\text{S1001}, \text{HST205A}), (\text{S1010}, \text{MTH103C}), (\text{S1002}, \text{MTH103C})\}$$

Here, the student ID represents the student entity, and the course number represents the class entity. Each ordered pair shows that a particular student is enrolled in a particular class. For example, (S1001,ART103A) shows that the student whose ID is S1001 is enrolled in the class with course number ART103A. The entire set is the relationship set, and each ordered pair is an instance of the relationship.

A relationship may involve more than two entity sets. For example, we could have a **ternary** relationship, involving three entity sets, linking students, classes, and faculty. Then the relationship set could be defined as a set of ordered triples, in which the first element represents a student, the second a class, and the third a faculty member. Using student IDs to represent student entities, course numbers to represent class entities, and faculty IDs to represent faculty entities, this relationship might appear as

$$\text{Student-Class-Faculty} = \{(\text{S1001}, \text{ART103A}, \text{F101}), (\text{S1020}, \text{CSC201A}, \text{F105}), (\text{S1002}, \text{CSC201A}, \text{F105}), (\text{S1010}, \text{ART103A}, \text{F101}), (\text{S1002}, \text{ART103A}, \text{F101}), (\text{S1020}, \text{MTH101B}, \text{F110}), (\text{S1001}, \text{HST205A}, \text{F115}), (\text{S1010}, \text{MTH103C}, \text{F110}), (\text{S1002}, \text{MTH103C}, \text{F110})\}$$

Here, each ordered triple is an instance that shows that a particular student is enrolled in a particular class which is taught by a particular professor. For example, the ordered triple (S1001,ART103A,F101) means that the student whose ID is S1001 is enrolled in the class whose course number is ART103A, which is taught by the professor whose ID is F101. The entity sets involved in a relationship set need not be distinct. For example, we could define a roommate relationship within the Student entity set. Assuming that only two students share a room, this would be a binary relationship called Roommate of the form

$$\text{Roommate} = \{(\text{Student1}, \text{Student2}) \mid \text{Student1} \in \text{Student entity set}, \text{Student2} \in \text{Student entity set and Student1 is the roommate of Student2}\}$$

Although most relationships in a data model are binary or at most ternary, we could define a relationship set linking any number of entity sets. Therefore, the general relationship set is an **n-ary** relation of the form

$$\{(e_1, e_2, ..., e_n) \mid e_1 \in E_1, e_2 \in E_2, ..., e_n \in E_n\}$$

where the E_i are entity sets, the e_i are entity instances, and each ordered n-tuple represents an instance of the relationship.

You may recognize this notation from mathematics as the cross-product or Cartesian product of sets. In fact, a relationship set is a subset of the Cartesian product of the entity sets involved; that is, if R is a relationship set and $E_1, E_2, ..., E_n$ are entity sets, then

$$R \subseteq E_1 \times E_2 \times \ldots \times E_n$$

A relationship set is represented in an E-R diagram by a diamond with the name of the relationship inside.

5.5.2 Attributes of Relationship Sets

In addition to the keys of the linked entities, a relationship set may have **descriptive attributes** that describe the relationship rather than the entities involved. For example, the attribute Grade is a descriptive attribute for the Enroll relationship set. Grade does not describe the Student entity, since each student may have several grades, nor does it describe the Class entity, since there are several grades given in a particular class. For a grade to have meaning, it must be associated with a particular student for a particular class. Since Grade is an attribute of Enroll, it can be described as a function that maps an instance of Enroll to the domain of Grade. Figure 5.3 shows Grade as a function mapping the instance (S1001,ART103A) to the domain of Grade. Note that the relationship Enroll is pictured as a set of ordered pairs. On an E-R diagram, we place a descriptive attribute of a relation in an oval and connect it to the relationship diamond. We do not need to rewrite the keys of the related entities, since it is understood that they are attributes of the relationship set.

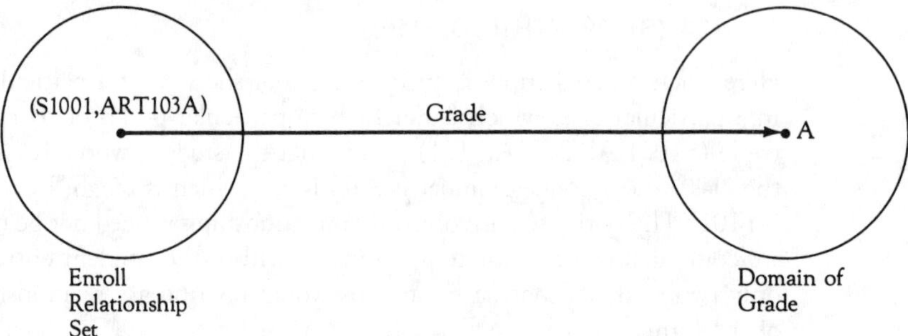

Figure 5.3

5.5.3 Cardinality of a Relationship

It is important to identify restrictions or constraints on relationships so that the possible extensions of the relation correspond to real-world connections or associations. One type of constraint on relationships is **cardinality**. The cardinality of a relationship is the number of entities to which another entity can map under that relationship. Let X and Y be entity sets and R a binary relationship from X to Y. If there are no cardinality constraints on R, any number of entities in X can map to any number of entities in Y. Usually, however, there are restrictions on the number of corresponding entities. We distinguish four types of mappings:

1. A mapping R from X to Y is **one-to-one** if each entity in X is associated with at most one entity in Y and, conversely, each entity in Y is associated with at most one entity in X. Figure 5.4(a) shows a one-to-one mapping. An example of a one-to-one mapping is the normal Chairperson to Department mapping. Each chairperson chairs at most one department, and each department has at most one chairperson. In family life, an example of a one-to-one mapping is the marriage relationship. At any given time, each husband can be married to at most one wife and each wife to at most one husband.

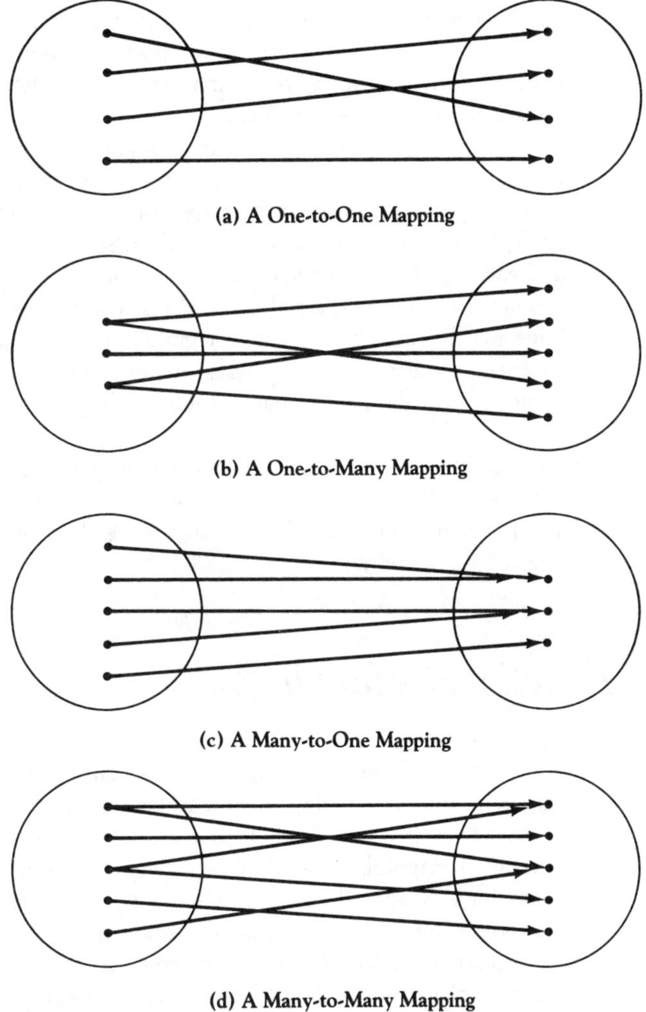

(a) A One-to-One Mapping

(b) A One-to-Many Mapping

(c) A Many-to-One Mapping

(d) A Many-to-Many Mapping

Figure 5.4

2. A mapping R from X to Y is **one-to-many** if each entity in X can be associated with many entities in Y but each entity in Y is associated with at most one entity in X. Figure 5.4(b) shows a one-to-many mapping. The relationship between a faculty

member and a class is one-to-many, assuming that there is no team teaching. Each faculty member can teach several classes, but each class is taught by only one faculty member. In a family, the usual mother-to-child relationship is one-to-many. A mother can have many children, but each child has only one mother.

3. A mapping R from X to Y is **many-to-one** if each entity in X is associated with at most one entity in Y, but each entity in Y can be associated with many entities in X. Figure 5.4(c) shows a many-to-one mapping. The relationship between student and major department is many-to-one, assuming that there are no double or triple majors. Each student can have at most one major, but a department can have many student majors enrolled in it. In family life, the child-to-mother relationship is many-to-one. Each child has at most one mother, but each mother can have many children. A many-to-one mapping is actually the same as a one-to-many, but viewed from the opposite side.
4. A mapping R from X to Y is **many-to-many** if each entity in X can be associated with many entities in Y and each entity in Y can be associated with many entities in X. Figure 5.4(d) shows a many-to-many mapping. The relationship between student and class is many-to-many. Each student can be enrolled in many classes, and each class can have many students enrolled in it. In a family, the grandparent-to-grandchild relationship illustrates a many-to-many mapping. A grandparent may have many grandchildren, and a grandchild may have many grandparents. The parent-to-child relationship is also many-to-many, since each child may have two parents, and each parent many children.

Note that the word "many" applies to the **possible** number of entities another is associated with. For a given instance, there might be zero, one, two, or more associated entities, but if it is ever possible to have more than one, we use the word "many" to describe the association.

5.5.4 *Functional Mappings*

Some mappings may satisfy the definition of mathematical functions. Figure 5.5 shows an example of such a mapping. If F is a mapping from X to Y and D is some subset of X such that for every x in D, there is a y in Y that is the image of x under F, then F is a **functional mapping**. Note that two x values may have the same y value, but no x value may have two y values. Also, the set D, called the domain of the function, may be some proper subset of X. The set of images in Y, the range of the function, may be a proper subset of Y. The functional mapping in Figure 5.5 is a one-to-many mapping.

A functional mapping from X to Y may be **total**, meaning that **every** x in set X must be mapped to at least one y in set Y or **partial**, meaning that **not every** x has to be mapped. In a total mapping, the domain of the function is the entire set X. The mapping from Student to Major department is partial if not every student has a major. Figure 5.6(a) illustrates this partial mapping. The mapping from Faculty to Department is total if every faculty member must be assigned to some department. Figure 5.6(b) illustrates this total mapping.

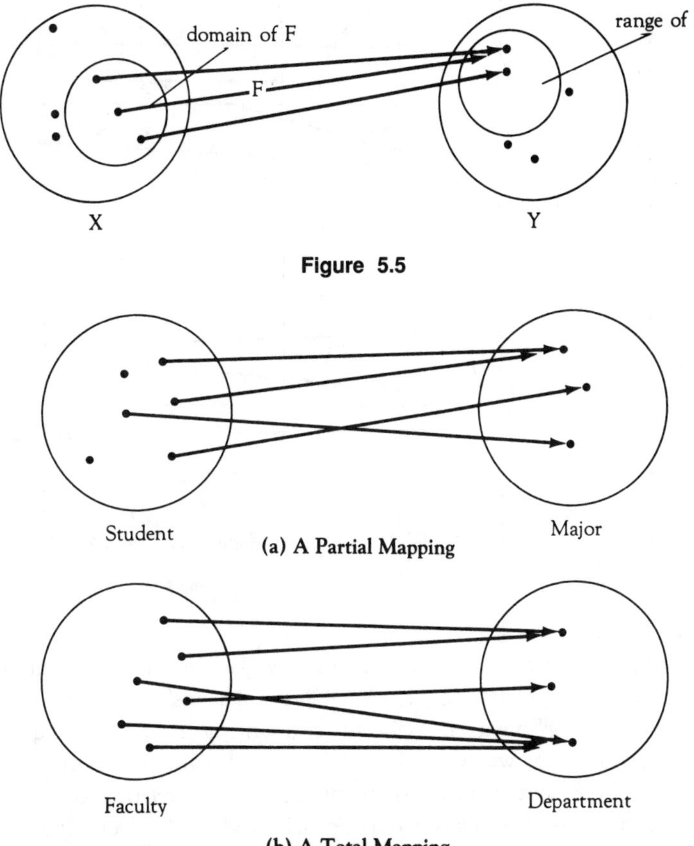

Figure 5.5

(a) A Partial Mapping

(b) A Total Mapping

Figure 5.6

A functional mapping from X to Y may or may not involve all the y values. If every y in Y is the image of some x in X, then the mapping is said to be **onto** Y. If there may be some y values that are not images of x values, then the mapping is said to be **into** Y. In an onto mapping, the range of the function is all of Y. Figure 5.7(a) shows a mapping of X onto Y, and Figure 5.7(b) shows a mapping of X into Y.

5.5.5 *Showing Cardinalities on an E-R Diagram*

In an E-R diagram, lines are used to represent mappings. Lines connect the rectangles representing entity sets to the diamonds representing the relationship sets that show their associations. There are several methods of showing the cardinality of the mapping. The traditional one is to put a "1" to show a "one" mapping cardinality and an "N" or "M" to show a many cardinality. Thus if one faculty member is associated with each class, the line between the Faculty entity set rectangle and the Faculty-Class relationship set

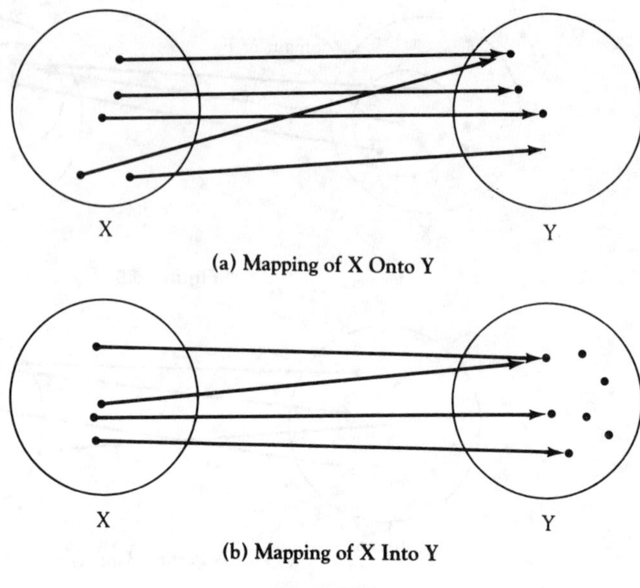

(a) Mapping of X Onto Y

(b) Mapping of X Into Y

Figure 5.7

diamond has a "1" on it. Since many classes can be associated with the faculty member, the line between the Faculty-Class relationship set diamond and the class rectangle has an "N" on it. If we were representing the one-to-one Chairperson-to-Department relationship, we would put a "1" on the line connecting the Chairperson rectangle to the Chairperson-Department relationship set diamond, and another "1" on the line connecting the relationship set diamond to the Department rectangle. For the Enroll relationship, we would have an "N" from the Student entity set rectangle to the Enroll diamond and an "M" from the Enroll diamond to the Class entity set rectangle. An alternative to the "1" is to put a single arrowhead on the line pointing to an entity set rectangle that participates as a "one" and a double arrowhead on the line pointing to an entity set that participates as a "many." Some authors use a single arrowhead for a "one" and no arrowhead for a "many," while others use a "big dot" at the end of a "many" line and nothing at the end of a "one" line. Figure 5.8 summarizes all four methods applied to our three examples. We will use the single arrow for a "one" and double arrow for a "many" because it seems most natural. This is shown as Method 2 in Figure 5.8.

Lines are also used to link attributes to entities or relationships on an E-R diagram. Therefore, there is a line to each attribute oval from either an entity rectangle or a relationship diamond. This line could be interpreted to be the mapping of the entity set to the domain of the attribute. It is understood to be a many-to-one mapping, meaning that each entity instance has one value for each attribute, but each value may be used for several entities. However, arrows are not usually used to show explicitly that it is one-to-many. If we wanted to be very strict, we would put the domain of the attribute in the oval, the name of the attribute on the line connecting the rectangle to the oval, and an indication of the cardinality by labeling or using arrows. This would allow us to represent the possibility that an attribute could have multiple values for an entity instance. For example, if a student could have a double major, then the mapping

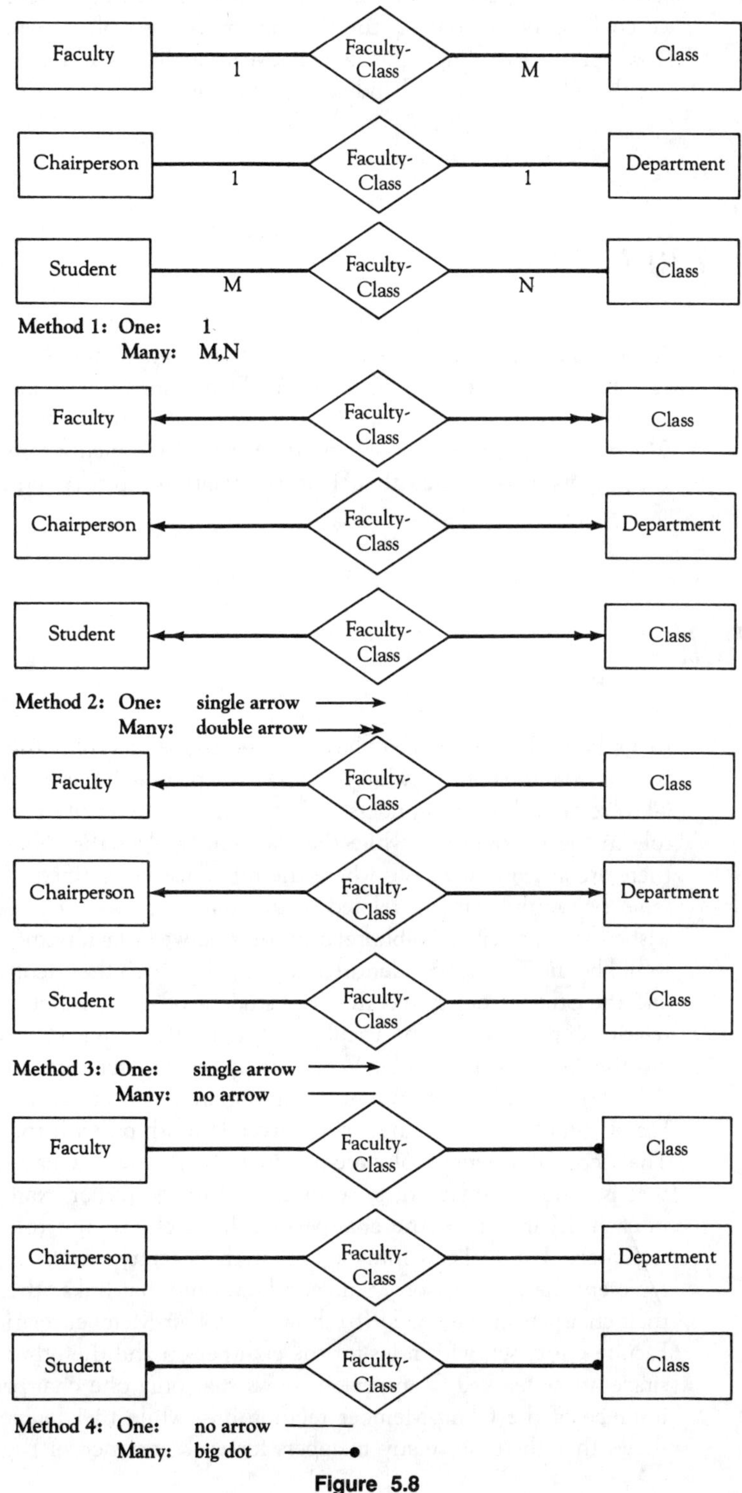
Faculty
Faculty-Class
Class
1
M
Chairperson
Faculty-Class
Department
1
1
Student
Faculty-Class
Class
M
N
Method 1: One: 1
Many: M,N
Faculty
Faculty-Class
Class
Chairperson
Faculty-Class
Department
Student
Faculty-Class
Class
Method 2: One: single arrow
Many: double arrow
Faculty
Faculty-Class
Class
Chairperson
Faculty-Class
Department
Student
Faculty-Class
Class
Method 3: One: single arrow
Many: no arrow
Faculty
Faculty-Class
Class
Chairperson
Faculty-Class
Department
Student
Faculty-Class
Class
Method 4: One: no arrow
Many: big dot

Figure 5.8

between the Student entity set and the domain of Major would be many-to-many, and we could indicate that on the diagram by two double arrows or "N" and "M" labels. However, we will simply put links between attributes and the entity sets or relationship sets they describe without indicating cardinality.

5.6 *Foreign Keys*

A **foreign key** is an attribute or combination of attributes of an entity that is the primary key of another entity. For example, FacID may appear as an attribute of the Class entity, and is not the primary key of Class. However, it is the primary key of the Faculty entity. When discussing the Class entity, then, FacID is called a foreign key. When a foreign key appears, it is a signal that there is a relationship between the entities involved.

5.7 *Roles*

In a relationship, each entity has a function called its **role** in the relationship. Usually it is clear from the context what role an entity plays in a relationship. Thus in the Faculty-Class relationship, it is understood that the faculty entity plays the "is the teacher of" role in the relationship, while the class entity plays the "is taught by" role. However, there are at least two cases where the role must be clarified. The first occurs when the same two entity sets are related in two different ways. For example, suppose that we wished to represent possible relationships between faculty members and students. One would be the Teacher-Student relationship, in which the Faculty entity has the "teaches" and the Student entity has the "is a student of" role. Another is the Advisor-Student relationship, in which the Faculty entity has the "advisor" role and the student entity has the "is advised by" role. When entity sets are connected by multiple relationships, the roles should be written on the appropriate links. Figure 5.9(a) shows two entity sets, Faculty and Student, connected by two relationships, with roles appearing on the links. The second case where roles are required occurs when we have a **recursive relationship**, that is, when a single entity set is related to itself. For example, one faculty member in each department is the chairperson. If we choose not to represent the chairperson separately, but to keep him or her in the Faculty entity set, then we may want to represent the Chairperson-Member relationship that links other department members to their chairperson. Figure 5.9(b) shows the Chair-Member relationship set defined on the Faculty entity set, with roles for the chairperson and the other members. Note that the single arrow marked Chairperson shows that only one chairperson is involved in each instance of the Chair-Member relationship, while the double arrow marked Member shows that there are many members for each instance of the relationship. Although

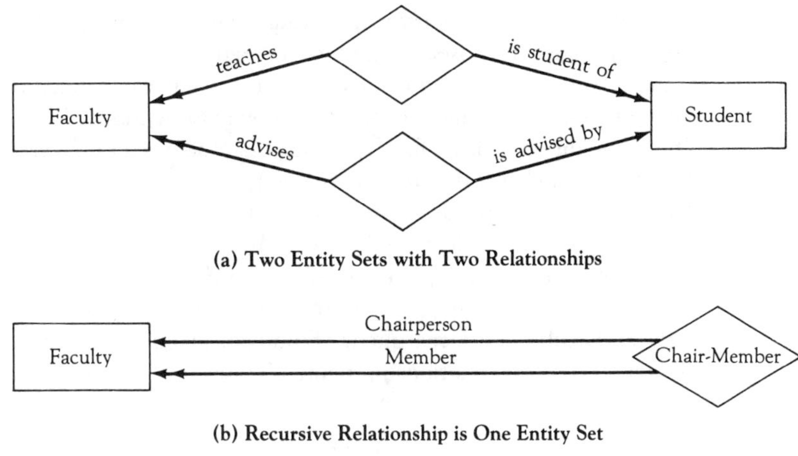

(a) Two Entity Sets with Two Relationships

(b) Recursive Relationship is One Entity Set

Figure 5.9

role names are required for the two cases discussed, we can use role names to help clarify any relationships, whether required or not.

5.8 *Dependencies*

We have already introduced the notion of a data **constraint** as a rule or condition that the data instances must obey. There are many types of constraints. For example, specifying the domain of an attribute allows us to state that only certain types of values will be permitted for the attribute. Giving the cardinality of a relationship specifies how many entities may be associated under that relationship. Identifying a superkey, candidate key, and primary key shows that the set of attributes involved must have unique values. Another constraint on primary keys is that no attribute may have a null value. Additional constraints that refer to relationships involve the entities that participate in them.

5.8.1 *Existence Dependency*

An **existence constraint** or **existence dependency** can occur between two entities. If *X* and *Y* are entities and each instance of *Y* must have a corresponding instance of *X*, we say that *Y* is existence dependent on *X*. This means a *Y* entity cannot exist without some *X* entity. A *Y* cannot enter the database unless its corresponding *X* is there, and if the *X* is dropped from the database, the *Y* must be dropped as well. *X* is referred to as the **strong, parent, owner,** or **dominant** entity and *Y* as the **weak, child, dependent,** or **subordinate** entity. Another way of expressing an existence dependency is to say that the relationship is a **total** mapping from set *Y* to set *X*. That means that if *y* in set *Y* exists, it must be related to some *x* in set *X*. For our university example, we can say that a faculty entity is existence dependent on a department entity, meaning that the faculty member cannot exist without a corresponding department. This would mean that no faculty member can be hired unless he or she is hired for some department, and if a department ceases to exist, the faculty members assigned to that department are dropped or are reassigned to another department. A faculty member is never allowed to "float free" in the database without a corresponding department. An existence dependency is depicted in the E-R diagram by a double rectangle for the weak entity. Figure 5.10(a) shows the E-R diagram depicting the existence dependency between Faculty and Department. Some authors also place an "E" in the relationship diamond above the relationship name to show an existence dependency.

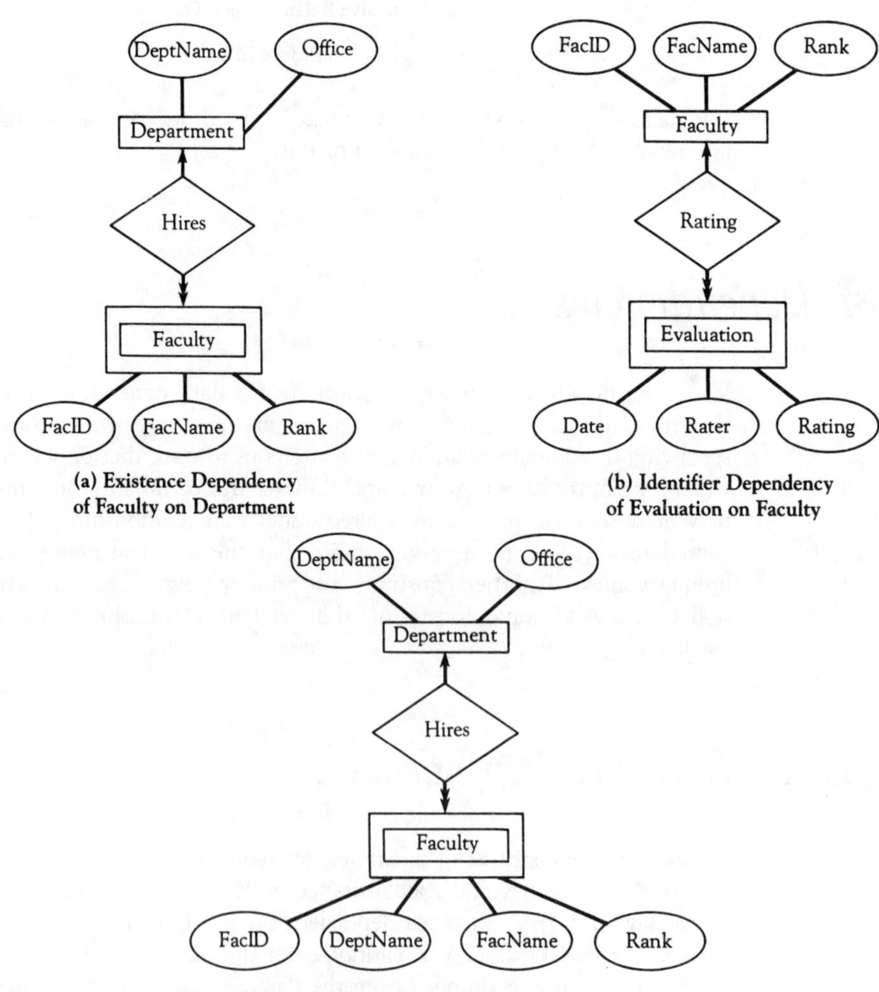

(a) Existence Dependency of Faculty on Department

(b) Identifier Dependency of Evaluation on Faculty

(c) Referential Dependency of Faculty on Department

Figure 5.10

5.8.2 *Identifier Dependency*

A special type of existence dependency, called an **identifier dependency,** occurs when the weak entity set does not have a candidate key, and its instances are indistinguishable without a relationship with another entity. Our previous example of Faculty and Department does not apply here, since the faculty entity set has FacId as a primary key. As an example of an identifier dependency, let us assume that evaluations are kept on faculty members. An evaluation entity instance has attributes Date, RaterName, and Rating. There may be several instances with identical values for all three attributes, so such an entity must be associated with the correct faculty instance to have meaning. Figure 5.10(b) shows the E-R diagram with the identifier dependency of Evaluation on Faculty. Some authors distinguish identifier dependencies from other existence dependencies by placing "ID" in the relationship diamond above the relationship name, replacing the "E" in the corresponding location for an existence dependency.

5.8.3 *Referential Dependency*

Another special type of existence dependency, called a **referential dependency**, occurs when a weak entity contains as a foreign key the primary key of the corresponding strong entity. This leads to an important type of constraint called a **referential constraint** which states that a nonnull value of the foreign key attribute in the weak entity instance must always equal the value of the primary key of an associated strong entity instance. For example, if DeptName appears as an attribute of the Faculty entity and Faculty is existence dependent on Department, then DeptName is a foreign key for Faculty. We are assuming, of course, that DeptName is the key of the Department entity. The constraint says that in every Faculty entity instance the value of DeptName must match the value of DeptName in some Department entity instance. Figure 5.10(c) shows the E-R diagram with a referential dependency of Faculty on Department. We could identify that this is a referential dependency by placing an "R" above the relationship name in the relationship diamond.

5.9 *A Sample E-R Diagram*

Figure 5.11 shows an E-R diagram incorporating many of the entities and relationships discussed in this chapter. The entities and attributes are

- **Student:** StuID, StuName, Major, Credits. We are assuming that each student has a unique ID and has at most one major.
- **Department:** DeptName, Office. We are assuming that each department has a unique name and that each department has one office designated as the departmental office.

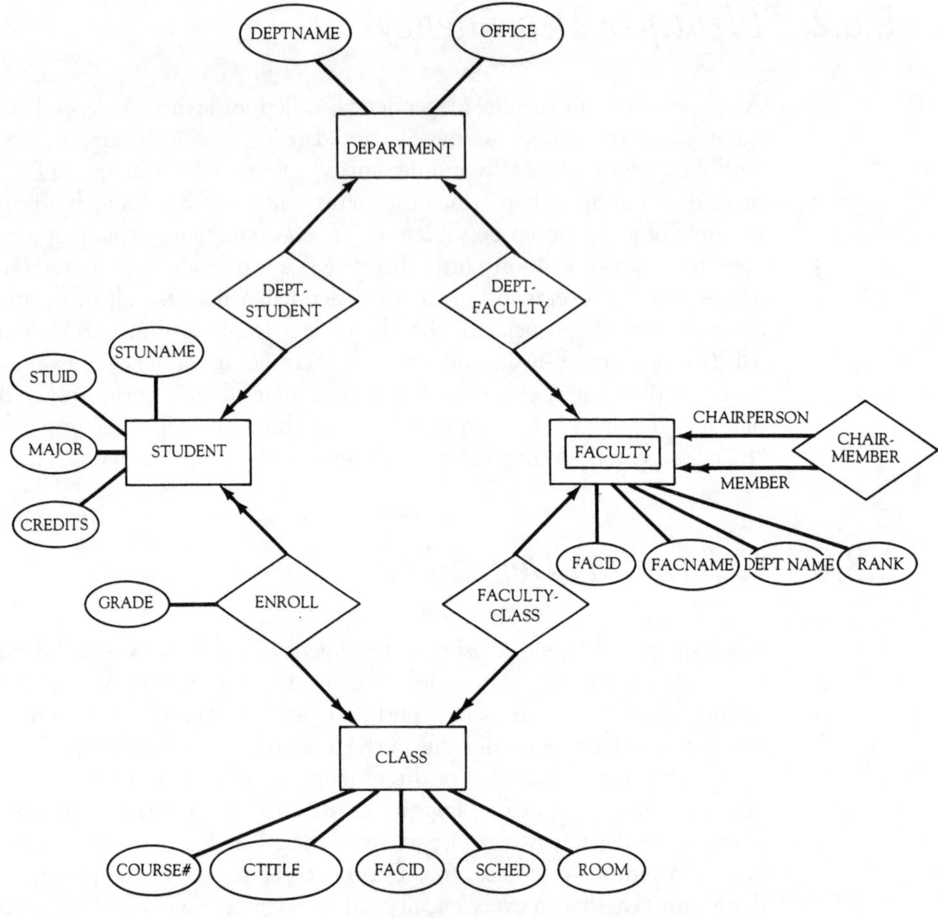

Figure 5.11

- **Faculty:** FacID, FacName, DeptName, Rank. We are assuming that FacID is unique and that every faculty member must belong to a department, so Faculty is a weak entity with a referential dependency on Department. One faculty member in each department is the chairperson.
- **Class:** Course#, CTitle, FacID, Sched, Room. We are assuming that the Course# consists of a department code, a number that identifies the course within the department, and a section code. We are keeping data for current classes only. If we wanted to store historical data about past class offerings or data about planned classes, we would need to add a Date attribute. We are assuming that each class is taught by only one faculty member; that is, there is no team teaching.

The relationship sets are

- **Dept-Student**, which is a one-to-many relationship that connects students to their major departments. We are assuming that students have only one major.

- **Enroll**, which is a many-to-many relationship that connects students to the classes in which they are enrolled. We are assuming that only current enrollments are kept. Grade is a descriptive attribute for this relationship set.
- **Dept-Faculty**, which is a one-to-many relationship that connects departments to faculty members assigned to them.
- **Faculty-Class**, which is a one-to-many relationship that connects faculty members to the classes they teach.
- **Chair-Member**, which is a one-to-many recursive relationship on Faculty that connects the chairperson of each department to the members of that department.

We chose to use two different binary relationships, Enroll and Faculty-Class, involving Class. We could have chosen to use a ternary relationship instead. It could be called Stu-Fac-Class and would connect the three entities involved, as pictured in Figure 5.12. The cardinalities are more difficult to identify in a ternary relationship than in a binary one, but the ones pictured preserve the meanings from Figure 5.11. Note that for each combination of Student and Faculty there are many classes, so we have a double arrow into Class. For each combination of Student and Class there is only one faculty member, so we have a single arrow into Faculty, and for each combination of Faculty and Class there are many students, so we have a double arrow into Student. However, this representation is not as good as the one using two binary relationships because the faculty data should not have to be associated with each combination of class and student data. We included it only to demonstrate a ternary relationship.

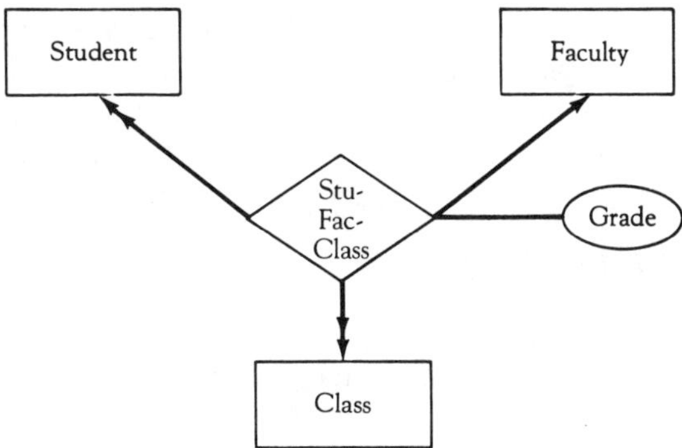

Figure 5.12

5.10 *Aggregation*

J. M. Smith and D. C. P. Smith have extended the entity–relationship model by adding two types of abstraction, called **aggregation** and **generalization**. These abstractions make the model more powerful by allowing the designer to express concepts that are not easily included in the basic model. The purpose of any type of abstraction is to allow different perceptions of the objects under discussion. The aggregation abstraction allows the designer to either **decompose** objects, breaking them into more detailed components, or to **aggregate** objects, grouping them together into higher-level objects. Decomposition is simply the opposite process to aggregation: Both processes are considered part of the aggregation abstraction.

Let us assume that the university has an institute that offers professional development seminars for industry. The seminars are offered periodically at various locations, either at the institute on campus or at training centers belonging to various companies. The seminars are taught by regular or adjunct faculty members of the university. We might decompose a seminar offering into components called Leader and Offering. Each seminar may be offered many times, and it may have different leaders. Both Leader and Offering could then be decomposed into their attributes, FacID and FacName for Leader, and Date, Time, Location, NumofParticipants, and Budget for Offering. The decomposition is shown by lines down from Seminar to its components and lines down from them to their attributes, as shown in Figure 5.13(a). To illustrate aggregation, we search for a higher-level object that can contain Seminar as a component. Since a seminar might be part of a training program, we aggregate it with other components of a training program. Figure 5.13(b) shows Seminar and Internship as components of Training-Program. The upward arrow in Figure 5.13(b) illustrates that the two lower-level components have been grouped together, or aggregated, to form the higher-level one. The aggregation or decomposition process can begin at any level. If we had started with Training-Program as our basic entity, we could have decomposed it into its two components and then decomposed them in turn. Conversely, we could have started with attributes such as the date and location of a seminar, aggregated them into a higher-level entity, and then continued aggregating until we reached the top level. Figure 5.13(c) illustrates the entire diagram and shows the direction of decomposition and aggregation.

5.11 *Generalization*

Another powerful abstraction is **generalization**. Generalization allows objects of different types to be considered as examples of a higher-level set or, conversely, objects in a set to be categorized into specialized types. Breaking up a set of objects into the various types it contains, or categorizing the objects in the set according to their roles in a relationship, is called **specialization**. Its inverse is generalization, which means combining different types of objects into a higher-level set. Just as aggregation and decomposition are opposites in the aggregation process, generalization and specialization are opposites in the generalization process. In the aggregation abstraction, we searched for "parts of" or components of objects. In the generalization abstraction, we search for "types of" or categorizations of objects. For example, if we start with the Seminar entity, we can generalize by saying that a seminar is a type of course. Other types of courses may be lecture courses, lab courses, or film courses. Note that here we are not identifying components of a single course, but different types of courses.

In a diagram, generalization is pictured on a different plane from aggregation. The *aggregation plane* is the plane of the paper. As pictured in Figure 5.13(c), aggregation is

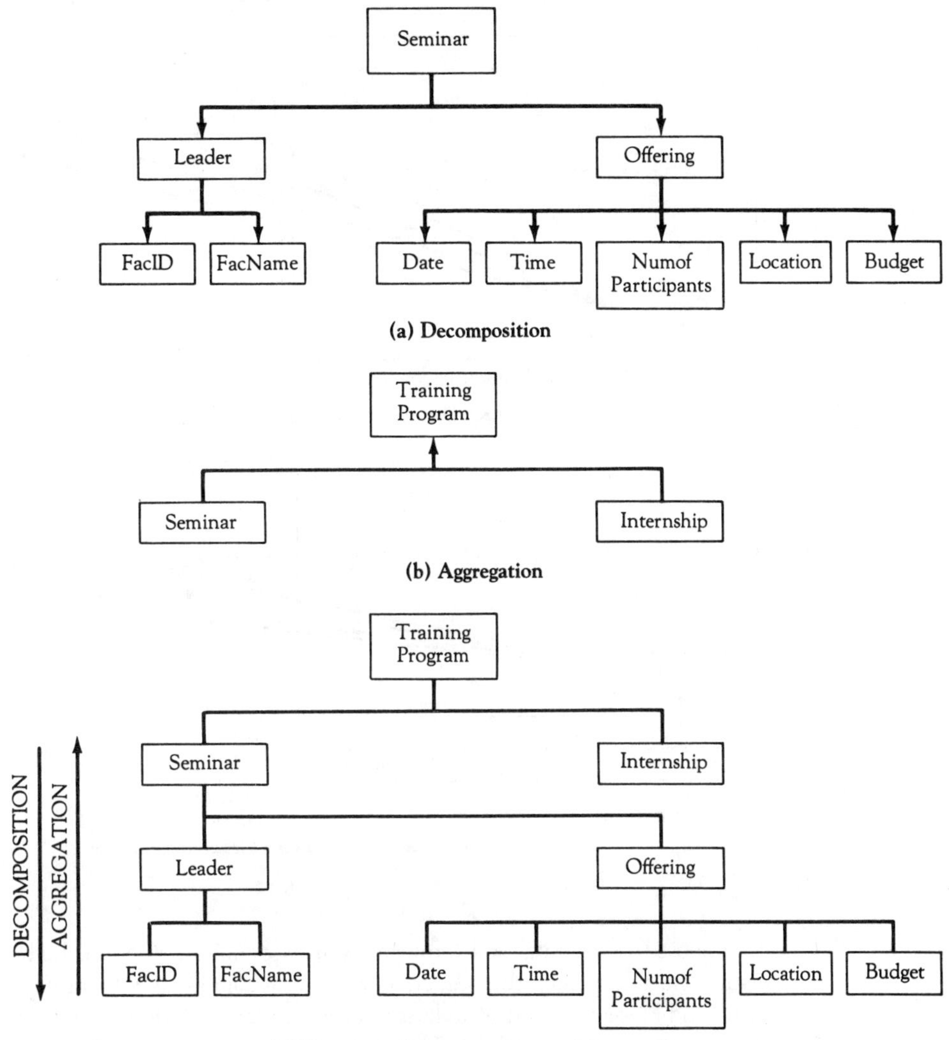

Figure 5.13

the upward direction and decomposition is the downward direction on the aggregation plane. The *generalization plane* is orthogonal to the paper, coming out of the paper toward the reader. On that plane, the direction toward the reader is the generalization direction, and the one toward the paper is the specialization direction. Figure 5.14(a) shows the three-dimensional representation of generalization. In the nearer plane, Course is the generalization of Seminar, Lecture, Lab, and Film, which appear on the more specialized plane.

Once a generalization plane has been established, aggregation and decomposition can be performed on that generalization level. Thus Seminar on the lower generalization plane could be decomposed into its parts. We have pictured them in Figure 5.14(b) as Leader and Offering. We could have decomposed these further, or we could have

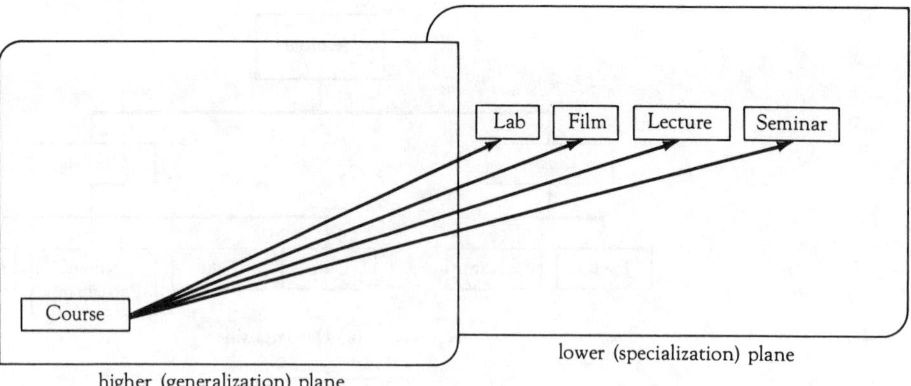

(a) Three-Dimensional Representation of Generalization

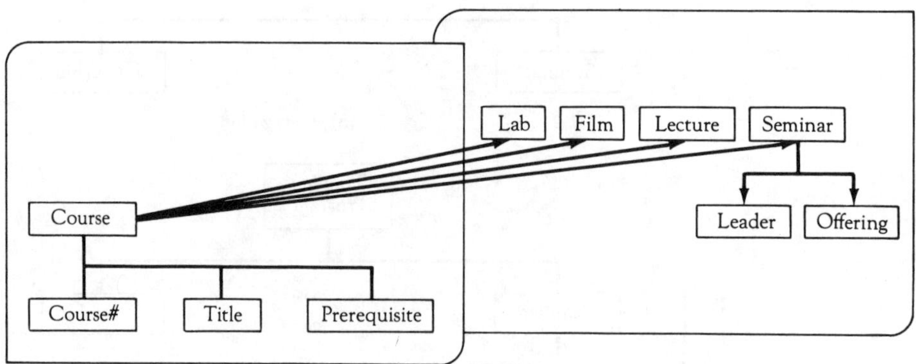

(b) Using Decomposition on a Generalization Plane

Figure 5.14

decomposed Lab, Film, or Lecture as well as Seminar. On the higher generalization plane, the one nearer the reader, Course is decomposed into its attributes, Course#, Title, and Prerequisite. It is understood that these are attributes of all courses, regardless of the type of course involved. Therefore, the generalization and aggregation abstraction model allows the designer to select any plane and decompose it to any desired depth, considering different aspects of objects at different levels.

5.12 *Representing Generalization and Aggregation on an E-R Diagram*

On an E-R diagram, generalization and specialization are pictured using a triangle containing the word *ISA* to connect the components to each other and to the higher-level entity. Figure 5.15 shows an E-R diagram in which Seminar, Lab, Lecture, and Film have been generalized into Course. Since each "is a" course (i.e., they are all types of courses), the *ISA* is used to show the generalization. If we read the diagram from the top down, we would be looking at a specialization of Course into these four types. We could have added the attributes Course#, Title, and Prerequisite to Course and descriptive attributes to each of the four types. For example, the attributes of Seminar are FacID, FacName, Date, NumofParticipants, Location, and Budget, but Lecture, Lab, and Film would also have their own attributes. It is understood that the attributes of the higher-level entity are "inherited" by the lower-level ones. This means that in addition to FacID, FacName, Date, and so on, Seminar also has attributes Course#, Title, and Prerequisite.

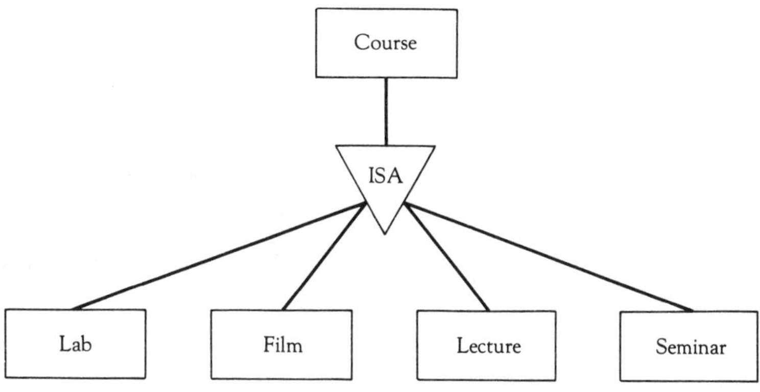

Figure 5.15

Aggregation and specialization can also be represented in an E-R diagram. If we wish to group together entities into a higher-level entity set, we simply draw a larger rectangle around them and name the rectangle. Figure 5.16(a) shows Seminar and Internship aggregated into Training-Program. Now the large rectangle can be treated as a single entity. We can use aggregation even when relationship sets are involved. For example, suppose that seminars and internships are related in a work-study relationship, and there are several field examinations that work-study participants must take. The field examinations are related to both seminars and internships, as shown in Figure 5.16(b), but they are actually more related to the combination of the two, so the relationships Requires and Work-Study should be connected in some way. The model does not allow relationship sets to be connected. Instead, we can use aggregation to group together the Seminar, Internship, and Work-Study sets into a Training-Program aggregate. We draw a rectangle to indicate that this is a higher-level entity, and now we can connect that rectangle to the Requires relationship, as shown in Figure 5.16(c).

5.13 *Chapter Summary*

The entity-relationship model uses **E-R diagrams** to represent an **enterprise schema**, a conceptual-level description that is independent of any DBMS. An **entity** is any

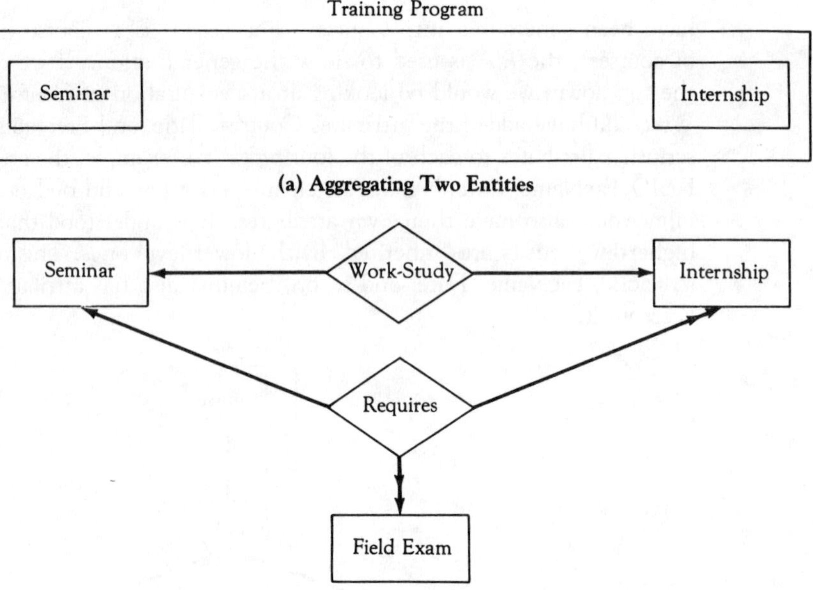

(a) Aggregating Two Entities

(b) Using a Ternary Relationship in Place of Aggregation

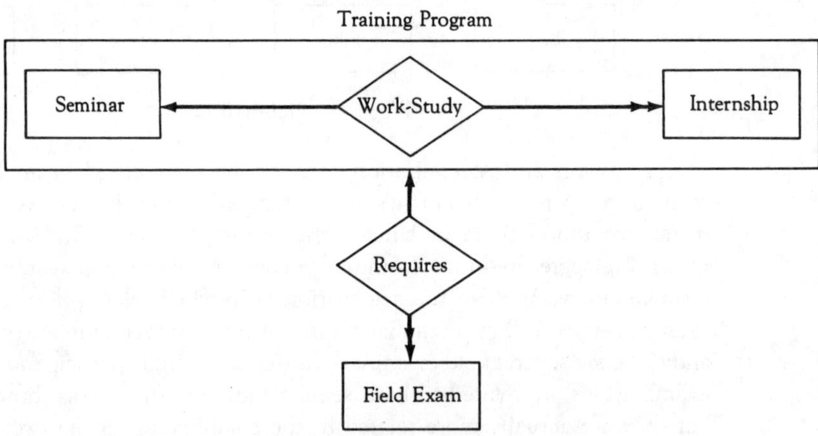

(c) Aggregation with a Relationship Set

Figure 5.16

distinguishable object in the real world. Entities are categorized into **entity types,** and a collection of entities of the same type forms an **entity set.** The individual entities that belong to the set at a given moment are **entity instances.** On an E-R diagram, a rectangle represents an entity set. **Attributes** are representations of properties of the real-world entities. The set of values permitted for an attribute is its **domain.** The attribute is actually a mapping of the entity set into the domain of the attribute. **Null values** occur when an entity instance is missing a value for a particular attribute.

A **superkey** is an attribute set that uniquely identifies entity instances. A minimal superkey, one with no proper subset that is also a superkey, is called a **candidate key.**

The **primary key** of an entity is the candidate key that the designer chooses for unique identification. The other candidate keys may become **alternate keys**. A **secondary key**, which provides another way to access records, may or may not have unique values. A **composite key** is one that has more than one attribute. No attribute of a primary key may have null values. A **foreign key** is an attribute of an entity that is the primary key of another entity.

A **relationship** is an association or interaction between entities. A **relationship set** consists of all relations of a given relationship type. Relationships may be **binary**, linking two entities, **ternary**, linking three entities, or ***n*-ary**, linking *n* entities. Binary relationship instances can be represented as ordered pairs, ternary instances as ordered triples, and *n*-ary instances as ordered *n*-tuples. A relationship set is a subset of the Cartesian product of the related entity sets. A diamond is used to represent a relationship set on an E-R diagram. A relationship set always has the primary keys of the related entity sets as attributes, but some also have **descriptive attributes** as well. On an E-R diagram, a descriptive attribute appears in an oval connected to the relationship diamond. Relationships have **cardinality** constraints, which specify how many entity instances may be related. These may be **one-to-one, one-to-many, many-to-one,** or **many-to-many**. Some relationships are also **mathematical functions**. A functional mapping may be described as **total** if its domain is the entire set, or **partial** if its domain is not the entire set. The function may be **onto** if its range is the entire set, or **into** if its range is not the entire set. Cardinalities may be shown on E-R diagrams in several ways. We use a line with a single arrow to represent a "one" and a double arrow to represent a "many."

If a relationship is **recursive**, defined on a single entity set, or if two entity sets are related in more than one way, the **role** or function that an entity plays in a relationship should be identified. This is done by placing the role name on the line representing the relationship on the E-R diagram.

An entity is **existence dependent** on another if it cannot exist in the database without a corresponding instance of the other entity. Such an entity is called **weak**. The entity it depends on is called **strong**. A weak entity is shown on an E-R diagram within a double rectangle. Special types of existence dependencies are **identifier** and **referential** dependencies.

Aggregation is an abstraction that allows us to group together objects into higher-level objects. Its inverse, **decomposition**, means breaking up an object into its detailed components. **Generalization** means allowing objects of different types to be considered as examples of a higher-level set. Its inverse, **specialization**, means breaking up a set into the various types of objects it contains. In aggregation and decomposition, we search for "parts of" higher-level objects. In generalization and specialization, we search for "types of" higher-level objects. These two abstractions may be used together to consider different aspects of objects at different levels. On an E-R diagram, generalization is represented by an *ISA* triangle connecting the higher-level entity to its types. Aggregation can be represented by placing a large labeled rectangle around the objects being aggregated, whether they are entity sets alone or include relationships.

5.14 *Exercises*

1. Consider the entity set Employee with attributes EmpID, SocSecNo, Empname, Dept, Jobtitle, Salary.
   (a) Show how the entity set and its attributes would be represented on an E-R diagram.
   (b) Describe the domain of the Salary attribute, making assumptions as needed.
   (c) Identify a superkey for the Employee entity set.
   (d) Identify all candidate keys for the entity set.
   (e) Identify a primary key for the entity set.

2. Assume that in the same enterprise as in Exercise 1 there is an entity set called Project with attributes ProjName, StartDate, EndDate, Budget.
   (a) Show how this entity set and its relationship to Employee would be represented on the E-R diagram. Assume that you wish to represent the number of hours an employee is assigned to work on a project, and show that in the diagram.
   (b) Stating any necessary assumptions, make a decision about the cardinality of the relationship, explain its meaning, and add appropriate symbols to the E-R diagram to show the cardinality.
   (c) Identify foreign key(s), if any, in either Employee or Project.
   (d) Identify any existence dependency, and if there is one, decide whether it is an identifier dependency, a referential dependency, or neither.

3. (a) Assume that the entity set Employees is specialized into Clerical, Sales, and Management. Show how the specialization is represented on an E-R diagram.
   (b) Assume that there is another entity set called Equipment, with attributes Equip-Name, Location, Cost. Suppose that Employees and Equipment are aggregated into an entity set called Resources. Show how the aggregation could be represented on an E-R diagram. [Note: Do not include the specialization of Employees from part (a).]
   (c) On an E-R diagram, show how Resources from part (b) could participate in a relationship with the Project entity set described in Exercise 2.

4. Define each of the following terms.
   (a) entity type
   (b) entity set
   (c) well-defined set
   (d) attribute
   (e) domain of an attribute
   (f) null value
   (g) superkey
   (h) candidate key
   (i) composite key
   (j) primary key
   (k) alternate key
   (l) secondary key
   (m) relationship type
   (n) relationship set
   (o) binary relationship
   (p) ternary relationship
   (q) n-ary relationship
   (r) cardinality of a relationship
   (s) functional mapping
   (t) total mapping
   (u) onto mapping
   (v) foreign key
   (w) recursive relationship
   (x) existence dependency
   (y) weak entity

5.15 *Bibliography*

Batini, C. (Ed.). Proceedings of the Seventh International Conference on Entity-Relationship Approach. Rome: November, 1988.

Brackett, M. *Developing Data Structured Databases.* Englewood Cliffs, NJ: Prentice-Hall, 1987.

Brathwaite, K. *Data Administration.* New York: John Wiley & Sons, 1985.

Chen, P. "The Entity-Relationship Model: Toward a Unified View of Data," ACM Transactions on Database Systems **1**:1 (March, 1976) pp. 9-36.

Chen, P. (Ed.) Proceedings of the First International Conference on Entity-Relationship Approach (December, 1979), North Holland 1980.

Chen, P. (Ed.) Proceedings of the Second International Conference on Entity-Relationship Approach (October, 1981), Elsevier Science, 1981.

Davis, C., S. Jajodia, P. Ng, and R. Yeh (Ed.). Proceedings of the Third International Conference on Entity-Relationship Approach (October, 1983) North-Holland, 1983.

Howe, D. *Data Analysis for Data Base Design.* London: Edward Arnold, 1983.

Kent, W. *Data and Reality.* Amsterdam: North-Holland, 1978.

Ng, P. "Further Analysis of the Entity-Relationship Approach to Database Design," IEEE Transactions on Software Engineering **SE7**:1 (January, 1981) pp. 85-98.

Sakai, H. "Entity-Relationship Approach to Conceptual Schema Design," Proceedings of the ACM SIGMOD International Conference on Management of Data (1980) pp. 1-8.

Smith, J. and D. Smith. "Database Abstractions: Aggregation and Generalization," ACM Transactions on Database Systems **2**:2 (June, 1977) pp. 105-133.

Tsichritzis, D. and F. Lochovsky. *Data Models.* Englewood Cliffs, NJ: Prentice-Hall, 1982.

Ullman, J. *Principles of Database and Knowledge-Base Systems Volume I.* Rockville, MD: Computer Science Press, 1988.

SAMPLE PROJECT: CREATING THE E-R DIAGRAM FOR CLERICALTEMPS

Step 5.1

Make a list of all entities and their associated attributes.

This may take several attempts, and different designers will arrive at different solutions. In identifying entities, we examine the data dictionary and the cross-reference table. The data items there represent attributes rather than entities. Our job is to try to use abstraction to group the attributes into entities. The cross-reference table can help here. If several attributes tend to appear together on reports, they may be attributes of the same entity. We should avoid the temptation to make all reports or transactions entities. Besides examining the documents we have already developed, we think about the enterprise and ask ourselves what are the persons, places, events, objects, or concepts that we need to keep information about. The original data dictionary may have some items that we need not store in the database. They can be dropped from the list of attributes. As a result of this analysis, we may have the following entities and attributes:

WORKER: EMPID, EMPNAME, SSN, EMPADD, EMPPHONE, DOB, SEX, DATEHIRED, LASTDATEWORKED, AVERRATING, WORDPROC, TYPING, FILING, BOOKKPING, STENO, AVAILCODE

CLIENT: CLID, CLNAME, CLADD, CLPHONE, CONTACT, BILLINGYTD, PAYMENTSYTD

JOB: JOB#, JOBTITLE, STARTDATE, EXPECTENDDATE, DAILYRATE, DAILYHOURS, REPORTTONAME, REPORTTOADD, REPORTTOPHONE, JOBSTATUS

BILL: INVOICE#, BILLDATE, OLDBAL, TOTCHARGES, NEWBAL, TOTPAID

PAYROLL: CHECK#, PAYDATE, GROSS, FED, FICA, STATE, LOCAL, NET, GROSSYTD, NETYTD, FEDYTD, FICAYTD, STATEYTD, LOCALYTD

Step 5.2

Make a list of relationships to be represented and any descriptive attributes for them. The following relationships exist:

ASSIGNMENT: connects Worker to Job. In addition to JOB# and EMPID, it has descriptive attributes EMPRATING, RATINGDATE, and RATERNAME.

CLIENT-JOB: connects Client to Job. Attributes are JOB# and CLID.

CLIENT-BILL: connects Client to Bill. Attributes are INVOICE# and CLID.

WORKER-PAYROLL: connects Worker to Payroll. Attributes are CHECK# and EMPID.

Note that we have decided not to store some of the items from the original data dictionary. The following items are not stored for the reasons indicated:

NUMDAYSWORKED. This item, used only to do the weekly payroll, is entered as a temporary data item for payroll.

All payroll totals (**WKTOTALFED** through **WKTOTALSTATEYTD** in the data dictionary). These are calculated for the payroll report and are not needed for any other purpose. If they are ever needed again, they could be recalculated.

Step 5.3

Draw an E-R diagram to represent the enterprise. Be sure to identify relationship cardinalities, any weak entity sets, and role names, if needed. Use generalization and aggregation as necessary to express relationships.

The E-R diagram for ClericalTemps is shown in Figure 5.17. Note that we have omitted the attributes.

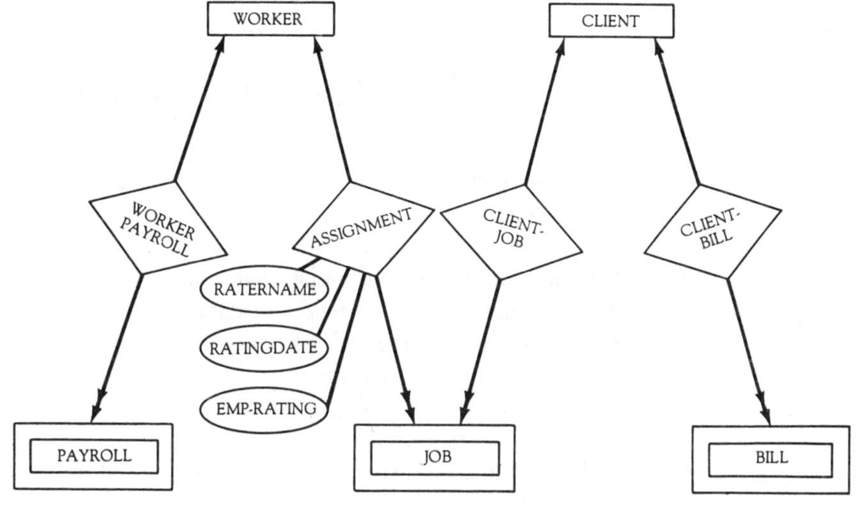

Figure 5.17

Student Project: Creating an E-R Diagram

For the project you have chosen, do the following:

Step 5.1

Make a list of all entities and their associated attributes.

Step 5.2

Make a list of relationships to be represented and any descriptive attributes for them.

Step 5.3

Draw an E-R diagram to represent the enterprise. Be sure to identify relationship cardinalities, any weak entity sets, and role names, if needed. Use generalization and aggregation as necessary to express relationships.

CHAPTER

6

The Relational Model

6 Chapter Objectives

In this chapter you will learn

- the origins of the relational model
- some advantages of the relational model
- how tables are used to represent data
- the connection between mathematical relations and relational model relations
- characteristics of database relations
- how to identify relation keys
- the meaning of entity integrity and referential integrity
- how to write out a relational scheme
- the categories of relational DMLs
- how to write queries in relational algebra
- how relational calculus queries are expressed
- how views are defined in the relational model
- some criteria for relational database management systems
- how to transform an E-R diagram into a relational model for a database

6.1 Brief History of the Relational Model

The relational model was first proposed by Codd in 1970, in a paper called "A Relational Model of Data for Large Shared Data Banks." Much of the early research on the model was done by him and his associates at the IBM Research Laboratory formerly in San Jose, California. At that time, the market was dominated by hierarchical and network model database management systems, which used complex structures and were difficult for users to understand, as Chapters 9 and 10 demonstrate. A prototype relational database management system, called **System R**, was developed by IBM researchers during the late 1970s. This project was designed to prove the practicality of the relational model by providing an implementation of its data structures and operations. It also proved to be an excellent source of information about implementation concerns such as concurrency control, query optimization, transaction management, data security and integrity, recovery techniques, human factors, and user interfaces, and led to many research papers and other prototypes. System R is the basis for IBM's two commercially available relational database management systems, DB2 and SQL/DS.

The model is also used by many other DBMSs for both mainframe and microcomputer environments. INGRES was an early relational model research project developed at the University of California at Berkeley at about the same time as the System R project. The research led to a "university" version of INGRES which runs under UNIX on DEC PDP machines. Relational Technology, Inc. has a commercial version of INGRES that runs under VMS or UNIX on DEC VAX machines, as well as on some other systems. ORACLE was developed and marketed by Relational Software, Inc. (now Oracle, Inc.) using many of the System R results. ORACLE runs under VMS and UNIX, as well as IBM MVS machines. Among microcomputer-based relational database management systems are dBaseIV from Ashton-Tate and R:base from Microrim.

Because of the popularity of the relational model, many nonrelational systems now provide a relational user interface, regardless of the underlying model. Computer Associates' IDMS, formerly the example of the network model, has become IDMS/R and IDMS/SQL, supporting a relational view of data. Other mainframe DBMSs that support some relational features are Computer Corporation of America's Model 204 and Software AG's ADABAS.

6.2 Advantages of the Relational Model

The relational model is based on the mathematical notion of a relation. Codd and others have extended the notion to apply to database design. Thus they were able to take advantage of the power of mathematical abstraction and of the expressiveness of mathematical notation to develop a simple but powerful structure for databases. The relational model is the subject of a large body of research literature, which is still growing rapidly. Much of the literature treats the model theoretically, developing aspects of the model by using the mathematical approach of theorem and proof. This abstract approach has the advantage that the results are general, meaning that they do not depend on a particular example and can be applied to many different applications. Fortunately, we can use the results of the theory to design relational models without necessarily following the intricate process of theorem proving. The theory assists in database design by identifying potential flaws in proposed designs, and providing tools to allow us to correct those flaws. Chapter 7 contains a detailed discussion of these techniques.

The basic structure of the relational model is simple, making it easy to understand on an intuitive level. It allows separation of the logical and physical levels, so that logical design can be performed without considering storage structures. Users and designers find that the model allows them to express logical data notions in a manner that is easily understood, unlike the two other record-based models, which require complicated data structures to express data relationships. Data operations are also easy to express and do not require that users be familiar with the storage structures used. The model uses a few very powerful commands to accomplish data manipulations that range from the simple to the complex. For these reasons, the relational model has taken the lead in development of new database management systems and new applications. Some relational systems do not yet have the performance capabilities of older hierarchical and network-based systems, but, with proper separation of physical and logical aspects, this disadvantage can be overcome.

6.3 *Relational Data Structures*

6.3.1 *Tables*

The relational model is based on the concept of a **relation**, which is physically represented as a **table**. In this model, tables are used to hold information about the objects to be represented in the database. Using the terms of the entity–relationship model, both entity sets and relationship sets are shown as tables. A relation is represented as a two-dimensional table in which the rows of the table correspond to individual records and the table columns correspond to attributes. For example, the STUDENT relation is represented by the STUDENT table, having columns for attributes STUID, STUNAME, MAJOR, and CREDITS. Figure 6.1 shows an instance of the STUDENT table. Note that the column names, STUID, STUNAME, MAJOR, and CREDITS, are the same as the attribute names. As you can see from this example, a column contains values of a single attribute; for example, the STUID column contains only IDs of students. The **domain** of an attribute is the set of allowable values for that attribute. Domains may be distinct, or two or more attributes may have the same domain. Each row of the table corresponds to an individual record or entity instance. In the relational model, each row is called a **tuple**.

A table that represents a relation has the following characteristics:

- Each cell of the table contains only one value.
- Each column has a distinct name, which is the name of the attribute it represents.

STUDENT	STUID	STUNAME	MAJOR	CREDITS
	S1015	Jones,Mary	Math	42
	S1005	Lee,Perry	History	3
	S1001	Smith,Tom	History	90
	S1010	Burns,Edward	Art	63
	S1002	Chin,Ann	Math	36
	S1013	McCarthy,Owen	Math	0
	S1020	Rivera,Jane	CSC	15

Figure 6.1 The STUDENT Table

- The values in a column all come from the same domain, since they are all values of the corresponding attribute.
- The order of columns is immaterial.
- Each tuple or row is distinct; there are no duplicate tuples.
- The order of tuples or rows is immaterial.

To show what these restrictions mean, we use our STUDENT table as an example. Since each cell should contain only one value, it is illegal to store two majors for a single student in a single cell. The column names written at the tops of the columns correspond to the attributes of the relation. The values in the STUID column are all from the domain of STUID; we would not allow a student's name to appear in this column. As long as we know from the column names which attribute each column represents, we can interchange columns. The table would represent the same relation if we were to put the CREDITS column before the MAJOR column. There can be no duplicate rows, because each individual student is represented just once. For example, the row (S1001, Smith,Tom, History, 90) appears only once. The rows can be interchanged at will, so the records of S1001 and S1002 can be switched, with no change in the relation.

6.3.2 *Mathematical Relations*

To understand the strict meaning of the term *relation*, we need to review some ideas from mathematics. Suppose that we have two sets, D_1 and D_2, with $D_1 = \{1, 3\}$ and $D_2 = \{2, 4, 6\}$. We could form the Cartesian product of these two sets, written $D_1 \times D_2$, which is the set of all ordered pairs such that the first element is a member of D_1 and the second element is a member of D_2 . Another way of thinking of this is to find all combinations of elements with the first from D_1 and the second from D_2. Thus we find

$$D_1 \times D_2 = \{(1,2),(1,4),(1,6),(3,2),(3,4),(3,6)\}$$

A relation is simply some subset of this Cartesian product. For example,

$$R = \{(1,2),(3,2)\}$$

is a relation. Often, we specify which ordered pairs will be in the relation by giving some rule for their selection. For example, R includes all those ordered pairs in which the second element is 2, so we could write R as

$$R = \{(x, y) \mid x \in D_1, y \in D_2, \text{ and } y = 2\}$$

Using these same sets, we could form another relation, S, in which the second element is always twice the first. Thus

$$S = \{(x, y) \mid x \in D_1, y \in D_2, \text{ and } y = 2x\}$$

Alternatively, $S = \{(1, 2), (3, 6)\}$, since there are only two ordered pairs in the Cartesian product that satisfy the condition. We could extend the notion of a relation to three sets in a natural way. Let D_1 , D_2 , and D_3 be three sets. Then the Cartesian product $D_1 \times D_2 \times D_3$ of these three sets is the set of all ordered triples such that the first element is from D_1, the second element is from D_2, and the third element is from D_3. A relation is then any subset of this Cartesian product. For example, suppose that we define the sets as

$$D_1 = \{1, 3\} \qquad D_2 = \{2, 4, 6\} \qquad D_3 = \{3, 6, 9\}$$

$$\begin{aligned} D_1 \times D_2 \times D_3 = \{&(1,2,3), (1,2,6), (1,2,9), (1,4,3), (1,4,6), (1,4,9), (1,6,3), \\ &(1,6,6), (1,6,9), (3,2,3), (3,2,6), (3,2,9), (3,4,3), (3,4,6), \\ &(3,4,9), (3,6,3), (3,6,6), (3,6,9)\} \end{aligned}$$

A relation is any subset of these ordered triples. For example, we could define a relation T as those ordered triples in which the third element is the sum of the first two. Then we have

$$T = \{(x, y, z) \mid x \in D_1, y \in D_2, z \in D_3, \text{ and } z = x + y\}$$

or

$$T = \{(1, 2, 3), (3, 6, 9)\}$$

We can go beyond three sets and define a general relation on n domains. Let $D_1, D_2, \ldots, D_n$ be n sets. Their Cartesian product is defined as

$$D_1 \times D_2 \times \cdots \times D_n = \{(d_1, d_2, ..., d_n) \mid d_1 \in D_1, d_2 \in D_2, \ldots, d_n \in D_n\}$$

The Cartesian product is usually written

$$\mathop{\times}_{i=1}^{n} D_i$$

A relation on the n sets is any set of n-tuples chosen from this Cartesian product. Notice that in defining our relations we had to specify the domains, or the sets from which we were choosing values.

6.3.3 *Database Relations*

Applying these concepts to databases, let $A_1, A_2, \ldots, A_n$ be attributes with domains $D_1, D_2, \ldots, D_n$. A **relation scheme** R is such a set of attributes with their corresponding domains. Thus set $\{A_1, A_2, \ldots, A_n\}$ with corresponding domains $\{D_1, D_2, \ldots, D_n\}$ is a relation scheme. A **relation** r on a relation scheme R is a set of mappings from the attribute names to their corresponding domains. Thus relation r is a set of n-tuples $(A_1 : d_1, A_2 : d_2, \ldots, A_n : d_n)$ such that $d_1 \in D_1, d_2 \in D_2, \ldots, d_n \in D_n$. Each element in the n-tuple consists of an attribute and a value of that attribute. Normally, when we write out a relation as a table, we list the attribute names as column headings and simply write out the tuples using values chosen from the appropriate domains, so we think of the n-tuples as having the form $(d_1, d_2, \ldots, d_n)$. In this way we can think of a relation in the relational model as any subset of the Cartesian product of the domains of the attributes. A table is simply a representation of such a relation.

For our university example, the relation STUDENT has attributes STUID, STUNAME, MAJOR, and CREDITS, each with its corresponding domain. The STUDENT relation is any subset of the Cartesian product of the domains, or any set of 4-tuples in which the first element is a student ID, the second is a student name, the third is a major, and the fourth is a number of credits. Some of the 4-tuples are

$$\{(\text{S1001, Smith, Tom, History, 90}), (\text{S1002, Chin, Ann, Math, 36}), \ldots\}$$

More properly, these 4-tuples are

$$\{(\text{STUID : S1001, STUNAME : Smith, Tom, MAJOR : History, CREDITS : 90}),$$
$$(\text{STUID : S1002, STUNAME : Chin, Ann, MAJOR : Math, CREDITS : 36}), \ldots\}$$

The STUDENT table is a convenient way of writing out all the 4-tuples that satisfy the relation at the moment. The 4-tuples are, of course, the rows of the table, which explains why table rows in the relational model are called tuples. The table, with all its rows written out, is an instance or extension of the relation. The structure of the table, together with a specification of the domains and any other restrictions on possible values, shows the intension of the relation.

6.3.4 *Properties of Relations*

Most of the characteristics specified for tables result from the properties of relations. Since a relation is a set, the order of elements does not count. Therefore, in a table, the order of rows is immaterial. In a set, no elements are repeated. Similarly, in a table, there are no duplicate rows. When we found the Cartesian products of sets with simple, single-valued elements such as integers, each element in each tuple was single-valued. Similarly, each cell of a table contains only one value. In a relation, the possible values for a given position are determined by the set or domain on which the position is defined. In a table, the values in each column must come from the same attribute domain. However, in a mathematical relation, the order of elements in a tuple is important. For example, the ordered pair (1,2) is quite different from the ordered pair (2,1). This is not the case for relations in the relational model, which specifically require that the order of columns be immaterial. The reason is that the column headings tell us to which attribute the value belongs. This means that the order of column headings in the intension is immaterial, but once the structure of the table is chosen, the order of elements within the rows of the extension must match the order of column names.

6.3.5 *Degree and Cardinality*

The number of columns in a table is called the **degree** of the relation. The degree of the STUDENT relation is four, since the STUDENT table has four columns. This means each row of the table is a 4-tuple, containing four values. A relation with only one column would have degree one and be called a **unary** relation. A relation with two columns is called **binary**, one with three columns is called **ternary,** and after that the term ***n*-ary** is usually used. The degree of a relation is part of the intension of the relation and never changes.

By contrast, the number of rows in a table, called the **cardinality** of the relation, changes as new tuples are added or old ones are deleted. The cardinality is a property of the extension of the relation, the particular instance of the relation at any given moment.

6.3.6 *Relation Keys*

Since a relation has no duplicate tuples, it is always possible to tell rows apart. This means that a relation always has a primary key. In the worst case, the entire set of attributes could serve as the primary key, but usually some smaller set is sufficient to distinguish among tuples. Applying our definitions from Chapter 5, a **superkey** for a relation is a set of attributes that uniquely identifies a tuple, a **candidate key** is a superkey such that no proper subset is a superkey, and a **primary key** is the candidate key that is actually chosen to identify tuples uniquely. Note that an instance of the table cannot be used to prove that an attribute or combination of attributes is a candidate key. The fact that there are no duplicates for the values that appear at a particular moment does not guarantee that duplicates are not possible. However, the presence of duplicates in an instance can be used to show that some attribute combination is not a candidate key. Identifying a candidate key requires that we consider the real-world meaning of the attribute(s) involved so that we can make a decision about whether duplicates are possible. Only by using this semantic information can we be sure that an attribute combination is a candidate key.

6.4 *Integrity Rules*

Since every attribute has an associated domain, there are constraints in the form of restrictions on the set of values allowed for attributes of relations. In addition, there are two important **integrity rules**, which are constraints or restrictions that apply to all instances of the database. The first, called **entity integrity**, states that in a relation **no attribute of a primary key can have a null value.** By definition, a primary key is a minimal identifier that is used to identify tuples uniquely. This means that no subset of the primary key is sufficient to provide unique identification of tuples. If we were to allow a null value for any part of the primary key, we would be demonstrating that not all of the attributes are needed to distinguish between tuples, which would contradict the definition.

The second integrity rule is called **referential integrity** and applies to foreign keys. Recalling the definition from Chapter 5, a foreign key is an attribute or attribute combination of a relation that is the primary key of another relation. We will call the relation in which the attribute or combination is the primary key its **home relation**. Referential integrity states that if a foreign key exists in a relation, either the foreign key value must match the primary key value of some tuple in its home relation or the foreign key value must be completely null.

6.5 Representing Relational Database Schemes

A relational database consists of any number of relations. We can represent relation schemes by giving the name of the relation, followed by the attribute names in parentheses. Normally, we will underline the primary key. For the university example, a simple database might contain relations for STUDENT, CLASS, FACULTY, and ENROLLMENT. The relation schemes would be written as

```
STUDENT (STUID, STUNAME, MAJOR, CREDITS)
CLASS (COURSE#, FACID, SCHED, ROOM)
FACULTY (FACID, FACNAME, DEPT, RANK)
ENROLLMENT (COURSE#, STUID, GRADE)
```

The conceptual model or schema is the set of all these schemes for the database. Figure 6.2 shows an instance of this database.

Notice that some attributes appear in more than one relation. For example, STUID appears in both STUDENT and ENROLLMENT. When we want to distinguish between the two appearances of STUID, we use **qualified names**, giving the relation name, followed by a period, followed by the attribute name. The two qualified names for STUID are STUDENT.STUID and ENROLLMENT.STUID. When an attribute appears in more than one relation, its appearance usually represents a relationship or interaction between tuples of the two relations. The inclusion of STUID in both of the relations is quite deliberate, and links students to their enrollment records. Similarly, the appearance of FACID in both FACULTY and CLASS links faculty members to the classes they teach. These common attributes play an important role in performing data manipulation, as we shall see in later sections.

6.6 Relational Data Manipulation Languages

There are a variety of languages used by relational database management systems. Some of them are **procedural**, meaning that the user tells the system exactly how to manipulate the data. Others are **nonprocedural**, which means that the user states what data is

STUDENT	STUID	STUNAME	MAJOR	CREDITS
	S1015	Jones,Mary	Math	42
	S1005	Lee,Perry	History	3
	S1001	Smith,Tom	History	90
	S1010	Burns,Edward	Art	63
	S1002	Chin,Ann	Math	36
	S1013	McCarthy,Owen	Math	0
	S1020	Rivera,Jane	CSC	15

CLASS	COURSE#	FACID	SCHED	ROOM
	ART103A	F101	MWF9	H221
	HST205A	F115	MWF11	H221
	CSC201A	F105	TuThF10	M110
	MTH101B	F110	MTuTh9	H225
	CSC203A	F105	MThF12	M110
	MTH103C	F110	MWF11	H225

FACULTY	FACID	FACNAME	DEPT	RANK
	F101	Adams	Art	Professor
	F115	Smith	History	Associate
	F105	Tanaka	CSC	Instructor
	F110	Byrne	Math	Assistant
	F221	Smith	CSC	Professor

ENROLLMENT	COURSE#	STUID	GRADE
	ART103A	S1001	A
	CSC201A	S1020	B
	CSC201A	S1002	F
	ART103A	S1010	
	ART103A	S1002	D
	MTH101B	S1020	A
	HST205A	S1001	C
	MTH103C	S1010	
	MTH103C	S1002	B

Figure 6.2 Instance of the University Database

needed but not exactly how it is to be located. Some languages are **graphical,** allowing the user to draw a picture or illustration of what data should be found. Another category is **fourth-generation language (4GL)**, which allows a complete customized application to be created using a few commands in a user-friendly, often menu-driven, environment. Some systems accept a variety of **natural language**, sometimes called a **fifth-generation language**, a restricted version of natural English. **Relational algebra** is an example of a procedural language that we will discuss. **Relational calculus** and **SQL** are nonprocedural languages that we will examine. **QBE** (Query-By-Example) is a graphical language that allows users to provide examples of data they would like retrieved. Some microcomputer-based database management systems such as **dBaseIV** have applications generators with fourth-generation languages, and some prototype **knowledge-based database management systems** accept fifth-generation or natural language, although this development is still in its infancy.

In this section we concentrate on relational algebra and relational calculus, which are both formal, non-user-friendly languages. Both have been used as the basis for other, higher-level data manipulation languages for relational databases. They are of interest because they illustrate the basic operations required of any data manipulation language and because they serve as the standard of comparison for other relational languages.

6.6.1 *Relational Algebra*

Relational algebra is a theoretical language with operators that work on one or two relations to produce another relation. Thus both the operands and the result are tables. There are several variations of syntax of relational algebra commands, and we will use a fairly simple one here and present it informally. We also include the symbolic notation for the commands. There are also many variations of the operations that are included in relational algebra. Date originally proposed eight operations, but several others have been developed. Three very basic operations, SELECT, PROJECT, and JOIN, allow us to perform most of the data retrieval operations that we are interested in. We will use the university database example from Figure 6.2 to illustrate these operations. We assume that we have the option of assigning the results to a table which we name in the command.

The SELECT Operator

The SELECT command works on a single table and takes rows that meet a specified condition, copying them into a new table. The general form is

```
SELECT table-name WHERE condition [GIVING new-table-name]
```

Symbolically, the form is

$$\sigma_{\text{predicate}}(\textit{table-name})$$

Note that the operation is performed on an existing table, named "table-name," and produces a new table which is a horizontal subset of the old one and which we can name "new-table-name." The square brackets indicate that the part of the statement enclosed in them is optional. The old table continues to exist under its old name, and both it and the new table are available for additional operations. If we simply wish to find and display the rows that satisfy the condition, but do not plan further operations on the new table, we omit its name.

For example, if we wished to find all information in the STUDENT table about student S1013, we would write

```
SELECT STUDENT WHERE STUID = 'S1013' GIVING RESULT
```

or symbolically

$$\sigma_{STUID='S1013'}(STUDENT)$$

The command produces a new table that we call RESULT, which looks like this:

RESULT	STUID	STUNAME	MAJOR	CREDITS
	S1013	McCarthy,Owen	Math	0

The SELECT operation can be used to find more than one row. For example, to find all classes that meet in room H225, we would write

```
SELECT CLASS WHERE ROOM = 'H225' GIVING ANSWER
```

or symbolically

$$\sigma_{ROOM='H225'}(CLASS)$$

This command produces the following table:

ANSWER	COURSE#	FACID	SCHED	ROOM
	MTH101B	F110	MTuTh9	H225
	MTH103C	F110	MWF11	H225

We can form more complicated conditions by using the following symbols, having their usual meaning:

```
<,  <=,  >,  >=,  =,  ~=,  AND,  OR,  NOT
```

For example, to find all math majors who have more than 30 credits, we write

```
SELECT STUDENT WHERE MAJOR = 'Math' AND CREDITS > 30
```

or symbolically

$$\sigma_{MAJOR='\text{Math}'\ AND\ CREDITS>30}(\text{STUDENT})$$

This command produces the following unnamed table:

STUID	STUNAME	MAJOR	CREDITS
S1015	Jones,Mary	Math	42
S1002	Chin,Ann	Math	36

The PROJECT Operator

The PROJECT command also operates on a single table, but it produces a vertical subset of the table, extracting the values of specified columns, eliminating duplicates, and placing the values in a new table. Its form is

```
PROJECT table-name OVER (col-name,...,col-name) [GIVING new-table-name]
```

or symbolically

$$\pi_{col\text{-}name,...,col\text{-}name}(table\text{-}name)$$

To illustrate projection over a single column, we find all the different majors that students have declared, by the command

```
PROJECT STUDENT OVER MAJOR GIVING TEMP
```

or

$$\pi_{MAJOR}(STUDENT)$$

The resulting table, TEMP, looks like this:

```
TEMP    MAJOR
        -----
        Math
        History
        Art
        CSC
```

Notice that we get all the values that appear in the MAJOR column of the STUDENT table, but duplicates have been eliminated.

When we project over two or more columns, duplicates of combinations of values are eliminated. For example, suppose that we want to find the rooms that faculty members teach in. We could do so by using the following command:

```
PROJECT CLASS OVER (FACID,ROOM)
```

or

$$\pi_{FACID,ROOM}(CLASS)$$

This gives the result

```
FACID   ROOM
------------
F101    H221
F115    H221
F105    M110
F110    H225
```

While we have repetition in the room values, with H221 appearing twice, we notice that the repeated values appear with different FACID values. As long as the combination has not appeared before, it is added to the projection. Notice that the last two rows of CLASS did not contribute to the projection result, since their combination of values for FACID and ROOM appeared previously.

We can combine the SELECT and PROJECT operations, but doing so requires two steps. For example, suppose that we would like the names and IDs of all history majors.

Since we want only history majors, we need to do a SELECT. However, since we want only certain columns, we need to do a PROJECT. We can express the query as

```
SELECT STUDENT WHERE MAJOR = 'History' GIVING TEMP
PROJECT TEMP OVER (STUNAME, STUID) GIVING RESULT
```

After the first command is executed, we have the table

```
TEMP    STUID   STUNAME         MAJOR      CREDITS
        ----------------------------------------
        S1005   Lee,Perry       History       3
        S1001   Smith,Tom       History      90
```

The second command is performed on this temporary table, and the result is

```
RESULT  STUNAME        STUID
        ------------------
        Lee,Perry      S1005
        Smith,Tom      S1001
```

Notice that the PROJECT operator allowed us to reverse the order of the two columns in the final result. We could have written the commands symbolically as

$$\pi_{STUNAME,STUID}(\sigma_{MAJOR='History'}(STUDENT))$$

Note that we can compose the operations, using the result of the first as the argument for the second. The intermediate table resulting from the selection operation, which we called TEMP when we used the English-like syntax, does not need a name when we use symbolic notation, since we use the expression instead.

The Product, Theta Join, Equijoin, Natural Join, Semijoin, and Outerjoin Operators

If we start with two tables, A and B, we can form their product, written A TIMES B or $A \times B$, in much the same way as we formed the Cartesian product of sets in Section 6.3.2. $A \times B$ is a table whose width is the width of A plus the width of B and whose columns are the columns of A followed by the columns of B. It can be formed in several ways. One method is to start with the first row of A, combine it with the first row of B, then with the second row of B, and so on, until all combinations of the first row of A with rows of B have been formed. Then the procedure is repeated for the second row of A, then the third row, and so on. If A has x rows and B has y rows, then $A \times B$ has xy rows.

Suppose that we form the product of STUDENT and ENROLLMENT, written STUDENT $\times$ ENROLLMENT. This table will have seven columns, but two of them will be called STUID. To distinguish these two, we use the qualified names from the original tables, STUDENT.STUID and ENROLLMENT.STUID. The product, which has 63 rows, is shown in Figure 6.3.

We can define several operations on the product of tables. The most general one is called the **THETA JOIN**. "Theta" is the Greek letter often used by mathematicians

STUDENT. STUDID	STUNAME	MAJOR	CREDITS	COURSE#	ENROLLMENT. STUID	GRADE
S1015	Jones,Mary	Math	42	ART103A	S1001	A
S1015	Jones,Mary	Math	42	CSC201A	S1020	B
S1015	Jones,Mary	Math	42	CSC201A	S1002	F
S1015	Jones,Mary	Math	42	ART103A	S1010	
S1015	Jones,Mary	Math	42	ART103A	S1002	D
S1015	Jones,Mary	Math	42	MTH101B	S1020	A
S1015	Jones,Mary	Math	42	HST205A	S1001	C
S1015	Jones,Mary	Math	42	MTH103C	S1010	
S1015	Jones,Mary	Math	42	MTH103C	S1002	B
S1005	Lee,Perry	History	3	ART103A	S1001	A
S1005	Lee,Perry	History	3	CSC201A	S1020	B
S1005	Lee,Perry	History	3	CSC201A	S1002	F
S1005	Lee,Perry	History	3	ART103A	S1010	
S1005	Lee,Perry	History	3	ART103A	S1002	D
S1005	Lee,Perry	History	3	MTH101B	S1020	A
S1005	Lee,Perry	History	3	HST205A	S1001	C
S1005	Lee,Perry	History	3	MTH103C	S1010	
S1005	Lee,Perry	History	3	MTH103C	S1002	B
S1001	Smith,Tom	History	90	ART103A	S1001	A
S1001	Smith,Tom	History	90	CSC201A	S1020	B
S1001	Smith,Tom	History	90	CSC201A	S1002	F
S1001	Smith,Tom	History	90	ART103A	S1010	
S1001	Smith,Tom	History	90	ART103A	S1002	D
S1001	Smith,Tom	History	90	MTH101B	S1020	A
S1001	Smith,Tom	History	90	HST205A	S1001	C
S1001	Smith,Tom	History	90	MTH103C	S1010	
S1001	Smith,Tom	History	90	MTH103C	S1002	B
S1010	Burns,Edward	Art	63	ART103A	S1001	A
S1010	Burns,Edward	Art	63	CSC201A	S1020	B
S1010	Burns,Edward	Art	63	CSC201A	S1002	F
S1010	Burns,Edward	Art	63	ART103A	S1010	
S1010	Burns,Edward	Art	63	ART103A	S1002	D
S1010	Burns,Edward	Art	63	MTH101B	S1020	A
S1010	Burns,Edward	Art	63	HST205A	S1001	C
S1010	Burns,Edward	Art	63	MTH103C	S1010	
S1010	Burns,Edward	Art	63	MTH103C	S1002	B
S1002	Chin,Ann	Math	36	ART103A	S1001	A
S1002	Chin,Ann	Math	36	CSC201A	S1020	B
S1002	Chin,Ann	Math	36	CSC201A	S1002	F
S1002	Chin,Ann	Math	36	ART103A	S1010	
S1002	Chin,Ann	Math	36	ART103A	S1002	D
S1002	Chin,Ann	Math	36	MTH101B	S1020	A
S1002	Chin,Ann	Math	36	HST205A	S1001	C
S1002	Chin,Ann	Math	36	MTH103C	S1010	
S1002	Chin,Ann	Math	36	MTH103C	S1002	B

Figure 6.3 Student Times Enrollment

S1013	McCarthy,Owen	Math	0	ART103A	S1001	A
S1013	McCarthy,Owen	Math	0	CSC201A	S1020	B
S1013	McCarthy,Owen	Math	0	CSC201A	S1002	F
S1013	McCarthy,Owen	Math	0	ART103A	S1010	
S1013	McCarthy,Owen	Math	0	ART103A	S1002	D
S1013	McCarthy,Owen	Math	0	MTH101B	S1020	A
S1013	McCarthy,Owen	Math	0	HST205A	S1001	C
S1013	McCarthy,Owen	Math	0	MTH103C	S1010	
S1013	McCarthy,Owen	Math	0	MTH103C	S1002	B
S1020	Rivera,Jane	CSC	15	ART103A	S1001	A
S1020	Rivera,Jane	CSC	15	CSC201A	S1020	B
S1020	Rivera,Jane	CSC	15	CSC201A	S1002	F
S1020	Rivera,Jane	CSC	15	ART103A	S1010	
S1020	Rivera,Jane	CSC	15	ART103A	S1002	D
S1020	Rivera,Jane	CSC	15	MTH101B	S1020	A
S1020	Rivera,Jane	CSC	15	HST205A	S1001	C
S1020	Rivera,Jane	CSC	15	MTH103C	S1010	
S1015	Rivera,Jane	CSC	15	MTH103C	S1002	B

Figure 6.3 *(continued)*

to represent any kind of operator, and it was used by the developers of this theory to represent any one of the comparison operators. The theta join is defined as the result of performing a SELECT operation using a comparison operator theta, which may be <, <=, and so on, on the product. For example, we might want only those tuples of the product where the CREDITS value is greater than 50. Here, theta is >, and we could write the query as

```
STUDENT TIMES ENROLLMENT WHERE CREDITS > 50
```

This is equivalent to

```
STUDENT TIMES ENROLLMENT GIVING TEMP
SELECT TEMP WHERE CREDITS > 50
```

or, symbolically

$$\sigma_{CREDITS>50}(STUDENT \times ENROLLMENT)$$

The symbol $|\times|_{\Theta}$ is sometimes used to stand for the theta join. In use, the Θ is replaced by the actual predicate used for selection. We note that for any two relations, X and Y, the theta join is defined symbolically as

$$A\,|\times|_{\Theta}\,B = \sigma_{\Theta}(A \times B)$$

Since the product is a slow operation requiring, in the example above, 63 concatenations, it would be more efficient to perform the selection first and then do the product, provided that sequence of operations gives the same result. A more efficient form, requiring only 18 concatenations, is

```
SELECT STUDENT WHERE CREDITS > 50 GIVING TEMP2
TEMP2 TIMES ENROLLMENT
```

or $(\sigma_{CREDITS>50}(STUDENT)) \times ENROLLMENT$

One may wonder why we are interested in forming concatenations of rows of STUDENT with rows of ENROLLMENT having a different STUID. The truthful answer is that usually we are not! Therefore, a more common operation involving the product of tables is the one in which we ask for only those rows of the product in which the values of the common columns are equal. When the theta is equality, we have the **EQUIJOIN** of tables. To form the equijoin, then, you start with two tables having a common column or columns. You compare each tuple of the first with each tuple of the second and choose only those concatenations in which the values in the common columns are equal. We would form the equijoin of STUDENT and ENROLLMENT by choosing those tuples of the product with matching STUID values. Figure 6.4 shows

```
STUDENT EQUIJOIN ENROLLMENT
```

written symbolically as

$$STUDENT \mid\times\mid_{STUDENT.STUID=ENROLLMENT.STUID} ENROLLMENT$$

Note that this is equivalent to

```
STUDENT TIMES ENROLLMENT GIVING TEMP3
SELECT TEMP3 WHERE STUDENT.STUID = ENROLLMENT.STUID
```

or

$$\sigma_{STUDENT.STUID=ENROLLMENT.STUID}(STUDENT \times ENROLLMENT)$$

If we had more than one common column, both sets of values would have to match.

STUDENT. STUID	STUNAME	MAJOR	CREDITS	COURSE#	ENROLLMENT. STUID	GRADE
S1001	Smith,Tom	History	90	ART103A	S1001	A
S1001	Smith,Tom	History	90	HST205A	S1001	C
S1010	Burns,Edward	Art	63	ART103A	S1010	
S1010	Burns,Edward	Art	63	MTH103C	S1010	
S1002	Chin,Ann	Math	36	CSC201A	S1002	F
S1002	Chin,Ann	Math	36	ART103A	S1002	D
S1002	Chin,Ann	Math	36	MTH103C	S1002	B
S1020	Rivera,Jane	CSC	15	CSC201A	S1020	B
S1020	Rivera,Jane	CSC	15	MTH101B	S1020	A

Figure 6.4 Student Equijoin Enrollment

You may notice that, by definition, we always have at least two identical columns in an equijoin. Since it seems unnecessary to include the repeated column, we define a **NATURAL JOIN** as an equijoin in which the repeated column is eliminated. This is the most common form of the JOIN operation, so common, in fact, that this is what is usually meant by JOIN. When we mean the natural join we simply write

```
table-name-1 JOIN table-name-2 [GIVING new-table-name]
```

or

```
JOIN table-name-1, table-name-2 [GIVING new-table-name]
```

We can use the symbol |×| for the natural join, as in

$$table\text{-}name\text{-}1 \ |\times| \ table\text{-}name\text{-}2$$

Although normally the JOIN is performed over columns with the same names, all that is really required is that the domains of the attributes be the same. Thus we could do a join in which the number of credits of a student is compared with the age of a faculty member, since they would have the same domain. Since this does not make much sense, we usually require that the columns have the same semantic meanings. If there is any confusion about the columns to be compared, we could include their names, using a command such as

```
JOIN table-name-1, table-name-2 OVER col-1, col-2
```

or symbolically

$$table\text{-}name\text{-}1 \ |\times|_{col\text{-}1, col\text{-}2} \ table\text{-}name\text{-}2$$

The natural join of STUDENT and ENROLLMENT would produce a table identical to the one in Figure 6.4, except that the second STUID column would be dropped. Since FACULTY and CLASS have a common column, FACID, we will find their natural join. The result of the command

```
JOIN FACULTY, CLASS
```

or

$$FACULTY \ |\times| \ CLASS$$

is shown in Figure 6.5.

FACID	FACNAME	DEPT	RANK	COURSE#	SCHED	ROOM
F101	Adams	Art	Professor	ART103A	MWF9	H221
F115	Smith	History	Associate	HST205A	MWF11	H221
F105	Tanaka	CSC	Instructor	CSC201A	TuThF10	M110
F105	Tanaka	CSC	Instructor	CSC203A	MThF12	M110
F110	Byrne	Math	Assistant	MTH101B	MTuTh9	H225
F110	Byrne	Math	Assistant	MTH103C	MWF11	H225

Figure 6.5 Natural Join of Faculty and Class

The resulting table gives us all the details about faculty members and the classes they teach. We do not keep the data about faculty and classes in a single table, because we would have a lot of repetition in the table. Notice that data about Tanaka and Byrne is repeated, because they each teach two classes. The join allows us to recombine pieces of information about an entity, even though they appear on different tables.

More complicated queries can require use of the SELECT, PROJECT, and JOIN commands. For example, suppose that we want to find the classes and grades of student Ann Chin. We notice that the STUDENT table contains the student's name, but not classes or grades, while the ENROLLMENT table contains the classes and grades, but not the name. Whenever we need to use more than one table to answer a query, we must use a JOIN. If the result should contain only some, not all, columns of the original tables, we need a PROJECT. If not all rows will be used, we need a SELECT. To decide what operations to do and in what order, examine the tables to see how you would answer the question "by hand" and then try to formulate the operations required in terms of relational algebra commands. Here, we would start with the STUDENT table and look up the STUID for Ann Chin. We would then consult the ENROLLMENT table, looking for records with that STUID and reading off the course numbers and grades. One way to find the data required is the following:

```
SELECT STUDENT WHERE STUNAME ='Chin,Ann' GIVING TEMP1
JOIN TEMP1, ENROLLMENT GIVING TEMP2
PROJECT TEMP2 OVER (COURSE#, GRADE) GIVING ANSWER
```

After the SELECT in the first line we have this result:

```
TEMP1    STUID    STUNAME        MAJOR    CREDITS
         --------------------------------------
         S1002    Chin,Ann       Math     36
```

After the JOIN in the second line we have this result:

```
TEMP2    STUID    STUNAME        MAJOR     CREDITS    COURSE#   GRADE
         ----------------------------------------------------------
         S1002    Chin,Ann       Math      36         CSC201A   F
         S1002    Chin,Ann       Math      36         ART103A   D
         S1002    Chin,Ann       Math      36         MTH103C   B
```

After the PROJECT in the third line, we have this result:

```
ANSWER   COURSE#     GRADE
         -----------------
         CSC201A     F
         ART103A     D
         MTH103C     B
```

Symbolically, the entire query could be expressed as

$$\pi_{CLASS,GRADE}((\sigma_{STUNAME='Chin,Ann'}(STUDENT)) \mid\times\mid ENROLLMENT)$$

You may have observed that all we really needed from TEMP1 was the STUID column, since this was used for the comparison for the join and none of the other columns was used later. Therefore, if we preferred, we could have used a PROJECT on TEMP1 to give us only the STUID column before doing the JOIN.

A different way to do the query is

```
JOIN STUDENT, ENROLLMENT GIVING TEMPA
SELECT TEMPA WHERE STUNAME = 'Chin,Ann' GIVING TEMPB
PROJECT TEMPB OVER (COURSE#, GRADE)
```

or

$$\pi_{COURSE\#,GRADE}(\sigma_{STUNAME='Chin,Ann'}(STUDENT \;|\times|\; ENROLLMENT))$$

As you may have observed, this method is less efficient, since the first line requires 54 comparisons to form a joined table, a relatively slow operation. Doing the selection first reduces the number of comparisons to nine, thus optimizing the query.

We can do joins of joined tables. Suppose that we wanted to find the IDs of all students in Professor Adams' classes. We would need data from the FACULTY, CLASS, and ENROLLMENT tables to answer this query. One method is

```
SELECT FACULTY WHERE FACNAME = 'Adams' GIVING TEMP1
JOIN TEMP1, CLASS GIVING TEMP2
JOIN TEMP2, ENROLLMENT GIVING TEMP3
PROJECT TEMP3 OVER STUID GIVING RESULT.
```

or symbolically

$$\pi_{STUID}(((\sigma_{FACNAME='Adams'}(FACULTY)) \;|\times|\; CLASS) \;|\times|\; ENROLLMENT)$$

In this example, TEMP2 has seven columns and TEMP3 has nine columns. Since only one of the FACULTY columns, FACID, is used for the join and none of its other columns is needed later, we could do a PROJECT before the first join. Alternatively, since only one of TEMP2's columns, COURSE#, is needed for the join and none of its other columns is used again, we could do a PROJECT between the two joins.

There are several other types of join operators that can be defined. One variation is the **SEMIJOIN** of two tables. If A and B are tables, then the semijoin of A by B can be found by taking the natural join of A and B and then projecting the result onto the attributes of A. For the STUDENT and ENROLLMENT shown in Figure 6.2, the semijoin of STUDENT by ENROLLMENT, written as

```
STUDENT SEMIJOIN ENROLLMENT
```

or symbolically

$$STUDENT \;|\times\; ENROLLMENT$$

is shown in Figure 6.6. Note that semijoin is not commutative. For example, STUDENT SEMIJOIN ENROLLMENT, shown in Figure 6.6, is different from ENROLLMENT SEMIJOIN STUDENT, which would be the projection onto the ENROLLMENT tables of the natural join. Its columns would be COURSE#, STUID, and GRADE.

Another type of join operation is the **OUTERJOIN**. This operation is an extension of a THETA JOIN, an EQUIJOIN, or a NATURAL JOIN operation. When forming a join, any tuple of one of the original tables for which there is no tuple in the second table that would allow the pair of tuples to satisfy the join condition does not enter the result. An outer theta join consists of all the rows that appear in the usual theta join, plus an additional row for each of the tuples from the original tables that do not participate in

STUID	STUNAME	MAJOR	CREDITS
S1001	Smith,Tom	History	90
S1010	Burns,Edward	Art	63
S1002	Chin,Ann	Math	36
S1020	Rivera,Jane	CSC	15

Figure 6.6 Semijoin of Student by Enrollment

the theta join. In these rows, we place the unmatched original tuple and extend it by assigning null values to the other attributes. For example, in an equijoin for tables with a common column, a row in the first table will not participate in the result unless there is a row in the second table with the same value for the common column. We saw, for example, that the row "S1015 Jones,Mary Math 42" from the STUDENT table was not represented in the STUDENT EQUIJOIN ENROLLMENT table shown in Figure 6.4, because there was no row of ENROLLMENT having S1015 as the STUID value. In an outerjoin, such unmatched rows appear, with null values for the other attributes in the result. For example, to form the outer equijoin of STUDENT and ENROLLMENT we include all the rows from STUDENT EQUIJOIN ENROLLMENT, and add in the rows from STUDENT that have no matching ENROLLMENT rows, by placing null values in the COURSE#, ENROLLMENT.STUID, and GRADE columns. We should also include any rows of ENROLLMENT for which the STUID value does not have a match in the STUDENT table, but we note that there are no such rows in the original tables shown in Figure 6.2. To illustrate the possibilities for the outer equijoin, we change our example slightly, by appending some rows to the ENROLLMENT table, as shown in Figure 6.7(a). We call the new table NEWENROLL and note that the records inserted are quite illegal. The last row, having a null value in one of the key fields, STUID, does not have entity integrity, and the row above it, having S2222 as the STUID, does not have referential integrity, since no such value exists in the STUDENT table. We ignore these flaws in this illustration for the purpose of showing the outer equijoin operation in Figure 6.7(b).

A variation of the outer equijoin shown is a **LEFT OUTER EQUIJOIN**, which means only unmatched rows from the first (left) table appear in the result. The left outer equijoin of STUDENT and NEWENROLL is shown in Figure 6.7(c). In a **RIGHT OUTER EQUIJOIN** we include unmatched rows from the second (right) table, as shown for STUDENT and NEWENROLL in Figure 6.7(d).

The outer natural join is similar to the outer equijoin, except that we drop the repeated column(s). If the joined rows have an equal value for a repeated column, we use that value. If both have null values, we use a null, and if one has a null value and the other not, we use the nonnull value in the result.

Set Operations: Union, Difference, Intersection

Since relations are basically sets of *n*-tuples, relational algebra includes a version of the basic set operations of union, intersection, and set difference. For these binary operations to be possible, the two relations on which they are performed must be **union compatible**. This means that they must have the same basic structure. In particular, they must have the same degree and the attributes in the corresponding position in

STUDENT	STUID	STUNAME	MAJOR	CREDITS
	S1015	Jones,Mary	Math	42
	S1005	Lee,Perry	History	3
	S1001	Smith,Tom	History	90
	S1010	Burns,Edward	Art	63
	S1002	Chin,Ann	Math	36
	S1013	McCarthy,Owen	Math	0
	S1020	Rivera,Jane	CSC	15

NEWENROLL	COURSE#	STUID	GRADE
	ART103A	S1001	A
	CSC201A	S1020	B
	CSC201A	S1002	F
	ART103A	S1010	-
	ART103A	S1002	D
	MTH101B	S1020	A
	HST205A	S1001	C
	MTH103C	S1010	-
	MTH103C	S1002	B
	MTH101B	S2222	-
	CSC203A	-	-

Figure 6.7(a): Tables for the Outerjoin

STUDENT. STUID	STUNAME	MAJOR	CREDITS	COURSE#	ENROLLMENT. STUID	GRADE
S1015	Jones,Mary	Math	42	-	-	-
S1005	Lee,Perry	History	3	-	-	-
S1001	Smith,Tom	History	90	ART103A	S1001	A
S1001	Smith,Tom	History	90	HST205A	S1001	C
S1010	Burns,Edward	Art	63	ART103A	S1010	-
S1010	Burns,Edward	Art	63	MTH103C	S1010	-
S1002	Chin,Ann	Math	36	CSC201A	S1002	F
S1002	Chin,Ann	Math	36	ART103A	S1002	D
S1002	Chin,Ann	Math	36	MTH103C	S1002	B
S1013	McCarthy,Owen	Math	0	-	-	-
S1020	Rivera,Jane	CSC	15	CSC201A	S1020	B
S1020	Rivera,Jane	CSC	15	MTH101B	S1020	A
-	-	-	-	MTH101B	S2222	-
-	-	-	-	CSC203A	-	-

Figure 6.7(b): Outer Equijoin of STUDENT and NEWENROLL

Figure 6.7 Outer Equijoin of Student and Newenroll

both relations must have the same domains. For example, the third column in the first table must have the same domain as the third column in the second table, although the column names may be different. The result of each of the set operations is a new table with the same structure as the two original tables. The four tables we have been working with all have different structures, so no pair of them is union compatible. Therefore,

STUDENT. STUID	STUNAME	MAJOR	CREDITS	COURSE#	ENROLLMENT. STUID	GRADE
S1015	Jones,Mary	Math	42	-	-	-
S1005	Lee,Perry	History	3	-	-	-
S1001	Smith,Tom	History	90	ART103A	S1001	A
S1001	Smith,Tom	History	90	HST205A	S1001	C
S1010	Burns,Edward	Art	63	ART103A	S1010	-
S1010	Burns,Edward	Art	63	MTH103C	S1010	-
S1002	Chin,Ann	Math	36	CSC201A	S1002	F
S1002	Chin,Ann	Math	36	ART103A	S1002	D
S1002	Chin,Ann	Math	36	MTH103C	S1002	B
S1013	McCarthy,Owen	Math	0	-	-	-
S1020	Rivera,Jane	CSC	15	CSC201A	S1020	B
S1020	Rivera,Jane	CSC	15	MTH101B	S1020	A

Figure 6.7(c): Left Outer Equijoin of STUDENT and NEWENROLL

STUDENT. STUID	STUNAME	MAJOR	CREDITS	COURSE#	ENROLLMENT. STUID	GRADE
S1001	Smith,Tom	History	90	ART103A	S1001	A
S1001	Smith,Tom	History	90	HST205A	S1001	C
S1010	Burns,Edward	Art	63	ART103A	S1010	-
S1010	Burns,Edward	Art	63	MTH103C	S1010	-
S1002	Chin,Ann	Math	36	CSC201A	S1002	F
S1002	Chin,Ann	Math	36	ART103A	S1002	D
S1002	Chin,Ann	Math	36	MTH103C	S1002	B
S1020	Rivera,Jane	CSC	15	CSC201A	S1020	B
S1020	Rivera,Jane	CSC	15	MTH101B	S1020	A
-	-	-	-	MTH101B	S2222	-
-	-	-	-	CSC203A	-	-

Figure 6.7(d): Right Outer Equijoin of STUDENT and NEWENROLL

Figure 6.7 *(continued)*

we will use the two tables in Figure 6.8(a) for set operations. We assume that the MAINFAC table contains records of faculty members teaching at the main campus, while the BRANCHFAC table contains records of those teaching at the branch campus of the university. Some faculty members teach at both locations.

The **union** of two relations is the set of tuples in either or both of the relations. For example, we can find the union of MAINFAC and BRANCHFAC as follows:

```
MAINFAC UNION BRANCHFAC
```

or symbolically

$$MAINFAC \cup BRANCHFAC$$

The result is shown in Figure 6.8(b).

The **intersection** of two relations is the set of tuples in both of the relations simultaneously. The intersection of MAINFAC and BRANCHFAC

MAINFAC	FACID	FACNAME	DEPT	RANK
	F101	Adams	Art	Professor
	F105	Tanaka	CSC	Instructor
	F221	Smith	CSC	Professor

BRANCHFAC	FACID	FACNAME	DEPT	RANK
	F101	Adams	Art	Professor
	F115	Smith	History	Associate
	F110	Byrne	Math	Assistant
	F221	Smith	CSC	Professor

Figure 6.8(a): Union Compatible Relations MAINFAC and BRANCHFAC

FACID	FACNAME	DEPT	RANK
F101	Adams	Art	Professor
F105	Tanaka	CSC	Instructor
F221	Smith	CSC	Professor
F115	Smith	History	Associate
F110	Byrne	Math	Assistant

Figure 6.8(b): MAINFAC UNION BRANCHFAC

FACID	FACNAME	DEPT	RANK
F101	Adams	Art	Professor
F221	Smith	CSC	Professor

Figure 6.8(c): MAINFAC INTERSECTION BRANCHFAC

FACID	FACNAME	DEPT	RANK
F105	Tanaka	CSC	Instructor

Figure 6.8(d): MAINFAC MINUS BRANCHFAC

Figure 6.8

```
MAINFAC INTERSECTION BRANCHFAC
```

or symbolically

$$MAINFAC \cap BRANCHFAC$$

is shown in Figure 6.8(c).

The **difference** between two relations is the set of tuples that belong to the first relation but not to the second. Therefore,

```
MAINFAC MINUS BRANCHFAC
```

or symbolically

$$MAINFAC - BRANCHFAC$$

is the table shown in Figure 6.8(d).

Division

Division is a binary operation that can be defined on two relations where the entire structure of one (the divisor) is a portion of the structure of the other (the dividend). It tells us which values in the rows of the dividend appear with all the rows of the divisor. For example, if we have a table S with $m+n$ columns and another table T with n columns, and the n columns of T have the same domains as the columns in the corresponding positions in the last n columns of S, then S can be divided by T. The result or quotient is a table with m columns representing the attributes of S that are not in T. The tuples in the rows of the quotient are the columns of the tuples in S that are not columns in T such that there is a tuple in S for all tuple values in T. To illustrate this operation, we show three examples in Figure 6.9. The division operation gives us all the classes for which every student in the STU table has enrolled. Examining Figure 6.9(a), we see that ENROLL can be divided by STU because the last two column names of ENROLL match the entire structure of STU. The quotient will have two columns, C# and FID. The quotient will contain values of C# and FID that appear in ENROLL with all the value combinations of SID and SNAME in the STU table. Since S1001 and S1005 both appear with ART103A and with CSC201A, these two classes will appear in the result. MTH101B will not appear in the result, since it does not appear in ENROLL, with S1005. Figure 6.9(b) and (c) use the same dividend, ENROLL, as it appears in Figure 6.9(a), but STU has different values. In all three cases, we are finding

```
ENROLL DIVIDEDBY STU
```

which can also be written as

$$ENROLL \div STU$$

Notice that this division is equivalent to the following operations:

```
PROJECT ENROLL OVER (C#,FID) GIVING TEMP1
TEMP1 TIMES STU GIVING TEMP2
TEMP2 MINUS ENROLL GIVING TEMP3
PROJECT TEMP3 OVER C#,FID GIVING TEMP4
TEMP1 MINUS TEMP4 GIVING QUOTIENT
```

6.6.2 Relational Calculus

Relational calculus is a nonprocedural formal relational data manipulation language in which the user simply specifies what data should be retrieved, but not how to retrieve it. It is an alternative standard for relational data manipulation languages.

The relational calculus is not related to the familiar differential and integral calculus in mathematics, but takes its name from a branch of symbolic logic called the **predicate calculus**. When applied to databases, it comes in two forms: **tuple-oriented relational calculus** and **domain-oriented relational calculus**. We will not give a formal definition

```
ENROLL:                                    STU:
C#       FID  SID   SNAME                  SID   SNAME
-----------------------------              ---------------
ART103A F101 S1001 Smith,Tom               S1001 Smith,Tom
ART103A F101 S1002 Chin,Ann                S1005 Lee,Perry
ART103A F101 S1013 McCarthy,Owen
ART103A F101 S1005 Lee,Perry               ENROLL DIVIDED BY STU:
CSC201A F105 S1001 Smith,Tom               C#          FID
CSC201A F105 S1005 Lee,Perry               --------------
MTH101B F110 S1001 Smith,Tom               ART103A    F101
MTH101B F110 S1002 Chin,Ann                CSC201A    F105
MTH101B F110 S1013 McCarthy,Owen
```

Figure 6.9(a): Example 1 of ENROLL DIVIDEDBY STU

```
ENROLL:                                    STU:
C#       FID  SID   SNAME                  SID   SNAME
-----------------------------              ---------------
ART103A F101 S1001 Smith,Tom               S1001 Smith,Tom
ART103A F101 S1002 Chin,Ann                S1002 Chin,Ann
ART103A F101 S1013 McCarthy,Owen           S1013 McCarthy,Owen
ART103A F101 S1005 Lee,Perry
CSC201A F105 S1001 Smith,Tom               ENROLL DIVIDED BY STU:
CSC201A F105 S1005 Lee,Perry               C#          FID
MTH101B F110 S1001 Smith,Tom               --------------
MTH101B F110 S1002 Chin,Ann                ART103A    F101
MTH101B F110 S1013 McCarthy,Owen           MTH101B    F110
```

Figure 6.9(b): Example 2 of ENROLL DIVIDEDBY STU

```
ENROLL:                                    STU:
C#       FID  SID   SNAME                  SID   SNAME
-----------------------------              ---------------
ART103A F101 S1001 Smith,Tom               S1001 Smith,Tom
ART103A F101 S1002 Chin,Ann                S1002 Chin,Ann
ART103A F101 S1013 McCarthy,Owen           S1013 McCarthy,Owen
ART103A F101 S1005 Lee,Perry               S1005 Lee,Perry
CSC201A F105 S1001 Smith,Tom
CSC201A F105 S1005 Lee,Perry               ENROLL DIVIDED BY STU:
MTH101B F110 S1001 Smith,Tom               C#          FID
MTH101B F110 S1002 Chin,Ann                --------------
MTH101B F110 S1013 McCarthy,Owen           ART103A     F101
```

Figure 6.9(c): Example 3 of ENROLL DIVIDEDBY STU

Figure 6.9 Examples of Division

of relational calculus, but will provide the flavor of it through examples. Note that this discussion deals with only a subset of relational calculus.

In logic, a **predicate** is a declarative sentence that can be either true or false. For example, the sentences "Mary Jones is a student" and "Mary Jones has 500 credits" are both predicates, since we can decide whether they are true or false. On the other hand, "What a day!" is not a predicate. If a predicate contains a variable, as in "x is a student", there must be an associated replacement set or **range** for x. When some values of the range are substituted for x, the predicate may be true; for other values, it may be false. For example, if the range is the set of all people and we replace x by Mary Jones, the resulting predicate, "Mary Jones is a student", is true. If we replace x by Professor Adams, the predicate is probably false.

If we use P to stand for a predicate, then

$$\{x \mid P(x)\}$$

will mean the set of all x such that P is true for x. We could have used Q, R, or any other letter for the predicate. Similarly, we could have used y, z, w, or any other letter to stand for the replacement set element, so

$$\{t \mid P(t)\}, \{s \mid Q(s)\}, \{x \mid R(x)\}$$

all mean the set of values for which the corresponding predicate is true.

We may connect predicates by the logical connectives AND ($\wedge$), OR ($\vee$), and NOT ($\sim$) to form **compound predicates** such as

```
P(x) AND Q(x)      P(x) OR NOT Q(x)      NOT P(x) OR Q(x)
```

which can be written as

$$P(x) \wedge Q(x) \qquad P(x) \vee \sim Q(x) \qquad \sim P(x) \vee Q(x)$$

A **conjunction** consists of predicates connected by AND, a **disjunction** consists of predicates connected by OR, and a **negation** is a predicate preceded by a NOT. The connectives have the same meanings and precedences as in programming. The expression

$$\{<x,y> \mid P(x) \text{ AND } Q(y)\}$$

means the set of all ordered pairs $< x, y >$ such that P is true for x and Q is true for y.

6.6.3 *Tuple-Oriented Relational Calculus*

In tuple-oriented relational calculus we are interested primarily in finding relation tuples for which a predicate is true. To do so, we need **tuple variables**. A tuple variable is a variable that takes on only the tuples of some relation or relations as its range of values. Please note that the word *range* here does not correspond to the mathematical use of range. It actually corresponds to a mathematical domain. We specify the range of a tuple variable by a statement such as

```
RANGE OF S IS STUDENT
```

Here, *S* is the tuple variable and STUDENT is the range, so that *S* always represents a tuple of STUDENT for this example. We express a query as

$\{S|P(S)\}$

which means "Find the set of all tuples *S* such that *P*(*S*) is true." For example,

```
RANGE OF R IS STUDENT
{R | R.CREDITS > 50}
```

means "Find the STUID, STUNAME, MAJOR, and CREDITS of all students having more than 50 credits." Note that R.CREDITS means the value of the CREDITS attribute for the tuple R. Similarly,

```
RANGE OF T IS STUDENT
{T.STUID | T.MAJOR='History' AND T.CREDITS < 30}
```

means "Find the STUID of all history majors with fewer than 30 credits."

In logic there are two **quantifiers** used with predicates to tell how many instances the predicate applies to. The **existential quantifier EXISTS** means "there exists." It is used in **assertions,** or statements that must be true for at least one instance, such as

```
RANGE OF E IS ENROLLMENT
EXISTS E (E.STUID = T.STUID AND E.GRADE ='F')
```

which means "There exists an ENROLLMENT tuple with the same STUID as the STUID of the current STUDENT tuple, *T*, and grade of *F*." The symbol ∃ is sometimes used for "There exists", as in

```
∃ E(E.STUID = T.STUID ∧ E.GRADE ='F')
```

The **universal quantifier FORALL** means "for all." It is sometimes written ∀. It is used in assertions about every instance, such as

```
RANGE OF S IS STUDENT
FORALL S (S.MAJOR ~= 'Music')
```

or

```
∀ S(S.MAJOR ~= 'Music')
```

meaning "For all STUDENT tuples, the major is not music." This is logically equivalent to

```
NOT EXISTS S (S.MAJOR = 'Music')
```

or

```
~∃ S(S.MAJOR = 'Music')
```

which means "There is no student with a music major."

Tuple variables that are used without quantifiers are called **free variables.** A tuple variable that is quantified by a FORALL or EXISTS is called a **bound variable.** A predicate may have some free and some bound variables. Formulas in predicate calculus are defined by the following rules

1. If P is a predicate symbol and $X_1, X_2, \ldots, X_n$ are either constants or variables, then $P(X_1, X_2, \ldots, X_n)$ is a formula.
2. If X_1 and X_2 are either constants or variables and Θ is one of the comparison operators <, <=, >, >=, =, ~=, then $X_1 \Theta X_2$ is a formula.

The formulas described by these two rules are called **atomic formulas**. Atomic formulas can be combined to produce additional formulas. For example, if F_1 and F_2 are formulas, so are their conjunction, $F_1 \wedge F_2$; their disjunction, $F_1 \vee F_2$; and the negation, $\sim F_1$. Also, if F is a formula with free variable X, then EXISTS X (F) and FORALL X (F) are both formulas.

In creating a formula, it is important that the conditions to be tested be restricted to a finite set of possibilities, so that we do not spend time trying to test a predicate that cannot be tested in a finite amount of time. We can guarantee that a formula is **safe** (i.e., it does not require testing of infinite sets) by ensuring that

1. The universal quantifier FORALL does not appear in the formula. If it does, we replace it by its logical equivalent, using the negation of the existential quantifier and the negation of the predicate. For example, the formula FORALL X (F) would be replaced by NOT EXISTS X (NOT F). That is,

$$\forall X(F) \text{ is logically equivalent to } \sim \exists X(\sim F)$$

2. In a disjunction of formulas, such as F_1 OR F_2, the formulas F_1 and F_2 have the same set of free variables.
3. If F is a maximal subformula that is the conjunction of one or more $F_1, F_2, \ldots, F_n$ (i.e., $F = F_1$ AND F_2 AND ...AND F_j), the free variables in the F_i's must be **limited**, under one of the following rules:
   a. If one of the F_i's has the form $X = c$, where c is a constant, then X is limited
   b. If X is free in one of the F_i's, and the F_i is not negated and is not an arithmetic comparison, then X is limited
   c. If Y limited, and one of the F_i's has the form $X = Y$, then X is limited.
4. If a formula is a conjunction as described above, then a NOT operator can only apply to a term in the conjunction. Specifically, if S is a subformula, then NOT S violates the rule unless it is a part of a larger formula such as

$$F_1 \text{ AND } F_2 \text{ AND} \ldots \text{AND } F_j \text{ AND (NOT } S) \text{ AND } F_{j+1} \text{ AND } \ldots \text{ AND } F_n$$

   where are least one of the F_i's is not a negation.

It can be demonstrated that the relational algebra is logically equivalent to the safe relational calculus, so that any expression in one can be translated into an equivalent expression in the other.

Examples of Tuple-Oriented Relational Calculus

We will assume throughout these examples that the following tuple variables have the specified ranges:

```
RANGE OF SX IS STUDENT
RANGE OF CX IS CLASS
RANGE OF FX IS FACULTY
RANGE OF EX IS ENROLLMENT
```

■ Example 1.

Find the names of all faculty members who are professors in the CSC Department.

```
{FX.FACNAME | FX.DEPT = 'CSC' AND FX.RANK ='Professor'}
```

■ Example 2.

Find the names of all students enrolled in CSC201A.

```
{SX.SNAME | EXISTS EX(EX.STUID = SX.STUID AND EX.COURSE# = 'CSC201A')}
```

■ Example 3.

Find the names of all students who are enrolled in at least one class that meets in room H221.

```
{SX.STUNAME |  EXISTS EX(EX.STUID = SX.STUID AND EXISTS
CX(CX.COURSE# = EX.COURSE# AND CX.ROOM = 'H221'))}
```

■ Example 4.

Find the names of faculty members who are in the CSC Department but do not teach CSC201A.

```
{FX.FACNAME | FX.DEPT = 'CSC' AND NOT EXISTS CX(CX.FACID =
FX.FACID AND CX.COURSE# = 'CSC201A')}
```

■ Example 5.

Find the names of students enrolled in every class offered.

```
{SX.SNAME | FORALL CX(EXISTS EX(EX.STUID = SX.STUID AND EX.COURSE#
= CX.COURSE#))}
```

Domain-Oriented Relational Calculus

In domain-oriented relational calculus, we use variables that take their values from domains instead of tuples of relations. If $P(x_1, x_2, \ldots, x_n)$ stands for a predicate with variables $x_1, x_2, \ldots, x_n$, then

$$\{< x_1, x_2, \ldots, x_n > | P(x_1, x_2, \ldots, x_n)\}$$

will mean the set of all domain variables $x_1, x_2, \ldots, x_n$ for which the predicate $P(x_1, x_2, \ldots, x_n)$ is true. In the domain-oriented relational calculus, we often want to test for a **membership condition**, to determine whether values belong to a relation. The expression $< x, y, z > \in X$ evaluates to true if and only if there is a tuple in relation X with values x, y, z for its three attributes.

In Examples 6 to 10 we will use the domain variables:

- SI for STUID
- SN for STUNAME
- MJ for MAJOR
- CR for CREDITS
- CN for COURSE#
- FI for FACID
- SH for SCHEDULE
- RM for ROOM
- FN for FACNAME
- DP for DEPT
- RK for RANK
- GR for GRADE

Notice that when an attribute such as SI appears in more than one relation we need only one domain variable for both of its appearances, since the same domain is used.

Examples of Domain-Oriented Relational Calculus

■ Example 6.

Find the names of all faculty members who are professors in the CSC Department.

```
{FN | EXISTS FI,DP,RK(<FI,FN,DP,RK> ∈ FACULTY AND RK = 'Professor'
AND DP = 'CSC')}
```

■ Example 7.

Find the names of all students enrolled in CSC201A.

```
{SN | EXISTS SI,MJ,CR(<SI,SN,MJ,CR> ∈ STUDENT AND EXISTS
CN,GR(<SI,CN,GR> ∈ ENROLLMENT AND CN = 'CSC201A'))}
```

■ **Example 8.**

Find the names of all students who are enrolled in at least one class that meets in room H221.

```
{SN | EXISTS SI,MJ,CR(<SI,SN,MJ,CR> ∈ STUDENT AND EXISTS
CN,GR(<SI,CN,GR> ∈ ENROLLMENT AND EXISTS FI,SH,RM(<CN,FI,SH,RM>
∈
CLASS AND RM = 'H221')))}
```

■ **Example 9.**

Find the names of faculty members who are in the CSC Department but do not teach CSC201A.

```
{FN | EXISTS FI,DP,RK(<FI,FN,DP,RK> ∈ FACULTY AND DP = 'CSC' AND
NOT EXISTS CN,SH,RM(<CN,FI,SH,RM> ∈ CLASS AND CN = 'CSC201A'))}
```

■ **Example 10.**

Find the names of students enrolled in every class offered.

```
{SN | EXISTS SI,MJ,CR(<SI,SN,MJ,CR> ∈ STUDENT AND FORALL CN EXISTS
GR(<SI,CN,GR> ∈ ENROLL))}
```

All of the queries included here are safe. However, relational calculus allows expressions that we cannot write using the subset of the language presented here. For example, we cannot write a simple query such as "Find all the faculty members who are associate professors and their departments" using this subset.

6.7 *Views*

In the standard three-level architecture, an external view is the structure of the database as it appears to a particular user. In the relational model, the word "view" has a slightly different meaning. Rather than being the entire external model of a user, a view is a **virtual table**, a table that does not actually exist but that can be constructed by performing operations such as relational algebra select, project, join or other calculations on the values of existing tables. Thus an external model can consist of both actual conceptual-level tables and views derived from tables.

The view mechanism is desirable because it allows us to hide portions of the database from certain users. The user is not aware of the existence of any attributes that are missing from his or her view. It also permits users to access data in a "customized" manner. The view should be designed to create an external model that the user finds familiar and comfortable. For example, a user might need Enrollment records that contain student names as well as the three attributes already in Enrollment. This view would be created by joining the Enrollment and Student tables and then projecting on the four attributes of interest. Another user might need to see Student records without the Credits attribute. For this user, a projection is done so that his or her view does not have the Credits column. Attributes may be renamed, so that the user accustomed to calling the ID of students by the name STUNUMBER may see that column heading, and the order of columns may be changed, so that STUNAME may appear as the first column instead of the second column in a view. Selection operations may also be used to create a view. For example, a department chairperson may see faculty records only for that department. Here, a select operation is performed so that only a horizontal subset of the FACULTY table is seen. View tables are not permanently stored as such. Instead, their definitions are stored in the data dictionary and the system creates the view dynamically as the user requests it. When the user finishes with a view, the view is erased, but the underlying tables from which it was created remain.

Although all of the previous examples demonstrate that a view provides logical independence, views allow more significant logical independence when the conceptual level is reorganized. If a new column is added to a table, existing users can be unaware of its existence if their views are defined to exclude it. If an existing table is rearranged or split up, a view may be defined so that users can continue to see their old models. In the case of splitting up a table, the old table can be recreated by defining a view from the join of the new tables, provided that the split is done in such a way that the original can be reconstructed. We can ensure that this is possible by placing the primary key in both of the new tables. Thus if we originally had a STUDENT table of the form

```
STUDENT(STUID, STUNAME, STUADD, MAJOR, CREDITS)
```

we could reorganize it into two new tables

```
PERSONALSTU(STUID, STUNAME, STUADD)
ACADEMICSTU(STUID, MAJOR, CREDITS)
```

Users and applications could still access the data using the old table structure, which would be recreated by defining a view called STUDENT as the natural join of PERSONALSTU and ACADEMICSTU, with STUID as the common column.

Many views act as "windows" into tables, allowing the user to see portions of actual tables. Others that contain joined, calculated, or summary information from actual tables are not windows, but more like "snapshots," pictures of the data as it existed when the view was invoked during the session. In the "window" case, the view is **dynamic**, meaning that changes made to the actual table that affect view attributes are immediately reflected in the view. When users make permitted changes to the view, those changes are made to the underlying tables. There are restrictions on the types of modifications that can be made through views. For example, a view that does not contain the primary key should not be updatable at all. Also, views constructed from summary information are not updatable. When a view user writes a DML command, he or she uses the view name, and the system automatically converts the command into an equivalent one on the underlying tables. The necessary external/conceptual mapping information is stored in the data dictionary. The operations are performed on the actual tables and the system returns results in the form that the user expects, based on the view used.

6.8 *Some Criteria for a Relational Database Management System*

In a 1985 article, Codd published rules or principles that a database management system must use to be considered "fully relational." The rules, which have been the subject of much debate, are summarized as follows:

Rule Zero:

A relational database management system must manage its stored data using only its relational capabilities.

Rule 1—Information Representation:

All information must be represented, at the logical level, only as values in tables.

Rule 2—Guaranteed Access:

It must be possible to access any data item in the database by giving its table name, column name, and primary key value.

Rule 3—Representation of Null Values:

The system must be able to represent null values in a systematic way, regardless of the data type of the item. Null values must be distinct from zero or any other number, and from empty strings.

Rule 4—Relational Catalog:

The system catalog that contains the logical description of the database must be represented in the same way as ordinary data.

Rule 5—Comprehensive Data Sublanguage:

Regardless of the number of other languages it supports, the database must include one language that allows statements expressed as character strings to support data definition, definition of views, data manipulation, integrity rules, user authorization, and a method of identifying units for recovery.

Rule 6—Updating Views:

Any view that is theoretically updatable can actually be updated by the system.

Rule 7—Insert, Delete and Update Operations:

Any relation that can be handled as a single operand for retrieval can also be handled that way for insertion, deletion, and update operations.

Rule 8—Physical Data Independence:

The application programs are immune to changes made to storage representations or access methods.

Rule 9—Logical Data Independence:

Changes made to the logical level that do not affect the information content at the logical level do not require modification of applications.

Rule 10—Integrity Rules:

Integrity constraints such as entity integrity and referential integrity must be specifiable in the data sublanguage and stored in the catalog. Application program statements should not be used to express these constraints.

Rule 11—Distribution Independence:

The data sublanguage should be such that if the database is distributed, the applications programs and users' commands need not be changed.

Rule 12—Nonsubversion:

If the system allows a language that supports record-at-a-time access, any program using this type of access cannot bypass the integrity constraints expressed in the higher-level language.

In addition to these 12 rules, Codd called for support for domain definition, 18 manipulative features including all the relational algebra operations described in this section, and three integrity features.

6.9 *Mapping an E-R Model to a Relational Model*

An E-R diagram can be converted to a relational model fairly easily. The entity sets represented by rectangles become relations represented by tables. The table name is the same as the entity name, which is the name written inside the rectangle. For strong entity sets, the attributes represented by ovals become attributes of the relation, or column headings of the table. Weak entity sets are also represented by tables, but may require additional attributes. In particular, an entity that is identifier dependent on another entity has no candidate key consisting of just its own attributes. Therefore, the primary key of the corresponding strong entity is used to show which instance of the strong entity a weak entity instance depends on. The weak entity itself should have some attribute or attribute set that, when coupled with the owner's primary key, enables us to tell instances apart. To represent the weak entity with an identifier dependency, we use a table whose attributes include all the attributes of the weak entity, plus the primary key of the owner entity. Weak entities that have their own primary keys are represented by tables whose columns are just the entity's attributes represented by ovals in the E-R diagram. These weak entity sets may have referential dependencies or general existence dependencies.

Relationship sets can be translated directly into tables as well. Although not explicitly represented on the E-R diagram, it is understood that a relationship set has the primary keys of the associated entities as attributes. The table for a relationship set has column headings consisting of the primary keys of the associated entities, plus columns for descriptive attributes, if any.

In some cases, we could choose not to represent relationship sets explicitly. For example, if we have an identifier dependency, the primary key of the strong entity is already in the table for the weak entity, so it is not necessary to use another table to represent the connection. If we have a referential dependency, the same argument applies, since the foreign key value already shows the relationship. Whenever the relationship is one-to-one or one-to-many, it is possible to use foreign keys to show the relationship. If the *A* to *B* relationship is one-to-one, we can put the key of either relation in the other table to show the connection. If *A* to *B* is one-to-many, we can place the key of *A* (the "one" side) in the table for *B* (the "many" side), where it becomes a foreign key. The only case where it is impossible to drop the relationship set is the many-to-many case. Here, the only way the connection can be shown is by a table.

Whenever we have a choice of representing relationships, how do we know whether or not to use a separate table? The answer may depend on the application. Having a separate relationship table gives maximum flexibility, allowing us to change the associations easily. However, it requires doing a join (or two) whenever the relationship is used, which may produce poor performance. The designer must choose between flexibility and efficiency, depending on the criteria for the application.

To convert our university E-R diagram to a relational model, we refer to Figure 4.11. The strong entity sets DEPT, STUDENT, and CLASS, can be represented immediately by the following tables

```
DEPT (DEPTNAME, OFFICE)
STUDENT (STUID, STUNAME, MAJOR, CREDITS)
CLASS (COURSE#, CTITLE, FACID, SCHED, ROOM)
```

Since FACULTY is existence dependent on DEPT, we are concerned about whether the primary key of DEPT needs to be inserted into its table. However, we see that FACULTY has its own primary key, FACID, so the dependency is not an identifier dependency. We also note that DEPT already appears as a foreign key among the attributes of FACULTY. Therefore, the FACULTY table has the scheme

```
FACULTY (FACID, FACNAME, DEPT, RANK)
```

There are five relationship sets represented in the diagram by diamonds. The STUDENT-DEPT relationship set has attributes DEPTNAME and STUID, the primary keys of the associated entity sets. Therefore, to represent the relationship as a table, we would use

```
STUDENT-DEPT (DEPTNAME, STUID)
```

We underline STUID as the primary key, since this attribute gives unique values for each tuple, while DEPTNAME does not. We could choose not to create this relationship table at all, since it represents a one-to-many relationship and STUDENT already contains MAJOR, an attribute that is actually a foreign key. Note that STUDENT is not a weak entity, since a student without a major can be represented in the database, by allowing the MAJOR attribute to be null. If we do decide to create the relationship table, we could drop the MAJOR attribute from the STUDENT table. Then we would need to do a join whenever we needed to find a student's major. Our choice will be to keep MAJOR in STUDENT and not use a separate table for this relationship.

The ENROLL relationship represents a many-to-many relationship, which requires a separate table. In addition, it has a descriptive attribute, the presence of which always indicates that a separate table is desirable. This table must contain the primary keys of the associated STUDENT and CLASS entities, STUID and COURSE#, respectively. The relationship table is

```
ENROLL (STUID, COURSE#, GRADE)
```

Note that in a many-to-many relationship, we need both primary keys as the primary key of the relationship.

FACULTY-CLASS is a one-to-many relationship set connecting the strong entity sets CLASS and FACULTY. This relationship could be represented by the table

```
FACULTY-CLASS (COURSE#, FACID)
```

We choose COURSE# as the key, since FACID does not give unique values for this combination of attributes. However, we notice that CLASS already contains FACID as a foreign key, so the relationship does not have to be represented as a separate table. If it were, we should remove the FACID attribute from the CLASS table, requiring a join whenever we need complete class information. We therefore choose not to use the separate relationship table.

DEPT-FACULTY is a one-to-many relationship that represents the association between a strong entity set and its corresponding weak entity set. This relationship is already represented by the presence of DEPT in the FACULTY table. We have the option of representing the relationship explicitly by the table

```
DEPT-FACULTY (DEPTNAME, FACID)
```

This choice does not show the existence dependency of FACULTY on DEPT as well as the foreign key option, so we choose not to use it, because the foreign key provides a better reflection of the semantics of the application.

CHAIR-MEMBER is a one-to-many recursive relationship on FACULTY. It can be represented by a table that shows pairs of FACID values, in which the first FACID represents a faculty member and the second represents the chairperson for that faculty member. The table therefore has the form

```
CHAIR-MEMBER (MEMBERFACID, CHAIRFACID)
```

The two attributes have the same domain, the set of FACID values, but we have renamed them to distinguish between members and chairpersons. The key is MEMBERFACID since each faculty member has only one chairperson, but a chairperson may be associated with several department members.

Our entire schema, then, is

```
DEPT (DEPTNAME, OFFICE)
STUDENT (STUID, STUNAME, MAJOR, CREDITS)
CLASS (COURSE#, CTITLE, FACID, SCHED, ROOM)
FACULTY (FACID, FACNAME, DEPT, RANK)
ENROLL (STUID, COURSE#, GRADE)
CHAIR-MEMBER (MEMBERFACID, CHAIRFACID)
```

The university E-R diagram did not illustrate either aggregation or generalization, so we still need to find ways to represent these structures by tables. In the case of generalization and specialization, the diagram contains an *ISA* triangle, as shown in Figure 5.15. There are two methods in use for converting an E-R diagram that includes specialization to tables. The first is to ignore the higher-level entity and simply create tables for the lower-level (specialized) entities. Each of these tables has columns for all the attributes of the lower-level entity, plus columns for all the attributes of the higher-level entity. Referring to Figure 5.15, the LAB table would have whatever attributes are peculiar to LAB, such as LAB#, LABTYPE, and so on, in addition to all the attributes for CLASS, such as COURSE#, CTITLE, FACID. Similarly, FILM, LECTURE, and SEMINAR would each be represented by a table having its own attributes with all the class attributes. There would be no separate table for CLASS. The second method is to create a separate CLASS table, having the common course attributes, COURSE#, CTITLE, and FACID, and separate tables for each of the specialized entities, with their own descriptive attributes and only the primary key attributes of the higher-level entity. Thus the LAB table would have columns for COURSE#, LAB#, LABTYPE, and so on.

Aggregation can be represented by the usual transformation of entity rectangles and relationship sets to tables. The fact that items have been grouped need not be expressed in the tables. Referring to Figures 5.17(b) and 5.17(c), we would have the usual tables for SEMINAR, INTERNSHIP, FIELDEXAM, WORK-STUDY, and REQUIRES. A table to represent the grouping would simply repeat the connection data already present in the relationship tables.

6.10 Chapter Summary

A mathematical **relation** is a subset of the Cartesian product of two or more sets. In database terms, a relation is any subset of the Cartesian product of the domains of the attributes. A relation is normally written as a set of n-tuples, in which each element is chosen from the appropriate domain. Relations are physically represented as **tables**, with the rows corresponding to individual records and the columns to attributes. The structure of the table, with domain specifications and other constraints, is part of the **intension** of the database, while the table with all its rows written out represents an instance or **extension** of the database. Properties of database relations are: each cell is single-valued, column names are distinct, column values come from the same domain, column order is immaterial, row order is immaterial, and there are no duplicate rows.

The **degree** of a relation is the number of attributes, while the **cardinality** is the number of tuples. A **unary** relation has one column, a **binary** relation has two, a **ternary** relation has three, and an **n-ary** relation has n columns. A **superkey** is a set of attributes that identifies tuples of the relation uniquely, while a **candidate key** is a minimal superkey. A **primary key** is the candidate key chosen for use in identification of tuples. A relation must always have a primary key. **Entity integrity** is a constraint which states that no attribute of a primary key may be null. **Referential integrity** states that foreign key values must match the primary key values of some tuple in the home relation or be completely null.

Relational data manipulation languages are sometimes classified as **procedural** or **nonprocedural**, **graphical**, **fourth-generation**, or **fifth-generation**. **Relational algebra** is a formal procedural language. Its operators include select, project, product, union, intersection, difference, division, and several joins, semijoins, and outerjoins. **Relational calculus** is a formal nonprocedural language that uses predicates. The most common type of query in tuple-oriented relational calculus has the form $\{x \mid P(x)\}$, which means "Find the set of all tuple variables x such that predicate $P(x)$ is true." A typical query in domain-oriented relational calculus has the form $\{< x_1, x_2, \ldots, x_n > \mid P(x_1, x_2, \ldots, x_n)\}$, which means "Find the set of all domain variables for which the predicate is true." Relational algebra is logically equivalent to a safe subset of relational calculus.

A **view** in the relational model is a **virtual table**. The view protects security and allows the designer to customize a user's model. Views are created dynamically for users.

In converting an E-R model into a relational model, strong entities become tables having a column for each of the entity's attributes. Tables for weak entities with an identifier dependency have columns for the key attributes of the associated strong entity as well as for the attributes of the weak entity. Other weak entities do not require the key of the associated strong entity. Relationship tables have columns for the primary key attributes of the related entities and a column for each descriptive attribute of the relationship. Many-to-many relationships require a separate table, but one-to-one and one-to-many relationships can often be represented by foreign keys instead of by separate relationship tables. When generalization has been used, there may be no table for the higher-level entity, but each lower-level entity table can contain columns for all the attributes of the higher-level entity in addition to columns for their own attributes. Alternatively, there may be a table for the higher-level entity that contains its attributes, and the tables for the lower-level entities contain columns for the key of the higher-level entity plus columns for their own attributes. Aggregation is not represented explicitly by tables.

6.11 Exercises

1. Let S = {red, yellow, green} and T = {plaid, stripe, dot}. Find the Cartesian product of S and T.

2. Let Q = {Tom, Mary, Jim} and R = {walking, running}. Create a relation with Q and R as domains.

3. Consider the relation scheme containing book data for a bookstore:

```
BOOK (TITLE, AUTHOR, ISBN, PUBLISHER, PUBDATE, CITY, QTY_ON_HAND)
```

   (a) Write out the table for an instance of this relation.
   (b) Identify a superkey, a candidate key, and the primary key, writing out any assumptions you need to make to justify your choice.

4. Consider the following database instance, which contains information about employees and the projects to which they are assigned:

```
EMP                 PROJECT                      ASSIGNMENT
EMPID  ENAME        PROJ#  PROJNAME  BUDGET      EMPID  PROJ# HOURS
------------        -----------------------      ------------------
E101   Smith        P10    Hudson    500000      E101   P10   200
E105   Jones        P15    Columbia  350000      E101   P15   300
E110   Adams        P20    Wabash    350000      E105   P10   400
E115   Smith        P23    Arkansas  600000      E110   P20   350
                                                 E110   P15   700
                                                 E115   P10   300
                                                 E115   P20   400
```

   (a) Show ALL the tables that would be produced by each of the following relational algebra commands.

   (i) SELECT EMP WHERE ENAME = 'Smith' GIVING T1
   JOIN T1, ASSIGNMENT GIVING T2
   or

$$(\sigma_{NAME='Smith'}(EMP)) \mid\times\mid ASSIGNMENT$$

   (ii) SELECT PROJECT WHERE BUDGET > 400000 GIVING T1
   JOIN T1, ASSIGNMENT GIVING T2
   PROJECT T2 OVER EMPID GIVING T3
   or

$$\pi_{EMPID}((\sigma_{BUDGET>40000}(PROJECT)) \mid\times\mid ASSIGNMENT)$$

(iii)
```
PROJECT ASSIGNMENT OVER PROJ# GIVING T1
JOIN T1, PROJECT GIVING T2
PROJECT T2 OVER BUDGET GIVING T3
```
or

$$\pi_{BUDGET}((\pi_{PROJ\#}(ASSIGNMENT)) \mid\times\mid PROJECT)$$

(b) Show what tuples would be produced by each of the following tuple relational calculus commands. Assume that the ranges are specified as follows:

```
RANGE OF EX IS EMP
RANGE OF PX IS PROJECT
RANGE OF AX IS ASSIGNMENT
```

(i) {EX.EMPID | EX.EMPNAME = 'Smith'}
(ii) {PX | PX.BUDGET < 40000}
(iii) {EX.ENAME | EXISTS AX(EX.EMPID = AX.EMPID AND AX.PROJ# = 'P10')}
(iv) {EX | EXISTS AX(EX.EMPID = AX.EMPID AND EXISTS PX(AX.PROJ# = PX.PROJ# AND PX.PROJNAME = 'Hudson'))}

5. Consider the following database schema:

```
DOCTOR (LICNO, DOCTORNAME, SPECIALTY)
PATIENT (PATID, PATNAME, ADDRESS, PHONE, DATE_OF_BIRTH)
VISIT (LICNO, PATID, TYPE, DATE, DIAGNOSIS, CHARGE)
```

This database is kept by a medical group which consists of several physicians. Each physician has only one specialty. Patient records are shared among the doctors. For each patient visit, information is stored about the type (regular office, hospital, after hours, house call, etc.), a single diagnosis for that visit, and the charge. The visit is identified by LICNO, PATID, and DATE, because a patient may visit more than one of the doctors on a particular day. We assume, however, that a patient never visits the same doctor more than once in one day.

Write relational algebra commands to do each of the following:
(a) Get a list of all the different specialties the physicians have.
(b) Find the names of all the doctors whose specialty is Pediatrics.
(c) Get complete PATIENT records (not VISIT records) of all patients who are over 65. Assume DATE_OF_BIRTH is stored as in the form yyyymmdd (e.g., 19900115).
(d) Find the LICNO of all doctors who saw patient Mary Adams.
(e) Find the names of all doctors who have made house calls.
(f) Get a list of the names and addresses of all patients who visited Dr. Hubert Jones on January 15, 1990
(g) Find the names and addresses of all patients who have been diagnosed as having peptic ulcers.
(h) Find the names and specialties of all doctors who have ever diagnosed a patient as having hypoglycemia.

(i) Get information on all doctors who have treated patients under 10 years of age.
(j) Find the names and IDs of all patients who have been treated by doctors whose specialty is Cardiology.

6. Design a relational database corresponding to the diagram shown in Figure 6.10.

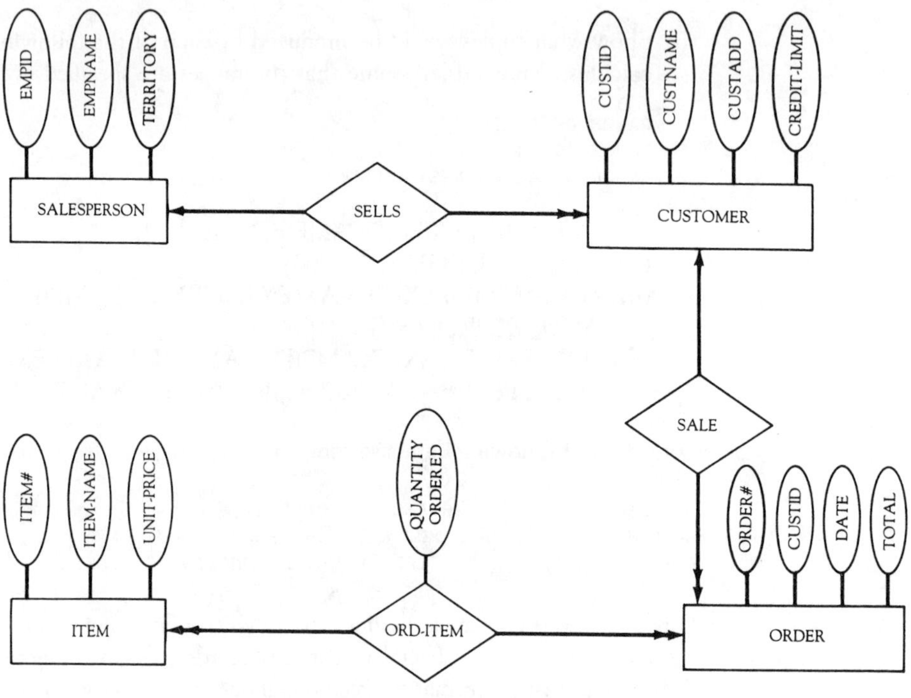

Figure 6.10

6.12 *Bibliography*

Aho, A. V., C. Beeri, and J. D. Ullman. "The Theory of Joins in Relational Databases," ACM Transactions on Database Systems, **4**:3 (September, 1979) pp. 297-314.

Bernstein, P. and N. Goodman. "The Power of Natural Semijoins," SIAM Journal of Computing, **10**:4 (December, 1981) pp. 751-771.

Boyce, R., D. Chamberlin, W. King, and M. Hammer. "Specifying Queries as Relational Expressions," Communications of the ACM, **18**:11 (November, 1975) pp. 621-628.

Chamberlin, D. "Relational Data-Base Management Systems," ACM Computing Surveys **8**:1 (March, 1976) pp. 43-66.

Codd, E. "A Relational Model for Large Shared Data Banks," Communications of the ACM **13**:6 (June, 1970) pp. 377-387.

Codd, E. "Extending the Data Base Relational Model to Capture More Meaning," ACM Transactions on Database Systems **4**:4 (December, 1979) pp. 397-434.

Codd, E. "The 1981 ACM Turing Award Lecture: Relational Database: A Practical Foundation for Productivity," Communications of the ACM **25**:2 (February, 1982) pp. 109-117.

Codd, E. "Is Your DBMS Really Relational?" Computerworld Oct 14, 1985.

Codd, E. "Does Your DBMS Run by the Rules?" Computerworld Oct 21, 1985.

Date, C. *An Introduction to Database Systems*. Reading, MA: Addison-Wesley, 1986.

Dayal, U. and P. Bernstein. "The Updatability of Relational Views," Proceedings of the International Conference on Very Large Data Bases (1978) pp. 368-377.

Elmasri, R. and S. Navathe. *Fundamentals of Database Systems*. Redwood City, CA: Benjamin/Cummings, 1989.

Gotlieb, L. "Computing Joins of Relations," Proceedings of the ACM SIGMOD International Conference on the Management of Data (1975) pp. 55-63.

Keller, A. "Algorithm for Translating View Updates into Database Updates for Views Involving Selections, Projections, and Joins," Proceedings of the Fourth ACM Symposium on Principles of Database Systems (1985) pp. 154-163.

Korth, H. and A. Silberschatz. *Database System Concepts*. New York: McGraw-Hill, 1986.

Maier, D. *The Theory of Relational Databases*. Rockville, MD: Computer Science Press, 1983.

Ozsoyoglu, G, Z. Ozsoyoglu, and V. Matos. "Extending Relational Algebra and Relational Calculus with Set Valued Attributes and Aggregate Functions," Transactions on Database Systems **12**:4 (December, 1987) pp. 566-592.

Reisner, P. "Use of Psychological Experimentation as an Aid to Development of a Query Language," IEEE Transactions on Software Engineering **SE3**:3 (May, 1977) pp. 218-229.

Reisner, P. "Human Factors Studies of Database Query Languages: A Survey and Assessment", ACM Computing Surveys **13**:1 (March, 1981).

Rissanen, J. "Independent Components of Relations," ACM Transactions on Database Systems **2**:4 (December, 1977) pp. 317-325.

Rissanen, J. "Theory of Joins for Relational Databases—a Tutorial Survey," Proceedings of the Symposium on Mathematical Foundations of Computer Science (1979) Berlin: Springer-Verlag pp. 537-551.

Schmidt, J. and J. Swenson. "On the Semantics of the Relational Model," Proceedings of the ACM SIGMOD International Conference on Management of Data (1975) pp. 9-36.

Stonebraker, M. (Ed.). *The INGRES Papers*. Reading, MA: Addison-Wesley, 1986.

Stonebraker, M. and L. Rowe. "The Design of POSTGRES," ACM SIGMOD International Conference on Management of Data (1986) pp. 340-355.

Todd, S. "The Peterlee Relational Test Vehicle – a System Overview," IBM Systems Journal **15**:4 (December, 1976) pp. 285-308.

Ullman, J. *Principles of Database and Knowledge-Base Systems Volume I*. Rockville, MD: Computer Science Press, 1988.

SAMPLE PROJECT: MAPPING THE E-R MODEL FOR CLERICALTEMPS TO A RELATIONAL MODEL

Step 6.1:

Map the E-R model developed at the end of Chapter 5 to a relational model, using the guidelines presented in Section 6.9.

The E-R diagram developed at the end of Chapter 5 showed the following entities and attributes:

WORKER: EMPID, EMPNAME, SSN, EMPADD, EMPPHONE, DOB, SEX, DATEHIRED, LASTDATEWORKED, AVERRATING, WORDPROC, TYPING, FILING, BOOKKPING, STENO, AVAILCODE

CLIENT: CLID, CLNAME, CLADD, CLPHONE, CONTACT, BILLINGYTD, PAYMENTSYTD

JOB: JOB#, JOBTITLE, STARTDATE, EXPECTENDDATE, DAILYRATE, DAILYHOURS, REPORTTONAME, REPORTTOADD, REPORTTOPHONE, JOBSTATUS

BILL: INVOICE#, BILLDATE, OLDBAL, TOTCHARGES, NEWBAL, TOTPAID

PAYROLL: CHECK#, PAYDATE, GROSS, FED, FICA, STATE, LOCAL, NET, GROSSYTD, NETYTD, FICAYTD, STATEYTD, LOCALYTD

Of these, WORKER and CLIENT are strong entities, PAYROLL is a weak entity dependent on WORKER, and JOB and BILL are weak entities dependent on CLIENT.

The relationship sets are

- **ASSIGNMENT**, one-to-many: connects WORKER to JOB. Descriptive attributes are RATERNAME, RATINGDATE, and EMPRATING.
- **CLIENT-JOB**, one-to-many: connects CLIENT to JOB. It has no descriptive attributes.
- **CLIENT-BILL**, one-to-many: connects CLIENT to BILL. It has no descriptive attributes.
- **WORKER-PAYROLL**, one-to-many: connects WORKER to PAYROLL. It has no descriptive attributes.

Converting the strong entities into tables, we have the following schemes:

WORKER (<u>EMPID</u>, EMPNAME, SSN, EMPADD, EMPPHONE, DOB, SEX, DATEHIRED, LASTDATEWORKED, AVERRATING, WORDPROC, TYPING, FILING, BOOKKPING, STENO, AVAILCODE)

CLIENT (<u>CLID</u>, CLNAME, CLADD, CLPHONE, CONTACT, BILLINGYTD, PAYMENTSYTD)

Since each of the weak entity sets is existence dependent but not identifier dependent on the corresponding strong entity sets, there is no need to include the key of the strong entity set in their relations. Therefore, we simply convert each of them into a table:

JOB (<u>JOB#</u>, JOBTITLE, STARTDATE, EXPECTENDDATE, DAILYRATE, DAILYHOURS, REPORTTONAME, REPORTTOADD, REPORTTOPHONE, JOBSTATUS)

BILL (<u>INVOICE#</u>, BILLDATE, OLDBAL, TOTCHARGES, NEWBAL, TOTPAID)

PAYROLL (<u>CHECK#</u>, PAYDATE, GROSS, FED, FICA, STATE, LOCAL, NET, GROSSYTD, NETYTD, FEDYTD, FICAYTD, STATEYTD, LOCALYTD)

Since the ASSIGNMENT relationship has descriptive attributes, we choose to represent it by a table:

ASSIGNMENT (<u>JOB#</u>, EMPID, EMPRATING, RATINGDATE, RATERNAME)

JOB# is the key since each JOB# has only one employee associated with it, but each EMPID is associated with many jobs.

The CLIENT-BILL relationship does not have descriptive attributes, so we could choose to represent it as a table having just the two keys of the related entities, CLID and INVOICE#, as attributes, or to eliminate the table and put the CLID in the BILL table. For the present, we will keep the relationship table:

CLIENT-BILL (<u>INVOICE#</u>, CLID)

We choose INVOICE# as our primary key because there is a unique CLID associated with each invoice, but there may be many invoices for each client. Therefore, INVOICE# has unique values for each tuple in this relation.

The CLIENT-JOB relation has JOB# and CLID, the keys of the two related entities, as its only attributes. We therefore have a choice of representing the relationship using a table with only these two columns, or placing the CLID in the JOB table and dropping the relationship table. For the present we will use the relationship table:

CLIENT-JOB (<u>JOB#</u>, CLID)

JOB# is the key because each job is for only one client, but a client may provide many jobs.

Similarly, the WORKER-PAYROLL relation could be represented by a table having the keys of the related entities as its only attributes. It could be eliminated by placing the EMPID in the PAYROLL table. We choose to keep it as a separate relationship table:

WORKER-PAYROLL (<u>CHECK#</u>, EMPID)

We choose CHECK# as the primary key, since we assume that check numbers are totally unique. For each check issued, there would be only one EMPID associated with that check.

The complete conceptual level relational schema consists of the relations whose schemes are written in boldface.

Student Project: Mapping to a Relational Model

Step 6.1

Examine the E-R diagram you developed at the end of Chapter 5 and map it to a relational model, following the guidelines discussed in Section 6.9 and illustrated in the Sample Project.

CHAPTER

7

Normalization

7 Chapter Objectives

In this chapter you will learn

- why relations should be normalized
- the meaning of functional dependency and its relationship to keys
- how inference rules for functional dependencies can be used
- the definition of first normal form and how to achieve it
- the meaning of full functional dependency
- the definition of second normal form and how to achieve it
- the meaning of transitive dependency
- the definition of third normal form and how to achieve it
- the definition of Boyce–Codd normal form and how to achieve it
- the meaning of multivalued dependencies
- the definition of fourth normal form and how to achieve it
- the definition of fifth normal form
- the meaning of join dependency
- the definition of domain-key normal form
- the difference between analysis and synthesis methods of developing normalized relations
- when to stop the normalization process

7.1 Objectives of Normalization

The basic objective of logical modeling is to develop a "good" description of the data, its relationships, and its constraints. For the relational model, this means that we must identify a suitable set of relations. However, the task of choosing the relations is a difficult one, because there are many options for the designer to consider. This chapter is devoted to explaining some methods of improving logical design. The techniques presented here are based on a large body of research into the logical design process generally called normalization.

The purpose of normalization is to produce a stable set of relations that is a faithful model of the operations of the enterprise. By following the principles of normalization, we can achieve a design that is highly flexible, allowing the model to be extended when needed to account for new attributes, entity sets, and relationships. We can also reduce redundancy in the database and ensure that the design is free of certain update, insertion, and deletion anomalies. An anomaly is an inconsistent, incomplete, or contradictory state of the database. If these anomalies were present, we would be unable to represent some information, we might lose information when certain updates were performed, and we would run the risk of having data become inconsistent over time.

Research into these anomalies was first done by Codd, who identified the causes and defined the first three "normal forms". A relation is in a specific normal form if it satisfies the set of requirements or constraints for that form. Note that the constraints we discuss are schema constraints, permanent properties of the relation, not merely of some instance of the relation. Later research by Boyce and Codd led to a refinement of the third of these forms. Additional research by Fagin and independently by Zaniolo resulted in the definition of three new normal forms. All of the normal forms are nested, in that each satisfies the constraints of the previous one but is a "better" form because each eliminates flaws found in the previous form. Figure 7.1 shows how the seven normal forms are related. The largest circle represents all relations. Among the set of all relations those that are in first normal form are represented by the next-largest circle. Of those in first normal form, there are some that qualify as second normal form as well; these fall into the next circle, and so on. Our design objective should be to put the schema in the highest normal form that is practical and appropriate for the application. "Normalization" means putting a relation into a higher normal form. Although there is still a great deal of research being done on this process, the last normal form, domain-key normal form, is the "final" one in a sense which we will discuss later. Normalization requires that we have a clear grasp of the semantics of the application. Merely examining an instance or extension is not sufficient, because an instance does not provide enough information about all the possible values or combinations of values for relation attributes.

In attempting to pinpoint the causes of update, insertion, and deletion anomalies, researchers have identified three important kinds of dependencies: **functional dependencies, multivalued dependencies** and **join dependencies**. Additional dependencies appear in the research literature.

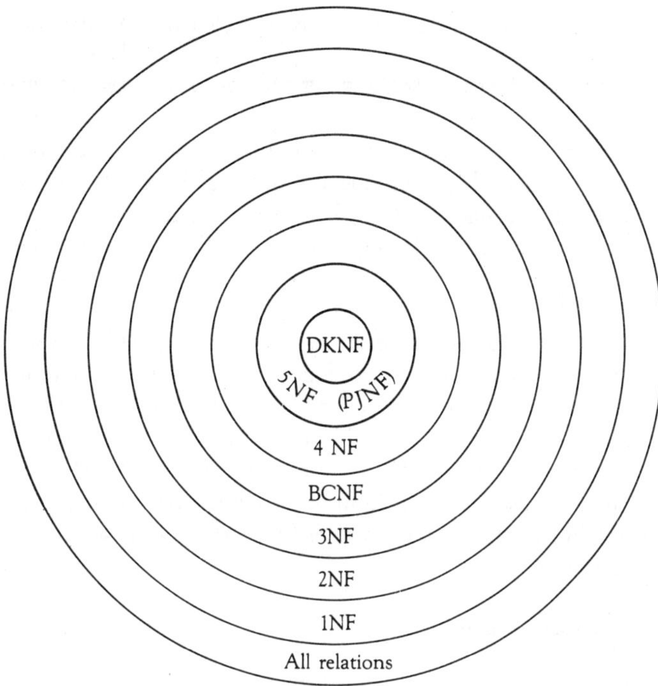

Figure 7.1

7.2 *Functional Dependency*

A functional dependency (FD) is a type of relationship between attributes, as described in the following definition:

Definition of Functional Dependency

DEFINITION: If *A* and *B* are attributes or sets of attributes of relation *R*, we say that *B* is **functionally dependent** on *A* if each value of *A* in *R* has associated with it exactly one value of *B* in *R*.

We write this as $A \rightarrow B$, read as "*A* functionally determines *B*" or "*A* determines *B*". (Note: If we want to be very explicit about which relation we are discussing, particularly in the case where *A* or *B* appears in another relation, we write the qualified names, as in $R.A \rightarrow R.B$.) This does not mean that *A* **causes** *B* or that the value of *B* can be calculated from the value of *A* by a formula, although sometimes that is the case. It simply means that if we know the value of *A* and we examine the table of relation *R*, we will find only one value of *B* in all the rows that have the given value of *A* at any one time. Thus when two rows have the same *A* value, they must also have the same *B* value. However, for a given *B* value, there may be several different *A* values. When a functional dependency exists, the attribute or set of attributes on the left side of the arrow is called a **determinant.**

To illustrate functional dependency, let us consider the following relation:

```
STUDENT(STUID, STUNAME, MAJOR, CREDITS, STATUS, SOCSECNO)
```

This relation stores information about students in a college. Here, we will assume that every student has a unique ID and social security number and that each student has at most one major. We will assume that names are not unique, so that two different students may have the same name. CREDITS means the number of credits completed, and STATUS refers to the year the student is in—freshman, sophomore, junior, or senior.

Figure 7.2 shows an instance of the table. Although we will use this instance to help us detect functional dependencies, we are trying to determine permanent characteristics of the relation, not simply of the instance. Examining the table, we see that if we are given a specific value of STUID, there is only one value of STUNAME associated with that particular STUID. For example, for STUID S1006, the associated STUNAME is Lee,Pamela. We know from our assumptions that this is a characteristic of the relation, not just of this instance, so STUNAME is functionally dependent on STUID, and we can write

```
STUID → STUNAME
```

However, for a given value of STUNAME there may be more than one STUID. We note that for the STUNAME Jones,Mary there are two STUID values, S1003 and S1060. Therefore we cannot turn the functional dependency around and write STUNAME → STUID. For each of the other attributes, there is only one value associated with a particular value of STUID, so all the attributes are functionally dependent on STUID. We write

```
STUID → STUNAME, MAJOR, CREDITS, STATUS, SOCSECNO
```

to indicate that each of the attributes on the right is functionally dependent on STUID. Similarly, we have

```
SOCSECNO → STUID, STUNAME, MAJOR, CREDITS, STATUS
```

Also note that STATUS is functionally dependent on CREDITS. For example, if the value of CREDITS is known to be 15, the STATUS is automatically freshman. We write

```
CREDITS → STATUS
```

However, we cannot write STATUS → CREDITS, since two freshmen may have a different number of credits, as we see in the records of S1006 and S1060. For this case of functional dependency, the determinant CREDITS does **not** functionally determine **all** the other attributes of the relation. Note also that the value of CREDITS is not necessarily unique. Several students could have the same number of credits, so uniqueness is not a necessary characteristic of determinants. The instance in Figure 7.2 did not really

STUID	STUNAME	MAJOR	CREDITS	STATUS	SOCSECNO
S1001	Smith,Tom	History	90	Sen	100429500
S1003	Jones,Mary	Math	95	Sen	010124567
S1006	Lee,Pamela	CSC	15	Fresh	088520876
S1010	Burns,Edward	Art	63	Jun	099320985
S1060	Jones,Mary	CSC	25	Fresh	064624738

Figure 7.2 STUDENT Table (Each student has at most one major)

demonstrate the lack of uniqueness of CREDITS, which shows that we must be careful in making judgments from instances only. We need to concentrate on the meanings of the attributes and their constraints in identifying functional dependencies.

7.3 *Superkeys, Candidate Keys, and Primary Keys*

Recall from Chapter 5 that a **superkey** is an attribute or a set of attributes that identifies an entity uniquely. In a table, a superkey is any column or set of columns whose values can be used to distinguish one row from another. Since a superkey identifies each entity uniquely, it functionally determines all the attributes of a relation. For the STUDENT table in Figure 7.2, STUID is a superkey. So is the combination of {STUID,STUNAME}. In fact, {STUID,any other attribute} is a superkey for this relation. The same is true for {SOCSECNO,any other attribute}.

A **candidate key** is a superkey such that no proper subset of its attributes is itself a superkey. Therefore, a candidate key must be a **minimal** identifier. In our example, the superkey {STUID,STUNAME} is not a candidate key because it contains a proper subset, STUID, that is a superkey. However, STUID by itself is a candidate key. Similarly, SOCSECNO is a candidate key. If no two students were permitted to have the same combination of name and major values, the combination {STUNAME,MAJOR} would also be a candidate key. A relation may have several candidate keys. We will use the term "composite key" to refer to a key that consists of more than one attribute. We will also drop the set brackets in showing sets of attributes.

A **primary key** is a candidate key that is used to identify tuples in a relation. In our example, STUID might be the primary key and SOCSECNO an alternate key. These two attributes functionally determine each other, and all of the attributes are functionally dependent on each of them. Although not explicitly stated in the definition, an important characteristic of a primary key is that none of its attributes may have null values. If we permitted null values in keys, we would be unable to tell records apart, since two records with null values in the same key field might be indistinguishable. It is also desirable to enforce the "no nulls" rule for candidate keys.

7.4 *Inference Rules*

Rules of inference for functional dependencies, called **inference axioms** or **Armstrong's axioms,** after their developer, can be used to find all the FDs logically implied by a set of FDs. These rules are **sound,** meaning that they are an immediate consequence of the definition of functional dependency and that any functional dependency that can be derived from a given set of FDs using them is true. They are also **complete,** meaning they can be used to derive every valid inference about dependencies, so that if a particular FD cannot be derived from a given set of FDs, the given set of FDs does not imply that particular FD.

Let A, B, C, and D be subsets of attributes of a relation R. The following axioms hold: (Note: AC means A and C.)

F1. Reflexivity

If B is a subset of A, then $A \rightarrow B$. This also implies that $A \rightarrow A$ always holds. Functional dependencies of this type are called **trivial functional dependencies.**

F2. Augmentation

If $A \rightarrow B$, then $AC \rightarrow BC$

F3. Transitivity

If $A \rightarrow B$ and $B \rightarrow C$, then $A \rightarrow C$.

The following rules can be derived from the previous three:

F4. Additivity or Union

If $A \rightarrow B$ and $A \rightarrow C$, then $A \rightarrow BC$.

F5. Projectivity or Decomposition

If $A \rightarrow BC$ then $A \rightarrow B$ and $A \rightarrow C$.

F6. Pseudotransitivity

If $A \rightarrow B$ and $CB \rightarrow D$, then $AC \rightarrow D$.

These rules can be used to develop a formal theory of functional dependencies, but we will concentrate instead on their practical applications.

If F is a set of functional dependencies for a relation R, the set of all functional dependencies that can be derived from F, $F+$, is called the **closure** of F. Armstrong's axioms are sufficient to compute all of $F+$; that is, if we were to apply these rules repeatedly, we would find all the functional dependencies in $F+$. However, the task would obviously be very complex and take a lot of time.

Given a set of functional dependencies F of a relation R, we are often interested in finding all the attributes in R that are functionally dependent on a certain attribute or set of attributes, A, in R. We call this set of attributes the closure of A or $A+$. Clearly, if $A+$ is all of R, then A is a superkey for R. We could find $A+$ by computing all of $F+$ and then choosing only those functional dependencies where A is the determinant, but there is a shortcut. The following algorithm can be used to find $A+$, given a set F of functional dependencies:

```
result := A;
while (result changes) do
     for each functional dependency B → C in F
     if B is contained in result then result := result ∪ C;
end;
A+ := result;
```

For example, let R be a relation with attributes W, X, Y, Z and functional dependencies

$$W \rightarrow Z$$

$$YZ \rightarrow X$$

$$WZ \rightarrow Y$$

Let us compute $WZ+$. We assign WZ to the result and enter the **while** for the first time. We look for an FD whose determinant is contained in **result**, which has only WZ at the moment. The FD $WZ \rightarrow Y$ satisfies this requirement, so we assign $WZ \cup Y$ to **result**. Since we had a change in **result**, we enter the **while** again. Now we look for an FD where W, Z, Y, or any combination of these three is a determinant. We can use $YZ \rightarrow X$, and now we assign $WZY \cup X$ to **result.** Since we have found that every attribute of R is in $WZ+$, WZ is a superkey.

To find $W+$, we assign W to **result** and enter the **while** for the first time. Using the FD $W \rightarrow Z$, we assign $W \cup Z$ to **result**. Since we had a change to **result**, we enter the **while** again. This time we use $WZ \rightarrow Y$ and we assign $WZ \cup Y$ to **result**. Now we look for an FD where any combination of WZY appears as the determinant. This time we can use $YZ \rightarrow X$, and we assign $WZY \cup X$ to **result**. Since we have found that every attribute of R is in $W+$, W is a superkey for this relation. Because it has no proper subset that is also a superkey, W is a candidate key as well. Note that we now know that WZ is not a candidate key.

It is easy to verify that YZ is not a superkey. We start with **result** := YZ. Using $YZ \rightarrow X$, **result** becomes YZX. Now we look for an FD where some combination of YZX is the determinant. Since there is none, we cannot add any new attributes to **result**. This means that $YZ+$ is only YZX, so W is not functionally dependent on YZ, which means that YZ is not a superkey.

Given a set of functional dependencies, we would like to be able to determine whether any of them is **redundant**, meaning that it can be derived from the others. To do so, we can use the following algorithm:

```
1.  Choose a candidate FD, say X → Y, and remove it from the set of FDs.
2.  result := X;
    while (result changes and Y is not contained in result) do
     for each FD, A → B, remaining in the reduced set of FDs,
```

```
        if A is a subset of result, then result := result ∪ B
    end
3.  If Y is a subset of result, then the FD X → Y is redundant
```

We could then remove the FD $X \rightarrow Y$ from the set, since it can be derived from the other FDs. By testing every FD in the set and removing any that can be derived from the others, we can find a nonredundant set of FDs equivalent to the original set.

For example, suppose that we have the following set of FDs:

(1) $W \rightarrow Z$

(2) $W \rightarrow Y$

(3) $YZ \rightarrow X$

(4) $WZ \rightarrow Y$

We begin by testing (1), $W \rightarrow Z$. We assign W to **result**. Now we search for an FD [other than (1)] in which W is the determinant. We find one in (2), $W \rightarrow Y$. Now we assign $W \cup Y$ to **result**. Searching for an FD having a determinant that is contained in WY, we find none. Therefore, we are unable to show that Z is contained in **result**, and we conclude that (1) is not redundant.

Next we test (2), $W \rightarrow Y$. We assign W to **result**. Searching for an FD other than (2) whose determinant is W, we find one in (1), so we can assign WZ to **result**. Now we seek an FD whose determinant is contained in WZ. We find (4), $WZ \rightarrow Y$, and now we can assign WZY to **result**. Since Y is now contained in **result**, we can exit the **while** and conclude that (2) is redundant. We now eliminate (2) from the set of FDs.

Testing (3), we assign YZ to **result**. We look for an FD other than (3) or (2) whose determinant is contained in YZ. Finding none, we conclude that (3) is not redundant.

Testing (4), we assign WZ to **result**. In (1), we see that the determinant, W, is contained in **result**, so we could add the right side of (1), Z, to **result**, but it is already there. There is no other FD whose determinant is contained in WZ, except for (2), which we have eliminated. Therefore, we conclude that (4) is not redundant in the reduced set of FDs since we are unable to get Y in **result**.

Sometimes we would like to be able to substitute one set of FDs for another. If F and G are two sets of FDs, then F is a **cover** or G if every FD in G is also in $F+$, which means that every FD in G can be derived from the FDs in F. In the special case where F is a cover for G and G is also a cover for F (i.e., $F+ = G+$), then F and G are said to be **equivalent**. A cover, F, for G, is said to be **nonredundant** if F is a cover for G but no proper subset of F is a cover for G.

G may have several nonredundant covers, so we would like to be able to find one that has the fewest number of FDs in it and is in a standard, or **canonical**, form in which each FD has a single attribute on the right side.

A set of FDs, F, is said to be **minimal** if

(1) F has no redundant FDs
(2) The right side of every FD in F has a single attribute
(3) No attribute on the left side of any FD in F is redundant.

This means that if $X \rightarrow Y$ is an FD in F, there is no proper subset S of X such that $S \rightarrow Y$ can be used in place of $X \rightarrow Y$ and the resulting set is equivalent to F. If F is minimal and equivalent to G, then F is a **minimal cover** for G. Intuitively, F is a minimal cover if the number of FDs in it is less than or equal to the number of FDs in any canonical set equivalent to it. A set of FDs may have several minimal covers.

7.5 *First Normal Form*

We will use a counterexample to describe first normal form. If we assume that a student is permitted to have more than one major, and we try to store multiple majors in the same field of the student record, our STUDENT table might appear as in Figure 7.3(a). This example violates the definition of first normal form, which is:

Definition of First Normal Form (1NF)

DEFINITION: A relation is in **first normal form** if and only if every attribute is single-valued for each tuple.

This means that each attribute in each row, or each "cell" of the table, contains only one value. No repeating fields or groups are allowed. An alternative way of describing first normal form is to say that the domains of the attributes of a relation are **atomic**, that is, they consist of single units that cannot be broken down further. In our table in Figure 7.3(a), we see this rule violated in the records of students S1006 and S1010, who now have two values listed for MAJOR. This is the first such example we have seen, because all the relations we considered until now were in first normal form. In fact, much of relational theory is based on relations in first normal form, although there is current research on non-first-normal-form relations. It is important to have first normal form so that the relational operators, as we have defined them, will work correctly. For example, if we perform the relational algebra operation SELECT STUDENT WHERE MAJOR ='Math' on the table in Figure 7.3(a), should the record of student S1006 be included? If we were to do a natural join with some other table using MAJOR as the joining column, would this record be paired with only those having both CSC and Math as MAJOR, or with those having either CSC or Math? What would happen on the join if another record had a double major listed as Math CSC? To avoid these ambiguities, we will insist that every relation be written in first normal form. If a relation is not already in 1NF, we can rewrite it, "flattening" it so that each of the multiple values appears in a different row. Therefore, we would rewrite the STUDENT table as in Figure 7.3(b). We also note that the key is no longer STUID, since any student with more than one major appears at least twice. Now we need STUID,MAJOR (or SOCSECNO,MAJOR) to identify a record uniquely.

STUID	STUNAME	MAJOR	CREDITS	STATUS	SOCSECNO
S1001	Smith,Tom	History	90	Sen	100429500
S1003	Jones,Mary	Math	95	Sen	010124567
S1006	Lee,Pamela	CSC Math	15	Fresh	088520876
S1010	Burns,Edward	Art English	63	Jun	099320985
S1060	Jones,Mary	CSC	25	Fresh	064624738

Figure 7.3(a) STUDENT Table (Students may have more than one major)

STUID	STUNAME	MAJOR	CREDITS	STATUS	SOCSECNO
S1001	Smith,Tom	History	90	Sen	100429500
S1003	Jones,Mary	Math	95	Sen	010124567
S1006	Lee,Pamela	CSC	15	Fresh	088520876
S1006	Lee,Pamela	Math	15	Fresh	088520876
S1010	Burns,Edward	Art	63	Jun	099320985
S1010	Burns,Edward	English	63	Jun	099320985
S1060	Jones,Mary	CSC	25	Fresh	064624738

Figure 7.3(b) STUDENT Table Rewritten in 1NF

Figure 7.3

7.6 *Full Functional Dependency*

Consider the relation

CLASS(<u>COURSE#, STUID</u>, STUNAME, FACID, SCHED, ROOM, GRADE)

In this example we will assume that COURSE# includes the department and section, and that there is only one faculty member for each class (i.e., no team teaching). The SCHED is a string that gives meeting days and time, and ROOM gives the building and room where the class always meets. An instance of this relation appears in Figure 7.4(a).

COURSE#	STUID	STUNAME	FACID	SCHED	ROOM	GRADE
ART103A	S1001	Smith,Tom	F101	MWF9	H221	A
ART103A	S1010	Burns,Edward	F101	MWF9	H221	
ART103A	S1006	Lee,Pamela	F101	MWF9	H221	B
CSC201A	S1003	Jones,Mary	F105	TUTHF10	M110	A
CSC201A	S1006	Lee,Pamela	F105	TUTHF10	M110	C
HST205A	S1001	Smith,Tom	F202	MWF11	H221	

Figure 7.4(a) CLASS Table

COURSE#	STUID	GRADE
ART103A	S1001	A
ART103A	S1010	
ART103A	S1006	B
CSC201A	S1003	A
CSC201A	S1006	C
HST205A	S1001	

CLASS2 Table

STUID	STUNAME
S1001	Smith,Tom
S1010	Burns,Edward
S1006	Lee,Pamela
S1003	Jones,Mary

STU Table

COURSE#	FACID	SCHED	ROOM
ART103A	F101	MWF9	H221
CSC201A	F105	TUTHF10	M110
HST205A	F202	MWF11	H221

COURSE Table

Figure 7.4(b) CLASS2, STU, and COURSE Tables

Figure 7.4

We have the following functional dependency

COURSE#, STUID → STUNAME, FACID, SCHED, ROOM, GRADE

Since there is no other candidate key, COURSE#,STUID is the (composite) key for the relation. Ignoring trivial functional dependencies, we also have the functional dependencies

COURSE# → FACID, SCHED, ROOM
STUID → STUNAME

In both of these cases, we find attributes that are functionally dependent on the combination COURSE#,STUID, but also functionally dependent on a subset of that combination. We say that such attributes are not **fully** functionally dependent on the combination.

Definition of Full Functional Dependence

DEFINITION: In a relation *R*, attribute *B* of *R* is **fully functionally dependent** on an attribute or set of attributes *A* of *R* if *B* is functionally dependent on *A* but not functionally dependent on any proper subset of *A*.

In our example, although STUNAME is functionally dependent on COURSE#,STUID, it is also functionally dependent on a proper subset of that combination, STUID. Similarly, FACID, SCHED, and ROOM are functionally dependent on the proper subset COURSE#. We note that GRADE is fully functionally dependent on the combination COURSE#,STUID.

7.7 *Second Normal Form*

Definition of Second Normal Form (2NF)

DEFINITION: A relation is in **second normal form** (2NF) if and only if it is in first normal form and all the nonkey attributes are fully functionally dependent on the key.

Clearly, if a relation is 1NF and the key consists of a single attribute, the relation is automatically 2NF. The only time we have to be concerned about 2NF is when the key is composite. From the definition, we see that the CLASS relation is not in second normal form. For example, STUNAME is not fully functionally dependent on the key COURSE#,STUID. Although there are other nonfull functional dependencies here, one is sufficient to show that the relation is not 2NF.

A relation that is not 2NF exhibits the update, insertion, and deletion anomalies that we referred to in Section 7.1. Suppose that we wish to change the schedule of ART103A to MWF12. It is possible we might update the first two records of the CLASS table but not the third, resulting in an inconsistent state in the database. It would then be impossible to tell the true schedule for that class. This is an update anomaly. An insertion anomaly occurs when we try to add information about a course for which no student has yet registered. Because the key is COURSE#,STUID, we are not permitted to insert a null value for STUID, so we are unable to record the course information, even though we may have the COURSE#, FACID, SCHED, and ROOM values available. Because we are not able to represent this information, we have an insertion anomaly. A similar problem occurs if we try to insert information about a student who has not yet registered for any course. A deletion anomaly occurs when we delete the record of the only student taking a particular course. For example, if student S1001 drops HST205A, we lose all information about that course. It is desirable to keep the course information, but we cannot do so without a corresponding STUID. Similarly, if a student drops the only course that he or she is taking, we lose all information about that student.

A 1NF relation that is not 2NF can be transformed into an equivalent set of 2NF relations. We perform **projections** on the original relation in such a way that it is possible to get back the original by taking the **join** of the projections. Projections of this type are called **lossless projections** and are discussed in more detail in Section 7.14. Essentially, to make a relation 2NF, you identify each nonfull functional dependency and form projections by removing the attributes that depend on each of the determinants so identified. These determinants are placed in separate relations along with their dependent attributes. The original relation still contains the composite key and any attributes that are fully functionally dependent on it. Even if there are no attributes fully functionally dependent on the key of the original relation, it is important to keep the relation (with only the key attributes) in order to be able to reconstruct the original relation by a join. This "connecting relation" shows how the projections are related.

Applying this method to our example

```
CLASS (COURSE#, STUID, STUNAME, FACID, SCHED, ROOM, GRADE)
```

we first identify all the functional dependencies that we are concerned about. They are

```
COURSE# → FACID, SCHED, ROOM
STUID   → STUNAME
COURSE#,STUID → GRADE ( and, of course, FACID, SCHED,ROOM,STUNAME)
```

Using projection, we break up the CLASS relation into the following set of relations:

```
CLASS2 (COURSE#, STUID, GRADE)
COURSE (COURSE#, FACID, SCHED, ROOM)
STU (STUID, STUNAME)
```

The resulting relations are shown in Figure 7.4(b). Note that we could reconstruct the original relation by taking the natural join of these three relations. Even if there were no GRADE attribute, we would need the relation CLASS2(COURSE#,STUID) in order to show which students are enrolled in which courses. Without it, we could not join COURSE and STU. Using these new relations, we have eliminated the update, insertion, and deletion anomalies discussed earlier. We can change the course schedule for ART103A by updating the SCHED column in a single record in COURSE. We can add new course information to COURSE without having any student registered in the course, and we can insert new student information by adding a record to STU, without having to insert course information for that student. Similarly, we can drop a registration record from CLASS2 and still retain the information about the course in COURSE and about the student in STU.

7.8 *Transitive Dependency*

Although second-normal-form relations are better than those in first normal form, they may still have update, insertion, and deletion anomalies. Consider the following relation:

```
STUDENT (STUID, STUNAME, MAJOR, CREDITS, STATUS)
```

Figure 7.5(a) shows an instance of this relation. Here, the only candidate key is STUID, so we will use that as the primary key. Every other attribute of the relation is functionally dependent on the key, so we have the following functional dependency, among others:

STUID → CREDITS

However, since the number of credits determines STATUS, as discussed in Section 7.2, we also have

CREDITS → STATUS

Thus STUID functionally determines STATUS in two ways–directly, and transitively, through STATUS:

(STUID → CREDITS) AND (CREDITS → STATUS) ⟹ (STUID → STATUS)

Recall that transitivity is the third of Armstrong's axioms. Thus a transitive dependency is one that "carries over" another attribute. Put simply, a transitive dependency occurs when one nonkey attribute determines another nonkey attribute. For third normal form, we concentrate on relations with only one candidate key, and we eliminate transitive dependencies.

7.9 *Third Normal Form*

Transitive dependencies cause insertion, deletion, and update anomalies. For example, in the STUDENT table in Figure 7.5, we cannot insert the information that any student with 30 credits has Soph status until we have such a student, because that would require inserting a record without a STUID, which is not permitted. If we delete the record of the only student with a certain number of credits, we lose the information about the status associated with those credits. If we have several records with the same CREDITS value and we change the status associated with that value (e.g., making 24 credits now have status of Soph), we may accidentally fail to update all of the records, leaving the database in an inconsistent state. Because of these problems, it is desirable to remove

STUID	STUNAME	MAJOR	CREDITS	STATUS
S1001	Smith,Tom	History	90	Sen
S1003	Jones,Mary	Math	95	Sen
S1006	Lee,Pamela	CSC	15	Fresh
S1010	Burns,Edward	Art	63	Jun
S1060	Jones,Mary	CSC	25	Fresh

Figure 7.5(a) STUDENT Table

STUID	STUNAME	MAJOR	CREDITS
S1001	Smith,Tom	History	90
S1003	Jones,Mary	Math	95
S1006	Lee,Pamela	CSC	15
S1010	Burns,Edward	Art	63
S1060	Jones,Mary	CSC	25

STU2 Table

CREDITS	STATUS
15	Fresh
25	Fresh
63	Jun
90	Sen
95	Sen

STATS Table

Figure 7.5(b) STU2 and STATS Tables

Figure 7.5

transitive dependencies and create a set of relations that satisfy the following definition (applied to relations with only one candidate key):

Definition of Third Normal Form (3NF)

DEFINITION: A relation is in **third normal form** (3NF) if it is in second normal form and no nonkey attribute is transitively dependent on the key.

Paraphrasing Kent (see the Bibliography), you can remember the characteristics of third normal form by saying that each nonkey attribute must depend on the key, the whole key, and nothing but the key.

In checking a second-normal-form relation for third normal form, we look to see if any nonkey attribute is functionally dependent on another nonkey attribute. If such a functional dependency exists, we remove the functionally dependent attribute from the relation, placing it in a new relation with its determinant. The determinant can remain in the original relation. For our STU example, since the undesirable dependency is CREDITS → STATUS, we form the set of relations

```
STU2 (STUID, STUNAME, MAJOR, CREDITS)
STATS (CREDITS, STATUS)
```

This decomposition is shown in Figure 7.5(b). In fact, we may decide not to store STATUS in the database at all, and calculate the STATUS for those views that need it. In that case, we simply drop the STATS relation.

This definition of third normal form is the original one developed by Codd. It is sufficient for relations that have a single candidate key, but was found to be deficient in cases where there are multiple candidate keys and where candidate keys are composite and overlapping. Therefore, an improved definition of third normal form, named for its developers, Boyce and Codd, was formulated to take care of all cases.

7.10 *Boyce–Codd Normal Form*

Definition of Boyce–Codd Normal Form (BCNF)

DEFINITION: A relation is in **Boyce–Codd normal form** (BCNF) if and only if every determinant is a candidate key.

For a relation with only one candidate key, third normal form and Boyce–Codd normal form are equivalent. In fact, some authors refer to this definition as the standard one for third normal form. Note that unlike previous forms that started with relations already in the lower normal form, this definition does not state that the relation must first be 2NF and then satisfy an additional condition. Therefore, to check for BCNF, we simply identify all the determinants and make sure that they are candidate keys. However, all relations that are BCNF are also 3NF.

Returning to our earlier examples to check directly for BCNF, we see that for our STUDENT relation of Section 7.8, shown in Figure 7.5(a), the determinants are STUID and CREDITS. Since CREDITS is not a candidate key, this relation is not BCNF. Performing the projections as we did in Section 7.9, the resulting relations are BCNF. For the relation CLASS in Section 7.7, shown in Figure 7.4(a), we found the determinant COURSE#, which is not (by itself) a candidate key, and STUID, also not a candidate key. Therefore, the CLASS relation is not BCNF. However, the relations resulting from the projections are BCNF.

Let us consider an example in which we have overlapping candidate keys:

```
FACULTY (FACNAME, DEPT, OFFICE, RANK, DATEHIRED)
```

For this example, we will assume that although faculty names are not unique, no two faculty members within a single department have the same name. We also assume that each faculty member has only one office, identified in OFFICE. A department may have several faculty offices, and faculty members from the same department may share offices. From these assumptions we see

```
OFFICE → DEPT
FACNAME,DEPT → OFFICE, RANK, DATEHIRED
FACNAME,OFFICE → DEPT, RANK, DATEHIRED
```

Our overlapping candidate keys are FACNAME,DEPT and FACNAME,OFFICE. If we choose FACNAME,DEPT as our primary key, we are left with a determinant, OFFICE, that is not a candidate key. This violates BCNF. (Note that the relation is 3NF. It is 1NF because each cell has a single value. It is 2NF because even though the key has two attributes, both are needed to determine the nonkey attributes, OFFICE, RANK, and DATEHIRED. It is 3NF because there is no transitive dependency. Even though OFFICE determines DEPT, the 3NF definition is not violated, since DEPT is part of the key.) To reach BCNF, we can decompose the FACULTY relation by projection into

```
FAC1 (DEPT, OFFICE)
FAC2 (FACNAME, OFFICE, RANK, DATEHIRED)
```

The key of the first relation is OFFICE, since a department may have several offices, but each office belongs to only one department. It is clearly BCNF, since the only determinant is the key. The key of the second is FACNAME,OFFICE. It is also BCNF, since its only determinant is the key. Note, however, that our final scheme does not show the functional dependency FACNAME,DEPT → OFFICE, RANK, DATEHIRED. (Note: If we had chosen FACNAME,OFFICE as the primary key of the original FACULTY relation, we would have OFFICE → DEPT. Since OFFICE is not a candidate key, the relation would not be BCNF. In fact, it would not be 2NF, since DEPT would not be fully functionally dependent on the key, FACNAME,OFFICE.)

A relation may have overlapping candidate keys and still be BCNF. For example, let us consider the relation

```
STU (STUNAME, STUADD, MAJOR, GPA)
```

Here, we will assume that a student can have only one major and that both of the combinations STUNAME,STUADD and STUNAME,MAJOR are unique, so we have two overlapping candidate keys. If we choose STUNAME,STUADD as the primary key, our only other determinant, STUNAME,MAJOR, is a candidate key. Therefore, the relation STU is already BCNF, and there is no need to decompose it.

Any relation that is not BCNF can be decomposed into BCNF relations by the method illustrated. However, it may not always be desirable to transform the relation into BCNF. In particular, if there is functional dependency that is not preserved when we perform the decomposition (i.e., the determinant and the attributes it determines end up in different relations), it is difficult to enforce the functional dependency in the database and an important constraint is lost. In that case, it is preferable to settle for 3NF, which always allows us to preserve dependencies. Our FACULTY relation provided an example in which we lost a functional dependency by normalizing to BCNF. In the resulting relations, the attributes FACNAME and DEPT appeared in different relations, and we had no way to express the fact that they determined all other attributes.

7.11 *Comprehensive Example of Functional Dependencies*

To summarize the various normal forms defined by functional dependencies, let us consider the following relation that stores information about projects in a large business:

WORK → (PROJNAME, PROJMGR, EMPID, HOURS, EMPNAME, BUDGET, STARTDATE, SALARY, EMPMGR, EMPDEPT, RATING)

PROJNAME	PROJMGR	EMPID	HOURS	EMPNAME	BUDGET	STARTDATE	SALARY	EMPMGR	EMPDEPT	RATING
Jupiter	Smith	E101	25	Jones	100000	890115	40000	Levine	10	9
Jupiter	Smith	E105	10	Adams	100000	890115	55000	Jones	12	
Jupiter	Smith	E110	10	Rivera	100000	890115	43000	Levine	10	8
Maxima	Lee	E101	15	Jones	200000	900301	40000	Levine	10	
Maxima	Lee	E105	30	Adams	200000	900301	55000	Jones	12	
Maxima	Lee	E120	15	Tanaka	200000	900301	45000	Jones	15	

Figure 7.6 WORK Table

Figure 7.6 shows an instance of this relation. Assume that:

1. Each project has a unique name, but names of employees and managers are not unique.
2. Each project has one manager, whose name is stored in PROJMGR.

3. Many employees may be assigned to work on each project, and an employee may be assigned to more than one project. HOURS tells the number of hours per week that a particular employee is assigned to work on a particular project.
4. BUDGET stores the amount budgeted for a project, and STARTDATE gives the starting date for a project.
5. SALARY gives the annual salary of an employee.
6. EMPMGR gives the name of the employee's manager, who is not the same as the project manager.
7. EMPDEPT gives the employee's department. Department names are unique. The employee's manager is the manager of the employee's department.
8. RATING gives the employee's rating for a particular project. The project manager assigns the rating at the end of the employee's work on that project.

Using the assumptions, we find the following functional dependencies to begin with:

```
PROJNAME → PROJMGR, BUDGET, STARTDATE
EMPID → EMPNAME, SALARY, EMPMGR, EMPDEPT
PROJNAME, EMPID → HOURS, RATING
```

Since we assumed that people's names were not unique, EMPMGR does not functionally determine EMPDEPT. However, since department names are unique and each department has only one manager, we add

```
EMPDEPT → EMPMGR
```

Because people's names are not unique, PROJMGR does not determine PROJNAME. You may ask whether PROJMGR → BUDGET. Although it may be the case that the manager determines the budget in the English sense of the word, meaning that the manager comes up with the figures for the budget, you should recall that functional dependency does not mean "causes" or "figures out." Similarly, although the project manager assigns a rating to the employee, there is no functional dependency between PROJMGR and RATING.

Since we see that every attribute is functionally dependent on the combination PROJNAME,EMPID, we will choose that combination as our primary key, and see what normal form we have.

First Normal Form: With our composite key, each cell would be single-valued, so WORK is 1NF.

Second Normal Form: We found partial (nonfull) dependencies,

```
PROJNAME → PROJMGR, BUDGET, STARTDATE
EMPID → EMPNAME, SALARY, EMPMGR, EMPDEPT.
```

We transform the relation into an equivalent set of 2NF relations by projection, resulting in

```
PROJ (PROJNAME, PROJMGR, BUDGET, STARTDATE)
EMP (EMPID, EMPNAME, SALARY, EMPMGR, EMPDEPT)
WORK1 (PROJNAME, EMPID, HOURS, RATING)
```

Third Normal Form: Using the set of projections, {PROJ,EMP,WORK1}, we test each relation for 3NF. PROJ is 3NF because no nonkey attribute functionally determines another nonkey attribute. In EMP we have a transitive dependency, EMPDEPT → EMPMGR. Therefore, we need to rewrite EMP as

```
EMP1 (EMPID, EMPNAME, SALARY, EMPDEPT)
DEPT (EMPDEPT, EMPMGR)
```

In WORK1, there is no functional dependency between HOURS and RATING, so that relation is already 3NF. Our new set of 3NF relations is therefore

```
PROJ (PROJNAME, PROJMGR, BUDGET, STARTDATE)
EMP1 (EMPID, EMPNAME, SALARY, EMPDEPT)
DEPT (EMPDEPT, EMPMGR)
WORK1 (PROJNAME, EMPID, HOURS, RATING)
```

Boyce–Codd Normal Form: Our new 3NF set of relations is also BCNF, since, in each relation, the only determinant is the primary key.

We already know that our original relation could not have been BCNF, since it was not even 2NF. To verify the fact that WORK was not BCNF, all we needed to do was find a determinant that was not a candidate key. Any one of EMPID, EMPDEPT, or PROJNAME is sufficient to show that the original WORK relation was not BCNF.

7.12 *Multivalued Dependencies*

Although Boyce–Codd normal form removes any anomalies due to functional dependencies, further research by Fagin led to the identification of another type of dependency called a multivalued dependency that can cause similar design problems. To illustrate the concept of multivalued dependencies, consider the following relation:

```
FACULTY (FACID, DEPT, COMMITTEE)
```

Here we will assume that a faculty member can belong to more than one department. For example, a professor can be hired jointly by the CSC and Math departments. A faculty member can belong to several college-wide committees, each identified by the committee name. There is no relationship between department and committee. Figure 7.7(a) shows an unnormalized version of this relation. To make the relation 1NF, we must rewrite it as shown in Figure 7.7(b). Notice that we are forced to write all the combinations of DEPT values with COMMITTEE values for each faculty member, or else it would appear that there is some relationship between DEPT and COMMITTEE.

For example, without the second row, it would appear that F101 is on the Budget committee only as a member of the CSC Department, but not as a member of the Math Department. Also note that the key of the relation is now FACID,DEPT,COMMITTEE. The resulting relation is BCNF, since the only determinant is the key. Although we have taken care of all functional dependencies, there are still update, insertion, and deletion anomalies. If we want to update a committee that F101 belongs to from Budget to Advancement, we need to make two changes or have inconsistent data. If we want to insert the record of a faculty member who belongs to one or more departments but who is not on any committee, we are unable to do so, since COMMITTEE is part of the key, so null values are not permitted in that column. This is an insertion anomaly. Similarly, if F221 drops membership on the Library committee, we lose all the rest of the information stored for him or her, since we are not permitted to have a null value for an attribute of the key. Earlier, we found that similar problems were caused by functional dependencies, but there are none in this example, so we need to identify a new cause. Although a faculty member is not associated with only one department, he or she is certainly associated with a particular set of departments. Similarly, a faculty member is associated with a specific set of committees at any given time. The set of departments for a particular FACID is independent of the set of committees for that faculty member. This independence is the cause of the problems. To see how we can correct them, we need another definition.

Definition of Multivalued Dependency

DEFINITION: Let R be a relation having attributes or sets of attributes A, B, and C. There is a **multivalued dependence** of attribute B on attribute A if and only if the set of B values associated with a given A value is independent of the C values.

We write this as $A \twoheadrightarrow B$ and read it as "A multidetermines B." If R has at least three attributes, A, B, and C, then in $R(A,B,C)$, if $A \twoheadrightarrow B$, then $A \twoheadrightarrow C$ as well.

Unlike rules for functional dependencies, which made certain tuples illegal in relations, multivalued dependencies make certain tuples essential in a relation. In the normalized FACULTY table shown in Figure 7.7 (b), we were forced to write certain tuples because we had included others. For example, when we wrote the combination of F101 with both the CSC and Math Department values, we had to write two tuples for each of the committee values, Budget and Curriculum, and place each department value in a tuple with each committee value. An alternative definition of multivalued dependency describes the tuples that must appear.

Alternative Definition of Multivalued Dependency

If R is a relation with multivalued dependency

$$A \twoheadrightarrow B$$

then in any table for R, if two tuples, $t1$ and $t2$, have the same A value, then there must exist two other tuples, $t3$ and $t4$, obeying these rules:

1. $t3$ and $t4$ have the same A value as $t1$ and $t2$.
2. $t3$ has the same B value as $t1$.
3. $t4$ has the same B value as $t2$.
4. If $R - B$ represents the attributes of R that are not in B, then $t2$ and $t3$ have the same values for $R - B$.
5. $t1$ and $t4$ have the same values for $R - B$.

The dependency $A \twoheadrightarrow B$ is called a **trivial multivalued dependency** if B is a subset of A or $A \cup B$ is all of R. Now we are ready to consider fourth normal form.

7.13 *Fourth Normal Form*

Definition of Fourth Normal Form (4NF)

DEFINITION: A relation is in **fourth normal form** (4NF) if and only if it is in Boyce–Codd normal form and there are no nontrivial multivalued dependencies.

Our FACULTY relation shown in Figure 7.7(b) is not in fourth normal form because of the two nontrivial multivalued dependencies

```
FACID ->> DEPT
FACID ->> COMMITTEE
```

When a relation is BCNF but not 4NF, we can transform it into an equivalent set of 4NF relations by projection. We form two separate relations, placing in each the attribute that multidetermines the others, along with one of the multidetermined attributes or sets of attributes.

For our FACULTY relation, we form the two projections

```
FAC1 (FACID, DEPT)
FAC2 (FACID, COMMITTEE)
```

These relations, shown in Figure 7.7(c) are both in 4NF.

7.14 *Lossless Decomposition*

In splitting relations by projection, we were very explicit about the method of decomposition to use. In particular, we were careful to use projections that could be "undone" by joining the resulting tables, so that the original table would result. By the term *original*

```
|FACID|DEPT|COMMITTEE |
|-----|----|----------|
|F101 |CSC |Budget    |
|     |Math|Curriculum|
|-----|----|----------|
|F221 |Bio |Library   |
|-----|----|----------|
|F330 |Eng |Budget    |
|     |    |Admissions|
------------------------
```

Figure 7.7(a) Unnormalized FACULTY Table

```
|FACID|DEPT|COMMITTEE |
|-----|----|----------|
|F101 |CSC |Budget    |
|-----|----|----------|
|F101 |Math|Budget    |
|-----|----|----------|
|F101 |CSC |Curriculum|
|-----|----|----------|
|F101 |Math|Curriculum|
|-----|----|----------|
|F221 |Bio |Library   |
|-----|----|----------|
|F330 |Eng |Budget    |
|-----|----|----------|
|F330 |Eng |Admissions|
------------------------
```

Figure 7.7(b) Normalized FACULTY Table Showing Multivalued Dependencies

```
|FACID|DEPT|
|-----|----|
|F101 |CSC |
|-----|----|
|F101 |Math|
|-----|----|
|F221 |Bio |
|-----|----|
|F330 |Eng |
------------
FAC1 Table
```

```
|FACID|COMMITTEE |
|-----|----------|
|F101 |Budget    |
|-----|----------|
|F101 |Curriculum|
|-----|----------|
|F221 |Library   |
|-----|----------|
|F330 |Budget    |
|-----|----------|
|F330 |Admissions|
------------------
FAC2 Table
```

Figure 7.7(c) FAC1 and FAC2 Tables in 4NF

Figure 7.7

table we do not mean merely the structure of the table (i.e., the column names) but the actual tuples as well. Such a decomposition is called a **nonloss** or **lossless** decomposition, because it preserves all the information in the original relation. Although we have used the word *decomposition*, we have not written a formal definition, and we do so now.

Definition of Decomposition

DEFINITION: A **decomposition** of a relation R is a set of relations $\{R1, R2, \ldots, Rn\}$ such that each Ri is a subset of R and the union of all of the Ri is R.

Note that the Ri need not be disjoint. Now we are ready to define lossless decomposition.

Definition of Lossless Decomposition

DEFINITION: A decomposition $\{R1, R2, \ldots, Rn\}$ of a relation R is called a **lossless decomposition** for R if the natural join of $R1$, $R2, \ldots, Rn$ produces exactly the relation R.

Not every decomposition is lossless. It is possible to produce a decomposition that is **lossy**, one that loses information. As an example, consider the relation

```
MARKS (STUID, COURSE#, GRADE)
```

with the instance pictured in Figure 7.8 (a). Each tuple in this table shows that a certain student received the specified grade in the course listed. Now we form the two relations

```
MARK1 (STUID, COURSE#)
MARK2 (COURSE#, GRADE)
```

by projecting over the columns indicated. The results are pictured in Figure 7.8 (b).

We now perform the natural join of these two relations, using the common column, COURSE#. We observe that the result, shown in Figure 7.8 (c), contains some tuples that were not in the original relation. These spurious tuples were introduced by the operations performed. Since, without the original table, we would have no way of identifying which tuples are genuine and which are spurious, we actually lose information (even though we have more tuples) if we substitute the projections for the original relation. We can guarantee that the decomposition is lossless by making sure that for each pair of relations that will be joined, the set of common attributes is a determinant of one of the relations. We can do this by placing functionally dependent attributes in a relation with their determinants and keeping the determinants themselves in the original relation. More formally, if R is decomposed into two relations $\{R1, R2\}$, the join is lossless if and only if either of the following holds in the closure of the set of FDs for R:

$$R1 \cap R2 \rightarrow R1 - R2$$

or

$$R1 \cap R2 \rightarrow R2 - R1$$

In the MARKS example, COURSE# was not a determinant for either GRADE or STUID, so the intersection of the two projections, COURSE#, did not functionally determine either projection. We saw several examples of lossless projection when we normalized relations. For example, when we projected CLASS into {STU,CLASS2, COURSE} the projection was lossless. Since CLASS2 ∩ COURSE is COURSE# and COURSE# → COURSE (i.e., COURSE# → COURSE#, FACID, SCHED, ROOM) we can form a lossless join of CLASS2 and COURSE. Then the join of that result with STU has STUID as its intersection. Since STUID → STUID, STUNAME, the second join is also lossless.

For a decomposition involving more than two relations, the previous test cannot be used, so we present an algorithm for the general case. Given a relation *R(A1, A2, . . . , An)*, a set of functional dependencies, *F*, and a decomposition of *R* into relations *R1*, *R2, . . . , Rm*, the following algorithm can be used to determine whether the decomposition has a lossless join:

1. Construct an *m* by *n* table, *S*, with a column for each of the *n* attributes in *R* and a row for each of the *m* relations in the decomposition.

STUID	COURSE#	GRADE
S1001	ART103A	A
S1001	HST205A	B
S1003	CSC201A	A
S1006	ART103A	B
S1010	ART103A	D

Figure 7.8(a) Original MARKS Table

STUID	COURSE#
S1001	ART103A
S1001	HST205A
S1003	CSC201A
S1006	ART103A
S1010	ART103A

MARK1 Table

COURSE#	GRADE
ART103A	A
HST205A	B
CSC201A	A
ART103A	B
ART103A	D

MARK2 Table

Figure 7.8(b) Projections of the MARKS Table

Figure 7.8

```
|STUID|COURSE#|GRADE|
|-----|-------|-----|
|S1001|ART103A|A    |
|-----|-------|-----|
|S1001|ART103A|B    |
|-----|-------|-----|
|S1001|ART103A|D    |
|-----|-------|-----|
|S1001|HST205A|B    |
|-----|-------|-----|
|S1003|CSC201A|A    |
|-----|-------|-----|
|S1006|ART103A|A    |
|-----|-------|-----|
|S1006|ART103A|B    |
|-----|-------|-----|
|S1006|ART103A|D    |
|-----|-------|-----|
|S1010|ART103A|A    |
|-----|-------|-----|
|S1010|ART103A|B    |
|-----|-------|-----|
|S1010|ART103A|D    |
---------------------
```

Figure 7.8(c) Join of MARK1 and MARK2 Tables

Figure 7.8 (Continued)

2. For each cell $S(i,j)$ of S,
   if the attribute for the column, Aj, is in the relation for the row, Ri, then place the symbol $a(j)$ in the cell
   else place the symbol $b(i,j)$ there
3. Repeat the following process until no more changes can be made to S:
   for each FD $X \rightarrow Y$ in F
   for all rows in S that have the same symbols in the columns corresponding to the attributes of X, make the symbols for the columns that represent attributes of Y equal by the following rule:
   if any row has an a value, $a(j)$, set the value of that column in all the other rows equal to $a(j)$
   if no row has an a value, then pick any one of the b values, say $b(i,j)$, and set all the other rows equal to $b(i,j)$
4. If, after all possible changes have been made to S, a row is made up entirely of a symbols, $a(1), a(2), \ldots, a(n)$, the join is lossless. If there is no such row, the join is lossy.

Example 1. Consider the relation $R(A, B, C, D, E)$ having decomposition consisting of $R1(A, C)$, $R2(A, B, D)$, and $R3(D, E)$ with FDs $A \rightarrow C$, $AB \rightarrow D$, and $D \rightarrow E$. Referring to Figure 7.9, we construct one row for each relation in the decomposition and one column for each of the five attributes of R. For each row, we place the value a with the

```
R(A,B,C,D,E)
Decomposition:  R1(A,C), R2(A,B,D), R3(D,E)
FDs:  A → C, AB → D, D → E
                 | A        B        C        D        E
-----------------------------------------------------------
R1(A,C)          | a(1)     b(1,2)   a(3)     b(1,4)   b(1,5)
R2(A,B,D)        | a(1)     a(2)     b(2,3)   a(4)     b(2,5)
R3(D,E)          | b(3,1)   b(3,2)   b(3,3)   a(4)     a(5)
```

Figure 7.9(a) Initial placement of values

```
                 | A        B        C        D        E
-----------------------------------------------------------
R1(A,C)          | a(1)     b(1,2)   a(3)     b(1,4)   b(1,5)
R2(A,B,D)        | a(1)     a(2)     a(3)     a(4)     a(5)
R3(D,E)          | b(3,1)   b(3,2)   b(3,3)   a(4)     a(5)
```

Figure 7.9(b) Table after considering all FDs

Figure 7.9 Testing for Lossless Join

column subscript in any column whose heading represents an attribute in that relation, and the value *b* with the usual row and column subscript in the column for any attribute not in that relation. For example, in the first row, for relation *R*1(*A*, *C*), we place *a*(1) in the first column, for *A*, and *a*(3) in the third column, for *C*. Since *B* does not appear in *R*1, we place *b*(1,2) in its column. Similarly, we place *b*(1,4) in the *D* column and *b*(1,5) in the *E* column, since these attributes do not appear in *R*1. Now we consider the FD *A* → *C*, and look for rows that agree on the value of the left-hand side, *A*. We find that rows 1 and 2 agree on the value *a*(1). Therefore, we can set the *C* values equal. We find that row 1 has an *a* value, *a*(3), in the *C* column, so we set the *C* column value of row 2 equal to *a*(3). Considering the second FD, *AB* → *D*, we cannot find any two rows that agree on both their *A* and *B* values, so we are unable to make any changes. Now considering the FD *D* → *E*, we find that row 2 and row 3 agree on their *D* values, *a*(4), so we can set their *E* values equal. Since row 3 has an E value of *a*(5), we change the *E* value of row 2 to *a*(5) as well. Now we find that the second row has all *a* values, and we conclude that the projection has the lossless join property.

7.15 *Fifth Normal Form*

We have progressed from each normal form to a higher one by decomposition. Fifth normal form, also called **Project-Join Normal Form**, is the final stage of that process.

Definition of Fifth Normal Form

DEFINITION: A relation is in **fifth normal form** (5NF) if no remaining nonloss projections are possible, except the trivial one in which the key appears in each projection.

If a design consists of relations that are all 5NF, then there is nothing to be gained by decomposing them further, since that would result in a loss of information. The relations are in their "simplest" useful form.

An alternative formulation of fifth normal form involves the notion of **join dependency**. A join dependency means that a relation can be reconstructed be taking the join of its projections. Thus if *R*(*A*,*B*,*C*) is decomposed into *R*1(*A*,*B*) and *R*2(*B*,*C*), a join dependency exists if we can get back *R* by taking the join of *R*1 and *R*2. As we have seen from our MARKS example, not all projections have this property. Using this formulation, a relation is in fifth normal form if and only if every join dependency is implied by the candidate keys. Fifth normal form is not as easily verified as lower normal forms. In fact, no systematic method exists for obtaining 5NF or for ensuring that a set of relations is indeed 5NF.

7.16 Domain-Key Normal Form

The final normal form defined by Fagin involves the concepts of domain, key, and constraint. Fagin demonstrated that a relation in this form cannot have update, insertion, or deletion anomalies. Therefore, this form represents the ultimate normal form with respect to these defects.

Definition of Domain-Key Normal Form (DKNF)

DEFINITION: A relation is in **domain-key normal form** (DKNF) if every constraint is a logical consequence of domain constraints or key constraints.

The definition uses the terms **domain, key,** and **constraint.** As usual, the domain of an attribute is the set of allowable values for that attribute. Fagin uses the word *key* to mean what we have described as a superkey, a unique identifier for each entity. *Constraint* is a general term meaning a rule or restriction that can be verified by examining static states of the database. For a constraint to exist, we must be able to state it as a logical predicate which we can verify by examining instances of the relation. Although functional dependencies, multivalued dependencies, and join dependencies are constraints, there are other types, called "general constraints", as well. We may have rules about relationships between attributes of a relation (intrarelation constraints) that are not expressed as dependencies. For example, consider the relation STUDENT (STUID,STUNAME,MAJOR,CREDITS). Suppose that we have a rule that the STUID has a prefix that changes as the student progresses; for example, all freshman have a "1," all sophomores a "2," and so on, at the beginning of their IDs. This could be expressed as the general constraint "If the first digit of STUID is 1, then CREDITS must be between 0 and 30. If the first digit of STUID is 2, ..." For a relation to be DKNF, intrarelation constraints must be expressible as domain constraints or key constraints. We could express our constraint on STUDENT by splitting STUDENT into four different relations. For example, for freshman, we might have

```
STU1(STUID, STUNAME, MAJOR, CREDITS) with the domain constraints
1.  STUID must begin with a 1
2.  CREDITS must be between 0 and 30.
```

We would then have STU2 with similar domain constraints for sophomores, STU3 for juniors, and STU4 for seniors. Fagin's definition does not extend to interrelation constraints such as referential integrity, since his objective was to define a form that would allow general constraints to be checked **within** a relation by checking only that relation's domain and key constraints. Since an interrelation constraint involves two relations, it is not considered in the definition of DKNF.

Unfortunately, although the concept of domain-key normal form is simple, there is no proven method of converting a design to this form, so it remains an ideal rather than a state that can readily be achieved.

7.17 *The Normalization Process*

As we stated at the beginning of this chapter, the objective of normalization is to find a stable set of relations that is a faithful model of the enterprise. We found that normalization eliminated some problems of data representation and resulted in a "good" schema for the database. Analysis and synthesis are two different processes that could be used to develop the set of normalized relations.

7.17.1 *Analysis*

The analysis or decomposition approach begins with a list of all the attributes to be represented in the database and assumes that all of them are in a single relation called the **universal relation** for the database. The designer then identifies functional dependencies among the attributes and uses the techniques of decomposition explained in this chapter to split the universal relation into a set of normalized relations. Our examples in previous sections were all decomposition examples. In particular, in Section 7.11 we considered an example in which we had a single relation called WORK. WORK was actually a universal relation containing all the attributes to be stored in the database. We wrote out our assumptions and identified four functional dependencies. The functional dependencies enabled us to perform lossless projections, so that we developed a set of relations in BCNF that preserved all functional dependencies. Since there were no multivalued dependencies, the relations are also in 4NF, and since there were no remaining nontrivial lossless projections, they are in 5NF. All the constraints expressed in our list of assumptions and all the dependencies we identified in our discussion were considered in developing the final set of relations. The constraints are represented as key constraints in the resulting relations, so we actually have a set of DKNF relations. This example illustrates the process of analysis from a universal relation. In practice, a designer often begins with some idea of what the basic entities are, and groups attributes into initial relations before beginning the decomposition process on these relations.

7.17.2 *Synthesis*

Synthesis is, in a sense, the "opposite" of analysis. In analysis we begin with a single big relation and break it up until we reach a set of smaller normalized relations. In synthesis we begin with attributes (no relation at all) and combine them into related groups, using functional dependencies to develop a set of normalized relations. If analysis is a "top-down" process, then synthesis is a "bottom-up" one. A synthesis algorithm for producing a set of 3NF relations from a set of attributes was developed by Bernstein. Although we do not use this method in this book, we will describe the basic steps:

(1) Make a list of all FDs.
(2) Group together those with the same determinant.
(3) Construct a relation for each such group.

Difficulties may be introduced in several possible ways. For example, some FDs have more attributes in the determinant than needed, and we must eliminate the extraneous attributes before grouping, or else we will not recognize that two groups actually have the same determinants and we may create a relation that is not 2NF. For example, consider the set of FDs:

$$AB \rightarrow C$$

$$A \rightarrow D$$

$$D \rightarrow B$$

From the second and third we see that, by transitivity, $A \rightarrow B$. This makes B an extraneous attribute in the first FD, since $A \rightarrow B$ by transitivity. Another problem is that some of the FDs may be redundant, meaning that we can derive them from other FDs. In that case we must eliminate the redundant FDs before grouping or third normal form will not result. An example of that occurs in the following:

$$A \rightarrow B$$

$$A \rightarrow C$$

$$B \rightarrow C$$

Here, the second FD can be derived from the first and third. A third problem is that two relations may appear to have different keys when, in fact, the keys are equivalent. Equivalent keys functionally determine each other. For example, if we had STUID and SOCSECNO as attributes of a relation STUDENT we might use STUID as the key of one group of attributes, and SOCSECNO as the key of another, and fail to realize that the two relations should be combined. This could occur in cases where the equivalence of the candidate keys is obvious, that is, where the list of FDs specifically states that they determine each other, or, worse, where the equivalence is not obvious but could be derived from the list of FDs. A final problem could be that new functional dependencies would be introduced when equivalent keys are found. These new FDs may make some of the existing ones redundant, and the resulting relations would not be 3NF. Once these difficulties are eliminated, the process of constructing relations from attribute groups with identical or equivalent keys can begin.

Regardless of the process used, the end result should be a set of normalized relations that preserve dependencies and form lossless joins over common attributes. An important question is how far to go in the normalization process. Ideally, we try to reach DKNF. However, if that results in a decomposition that does not preserve dependencies, then we settle for less. Similarly, if we try for 5NF, 4NF, or BCNF, we may not be able to get a decomposition that preserves dependencies, so we would settle for 3NF in that case. It is always possible to find a dependency-preserving decomposition in 3NF. Even so, there may be valid reasons for choosing not to implement 3NF as well. For example, if we have attributes that are almost always used together in applications and they end up in different relations, then we will almost always have to do a join operation when we retrieve them. A familiar example of this occurs in storing addresses. Let us assume that we are storing an employee's name and address, in the relation

```
EMP (EMPID, NAME, STREET, CITY, STATE, ZIP)
```

As usual we assume that names are not unique. We have the functional dependency

```
ZIP → CITY, STATE
```

which means that the relation is not 3NF. We could normalize it by decomposition into

```
EMP1 (EMPID, NAME, STREET, ZIP)
CODES (ZIP, CITY, STREET)
```

However, this would mean that we would have to do a join whenever we want a complete address for a person. In this case we would settle for 2NF and implement the original EMP relation. In general, performance requirements must be taken into account in deciding what the final form will be.

7.18 *Chapter Summary*

In this chapter we dealt with a method for developing a suitable set of relations for the logical model. Three types of dependencies, **functional dependencies, multivalued dependencies,** and **join dependencies**, were found to produce problems in representing information in the database. Many problems involved **update, insertion, and deletion anomalies.** An attribute *B* is said to be **functionally dependent** on an attribute *A* in a relation *R* if each *A* value has exactly one *B* value associated with it. Functional dependencies can be manipulated by using **Armstrong's axioms** or rules of inference. The set *F+* of all functional dependencies logically implied by a given set *F* of functional dependencies is called its **closure.** Similarly, the closure, *A+*, of an attribute *A* in a set of functional dependencies is the set of all attributes that it functionally determines. We can compute *A+* by a simple algorithm.

First normal form means that a relation has no multiple-valued attributes. We can normalize a relation that is not already in 1NF by flattening it. Relations in 1NF can have update, insertion, and deletion anomalies, due to **partial dependencies** on the key. If a nonkey attribute is not **fully functionally dependent** on the entire key, the relation is not in **second normal form**. In that case we normalize it by **projection**, placing each determinant that is a proper subset of the key in a new relation with its dependent attributes. The original composite key must also be kept in another relation. Relations in 2NF can also have update, insertion, and deletion anomalies. **Transitive dependencies**, which allow one nonkey attribute to functionally determine another nonkey attribute, cause such anomalies. In relations with only one candidate key, **third normal form** is achieved by using projection to eliminate transitive dependencies. The determinant causing the transitive dependency is placed in a separate relation with the attributes it determines. It is also kept in the original relation. In third normal form, each nonkey attribute is functionally dependent on the key, the whole key, and nothing but the key.

Boyce–Codd normal form requires that every determinant be a candidate key. This form is also achieved by projection, but in some cases the projection will separate determinants from their functionally dependent attributes, resulting in the loss of an important constraint. If this happens, 3NF is preferable.

Multivalued dependencies can occur when there are at least three attributes in the key and two of them have independent multiple values. **Fourth normal form** requires that a relation be BCNF and have no multivalued dependencies. We can achieve 4NF by projection, but we do so only if the resulting projections preserve all functional dependencies. Some projections can lose information because when they are undone by a join, spurious tuples can result. We can be sure that a decomposition is **lossless** if the intersection of the two projections is a determinant for one of them. A relation is in **fifth normal form** if there are no remaining nontrivial nonloss projections. Alternatively, a relation is in fifth normal form if every join dependency is implied by the candidate keys. There is no proven method for achieving fifth normal form. **Domain-key normal form** requires that every constraint be a consequence of domain constraints or key constraints. No proven method exists for producing domain-key normal form.

In **analysis** we begin with a universal relation, identify dependencies, and use projection to achieve a higher normal form. The opposite approach, called **synthesis**, begins with attributes, finds functional dependencies, and groups together functional dependencies with the same determinant, forming relations.

In deciding what normal form to choose for implementation, we consider lossless projection and dependency preservation. We generally choose the highest normal form that allows for both of these. We must balance performance against normalization in implementation.

7.19 *Exercises*

1. Consider the following universal relation that holds information about books in a bookstore:

```
BOOKS (TITLE, ISBN, AUTHOR, PUBLISHER_NAME, PUBLISHER_ADD,
TOTAL_COPIES_ORDERED, COPIES_IN_STOCK, PUBLICATION_DATE, CATEGORY,
SELLING_PRICE, COST)
```

Assume that:

- 1. The ISBN identifies a book uniquely. (It does not identify each copy of the book, however.)
- 2. If a book has more than one author, only the first is listed.
- 3. An author may have more than one book.
- 4. Each publisher name is unique. Each publisher has one unique address, the address of the firm's headquarters.
- 5. Titles are not unique.
- 6. TOTAL_COPIES_ORDERED is the number of copies of a particular book that the bookstore has ever ordered, while COPIES_IN_STOCK is the number still unsold in the bookstore.
- 7. Each book has only one publication date. A revision of a book is given a new ISBN.
- 8. The category may be biography, science fiction, poetry, and so on. The title alone is not sufficient to determine the category.
- 9. The SELLING_PRICE, which is the amount the bookstore charges for a book, is always 20 percent above the COST, which is the amount the bookstore pays the publisher or distributor for the book.

   (a) Using these assumptions and stating any others you need to make, list all the nontrivial functional dependencies for this relation.
   (b) What are the candidate keys for this relation? Identify the primary key.
   (c) Is the relation in third normal form? If not, find a 3NF lossless join decomposition of BOOK that preserves dependencies.
   (d) Is the relation or resulting set of relations in Boyce–Codd normal form? If not, find a lossless join decomposition that is in BCNF, if possible.

2. Consider the following relation that stores information about students living in dormitories at a college:

```
COLLEGE (STUNAME, STUID, HOMEADD, HOMEPHONE, DORMROOM, ROOMMATE_NAME,
DORMADD, STATUS, MEALPLAN, ROOMCHARGE, MEALCHARGE)
```

Assume that

- 1. Each student is assigned to one dormitory room and has at most one roommate. Names of students are not unique.
- 2. The college has several dorms. DORMROOM contains a code for the dorm and the number of the particular room assigned to the student. For example, A221 means Adams Hall, room 221. Dorm names are unique.
- 3. The DORMADD is the address of the dorm building. Each building has its own unique address. For example, Adams Hall may be 123 Main Street, Anytown, NY 10001.
- 4. STATUS tells the student's status: Freshman, Sophomore, Junior, Senior, or Graduate Student.
- 5. MEALPLAN tells how many meals per week the student has chosen. Each meal plan has a single MEALCHARGE associated with it.
- 6. The ROOMCHARGE is different for different dorms, but all students in the same dorm pay the same amount.

For this example, answer parts (a)-(d) as in Exercise 1.

3. Consider the following relations and identify the highest normal form for each, as given, stating any assumptions that you need to make:

```
(a) WORK1 (EMPID, EMPNAME, DATE_HIRED, JOB_TITLE, JOB_LEVEL)
(b) WORK2 (EMPID, EMPNAME, JOB_TITLE, RATING_DATE, RATER_NAME,
     RATING)
(c) WORK3 (EMPID, EMPNAME, PROJECT#, PROJECT_NAME, PROJ_BUDGET,
     EMP_MANAGER, HOURS_ASSIGNED)
(d) WORK4 (EMPID, EMPNAME, SCHOOL_ATTENDED, DEGREE, GRADUA-
     TION_DATE)
(e) WORK5 (EMPID, EMPNAME, SOCIAL_SECURITY_NUMBER, DEPENDENT_NAME,
     DEPENDENT_ADDRESS, RELATION_TO_EMP)
```

4. For each of the relations in Exercise 3, identify a primary key and

(a) if the relation is not in third normal form, find a 3NF lossless join decomposition that preserves dependencies.
(b) if the relation or resulting set of relations is not in Boyce–Codd normal form, find a lossless join decomposition that is in BCNF.

5. Consider instances of relation $R(A,B,C,D)$ shown in Figure 7.10. For each of the following sets of FDs, determine whether each of the instances is consistent with the FDs given.

(a) $A \rightarrow B,C$
$B \rightarrow D$
(b) $AB \rightarrow C$
$B \rightarrow D$
(c) $AB \rightarrow C,D$
$AC \rightarrow B$

Instance 1:

A	B	C	D
a1	b1	c1	d1
a2	b2	c1	d2
a3	b1	c2	d3
a4	b3	c2	d3

Instance 2:

A	B	C	D
a1	b1	c1	d1
a2	b1	c2	d1
a3	b2	c1	d2
a4	b2	c2	d2

Instance 3:

A	B	C	D
a1	b1	c1	d1
a2	b1	c2	d1
a1	b2	c3	d2
a2	b2	c4	d2

Figure 7.10 Instances of R(A,B,C,D)

6. Given the following set, S, of FDs:

$$S = \{A \rightarrow B, B \rightarrow C, AC \rightarrow D\}$$

   (a) Find the closure of A, $A+$
   (b) Find the closure of the set of FDs, $S+$

7. Examine each of the following sets of FDs and find any redundant FDs in each. Give a minimal covering for each.

   (a) $B \rightarrow D$
   $E \rightarrow C$
   $AC \rightarrow D$
   $CD \rightarrow A$
   $BE \rightarrow A$
   (b) $A \rightarrow C, D, E$
   $B \rightarrow C, E$
   $AD \rightarrow E$
   $CD \rightarrow F$
   $BD \rightarrow A$
   $CED \rightarrow A, B, D$
   (c) $D \rightarrow C$
   $AB \rightarrow C$
   $AD \rightarrow B$
   $BD \rightarrow A$
   $AC \rightarrow B$

8. Consider the relation

$$R(A, B, C, D, E)$$

with FDs

$$A \rightarrow B$$

$$BC \rightarrow D$$

$$D \rightarrow B, C$$

$$C \rightarrow A$$

(a) Identify the candidate keys of this relation.
(b) Suppose that the relation is decomposed into

$$R1(A, B)$$

$$R2(B, C, D)$$

Does this decomposition have a lossless join?

7.20 *Bibliography*

Armstrong, W. W. "Dependency Structures of Data Base Relationships," Proceedings of the IFIP Congress (1974) pp. 580-583.

Beeri, C., R. Fagin, and J. Howard. "A Complete Axiomatization for Functional and Multivalued Dependencies," ACM SIGMOD International Conference on Management of Data (1977) pp. 47-61.

Bernstein, P. "Synthesizing Third Normal Form Relations from Functional Dependencies," ACM Transactions on Database Systems **1**:4 (December, 1976) pp. 277-298.

Bernstein, P. and N. Goodman. "What Does Boyce–Codd Normal Form Do?" Proceedings of the International Conference on Very Large Data Bases (1980) pp. 245-259.

Biskup, J., U. Dayal, and P. Bernstein. "Synthesizing Independent Database Schemas," ACM SIGMOD Conference on Management of Data (1979) pp. 143-152.

Codd, E. "Further Normalization of the Data Base Relational Model," in Rustin, R. (Ed.) *Data Base Systems*. Englewood Cliffs, NJ: Prentice-Hall, 1972 pp. 33-64.

Date, C. *An Introduction to Database Systems*. Reading, MA: Addison-Wesley, 1986.

Elmasri, R. and S. Navathe. *Fundamentals of Database Systems*. Redwood City, CA: Benjamin/Cummings, 1989.

Fagin, R. "Multivalued Dependencies and a New Normal Form for Relational Databases," ACM Transactions on Database Systems **2**:3 (September 1977) pp. 262-278.

Fagin, R. "A Normal Form for Relational Databases That is Based on Domains and Keys," ACM Transactions on Database Systems **6**:3 (September, 1981) pp. 387-415.

Gottlob, G. "Computing Covers for Embedded Functional Dependencies," Proceedings of the Sixth ACM Symposium on Principles of Database Systems (1987) pp. 58-69.

Jaeschke, G. and H. Scheck. "Remarks on the Algebra of Non First Normal Form Relations," Proceedings of the First ACM Symposium on Principles of Database Systems (1982) pp. 124-138.

Kent, W. *Data and Reality*. Amsterdam: North-Holland, 1978.

Korth, H. and A. Silberschatz. *Database System Concepts*. New York: McGraw-Hill, 1986.

Liu, L. and A. Demers. "An Algorithm for Testing Lossless Joins in Relational Databases," Information Processing Letters **11**:1 (1980) pp. 73-76.

Maier. D. *The Theory of Relational Databases*. Rockville, MD: Computer Science Press, 1983.

Mendelzon, A. and D. Maier. "Generalized Mutual Dependencies and the Decomposition of Database Relations," Proceedings of the International Conference on Very Large Data Bases (1979) pp. 75-82.

Mitchell, J. "Inference Rules for Functional and Inclusion Dependencies," Proceedings of the Second ACM Symposium on Principles of Database Systems (1983) pp. 58–69.

Nicolas, J. "Mutual Dependencies and Some Results on Undecomposable Relations," Proceedings of the International Conference on Very Large Data Bases (1978) pp. 360-367.

Ozsoyoglu, Z. and L. Yuan. "A New Normal Form for Nested Relations," Transactions on Database Systems **12**:1 (March, 1987) pp. 111-136.

Sadri, F. and J. Ullman. "Template Dependencies: A Large Class of Dependencies in Relational Databases and Their Complete Axiomatization," Journal of the ACM **29**:2 (April, 1982) pp. 363-372.

Sciore, E. "A Complete Axiomatization for Full Join Dependencies," Journal of the ACM **29**:2 (April, 1982) pp. 373-393.

Ullman, J. *Principles of Database and Knowledge-Base Systems Volume I*. Rockville, MD: Computer Science Press, 1988.

Vassiliou, Y. "Functional Dependencies and Incomplete Information," Proceedings of the International Conference on Very Large Data Bases (1980) pp. 260-269.

SAMPLE PROJECT: CREATING A NORMALIZED RELATIONAL MODEL FOR CLERICALTEMPS.

In the Sample Project section of Chapter 5 we created an E-R diagram for ClericalTemps. At the end of Chapter 6 we saw how to map that diagram to tables. In the present section we want to normalize the relations.

Step 7.1:

Make a list of all attributes to be stored in the database.
Our universal relation consists of the following attributes:

$U = \{$ AVAILCODE, AVERRATING, BILLDATE, BILLINGYTD, BOOKKPING, CHECK#, CLADD, CLID, CLNAME, CLPHONE, CONTACT, DAILYHOURS, DAILYRATE, DATEHIRED, DOB, EMPADD, EMPID, EMPNAME, EMPPHONE, EMPRATING, EXPECTENDDATE, FED, FEDYTD, FICA, FICAYTD, FILING, GROSS, GROSSYTD, INVOICE#, JOB#, JOBSTATUS, JOBTITLE, LASTDATEWORKED, LOCAL, LOCALYTD, NET, NETYTD, NEWBAL, OLDBAL, PAYDATE, PAYMENTSYTD, RATERNAME, RATINGDATE, REPORTTOADD, REPORTTONAME, REPORTTOPHONE, SEX, STATE, STATEYTD, SSN, STARTDATE, STENO, TOTCHARGES, TOTPAID, TYPING, WORDPROC$\}$

Although we could begin by trying to isolate functional dependencies among all these attributes, we can make our job easier by using the entities and relationships we identified in Chapter 5 and the tables to which they mapped at the end of Chapter 6.

Step 7.2:

Make a list of entities and relationships using the E-R diagram developed at the end of Chapter 5. Make a list of the tables that the entities and relationships mapped to naturally, from the Sample Project section of Chapter 6.

The entities are WORKER, CLIENT, JOB, PAYROLL, and BILL. There is a one-to-many relationship between WORKER and JOB having descriptive attributes EMPRATING, RATERNAME, and RATINGDATE. There are one-to-many relationships with no descriptive attributes between CLIENT and JOB, between CLIENT and BILL, and between WORKER and PAYROLL.

The following tables resulted:

WORKER (EMPID, EMPNAME, SSN, EMPADD, EMPPHONE, DOB, SEX, DATEHIRED, LASTDATEWORKED, AVERRATING, WORDPROC, TYPING, FILING, BOOKKPING, STENO, AVAILCODE)

CLIENT (CLID, CLNAME, CLADD, CLPHONE, CONTACT, BILLINGYTD, PAYMENTSYTD)

JOB (JOB#, JOBTITLE, STARTDATE, EXPECTENDDATE, DAILYRATE, DAILYHOURS, REPORTTONAME, REPORTTOADD, REPORTTOPHONE, JOBSTATUS)

BILL (INVOICE#, BILLDATE, OLDBAL, TOTCHARGES, NEWBAL, TOTPAID)

PAYROLL (CHECK#, PAYDATE, GROSS, FED, FICA, STATE, LOCAL, NET, GROSSYTD, NETYTD, FEDYTD, FICAYTD, STATEYTD, LOCALYTD)

ASSIGNMENT (JOB#, EMPID, RATERNAME, RATINGDATE, EMPRATING)

CLIENT-JOB (JOB#, CLID)

CLIENT-BILL (INVOICE#, CLID)

WORKER-PAYROLL (CHECK#, EMPID)

Step 7.3:

For each table identified in the preceding step, identify functional dependencies, multivalued dependencies, and join dependencies, and normalize the relation. Then decide whether the table should be implemented in the highest normal form. If not, explain why.

Working first with the WORKER table, we find the following functional dependencies:

- EMPID → all other attributes
- SSN → all other attributes
- EMPPHONE → EMPADD (We assume that two different workers could have the same telephone number. For example, two members of the same household might both work for ClericalTemps. Therefore, EMPPHONE is not a candidate key.)

We could decompose WORKER into the following tables:

```
WORKER1 (EMPID, EMPNAME, SSN, EMPPHONE, DOB, SEX, DATEHIRED,
LASTDATEWORKED, AVERRATING, WORDPROC, TYPING, FILING, BOOKKPING,
STENO, AVAILCODE)

WORKER2 (EMPPHONE, EMPADD)
```

WORKER1 is in BCNF because both determinants, EMPID and SSN, are candidate keys. WORKER2 is also BCNF. However, because we would normally want a worker's address when we retrieve his or her record, we would have to do joins of these tables quite often. Therefore, we will combine them and leave the WORKER table in its original state. Note this means we are satisfied with 2NF in this case.

Now we work with the CLIENT table. We find the following functional dependencies:

- CLID → all other attributes
- CLPHONE → all other attributes (Unlike workers, clients would have unique telephone numbers. We assume that we store only one telephone number per client.)

The CLIENT relation is already in BCNF because both determinants are candidate keys.

We move on to the JOB table. The following functional dependencies exist:

- JOB# → all other attributes
- JOBTITLE → DAILYRATE (We assume that JOBTITLE has both a job name and a level, e.g., JUNIOR TYPIST, EXPERT WORDPROC)
- REPORTTOPHONE → REPORTTOADD

Because of the transitive dependencies we could break up this relation into

```
JOB1 (JOB#, JOBTITLE, STARTDATE, EXPECTENDDATE, DAILYHOURS, REPORTTONAME,
REPORTTOPHONE, JOBSTATUS)

JOB2 (REPORTTOPHONE, REPORTTOADD)

JOB3 (JOBTITLE, DAILYRATE)
```

However, because we would normally want the REPORTTOADDRESS with the job record, we will leave it in the record. Similarly, the rate is a piece of information that would be integral to a job record, so we will choose to leave the rate in the record as well. This means that the original JOB record, which is only 2NF, will be used.

Now we work with the PAYROLL relation. We find the functional dependencies:

- CHECK# → all other attributes
- GROSS,FED,FICA,STATE,LOCAL → NET
- GROSSYTD, FEDYTD, FICAYTD, STATEYTD, LOCALYTD → NETYTD

We could break up this relation into the following relations

```
PAYROLL1 (CHECK#,PAYDATE, GROSS, FED, FICA, STATE, LOCAL,
GROSSYTD, FEDYTD, FICAYTD, STATEYTD, LOCALYTD)

PAYROLL2 (GROSS, FED, FICA, STATE, LOCAL, NET)

PAYROLL3 (GROSSYTD, FEDYTD, FICAYTD, STATEYTD, LOCALYTD, NETYTD)
```

We note that the only nonkey attribute in PAYROLL2, NET, can be calculated by a simple formula from the other attributes. The same is true of NETYTD in PAYROLL3. Since all the key attributes in these two relations are already present in PAYROLL1, this is the only relation we need to store for PAYROLL. We will calculate net as needed.

Working now with the BILL relation, we find the following functional dependencies:

- INVOICE# → all other attributes
- OLDBAL, TOTCHARGES → NEWBAL

We can split this up into the following tables

```
BILL1 (INVOICE#, BILLDATE, OLDBAL, TOTCHARGES, TOTPAID)

BILL2 (OLDBAL, TOTCHARGES, NEWBAL)
```

Since NEWBAL is simply the sum of OLDBAL and TOTCHARGES, it can be calculated when needed, so we will not store it. This means that we do not need BILL2.

The ASSIGNMENT relation connects the JOB with the WORKER. Since there is only one employee per JOB#, we have the following functional dependency:

```
JOB# → EMPID, RATERNAME, RATINGDATE, EMPRATING
```

This relation is already in 5NF.

The CLIENT-JOB relation connects the CLIENT with the JOB. It has the following functional dependency

```
JOB# → CLID
```

Therefore, it is already in 5NF. We note that this relationship table has no descriptive attributes and its only function is to show which client has generated a particular job.

By introducing CLID as a foreign key into the existing JOB table, we are not creating any normalization problems for that table, since JOB#, the key of that table, functionally determines CLID, and there are no additional functional dependencies introduced by CLID. We also note that this choice would reduce the number of joins required, so we will decide to drop the CLIENT-JOB relationship table.

The CLIENT-BILL relation connects the CLIENT with the BILL. The only functional dependency is

```
INVOICE# → CLID
```

so the relationship is in 5NF. Since we have no descriptive attributes, and since the introduction of CLID as a foreign key in BILL causes no problems, we will choose to drop the CLIENT-BILL table and include CLID in the BILL table.

The last relation is WORKER-PAYROLL. It consists only of the keys, CHECK# and EMPID, of the two relations it connects. The functional dependency is

```
CHECK# → EMPID
```

Since there are no descriptive attributes, we will keep the connection by placing EMPID as a foreign key in the PAYROLL record, and drop the WORKER-PAYROLL relation completely.

Our final set of normalized tables is the following:

WORKER (<u>EMPID</u>, EMPNAME, SSN, EMPADD, EMPPHONE, DOB, SEX, DATEHIRED, LASTDATEWORKED, AVERRATING, WORDPROC, TYPING, FILING, BOOKKPING, STENO, AVAILCODE)

CLIENT (<u>CLID</u>, CLNAME, CLADD, CLPHONE, CONTACT, BILLINGYTD, PAYMENTSYTD)

JOB (<u>JOB#</u>, CLID, JOBTITLE, STARTDATE, EXPECTENDDATE, DAILYRATE, DAILYHOURS, REPORTTONAME, REPORTTOADD, REPORTTOPHONE, JOBSTATUS)

PAYROLL (<u>CHECK#</u>, EMPID, PAYDATE, GROSS, FED, FICA, STATE, LOCAL,

GROSSYTD, FEDYTD, FICAYTD, STATEYTD, LOCALYTD)

BILL (<u>INVOICE#</u>, CLID, BILLDATE, OLDBAL, TOTCHARGES, TOTPAID)

ASSIGNMENT (<u>JOB#</u>, EMPID, RATERNAME, RATINGDATE, EMPRATING)

Student Project: Creating a Normalized Relational Model

Step 7.1

Make a list of all attributes to be stored in the database.

Step 7.2

Make a list of entities and relationships using the E-R diagram developed at the end of Chapter 5. Make a list of the tables that the entities and relationships mapped to naturally, from the Student Project section of Chapter 6.

Step 7.3

For each table identified in Step 7.2, identify functional dependencies, multivalued dependencies, and join dependencies, and normalize the relation. Be sure that every attribute listed in Step 7.1 appears in at least one table. Then decide whether each table should be implemented in the highest normal form. If not, explain why.

PART III

DESIGNING THE PHYSICAL MODEL

CHAPTER

8

A Relational Database Management System: DB2

8 Chapter Objectives

In this chapter you will learn

- the history of DB2 and SQL
- how the three-level architecture is implemented in DB2
- how to create and modify a conceptual-level database structure in DB2
- how to retrieve and update data in a DB2 database
- how to create external views in DB2
- how to perform operations on views
- the structure and functions of the DB2 system catalog
- the functions of the various components of a DB2 environment

8.1 *Background of DB2*

Because the relational model is both theoretically and practically important, in this chapter we examine an implementation that is relatively faithful to the abstract model. The system we will study is IBM's **Database 2**, or **DB2**. This database management system is an outgrowth of work begun at the IBM Research Laboratory, then in San Jose, California, in the early 1970s. As mentioned in Chapter 6, the relational model was first proposed by E. F. Codd in 1970. D. D. Chamberlin and others at the San Jose Research Laboratory developed a language now called **SQL**, or **Structured Query Language**, as a data sublanguage for the relational model. Originally spelled SEQUEL, and still pronounced that way, the language was described in a series of papers starting in 1974. It was used in a prototype relational system called **System R**, which was developed by IBM in the late 1970s and was evaluated and refined over a period of several years. It became the basis for IBM's first commercially available relational database management system, **SQL/DS,** which was announced in 1981. The announcement of DB2 followed in 1983. Both SQL/DS and DB2 use the SQL language, although there are minor differences in the two implementations. In addition, SQL has been adopted by other vendors for use in relational systems, and even in nonrelational systems with a relational interface. It has been approved by the American National Standards Institute, **ANSI**, as a standard relational database language. SQL has a complete data definition language (DDL), data manipulation language (DML), and an authorization language. Different implementations of SQL vary slightly from the DB2 syntax presented here, but the basic notions are the same.

8.2 *Architecture of DB2*

DB2 supports the standard **three-level architecture** for databases, as shown in Figure 8.1. It is one of the few products that provide a high degree of both logical and physical data independence. The conceptual level consists of **base tables**, which are physically stored tables. These tables are created by the Database Administrator using a CREATE TABLE command, as explained in Section 8.3. Once the base tables have been created, the DBA can create "views" for users. A **view** may be a subset of a single base table or may be created by combining base tables or performing other operations on them. Views are "virtual tables," not permanently stored, but merely created when the user needs to access them. Users are unaware of the fact that their views are not physically stored in table form. DB2 uses the word *view* to mean a single virtual table. This is not exactly the same as our term *external view*, which means the database as it appears to a particular user. In our terminology, an external view may consist of several DB2 base tables and/or DB2 views. A base table may have any number of indexes, one of which may be a clustered index.

On the physical level, the base tables and their indexes are represented in **entry-sequenced VSAM files**. The physical representation of the tables may not correspond

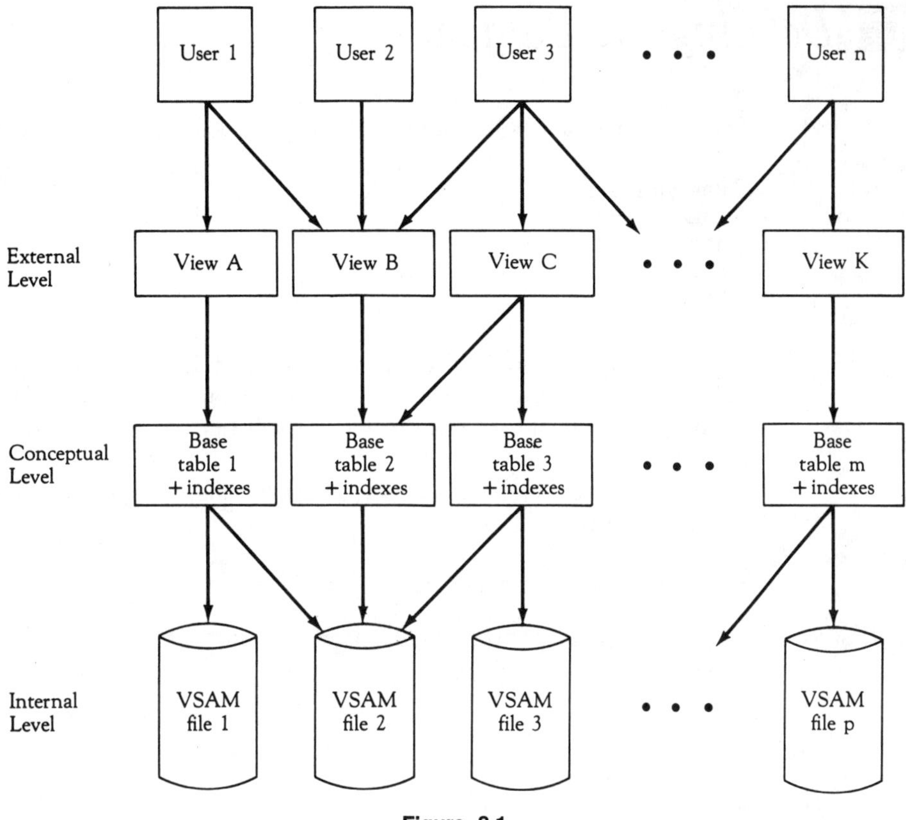

Figure 8.1

exactly to our notion of the base table as a two-dimensional object consisting of rows and columns. However, the rows of the table do correspond to physically stored records, although their order and other details of storage may be changed. VSAM is used only as the disk manager, while DB2 acts as the file manager. DB2 uses B trees for indexes, and DB2, not VSAM, controls the internal structure of both the data files and the indexes. The user is generally unaware of what indexes exist and has no control over which index will be used in locating a record.

One of the most useful features of DB2 is that it permits **dynamic database definition**. The DBA and users that he or she authorizes to do so may create new tables, add columns to old ones, create new indexes, define views, and drop any of these objects at any time. This is in contrast to many other systems, which require that the entire database structure be defined at creation time and that the entire system be halted and reloaded when any structural changes are made. The flexibility of DB2 encourages users to experiment with various structures and allows the system to be modified to meet their changing needs. This enables the DBA to ensure that the database is a useful model of the enterprise throughout its life cycle.

8.3 *Defining the Database*

The most important SQL Data Definition Language commands are the following:

```
CREATE TABLE
CREATE INDEX
ALTER TABLE
DROP TABLE
DROP INDEX
```

These statements are used to create, change, and destroy the logical structures that make up the conceptual model. Additional commands are available to the DBA to specify physical details of storage, but we will not discuss them here, since they are specific to the system.

We will apply these commands to the following example, which we have used in previous chapters:

```
STUDENT(STUID, STUNAME, MAJOR, CREDITS)
FACULTY(FACID, FACNAME, DEPT, RANK)
CLASS(COURSE#, FACID, SCHED, ROOM)
ENROLL(COURSE#, STUID, GRADE)
```

8.3.1 *Create Table*

This command is used to create the base tables that form the heart of the DB2 database. Since this command can be used at any time during the life cycle of the system, the DBA can start with a small number of tables and add to them as additional applications are planned and developed. A base table is fairly close to the abstract notion of a relational table. It consists of one or more **column headings**, with the specified **column name** and **data type**, and zero or more **data rows**, which contain one data value of the specified data type for each of the columns. As in the abstract relational model, the rows are considered to be unordered. However, in a departure from the abstract model, the columns are ordered left to right, to match the order of column definitions in the CREATE TABLE command. The form of the command is

```
CREATE TABLE base-table-name (col-name data-type [NOT NULL
[WITH DEFAULT]][,col-name date-type [NOT NULL [WITH DEFAULT]]]...,
[PRIMARY KEY (col-name [,col-name]...)], [FOREIGN KEY (col-name
[,col-name]...) REFERENCES (other-base-table-name)])[storage-
specifications];
```

Here, base-table-name is a unique user-supplied name of at most 18 characters. Its first character must be alphabetic, which means a letter of the alphabet or one of the "alphabetic" characters $,#,@. Each remaining character can be alphabetic, numeric

(0–9), or an underscore. No spaces or other special characters are permitted and no SQL keywords may be used as table names.

For each column, the user must define a name that is unique within the table and that follows the same rules as table names. Permitted data types are the following:

- **SMALLINT**: A halfword binary integer, with 15-bit precision, and sign.
- **INTEGER**: A fullword binary integer, with 31-bit precision, and sign.
- **DECIMAL(p,q)**: A signed packed decimal number with a total of p digits, where $p < 16$, of which q are to the right of the assumed decimal point. Note that $q <= p$, and if $q = 0$, it may be omitted.
- **FLOAT(p)**: A floating-point number having precision of p binary digits, where $p <= 54$. Single precision is used if $p < 22$; double precision if $p >= 22$.
- **CHAR(n)**: A character string of fixed length $n < 255$.
- **VARCHAR(n)**: A varying-length character string with a maximum of n characters, where $n < 255$.
- **LONG VARCHAR**: A varying-length character string of length up to 32,767.
- **GRAPHIC, VARGRAPHIC**, and **LONG VARGRAPHIC**: Used with special character sets that use two bytes to represent data, such as certain foreign languages.
- **DATE**: A date in the form yyyymmdd.
- **TIME**: A time in the form hhmmss.
- **TIMESTAMP**: A value consisting of a date and a time, including microseconds, of the form yyyymmddhhmmssnnnnnn.

DB2 allows data items to have null values, so that the user can insert records that have unknown values for some fields. When a null value is given, the system is able to distinguish it from a blank or zero and treats it differently in computations and logical comparisons. It is desirable to be able to insert null values in certain situations; for example, when a college student has not yet declared a major, we might want to set the MAJOR field to null. However, the use of null values can create complications, especially in operations such as joins. It is very important to ensure that null values are not permitted for the key, since we could not distinguish between two different records if they both had null key values. For such special fields, we should specify NOT NULL when we create the table. In fact, we are permitted to make that specification for any column or columns we choose. The system automatically checks each record we try to insert to ensure that data items for columns that have been described as NOT NULL have actual values. If not, it will reject the insertion. If we specify NOT NULL WITH DEFAULT, the system automatically assigns an appropriate default value if we do not specify a value for that data item when we insert a record. The default value is determined by the data type, with 0 assigned for numeric data, a string of blanks for fixed-length character or graphic data, a null string for variable-length data, and the current date and the current time for their corresponding data types.

We can identify the primary key for the table by using the option PRIMARY KEY, followed by the name of the column or columns used as the primary key. These columns must have the NOT NULL option and must have unique values. We can ensure the values are unique by creating a unique index on these columns, as described in Section

8.3.2. A serious flaw in DB2 is the inability to specify domains. Beyond giving data type, the DDL provides no way to restrict the range of data values and thereby protect the integrity of data entered.

The optional storage specifications section of the CREATE TABLE allows the DBA to name the exact physical location of the space where the table will be stored. If this is not specified, DB2 will create a default space for the table. This feature allows those who wish to do so to ignore system details and those who desire more control to be very specific about storage areas.

If a table contains a foreign key, we can enforce referential integrity by naming the column or columns that make up the foreign key and identifying the home relation in which they are the primary key. If the table contains more than one foreign key, we simply repeat the specification for those columns. We also have the option of specifying how referential integrity is to be maintained when tables are updated. This topic will be discussed in Chapter 13.

For our example, the following statement creates the STUDENT table

```
CREATE TABLE STUDENT
    (STUID     CHAR(6)    NOT NULL,
    STUNAME    CHAR(20)   NOT NULL,
    MAJOR      CHAR(10),
    CREDITS    SMALLINT,
    PRIMARY KEY (STUID));
```

The CLASS table is created by the following

```
CREATE TABLE CLASS
    (COURSE#     CHAR(7) NOT NULL,
    FACID        CHAR(4),
    SCHED        CHAR(7),
    ROOM         CHAR(4),
    PRIMARY KEY (COURSE#),
    FOREIGN KEY (FACID) REFERENCES FACULTY);
```

Notice that we specified both primary keys, STUID and COURSE#, as NOT NULL. We also chose to make STUNAME NOT NULL. We identified FACID, the primary key of the FACULTY table, as a foreign key in the CLASS table. The system will check to ensure that the FACID of every CLASS record inserted matches some FACID in the FACULTY table. We added optional extra spaces within and between column definitions to make the statements more readable. The remaining two tables for our example are created using similar statements.

8.3.2 *Create Index*

DB2 allows any number of **indexes** for a base table. All DB2 indexes are **B trees**, which are stored in separate index files, usually close to the tables they index. Indexes can be created on single fields or combinations of fields. The presence of an index, especially a clustered one, can have a tremendous effect on performance. However, since indexes must be updated by the system every time the underlying tables are updated, additional overhead is required. Aside from choosing which indexes will exist, users have no control over the use or maintenance of indexes. The system chooses which index, if any, to use in searching for records.

The command for creating an index is

```
CREATE [UNIQUE] INDEX index-name ON base-table-name
(col-name [order] [,col-name [order]]...) [CLUSTER] ;
```

If the UNIQUE specification is used, uniqueness of the indexed field or combination of fields will be enforced by the system. We certainly want this specification for our primary key, and possibly for other fields as well—for example, for candidate keys. Although indexes can be created at any time, we may have a problem if we try to create a unique index after the table has records stored in it, because the values stored for the indexed field or fields may already contain duplicates. In this case the system will not allow the unique index to be created. Therefore, we should make it a practice to create unique indexes at least for key fields at the same time we create the tables. For the STUDENT table, then, we should create at least the following index:

```
CREATE UNIQUE INDEX XSID ON STUDENT (STUID);
```

Index names follow the same rules as table names, but it is a good idea to begin with an X. This helps the reader to see that a particular file is an index file rather than a data file. In addition, the name should be chosen to indicate which field or fields are used in the index.

Any number of columns, regardless of where they appear in the table, may be used in an index. The first column named determines major order, the second gives minor order, and so on. For each column, we may specify that the order is ascending, ASC, or descending, DESC, with ASC being the default. If we write

```
CREATE INDEX XFDPTFNAME ON FACULTY (DEPT, FACNAME);
```

then an index file called XFDPTFNAME will be created for the FACULTY table. Entries will be in alphabetical order by department and by faculty name within each department.

The optional CLUSTER specification may be used for only one index for each table. Using this option, the system will store records with the same or similar values for the indexed field(s) close together physically—on the same page, on the same cylinder, or on adjacent cylinders, if possible. If a second clustered index were permitted, it would require a different physical placement of records in storage, so we are necessarily limited to one such index. If we create a clustered index for the field(s) used most often for retrieval, we can substantially improve performance for those applications needing that particular order of retrieval, since seek time and read time will be minimized.

8.3.3 *Alter Table*

Once a table has been created, users may find that it would be more useful if it contained an additional data item. The dynamic nature of DB2 makes it easy to change existing base tables by adding a new column on the right. The form of the command is

```
ALTER TABLE base-table-name ADD column-name data-type;
```

Notice the absence of the NOT NULL specification for the column. An ALTER TABLE command causes the new field to be added to all records already stored in the table, and null values to be assigned to that field in all existing records. Newly inserted records, of course, will have the additional field, but we are not permitted to specify no nulls even for them.

To add a new column, CTITLE, to our CLASS table, we write

```
ALTER TABLE CLASS
     ADD  CTITLE      CHAR(30);
```

The format of the CLASS table is now

```
CLASS(COURSE#,FACID,SCHED,ROOM,CTITLE)
```

All old CLASS records now have null values for CTITLE, but we can fill in a title for any new CLASS records we insert, and update old CLASS records by adding titles to them.

8.3.4 *Drop Table*

DB2 allows a table to be dropped at any time by the SQL command

```
DROP TABLE base-table-name;
```

When this statement is executed, the table itself and all records contained in it are removed. In addition, all indexes and, as we shall see later, all views that depend on it are dropped. Naturally, the DBA would wish to confer with potential users of the table before taking such a drastic step.

8.3.5 *Drop Index*

Any existing index can be destroyed by the command

```
DROP INDEX index-name;
```

The effect of this change may or may not be seen in performance. Recall that users cannot specify when the system is to use an index. Therefore, it is possible that an index exists which is never actually used, and its destruction would have no effect on performance. However, the loss of an efficient index that is used by the system for many retrievals would certainly affect performance. When an index is dropped, any access plans that depend on it are marked as invalid. When an application calls them, a new access plan is devised to replace the old one.

8.4 *Manipulating the Database*

The SQL DML statements are

```
SELECT
UPDATE
INSERT
DELETE
```

8.4.1 *Introduction to the SELECT Statement*

The SELECT statement is used for retrieval of data. It is a very powerful command, performing the equivalent of relational algebra's SELECT, PROJECT, and JOIN, as well as other functions, in a single simple statement. There are, however, some relational algebra operations, such as the outerjoin, that are not included in current implementations of SQL. The general form of SELECT is

```
SELECT [DISTINCT] col-name [,col-name]...
FROM table-name [,table-name]...
[WHERE predicate]
[GROUP BY col-name [,col-name]...[HAVING predicate]]
[ORDER BY col-name [,col-name]...];
```

Notice that this statement is nonprocedural because it specifies what is to be retrieved, not how it is to be done. The system, not the user, is responsible for navigating the database. The result of the query is a table, because the system is closed under the SELECT operation. The many variations of this statement will be illustrated by the examples that follow. All of these use the STUDENT, FACULTY, CLASS, and/or ENROLL tables as they appear in Figure 8.2.

■ Example 1. Simple Retrieval with Condition

PROBLEM: Get names, IDs, and number of credits of all math majors.

SOLUTION: The information requested appears on the STUDENT table. From that table we will select only the rows that have a value of 'Math' for MAJOR.

STUDENT	STUID	STUNAME	MAJOR	CREDITS
	S1001	Smith,Tom	History	90
	S1010	Burns,Edward	Art	63
	S1015	Jones,Mary	Math	42
	S1002	Chin,Ann	Math	36
	S1020	Rivera,Jane	CSC	15
	S1013	McCarthy,Owen	Math	9

FACULTY	FACID	FACNAME	DEPT	RANK
	F101	Adams	Art	Professor
	F202	Smith	History	Associate
	F105	Tanaka	CSC	Instructor
	F110	Byrne	Math	Assistant
	F221	Smith	CSC	Professor

CLASS	COURSE#	FACID	SCHED	ROOM
	ART103A	F101	MWF9	H221
	CSC201A	F105	TUTHF10	M110
	MTH101B	F110	MTUTH9	H225
	HST205A	F202	MWF11	H221
	MTH103C	F110	MWF11	H225
	CSC203A	F105	MTHF12	M110

ENROLL	COURSE#	STUID	GRADE
	ART103A	S1001	A
	CSC201A	S1020	B
	CSC201A	S1002	F
	ART103A	S1010	
	ART103A	S1002	D
	MTH101B	S1020	A
	HST205A	S1001	C
	MTH103C	S1010	
	MTH103C	S1002	B

Figure 8.2 Tables for DML Commands

For those rows, we will display only the STUNAME, STUID, and CREDITS columns. Notice that we are doing the equivalent of relational algebra's SELECT (in finding the rows) and PROJECT (in displaying only certain columns). We are also rearranging the columns.

SQL QUERY:

```
SELECT    STUNAME, STUID, CREDITS
FROM      STUDENT
WHERE     MAJOR = 'Math';
```

RESULT:

```
STUNAME          STUID   CREDITS
----------       -----   -------
Jones,Mary       S1015   42
Chin,Ann         S1002   36
McCarthy,Owen    S1013   9
```

■ Example 2. Use of Asterisk Notation

PROBLEM: Get all information about CSC faculty.

SOLUTION: We want the entire FACULTY record of any faculty member with DEPT value of 'CSC'. Since many SQL retrievals require all columns of a single table, there is a short way of expressing "all columns," by using an asterisk in place of the column names in the SELECT line.

SQL QUERY:

```
SELECT *
FROM   FACULTY
WHERE  DEPT = 'CSC';
```

RESULT:

```
FACID   FACNAME DEPT    RANK
------  ------- ----    ----
F105    Tanaka  CSC     Instructor
F221    Smith   CSC     Professor
```

The query is exactly the same as

```
SELECT FACID, FACNAME, DEPT, RANK
FROM   FACULTY
WHERE  DEPT = 'CSC';
```

Users who access a DB2 database through a host language are usually advised to avoid using the asterisk notation. The danger is that an additional column might be added to a table after a program has been written. The program will then retrieve the value of that new column with each record and will not have a matching program variable for the value, causing a loss of correspondence between database variables and program variables.

■ Example 3. Retrieval Without Condition, Use of "Distinct," Use of Qualified Names

PROBLEM: Get the course number of all courses in which students are enrolled.

SOLUTION: We go to the ENROLL table rather than the CLASS table, because it is possible that there is a CLASS record for a planned class in which no one is enrolled. From the ENROLL table, we will list all the COURSE# values.

SQL QUERY:

```
SELECT COURSE#
FROM   ENROLL;
```

RESULT:

```
COURSE#
-------
ART103A
CSC201A
CSC201A
ART103A
ART103A
MTH101B
HST205A
MTH103C
MTH103C
```

Since we did not need a predicate, we did not use the WHERE line. Notice that there are several duplicates in our result because, unlike the relational algebra PROJECT, the SQL SELECT does not eliminate duplicates when it "projects" over a column or columns. To eliminate the duplicates, we use the DISTINCT option in the SELECT line. If we wrote

```
SELECT DISTINCT COURSE#
FROM   ENROLL;
```

the result would be

```
COURSE#
------
ART103A
CSC201A
MTH101B
HST205A
MTH103C
```

In any retrieval, especially if there is a possibility of confusion because the same column name appears on two different tables, we can use qualified names for the columns. We do this by specifying "table-name.col-name". In this example, we could have written

```
SELECT  DISTINCT  ENROLL.COURSE#
FROM    ENROLL;
```

In this example, it is not necessary to use the qualified name, since the FROM line tells the system to use the ENROLL table, and column names are always unique within a table. However, it is never wrong to use a qualified name, and it is sometimes necessary to do so when two or more tables appear in the FROM line.

■ Example 4. Retrieving a Table

PROBLEM: Get all information about all students.

SOLUTION: Since we want all columns of the STUDENT table, we will use the asterisk notation. Since we want all the records in the table, we omit the WHERE line.

SQL QUERY:

```
SELECT *
FROM   STUDENT;
```

RESULT: The result is the entire STUDENT table.

■ Example 5. Use of ORDER BY

PROBLEM: Get names and IDs of all faculty members, arranged in alphabetical order by name.

SOLUTION: The ORDER BY option in the SQL SELECT allows us to order the retrieved records in ascending (ASC) or descending (DESC) order on any field or combination of fields, regardless of whether that field appears in the result.

SQL QUERY:

```
SELECT     FACNAME, FACID
FROM       FACULTY
ORDER BY   FACNAME;
```

RESULT:

```
FACNAME          FACID
--------         -----
Adams            F101
Byrne            F110
Smith            F202
Smith            F221
Tanaka           F105
```

Note the duplicate name of 'Smith'. Since we did not specify minor order, the system will arrange these two in any order it chooses. We could break the "tie" by giving a minor order, as follows:

```
SELECT    FACNAME, FACID
FROM      FACULTY
ORDER BY  FACNAME, DEPT;
```

Now the Smith records will be reversed, since F221 is assigned to CSC, which is alphabetically before History.

■ Example 6. Use of Multiple Conditions

PROBLEM: Get names of all math majors who have more than 30 credits.

SOLUTION: From the STUDENT table, we choose those rows where the major is 'Math' and the number of credits is greater than 30. We express these two conditions by connecting them with AND.

SQL QUERY:

```
SELECT  STUNAME
FROM    STUDENT
WHERE   MAJOR = 'Math' AND CREDITS > 30;
```

RESULT:

```
STUNAME
-------
Jones,Mary
Chin,Ann
```

The predicate can be made as complicated as needed by using the standard comparison operators =, >, <, >=, <=, ~=, ~>, ~<, and the standard logical operators AND, OR, and NOT, with parentheses, if needed or desired, to show order of evaluation.

8.4.2 *SELECT Using Multiple Tables*

■ Example 7. Natural Join

PROBLEM: Find IDs and names of all students taking ART103A.

SOLUTION: This question requires the use of two tables. We first look in the ENROLL table for records where the COURSE# is 'ART103A'. We then look up the STUDENT table for records with matching STUID values and join those records into a new table. From this table we find the STUNAME. This is similar to the JOIN operation in relational algebra. SQL allows us to do a natural join (Chapter 6) by naming the tables involved and expressing in the predicate the condition that the records match on the common field.

SQL QUERY:

```
SELECT    ENROLL.STUID, STUNAME
FROM      STUDENT, ENROLL
WHERE     COURSE# = 'ART103A'
          AND ENROLL.STUID = STUDENT.STUID;
```

RESULT:

```
STUID            STUNAME
-------          ---------
S1001            Smith,Tom
S1010            Burns,Edward
S1002            Chin,Ann
```

Notice that we use the qualified name for STUID in the SELECT line. We could have written STUDENT.STUID instead of ENROLL.STUID, but we need to use the table name, since STUID appears on both of the tables in the FROM line. We do not need to use the qualified name for COURSE# since it does not appear on the STUDENT table. The fact that it appears on the CLASS table is irrelevant, since that table is not mentioned in the FROM line. Of course, we must write both qualified names for STUID in the WHERE line.

You may wonder whether the condition "ENROLL.STUID=STUDENT.STUID" is necessary. The answer is that it is essential. When DB2 performs a join, it acts as if it first forms a Cartesian product (Chapter 5), so an intermediate table containing the combinations of all records from the STUDENT table with the records of the ENROLL table is (theoretically) formed. Even if the system restricts itself to records in ENROLL that satisfy the condition "COURSE#='ART103A'", the intermediate table numbers 6 * 3 or 18 records. For example, one of those intermediate records is

```
S1015 Jones,Mary Math 42 ART103A S1001 A
```

We are not interested in this record, since this student is not one of the people in the ART103A class. Therefore, we add the condition that the STUID values must be equal. This reduces the intermediate table to three records.

■ Example 8. Natural Join with Ordering

PROBLEM: Find STUID and GRADE of all students taking any course taught by the faculty member whose FACID is F110. Arrange in order by STUID.

SOLUTION: We need to look at the CLASS table to find the COURSE# of all courses taught by F110. We then look at the ENROLL table for records with matching COURSE# values and form the join of the tables. From this we find the corresponding STUID and GRADE. Since we are using two tables, we will write this as a join.

SQL QUERY:

```
SELECT    STUID,GRADE
FROM      CLASS,ENROLL
WHERE     FACID = 'F110' AND CLASS.COURSE# = ENROLL.COURSE#
ORDER BY STUID ASC;
```

RESULT:

```
STUID   GRADE
------  -----
S1002   B
S1010
S1020   A
```

■ Example 9. Natural Join of Three Tables

PROBLEM: Find course numbers and the names and majors of all students enrolled in the courses taught by faculty member F110.

SOLUTION: As in Example 8, we need to start at the CLASS table to find the COURSE# of all courses taught by F110. We then compare these with COURSE# values in the ENROLL table to find the STUID values of all students in those courses. Now we look at the STUDENT table to find the names and majors of all those students.

SQL QUERY:

```
SELECT   ENROLL.COURSE#, STUNAME, MAJOR
FROM     CLASS, ENROLL, STUDENT
WHERE    FACID = 'F110'
         AND CLASS.COURSE# = ENROLL.COURSE#
         AND ENROLL.STUID = STUDENT.STUID;
```

RESULT:

```
COURSE# STUNAME          MAJOR
------- ---------        -------
MTH101B Rivera,Jane      CSC
MTH103C Burns,Edward     Art
MTH103C Chin,Ann         Math
```

This was a natural join of three tables, and required two sets of common columns. We used the condition of equality for both of the sets in the WHERE line. You may have noticed that the order of the table names in the FROM line corresponded to the order in which they appeared in our plan of solution, but that is not necessary. SQL ignores the order in which we name the tables in the FROM line. The same is true of the order in which we write the various conditions that make up the predicate in the WHERE line. DB2 makes its own decisions about which table to use first and which condition to check first. It has an optimizer that identifies the most efficient method of accomplishing any retrieval before choosing a plan.

■ Example 10. Use of Aliases

PROBLEM: Get a list of all courses that meet in the same room, with their schedules and room numbers.

SOLUTION: This query requires comparing the CLASS table with itself, and it would be handy if there were two copies of the table so that we could do a natural join. DB2 allows us to pretend that there are two copies of a table by giving it two "aliases," for example, COPY1 and COPY2, and then treating these names as if they were the names of two distinct tables. We introduce the "aliases" in the FROM line by writing them immediately after the real table names. Then we have the aliases available for use in the other lines of the query.

SQL QUERY:

```
SELECT COPY1.COURSE#, COPY1.SCHED, COPY1.ROOM,
       COPY2.COURSE#, COPY2.SCHED
FROM   CLASS COPY1, CLASS COPY2
WHERE  COPY1.ROOM = COPY2.ROOM
       AND COPY1.COURSE# < COPY2.COURSE# ;
```

RESULT:

COPY1.COURSE#	COPY1.SCHED	COPY1.ROOM	COPY2.COURSE#	COPY2.SCHED
ART103A	MWF9	H221	HST205A	MWF11
CSC201A	TUTHF10	M110	CSC203A	MTHF12
MTH101B	MTUTH9	H225	MTH103C	MWF11

Notice that we had to use the qualified names in the SELECT line even before we introduced the "aliases." This was necessary because every column in the CLASS table now appears twice, once in each copy. We added the second condition, "COPY1.COURSE# < COPY2.COURSE#", to keep every course from being included, since every course obviously satisfies the requirement that it meets in the same room as itself. It also keeps records with the two courses reversed from appearing—for example, since we have

```
ART103A MWF9   H221 HST205A MWF11
```

we do not need the record

```
HST205A MWF11  H221 ART103A MWF9
```

We can introduce aliases in any SELECT, even when they are not required.

■ Example 11. Join Without Equality Condition

PROBLEM: Find all combinations of students and faculty where the student's major is different from the faculty member's department.

SOLUTION: This unusual request is to illustrate a join in which the condition is not equality on a common field. As in relational algebra, a join can be done on any two tables simply by forming the Cartesian product. Although we usually want the natural join as in our previous examples, we might use any type of predicate as the condition for the join. If we want to compare two columns, however, they must have the same domains. In this case the fields we are examining, MAJOR and DEPT, do not have the same name but they have the same domain. Since we are not told which columns to show in the result, we use our judgment.

SQL QUERY:

```
SELECT STUID, STUNAME, MAJOR, FACID, FACNAME, DEPT
FROM   STUDENT, FACULTY
WHERE  STUDENT.MAJOR  ~=  FACULTY.DEPT;
```

RESULT:

```
STUID  STUNAME          MAJOR     FACID   FACNAME  DEPT
-----  ---------        -------   ------  -------  ----
S1001  Smith,Tom        History   F101    Adams    Art
S1001  Smith,Tom        History   F105    Tanaka   CSC
S1001  Smith,Tom        History   F110    Byrne    Math
S1001  Smith,Tom        History   F221    Smith    CSC
S1010  Burns,Edward     Art       F202    Smith    History
.......................................................
.......................................................
.......................................................
S1013  McCarthy,Owen    Math      F221    Smith    CSC
```

Notice that we used qualified names in the WHERE line. This was not really necessary, since each column name was unique, but we did so to make the condition easier to follow.

■ Example 12. Using a Subquery with Equality

PROBLEM: Find the numbers of all the courses taught by Byrne of the Math Department.

SOLUTION: We already know how to do this by using a natural join, but there is another way of finding the solution. Instead of imagining a join from which we choose records with the same FACID, we could visualize this as two separate queries. For the first one, we go to the FACULTY table and find the record with FACNAME of Byrne and DEPT of Math. We make a note of the corresponding FACID. Then we take the result of that query, namely F110, and search the CLASS table for records with that value in FACID. Once we find them, we display the COURSE#. SQL allows us to sequence these queries so that the result of the first can be used in the second, as follows:

SQL QUERY:

```
SELECT  COURSE#
FROM    CLASS
WHERE   FACID  =
        (SELECT FACID
        FROM    FACULTY
        WHERE   FACNAME = 'Byrne'
                AND DEPT = 'Math');
```

RESULT:

```
COURSE#
------
MTH101B
MTH103C
```

Note that this result could have been produced by the following SQL query, using a join:

```
SELECT  COURSE#
FROM    CLASS, FACULTY
WHERE   FACNAME = 'Byrne'
        AND DEPT = 'Math'
        AND CLASS.FACID = FACULTY.FACID;
```

A subquery can be considered in place of a join if the result to be displayed is contained in a single table and the data retrieved from the subquery consists of only one column. The subquery, which is done first, is the one in parentheses, following the WHERE line. The main query is performed using the result of the subquery. Normally, you name only one table in the subquery and another table in the main query, and you want the value of some field in the table mentioned in the main query to match the value of some field from the table in the subquery. In this example we knew we would get only one value from the subquery, since FACID is the key of FACULTY, so a unique value would be produced. However, conditions other than equality could be used. Any single comparison operator can be used in a subquery from which you know a single value will be produced. Since the subquery is performed first, the SELECT...FROM...WHERE of the subquery is actually replaced by the value retrieved, so the main query is equivalent to the following:

```
SELECT  COURSE#
FROM    CLASS
WHERE   FACID = ('F110');
```

■ Example 13. Subquery Using IN

PROBLEM: Find the names and IDs of all faculty members who teach a class in room H221.

SOLUTION: First we notice that we need two tables, CLASS and FACULTY, to answer this question. We also observe that the names and IDs both appear on the FACULTY table, so we have a choice of a join or a subquery. If we use a subquery, we begin with the CLASS table to find FACID values for any courses that meet in Room H221. We find two such entries, so we make a note of those values. Then we go to the FACULTY table and compare the FACID value of each record on that table with the two ID values from CLASS, and display the corresponding FACID and FACNAME.

SQL QUERY:

```
SELECT  FACNAME, FACID
FROM    FACULTY
WHERE   FACID  IN
        (SELECT FACID
        FROM    CLASS
        WHERE   ROOM = 'H221');
```

RESULT:

```
FACNAME FACID
------- -----
Adams   F101
Smith   F202
```

In the WHERE line of the main query, we used IN rather than =, because the result of the subquery is a set of values rather than a single value. We are saying that we want the FACID in FACULTY to match any member of the set of values we obtain from the subquery. When the subquery is replaced by the values retrieved, the main query becomes

```
SELECT  FACNAME, FACID
FROM    FACULTY
WHERE   FACID IN ('F101','F202');
```

The IN is a more general form of a subquery than the comparison operator, which is restricted to the case where a single value is produced. We can also use the negative form NOT IN, which will evaluate to true for any record having a value for the specified field that is not in the set of values retrieved by the subquery.

■ Example 14. Nested Subqueries

PROBLEM: Get an alphabetical list of names and IDs of all students in any class taught by F110.

SOLUTION: We need three tables, STUDENT, ENROLL, and CLASS, to answer this question. However, the values to be displayed appear on one table, STUDENT, so we will try a subquery. First we check the CLASS table to find the COURSE# of all courses taught by F110. We find two values, MTH101B and MTH103C. Next we go to the ENROLL table to find the STUID of all students in either of these courses. We find three values, S1020, S1010, and S1002. We now look at the STUDENT table to find the records with matching STUID values, and display both the STUID and STUNAME, in alphabetical order by name.

SQL QUERY:

```
SELECT  STUNAME, STUID
FROM    STUDENT
WHERE   STUID  IN
        (SELECT STUID
        FROM    ENROLL
        WHERE   COURSE#  IN
                (SELECT COURSE#
                FROM    CLASS
                WHERE FACID = 'F110'))
ORDER BY STUNAME ASC;
```

RESULT:

```
STUNAME          STUID
------------     -----
Burns,Edward     S1010
Chin,Ann         S1002
Rivera,Jane      S1020
```

In execution, the most deeply nested SELECT is done first, and it is replaced by the values retrieved, so we have

```
SELECT  STUNAME, STUID
FROM    STUDENT
WHERE   STUID  IN
        (SELECT STUID
        FROM    ENROLL
        WHERE   COURSE# IN
                ('MTH101B', 'MTH103C'))
ORDER BY STUNAME ASC;
```

Next the subquery on ENROLL is done, and we get

```
SELECT  STUNAME, STUID
FROM    STUDENT
WHERE   STUID  IN
        ('S1020', 'S1010', 'S1002')
ORDER BY STUNAME ASC;
```

Note that the ordering refers to the final result, not to any intermediate steps.

■ Example 15. Query Using EXISTS

PROBLEM: Find the names of all students enrolled in CSC201A.

SOLUTION: We already know how to write this using a join or a subquery with IN. However, another way of expressing this query is to use the existential quantifier, EXISTS, with a subquery.

SQL QUERY:

```
SELECT  STUNAME
FROM    STUDENT
WHERE   EXISTS
        (SELECT *
        FROM    ENROLL
        WHERE   STUDENT.STUID = ENROLL.STUID
        AND COURSE# = 'CSC201A');
```

RESULT:

```
STUNAME
------------
Rivera, Jane
Chin,Ann
```

This query could be phrased as "Find the STUNAME of all students such that there exists an ENROLL record containing their STUID and COURSE# of CSC201A." The test for inclusion is the existence of such a record. If it exists, the "EXISTS (SELECT* FROM...);" evaluates to true. Notice that we needed to use the name of the main-query-table (STUDENT) in the subquery to express the condition STUDENT.STUID = ENROLL.STUID. In general, we avoid mentioning a table not listed in the FROM for that particular query, but it is necessary and permissible to do so in this case.

■ Example 16. Query Using NOT EXISTS

PROBLEM: Find the names of all students who are not enrolled in CSC201A.

SOLUTION: Unlike Example 15, we cannot readily express this using a join or an IN subquery. Instead, we will use NOT EXISTS.

SQL QUERY:

```
SELECT  STUNAME
FROM    STUDENT
WHERE   NOT EXISTS
        (SELECT *
        FROM ENROLL
        WHERE STUDENT.STUID = ENROLL.STUID
        AND COURSE# = 'CSC201A');
```

RESULT:

```
STUNAME
----------
Smith,Tom
Burns,Edward
Jones,Mary
McCarthy,Owen
```

We could phrase this query as "Select student names from the STUDENT table such that there is no ENROLL record containing their STUID values with COURSE# of CSC201A."

8.4.3 *SELECT with Other Operators*

■ Example 17. Query Using UNION

PROBLEM: Get the IDs of all faculty who are assigned to the History Department at either the main campus or the branch campus. Assume tht BRANCHFAC contains data about faculty at the branch campus and that it contains a record with FACID of F500 and DEPT of History.

SOLUTION: It is easy to write a query for either of the conditions, and we can combine the results from the two queries by using a UNION operator. The UNION in SQL is the standard relational algebra operator for set union, and works in the expected way, eliminating duplicates.

SQL QUERY:

```
SELECT  FACID
FROM    FACULTY
WHERE   DEPT = 'History'
UNION
SELECT  FACID
FROM    BRANCHFAC
WHERE   DEPT = 'History';
```

RESULT:

```
FACID
-----
F202
F500
```

■ Example 18. Using Functions

PROBLEM: Find the total number of students enrolled in ART103A.

SOLUTION: Although this is a simple problem, we are unable to express it as an SQL query at the moment, because we have not yet seen any way to operate on collections of rows or columns. We need some functions to do so. SQL has five built-in functions: COUNT, SUM, AVG, MAX, and MIN. The one we want is COUNT, which returns the number of values in a column.

SQL QUERY:

```
SELECT  COUNT(DISTINCT STUID)
FROM    ENROLL
WHERE   COURSE# = 'ART103A';
```

RESULT:

```
3
```

The built-in functions operate on a single column of a table. Each of them eliminates null values first, and operates only on the remaining nonnull values. The functions return a single value, defined as follows:

- COUNT returns the number of values in the column.
- SUM returns the sum of the values in the column.
- AVG returns the mean of the values in the column.
- MAX returns the largest value in the column.
- MIN returns the smallest value in the column.

COUNT, MAX, and MIN apply to both numeric and nonnumeric fields, but SUM and AVG may be used on numeric fields only. The collating sequence is used to determine order of nonnumeric data. If we want to eliminate duplicate values before starting, we use the word DISTINCT before the column name in the SELECT line. COUNT(*) is a special use of COUNT. Its purpose is to count all the rows of a table, regardless of whether null values or duplicate values occur. Except for COUNT(*) we must always use DISTINCT with the COUNT function, as we did in the previous example. If we use DISTINCT with MAX or MIN, it will have no effect, since the largest or smallest value remains the same even if two tuples share it. However, DISTINCT usually has an effect on the result of SUM or AVG, so the user should understand whether or not duplicates should be included in computing these. Function references appear in the SELECT line of a query or a subquery.

ADDITIONAL FUNCTION EXAMPLES:

1. Find the number of departments that have faculty in them. Since we do not wish to count a department more than once, we use DISTINCT here.

```
SELECT   COUNT(DISTINCT DEPT)
FROM     FACULTY;
```

2. Find the average number of credits students have. We do not want to use DISTINCT here, since if two students have the same number of credits, both should be counted in the average.

```
SELECT   AVG(CREDITS)
FROM     STUDENT;
```

3. Find the student with the largest number of credits. Since we want the student's credits to equal the maximum, we need to find that maximum first, so we use a subquery to find it.

```
SELECT   STUID, STUNAME
FROM     STUDENT
WHERE    CREDITS =
         (SELECT MAX(CREDITS)
         FROM STUDENT);
```

4. Find the ID of the student(s) with the highest grade in any course. Since we want the highest grade, it might appear that we should use the MAX function here. A closer look at the table reveals that the grades are letters such as A, B, C, and so on. For this scale, the best grade is the one that is earliest in the alphabet, so we actually want MIN.

```
SELECT   STUID
FROM     ENROLL
WHERE    GRADE =
         (SELECT MIN(GRADE)
         FROM  ENROLL);
```

5. Find names and IDs of students who have less than the average number of credits.

```
SELECT  STUNAME, STUID
FROM    STUDENT
WHERE   CREDITS <
        (SELECT AVG(CREDITS)
        FROM    STUDENT);
```

■ Example 19. Using an Expression

PROBLEM: Assuming that each course is three credits, list, for each student, the number of courses that he or she has completed.

SOLUTION: We can calculate the number of courses by dividing the number of credits by 3. We can use the expression CREDITS/3 in the SELECT to display the number of courses. Since we have no such column name, we will use a string constant as a label. String constants that appear in the SELECT line are simply printed in the result.

SQL QUERY:

```
SELECT  STUID,'Number of courses =', CREDITS/3
FROM    STUDENT;
```

RESULT:

```
STUID
-----   -------------------   ---
S1001   Number of courses =   30
S1010   Number of courses =   21
S1015   Number of courses =   14
S1002   Number of courses =   12
S1020   Number of courses =   5
S1013   Number of courses =   3
```

By combining constants, column names, arithmetic operators, built-in functions, and parentheses, the user can customize retrievals.

■ Example 20. Use of GROUP BY

PROBLEM: For each course, show the number of students enrolled.

SOLUTION: We want to use the COUNT function, but need to apply it to each course individually. The GROUP BY allows us to lump together all the records with a single value in the specified field. Then we can apply any function to any field in each group, provided that the result is a single value for the group.

SQL QUERY:

```
SELECT    COURSE#, COUNT(*)
FROM      ENROLL
GROUP BY  COURSE#;
```

RESULT:

```
COURSE#
-------  --
ART103A  3
CSC201A  2
MTH101B  1
HST205A  1
MTH103C  2
```

Note that we could have used COUNT(DISTINCT STUID) in place of COUNT(*) in this query.

■ Example 21. Use of HAVING

PROBLEM: Find all courses in which fewer than three students are enrolled.

SOLUTION: This is a question about a characteristic of the groups formed in Example 20. HAVING is used to determine which groups have some quality, just as WHERE is used with tuples to determine which records have some quality. You are not permitted to use HAVING without a GROUP BY, and the predicate in the HAVING line must have a single value for each group.

SQL QUERY:

```
SELECT     COURSE#
FROM       ENROLL
GROUP BY   COURSE#
HAVING     COUNT(*) < 3 ;
```

RESULT:

```
COURSE#
--------
CSC201A
MTH101B
HST205A
MTH103C
```

■ Example 22. Use of LIKE

PROBLEM: Get details of all MTH courses.

SOLUTION: We do not wish to specify the exact course numbers, but we want the first three letters of COURSE# to be MTH. SQL allows us to use LIKE in the predicate to show a pattern string for character fields. Records whose specified columns match the pattern will be retrieved.

SQL QUERY:

```
SELECT *
FROM CLASS
WHERE COURSE# LIKE 'MTH%' ;
```

RESULT:

```
COURSE#   FACID   SCHED        ROOM
--------  ------  ------------ ----
MTH101B   F110    MTUTH9       H225
MTH103C   F110    MWF11        H225
```

In the pattern string, we can use the following symbols:

- % The percent character stands for any sequence of characters of any length >= 0.
- _ The underscore character stands for any single character.

All other characters in the pattern stand for themselves.

EXAMPLES:

- **COURSE# LIKE 'MTH%'** means that the first three letters must be MTH, but the rest of the string can be any characters.
- **STUID LIKE 'S____'** means that there must be five characters, the first of which must be an S
- **SCHED LIKE '%9'** means any sequence of characters, of length at least 1, with the last character a 9.
- **COURSE# LIKE '%101%'** means a sequence of characters of any length containing 101. Note the 101 could be the first, last, or only characters, as well as being somewhere in the middle of the string.
- **FACNAME NOT LIKE 'A%'** means that the name cannot begin with an A.

■ Example 23. Use of NULL

PROBLEM: Find the STUID and COURSE# of all students whose grades in that course are missing.

SOLUTION: We can see from the ENROLL table that there are two such records. You might think they could be accessed by specifying that the grades are not A, B, C, D, or F, but that is not the case. A null grade is considered to have "unknown" as a value, so it is impossible to judge whether it is equal to or not equal to another grade. If we put the condition "WHERE GRADE ~='A' AND GRADE ~='B' AND GRADE ~='C' AND GRADE ~='D' AND GRADE ~='F'" we would get an empty table back, instead of the two records we want. SQL uses the logical expression

```
column-name IS [NOT] NULL
```

to test for null values in a column.

SQL QUERY:

```
SELECT   COURSE#,STUID
FROM     ENROLL
WHERE    GRADE IS NULL;
```

RESULT:

```
COURSE#          STUID
--------         ------
ART103A          S1010
MTH103C          S1010
```

Notice that it is illegal to write "WHERE GRADE = NULL", because a predicate involving comparison operators with NULL will evaluate to "unknown" rather than "true" or "false." Also, the WHERE line is the only one on which NULL can appear in a SELECT statement.

8.4.4 *The UPDATE Operator*

The UPDATE operator is used to change values in records already stored in a table. It is used on one table at a time, and can change zero, one, or many records, depending on the predicate. Its form is

```
UPDATE table-name SET column-name = expression [column-name =
expression]... [WHERE predicate];
```

Notice it is not necessary to specify the present value of the field, although the present value may be used in the expression to determine the new value. The SET statement is actually an assignment statement and works in the usual way.

■ Example 24. Updating a Single Field of One Record

Change the major of S1020 to Music.

```
UPDATE STUDENT
SET    MAJOR = 'Music'
WHERE  STUID  =  'S1020';
```

■ Example 25. Updating Several Fields of One Record

Change Tanaka's department to MIS and rank to Assistant.

```
UPDATE  FACULTY
SET     DEPT = 'MIS'
        RANK = 'Assistant'
WHERE   FACNAME = 'Tanaka';
```

■ Example 26. Updating Using NULL

To insert a null value into a field that already has an actual value, we must use the form

```
SET column-name = NULL
```

Change the major of S1013 from Math to NULL.

```
UPDATE STUDENT
SET    MAJOR = NULL
WHERE  STUID = 'S1013';
```

■ Example 27. Updating Several Records

Change grades of all students in CSC201A to A.

```
UPDATE ENROLL
SET    GRADE = 'A'
WHERE  COURSE# = 'CSC201A';
```

■ Example 28. Updating All Records

Give all students three extra credits.

```
UPDATE STUDENT
SET    CREDITS = CREDITS + 3;
```

Notice that we do not need the WHERE line, since all records are to be updated.

■ Example 29. Updating with a Subquery

Change the room to B220 for all courses taught by Tanaka.

```
UPDATE CLASS
SET    ROOM = 'B220'
WHERE  FACID =
        (SELECT FACID
       FROM    FACULTY
       WHERE   FACNAME = 'Tanaka');
```

8.4.5 *The INSERT Operator*

The INSERT operator is used to put new records into a table. Normally, it is not used to load an entire table, since DB2 has a load utility to handle that task. However, the INSERT is useful for adding a small number of records to a table. Its form is

```
INSERT INTO table-name [(col-name [,col-name]...)] VALUES
(constant [,constant]...);
```

■ Example 30. Inserting a Single Record

Insert a new faculty record with ID of F330, name of Jones, department of CSC, and rank of Instructor.

```
INSERT
INTO    FACULTY (FACID, FACNAME, DEPT, RANK)
VALUES ('F330',  'Jones', 'CSC', 'Instructor');
```

Since we are inserting values for all fields, it is not necessary to list the fields, and we could have written

```
INSERT
INTO    FACULTY
VALUES ('F330',   'Jones', 'CSC', 'Instructor');
```

■ Example 31. Inserting a Record with Null Value in a Field

Insert a new student record with ID of S1031, name of Maria Bono, 0 credits, and no major.

```
INSERT
INTO    STUDENT (STUNAME, STUID, CREDITS)
VALUES ( 'Maria Bono', 'S1031', 0);
```

Notice that we rearranged the field names, but there is no confusion since it is understood the order of values matches the order of fields named in the INTO, regardless of their order in the table. Also notice that the zero is an actual value for CREDITS, not a null value. MAJOR will be set to null, since we excluded it from the field list in the INTO line.

■ Example 32. Inserting Multiple Records into a New Table

Create and fill a new table that shows each course and the number of students enrolled in it.

```
CREATE  TABLE ENROLLMENT
        (COURSE#  CHAR(7) NOT NULL,
        STUDENTS SMALLINT);
```

```
INSERT
INTO        ENROLLMENT (COURSE#, STUDENTS)
SELECT      COURSE#, COUNT(*)
FROM        ENROLL
GROUP BY    COURSE#;
```

Here, we created a new table, ENROLLMENT, and filled it by taking data from an existing table, ENROLL. If ENROLL is as it appears in Figure 8.2, ENROLLMENT now looks like this:

```
ENROLLMENT  COURSE#    STUDENTS
            -------------------------
            ART103A     3
            CSC201A     2
            MTH101B     1
            HST205A     1
            MTH103C     2
```

The ENROLLMENT table is now available for the user to manipulate, just as any other table would be. It can be updated as needed, but it will not be updated automatically when the ENROLL table is updated.

8.4.6 *The DELETE Operator*

The DELETE is used to erase records. The number of records deleted may be zero, one, or many, depending on how many satisfy the predicate. The form of this command is

```
DELETE FROM table-name WHERE predicate;
```

■ Example 33. Deleting a Single Record

Erase the record of student S1020.

```
DELETE
FROM     STUDENT
WHERE    STUID = 'S1020';
```

■ Example 34. Deleting Several Records

Erase all enrollment records for student S1020.

```
DELETE
FROM     ENROLL
WHERE    STUID = 'S1020';
```

■ Example 35. Deleting All Records from a Table

Erase all the class records.

```
DELETE
FROM    CLASS;
```

The CLASS table is now empty, but its structure still remains, so we can add new records to it at any time. You may recall that the DROP TABLE command erases the structure as well as the records.

■ Example 36. DELETE with a Subquery

Erase all enrollment records for Owen McCarthy.

```
DELETE
FROM    ENROLL
WHERE   STUID =
        (SELECT STUID
        FROM    STUDENT
        WHERE   STUNAME = 'Owen McCarthy');
```

Since there are no such records shown in Figure 8.2, this statement has no effect on the present instance of ENROLL.

8.5 *External Views*

As explained in Section 8.2, a DB2 **view** does not correspond exactly to the general external view, but is a **virtual table** derived from one or more underlying base tables. It does not exist in storage in the sense that the base tables do, but is created by selecting specified rows and columns from the base tables, and possibly performing operations on them. The view is **dynamically produced** as the user works with it. To make up a view, the DBA decides which attributes the user needs to access, determines what base tables contain them, and constructs one or more DB2 views to display in table form the values the user should see. An advantage of DB2 is the ease with which the dynamic external model can be created for the user. The reasons for providing views rather than allowing all users to work with base tables are that

- Views allow different users to see the data in different forms, permitting an external model that differs from the conceptual model.
- The view mechanism provides a simple authorization control device, easily created and automatically enforced by the system. View users are unaware of, and cannot access, certain data items.
- Views can free users from complicated DML operations, especially in the case where the views involve joins. The user writes a simple SELECT statement using the view as the named table, and the system takes care of the details of corresponding, more complicated, operations on the base tables to support the view.

- If the database is restructured on the conceptual level, a view may be used to keep the user's model constant. For example, if a table is split by nonloss projection, the original table can always be reconstructed when needed by defining a view that is the join of the new tables.

The following is the most common form of the command used to create a view:

```
CREATE VIEW view-name [(view-col-name [,view-col-name]...)]
AS SELECT col-name [,col-name]... FROM base-table-name [,base-
table-name]... [WHERE predicate];
```

The view name is chosen using the same rules as the table name, and should be unique. Column names in the view can be different from the corresponding column names in the base tables, but they must obey the same rules of construction. If we choose to make them the same, we need not specify them twice, so we leave out the view-col-name line. In the AS SELECT line, we list the names of the columns from the underlying base tables that we wish to include in the view. The order of these names should correspond exactly to the view-col-names, if those are specified. However, columns chosen from the base tables may be rearranged in any desired manner in the view. As in the usual SELECT, the predicate expresses some restriction on the records to be included. A more general form of the CREATE VIEW uses any valid subquery in place of the SELECT we have described.

■ Example 37. Choosing a Vertical and Horizontal Subset of a Table

To create a view for a user who needs to see IDs and names of all history majors, we write

```
CREATE VIEW HISTMAJ (STUDENT-NAME,STUDENT-ID)
AS      SELECT STUNAME,STUID
        FROM STUDENT
        WHERE MAJOR = 'History';
```

Here we renamed the columns from our base table. The user of this view need not know the actual column names.

■ Example 38. Choosing a Vertical Subset of a Table

To obtain a table of all courses with their schedules and rooms we write

```
CREATE VIEW CLASSLOC
AS      SELECT COURSE#,SCHED,ROOM
        FROM CLASS;
```

Notice we did not need a condition here, since we wanted to include all CLASS records. This time we kept the names of the columns as they appear in the base table.

■ Example 39. A View Using Two Tables

Assume that a user needs a table containing the IDs and names of all students in course CSC101. The virtual table can be created by choosing records in ENROLL that have COURSE# of CSC101, matching the STUID of those records with the STUID of the STUDENT records, and taking the corresponding STUNAME from STUDENT. We could express this as a join or a subquery.

```
CREATE VIEW CLASS-LIST
AS      SELECT STUID,STUNAME
        FROM   ENROLL,STUDENT
        WHERE  COURSE# = 'CSC101'
               AND ENROLL.STUID = STUDENT.STUID;
```

■ Example 40. A View of a View

DB2 allows us to define a view derived from a view. For example, we can ask for a subset of the CLASSLOC view by writing

```
CREATE VIEW CLASSLOC2
AS      SELECT    COURSE#, ROOM
        FROM      CLASSLOC;
```

■ Example 41. A View Using a Function

In the SELECT statement in the AS line we can include built-in functions and GROUP BY options. For example, if we want a view of ENROLL that gives COURSE# and the number of students enrolled in each class, we write

```
CREATE VIEW CLASSCOUNT (COURSE#, TOTCOUNT)
AS      SELECT     COURSE#, COUNT(*)
        FROM       ENROLL
        GROUP BY   COURSE#;
```

Notice that we had to supply a name for the second column of the view, since there was none available from the base table.

■ Example 42. Operations on Views

Once a view is created, the user can write SELECT statements to retrieve data through the view. The system maps the user names to the underlying base table names and column names, and performs whatever functions are required to produce the result in the form the user expects. Users can write SQL queries that refer to joins, ordering, grouping, built-in functions, and so on, of views just as if they were operating on base tables. Since the SELECT operation does not change the underlying base tables, there is no restriction on using it with views. The following is an example of a SELECT operation on the CLASSLOC view:

```
SELECT  *
FROM    CLASSLOC
WHERE   ROOM LIKE 'H%';
```

INSERT, DELETE and UPDATE may present problems with views. For example, suppose that we had a view of student records of the form

```
STUDENTVW1(STUNAME, MAJOR, CREDITS)
```

If we were permitted to insert records, any records created through this view would actually be STUDENT records, but would not contain STUID, which is the key of the STUDENT table. Since we would have specified NOT NULL for STUID, we would have to reject any records without this field. However, if we had the view

```
STUDENTVW2(STUID,STUNAME,CREDITS)
```

we would have no problem inserting records, since we would be inserting STUDENT records with a null major field, which is allowable. We could accomplish this by writing a command such as the following

```
INSERT
INTO     STUDENTVW2
VALUES   ('S1040', 'Adam Levine', 30);
```

Now let us consider inserting records into the view CLASSCOUNT, as described in Example 41. This view used the COUNT function on groups of records in the ENROLL table. Obviously, this table was meant to be a dynamic summary of the ENROLL table, rather than being a row and column subset of that table. It would not make sense for us to permit new CLASSCOUNT records to be inserted, since these do not correspond to individual rows or columns of a base table.

The problems we have identified for INSERT apply with minor changes to UPDATE and DELETE as well. As a general rule, DB2 allows these three operations to be performed on views that consist of actual rows and columns of underlying base tables, provided that the primary key is included in the view, and no other NOT NULL problems occur. However, there are other situations in which updates should be allowed, but they are not permitted in DB2's present implementation. This is an area that needs additional refinement.

8.6 The System Catalog

The DB2 catalog can be thought of as a database of information about a database. It contains a summary of the structure of the database as it appears at a given time. The information is kept in table form. Whenever a base table or view is created, entries are automatically made in the catalog about its name, each of its columns, and its creator. When an index is created, similar entries are made, to be used by the optimizer in choosing access plans. Authorization information, telling what privileges each user has, is also stored in the catalog and used by the authorization subsystem, as described in Chapter 13. You can think of the catalog as a system-oriented data dictionary. Some of the important tables in the catalog are the following

```
SYSTABLES(NAME, CREATOR, COLCOUNT, <other data>)
SYSCOLUMNS(NAME, TBNAME, COLTYPE, <other data>)
SYSINDEXES(NAME, TBNAME, CREATOR, <other data>)
```

Figure 8.3 shows the contents of these tables after the sample database in Figure 8.2 has been created.

SYSTABLES	NAME	CREATOR	COLCOUNT	<other data>
	STUDENT	DBA	4	...
	FACULTY	DBA	4	...
	CLASS	DBA	4	...
	ENROLL	DBA	3	...

SYSCOLUMNS	NAME	TBNAME	COLTYPE	<other data>
	STUID	STUDENT	CHAR	...
	STUNAME	STUDENT	CHAR	...
	MAJOR	STUDENT	CHAR	...
	CREDITS	STUDENT	SMALLINT	...
	FACID	FACULTY	CHAR	...
	FACNAME	FACULTY	CHAR	...
	DEPT	FACULTY	CHAR	...
	RANK	FACULTY	CHAR	...
	COURSE#	CLASS	CHAR	...
	FACID	CLASS	CHAR	...
	SCHED	CLASS	CHAR	...
	ROOM	CLASS	CHAR	...
	COURSE#	ENROLL	CHAR	...
	STUID	ENROLL	CHAR	...
	GRADE	ENROLL	CHAR	...

SYSINDEXES	NAME	TBNAME	CREATOR	<other data>
	XSID	STUDENT	DBA	...
	SFID	FACULTY	DBA	...
	SC#	CLASS	DBA	...
	SC#SID	ENROLL	DBA	...

Figure 8.3 The System Catalog

In DB2, the catalog can be queried using SQL SELECT statements, so it is possible for a user to try to find the true conceptual structure of the database using queries such as

```
SELECT  *
FROM    SYSTABLES ;
```

or

```
SELECT  *
FROM    SYSCOLUMNS;
```

In this way, a user whose view includes only a small portion of the database could discover what tables and columns are hidden and possibly gain unauthorized access to them. It is, therefore, important for the DBA to restrict even read access to the system catalog. This authorization information is, of course, stored in the catalog itself.

The catalog is automatically updated by the system when the database structure or authorization information is changed. The usual UPDATE, INSERT, and DELETE commands cannot be used on catalog tables. A form of updating is permitted for a special column of SYSTABLES and SYSCOLUMNS, called the COMMENT column. This column is part of the <other data> section of the tables pictured in Figure 8.3. Each row of these tables has room for a COMMENT, which is a string that can contain whatever information the user chooses. This is a natural place to insert user-oriented definitions of the objects, much as we did in our sample project data dictionary at the end of Chapter 2. The following statements show how to insert or update comments for tables and columns:

```
COMMENT ON TABLE STUDENT IS
     'Each row is one student record.  STUID is the key.'
COMMENT ON ENROLL.GRADE IS
     'The letter grade earned by the student in each course.
      Valid entries are A,B,C,D,F,I,W, and null.'
```

8.7 DB2 Internals

DB2 is designed to run under the MVS operating system, interacting with IMS, CICS, or TSO. It can use the communications facilities of IMS or CICS for on-line applications, or TSO for both on-line and batch. If either IMS or CICS is used, the DB2 application can access both DB2 and IMS databases, which are discussed in Chapter 10. The data sublanguage, SQL, is available in interactive form, as demonstrated in this chapter, and embedded form, with a host programming language. Embedded SQL statements can be placed where needed in programs and are preceded by the words "EXEC SQL," to distinguish them from host language statements. When the program is submitted for compilation, the SQL Precompiler picks out the SQL statements and substitutes host-language CALL statements for them. Then the rest of the host-language program is compiled as usual and link-edited, producing a load module for the (stripped) host-language program.

Meanwhile, the SQL statements are used by the Precompiler to construct a DBRM, Database Request Module, which contains a parsed version of the SQL statements. The DBRM is then used by the Bind component, an optimizing compiler that converts the parsed SQL requests into an application plan, to produce optimized System/370 object code. This application plan is kept in the catalog. At execution time, the load module (created from the stripped host-language program) and the application plan (created from the SQL statements by the Bind component) are both needed. The load module executes first until a CALL statement is reached. The Runtime Supervisor then takes over, fetches the application plan from the catalog, loads it, and passes control to it. The application plan contains machine-code instructions that direct actual I/O operations on the database. These are performed by a DB2 component called the Stored Data Manager. After the application plan is executed, results are passed back to the program, and control goes back to the load module.

One of the best features of DB2 is that all of the interactive SQL queries can be used, with minor modifications, in embedded form. An important modification is that the programmer must specify the program variables (called **host variables**) that are to receive values from the database. The data types of host variables and their corresponding database variables must be compatible, although their names may be different. To distinguish a host variable from a database variable in an SQL statement, the host variable is preceded by a colon. In a SELECT statement, an INTO line tells which host variables should receive values from the database. For example, the following statement, embedded in a PL/1 program, retrieves the STUNAME, MAJOR, and CREDITS from the student record whose STUID matches the host variable :STUDENT# and places those values in the program variables :STUNAME, :STUMAJOR, and :CREDITS.

```
EXEC SQL  SELECT  STUNAME, MAJOR, CREDITS
          INTO    :STUNAME, :STUMAJOR, :CREDITS
          FROM    STUDENT
          WHERE   STUID = :STUDENT#;
```

An alternative method, used when more than one row will be accessed by a program, is to create a structure containing the host variables and to use a **cursor** or pointing device to access the rows one at a time and bring the data into the structure. The cursor is identified with a SELECT statement that retrieves a row of data. The program must have a statement that opens the cursor, a statement that fetches a row at a time, and a statement that closes the cursor.

Whether embedded or interactive, SQL is compiled rather than interpreted and always uses an optimizer to make access as efficient as possible. Some of the components of a DB2 system mentioned here and others that users may be interested in are the following:

- **The DB2 Precompiler** is an integral part of DB2. It is a preprocessor that examines applications programs for SQL statements, replaces them with CALLs, and generates the Database Request Module (DBRM) that is used as input by the Bind component.

- **The Bind component** takes the DBRM and uses its knowledge of table size, indexes, data placement, and the query conditions to produce optimized machine code, called the application plan, which is stored in the system catalog.
- **The Runtime Supervisor** is in main memory when an applications program is running, and oversees its execution. When the program reaches a CALL, the Runtime Supervisor gets control and it then sends control to the application plan, which calls the Stored Data Manager to perform the required I/O operation.
- **The Stored Data Manager** acts as the access method for the stored database. It does the searching, retrieving, updating, index maintenance, and so on, normally done by the access method. Recall that VSAM is used as the disk manager, while DB2 does actual file management. Other operating-system components do locking, buffering, logging, sorting, and so on, as directed by the Stored Data Manager.
- **DB2I, DB2 Interactive**, is an interactive interface that, among other things, allows a user to enter DB2 queries at a terminal, invokes DB2, and sends the results back to the user's terminal. It is a TSO on-line program using ISPF as a screen manager. Besides executing interactive SQL statements, DB2I also permits users to run stored applications programs, to run utility programs, to prepare applications programs, to use BIND, REBIND, or FREE commands to manipulate DBRM application plans, and to issue certain console operator commands, as well as other options.
- **QMF, Query Management Facility**, is another TSO application that can be used as an optional front-end query and report writer for DB2. It is also available for SQL/DS. Although not an integral part of DB2, it is an attractive option that provides support for end users by means of help facilities and easy-to-use commands. In addition to the standard SQL interface, QMF provides a Query-By-Example (QBE) interface that permits users to express their queries by filling in blanks on table forms. Unlike DB2I, QMF has extensive report formatting and writing facilities.
- **DXT, Data Extract**, is another separate product that can be used with DB2 or SQL/DS. Its purpose is to copy data stored in an IMS database or a SAM or VSAM data set into a sequential file that can then serve as input for a DB2 or SQL load module. It can simplify and speed conversion to a DB2 environment.

8.8 Chapter Summary

IBM's **DB2** and **SQL/DS** are two relational database management systems that use **SQL**, a standard relational DDL and DML. DB2 uses **base tables** on the conceptual level; each base table represents a single relation. The external level consists of **views**, which are created from subsets, combinations, or other operations on the base tables. A base table may have **indexes**, one of which may be a **clustered index**, defined on it. Base tables and indexes are represented internally by **entry-sequenced VSAM files.** DB2's **dynamic database definition** allows the structure to be changed at any time.

SQL DDL commands **CREATE TABLE** and **CREATE INDEX** are used to create the base tables and their indexes. The **ALTER TABLE** command allows a new column to be added to the right of an existing base table. **DROP TABLE** and **DROP INDEX** remove tables and indexes from the database.

The **DML** commands are **SELECT, UPDATE, INSERT,** and **DELETE**. The SELECT command has several forms, and it performs the equivalent of the relational algebra SELECT, PROJECT, and JOIN operations. Options include **GROUP BY, ORDER BY, GROUP BY...HAVING, LIKE,** and built-in functions **COUNT, SUM, AVG, MAX,** and **MIN**. Expressions and set operations are also possible. The UPDATE command may be used to update one or more fields in one or more records. The INSERT command can insert one or more records, possibly with null values for some fields. The DELETE operator erases records, while leaving the table structure intact.

The **CREATE VIEW** command is used to define a virtual table, by selecting fields from existing base tables or previously defined views. The SELECT operation can be used on views, but the other DML commands are restricted to certain types of views. The DB2 **System Catalog** is a database containing information about the user's DB2 database. It keeps track of the tables, columns, indexes, and views that exist, as well as authorization information and other data. The system automatically updates the catalog when structural changes and other modifications are made.

DB2 runs under **MVS**, using **IMS, CICS**, or **TSO**. SQL can be used in either **interactive** or **embedded** form. System components include the **Precompiler**, the **Bind** component, the **Runtime Supervisor,** and the **Stored Data Manager.** Other options include **DB2I, QMF,** and **DXT.**

8.9 *Exercises*

1. Write the commands needed to create the FACULTY and CLASS tables for the examples used in this chapter.

2. Write the commands needed to create the required indexes for the FACULTY, CLASS, and ENROLL tables in this chapter.

3. For each of the join examples in this chapter (Examples 7 to 11), replace the join by a subquery, if possible. If not possible, explain why not.

Directions for Exercises 4–21: Use the following tables and write the indicated commands in SQL:

```
WORKER  (EMPID, EMPNAME, EMPMGR, DEPT, BIRTHDATE, HIREDATE, SALARY)

PROJECT (PROJ#, PROJNAME, PROJMGR, BUDGET, STARTDATE, EXPECTED-DURATION)

ASSIGN  (PROJ#, EMPID, HOURS-ASSIGNED, RATING)
```

4. Get the names of all workers in the accounting department.

5. Get an alphabetical list of names of all workers assigned to project P12.

6. Get details of the project with the highest budget.

7. Get the names and departments of all workers on project P20.

8. Get an alphabetical list of names and corresponding ratings of all workers on any project that is managed by Jones.

9. Create a view that has the project number and manager of each project, along with the IDs and names of all workers assigned to it.

10. Using the view created in Exercise 9, find the project number and project manager of all projects to which employee E101 is assigned.

11. Add a new worker named Jack Smith with ID of 101 to the sales department.

12. Change the hours that employee E101 is assigned to project P25 from 100 to 150.

13. For all projects with starting date after January 1, 1990, find the project number and the IDs and names of all workers assigned to them.

14. For each project, list the project number and how many workers are assigned to it.

15. Find the employee names and manager names of all workers who are not assigned to any project.

16. Find the details of any project with the word STAR anywhere in its name.

17. Get a list of project numbers and names and starting dates of all projects that have the same starting date.

18. Add a field called STATUS to the PROJECT table.

19. Get the employee IDs and project numbers of all employees who have no ratings.

20. Assuming that SALARY now contains annual salary, write each worker's ID, name, and monthly salary.

21. Write out the system catalog entries for this example.

22. Using the tables in Exercise 21, write a catalog query to tell how many tables John has created.

23. Using the tables in Exercise 21, write a catalog query to find out how many columns are named PROJ#.

24. Using the tables in Exercise 21, write a list of names of people who have created tables, along with the number of tables each has created.

25. Using the tables in Exercise 21, write the names of tables that have more than two indexes.

8.10 *Bibliography*

American National Standards Institute. "The Database Language SQL," Document X3.135, ANSI, 1986.

Astrahan, M. M. et al. "System R: A Relational Approach to Data Management," ACM Transactions on Database Systems **1**:2 (June, 1976) pp. 97-137.

Astrahan, M. M. et al. "System R: A Relational Database Management System," Computer **12**:5 (May, 1979) pp. 43-48.

Blasgen, M. et al. "System R: An Architectural Overview," IBM Systems Journal **20**:1 (January, 1981) pp. 41-62.

Chamberlin, D. "Relational Data-Base Management Systems," ACM Computing Surveys **8**:1 (March, 1976) pp. 43-66.

Chamberlin, D. et al. "SEQUEL 2: A Unified Approach to Data Definition, Manipulation, and Control," IBM Journal of Research and Development **20**:6 (November, 1976) pp. 560-575.

Chamberlin, D. "A Summary of User Experience with the SQL Data Sublanguage," Proceedings of the International Conference on Very Large Data Bases (July, 1980) pp 181-203.

Chamberlin, D. et al. "A History and Evaluation of System R," Communications of the ACM **24**:10 (October, 1981) pp 632-646.

Date, C. *An Introduction to Database Systems Volume II* (3rd ed). Reading, MA: Addison-Wesley, 1984.

Date, C. *An Introduction to Database Systems Volume I* (4th ed). Reading, MA: Addison-Wesley, 1986.

Date, C. *A Guide to INGRES*. Reading, MA: Addison-Wesley, 1987.

Date, C. and C. White. *A Guide to DB2* (2nd ed). Reading, MA: Addison-Wesley, 1988.

Date, C. and C. White. *A Guide to SQL/DS*. Reading, MA: Addison-Wesley, 1988.

Korth, H. and A. Silberschatz. *Database System Concepts*. New York: McGraw-Hill, 1986.

Martin, J., K. Chapman, and J. Leben. *DB2: Concepts, Design, and Programming*. Englewood Cliffs, NJ: Prentice-Hall, 1989.

Stonebraker, M. (Ed.) *The INGRES Papers*. Reading, MA: Addison-Wesley, 1986.

Stonebraker, M. and L. Rowe. "The Design of POSTGRES," ACM SIGMOD International Conference on Management of Data (1986) pp. 340-355.

Zloof, M. "Query-by-Example: A Data Base Language," IBM Systems Journal **16**:4 (1977) pp. 324-343.

SAMPLE PROJECT: CREATING AND MANIPULATING A DB2 DATABASE FOR CLERICALTEMPS

In the Sample Project section of Chapter 7, we created a normalized relational model for the ClericalTemps application. We concluded that the following model should be implemented:

```
WORKER (EMPID, EMPNAME, SSN, EMPADD, EMPPHONE, DOB, SEX, DATEHIRED,
LASTDATEWORKED, AVERRATING, WORDPROC, TYPING, FILING, BOOKKPING, STENO,
AVAILCODE)

CLIENT (CLID, CLNAME, CLADD, CLPHONE, CONTACT, BILLINGYTD,
PAYMENTSYTD)

JOB (JOB#, CLID, JOBTITLE, STARTDATE, EXPECTENDDATE, DAILYRATE,
DAILYHOURS, REPORTTONAME, REPORTTOADD, REPORTTOPHONE, JOBSTATUS)

PAYROLL (CHECK#, EMPID, PAYDATE, GROSS, FED, FICA, STATE, LOCAL,
GROSSYTD, FEDYTD, FICAYTD, STATEYTD, LOCALYTD)

BILL (INVOICE#, CLID, BILLDATE, OLDBAL, TOTCHARGES, TOTPAID)

ASSIGNMENT (JOB#, EMPID, RATERNAME, RATINGDATE, EMPRATING)
```

Step 8.1

Write SQL statements to create all tables and indexes needed to implement this design in DB2:

```
CREATE TABLE WORKER
        (EMPID CHAR(5) NOT NULL, EMPNAME VARCHAR(20) NOT NULL, SSN
CHAR(9), EMPADD VARCHAR(40), EMPPHONE CHAR(10), DOB DATE, SEX
CHAR(1), DATEHIRED DATE, LASTDATEWORKED DATE, AVERRATING
DECIMAL (3,2), WORDPROC CHAR (1), TYPING CHAR (3), FILING
CHAR(1), BOOKKPING CHAR(1), STENO CHAR(1), AVAILCODE CHAR(8),
PRIMARY KEY (EMPID));

CREATE UNIQUE INDEX XWORKEID ON WORKER (EMPID);
```

```
CREATE TABLE CLIENT
        (CLID CHAR(5) NOT NULL, CLNAME VARCHAR(25) NOT NULL, CLADD
VARCHAR(40), CLPHONE CHAR(10), CONTACT VARCHAR(20), BILLINGYTD
DECIMAL(10,2), PAYMENTSYTD DECIMAL(10,2), PRIMARY KEY (CLID));

CREATE UNIQUE INDEX XCLCLID ON CLIENT (CLID);

CREATE TABLE JOB
        (JOB# CHAR(8) NOT NULL, CLID CHAR(5) NOT NULL, JOBTITLE
CHAR(15), STARTDATE DATE, EXPECTENDDATE DATE, DAILYRATE
DECIMAL(5,2), DAILYHOURS CHAR(9), REPORTTONAME VARCHAR(20),
REPORTTOADD(VARCHAR(40), REPORTTOPHONE CHAR(10), JOBSTATUS
CHAR(1), PRIMARY KEY(JOB#), FOREIGN KEY(CLID) REFERENCES CLIENT);

CREATE UNIQUE INDEX XJOBJOB# ON JOB (JOB#);

CREATE TABLE PAYROLL
        (CHECK# INTEGER NOT NULL, EMPID CHAR(5) NOT NULL, PAYDATE
DATE, GROSS DECIMAL(6,2), FED DECIMAL(6,2), FICA DECIMAL(5,2),
STATE DECIMAL(5,2), LOCAL DECIMAL(5,2), GROSSYTD DECIMAL (8,2),
FICAYTD DECIMAL (7,2), STATEYTD DECIMAL (7,2), LOCALYTD DECIMAL
(7,2), PRIMARY KEY (CHECK#), FOREIGN KEY (EMPID) REFERENCES WORKER);

CREATE UNIQUE INDEX XPAYCHK# ON PAYROLL (CHECK#);

CREATE TABLE BILL
        (INVOICE# INTEGER NOT NULL, CLID CHAR (5) NOT NULL, BILLDATE
DATE, OLDBAL DECIMAL(8,2), TOTCHARGES DECIMAL (7,2), TOTPAID
DECIMAL (7,2), PRIMARY KEY (INVOICE#), FOREIGN KEY (CLID) REFERENCES CLIENT);


CREATE UNIQUE INDEX XBILLINV# ON BILL (INVOICE#);

CREATE TABLE ASSIGNMENT
        (JOB# INTEGER NOT NULL, EMPID CHAR(5) NOT NULL, RATERNAME
CHAR(20), RATINGDATE DATE, EMP_RATING SMALLINT PRIMARY KEY (JOB#), FOREIGN
KEY (EMPID) REFERENCES WORKER);

CREATE UNIQUE INDEX XASNJOB# ON JOB (JOB#);
```

Step 8.2

Write SQL statements that will process five nonroutine requests for information from the database just created. For each, write the request in English, followed by the corresponding SQL command.

1. Request: Get the names and average ratings of all workers who have worked for client C1001.

SQL Query:

```
SELECT EMPNAME, AVERRATING
FROM   WORKER
WHERE  EMPID IN
       (SELECT EMPID
       FROM ASSIGNMENT
       WHERE JOB# IN
              (SELECT JOB#
              FROM JOB
              WHERE CLID = 'C1001'));
```

2. Request: Get a list of all assignments, including job title, job rating, client ID, and client name, for worker Jane Logan.

SQL Query:

```
SELECT CLIENT.CLID, CLNAME, JOBTITLE, EMPRATING
FROM   CLIENT, JOB, ASSIGNMENT, WORKER
WHERE  WORKER.EMPNAME = 'Logan,Jane'
       AND  CLIENT.CLID = JOB.CLID
       AND  JOB.JOB# = ASSIGNMENT.JOB#
       AND  ASSIGNMENT.EMPID = WORKER.EMPID;
```

3. Request: Get an alphabetical list of names and addresses of all employees who have earned over $50,000 gross so far this year.

SQL Query:

```
SELECT EMPNAME, EMPADD
FROM   WORKER
WHERE  EMPID IN
       (SELECT EMPID
       FROM PAYROLL
       WHERE GROSSYTD > 50000)
ORDER BY EMPNAME;
```

4. Request: Get a list of client IDs along with the number of jobs each has offered.

SQL Query:

```
SELECT     CLID, COUNT(*)
FROM       JOB
GROUP BY   CLID;
```

5. Request: Get a list of clients, including ID, name, and address, of all clients who have unpaid or partially paid bills.

SQL Query:

```
SELECT CLID, CLNAME, CLADD
FROM   CLIENT, BILL
WHERE  (TOTPAID < TOTCHARGES OR TOTPAID IS NULL)
       AND CLIENT.CLID = BILL.CLID;
```

Student Project: Creating a DB2 Database

For the normalized tables you developed at the end of Chapter 7 for the application you have chosen, carry out the following steps to implement the design using DB2:

Step 8.1

Write SQL statements to create all tables and indexes needed to implement the design in DB2. In addition to the unique indexes for primary keys, create any others you can justify.

Step 8.2

Write SQL statements that will process five nonroutine requests for information from the database just created. For each, write the request in English, followed by the corresponding SQL command.

CHAPTER

9

The Network Model

9 Chapter Objectives

In this chapter you will learn

- how the network model originated
- the role of the CODASYL DBTG in developing standards
- how the network model fits the standard three-level architecture
- how network structures represent data
- the meaning of **record**, **data item**, and **set** in the DBTG model
- how data structure diagrams represent network database structures
- how sets represent relationships
- the meaning of **essential set**, **value-based set**, **multimember set**, **singular set**, and **dynamic set**
- how to write a schema for a DBTG database
- how to write a DBTG subschema
- some forms of the DML commands for the DBTG model
- the basic structure and operations of IDMS/R
- how to map an E-R model to a network model

9.1 History of the Network Model

The network model was the basis of one of the oldest database management systems, Integrated Data Store (**IDS**), developed by Bachman at General Electric during the 1960s. Together with IBM's IMS, this database management system influenced the development of the database area for many years. The Conference on Data Systems Languages (**CODASYL**) is an organization consisting of representatives of major hardware and software vendors and users. This group was responsible for the development and standardization of the COBOL language, and in the late 1960s it formed a subgroup called the Database Task Group (**DBTG**) to address the question of standardization for database management systems. Influenced by IDS, the group proposed a network-based model and specifications for data definition and data manipulation languages. The tentative report was published in 1969 and resulted in many suggestions for changes from its readers. The DBTG reconsidered its proposal and published its first official report in 1971. This landmark document was submitted to the American National Standards Institute (**ANSI**) in the hope that its specifications would be accepted as a standard for database management systems. However, ANSI refused to accept or reject the proposed standard. The 1971 report was followed by several newer versions, notably in 1973, 1978, 1981, and 1984, but it remains the principal document describing a network-based model generally referred to as the CODASYL model or the DBTG model. In addition, it provided the vocabulary and framework for discussion of database issues, establishing for the first time the notion of a layered database architecture and common terminology. The DBTG evolved in 1972 into a permanent CODASYL committee, the **DDLC**, or Data Description Language Committee, which continued to operate and to publish its findings periodically in its **Journals of Development** until 1984, when its function was taken over by the **ANSI X3H2** committee for standardization.

Despite the fact that the DDLC continued to make changes to the CODASYL model, the 1971 proposal was used by several major vendors as the basis of their database management systems. The most widely used of these network-based systems is **IDMS/R** from Computer Associates, which also offers a companion product, **IDMS/SQL**. Others include **PRIME DBMS** from PRIME Computer, **IDS II** from Honeywell, **DMS 170** from CDC, **DMSII** and **DMS 1100** from UNISYS, and **DBMS 10** and **DBMS 11** from Digital Equipment Corporation. Popular systems that are partially network-based include **TOTAL** from CINCOM and **IMAGE** from Hewlett-Packard.

9.2 DBTG Model and Terminology

The DBTG model proposed the standard three-level database architecture. It introduced **data definition language** (DDL) for each of the levels. The external level or view is specified in the **subschema**, a description written in the **subschema data description language** (subschema DDL). The conceptual level is specified in the **schema**, whose description is written in the **schema data description language** (schema DDL). The **data**

storage definition language (DSDL) was added in 1978 to specify the internal model and physical details of storage. In earlier reports, a **device media control language** (DMCL) was recommended, with implementation details left to vendors. Early versions did not completely separate the conceptual level from the physical level, so that some storage information was actually represented in the schema. Although later proposals removed most of these peculiarities, the DBMS products that were based on the early proposals retained them. The DBTG proposals also contained specifications for a DML for both COBOL and FORTRAN host languages, but not for on-line queries, because it was assumed that users would be programmers. Figure 9.1 shows the architecture of a DBTG database system. The User Work Area (UWA) that appears at the top level is a buffer through which the programmer or user communicates with the database.

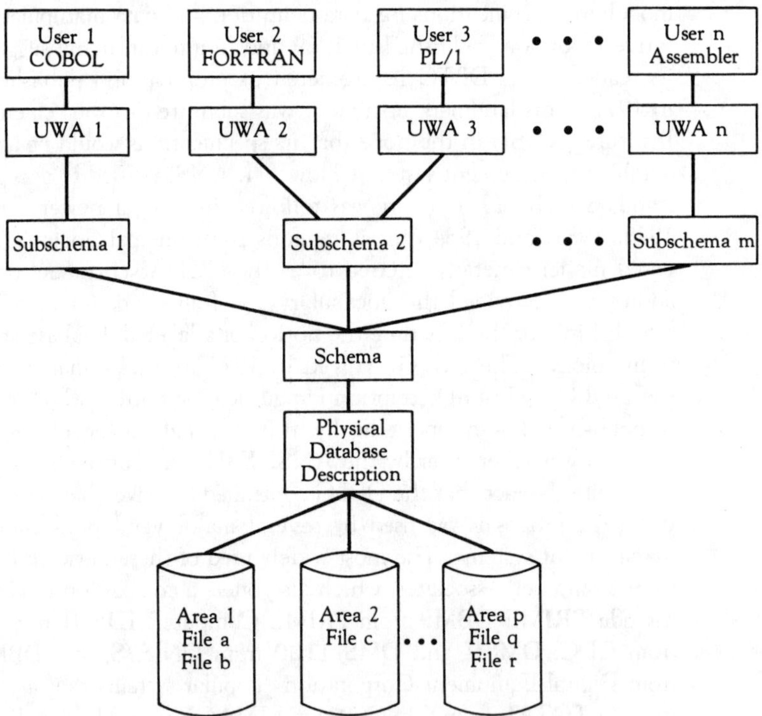

Figure 9.1 Architecture of DBTG System

The network model uses the **network** or **plex** structure as its basic data structure. A network is a directed graph consisting of **nodes** connected by **links** or directed arcs. The nodes correspond to **record types** and the links to **pointers**. Using E-R terms, the DBTG network model uses records to represent entities and links or pointers between records to represent relationships. Only binary one-to-one or one-to-many relationships can be represented directly by links. The network data structure looks very much like a tree structure, except that a dependent node, called a child or **member**, may have more than one parent or **owner** node. Figure 9.2 shows a network structure. Compare it with Figure 3.27, which shows a tree structure.

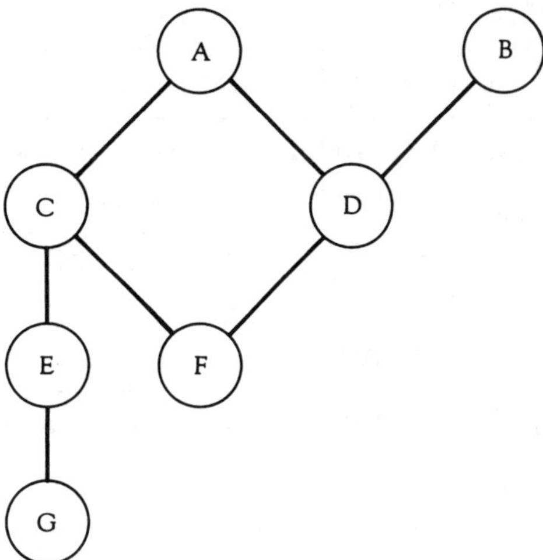

Figure 9.2 A Network Structure

9.3 *Records and Sets*

A network database consists of any number of named **record types** whose structures are completely described in the schema. A record consists of any number of **data items** or fields. A data item is the smallest named unit of data. Each data item has a specific data type associated with it. Each data item corresponds to an attribute, and the record corresponds to an entity. The model allows data items to be grouped within a record. A record may consist of **elementary data items**, which are single-valued fields, and/or **data aggregates**, which are named groups of elementary data items. There are two special types of data aggregates: **vector data aggregates**, which are composed of several related elementary data items all of the same data type and referenced by a common name, and **repeating group data aggregates**, which are named groups of related data items that may be of different types. Data aggregates may be nested. Figure 9.3 shows diagrams of record types containing different kinds of data items.

We will use a **data structure diagram**, as shown in Figure 9.4, to represent a network database structure. This diagram corresponds to a network graph in which nodes have been replaced by rectangles that represent records and links are shown by lines connecting the rectangles. When we need to specify them explicitly, rectangles will be subdivided to show data items. It is understood that the links, despite the fact that they are represented by a single-headed arrow, are one-to-many, although one-to-one relationships are permitted. This type of diagram is sometimes called a **Bachman diagram.** In a Bachman diagram, the base of the arrow comes from the owner node and the head of the arrow points to the member or dependent node.

A distinguishing feature of the DBTG model is the concept of named **sets** to express relationships. The DBTG term *set* does not mean the same as the mathematical term. A **set type** consists of a single **owner** node type and one or more dependent node types

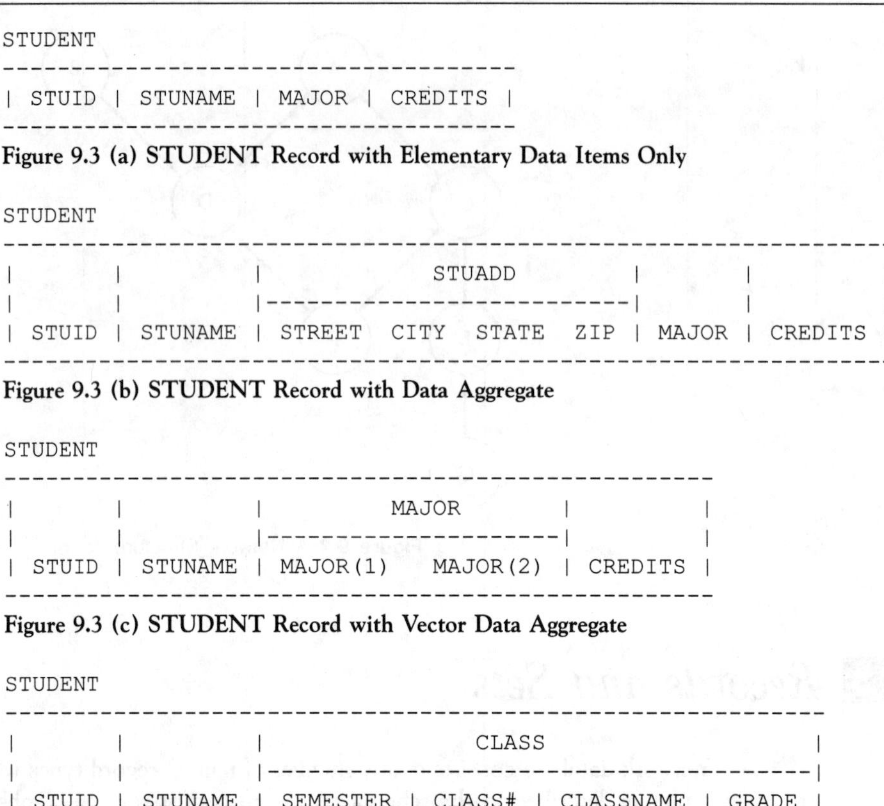

```
STUDENT
--------------------------------------
| STUID | STUNAME | MAJOR | CREDITS |
--------------------------------------
```

Figure 9.3 (a) STUDENT Record with Elementary Data Items Only

```
STUDENT
------------------------------------------------------------------
|       |         |           STUADD           |        |         |
|       |         |----------------------------|        |         |
| STUID | STUNAME | STREET  CITY  STATE  ZIP | MAJOR | CREDITS |
------------------------------------------------------------------
```

Figure 9.3 (b) STUDENT Record with Data Aggregate

```
STUDENT
----------------------------------------------------
|       |         |          MAJOR        |         |
|       |         |-----------------------|         |
| STUID | STUNAME | MAJOR(1)    MAJOR(2) | CREDITS |
----------------------------------------------------
```

Figure 9.3 (c) STUDENT Record with Vector Data Aggregate

```
STUDENT
------------------------------------------------------------
|       |         |                 CLASS                   |
|       |         |-----------------------------------------|
| STUID | STUNAME | SEMESTER | CLASS# | CLASSNAME | GRADE |
------------------------------------------------------------
                          repeats n times
```

Figure 9.3 (d) STUDENT Record with Repeating Group Data Aggregate

Figure 9.3 STUDENT Record Structures

to which it is related, called **member types.** Normally, there is only one member type for a given set type. For example, a typical set type is shown in Figure 9.5, in which DEPT is the owner and STU is the member type. We will call this the DEPT-STU set type, and write the set name, which is completely arbitrary, along the link from the owner to the member. This set represents a one-to-many relationship between DEPT and STU records. An **occurrence of a set** is a collection of records having one owner occurrence and any number of associated member occurrences. Therefore, there is an occurrence of DEPT-STU for each occurrence of DEPT in the database. Some of these occurrences are pictured in Figure 9.6. If there is some department with no students, we have an occurrence with an owner and no members. Such a set occurrence is said to be **empty.** A strict rule for sets is that a record cannot be a member of two occurrences of the same set type. For our example, this means that a student cannot belong to more than one department. However, a record may belong to more than one set type. For example, our students may also be associated with dorms, so a student record could also be owned by a dorm record in a DORM-STU set occurrence. A record type can be an owner type in one set and a member type in another. For example, using the data

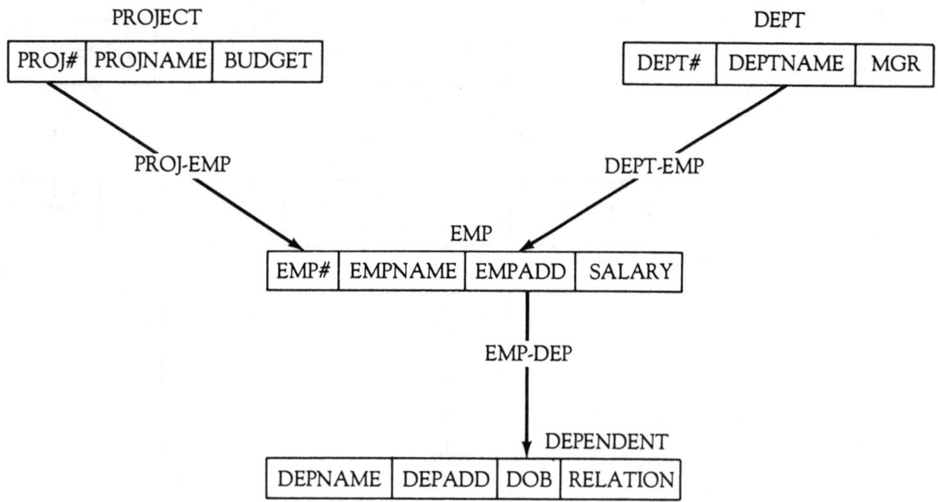

Figure 9.4 Network Data Structure Diagram

structure diagram of Figure 9.4, EMP would be a member of two set types, which we will call PROJ-EMP and DEPT-EMP, and an owner of one set type, EMP-DEP. Therefore, a particular EMP record could be connected with one PROJECT record, one DEPT record, and several DEPENDENT records.

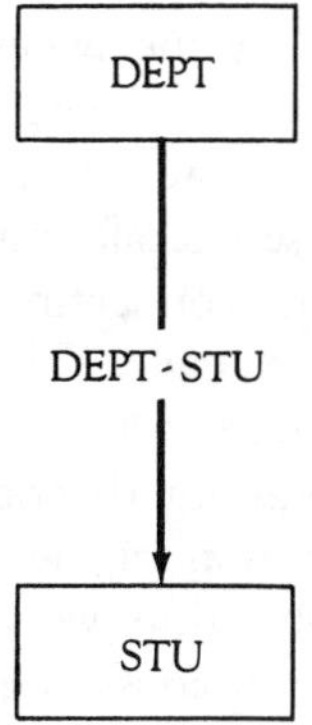

Figure 9.5 The DEPT-STU Set Type

Using the DEPT-STU set in Figure 9.5, it is possible to tell what major department a student belongs to by knowing what occurrence of the DEPT-STU set the STU record is in. Therefore, we no longer need to include the MAJOR field in the STU record. Such a set is called an **information-bearing** or **essential** set. It conveys information by keeping a logical connection because of its existence. The alternative to an essential set is to keep the value of one or more fields of the owner record occurrence in the member occurrence. Normally, this field is a foreign key, as in the case of storing MAJOR in the student records. A set with such information in the member records is called a **value-based** set. When we have a choice, do we pick essential or value-based

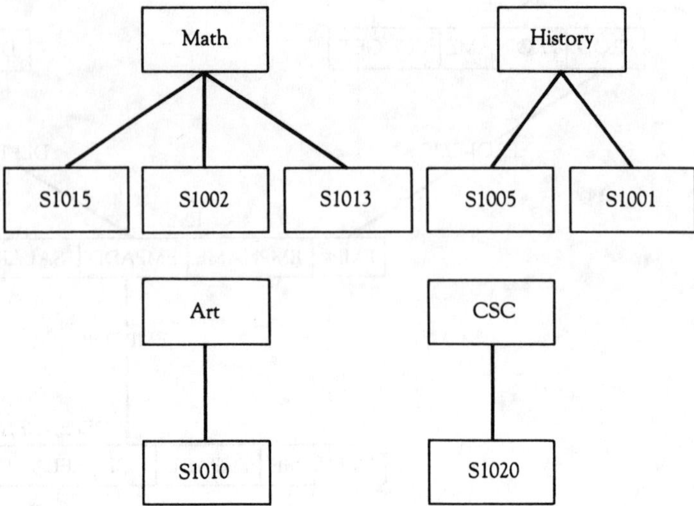

Figure 9.6 Occurrences of DEPT-STU Set

sets? The answer depends on what criteria we use. If we want to reduce redundancy in order to ensure data integrity and preserve space, we choose essential sets. If we are concerned that set-membership information may be accidentally lost or destroyed, we choose value-based sets.

Because sets are the only method of showing relationships between records, and because a set can have only one owner, there is no direct way to represent a many-to-many relationship in this model. Therefore, we have no way to represent the STU-CLASS relationship shown in Figure 9.7(a) directly. However, there is an indirect way to handle the many-to-many case. Recall that in the E-R model we represented many-to-many relationships as diamonds connecting the associated entity sets, as shown in Figure 9.7(b) for our STU-CLASS example. When we translated such relationships into tables for the relational model, we formed a table whose columns consisted of the primary keys of the associated entities, plus any descriptive attributes, as shown in Figure 9.7(c). We can borrow that representation for the network model as well. When two record types have a many-to-many relationship, we will create a new record type, called an **intersection record** or a **link record**, consisting of just the keys of the associated records, plus any intersection information, that is, any descriptive attributes whose values depend on the association. Figure 9.7(d) shows the intersection record created for each interaction between a STU record and a CLASS record. This diagram shows three record types and two set types. Each intersection record belongs to two sets, one owned by STU and one owned by CLASS.

As another example of the need for an intersection record, let us reconsider the model shown in Figure 9.4. Since we had a PROJ-EMP set, we were assuming each employee was assigned to only one project. Suppose, instead, that an employee could work on several projects simultaneously. The resulting many-to-many relationship could not be represented directly. Instead, we would have to create an intersection record type, called P-E INTERSECT, to keep the connection between an employee and all of his or her projects. This record would contain the PROJ#, EMPID, and any intersection data, such

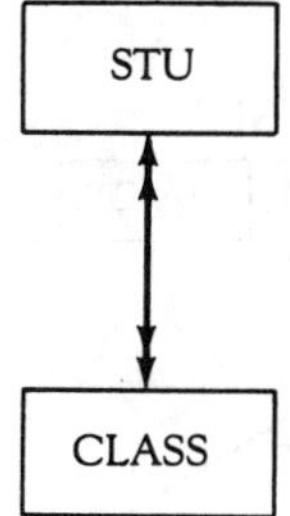

Figure 9.7(a) The Many-to-Many STU to CLASS Relationship

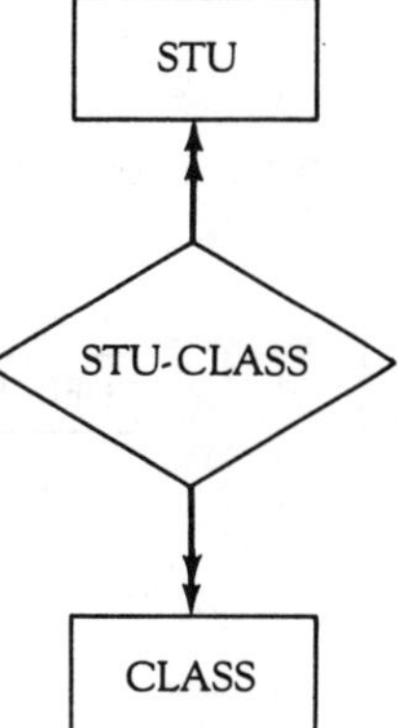

Figure 9.7(b) E-R Representation of Many-to-Many Relationship

ENROLL

CLASS#	STUID	GRADE
ART103A	S1001	A
CSC201A	S1020	B
CSC201A	S1002	F
ART103A	S1010	
ART103A	S1002	D
MTH101B	S1020	A
HST205A	S1001	C
MTH103C	S1010	
MTH103C	S1002	B

Figure 9.7(c) Table Representing Many-to-Many Relationship

as the number of hours an employee is assigned to work on the project or the rating the employee receives for work on that project. Figure 9.8 shows the model revised to handle the many-to-many case.

In the DBTG model, all sets are implemented by pointers. Usually, a linked list is created in which the owner occurrence is the head. The owner points to the first member, which points to the second, and so on, until the last member is reached. The last member then points back to the owner, forming a chain. Figure 9.9(a) shows how one occurrence of the DEPT-STU set is represented, and Figure 9.9(b) shows how all

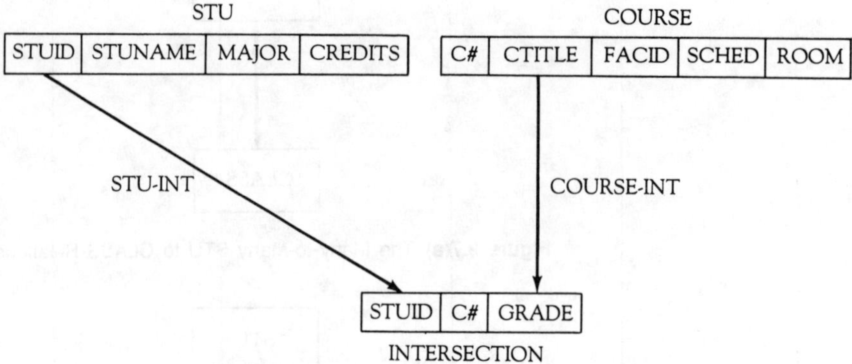

Figure 9.7(d) Intersection Record for Many-to-Many Relationship

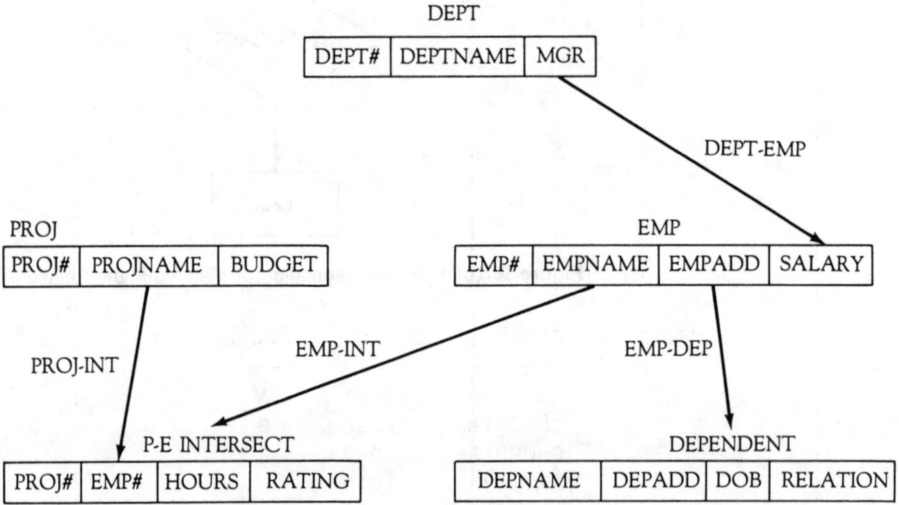

Figure 9.8 Using an Intersection Record for Many-to-Many PROJ-EMP Relationship

the DEPT-STU occurrences appear. Note that DEPT and STU are simply two separate files with pointers connecting them. Although we have pictured the pointers as arrows, they are, of course, logical addresses or keys of the target records. Suppose that we asked the question "What students are majoring in Math?" To answer, we would start at the Math record in the DEPT file and follow its STU pointer to the STU record of S1015. This points to S1002, which points to S1013, which points back to the Math record in the DEPT file. Once we get back to the head or owner, we know that we have reached all the member records. Suppose that we asked "What department does S1005 belong to?" This time, we would start in the STU file at the record of S1005, follow its DEPT pointer to the next STU record for the same department, S1001, and follow its pointer, which goes to the History record in the DEPT file. Thus we eventually get back to the correct owner record. However, the linked list could be long for departments with many students, so we have the option of creating **owner pointers** directly in member records. If we choose this option, we double the number of pointers required for a given set, but we make it easy to answer our second question. Another option is to make the linked list two-way, by placing a **prior pointer** in each record. Thus a set member record might have three pointers: one to the next record, one to the prior record, and one to the owner.

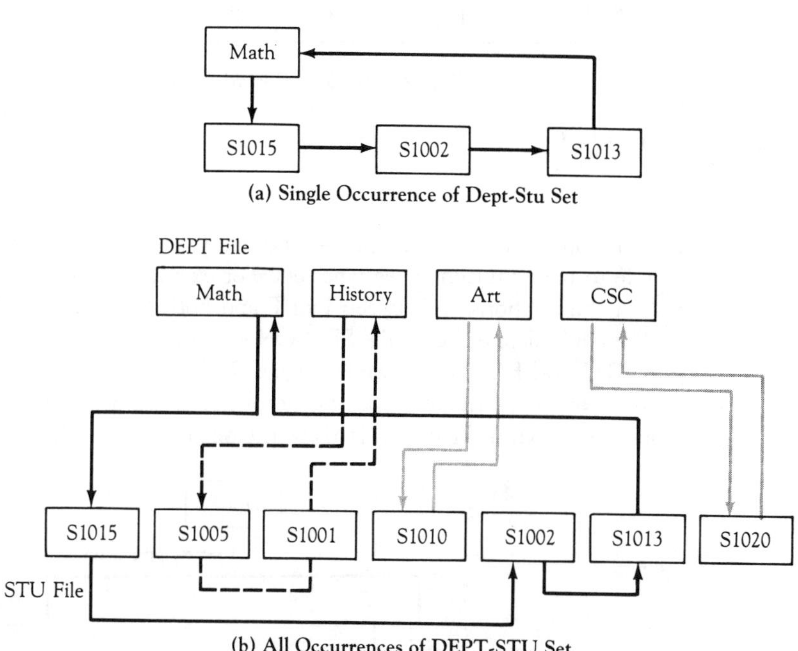

Figure 9.9 Linked List Implementation of Sets

Even if only next pointers are used, if a record belongs to several sets, it will contain several pointers to show its place in each of the sets. Thus if we were also representing the DORM-STU set, each STU record would contain an additional pointer to show to what occurrence of DORM-STU it belonged. Belonging to two sets requires a minimum of two pointers, but we could easily have six pointers if we choose the owner and prior pointer options. Figure 9.10 shows a STU record with six pointers. The first points to the next student in the same department, the second to the owner department, the third to the previous student in the same department, the fourth to the next student in the same dorm, the fifth to the owner dorm, and the sixth to the previous student in the same dorm. As you can see, the pointer overhead required for even a simple application can be quite heavy. In some network systems, the designer can choose the types of pointers by specifying them in the schema as the "mode" in the set description.

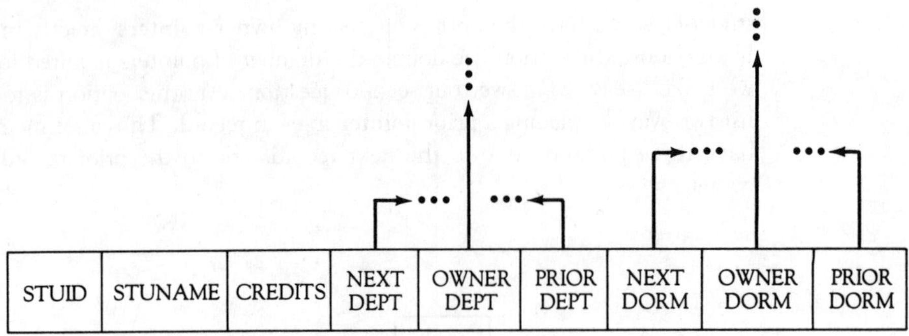

Figure 9.10 STU Record Containing 6 Pointers

9.4 *Special Sets*

A set has one owner record type and, normally, only one member record type, but it is possible to have **multimember** type sets. For example, suppose that we wished to keep track of the relationship between DEPT and both STU and FAC records in the same set. We could define the DEPT-PERSON set as having owner type DEPT and member types STU and FAC, as shown in Figure 9.11(a). In each occurrence of this set, we will have one department record as the owner and any number of student and faculty records, as shown in Figure 9.11(b) for the occurrence in which Math is the owner.

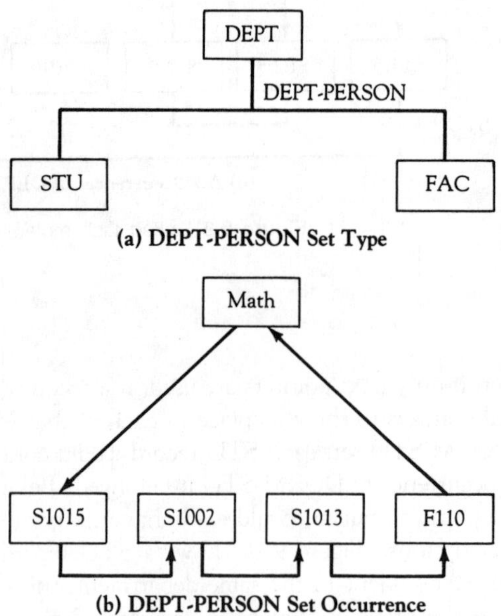

Figure 9.11 Multi-Member DEPT-PERSON Set

Another special set type is a **singular set**. This is used when we wish to treat all the records of a particular type as if they were members of a set, because set membership can be used to impose an ordering that can be useful for data manipulation. Since all the records in the set are of the same type (i.e., all members) there is no real owner record, so we specify that the set is **system-owned**. There can be only one occurrence of each system-owned set.

Another type of special set is a **dynamic** set. A dynamic set is one that has no member records "permanently" assigned to it. At execution time, an application program chooses whatever records it needs to include in the set. When the program ends, the records no longer belong to the set. This special set type was eliminated in the 1978 DBTG specifications.

9.5 *The DBTG DDL*

The DBTG schema has changed over the years as newer reports were issued by the DBTG and DDLC. The basic thrust of the changes has been to remove storage information from the schema. However, many network-based commercial systems were based on the earlier versions, so we show a schema that includes some of this information.

9.5.1 *The Schema*

A schema has four major sections, which are

1. **The Schema Section.** This is an introductory section naming the schema.
2. **The Area Section.** This section identifies storage areas and gives other physical information.
3. **The Record Section.** This section gives a complete description of each record structure with all its data items and details of record location.
4. **The Set Section.** This section identifies all the sets, the owner and member types for each, and other details such as ordering.

We will use a version of the university example, with data structure diagram pictured in Figure 9.12. The schema appears in Figure 9.13. We have numbered the lines for convenience in discussing the schema. Many of the lines in the example are optional and, within lines, many of the specified items are optional.

The Schema Section

Line 1, the schema section, identifies this as a schema description and gives the name of the database, UNIVDATA, which is a user-supplied name. If we wished, we could have provided a lock for the entire schema, by specifying PRIVACY LOCK IS <name>.

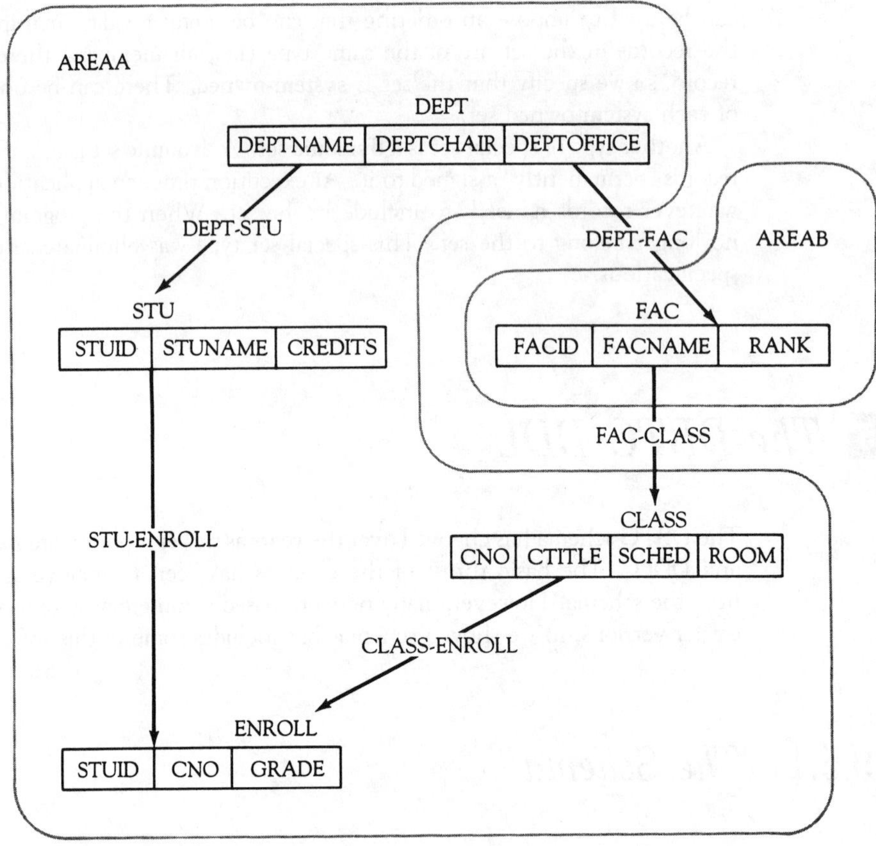

Figure 9.12 Network Data Structure Diagram for University Example

The Area Section

Line 2 begins the area section, which provides a list of the storage areas for the database. In this case we have two areas, called AREAA and AREAB, as shown in Figure 9.12. The area section was removed in the 1981 proposal because it provides physical storage information, but it still appears in some commercial products. An area is sometimes called a **realm.** The records and sets of the database are split into areas that are allocated to different physical files or devices. One purpose of this option is to allow the designer to specify which records should be placed on the same device or page, to permit efficient access to records that are logically related. For example, the owner and members of a set might be placed in the same area if they are usually accessed together. Areas that are accessed frequently would be placed on faster devices, while those that are not in such demand might be on slower ones. Another benefit is that different areas can have different security restrictions, so that entire areas can be hidden from certain users, or areas can be locked to simplify concurrency control. For example, on line 4 we have provided a privacy lock, HUSH, for AREAB. We did not specify the activities for which the privacy lock is used, but we could have done so. Our choices are UPDATE and/or RETRIEVAL or some support functions available to the DBA, and we could have either

```
SCHEMA NAME IS UNIVDATA
AREA NAME IS AREAA
AREA NAME IS AREAB
PRIVACY LOCK IS HUSH
RECORD NAME IS DEPT
      PRIVACY LOCK IS DEAN
      WITHIN AREAA
      LOCATION MODE IS CALC HASHDEPT USING DEPTNAME
      01  DEPTNAME  PIC IS X(10)
      01  DEPTCHAIR PIC IS X(15)
      01  DEPTOFFICE PIC IS X(4)
RECORD NAME IS STU
      WITHIN AREAA
      LOCATION MODE IS CALC HASHSTU USING STUID
      01  STUID  PIC IS 9(5)
      01  STUNAME TYPE IS CHARACTER 25
      01  CREDITS PIC IS 999
RECORD NAME IS FAC
      WITHIN AREAB
      PRIVACY LOCK IS CHAIR
      LOCATION MODE IS VIA DEPT-FAC SET
      01  FACID PIC IS 9(5)
      01  FACNAME TYPE IS CHARACTER 25
      01  RANK PIC IS X(10)
RECORD NAME IS CLASS
      WITHIN AREAA
      PRIVACY LOCK IS REGISTRAR
      LOCATION MODE IS CALC HASHCRS USING CNO
      01  CNO  PIC IS X(6)
      01  CTITLE TYPE IS CHARACTER 50
      01  SCHED PIC IS X(7)
      01  ROOM PIC IS X(4)
RECORD NAME IS ENROLL
      WITHIN AREAA, AREAB
      PRIVACY LOCK IS ADVISE
      LOCATION MODE IS VIA STU-ENROLL SET
      01  STUID  PIC IS 9(5)
      01  CNO PIC IS X(6)
      01  GRADE PIC IS X
SET NAME IS DEPT-STU
      MODE IS CHAIN
      ORDER IS SORTED INDEXED BY DEFINED KEY
      OWNER IS DEPT
      MEMBER IS STU MANUAL OPTIONAL
      ASCENDING KEY IS STUID
      SET OCCURRENCE SELECTION IS THRU CURRENT OF SET
SET NAME IS DEPT-FAC
      MODE IS CHAIN LINKED TO OWNER
      ORDER IS SORTED INDEXED BY DEFINED KEY
```

Figure 9.13 DBTG Schema for University Example

```
50      OWNER IS DEPT
51      MEMBER IS FAC AUTOMATIC MANDATORY
52      ASCENDING KEY IS FACID
53      SET OCCURRENCE SELECTION IS THRU CURRENT OF SET
54 SET NAME IS CLASS-ENROLL
55      MODE IS CHAIN
56      ORDER IS LAST
57      OWNER IS CLASS
58      MEMBER IS ENROLL AUTOMATIC FIXED
59      SET OCCURRENCE SELECTION IS BY VALUE OF CNO
60 SET NAME IS FAC-CLASS
61      MODE IS CHAIN
62      ORDER IS FIRST
63      OWNER IS FAC
64      MEMBER IS CLASS MANUAL OPTIONAL
65      SET OCCURRENCE SELECTION IS THRU CURRENT OF SET
66 SET NAME IS STU-ENROLL
67      MODE IS CHAIN
68      ORDER IS FIRST
69      OWNER IS CLASS
70      MEMBER IS ENROLL AUTOMATIC FIXED
71      SET OCCURRENCE SELECTION IS BY VALUE OF STUID
```

Figure 9.13 *(continued)*

EXCLUSIVE or PROTECTED locking for those activities. We would specify the exact type of lock by replacing line 4 with a specification such as PRIVACY LOCK FOR EXCLUSIVE UPDATE IS PROCEDURE KEEPOUT. This exclusive lock would allow a user obtaining the lock for update purposes to exclude other users completely so that they would not have concurrent access to this area. In the schema, we used the literal HUSH as our lock. We could have chosen a lock name or a procedure name instead.

The Record Section

Lines 5-39 contain the record section. Each record type is identified by name, as shown on lines 5, 12, 18, 25, and 33. If areas are used, the area names should be included somewhere within the description of each record. We have put the area placement data immediately after the record identification line in each case, by specifying "WITHIN AREAA" or "WITHIN AREAB". Line 6 gives the privacy lock, DEAN, for the DEPT file. If we wish, we can provide locks at the record level. For each record lock, we have a choice of specifying a value, a lock name, or a lock procedure name. We can apply the lock to all activities involving a record, or only to some. The activities, which will be explained in Section 9.6, are CONNECT, DISCONNECT, RECONNECT, ERASE, STORE, MODIFY, FIND, and GET. We can specify which of the activities require a lock by replacing line 6 with a specification such as PRIVACY LOCK FOR INSERT IS PROCEDURE SECRET.

Line 8 shows the **location mode**, CALC, for the DEPT record. The location mode for a record type is the method used by the DBMS to place the record in storage. Since this is physical storage information, the LOCATION MODE line was dropped in later versions of the DBTG proposal. However, it continues to exist in commercial systems, so we include it here. Location mode options include **CALC, VIA,** and **DIRECT**.

1. **CALC**, which is the method chosen for the DEPT record, means that the DBMS must use a hashing scheme on a key field to determine the proper physical address for the record. In this case, the hashing scheme is named HASHDEPT, and it is performed on the field DEPTNAME. If we wish to indicate that the field on which the hashing is performed, called the CALC key, is to be unique, we add DUPLICATES ARE NOT ALLOWED. The CALC option allows us to access a record directly based on the value of the CALC key field. Line 14 shows that we are placing STU records according to the value of STUID, using the hashing procedure HASHSTU, and line 28 shows that we are placing CLASS records by using the procedure HASHCRS to calculate addresses from the CNO field. Actually, the clause DUPLICATES ARE NOT ALLOWED FOR <field-name> can be used for any field whose values should be unique, not just for CALC key fields. This is one way of enforcing a uniqueness constraint.
2. The **VIA** option, which is used for FAC and ENROLL records, places records according to their membership in some set. In this case, the DBMS will place a record instance close to its owner instance in one specified set. For the FAC records, since DEPT-FAC is the only set they belong to, each FAC record will be placed close to the record of the associated department, as specified in line 21 by VIA DEPT-FAC SET. This makes it easy to find all the members of a department. For ENROLL records, which belong to two sets, we specified in line 36 that those records should be placed via the STU-ENROLL set, which means that enrollment records of a student will be placed on the same page as the student's STU record. This will make it easy to find the course numbers and grades for all courses the student has taken, by going through the student's record. It is not possible to access enrollment records directly by key value.
3. **DIRECT**, the third option, means that the address will be specified by the programmer when the record is to be inserted. To retrieve the record directly, the user must specify its address. This means that the programmer is accepting responsibility for a task that is normally done by the DBMS, thereby losing some physical data independence. It is best to avoid the DIRECT option and let the database take over physical placement, and most systems no longer allow this option. In choosing between CALC and VIA, the designer normally chooses CALC when there is a key and direct access is needed, and chooses VIA when direct access is not needed, or when the usual question is "What are all the members of this set occurrence?"

The individual data items are described next. For DEPT, these are DEPTNAME, DEPTCHAIR, and DEPTOFFICE. Each elementary item is assigned a data type, which may be given in a PIC (or PICTURE) clause showing a data type and (optional) repetition factor, or a TYPE IS clause. The usual data types and format items included in the host language are available. Notice the level numbers that precede each item. We choose any number to indicate the highest level and use a higher number for a sublevel. For example, if DEPTOFFICE consisted of two fields, BUILDING and ROOM, we would have written

```
01 DEPTOFFICE
   02 BUILDING PIC IS X
   02 ROOM PIC IS 999
```

This is an example of a nonrepeating data aggregate. To show a repeating data item or data aggregate, we need to show the number of repetitions, which may be a constant or a variable. For example, if we decided to store the clubs a student belongs to in the student record, we would write

```
01  STUID  PIC IS 9(5)
01  STUNAME  TYPE IS CHARACTER 15
01  CREDITS  PIC IS 999
01  NUM-TIMES  PIC IS 99
01  CLUBS OCCURS NUM-TIMES TIMES
      02  CLUB-NAME TYPE IS CHARACTER 20
      02  OFFICE-HELD TYPE IS CHARACTER 15
```

In this case, the number of clubs is a variable whose value is stored in NUM-TIMES. If the number of repetitions were constant, we could eliminate the NUM-TIMES field and simply write

```
01 CLUBS OCCURS 5 TIMES
```

followed by the CLUB-NAME and OFFICE-HELD lines.

The 1981 proposal suggested adding some domain constraints by using a CHECK option to restrict the set of allowable values for a data item, as in

```
01 CREDITS  PIC IS 999  CHECK IS LESS THAN 150
```

This method can also be used to enforce no-nulls rules, as in

```
01 STUID  PIC IS 9(5) CHECK IS NOT NULL.
```

The Set Section

Once all records have been described, we define the sets. The set section in Figure 9.13 begins on line 40. There are only three lines absolutely required for a set. These are

```
SET NAME IS <set-name>
      OWNER IS <owner-record-name>
      MEMBER IS <member-record-name>
```

However, it is usual to add other information about the set. For example, the **mode**, the method used to link records in the same set occurrence, is often specified, although this information was dropped from later proposals. There are two basic methods for connecting the set owner to the members and the members to one another. The first is the one illustrated in Figure 9.9, the linked list implementation, in which the owner points to the first member, which points to the next, and so on, with the last member pointing back to the owner. This is indicated by the entry

```
MODE IS CHAIN
```

Recall that it is possible to have direct pointers back to the owner as well as to the next member, in which case we specify

```
MODE IS CHAIN LINKED TO OWNER
```

It is also possible to have a two-way linked list, with each member pointing to the previous one, when we specify

```
MODE IS CHAIN LINKED TO PRIOR
```

The second basic method of linking set members is to have an array of pointers in the owner record, pointing directly to each member. This is pictured in Figure 9.14 and is specified by

```
MODE IS ARRAY [DYNAMIC]
```

The dynamic option allows the array to grow as needed, using dynamic storage allocation. With the array mode, set members are not linked to each other directly.

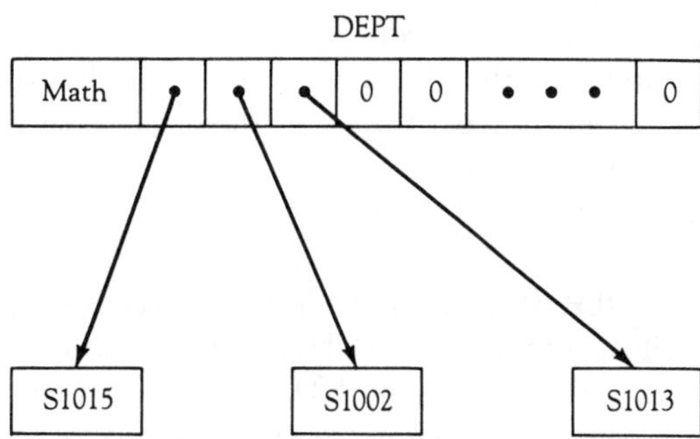

Figure 9.14 Mode is Array

Another piece of information that occurs in many implementations but has been dropped from the proposals is the ORDER specification. Please note that this order is the **logical order of the member records within a set occurrence**. It is independent of the location mode of the record and simply refers to the logical order created by the pointers within the set. There are two basic choices, **chronological** and **sorted**, each with subchoices. Chronological order means that the logical position of a record within a set is determined by the time the record is put into the set. Within chronological order, there are five choices:

1. **ORDER IS FIRST.** This means that a new member record is inserted at the beginning of the pointer chain, so that the owner points to it first. This is appropriate when the newest records are of the most interest.

2. **ORDER IS LAST.** This means that when a new record is inserted, it becomes the last in the pointer chain, and points back to the owner. This is used when the newest records are not as likely to be retrieved as the oldest ones.
3. **ORDER IS NEXT.** This option is used when new records are to be inserted by an applications program. A new record will be placed right after the most recently accessed set member.
4. **ORDER IS PRIOR.** This option means that when a new record is inserted by an applications program it will be placed right before the most recently accessed set member.
5. **ORDER IS IMMATERIAL.** This option, which is not available on all systems, means that we allow the system to decide what position in the set a new member will have, placing it in the most efficient manner.

SORTED order means that records are placed on the chain according to increasing or decreasing value of some sort key, which we identify. If the set is a single-member type, the options are simple. We write

```
ORDER IS SORTED BY DEFINED KEY
ASCENDING (or DESCENDING) KEY IS <sort-key-field-name>
DUPLICATES ARE ((NOT) ALLOWED) or (FIRST) or (LAST)
```

The sort key field need not have unique values. If the values are unique, we say that duplicates are not allowed. If they are not unique, we may choose whether to put the duplicate before the old values (FIRST) or after the old values (LAST). If the set is a multimember set type, there are three additional choices. Recall our multimember set example, DEPT-PERSON, consisting of owner DEPT and members STU and FAC, as shown in Figure 9.11. The choices are

1. **ORDER IS SORTED BY RECORD NAME.** This means that all FAC records will appear before any STU records, because the record name FAC is alphabetically before the record name STU. Within each record type, individual records are sorted by defined keys, so we need additional lines to identify the sort keys. We should add

```
ASCENDING (or DESCENDING) KEY IS <sort-key-field-name >
DUPLICATES ARE (NOT ALLOWED) or (FIRST) or (LAST)
```

For the DEPT-PERSON example, we would write

```
SET NAME IS DEPT-PERSON
ORDER IS SORTED BY RECORD NAME
OWNER IS DEPT
MEMBER IS FAC AUTOMATIC MANDATORY
ASCENDING KEY IS FACID
DUPLICATES ARE NOT ALLOWED
MEMBER IS STU MANUAL OPTIONAL
ASCENDING KEY IS STUID
DUPLICATES ARE NOT ALLOWED
```

2. **ORDER IS SORTED BY DEFINED KEYS.** This can be used only if all member record types have a field with a common domain. For example, if both record types have a DATE field, we can compare dates. For DEPT-PERSON, we might choose to arrange records in the same department in alphabetical order by the name. We would do this by specifying

```
ORDER IS SORTED BY DEFINED KEYS
DEFINED KEYS ARE FACNAME, STUNAME
```

In this case student and faculty records will appear in the set occurrence mixed together, but in strict alphabetical order by name. If we wanted to state what should be done with duplicates, if allowed, we could specify each key separately, followed by the DUPLICATES... line for each.

3. **ORDER IS SORTED WITHIN RECORD NAME.** This option allows the member types to be mixed together but sorted order to be maintained within each type. We will find FAC records among STU records (in the set occurrence, not necessarily physically), but the FAC records will be in order by FACID and the STU records will be in order by STUID, provided that we identify those fields as the key fields. We write

```
ORDER IS SORTED WITHIN RECORD NAME
ASCENDING KEY IS FACID
DUPLICATES ARE NOT ALLOWED
ASCENDING KEY IS STUID
DUPLICATES ARE NOT ALLOWED
```

Another option we identify is the class of membership. We must choose two items: **set insertion class** and **set retention class**. Set insertion is concerned with how a member gets placed in the set occurrence, while set retention is concerned with whether, once placed in a set, the member is allowed to leave the set. For set insertion the choices are

- **MANUAL**, which means that the member must be placed in a set by a program or user using a CONNECT command to link it to the proper set occurrence.
- **AUTOMATIC**, which means that when a new member record enters the database, the DBMS will automatically connect it to the proper set occurrence, setting up the necessary pointers.

For set retention, the choices are

- **FIXED**, which means once a member has been placed in a set occurrence, it cannot ever be removed from that particular occurrence unless the record is deleted from the database.
- **MANDATORY**, which means that once a member has been placed in a set occurrence, it must remain in some occurrence of that set, but not necessarily the same occurrence.

- **OPTIONAL**, which means that the member record can be disconnected from the set entirely and allowed to "float free" in the database.

To understand set insertion and retention, imagine the possible ways that students can become and remain connected to major departments. If a student must have declared a major before entering the university (i.e., a student record has to be connected to a department in order to be placed in the database), we have automatic insertion. If the student record can enter the database without being connected to a major and "float free" until a major is chosen and then be connected to a department, we have manual insertion. Regardless of how the student was originally connected to a department, retention has to do with whether he or she can change or drop a major. If the student must keep the same major and cannot change to another major without dropping out of the university, we have fixed retention. If the student can switch majors but never go back to undeclared, we have mandatory retention. If the student can drop a major without declaring another one immediately, we have optional retention.

For our schema in Figure 9.13, we see from line 44 that the DEPT-STU set showed the set insertion class as MANUAL and the retention class as OPTIONAL. This means that the student can enter without a major and can drop a major without declaring a new one. For the DEPT-FAC set we see from line 51 that the insertion is AUTOMATIC and the retention is MANDATORY. This means that no faculty member can be hired unless he or she belongs to a department, but that a faculty member can change departments. The ENROLL records have AUTOMATIC FIXED membership in both of the sets in which they participate. By the nature of the enrollment records, which are intersection records, they must be logically tied to a particular student and a particular course.

The SET OCCURRENCE SELECTION clause tells what method is used to determine to which occurrence of a set a member record should belong. To understand some of the options here, we need the notion of **currency indicators.** As explained in Section 9.2, the User Work Area is a buffer through which the programmer or user communicates with the database. It contains, among other things, currency indicators, pointers to the database records of various types most recently accessed by the program. Some of these pointers may be used in set occurrence selection.

There are many options for set selection, including:

1. **SET OCCURRENCE SELECTION IS THRU CURRENT OF SET.** This option was chosen for the DEPT-STU and DEPT-FAC sets. It means that when a new member record is to be inserted, the DBMS should choose the last occurrence of the owner record type as the owner.
2. **SET SELECTION IS BY VALUE OF <field-name>.** With this option, the DBMS will determine the current value of the named field from the user work area and use it as a key to find the correct owner record for the new member.
3. **SET SELECTION IS STRUCTURAL <owner.field=member.field>.** In this case the DBMS is to look at the specified field in the member record and use that value to identify the correct occurrence of the owner record.
4. **SET OCCURRENCE SELECTION IS THRU PROCEDURE <procedure-name>.** Here, the named program is responsible for finding the correct owner occurrence and inserting the member in that occurrence. Often, the set selection

line is accompanied by a CHECK line that ensures that some constraint involving the set owner and member is satisfied. For example, we might have

```
CHECK IS STU.STUID=ENROLL.STUID
```

This is not necessary when we use the STRUCTURAL selection option, because it is checked automatically in that case.

9.5.2 *The Subschema*

The subschema is a description of the external view of a particular user or set of users. It provides data independence by allowing certain items to differ from the schema. In particular, we can omit areas, records, sets, and data items from the subschema, rename data items, records, and sets, change the order of data items in a record, group elementary data items that were not grouped in the schema, split up grouped items into individual data items, change the data type of items by changing the PIC, TYPE, or length specifications, and form virtual records by choosing data items from separate conceptual records. The exact format of the subschema DDL depends on the host language, so there is no single form used. The forms described for various languages have changed over the years and differ slightly from the forms used by commercial products. However, subschemas usually contain the following divisions:

1. **TITLE Division**, which gives the name of the subschema and of the associated schema.
2. **MAPPING Division**, which gives the changes in names from the schema to the subschema, if any.
3. **STRUCTURE Division**, which is subdivided into **AREA, RECORD,** and **SET Sections**. The Area Section gives the names of areas to be included in the subschema. The Record Section identifies the records and data items within them that are to be included, possibly with their new names (from the Mapping Division) and data types. The Set Section lists all the sets that are to be included. Figure 9.15 shows a subschema for the University database.

9.6 *DBTG Data Manipulation*

The DBTG DML is a procedural language that requires the user to be familiar with the structure of the database. There are many options available, and the skilled programmer

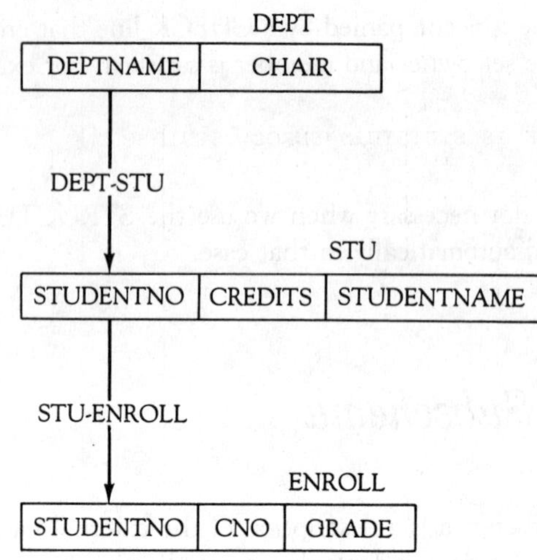

Figure 9.15(a) Structure of COLLEGE Subschema

```
TITLE DIVISION
SS  COLLEGE WITHIN UNIVDATA
MAPPING DIVISION
ALIAS SECTION
AD       STUDENTNO IS STUID
AD       STUDENTNAME IS STUNAME
STRUCTURE DIVISION
RECORD SECTION
01       DEPT
         02       DEPTNAME       PIC X(10)
         02       DEPTCHAIR      PIC X(15)
01       STU
         02       STUDENTNO      PIC 9(5)
         02       CREDITS        PIC 999
         02       STUDENTNAME    PIC X(25)
01       ENROLL ALL
SET SECTION
SD       DEPT-STU
SD       STU-ENROLL
```

Figure 9.15 (b) Written Subschema for University Example

Figure 9.15 Subschema for University Example

can use them to navigate the database very efficiently. We will consider only a small subset of the many DML commands available. To understand the basic workings of these commands, we need to discuss the User Work Area again. You recall that the User Work Area or program work area is a buffer assigned to a program. It contains

1. **Currency indicators**, a set of pointers that identify the records most recently accessed by the program in the following categories:
   a. **Current of run unit**, a pointer to the most recent record of any type accessed by the program.
   b. **Current of the record type**. For each record type identified in the subschema for the program, the work area contains the address of the record of that type most recently accessed by the program.
   c. **Current of the set type.** For each set type, the work area contains the address of the most recent record of that set, whether the owner or a member of an occurrence.
   d. **Current of the area**. For each area or realm, the work area shows the address of the most recently accessed record from that area, regardless of its type. Since areas were dropped in the newer versions of the proposal, these indicators were also dropped. However, they appear in some commercial systems.

	Time t = 1	t = 2	t = 3
Current of:	FIND HISTORY	FIND F101	FIND S1001
run unit	History	F101	S1001
DEPT	History	History	History
STU			S1001
FACULTY		F101	F101
CLASS			
ENROLL			
DEPT-STU	History	History	S1001
DEPT-FAC	History	F101	F101
STU-ENROLL			S1001
FAC-CLASS		F101	F101
CLASS-ENROLL			
AREAA	History	History	S1001
AREAB		F101	F101

Figure 9.16 Currency Indicators for University Application

For example, Figure 9.16 shows the currency indicators for a program that has access to the entire university database. For this application, we would have a current of the run unit, current of record types DEPT, STU, FACULTY, CLASS, and ENROLL, current of the set types DEPT-STU, DEPT-FAC, STU-ENROLL, FAC-CLASS, and CLASS-ENROLL, and current of the two areas, AREAA and AREAB. In the figure we picture the changes to the indicators as the program accesses different records at time 1, 2, and 3. When the program starts, all currency indicators are null. When the record of the History Department is found at time $t = 1$, the current of the run unit, the DEPT record type, the DEPT-STU set, the DEPT-FAC set, and AREAA are all set to point to the History Department record. The currency indicators for other record types (STU, FACULTY, CLASS, ENROLL), the currency indicators for the sets in which DEPT does not participate (STU-ENROLL, FAC-CLASS, CLASS-ENROLL), and the currency indicator for any area that does not contain a DEPT record (AREAB) are not affected. Next the program finds the record of faculty member F101 at time $t = 2$. This becomes the current of the run unit, the FACULTY record type, the DEPT-FAC set, the FAC-CLASS set, and AREAB. No other currency indicators are affected. Finally, the program finds the record of student S1001 at time $t = 3$. It becomes the current of the run unit, the STU record type, the DEPT-STU set, the STU-ENROLL set, and AREAA, but no other pointers are affected.

2. **Record templates**, one for each record type that the program can access. As database records are brought into the buffer, they must be placed in the appropriate record templates. For the university database, there would be templates for DEPT, STU, FACULTY, CLASS, and ENROLL records.
3. **Status flags**, which contain values that indicate whether the last attempted database operation was successful. A value of 0 means success, while other values indicate errors of various types.

The DBTG DML commands we will consider are the following:

- **OPEN**: opens area(s) for processing.
- **CLOSE**: closes area(s) when processing is complete.
- **FIND**: finds the location of a database record.
- **GET**: brings the previously found record into the work area.
- **MODIFY**: stores changes to a record updated in the work area.
- **ERASE**: erases a record from the database.
- **STORE**: adds a new record to the database.
- **CONNECT**: places a new member in a set occurrence.
- **DISCONNECT**: removes a member from a set occurrence.
- **RECONNECT**: moves a member from one set occurrence to another.

These are the major commands for processing the database, but each has many different forms and many options within each form. The OPEN (or READY) and CLOSE (or FINISH) commands refer to areas and no longer appear in the proposals. If required, an OPEN command should be written to open all the areas that will be accessed by the program, and a CLOSE command should appear when processing is complete. We will consider a few relatively simple operations using the other commands.

FIND: This command merely locates a record in the database. It does not bring the record into the work area template but causes the relevant currency indicators to be changed to reflect the address of the found record. The found record becomes the current of the run unit, record type, and set type for all sets in which it participates as either owner or member. The FIND command is usually followed by GET, MODIFY, or ERASE. In one version of the FIND, we must first specify the value of the CALC field in a record whose location mode is CALC and then ask the system to FIND a record with a matching value. We would use the host language to assign the field value and then write the FIND:

```
STUID = "S1015";
FIND ANY STU USING STUID
```

The first line, in the host language, establishes the value of STUID, and the second line asks the database management system to locate the first STU record with a matching STUID. So FIND ANY really means "find the first." If we specify that duplicates are allowed and wish to continue searching for a second or subsequent records after the first record is found, we write

```
FIND DUPLICATE STU USING STUID
```

This command may be used in a loop to continue the search. If we intend to update a record, we use a slightly different form of the FIND, namely

```
FIND FOR UPDATE ANY STU USING STUID    or
FIND FOR UPDATE DUPLICATE STU USING STUID
```

The FIND command can also locate records according to set membership, especially useful when the location mode is VIA. There are several methods of locating set members, but a simple one involves finding the owner of a set occurrence, and then asking for the FIRST, NEXT, PRIOR, Nth, or LAST member. The following segment illustrates how we could use a STU record to find the associated ENROLL records:

```
MOVE "S1002" TO STUID IN STU
FIND ANY STU USING STUID
FIND FIRST ENROLL WITHIN STU-ENROLL
DOWHILE DBSTATUS = 0
        {Bring the record into the work area and process it}
        FIND NEXT ENROLL WITHIN STU-ENROLL
ENDDO
```

Once we have a set member, we can ask for its owner within any set. For example, when we have any of the ENROLL records in the segment above, we could have asked for the associated CLASS by

```
FIND OWNER WITHIN CLASS-ENROLL
```

GET: This command, which follows a FIND, brings the found record into the work area, where the user can do additional processing. As an example of the GET, suppose that we wanted to print out a list of IDs and names of all math majors. Using PL/1, we would write

```
DEPT.DEPTNAME = 'Math';
FIND ANY DEPT USING DEPTNAME;
FIND FIRST STU WITHIN DEPT-STU;
DO WHILE (DBSTATUS = 0);
        GET STU;
        PUT LIST (STUID, STUNAME);
        FIND NEXT STU WITHIN DEPT-STU;
END;
```

MODIFY: If a record is to be updated, we use a special form of the FIND command, FIND FOR UPDATE. Then we do a GET to bring the record into the work area, where we use the host language to make changes. After the record has been updated in the work area, we use the MODIFY command to replace it in the database. To update the rank of faculty member F105, we write

```
FAC.FACID = 'F105';
FIND FOR UPDATE ANY FAC USING FACID;
GET FAC;
RANK = 'Assistant';
MODIFY FAC;
```

ERASE: To use the ERASE command, we must FIND FOR UPDATE the targeted record. Once the record is found, we delete it from the database by writing ERASE, as shown in the following segment using COBOL:

```
MOVE 'ART103A' TO CNO IN CLASS
FIND FOR UPDATE ANY CLASS USING CNO
ERASE
```

When we erase a record that is an owner of a set occurrence, what happens to the set members? This problem arises when we erase the record of ART103A, since there are some enrollment records with this course number, so there is a possibility of losing data integrity. We can be sure that all members of any set occurrence owned by a record are erased by writing ERASE ALL in place of ERASE. If we write only ERASE, as in the segment above, the command will have different effects on different sets, depending on the retention status of the member records. If we specified FIXED in the schema, all members will be erased when the owner is erased. This is the case for CLASS-ENROLL, so we will automatically lose all enrollment records when a course is deleted. If the retention class is MANDATORY, the ERASE is illegal and the system will refuse to execute it until all set members have been removed and reconnected to another occurrence. For an OPTIONAL retention class, the owner is erased and the members are released from the occurrence, but remain in the database. Since a record could be an owner of several different sets, each with its own retention class, its deletion could have different effects on different sets. If a deleted record is only a set member, not an owner, pointers are simply readjusted to connect the remaining members.

STORE: This command inserts new records into the database. First we must build the record in the work area, using the host language, and then we place it in the database by STORE. To create a new STU record, we write

```
STU.STUID = 'S1050';
STU.STUNAME = 'Marks,Joseph';
CREDITS = 0;
STORE STU;
```

When we insert this record, it does not belong to any set occurrence. Placing the student record in the appropriate DEPT-STU set occurrence requires a CONNECT command.

CONNECT: If a member type record is already in the database but not connected to a set, either because its insertion class is MANUAL or because its retention class is OPTIONAL and it has been disconnected from a set occurrence, the CONNECT command can be used to place it in a set occurrence. The following segment would cause the student record just created to be inserted in the DEPT-STU set occurrence for the History Department:

```
DEPT.DEPTNAME = 'History';
FIND ANY DEPT USING DEPTNAME;
CONNECT STU TO DEPT-STU;
```

In general, to connect a member to an occurrence, we must have the occurrence owner as the current of its record type. The effect of the CONNECT is to adjust pointers so that the record is placed in the correct logical position in the correct occurrence.

DISCONNECT: This command works only for a set member whose retention class is OPTIONAL. It removes the record from the set occurrence, while leaving it in the database. The record may still be a member of other sets or may belong to no set. To remove a student from a department, we write

```
STU.STUID = 'S1050';
FIND FIRST STU USING STUID;
DISCONNECT STU FROM DEPT-STU;
```

This operation is permitted since STU has OPTIONAL retention class in DEPT-STU.

RECONNECT: If a member has MANDATORY or OPTIONAL retention, it can be moved from one set occurrence to another by a RECONNECT command. The following segment moves F105 from CSC to Math:

```
FAC.FACID = 'F105';
FIND FIRST FAC USING FACID;
DEPT.DEPTNAME = 'Math';
FIND FIRST DEPT USING DEPTNAME;
RECONNECT FAC IN DEPT-FAC;
```

9.7 An Example: IDMS/R

IDMS/R, or Integrated Database Management System/Relational, is a network-based mainframe database management system from Computer Associates. The "R" was added in 1983, when a relational user interface was added to the product. In 1988, IDMS/SQL, a similar product for the Digital Equipment Corporation VAX environment, was released. However, the underlying structure of an IDMS database remains very close to the CODASYL model, particularly to the 1971 DBTG proposal. The result is that the strong performance traditionally associated with the network model is still available, but the user sees a simple relational view, although not all relational functions are present. The designer, however, needs to think of IDMS in DBTG terms.

We have included most of the structural and functional features of IDMS/R in our discussion of the network model, since we attempted to discuss both the 1971 and later DBTG proposals throughout previous sections of this chapter. IDMS/R is a large set of integrated products. The heart of the system is the **IDMS/R Engine** and the **Integrated Data Dictionary (IDD)**, which is an active data dictionary. Supporting systems include an applications program generator, report writers, data definition facilities, and other tools. The engine consists of the core database management system which uses a network model. The IDD stores the schema, subschemas, security information, user profiles, and other system information. The designer can use IDD utilities to define data items and records. These entries can be used to complete the schema and subschema, which are then compiled. IDMS/R has its own **DMCL** (Device Media Control Language), which is used to provide a complete written description of storage. The system has precompilers for PL/1, COBOL, Fortran, and Assembler.

IDMS/R uses the basic network structures of **record, data item,** and **set**, as they appear in the CODASYL proposals. The notion of **areas** that appeared in the early DBTG proposals is used as well. An area is a storage division that contains one or more record types. An area may be assigned one or more direct access files. A file may contain only a part of an area, a complete area, or several areas. Each file is divided into fixed-length **pages**. A page may contain variable-length records, possibly of different types. Each page contains a **header** giving overhead information about the page, and a **footer**, giving information about the database records on that page, including the position of the record relative to the start of the page and the record length.

Each record type must be assigned to a single area. On storage, each record occurrence is assigned a unique **database key (DBKEY)**, which consists of the page number and the relative position of the record on that page. Thus if a record is the fifth record on page 100 its DBKEY is 100:5. The DBKEY becomes the pointer that is used for connecting records in sets. Although stored records rarely move, if a record is moved for any reason, its DBKEY value will be changed, requiring that all the pointers to the record be changed accordingly. The location mode must be given for each record type. Location modes for ordinary database records are CALC, VIA, or DIRECT. If direct is chosen, the user specifies the page on which the record should be stored, and the system returns the DBKEY value to the user. The user must supply the DBKEY value when he or she uses the FIND command for that record.

Sets are implemented using either **indexes** or linked lists, which are called **chains.** A linked list can have owner and/or prior pointers, all of which are DBKEY values. An index is similar to the B+ tree indexes discussed in Chapter 3. The owner points to a chain of index records, which point to member records. The set description in the schema must include the mode, which is either CHAIN or INDEXED. There is no SET OCCURRENCE SELECTION clause in the schema. The user is responsible for establishing the correct currency indicators for the sets in which a record has automatic membership when a new record is stored as well as when he or she connects a member to a set manually. There is no CHECK facility to enforce referential integrity between set owners and members. Retention status is limited to MANDATORY or OPTIONAL, with no FIXED option. IDMS/R allows SYSTEM-owned sets.

The **IDMS/R schema** has some additional sections. It opens with the usual **SCHEMA DESCRIPTION** section. The **FILE DESCRIPTION** defines IDMS files and assigns them to external files. The **AREA DESCRIPTION** assigns pages of the files to particular areas. The **RECORD DESCRIPTION** and **SET DESCRIPTION** sections are the usual ones, with the modifications mentioned.

The subschema also has some slight changes. There is no **MAPPING** division, because aliases are not allowed for records, sets, or data items, except when the host-language syntax does not accept the database names as identifiers. There is an **AREA** division naming the areas to be included. The **RECORD** division is similar to the DBTG record division. If the complete record appears in the subschema, we specify ELEMENTS ARE ALL. If only selected data items appear, we list them in the specification ELEMENTS ARE <item>, <item>, ..., <item>, rearranging them as desired. The **SET** division names the sets to be included. Because of different set retention classes and various forms of the ERASE, there are some restrictions on which records should be included in a subschema, with IDMS requiring that sets that might be erased by deleting an owner record be present in any subschema containing the record. This requirement concerns not only the members of a set owned by the record, but sets owned by those members as well, down any number of levels. Two extra sections may appear after the set division. The first is the **LOGICAL RECORD** section, which names the logical record type and the source records from which it is to be created. The second is the **PATH GROUP** section, which tells the system how to do the joins that must be performed to create the logical records named in the preceding section.

The DML is very similar to the DBTG DML, with many different options for the various commands. Because the FIND...GET combination is used so often, IDMS/R allows the single command **OBTAIN** to perform the function of this combination. The **ERASE** command has more forms than the corresponding DBTG ERASE. IDMS/R requires the use of **READY** to open an area for processing, and **FINISH** to close the area. When an area is opened, we have the option of requesting locking on the area level. If we do not make such a request, the system will do only record-level locking. The READY command allows us to specify whether we are planning to do RETRIEVAL or UPDATE, and whether we require PROTECTED or EXCLUSIVE access, by a command such as READY AREAA EXCLUSIVE UPDATE. With the EXCLUSIVE option, no concurrent user is permitted to access the area in any way, while the PROTECTED option permits concurrent access but not updates. An area lock can seriously hinder performance, so the usual lock is at the record level. Record locks may be shared or exclusive. A user requests a record lock by adding the word KEEP to a FIND or OBTAIN command, such as OBTAIN KEEP EXCLUSIVE STU WITHIN AREAA. If the word EXCLUSIVE is omitted, the lock will be shared, allowing concurrent access but not update.

9.8 *Mapping an E-R Model to a Network Model*

To map an E-R diagram to a network data structure diagram, our basic plan is to make each entity a record type, each attribute a data item in a record, and each relationship a set type. However, there are some difficulties introduced by nonbinary relationships, many-to-many relationships, descriptive attributes of relationships, existence dependencies, and generalization abstraction.

1. For the simple case in which strong entities are related by a binary one-to-many relationship with no descriptive attributes, each entity becomes a record type and the relationship is kept by making the "one" entity the owner of a set type in which the "many" entity is a member.
2. If there is a one-to-one binary relationship with no descriptive attributes, we have a choice of combining the two entities into a single record type or creating a set type with one entity as the owner record and the other as the member record type.
3. To resolve a binary many-to-many relationship, we construct intersection records consisting of the keys of the associated entities and any descriptive attributes. The original entities become owner records of sets in which the intersection record is the member type. This technique is described in detail in Section 9.3.
4. For either one-to-one or one-to-many binary relationships with intersection information, since the set pointer cannot contain any data, we create a new record type, called a **link** or **junction** record, which consists of only the descriptive attributes as data fields. This link record will become the member type in two set types, each owned by the original entity records. We may wish to place direct parent pointers in link records.
5. To resolve ternary relationships, there are two techniques. The simplest method, usable if there are no descriptive attributes, is to substitute two or three binary relationships for the ternary one. Thus if entities *A*, *B*, and *C* are related, we might preserve the information by forming the two binary relationships *A* to *B* and *B* to *C*, or the three binary relationships *A* to *B*, *A* to *C*, and *B* to *C*. The other possibility is to create a new record type, called a **link** or **dummy** record, consisting of just pointers with no data fields or with a system-generated surrogate field. If there are descriptive attributes for the relationship, fields for them may be added to the link record. Each of the entities then becomes a record which is an owner of a set in which the link record is the member type.
6. For general *n*-ary relationships, we extend the method described in step 5 for ternary relationships.

7. For identifier existence dependencies, we can use essential sets to connect owner entities to weak member entities, or "migrate" the key of the strong entity into the weak entity record and use a structural constraint, if available, to enforce integrity.
8. When the E-R diagram contains a generalization relationship, as shown by an ISA triangle, there are three ways to proceed. The first is to let each entity become a record type, and let the higher-level entity become the owner of a multimember set type in which the lower-level entity records are the members. The set should have AUTOMATIC FIXED or AUTOMATIC MANDATORY class. Alternatively, we let each entity become a record type and have separate set types for each of the subtype entities. A second possibility is to have a single record type for the entire generalization, with the higher-level entity represented by common attributes and the subtype entities represented by variant fields. How this is done depends on the host language. For COBOL, for example, a "REDEFINES" clause allows us to describe alternative structures within a record. In PL/1, we use a tag field to specify which structure will be used in a record. The third alternative is to create record types only for the subtypes, repeating the attributes of the higher-level entity in the record of each subtype. Each of these choices loses some information about the relationship between the elements of the generalization.

Except for these situations, the transformation of an E-R diagram into a network data structure diagram is quite straightforward, with records replacing entities and sets replacing relationships.

9.9 *Chapter Summary*

The network model grew out of **IDS**, a DBMS developed during the 1960s at GE. It influenced the **CODASYL DBTG**, a committee formed to propose national standards for database systems. Various DBTG and later **DDLC** proposals were published periodically and many commercial products are based on the reports, especially the 1971 version.

The DBTG model supports the three-level architecture. It uses a **network** or **plex** structure, a directed graph consisting of **nodes** and **links**. The nodes become **record** types and the links become **pointers**. Records consist of **data items**, and relationships are represented by **sets**. A **set type** consists of one **owner** record type and one or more **member** record types. Many-to-many relationships require an **intersection** record consisting of the keys of the related entity instances. Similar **link** records are needed to handle ternary or general *n*-ary relationships and relationships with descriptive attributes.

All sets are implemented with chains or arrays of **pointers**. Options include **owner** and **prior** pointers. **Essential** or **information-bearing sets** use pointers alone to show the relationship, while **value-based** sets contain data that identifies the owner. Special set types include **multimember, singular (system-owned)**, and **dynamic** sets.

The major sections of a DBTG schema are **the schema section, the area section, the record section,** and **the set section.** There may be locks for various operations on the schema, area, record, or data item level. The **location mode** of a record, the method used to store it, may be **calc, via** a set, or **direct.** The **mode** of a set is the pointer method used. The **order** is the order of the member records within a set occurrence. **Chronological order** may be **first, last, next, prior,** or **immaterial. Sorted order** for single-member sets is by **defined key.** For multimember set types, order may be **sorted by record name, sorted by defined keys,** or **sorted within record name.** Set **insertion classes** are **manual** or **automatic.** Set **retention classes** are **fixed, mandatory,** or **optional.** Set **occurrence selection** is the method used to determine to what occurrence of a set a member should belong. Options are **thru current of set, by value of a field, structural,** and **through a procedure.** The **subschema** is a description of the external model of a user. Sections in the subschema are **the title division, the mapping division,** and **the structure division.**

The user work area contains **currency indicators** for the current of the **run unit, each record type, each set type,** and **each area.** It has **record templates** to hold retrieved records. It also has **status flags** that indicate the status of attempted operations. Some DML commands are **open, close, find, get, modify, erase, store, connect, disconnect,** and **reconnect.**

IDMS/R is a network-based DBMS with a relational user interface. It consists of a large set of integrated products, with the heart being the **IDMS/R Engine** and the Integrated Data Dictionary, **IDD.** The DML is similar to the DBTG DML, but requires a READY to open a realm and a FINISH to close it. A single command, OBTAIN, is a combination of the FIND and GET, both of which still exist.

The mapping of an E-R model to a network model is usually fairly straightforward, with the E-R diagram and the data structure diagram being almost identical.

9.10 *Exercises*

1. Draw data structure diagram representations of the following associations in a college.
   (a) Each student has only one major department, but a department has many students.
   (b) Each student may have more than one major, and a department has many students.
   (c) Each department has several faculty members, and each faculty member may belong to more than one department.
   (d) A student may belong to several clubs, each of which has many students.
   (e) Each faculty member teaches three courses, and each student takes up to five courses.

2. Explain the meaning of the set insertion and set retention classes in the context of voter registration and belonging to a political party.

3. For the E-R diagram in Figure 9.17, draw a corresponding data structure diagram.

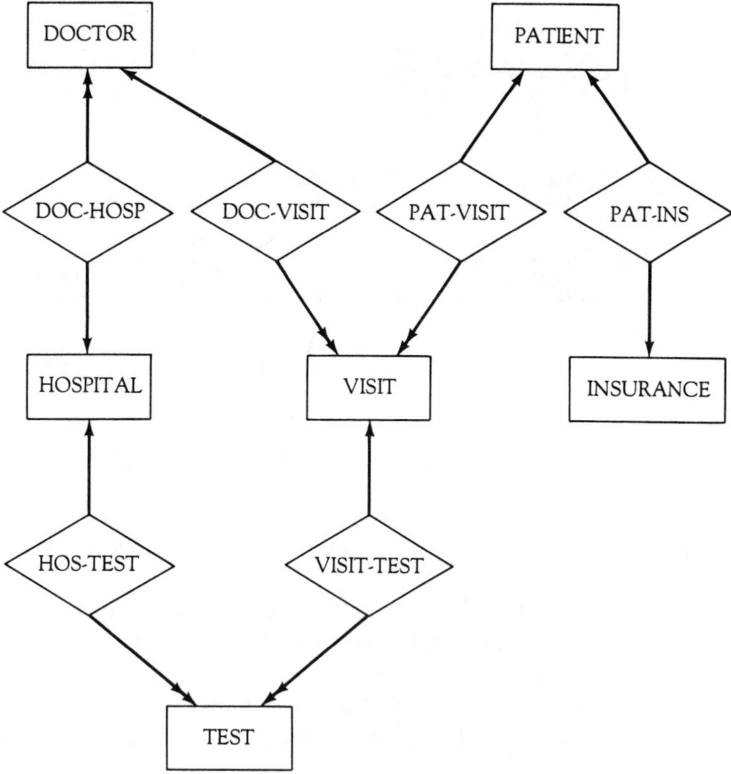

Figure 9.17 E-R Diagram

4. For the data structure diagram in Figure 9.18, write a DBTG schema, making assumptions about data types, location mode, set order, set selection, and so on, as needed.

5. For the schema in Exercise 4, write a subschema for a user who sees only PROJECT, TASK, and PART records, with CONSISTSOF and TASK-PART sets.

6. Make a list of currency indicators for the schema in Exercise 4 using Figure 9.16 as a model. Show what changes occur as the following records are accessed by a program.
   (a) Employee E1001.
   (b) Part P15 in the Midtown store in New York.
   (c) Project J20.
   (d) Task T300 in project J40.
   (e) Part number P30 in the Uptown store in Houston.

7. Assuming that the user's schema includes the entire database as pictured in Figure 9.18, write DML statements to do each of the following.
   (a) Get a list of the names of all employees in Denver.

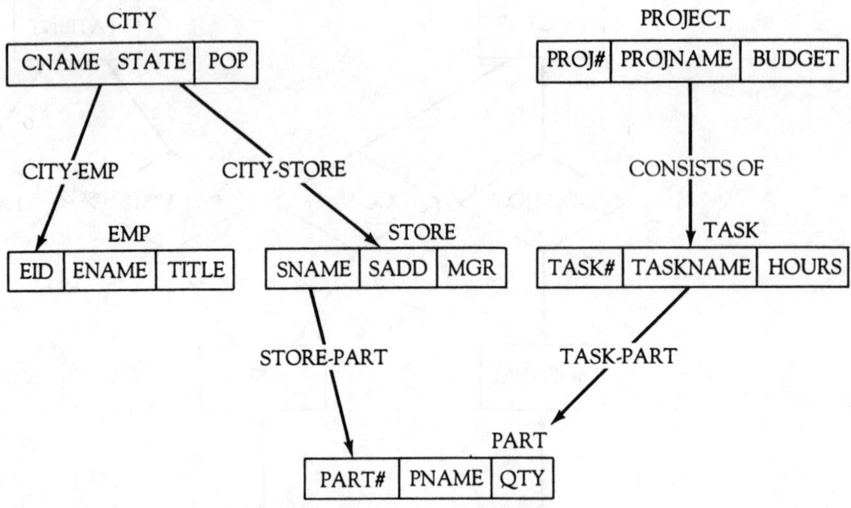

Figure 9.18 Data Structure Diagram

(b) Find all the stores in Chicago that have part P20.
(c) Find the names and hours of all tasks for the J300 project.
(d) Find out what tasks use part P20.
(e) Insert the record of a new employee, making up data.
(f) Increase the quantity of part P20 in the Downtown store in Baltimore by 500.

8. Given the schema shown in Figure 9.19, draw the corresponding data structure diagram.

```
SCHEMA NAME IS ABSDATA
AREA NAME IS AREA1, AREA2, AREA3
RECORD NAME IS RECA
WITHIN AREA1
LOCATION MODE IS CALC USING A1
DUPLICATES ARE ALLOWED
02   A1   PIC IS X(4)
02   A2   TYPE IS DECIMAL(5,2)
RECORD NAME IS RECB
WITHIN AREA2
LOCATION MODE IS CALC USING B1
DUPLICATES ARE NOT ALLOWED
02   B1   PIC IS 9999V99
02   B2   PIC IS X(5)
02   B3   TYPE IS DECIMAL(6,1)
RECORD NAME IS RECC
WITHIN AREA2
LOCATION MODE IS CALC USING C1
02   C1   PIC IS X(5)
```

Figure 9.19 Schema for Data Structure Diagram

```
02   C2   OCCURS 3 TIMES
     03   C21  PIC IS 99V99
     03   C22  PIC IS X(5)
     03   C23  PIC IS 999
02   C3   TYPE IS DECIMAL(6,2)
RECORD NAME IS RECD
WITHIN AREA1
LOCATION MODE IS VIA X SET
02   D1   TYPE IS INTEGER(5)
02   D2   TYPE IS INTEGER(2)
02   D3   OCCURS D2 TIMES
     03   D31  PIC IS 99V99
     03   D32  PIC IS X(4)
     03   D33  PIC IS 999
RECORD NAME IS RECE
WITHIN AREA2,AREA3
LOCATION MODE IS VIA Z SET
02   E1   PIC IS X(6)
02   E2   TYPE IS DECIMAL(6,1)
RECORD NAME IS RECF
WITHIN AREA1
LOCATION MODE IS CALC USING F1
DUPLICATES ARE NOT ALLOWED
02   F1   PIC IS 999V9
02   F2   TYPE IS FLOAT(6)
RECORD NAME IS RECG
WITHIN AREA3
LOCATION MODE IS CALC USING G1
DUPLICATES ARE NOT ALLOWED
02   G1   PIC IS 999V9
02   G2   PIC IS X(8)
02   G3   PIC IS 9(5)
RECORD NAME IS RECH
WITHIN AREA3
LOCATION MODE IS VIA T SET
02   H1   TYPE IS DECIMAL(6,2)
02   H2   TYPE IS FLOAT(8)
RECORD NAME IS RECI
WITHIN AREA3
LOCATION MODE IS CALC USING I2
02   I1   PIC IS 9(4)
02   I2   TYPE IS CHAR(8)
SET NAME IS X
MODE IS CHAIN
OWNER IS RECA
MEMBER IS RECD AUTOMATIC FIXED
SET NAME IS Y
MODE IS ARRAY DYNAMIC
OWNER IS RECB
MEMBER IS RECD MANUAL OPTIONAL
```

Figure 9.19 Continued

```
SET NAME IS Z
MODE IS ARRAY
OWNER IS RECB
MEMBER IS RECE AUTOMATIC MANDATORY
SET NAME IS W
OWNER IS SYSTEM
MEMBER IS RECC
SET NAME IS V
OWNER IS RECD
MEMBER IS RECF AUTOMATIC MANDATORY
MEMBER IS RECG AUTOMATIC MANDATORY
ORDER IS SORTED BY DEFINED KEYS
ASCENDING KEY IS F1
DUPLICATES ARE NOT ALLOWED
ASCENDING KEY IS G1
DUPLICATES ARE NOT ALLOWED
SET NAME IS U
MODE IS CHAIN
OWNER IS RECG
MEMBER IS RECI MANUAL OPTIONAL
ORDER IS FIRST
SET NAME IS T
MODE IS ARRAY
OWNER IS RECE
MEMBER IS RECH AUTOMATIC OPTIONAL
ORDER IS LAST
SET NAME IS S
MODE IS CHAIN
OWNER IS RECC
MEMBER IS RECE AUTOMATIC FIXED
ORDER IS NEXT
```

Figure 9.19 Continued

9.11 *Bibliography*

American National Standards Institute. "Study Group on Data Base Management Systems: Interim Report," FDT 7:2 (1975) New York: ACM.

Bachman, C. "Data Structure Diagrams," Data Base, Journal of the ACM SIGBDP 1:2 (March, 1969) pp. 4-10.

Bachman, C. "The Programmer as Navigator," Communications of the ACM 16:1 (November, 1973), pp. 653-658.

Bradley, J. *File and Data Base Techniques*. New York: Holt, Rinehart and Winston, 1982.

CODASYL. *CODASYL Data Base Task Group April 71 Report*. New York: ACM, 1971.

CODASYL. *CODASYL Data Description Language Journal of Development*. Ottawa, Ontario: Material Data Management Branch, Dept. of Supply and Services, 1978.

Jardine, D. (Ed.) *The ANSI/SPARC DBMS Model.* Amsterdam: North Holland, 1977.

Schenk, J. "Implementation Aspects of the DBTG Proposal," Proceedings of the IFIP Working Conference on Database Management Systems (1974).

Taylor, R. and R. Frank. "CODASYL Data Base Management Systems," ACM Computing Surveys 8:1 (March, 1976) pp. 67-103.

Tsichritzis, D. and A. Klug (Ed.). *The ANSI/X3/SPARC Framework.* Montvale, NJ: AFIPS Press, 1978.

Tsichritzis, D. and F. Lochovsky. *Data Models.* Englewood Cliffs, NJ: Prentice-Hall, 1982.

SAMPLE PROJECT: (1) MAPPING THE E-R MODEL FOR CLERICALTEMPS TO A NETWORK DATA MODEL AND (2) CREATING AND MANIPULATING AN IDMS DATABASE FOR CLERICALTEMPS

Step 9.1

Convert the E-R diagram to a network data structure diagram.

a. Make each strong entity a record type.
b. Migrate keys to identifier-dependent weak entities and make each a record type, or construct essential sets to connect each weak entity record to the associated strong entity record. If you migrated the keys, construct value-based sets to keep the connection. Make other types of weak entities record types, and construct value-based sets to connect them to their owner records.
c. Convert one-to-many binary relationships with no descriptive attributes to set types.
d. For binary relationships with descriptive attributes, and ternary or *n*-ary relations with or without descriptive attributes, construct link records, and define appropriate sets.
e. For one-to-one relationships, decide whether to combine records into a single record type or construct a set type with a single owner and single member occurrence in each.
f. For many-to-many binary relationships, construct intersection record types and set types for each owner type.
g. For generalizations, decide which of the three possible representations you wish to use, and construct the appropriate record types and/or sets.

Applying these steps to the E-R diagram for ClericalTemps that we developed at the end of Chapter 5, we see the following:

a. We will have the following records that represent strong entities:

WORKER - EMPID, EMPNAME, SSN, EMPADD, EMPPHONE, DOB, SEX, DATEHIRED, LASTDATEWORKED, AVERRATING, WORDPROC, TYPING, FILING, BOOKKPING, STENO, AVAILCODE
CLIENT - CLID, CLNAME, CLADD, CLPHONE, CONTACT, BILLINGYTD, PAYMENTSYTD

b. There are three weak entity sets, PAYROLL, JOB, and BILL. We could choose to put EMPID in PAYROLL, and CLID in JOB and BILL, or simply to construct three essential sets, which we name WORKER-PAYROLL, CLIENT-JOB, and CLIENT-BILL. We will choose to migrate the keys and construct value-based sets. We therefore have the following records:

PAYROLL - EMPID, CHECK#, PAYDATE, GROSS, FED, FICA, STATE, LOCAL, NET, GROSSYTD, NETYTD, FEDYTD, FICAYTD, STATEYTD, LOCALYTD

JOB - CLID, JOB#, JOBTITLE, STARTDATE, EXPECTENDDATE, DAILYRATE, DAILYHOURS, REPORTTONAME, REPORTTOADD, REPORTTOPHONE, JOBSTATUS

BILL - CLID, INVOICE#, BILLDATE, OLDBAL, TOTCHARGES, NEWBAL, TOTPAID

We also need the following sets to associate these records with their owners:

WORKER-PAYROLL SET: Owner is WORKER, Member is PAYROLL
CLIENT-JOB SET: Owner is CLIENT, Member is JOB
CLIENT-BILL SET: Owner is CLIENT, Member is BILL

c. There are no additional one-to-many binary relationships without descriptive attributes.

d. The relationship set connecting WORKER to JOB is one-to-many with three descriptive attributes. We therefore create a link record, which we call ASSIGN, having attributes RATERNAME, RATINGDATE, and EMP-RATING. ASSIGN will be a member of an essential set owned by WORKER which links all assignments with the worker, and also a member of an essential set owned by JOB. The JOB-ASSIGN set will be one-to-one. The following records and sets result:

ASSIGN - RATERNAME, RATINGDATE, EMP-RATING
WORKER-ASSIGN SET: Owner is WORKER, Member is ASSIGN
JOB-ASSIGN SET: Owner is JOB, Member is ASSIGN

To enable us to link the essential set member occurrences directly to their owners, we will insert OWNER pointers in them. Note that we could have made both of the sets value-based if we had chosen to place EMPID and JOB# in ASSIGN.

e. There are no one-to-one relationships pictured in the E-R diagram.

f. There are no many-to-many relationships.

g. There are no generalization relationships.

The resulting data structure diagram is pictured in Figure 9.20. Note that we have omitted fields and areas, to simplify the diagram.

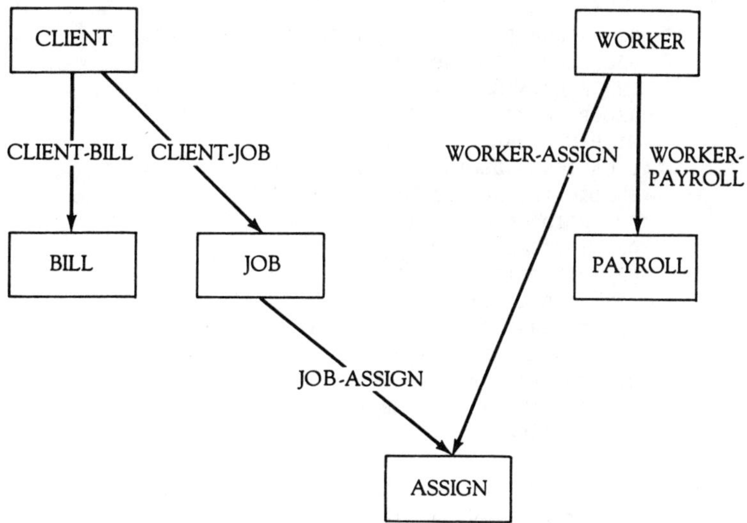

Figure 9.20 Schema for Data Structure Diagram

Step 9.2

Write a schema for the network database.

For our ClericalTemps data structure diagram, we have the following schema:

```
SCHEMA NAME IS TEMPSDATA
AREA NAME IS AREAA
PRIVACY LOCK IS EMP
AREA NAME IS AREAB
PRIVACY LOCK IS HUSH
RECORD NAME IS CLIENT
WITHIN AREAB
LOCATION MODE IS CALC USING CLID
DUPLICATES ARE NOT ALLOWED
02  CLID  PIC IS X(5)
02  CLNAME  PIC IS X(25)
02  CLADD  PIC IS X(40)
02  CLPHONE PIC IS X(10)
02  CONTACT  PIC IS X(20)
02  BILLINGYTD  TYPE IS DECIMAL(10,2)
02  PAYMENTSYTD  TYPE IS DECIMAL(10,2)
RECORD NAME IS JOB
WITHIN AREAA
LOCATION MODE IS CALC USING CLID
DUPLICATES ARE FIRST
02  CLID  PIC IS X(5)
02  JOB#  PIC IS X(8)
02  JOBTITLE PIC IS X(15)
02  STARTDATE  PIC IS X(8)
02  EXPECTENDDATE PIC IS X(8)
02  DAILYRATE TYPE IS INTEGER
02  DAILYHOURS  PIC IS X(9)
02  REPORTTONAME  PIC IS X(20)
```

```
02  REPORTTOADD  PIC IS X(40)
02  REPORTTOPHONE  PIC IS X(10)
02  JOBSTATUS  PIC IS X
RECORD NAME IS BILL
WITHIN AREAA
LOCATION MODE IS CALC USING CLID
DUPLICATES ARE FIRST
02  CLID  PIC IS X(5)
02  INVOICE#  PIC IS X(6)
02  BILLDATE  PIC IS X(8)
02  OLDBAL  PIC IS 9999V99
02  TOTCHARGES  PIC IS 9999V99
02  NEWBAL  PIC IS 9999V99
02  TOTPAID  PIC IS 9999V99
RECORD NAME IS WORKER
WITHIN AREAB
LOCATION MODE IS CALC USING EMPID
DUPLICATES ARE NOT ALLOWED
02  EMPID  PIC IS X(5)
02  EMPNAME  PIC IS X(20)
02  SSN  PIC IS X(9)
02  EMPADD PIC IS X(40)
02  EMPPHONE  PIC IS X(10)
02  DOB  PIC IS X(8)
02  SEX  PIC IS X
02  DATEHIRED  PIC IS X(8)
02  LASTDATEWORKED  PIC IS X(8)
02  AVERRATING  TYPE IS DECIMAL(3,2)
02  WORDPROC  PIC IS X(5)
02  TYPING  TYPE IS INTEGER
02  FILING  PIC IS X
02  BOOKKPING  PIC IS X
02  STENO  PIC IS X
02  AVAILCODE  PIC IS X(8)
RECORD NAME IS PAYROLL
WITHIN AREAB
LOCATION MODE IS CALC USING EMPID
DUPLICATES ARE FIRST
02  EMPID  PIC IS X(5)
02  CHECK#  TYPE IS INTEGER
02  PAYDATE  PIC IS X(8)
02  GROSS  TYPE IS DECIMAL(6,2)
02  FED  TYPE IS DECIMAL(6,2)
02  FICA  TYPE IS DECIMAL(5,2)
02  STATE  TYPE IS DECIMAL(5,2)
02  LOCAL  TYPE IS DECIMAL(5,2)
02  NET  TYPE IS DECIMAL(6,2)
02  GROSSYTD  TYPE IS DECIMAL(8,2)
02  NETYTD  TYPE IS DECIMAL(8,2)
02  FEDYTD TYPE IS DECIMAL(8,2)
02  FICAYTD  TYPE IS DECIMAL(6,2)
02  STATEYTD  TYPE IS DECIMAL(7,2)
02  LOCALYTD  TYPE IS DECIMAL(7,2)
RECORD NAME IS ASSIGN
WITHIN AREAB
```

```
LOCATION MODE IS VIA WORKER-ASSIGN SET
02  RATERNAME TYPE IS CHAR20
02  RATINGDATE PIC IS X(8)
02  EMPRATING  TYPE IS DECIMAL(3,2)
SET NAME IS CLIENT-JOB
MODE IS CHAIN
ORDER IS FIRST
OWNER IS CLIENT
MEMBER IS JOB AUTOMATIC FIXED
SET NAME IS CLIENT-BILL
MODE IS CHAIN
ORDER IS FIRST
OWNER IS CLIENT
MEMBER IS BILL AUTOMATIC FIXED
SET NAME IS WORKER-PAYROLL
MODE IS CHAIN
ORDER IS FIRST
OWNER IS WORKER
MEMBER IS PAYROLL AUTOMATIC FIXED
SET NAME IS JOB-ASSIGN
MODE IS CHAIN LINKED TO OWNER
ORDER IS FIRST
OWNER IS JOB
MEMBER IS ASSIGN AUTOMATIC FIXED
SET NAME IS WORKER-ASSIGN
MODE IS CHAIN LINKED TO OWNER
ORDER IS FIRST
OWNER IS WORKER
MEMBER IS ASSIGN AUTOMATIC FIXED
```

Step 9.3

Write a subschema for the database.

For our ClericalTemps application, we will choose a subschema that consists of all the information about workers, including their job assignments.

```
TITLE DIVISION
SS WORKS WITHIN TEMPSDATA
MAPPING DIVISION
STRUCTURE DIVISION
RECORD SECTION
01  WORKER ALL
01  PAYROLL ALL
01  ASSIGN ALL
SET SECTION
SD  WORKER-PAYROLL
SD  WORKER-ASSIGN
```

Step 9.4

Write out DDL commands for five nonroutine queries against the database.

1. Print out the number, title, start and end dates, and status of all the jobs from client C1000.

```
CLID = 'C1000';
FIND ANY CLIENT USING CLID;
FIND FIRST JOB WITHIN CLIENT-JOB
DO WHILE (DBSTATUS = 0);
   GET JOB;
   PUT LIST (JOB#, JOBTITLE, STARTDATE, EXPECTENDDATE, JOBSTATUS);
   FIND NEXT JOB WITHIN CLIENT-JOB;
END;
```

2. Find all the ratings earned by worker E2001.

```
EMPID = 'E2001';
FIND ANY WORKER USING EMPID;
FIND FIRST ASSIGN WITHIN WORKER-ASSIGN;
DO WHILE (DBSTATUS=0);
    GET ASSIGN;
    PUT LIST (EMPRATING);
    FIND NEXT ASSIGN WITHIN WORKER-ASSIGN;
END;
```

3. Find the name and address of all clients for whom E2001 has worked.

```
EMPID = 'E2001';
FIND ANY WORKER USING EMPID;
FIND FIRST ASSIGN WITHIN WORKER-ASSIGN;
DO WHILE (DBSTATUS=0);
     FIND OWNER WITHIN JOB-ASSIGN;
     FIND OWNER WITHIN CLIENT-JOB;
     PUT LIST (CLNAME, CLADD)
     FIND NEXT ASSIGN WITHIN WORKER-ASSIGN;
END;
```

4. Increase the amount paid on the most recent invoice of client C1000 by $250.00.

```
CLID = 'C1000';
FIND FIRST CLIENT USING CLID;
FIND FOR UPDATE FIRST BILL WITHIN CLIENT-BILL;
GET BILL;
AMTPAID = AMTPAID + 250.00;
MODIFY BILL;
```

5. Insert a new job record for client C1000.

```
CLID = 'C1000';
JOB# = 'J1001001';
JOBTITLE = 'Bookkeeping';
STARTDATE = '900415';
EXPECTENDDATE = '900430';
DAILYHOURS = '9:30-5:00';
REPORTTONAME = 'Johnson,Jim';
REPORTTOADD = '10 Main Street, Greenville, NY 10101';
REPORTTOPHONE = '2001234567';
JOBSTATUS = '0';
STORE JOB;
```

Student Project: Creating a Network Database

Follow the steps of the Sample Project to construct a data structure diagram for your project. Write the schema, a subschema, and five queries.

CHAPTER

10

The Hierarchical Model

10 Chapter Objectives

In this chapter you will learn

- the history of IMS
- how to traverse a tree using preorder
- how a tree can be used to represent data and relationships
- how a tree can be represented in storage
- how IMS fits the three-level architecture
- how to create physical and logical IMS databases
- how to retrieve and update data in an IMS database
- how IMS databases are represented internally
- why and how to create secondary data set groups in IMS
- when and how to create secondary indexes in IMS

10.1 *Hierarchical Data Structure*

The hierarchical model is the oldest of the three record-based data models, dating from the 1960s. Unlike the relational model, which was firmly grounded in theoretical research, and the network model, which developed along with carefully written specifications, the hierarchical model simply grew out of practice. It was an "ad hoc" solution to immediate needs of real applications. The oldest hierarchical database management system, IBM's IMS, was developed to organize and store information needed by the space program for the Apollo moon landing project. North American Aviation (which became Rockwell) and IBM worked jointly to produce the first version of IMS, which was released in 1968. Since then IMS has been the dominant hierarchical database management system in the marketplace; in fact, as of this writing, it is the most widely used of all DBMSs, although relational products, particularly DB2, are rapidly gaining ground. Several improvements have been made to IMS since 1968, resulting in new releases to take advantage of hardware and software improvements, provide new features, and maximize performance. IMS is known as a "workhorse," capable of processing large amounts of data efficiently. It uses a structure familiar to programmers who are accustomed to working with files, and provides predictable performance, since all access paths are known in advance. However, it is not as flexible or as easy to understand as relational systems. The current version, IMS/VS, runs under MVS. Another important hierarchical DBMS is System 2000 from Intel Corporation. Both use the same basic data structures.

The hierarchical model uses the **tree** as its basic structure. As explained in Chapter 3, a tree is a data structure that consists of a **hierarchy of nodes**, with a single node, called the **root**, at the highest level. A node may have any number of **children**, but each child node may have only one **parent** node on which it is dependent. The parent-to-child relationship in a tree is thus a one-to-many relationship, but the child-to-parent is one-to-one. Parent-child relationships are shown by drawing a line or an **edge** between the parent and child nodes. Figure 10.1, which is a repetition of Figure 3.27, represents an example of a tree structure. A node that has no children is called a **leaf**; note that leaves can occur on different levels. Nodes that are children of the same parent are called **siblings**. For any node, there is a single path, called the **hierarchical path**, from the root to that node. The nodes along this path are called that node's **ancestors**. Similarly, for a given node, any node along a path from that node to a leaf is called its **descendant**. If you visualize a node as if it were the root node in a new tree, the node and all its descendants form a **subtree** of the original tree. The **height** of a tree is the number of nodes on the longest hierarchical path from the root to a leaf. The tree in Figure 10.1 has height of 4. A tree is said to be **balanced** if every path from the root node to a leaf has the same length. The tree in our example is not balanced, since the path from *A* to *F* has length 3, while the path from *A* to *K* has length 4. A **binary** tree is one in which each node has no more than two children. Our example is clearly not a binary tree, since both *A* and *D* have three children.

We can represent a tree in storage in a "**flat**" or **tape-like** form by showing dependent node data after the parent node data. We will use a method of visiting and listing all nodes of the tree called **preorder traversal** which can be summarized by the following

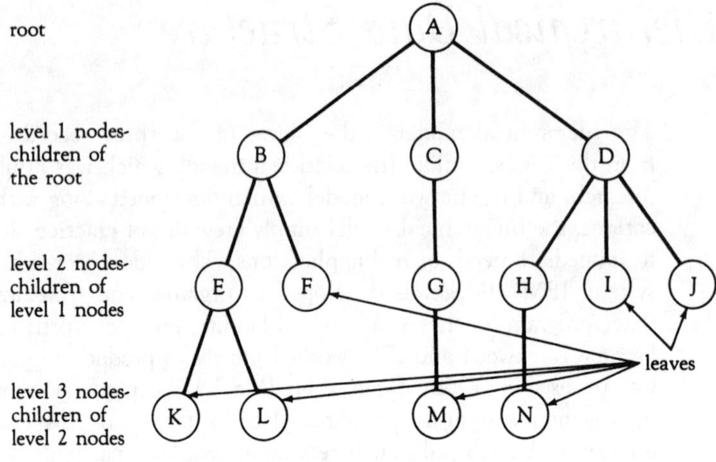

Figure 10.1

rules, starting with the root:

1. Visit the node if it has not already been visited,
2. Else visit the leftmost child that has not already been visited,
3. Else, if no descendants remain to be visited, return to the parent node and repeat this procedure on it.

Thus we start at the root and traverse its subtrees from left to right, recursively. Starting at the root, we visit the leftmost child, then its leftmost child, and continue in this fashion until we reach a leaf on the leftmost branch. We then move up one level to that leaf's parent, and from there proceed to its leftmost unvisited child. We continue until we have visited every node. When we visit a node for the first time, we print its name. Preorder traversal of the tree in Figure 10.1 gives us

A B E K L F C G M D H N I J

In the hierarchical database model, a database consists of a **collection of occurrences of a single type of tree** (i.e., a single tree structure diagram). The tree need not be either binary or balanced. In this model, each named node or **segment** contains one or more named **fields** or data items that represent **attributes** describing an **entity**. The entire tree may be a description of a single entity, or different segments within a tree may be used to represent different, but related, entities. Figure 10.2 shows a possible data structure diagram for a tree representing the STUDENT, FACULTY, CLASS, and ENROLL example. In this structure, we have chosen to make FACULTY the root node or segment. Its fields are FACID, FACNAME, DEPT, and RANK. We have represented CLASS as a child of FACULTY, which shows that there is a one-to-many relationship between each FACULTY record and its associated CLASS records. It is possible to visualize this relationship by saying that CLASS records do not exist independently, but are nested within FACULTY records. Note that we omitted the FACID field from the CLASS segment. Since the class is within a particular faculty record, there is no need to repeat the FACID. Its value is "inherited" from the parent. We also made the

STUDENT record a segment of the tree, and represented it as a child of CLASS. We added GRADE to the STUDENT segment since there is no ambiguity about which course the student's grade is for. Again, we are implying a one-to-many relationship between CLASS and STUDENT. We can visualize the STUDENT record as nested inside the CLASS record. By placing the STUDENT record inside the CLASS record, which is, in turn, inside the FACULTY record, we are showing which classes a faculty member teaches and which students are enrolled in those classes, so we no longer need the ENROLL records. Relationships are represented in the hierarchical model by **physical record placement** or by pointers that simulate such placement, rather than by the data itself.

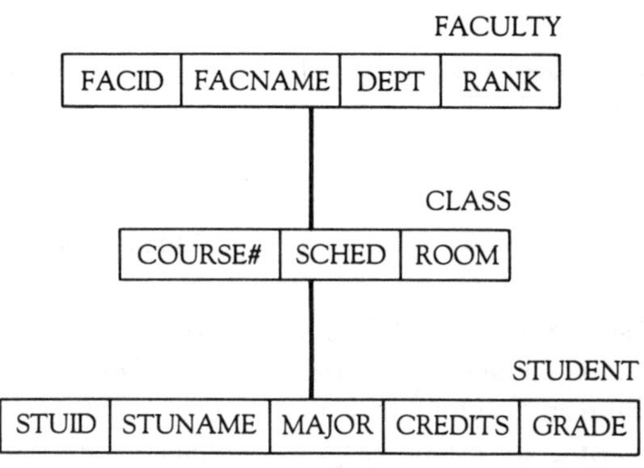

Figure 10.2

Figure 10.3 shows an occurrence of the FACULTY-CLASS-STUDENT tree. In an occurrence, a child node may appear zero, one, or many times, even though it appears exactly once in the tree structure diagram. In our example, for a given FACULTY record, there may be as many CLASS segments as needed, and each of these may have an arbitrary number of STUDENT segments. Multiple occurrences of the same child node type within the same parent segment occurrence are called **twins**. In a tree occurrence, **siblings** are segments that are of different types but have the same parent segment occurrence. Therefore, the two CLASS segments are twins, since they have the same parent segment occurrence, the FACULTY segment of F110. Also, the records of Students S1002 and S1010 are twins, since they have the same parent, MTH103C. However, the record of Student S1020 is not their twin, since it has a different parent occurrence, namely MTH101B. If a particular segment does not appear in an occurrence, none of its dependent segments may appear either. For our example, this means that no student segments can appear without a corresponding class segment, nor can a class appear without a corresponding faculty segment.

We can represent an occurrence in storage by using **preorder traversal** to get a flat representation of the tree, as shown in Figure 10.4. In that representation, we see that the FACULTY segment appears first, followed by the first CLASS segment, which is followed by the first STUDENT in that class. Since there is only one student in the class, we continue with the second CLASS segment, followed by the first STUDENT in that class, then the second STUDENT. If there were another CLASS segment for this faculty member, it would appear next. Since there are no more classes for Professor

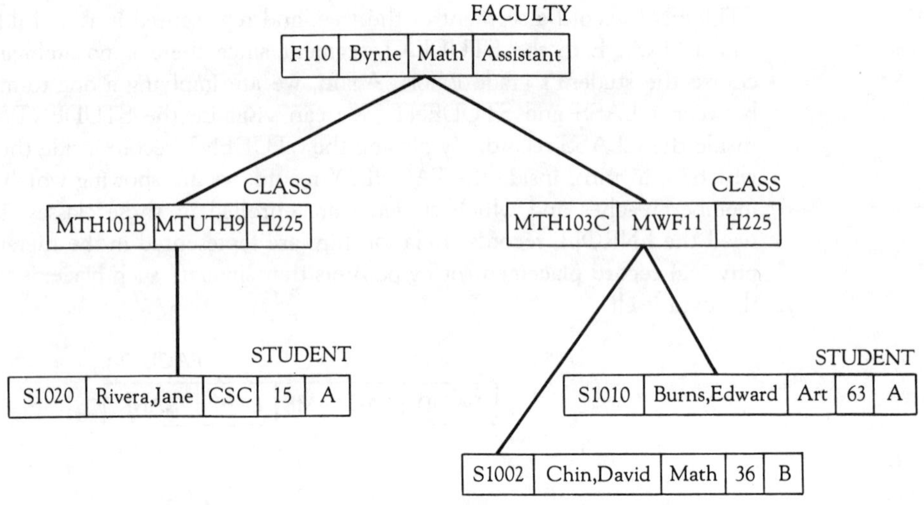

Figure 10.3

Byrne, the next FACULTY record follows. Notice that each new root segment signals the start of a new occurrence of the tree. For our example, there are as many occurrences as there are faculty members. You may wonder how the DBMS knows that a particular segment is, for example, a faculty segment rather than another student segment. In the hierarchical model, each segment type is assigned a unique **type code**, according to its position in the tree structure diagram. The type codes are determined by the preorder traversal of the tree structure, so the root has type code 1, its leftmost child has type code 2, the leftmost child of that child has type code 3, and so on. For the example in Figure 10.2, FACULTY has type code 1, CLASS has type code 2, and STUDENT has type code 3. For the tree structure in Figure 10.1, the type codes are as follows:

NODE	*A*	*B*	*E*	*K*	*L*	*F*	*C*	*G*	*M*	*D*	*H*	*N*	*I*	J
TYPE CODE	1	2	3	4	5	6	7	8	9	10	11	12	13	14

In storage, the type code, along with other overhead information, is stored as a **prefix** for the segment, but is not seen by the user. This enables the DBMS to distinguish segments from one another. Each new tree occurrence starts with a type code of 1.

The structure we have chosen represents all records in the database as information about faculty members. There are no independent CLASS or STUDENT records, since these are dependent segments of a tree in which FACULTY is the root node. The relationships among these segments are represented by positions in the tree. The structure in this example makes it easy to answer the questions "Find information about all classes taught by Professor *X*" and "Find information about all students in Professor *X*'s classes." All we need to do to answer either of these is to find Professor *X*'s record and look inside. However, it is very difficult to answer the question "Find information about Student *Y*." To do so, we would have to search sequentially to find the FACULTY record for a teacher who has Student *Y* in class. This gives us *Y*'s ID, name, major, and credits, as well as the grade for that course. We would need to continue searching

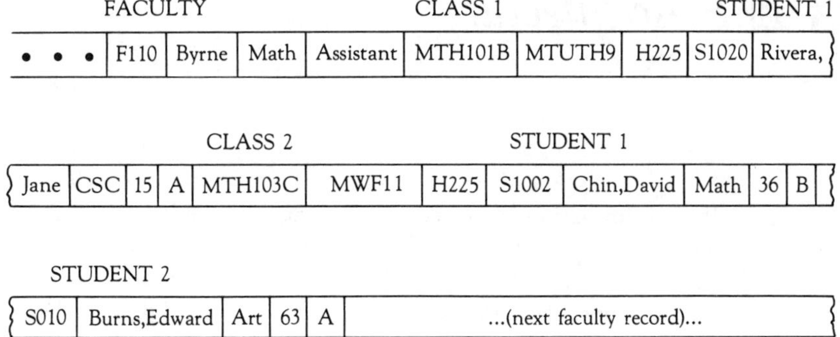

Figure 10.4

to get all of *Y*'s grades, however. Notice that the student information is duplicated for every class in which the student is enrolled. Not only does this waste space, but it creates consistency problems if one occurrence is updated and others are not. We could make our question about Student *Y* easier to answer by choosing a different structure for our tree. An alternative tree structure diagram is shown in Figure 10.5. Now the database contains student information, with the faculty and class data subordinate to the student data. While our student question becomes easier to answer, the question "Find information about Professor *X*" is harder, since we must search student records to find a student who has Professor *X* as a teacher. This time, the faculty information is repeated for every student who has a particular faculty member as a teacher. The question "Find information about all students in Professor *X*'s classes" is even worse, since we must search the entire database, looking in each student record to see if Professor *X* appears as the teacher, and, if so, backing up to read the student information. This illustrates the type of trade-off we have to consider in choosing a particular structure for the hierarchical model. Since the root node dominates all others, we should choose the structure that matches the most frequently asked or important questions.

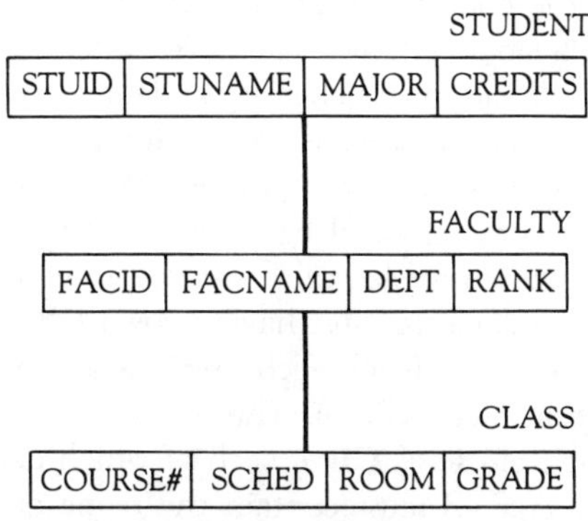

Figure 10.5

10.2 *IMS Architecture*

IMS, **Information Management System**, uses the hierarchical model. Several improvements have been made to IMS since the first version was released, resulting in a structure that is slightly more flexible than a strict hierarchical one, through the use of **logical relationships**. IMS uses a data sublanguage called **DL/1**, or **Data Language One**. DL/1 was originally designed for batch processing only, so its basic form is embedded in a host language, but it now allows on-line queries as well.

IMS was developed before abstract data models were defined, so it does not illustrate perfectly the three-level architecture for databases. However, it is possible to discuss IMS in the context of the abstract model. Figure 10.6 shows the basic IMS architecture. Roughly speaking, at the **conceptual level**, an IMS environment may have several **physical databases**. Each database is a set of physical database records, all occurrences of a single tree structure. For our example, we might have the FACULTY database, which would contain all occurrences of FACULTY records, containing faculty, class, and student data within them. There could be other physical databases containing information about buildings, equipment, financial data, and so on. Each physical database record consists of a hierarchical arrangement of segments occurrences, strictly sequenced, as shown in Figure 10.3. The physical representation may be as shown in Figure 10.4 or this arrangement may be simulated with pointers.

For each of the physical databases, a complete definition, called the **DBD** or **Database Description**, is written. These physical DBDs are stored in object form for use by IMS. The physical DBDs must obey all the restrictions for trees; in particular, no node may have more than one parent.

Users of IMS soon discovered that this restriction made it difficult to deal with segments that were dependent on more than one other segment, so IMS now allows **logical databases** as well as physical ones. We can think of logical databases as somewhere between the conceptual and the external level for IMS. A logical database can be a subset of a single physical database, or it can be formed by combining segments from two physical databases. The logical database is not stored in the usual hierarchical form as such, but its structure is created from the underlying physical databases, by the use of pointers. Note that the pointers themselves are actually stored with the segments, so there is some physical basis for the structure. There are severe restrictions on the segments chosen for logical databases, some of which we will discuss in Section 10.4. Each logical database must have its own DBD.

At the external level, each user has a view of the database known as the **program specification block (PSB)**. The user's PSB is made up of one or more **program communication blocks (PCBs)**, each of which defines an **external schema** for a particular program. A PCB must contain the name of the DBD, either physical or logical, on which it is based, so a PCB is really a subset or minor reorganization of a DBD. At the physical level, each physical database is stored in a **physical data set**. Details of the access methods and corresponding organizations are presented in Section 10.8.

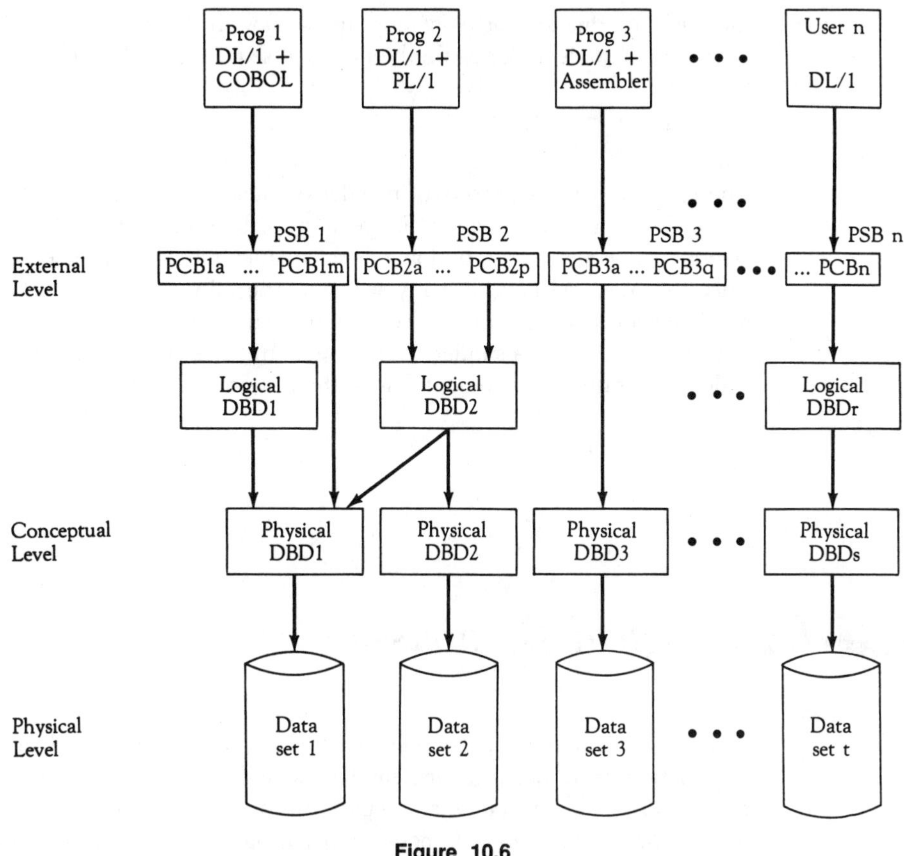

Figure 10.6

10.3 *IMS Physical Databases*

An IMS physical database is simply a **hierarchical arrangement of physical segments,** each of which consists of a set of **fields**. The structure of the physical database records is determined by the tree structure diagram, which fixes the type codes. IMS allows at most 255 segment types and 15 levels in the tree structure. Each physical database record begins with a root (type code 1) node. The order of segments of the same type is determined by a field called the **sequence field,** which can be thought of as a (possibly nonunique) key. For the tree structure diagram in Figure 10.2, we might use FACID as the sequence field for FACULTY, COURSE# as the sequence field for CLASS, and STUID as the sequence field for STUDENT. The physical database records are then stored in order by FACID, which is the sequence field for the root nodes. Within a particular faculty record, the classes are in order by COURSE#. Within a particular class record, the students are in order by STUID. The entire database is in order by the combination of type code and sequence field values. For any segment, we can define the **hierarchical sequence key value** as the type code and sequence field value of that segment, preceded by the type code and sequence field value of its parent, preceded by the same information for its parent, and so on, all the way back to the root node. For example, for student Burns, the hierarchical sequence key value is

```
1 F110 2 MTH103C 3 S1010
```

The physical database is stored in order by hierarchical sequence key values, either in physical sequence as shown in Figure 10.4, or by using pointers or other techniques to create that sequence. A notion related to hierarchical sequence key value is that of **fully concatenated key**. For any segment, the fully concatenated key is the sequence field value of that segment, preceded by the sequence field value of its parent, and so on back to the root. It is similar to the hierarchical sequence key value, except that type codes are omitted. For student Burns, the fully concatenated key is

```
F110 MTH103C S1010
```

10.4 *IMS Logical Databases*

As an example of the need for **logical databases**, let us consider a database that is to keep information about departments, employees, and projects. A department may have any number of employees, but each employee is assigned to only one department, so there is a parent-child relationship between department and employee. Similarly, we assume that each project may have many employees, but each employee is assigned to only one project, so there is a parent-child relationship between project and employee as well. There is no relationship between an employee's department and project. Each employee has many skills, and each project has many expenditures. We could represent this data by using two trees, as shown in Figure 10.7. Notice that we are wasting space by storing each employee record and associated skill records twice. In addition, this organization would eventually lead to data inconsistency, as employee data might be updated in one database and not the other. IMS allows us to replace the physical EMP segment in one tree by a **pointer** to the corresponding EMP segment in the other. We will choose to leave the EMP record in the DEPT tree, and replace the one in the PROJECT tree with a pointer, as shown in Figure 10.8. We now have two physical databases, the DEPT-EMP-SKILL one consisting of DEPT as the root, EMP as the physical child, and SKILL as the grandchild, and the PROJECT-EXPEND one which consists of PROJECT as a root node and EXPEND as its child. We also have a logical database, with PROJ as the root, EXPEND as its physical child, EMP as its logical child, and SKILL as the child of EMP. The three databases are shown in Figure 10.9. The logical database is made possible by the pointers shown in Figure 10.8. In the logical database, PROJ (or PROJECT) is the logical parent and EMP is the logical child. This means that EMP has two parents—DEPT, which is its physical parent, and PROJ, which is its logical parent. Programs that use either of the physical trees have PCBs that refer to one of the two

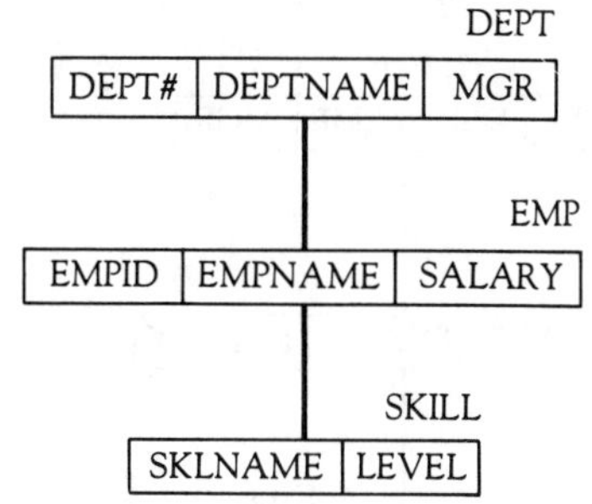

(a) The DEPT-EMP-Skill Database

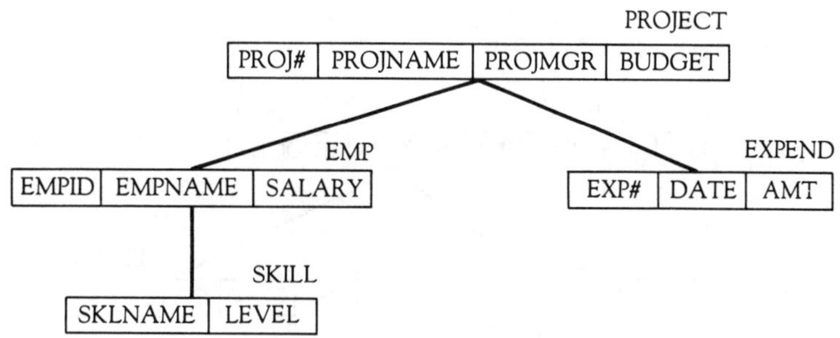

(b) The PROJECT-EMP-SKILL-EXPEND Database

Figure 10.7

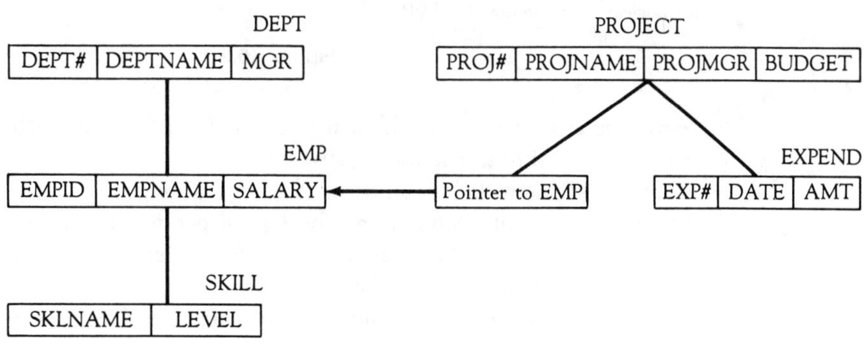

Figure 10.8

physical DBDs, and programs that use the logical tree have PCBs that are based on the logical DBD for PROJ-EMP-SKILL-EXPEND.

There are some rules concerning segments in logical databases, including the following:

1. The root of a logical database must be the root of some physical database.
2. A segment cannot be both a logical child and a logical parent.

Physical Data Bases:

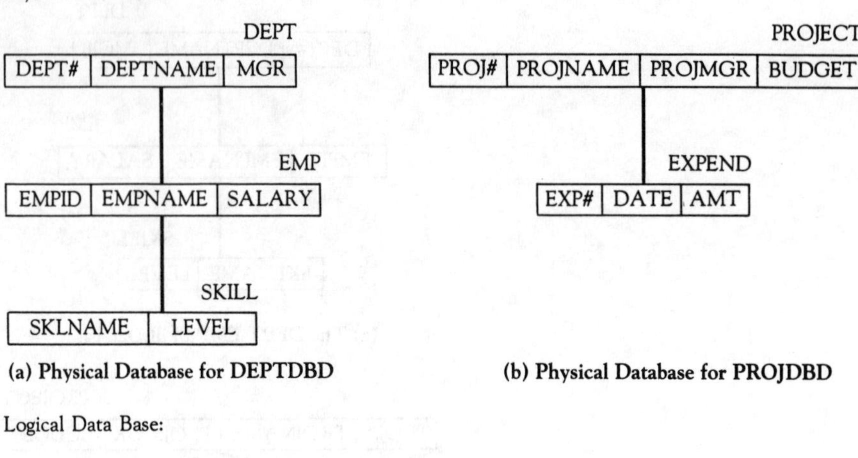

(a) Physical Database for DEPTDBD

(b) Physical Database for PROJDBD

Logical Data Base:

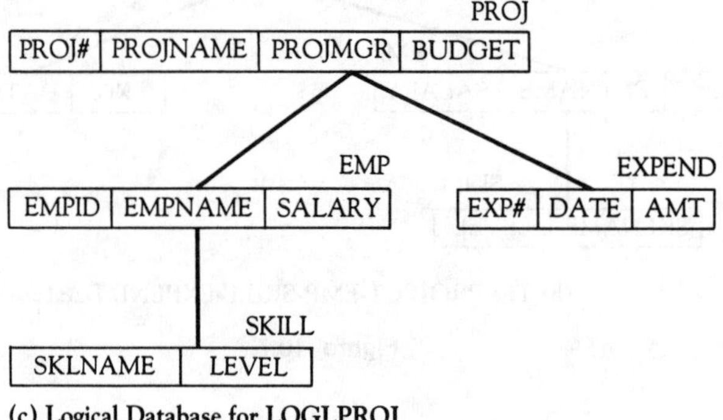

(c) Logical Database for LOGLPROJ

Figure 10.9

3. Any segment type in the physical tree structure, together with all its dependents, can be omitted from the logical structure.
4. Within a segment, fields can be omitted or rearranged.
5. In the physical DBD containing the logical parent, the segment description must name the logical child and the physical DBD where it can be found, before any of the segment's fields are described.
6. In the physical DBD containing the logical child, both the physical and logical parents must be named.
7. The logical child segment can contain "intersection data," that is, information that is functionally dependent on the combination of its physical and logical parents. We know that the segment already contains enough data to give us the fully concatenated key of its physical parent, so all we need to add is the fully concatenated key of its logical parent for the intersection data to be meaningful.

A segment type that is included in a logical database is called a **sensitive** segment—one that the user of the logical database is aware of. Within a sensitive segment, fields that are included in the logical database are called **sensitive fields**.

10.5 Control Blocks

IMS database definition is implemented by means of **control blocks**, descriptions that create physical databases, logical databases, and program communication blocks. These descriptions are written by the DBA and are compiled and stored in object form for use by the IMS control program.

10.5.1 Physical DBDs

For each physical database, a **physical DBD** gives a full description of the tree structure. Figure 10.10 shows the DBD for the FACULTY-CLASS-STUDENT database. The DBD itself is given a name containing at most eight characters. Each segment, together with its parent in the tree, and each of the segment's fields, with length, position within the segment, and (optional) type is identified. Permitted types are C (character), P (packed decimal), and X (hexadecimal), with C as the default. The order of the segments within the DBD is determined by preorder traversal of the tree structure. Each segment has a field called the sequence field, which may have unique (U) or nonunique (M) values within the parent occurrence, with unique being the default. The sequence field determines the order of twins, two occurrences of the same segment within a parent, or two occurrences of the root, which may be considered twins within the database. The first two lines of the DBD also identify the access method to be used (HSAM, HISAM, HDAM, or HIDAM), and the physical data set to be used. Each segment line contains the frequency (number of occurrences) and type of pointers used, but we will omit these details.

```
DBD      NAME=FACDBD,ACCESS=HDAM...
DATASET  (...details of physical device storage...)
SEGM     NAME=FACULTY,BYTES=39,...,PARENT=0
FIELD    NAME=(FACID,SEQ,U),BYTES=4,START=1,TYPE=C
FIELD    NAME=FACNAME,BYTES=20,START=5,TYPE=C
FIELD    NAME=DEPT,BYTES=10,START=25,TYPE=C
FIELD    NAME=RANK,BYTES=5,START=35,TYPE=C
SEGM     NAME=CLASS,BYTES=18,...,PARENT=FACULTY
FIELD    NAME=(COURSE#,SEQ,U),BYTES=7,START=1,TYPE=C
FIELD    NAME=SCHED,BYTES=7,START=8,TYPE=C
FIELD    NAME=ROOM,BYTES=4,START=15,TYPE=C
SEGM     NAME=STUDENT,BYTES=39,...,PARENT=CLASS
FIELD    NAME=(STUID,SEQ,U),BYTES=6,START=1,TYPE=C
FIELD    NAME=STUNAME,BYTES=20,START=7,TYPE=C
FIELD    NAME=MAJOR,BYTES=10,START=27,TYPE=C
FIELD    NAME=CREDITS,BYTES=2,START=37,TYPE=P
FIELD    NAME=GRADE,BYTES=1,START=39,TYPE=C
```

Figure 10.10 Physical DBD for FACULTY-CLASS-STUDENT Tree Structure

Figure 10.10 shows a simplified DBD for the database in Figure 10.2, the FACULTY-CLASS-STUDENT example.

10.5.2 *Logical DBDs*

A **logical DBD** is similar to a physical DBD, in that it shows a hierarchical structure of segments. However, the segments are taken from one or more physical databases, so we need to identify their sources in the logical DBD. We may change the names of segments, or keep the names as they appear in the sources. Since we can reorganize the physical trees, we must identify the parent, relative to the logical database, of each segment. In an occurrence of a logical tree, two segments of the same type that have the same logical parent are called **logical twins**. In addition to writing the logical DBD, we must modify the physical DBDs containing the logical parent and the logical child to show the logical relationships. To do this, we add an LCHILD line immediately after the SEGM line for the logical parent, and we identify both physical and logical parents in the SEGM line for the logical child. This is done so that room can be saved for the pointers necessary to create the logical relationship. Readers can distinguish a logical DBD from a physical one by examining the first two lines of the description. The first line contains the phrase ACCESS=LOGICAL and the second specifies DATASET LOGICAL. The DBD for the logical PROJ-EMP-SKILL-EXPEND database, and the modified physical DBDs for the underlying physical databases are shown in Figure 10.11. Again, some details are omitted for the sake of simplicity.

10.5.3 *PCBs*

An application program is presented with a subset of a physical or logical database through the use of the **program communication block (PCB)**. The PCB names the underlying database and lists each **sensitive segment** to be included in that program's external view. If some fields of a segment are not to be included, it lists only the **sensitive fields** and their relative positions. If no fields are listed, the entire segment is sensitive. If a segment is omitted from the PCB, none of its dependents can be included. The **processing options, PROCOPT**s, specify the operations the program may perform. They include **G** (get), **I** (insert), **R** (replace), **D** (delete), and **L** (load). If a program needs a segment to be included in order to provide a hierarchical path to a descendant, but is not actually permitted to see the data in that segment, we permit the program to have **key sensitivity** only and write **PROCOPT=K** for that segment. When a segment is used by a program, IMS keeps track of its location in the database by recording its **fully concatenated key**. To reserve space for the **key feedback area** where this is stored, we specify in KEYLEN=xxx, the length of the longest fully concatenated key the program can access. We calculate this by considering all possible hierarchical paths in the PCB. Figure 10.12 shows a PCB for a program that accesses parts of the FACULTY-CLASS-STUDENT database, whose DBD appears in Figure 10.10. On the first line,

```
DBD      NAME=DEPTDBD,ACCESS=HIDAM...
DATASET (...details of physical device storage...)
SEGM     NAME=DEPT,BYTES=39,...,PARENT=0
FIELD    NAME=(DEPT#,SEQ,U),BYTES=4,START=1,TYPE=C
FIELD    NAME=DEPTNAME,BYTES=15,START=5,TYPE=C
FIELD    NAME=MGR,BYTES=20,START=20,TYPE=C
SEGM     NAME=EMP,BYTES=29,...,PARENT=(DEPT,(PROJECT,PROJDBD))
FIELD    NAME=(EMPID,SEQ,U),BYTES=5,START=1,TYPE=C
FIELD    NAME=EMPNAME,BYTES=20,START=6,TYPE=C
FIELD    NAME=SALARY,BYTES=4,START=26,TYPE=P
SEGM     NAME=SKILL,BYTES=11,...,PARENT=EMP
FIELD    NAME=(SKLNAME,SEQ,U),BYTES=10,START=1,TYPE=C
FIELD    NAME=LEVEL,BYTES=1,START=11,TYPE=C
```

(a) DEPTDBD DBD

```
DBD      NAME=PROJDBD,ACCESS=HDAM...
DATASET (...details of physical device storage...)
SEGM     NAME=PROJECT,BYTES=43,...,PARENT=0
LCHILD   NAME=(EMP,DEPTDBD)...
FIELD    NAME=(PROJ#,SEQ,U),BYTES=4,START=1,TYPE=C
FIELD    NAME=PROJNAME,BYTES=15,START=5,TYPE=C
FIELD    NAME=PROJMGR,BYTES=20,START=20,TYPE=C
FIELD    NAME=BUDGET,BYTES=4,START=40,TYPE=P
SEGM     NAME=EXPEND,BYTES=14,...PARENT=PROJECT
FIELD    NAME=(EXP#,SEQ,U),BYTES=5,START=1,TYPE=C
FIELD    NAME=DATE,BYTES=6,START=6,TYPE=C
FIELD    NAME=AMT,BYTES=3,START=12,TYPE=P
```

(b) PROJDBD DBD

```
DBD      NAME=LOGLPROJ,ACCESS=LOGICAL
DATASET LOGICAL
SEGM     NAME=PROJ,SOURCE=(PROJECT,PROJDBD)
SEGM     NAME=EMP,SOURCE=(EMP,DEPTDBD),PARENT=PROJ
SEGM     NAME=SKILL,SOURCE=(SKILL,DEPTDBD),PARENT=EMP
SEGM     NAME=EXPEND,SOURCE=(EXPEND,PROJDBD),PARENT=PROJ
```

(c) LOGLPROJ DBD

Figure 10.11 Modified Physical DBDs and Logical DBD for the DEPT-PROJECT-EMP Example in Figure 10.9

the phrase TYPE=DB indicates that this PCB is for a database definition rather than an on-line transaction. The program using this PCB has access to the entire FACULTY and CLASS segments, but is not permitted to see the MAJOR, CREDITS, or GRADE fields of the STUDENT segment. Note that if we had chosen to reverse the ID and NAME fields in the student segment, we could have done so.

```
PCB      TYPE=DB,DBDNAME=FACDBD,KEYLEN=17
SENSEG   NAME=FACULTY,PROCOPT=G
SENSEG   NAME=CLASS,PARENT=FACULTY,PROCOPT=(G,I)
SENSEG   NAME=STUDENT,PARENT=CLASS,PROCOPT=(G,I,R,D)
SENFLD   NAME=STUID,START=1
SENFLD   NAME=STUNAME,START=7
```

Figure 10.12 A PCB for the FACULTY-CLASS-STUDENT Data Base

Figure 10.13 shows a PCB for the logical PROJ-EMP-SKILL-EXPEND database whose DBD appears in Figure 10.11(c). In this example, we are not permitting the program to read the PROJ record at all, but we need its key so that we have a hierarchical path to the EMP, SKILL, and EXPEND segments, so we give key sensitivity on this segment to the PCB. We are hiding the employee's SALARY field from this program, but including all of the SKILL and EXPEND segments.

```
PCB      TYPE=DB,DBDNAME=LOGLPROJ,KEYLEN=19
SENSEG   NAME=PROJ,PROCOPT=K
SENSEG   NAME=EMP,PARENT=PROJ,PROCOPT=G
SENFLD   NAME=EMPID,START=1
SENFLD   NAME=EMPNAME,START=6
SENSEG   NAME=SKILL,PARENT=EMP,PROCOPT=G
SENSEG   NAME=EXPEND,PARENT=PROJ,PROCOPT=G
```

Figure 10.13 A PCB for the Logical PROJECT-EMP-SKILL Data Base

10.6 *DL/1 Commands: GU, GN, GNP, GHU, GHN, GHNP, ISRT, DLET, REPL*

The **data manipulation language** for IMS, called **DL/1**, is basically an embedded language, invoked from a host-language program. As with any call, several parameters must be passed when IMS is called from such a program. Ignoring these difficulties, we will discuss some DL/1 commands, considering a simplified version of the language.

We will assume that each application program that is accessing an IMS database through a PCB has a program work area, in which the following are stored:

- **Currency pointers,** which give the fully concatenated key of the segment most recently accessed by the PCB.
- **Templates**, or record structures for each sensitive segment type in the database. As segments are retrieved, these templates are filled with the corresponding data.
- A **STATUS** flag, which indicates whether the last operation requested was successful. We will assume that a zero value means the last operation succeeded.

Regardless of the actual storage organization used, DL/1 always acts as if the database were stored in a strictly sequential tape-like form, as illustrated in Figure 10.4. Thus it appears to travel through the database by starting with the first tree occurrence, as determined by the sequence field of the root node, going through that first occurrence in preorder traversal, continuing with the second occurrence, traversing it in the same manner, and so on through the last tree occurrence in the database.

The retrieval operation is a **GET** command. It has several forms, as shown in Figure 10.14. When a GET is executed, IMS finds the requested segment in the database, sets a currency pointer to its fully concatenated key, copies the segment into the corresponding program area template, and sets the STATUS to a zero value to indicate a successful operation.

```
DL/1       MEANING                   OPERATION
----  ---------------           ------------------------------

GU    Get Unique                Retrieves the first segment that
                                satisfies the condition

- -   - - - - - - - - - - -     - - - - - - - - - - - - - - - -

GN    Get Next                  Retrieves the next segment,using
                                preorder traversal

- -   - - - - - - - - - - -     - - - - - - - - - - - - - - - -

GNP   Get next within Parent Retrieves the next segment, but
                                only within the current parent

- -   - - - - - - - - - - -     - - - - - - - - - - - - - - - -

GHU   Get Hold Unique           As above, but allow subsequent
GHN   Get Hold Next             DLET and REPL
GHNP  Get Hold Next within
              Parent

- -   - - - - - - - - - - -     - - - - - - - - - - - - - - - -

ISRT  Insert                    Inserts a new segment

- -   - - - - - - - - - - -     - - - - - - - - - - - - - - - -

DLET  Delete                    Deletes existing segment being
                                held

- -   - - - - - - - - - - -     - - - - - - - - - - - - - - - -

REPL  Replace                   Replaces existing segment being
                                held

-------------------------------------------------------------
```

Figure 10.14 DL/1 DML Commands

DL/1 uses **segment search arguments** (**SSA**s) to identify targeted segments. An SSA consists of the name of a segment and, possibly, a set of parentheses in which we write a condition. The condition may include the usual comparison and Boolean operators to express a restriction on the value of any field in the segment. For the GU and ISRT operations, in general, SSAs must give a complete hierarchical path from the root down. The GN and GNP operations do not necessarily require any SSA, but if a path is given, it must be a hierarchical one, but not necessarily starting with the root. These rules also apply to the GET HOLD versions of the same commands.

When a GET is written, the segment named in the last SSA is the one that is retrieved and copied into the template. The examples that follow show operations on the logical PROJ-EMP-SKILL-EXPEND database. We will assume that the PCB allows all fields of all segments to be accessed and other operations to be performed, as follows:

```
PCB     TYPE=DB,DBDNAME=LOGLPROJ,KEYLEN=19
SENSEG NAME=PROJ,PROCOPT=(G,I,R,D)
SENSEG NAME=EMP,PARENT=PROJ,PROCOPT=(G,R)
SENSEG NAME=SKILL,PARENT=EMP,PROCOPT=(G,R)
SENSEG NAME=EXPEND,PARENT=PROJ,PROCOPT=(G,I,R,D)
```

Even though we know this is a logical database, IMS acts as if it were a physical one—that is, it pretends there are physical trees, represented in tape-like form, corresponding to this structure.

10.6.1 *Get Unique*

This command is used to get an initial position in the database. It must be used first in order for GN or GNP to have meaning. It could be thought of as "Get the first segment that satisfies the following SSAs." Each SSA consists of a segment name, possibly followed by parentheses in which we write the condition to be satisfied. If the required segment is a root node, there is only one segment named, as in the following example:

■ Example 1. Use of GU with Single SSA

PROBLEM: Find the record of the project managed by Smith.

SOLUTION: We look through the database, examining root nodes until we find one where the PROJMGR is 'Smith' and retrieve that record. Notice that we will stop at the first such project. If there is a second project managed by Smith, we will not find it. Also notice that we are not retrieving the entire tree, only the root or PROJ node.

DL/1 COMMAND:

```
GU PROJ (PROJMGR='Smith');
```

RESULT: The PROJ template in the program work area now contains a record like the following

```
PROJ#    PROJNAME        PROJMGR        BUDGET
------------------------------------------
|P101   | Jupiter     |  Smith      |    100000|
------------------------------------------
```

In addition, a currency pointer now points to this segment, and the status flag is set to zero.

■ Example 2. Use of GU with More Than One SSA

PROBLEM: Find all expenditures for the Jupiter project.

SOLUTION: With this structure, the only way to get expenditure records is by going through the PROJ records, so we must write SSAs for the complete hierarchical path, starting with PROJ. Once we have located the correct PROJ record, we can find the first EXPEND record by using the GU. Notice that this does not quite answer our question.

DL/1 COMMAND:

```
GU     PROJ (PROJNAME='Jupiter'),
       EXPEND;
```

RESULT: This command finds only the first expenditure for the Jupiter project. That segment will be brought into the EXPEND template in the program work area. If we were to repeat the GU above, we would simply get the same segment again, so we need a different command to move forward in the database. We will return to this problem later.

■ Example 3. GU with Multiple SSAs and No Conditions

PROBLEM: Find the first skill of the first employee listed.

SOLUTION: Since we do not know what project we want, we must give an SSA for PROJ with no condition. This makes IMS go to the first project record. Similarly, we write an SSA for EMP without a condition, which will take us to the first employee segment, if any, for that project. Then we will take the first skill segment for that employee, provided it exists.

DL/1 COMMAND:

```
GU    PROJ,
      EMP,
      SKILL;
```

RESULT: The first skill record will be brought into the SKILL template in the program work area, and a currency pointer will be changed to point to the skill record. The template may look like this:

```
SKLNAME         LEVEL
----------------------
| WordProc      |  5 |
----------------------
```

■ Example 4. GU with Multiple SSAs and Conditions

PROBLEM: Find the level of typing skill for employee E101, who is assigned to project P1001.

SOLUTION: We search forward until we find the PROJ segment for P1001, then continue within that occurrence until we find the EMP record for E101, and within that, find the SKILL record for Typing.

DL/1 COMMAND:

```
GU    PROJ (PROJ#='P1001'),
      EMP (EMPID='E101'),
      SKILL(SKLNAME='Typing');
```

RESULT: The targeted SKILL segment will be brought into the program work area, and the currency pointer set to it.

From these examples, we see that GU always finds the first occurrence that satisfies the predicate. Normally, a complete hierarchical path, starting with the root node, must be specified, but we need not write a condition next to the name of every segment along the path. If we want to specify segments exactly, we write a condition for some field, not necessarily the sequence field, of the segment. Only the bottom segment named is retrieved, not all the segments along the path.

10.6.2 *Get Next*

Once a position has been established in the database by means of a GU, GN retrieves the next targeted segment, relative to the current one. Recall that the tape-like model is used to determine what "next" means. For retrieval of several segments, the programmer may use GN within a loop, which is written in the host language.

■ Example 5. Use of GN for Single Retrieval

PROBLEM: Find the second employee for the Jupiter project.

SOLUTION: We use a GU to find the first employee, and follow that by a GN to find the second.

DL/1 COMMAND:

```
GU    PROJ (PROJNAME='Jupiter'),
      EMP;
GN    EMP;
```

RESULT: If there is a second employee assigned to the Jupiter project, this will bring his or her record into the EMP template in the program work area. If not, IMS will simply keep searching along the tape until it finds the next EMP segment, regardless of what project that employee is assigned to. The programmer will be unaware of the fact that the system has entered another project occurrence. We are not permitted to add a condition such as "PROJNAME='Jupiter'" to the GN EMP line, since that condition refers to a field that is not contained in the EMP segment. However, we will learn how to correct this situation when we discuss GNP.

■ Example 6. GN in a Loop

PROBLEM: Find all project records, starting with the first project having a budget over $10,000.

SOLUTION: We want only PROJ segments to be retrieved, one at a time. We use the condition given to write a GU and then write a loop in the host language, using GN to find all the remaining PROJ segments.

DL/1 COMMAND:

```
GU    PROJ (BUDGET>10000);
do while (STATUS=0);
      GN PROJ;
end;
```

RESULT: The GU finds the first PROJ record where the budget has the required value and brings it into the PROJ template. Assuming that the retrieval is successful, STATUS has a zero value and the program will enter the loop. When the GN is executed, IMS will move forward to find the next PROJ record. Since we have no condition on this segment, IMS will retrieve it regardless of the size of the budget. This segment will now be brought into the PROJ template, erasing the previous entries. If this retrieval is successful, the program will enter the loop again, rewriting the template. This process continues until there are no more PROJ records, at which time STATUS will have a nonzero value.

■ Example 7. GN in a Loop with Additional Processing

PROBLEM: Find all EXPEND segments, print each, and total their amounts.

SOLUTION: We will position ourselves in the database by using a GU to find the first EXPEND segment. Once there, we will use GN in a loop to find all EXPEND segments. We will print each and use an accumulator to add the amounts.

DL/1 COMMAND:

```
TOTAMT = 0;
GU   PROJ,
     EXPEND;
do while (STATUS=0);
     TOTAMT = TOTAMT + AMT;
     put list (EXP#, DATE, AMT);
     GN EXPEND;
end;
put list (TOTAMT);
```

RESULT: The GU gets us to the first EXPEND segment within the first PROJ record containing an EXPEND. The GN moves us forward to the next EXPEND segment, regardless of the PROJ involved.

■ Example 8. GN with No SSAs

PROBLEM: Get all segments in the database.

SOLUTION: We know that the first segment must be a PROJ one. After that, we want to retrieve every segment we encounter, regardless of its type, so we use GN with no SSA.

DL/1 COMMAND:

```
GU   PROJ;
do while (STATUS=0);
     GN;
end;
```

RESULT: Every segment will be retrieved, but the programmer will have to inspect the program work area (I/O area) to see what has been brought in.

10.6.3 *Get Next within Parent*

■ Example 9. Use of GNP with One SSA

PROBLEM: Find all expenditures for the Jupiter project.

SOLUTION: Recall that we attempted to answer this question earlier (in Example 2) and found that we were unable to do so. We had to be satisfied with finding the first expenditure for the project. We know now that if we used

```
GU   PROJ (PROJNAME='Jupiter');
do while (STATUS=0);
     GN EXPEND;
end;
```

we would retrieve all expenditure records, regardless of project. Also, we are unable to add a condition as in

```
GN EXPEND (PROJNAME='Jupiter');
```

to the GN line, since the condition must refer to the segment named in the line. We can get around this by using GNP, which retrieves the segment named in the SSA, provided that it exists, inside the current parent. GNP will not allow IMS to move outside the current parent occurrence.

To solve this problem, then, we position ourselves in the record of the Jupiter project and ask for all EXPEND segments within that parent. We "fix" the parent by a GU in this example.

DL/1 COMMAND:

```
GU   PROJ (PROJNAME='Jupiter');
do while (STATUS=0);
     GNP EXPEND;
end;
```

■ Example 10. Use of GNP with Multiple SSAs

PROBLEM: Find all employees having salaries over $50,000 assigned to the Jupiter project.

SOLUTION: This is very much like Example 9, except that we add a condition to the EMP segments within the Jupiter PROJ record.

DL/1 COMMAND:

```
GU   PROJ (PROJNAME='Jupiter');
do while (STATUS=0);
     GNP EMP(SALARY>50000);
end;
```

RESULT: This retrieves only those employees on the Jupiter project with the specified salary. We could easily find the second employee in the Jupiter project, as we tried to do in Example 5, by writing

```
GU PROJ(PROJNAME='Jupiter');
GNP EMP;
GNP EMP;
```

The use of GNP for both EMP segments ensures that both employees are actually children of the Jupiter segment.

■ Example 11. GNP Using a "Grandparent"

PROBLEM: Find all the skills belonging to all employees assigned to the Jupiter project.

SOLUTION: The "parent" in GNP is always the segment last accessed by a GU or a GN. Once that segment has been chosen, the "parent pointer" value is set and any descendant can be retrieved by a GNP, regardless of the level of the tree involved.

DL/1 COMMAND:

```
GU   PROJ(PROJNAME='Jupiter');
do while (STATUS=0);
     GNP SKILL;
end;
```

■ Example 12. Using GN and GNP Together to Cross Segments

PROBLEM: Get all skills of employees making under $20,000.

SOLUTION: Once we position ourselves at the start of the database, we use a loop with a GN to go to each targeted EMP segment in turn. When we get such a segment, we fix it as the parent and, using a nested loop, ask for each of its SKILL child segments.

DL/1 COMMAND:

```
GU   PROJ;
do while (more EMP);
     GN  EMP(SALARY < 20000);
     do while (more SKILL);
          GNP SKILL;
     end;
end;
```

10.6.4 *Get Hold Unique, Get Hold Next, Get Hold Next within Parent*

These commands are used in exactly the same way as GU, GN, and GNP, respectively, except that they must be used in place of the those commands when the segments retrieved are going to be updated or deleted.

10.6.5 *REPL, DLET, and ISRT*

The replacement (**REPL**) statement is used when a segment is updated. First, the segment is retrieved using a GHU, GHN, or GHNP command. Once it is in the I/O area, the segment can be modified as needed, using host language statements. Any field except the sequence field may be changed. It is then replaced in the database by the REPL command.

■ Example 13. Updating a Record

PROBLEM: For employee E120 in project P20, change the level of the bookkeeping skill to 4.

SOLUTION: We use a GHU to target the required SKILL segment and hold it for processing. We use the host language to update the LEVEL value. Then we replace the segment.

DL/1 COMMAND:

```
GHU  PROJ(PROJ#='P20'),
     EMP(EMPID='E120'),
     SKILL(SKLNAME='Bookkeeping');
/* Change the skill level in the I/O area  */
     LEVEL = 4;
/*   Now replace the segment in the database  */
REPL;
```

RESULT: This will update only the first occurrence of this segment. To keep the database consistent, if we had assumed that employees could be assigned to more than one project, we should find every SKILL segment for this employee, regardless of PROJ. To do so, we would need to create a loop, as follows:

```
GHU  PROJ
     EMP(EMPID='E120'),
     SKILL(SKLNAME='Bookkeeping');
do while (STATUS=0);
/*  Change the skill level in the I/O area and replace   */
     LEVEL = 4;
     REPL;
/*  Continue to retrieve all SKILL segments for this EMP  */
     GHN  PROJ,
          EMP(EMPID='E120'),
          SKILL(SKLNAME='Bookkeeping');
end;
```

■ Example 14. Deleting a Record

PROBLEM: Delete the record of Employee E101 from project P25.

SOLUTION: We use a GHU to locate the targeted record, followed by a **DLET** command to erase it.

DL/1 COMMAND:

```
GHU  PROJ(PROJ#='P25'),
     EMP(EMPID='E101');
DLET
```

RESULT: When a segment is deleted, all of its descendants are also deleted, which means that the SKILL records for this employee in this occurrence would also be deleted. Although our plan is good, this would not actually work, since the PCB shows that we do not have the D procopt for the EMP segment. Therefore, our request would be rejected.

■ Example 15. Inserting a Segment

PROBLEM: Insert a new SKILL segment for employee E220 in project P30. The employee should be given a skill level of 2 for stenography.

SOLUTION: First we create the new segment in the I/O area. We then **insert** the segment, giving a complete hierarchical path, using conditions on the SSAs sufficient to guarantee that the segment will be inserted in the correct occurrence. Since we are providing the values of the (unique) sequence fields, we know that there is only one such occurrence.

DL/1 COMMAND:

```
/* Create the skill record */
SKLNAME = 'Steno';
LEVEL = 2;
/* Now insert it */
ISRT  PROJ(PROJ#='P30'),
      EMP(EMPID='E220'),
      SKILL;
```

RESULT: Unfortunately, because we do not have the I procopt for the SKILL segment, this will fail. However, if we had that procopt, these commands would cause a new segment to be inserted, provided the parent segment already exists. IMS is responsible for checking the sequence field of the segment so that it will be inserted in the correct order among the child SKILL segments for the specified parent. Again, if necessary, we should write a loop to update all records for this employee, regardless of PROJECT.

10.7 *Command Codes D, F, and V*

One of the major difficulties in manipulating an IMS database is that the system is designed to search **forward**—going on from a present position to traverse a tree using preorder. It is difficult to go back up a tree. The use of command codes allows us to "back up." This is possible because IMS actually keeps more than one currency indicator. We already know that the last segment accessed is considered the current segment, but in addition, each of its ancestors is the **current segment of its type**. Using our PROJ-EMP-SKILL-EXPEND example, if we have just retrieved a SKILL segment, then the EMP segment that is its parent is the current of EMP, and the PROJ that is its grandparent is the current of PROJ. This is true even if we did not specify values for them in the SSA. **Command codes** take advantage of these currency indicators. Command codes may be inserted after the segment name in an SSA by adding an asterisk and the appropriate letter or letters. We illustrate the command codes D, F, and V, using the PROJ-EMP-SKILL-EXPEND example, but note that the PCB procopts would need to be modified for some of these to work correctly.

■ Example 16. Use of Command Code D

The command code D is used when we want to retrieve **ancestors of a node**. For any segments on the hierarchical path for which we write *D, the data from those segments will be concatenated and placed in the I/O area, along with the data for the segment at the bottom of the path.

PROBLEM: Find the first project to which employee E133 is assigned.

SOLUTION: If we were to write the usual GU, as follows

```
GU PROJ,
EMP(EMPID='E133');
```

only the EMP segment would be retrieved, so we would be unable to read the PROJ record that is the parent. We really want to read sequentially until we reach the proper EMP segment and then back up and see which PROJ is the parent, which is what the D code allows.

DL/1 COMMAND:

```
GU  PROJ*D,
EMP(EMPID='E133');
```

RESULT: Both the PROJ and EMP segments are now in the I/O area. Note if we had a long hierarchical path, we could use *D for those segments we wanted retrieved, and not for others. For example, if a tree had nodes *W*, *X*, *Y*, and *Z* along a hierarchical path, and we wanted only *W*, *Y*, and *Z*, we could write

```
GU W*D,
X,
Y*D,
Z(predicate);
```

Note that the bottom segment does not require a *D, since it is always retrieved.

■ Example 17. Use of Command Code F

This command is used to "back up" **within a current parent** record to find the **first occurrence of the segment type** specified.

PROBLEM: Find the first employee assigned to the project for which expenditure number X500 was made.

SOLUTION: We can use a GU to find the targeted EXPEND segment and would be able to find the associated parent by using a D command code. However, we are not looking for the parent, but for a sibling. Because we have already traversed the EMP segment to reach the EXPEND segment, we need to "back up" under the current parent.

DL/1 COMMAND:

```
GU   PROJ,
     EXPEND(EXP#='X500'),
GNP  EMP*F;
```

RESULT: The GU positions us in the correct PROJ record. The *F causes IMS to back up to the beginning of the current parent record (i.e., the current PROJ). Once there, the GNP EMP gets the first EMP segment.

■ Example 18. Use of Command Code V to Replace GNP

The V command code keeps IMS **within the current segment of the type indicated** in trying to satisfy a request. It can usually be used in place of GNP, but it is actually a more general technique than GNP.

PROBLEM: Get all skills of employee E144 of the Jupiter project.

DL/1 COMMAND:

```
GU   PROJ(PROJNAME='Jupiter'),
     EMP(EMPID='E144');
do while (more skill segments);
GN   EMP*V,
     SKILL;
end;
```

RESULT: We would get exactly the same result if we had written the loop as

```
do while (more skill segments);
GNP SKILL;
end;
```

■ Example 19. More General Example of Command Code V

PROBLEM: Get the first employee for the project with expenditure number X500.

SOLUTION: Although we did this problem in Example 17, we will tackle it now by using the V command code. We will use a GU to find the EXPEND segment, and then use a V command code to find and stay within the current of the PROJ segment type, while we step back using an F command code to find the first EMP segment within that PROJ.

DL/1 COMMAND:

```
GU EXPEND(EXP#='X500');
GN PROJ*V,
   EMP*F;
```

RESULT: This is simpler than the previous method, because we were able to use a GU to ask for the first EXPEND segment that satisfied the condition without specifying the PROJ. In previous examples, we gave a complete hierarchical path to a segment in order to establish currency indicators for its ancestors. Now we can use GU to ask for any type of segment directly and then use the V command code to establish a current parent. Note that the GN PROJ*V EMP*F means "staying within the current PROJ record, back up to find the first EMP segment."

In general, command codes result in more efficient access than GNP, so they should be used whenever possible.

10.8 *Internal Level of IMS*

IMS/VS, or Information Management System/Virtual Storage, is designed to run under the **MVS** operating system. The underlying access method may be **SAM, VSAM, ISAM,** and/or a special access method designed for use with IMS called **OSAM,** Overflow Sequential Access Method. These provide the **stored record interface** for IMS. In addition, IMS allows four major storage structures for the database itself and provides for the management of these structures with four corresponding IMS "access methods." In all four structures, physical databases are represented by actual, physically stored occurrences of segments, which contain the data plus overhead information. However, the four structures differ in the way the segments are tied together into a tree structure and the way the tree occurrences are tied together to form a database. The four IMS "access methods" are **HSAM, HISAM, HDAM**, and **HIDAM**. The access method chosen is identified in the DBD by the entry "ACCESS=..." on the DBD line. In addition, some of the details of physical storage are given in the DATASET line, while others are in the DBD line.

10.8.1 *HSAM*

HSAM, **Hierarchical Sequential Access Method**, is used with **SAM**. The storage structure for HSAM is exactly as we have described in previous sections of this chapter and as pictured in Figure 10.4. Fixed-length stored records in a SAM data set are used to hold stored segments, which are in physical sequence as determined by hierarchical sequence key values. Stored records contain any number of stored segments, but segments are not permitted to be split across stored records (i.e., not spanned). This structure is quite inflexible, and once the database has been loaded, updating is not possible without generating a new version of the database. It is appropriate only for reading data.

10.8.2 *HISAM*

HISAM, **Hierarchical Indexed Sequential Access Method**, can be used with **VSAM** or a combination of **ISAM** and **OSAM**. As in HSAM, the database records are stored as physically contiguous segments. Each stored record begins with a root node and the dependent nodes follow the root in the usual order. If the database record is too long for a single stored record, a second one is assigned and chained to the first by a pointer. An **index** on the sequence field of the root node provides access to the root.

If **ISAM/OSAM** is used, there are two data sets, an ISAM one and an OSAM one, both consisting of fixed-length stored records. When the database is loaded, database records are arranged in hierarchical sequence. Each root segment is assigned an ISAM stored record, in which the root and its dependent nodes are stored in hierarchical sequence. If there is not enough room for the entire occurrence, an OSAM record is used to store the remaining dependent segments, and a pointer is placed at the end of the ISAM record. If the OSAM record is not long enough to hold the rest of the database record, a second OSAM record is assigned to hold the remaining segments, and a pointer is placed at the end of the first OSAM record. This process continues until the entire record is stored. Normally, there will be some free space at the end of the record, which may be used for subsequent insertions of dependent nodes. Segments are deleted by setting a deletion flag in the segment's prefix, and their space is not reclaimed. Insertion of new root nodes is a problem, since the ISAM data set is maintained in order by sequence field values of the roots. Therefore, the new root is inserted in the OSAM data set, and a pointer to it is placed in the "root overflow pointer" area at the beginning of the ISAM record that is its successor. The OSAM record will be filled with the inserted root and its dependents. A second OSAM record will be assigned if they do not all fit in the first, with an appropriate pointer inserted in the first record. If a second root node, with a sequence field value close to but less than the first, must be inserted, another OSAM record will be created for it, the "root overflow pointer" of the ISAM record will now point to this new root, and the OSAM record for the new root will point to the first insertion. This results in a chain of pointers, starting with an ISAM record, which keep inserted root segments in order by sequence field value. The ISAM index, which is nondense, is not changed. Insertion of new dependent nodes is easy if there is enough free space in the ISAM or OSAM record. In that case the new segment is inserted in its proper position, after other segments have been moved to the right to make room for it. If there is not enough free space, a new OSAM record will be created to hold the overflow and a pointer set to keep track of its location.

If **VSAM** is used instead of ISAM/OSAM, root nodes are placed in a VSAM key-sequenced data set, and overflow segments for each root are placed in a VSAM entry-sequenced data set, with a pointer to the overflow record placed at the beginning of the corresponding key-sequenced data set record. New root nodes are inserted in the key-sequenced data set, and the VSAM index is updated to keep track of them.

10.8.3 *HDAM*

HDAM, **Hierarchical Direct Access Method**, provides hashed access to roots. Parent–child and twin relationships are represented by pointers rather than by physical contiguity. This method provides fast access to roots but does not permit sequential access, since the records are in random order and, ordinarily, no index exists. The hashing scheme for the sequence field must be carefully chosen to minimize collisions (instances where two different keys generate the same target address) and to provide a relatively uniform distribution of records in the data set. In addition, the number of database records per address (bucket size) may be adjusted to hold the optimal number of records. However, since some collision overflow is unavoidable, HDAM provides collision chains to allow insertion and retrieval of such records.

The pointers that tie together segments of an occurrence may be either **hierarchical** or **child-and-twin**. In either case, they are stored in the prefix of the segment. If hierarchical pointers are used, each segment points to its successor in hierarchical order (preorder traversal). The pointers can be two-way, with each segment pointing to its predecessor as well. Even then, segments will normally have only two hierarchical pointers. If child-and-twin pointers are used, each segment points to the first occurrence of each of its child types. Each child, in turn, points to the next occurrence of its own type within the parent occurrence—its twin. The last occurrence of a particular child type within a parent has a null twin pointer. Root nodes also contain twin pointers, which are used to chain together colliding roots in ascending sequence field order. Twin pointers can be made two-way, with each child occurrence pointing to both its successor and its predecessor. Parent-child pointers may be made two-way by having the parent point to its last as well as its first child of each type. If two-way child-and-twin pointers are used in a "bushy" tree, a segment may have several pointers, which occupy space

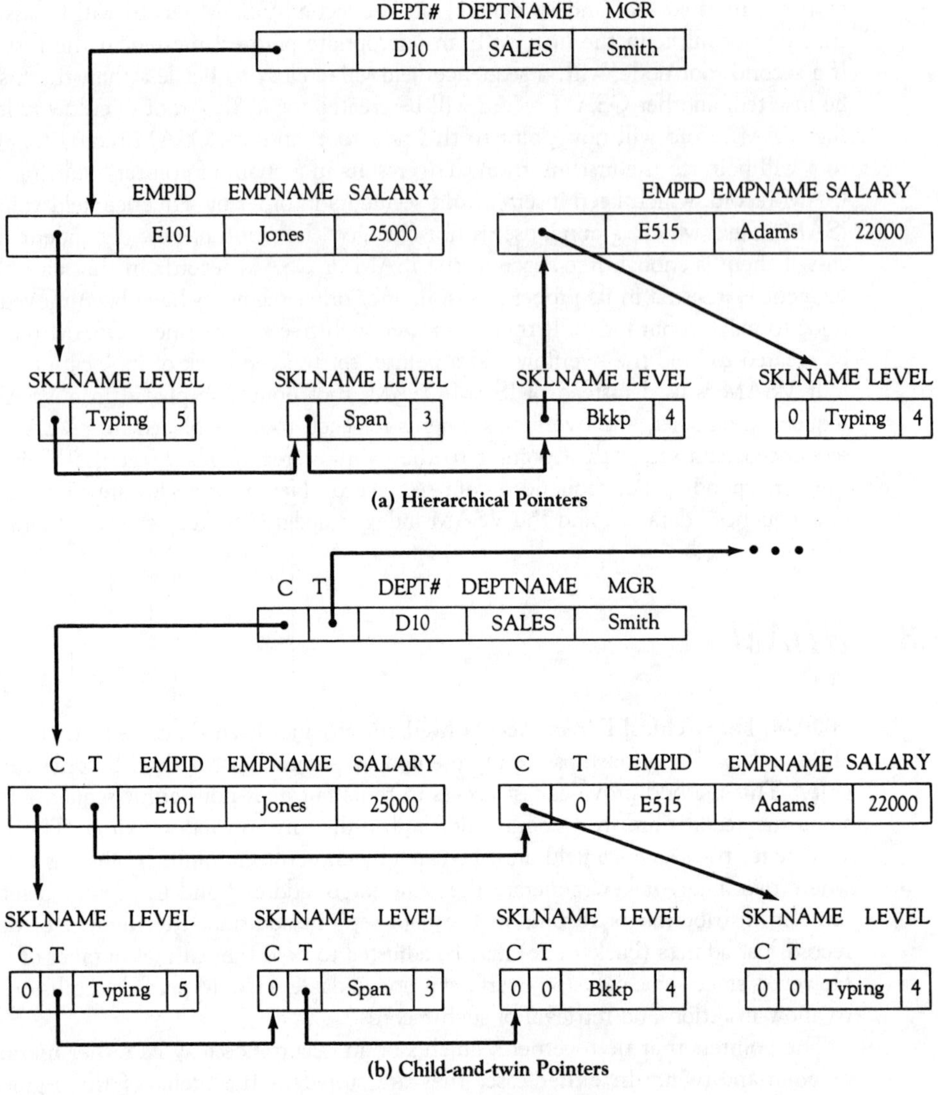

(a) Hierarchical Pointers

(b) Child-and-twin Pointers

Figure 10.15

and are hard to maintain when insertions or deletions are made. Figure 10.15 illustrates both hierarchical and child-and-twin pointers.

An HDAM database is stored in either an **OSAM data set** or a **VSAM entry-sequenced data set**, which is divided into two parts—a **root segment addressable area** and an **overflow area** . The database is initially loaded into the root segment addressable area, using the hashing algorithm to determine the target address for each root. If that location is already filled, IMS will search forward a predetermined number of spaces and try to insert the root close to its correct address. If that is not possible, the root will be placed in the overflow area, with a pointer from the record in its correct address. As additional collisions occur, a lengthy collision chain, tying together roots that hashed to the same address, may occur, resulting in poor performance. Dependent segments are placed as close to the root as possible, to try to provide fast access to the entire record. If the record is too long, some dependent segments will be placed in the overflow area. Regardless of their location, root nodes and dependent nodes are tied together by hierarchical or child-and-twin pointers. Deletions cause pointers to be reset and space to be freed for reuse. This organization has the advantage of fast access to records, provided that collision chains are not too long, and the disadvantage of potentially heavy pointer maintenance. The DBD must give the name of the hashing routine and identify the types of pointers used.

10.8.4 *HIDAM*

HIDAM, **Hierarchical Indexed Direct Access Method**, allows indexed access to roots and pointer access to dependent segments. The data itself is stored in a **VSAM entry-sequenced data set** or an **OSAM data set**. A **dense index** containing sequence field values and addresses of all root segments is stored in either a **VSAM key-sequenced data set** or **ISAM/OSAM data sets**, and is maintained by IMS, not by the access method. This **INDEX database** requires its own DBD. When the database is loaded, in strict hierarchical order, an entry is made in the index set for each root segment, and pointers are inserted in all segments. New segments are stored as close as possible to their correct hierarchical position, and pointers are adjusted so that they can be retrieved in their correct order. When segments are deleted, their space is reclaimed, and pointers are adjusted. This method therefore combines the advantages and disadvantages of both sequential and direct access.

Figure 10.16 summarizes the four IMS storage structures. The choice of storage structure and the options available with some of them obviously have a tremendous effect on performance. The DBA can use his or her knowledge of the environment to tune the system, choosing the options that favor the most important applications. The IMS "access method" for a physical database and other storage details are specified on the first line of the DBD, as shown in Figures 10.10 and 10.11. The corresponding data set information is shown on the second line, which begins DATASET. The pointer choice is shown on the segment line, because different choices can be made for different segments within the same database.

10.9 *Secondary Data Set Groups*

Instead of storing the entire database in a single data set, it is sometimes desirable to spread it across several. For example, if certain segment types are more active than others, we might want to put them on faster devices. If we choose HISAM as our organization, access to top-left segments is much faster than access to bottom-right segments. We could improve access to these "less favored" segments by placing them

IMS STRUCTURE	ACCESS METHOD	ACCESS TYPE
HSAM	SAM	sequential
HISAM	VSAM (key sequenced + entry sequenced) or ISAM/OSAM	indexed access to roots, using ISAM or VSAM index; pointer access to overflow dependent segments or roots
HDAM	VSAM (entry sequenced) or OSAM	hashed access to roots; pointer (hierarchical or child-and-twin) access to dependent segments
HIDAM	for data: OSAM or VSAM (entry sequenced) for index: ISAM/OSAM or VSAM (key sequenced)	indexed access to roots, using IMS HIDAM index; pointer (hierarchical or child-and-twin) access to dependent segments

Figure 10.16 Summary of IMS Storage Structures

in a separate data set. If we choose HDAM or HIDAM, we would like to be able to reuse space reclaimed by deletions, so it would be handy if segments in the data set had approximately the same length.

Secondary data set groups allow us to attain those objectives, provided that the access is HISAM, HDAM, or HIDAM. For HISAM, we create a secondary data set group by starting at a child of the root and taking that segment and all of the segments that follow it in the hierarchical structure and placing them in a second data set. The root node and those that remain with it (i.e., the nodes to the left) make up the primary data set group, while the nodes split off (i.e., those on the right) make up the secondary data set group. To tie the secondary data set group to the proper root node, the sequence field of the root segment appears at its start. This value is used to construct an ISAM index to the secondary data set group, giving us quick, indexed access to the rightmost nodes on the basis of the root's value. For HDAM and HIDAM, any segment types, not just the rightmost ones, can be chosen for the secondary data set group. However, the pointer scheme connecting segments across different data set groups must be child-and-twin, not hierarchical. For HDAM, the secondary data set group will consist entirely of an overflow area—no root segment addressable area. There can be at most nine secondary data set groups. The data sets involved are specified by DATASET statements in the DBD.

10.10 *Secondary Indexes*

Because of the hierarchical nature of IMS databases, certain types of searches are difficult. For example, dependent segments are normally accessed by going through the root, so it is difficult to find a record on the basis of a value of a dependent segment, as we saw in the DL/1 examples. Also, because HISAM and HIDAM indexes are defined on the sequence field of the root segment and the hashing algorithm for HDAM is performed on the sequence field, access to the root on the basis of the value of any other field requires a sequential search of the database. To overcome these problems, IMS allows secondary indexes to provide access in any of four ways:

1. Access to a root, using a field other than the sequence field.
2. Access to a root, using a field in a dependent segment.
3. Access to a dependent segment, using a field in that dependent.
4. Access to a dependent segment, using a field in a lower-level dependent.

If we wish to create a secondary index for a physical HISAM, HDAM, or HIDAM database, we must create an **INDEX database**, using VSAM. HSAM databases do not have secondary indexes. We may use a concatenation of up to five fields within a segment as the basis of the index. The INDEX database requires its own DBD, and the DBD for the original database must be modified. In the case of indexing the root on a field other than the sequence field, the modification consists of two lines within the description of the segment containing the field(s) to be indexed, but following any logical child line and the sequence field line. The first is an LCHILD line that shows the name of the index segment, the DBD where it is to be found, and the fact that an index pointer exists. The second is an XDFLD or "indexed field" statement that tells which field is being used for the index and gives a new field name or alias to be used when the index is invoked. For example, suppose that we decide to index the DEPT segment in the physical DEPT-EMP-SKILL database pictured in Figure 10.9(a) on the DEPTNAME field. The physical DBD for this database appears in Figure 10.11(a). We modify the DEPT segment by adding these two lines after the FIELD line for DEPTNAME:

```
LCHILD  NAME=(DPTNMNDX,DPTNMDBD),POINTER=INDEX
XDFLD NAME=XDEPTNAM,SRCH=DEPTNAME
```

The first line says that the department database is being indexed by an index segment called DPTNMNDX, which is described in the DBD called DPTNMDBD. The POINTER=INDEX entry says that this "logical child" is not a data segment, but an index. The next line specifies that DEPTNAME is the indexed field, and that it is to be known as XDEPTNAM when we wish to use the index. This is the name that would be used if we wanted to retrieve a DEPT segment using the index, as follows:

```
GU DEPT(XDEPTNAM='Sales');
```

In addition to this modification of the DEPTDBD, we must write the DBD for the index database. This consists of four lines, as follows:

```
DBD     NAME=DPTNMDBD,ACCESS=INDEX
SEGM    NAME=DPTNMNDX,BYTES=15
FIELD   NAME=DEPTNAME,BYTES=15,START=1
LCHILD  NAME=(DEPT,DEPTDBD),INDEX=XDEPTNAM
```

The first line states that the database is named DPTNMDBD and it is an index database. The second says that it consists of a single segment called DPTNMNDX. Both of these must agree with the previous LCHILD statement. The third line identifies the field on which the index is defined, DEPTNAME. It is the only field in the index database. The last line connects this database with the DEPTNAME (or XDEPTNAM) field in the DEPT segment of the DEPTDBD. IMS is responsible for loading and maintaining the index database, but the user is responsible for invoking the index when appropriate, as we did in the GU command above. In addition, the PCB should be modified to state that the processing sequence should be by values of DEPTNAME rather than by the sequence field, DEPT#. This is done by adding the following to the PCB line:

```
PROCSEQ=DPTNMDBD
```

When this secondary processing sequence is used, the database appears to be in order by DEPTNAME, rather than by the sequence field, DEPT#, which is the ordinary, primary sequence. This will obviously have an effect on the meaning and efficiency of GU and GN operations.

Similar modifications would be needed to create secondary indexes in the other three cases. For example, if we wanted to create an index to the root on the basis of a field in a dependent, we could create an index to access DEPT on the basis of EMPID in the EMP segment, making it easy to answer the question "Find the department to which employee E101 is assigned." If we create an index to a dependent node on a field in that dependent, we create a secondary data structure, in which the dependent node becomes the root. For example, if we create an index to EMP using EMPNAME as the indexed field, and use that as our processing sequence, the database appears to have the structure EMP-DEPT-SKILL rather than DEPT-EMP-SKILL. The (old) root segment appears to be the leftmost child of the indexed segment. Finally, we can create an index to a dependent segment based on the value of a field in a lower-level dependent. To illustrate this, we use SKLNAME to index the EMP segment. This also results in the secondary data structure EMP-DEPT-SKILL, with the original root now being seen as the leftmost child of EMP. This makes it easy to answer the question "Find all employees with skill of word processing." Figure 10.17 illustrates the use of indexes in the four cases we have discussed.

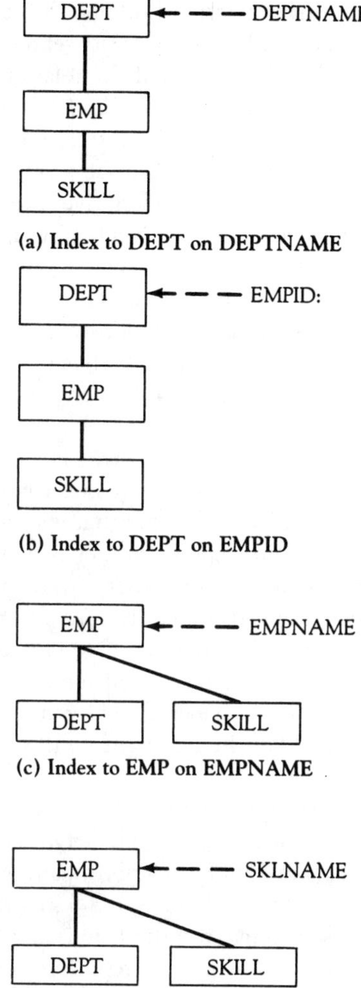

Figure 10.17

10.11 *Mapping an E-R Model to a Hierarchical Model*

To map an E-R model to a hierarchical model, the E-R diagram must be converted to tree structure diagrams. The general method of doing so is to change each entity into a segment type, each attribute of an entity into a field of a segment, and each relationship into a parent-child relationship. The results are then combined into one or more tree structures. There is no single "best method" of doing the mapping from an E-R diagram to a tree diagram.

The following steps can be used in most cases to make the transformation:.

1. Using the E-R diagram, identify **pairs of entity sets** *A* and *B* that have a **one-**

to-many binary relationship, and draw two-level tree structure diagrams for those relationships, making each entity set a segment type and making the one-to-many a parent-child relationship. If the relationship itself has descriptive attributes, create another segment type, *I*, to hold that data, and put the segment between the parent and child, giving a three-level tree. For example, if you had chosen *A* as the parent, you would now have the three-level tree structure *A* to *I* to *B*. If you prefer, you may "migrate" the descriptive attributes to the child segment. For entity set pairs that have a one-to-one relationship, represent the relationship as parent-child, choosing either entity as the parent, and proceed as for the one-to-many case. If you prefer, you can combine such entities into a single segment, provided that neither participates in another relationship.

2. For **entity set pairs** *A* and *B* that have a **many-to-many** relationship with **no intersection data**, draw two different one-to-many relationships, *A* to *B* and *B* to *A*. Picture the occurrences that would result, and try to estimate the number of repetitions that each would involve. For example, in the *A* to *B* representation, each *A* segment would appear only once, but the *B* segments would be repeated. Also consider the types of queries that will be used. After studying these factors, decide which of the two representations is better, and keep that one. You may decide to keep or to eliminate the other. An alternative is to create an intersection segment type, which would ordinarily contain only the keys (sequence field values) of the related entities. If you make this a physical child of one of them, it need not contain that parent's key, since the fully concatenated key of the segment will automatically have the parent's sequence field value. If you then make the intersection segment a logical child of the other entity, the logical parent's key value can be replaced by a pointer.
3. For **entity set pairs** *A* and *B* that have a **many-to-many** relationship **with intersection data**, create a new segment type, *I*, which will contain the intersection data. You can represent the many-to-many relationship between *A* and *B* by choosing either to be the parent, as you did in step 2. For the present, let us assume that you have chosen to make *A* the parent and *B* the child. Place the intersection data in between the two segments, resulting in a three-level diagram *A* to *I* to *B* with two parent-child relationships, *A* to *I* and *I* to *B*. Realizing that the intersection data and the *B* data will be repeated, decide whether the *A* to *I* relationship is one-to-one or one-to-many. If it is one-to-one, decide whether to combine the *A* and *I* data. Similarly, decide whether the *I* to *B* relationship is now one-to-one and make a decision about combining those segments. An alternative is to let the intersection data be a physical child of one of the original entities and a logical child of the other, as discussed in step 2. This time the intersection segment contains data as well as pointers.
4. For **entity sets** *A*, *B*, *C* that participate in **ternary relationships**, first determine whether any of the three lines coming out of the relationship is a "one." If so, choose the associated entity set as the root of the tree, make one of the remaining entity sets its child, and the second its grandchild. Picture the repetition involved to decide which is the child and which the grandchild. If the relationship has any intersection data, place it in a new segment type, and insert it in the diagram between the appropriate parent and child, as you did in step 3. If none of the three

relationship lines, or more than one of them, represents a "one," then choose any of the three entity sets as your root segment, and visualize the repetition and the types of queries your choice favors until you are satisfied with your choice. This method can be extended to any *n*-ary relationship, resulting in an *n*-level tree.

5. If an **entity set** participates in **two relationships**, you may need to represent the relationships by two trees, with repetition of the entity set involved. This method can be applied repeatedly if the entity set participates in several relationships.
6. If you have used **generalization** or **specialization**, you can choose to make the generic entity the parent and the subtypes the children. A second solution is to eliminate the subtype and redefine the generic entity by including in it all attributes of all subtypes. This results in a single segment type. A third method is to eliminate the generic entity and redefine the subtype entities to include its attributes. This results in several distinct segment types, having some fields in common. Aggregation is not represented explicitly.
7. Once all entities have been represented by segments, and all relationships by parent-child relationships, you will have several individual tree structures. Now you have to try to combine these into **one tree structure**, if possible. To do so, observe which entities appear in more than one tree and see if you can put those trees together. If you have an entity that appears as a parent in one diagram and a child in another, combine those into one three-level tree. If an entity appears as a parent in two diagrams, combine the diagrams so that the entity is now a parent of two child types. If an entity appears as a child in two diagrams, you have a problem of multiple parentage. In IMS, you can choose to make one of the parents physical and the other logical. In doing so, choose as the physical parent the segment that you will want to process through most often. If an entity appears as a child in three or more diagrams, you cannot use logical relationships to represent all of these connections, so you will have to repeat the segment, or choose not to represent one of the relationships. Repeat these steps until you have taken care of all related segments. If any segments are totally unrelated, they belong in separate tree structures.

10.12 *Chapter Summary*

The hierarchical data model uses a tree structure consisting of nodes and branches. **Preorder traversal** is a method of visiting and listing all nodes of a tree. In the hierarchical database model, each node is a **segment** consisting of one or more **fields**, which represent attributes. Relationships between entities are represented as parent-child relationships in a tree. Since all access is through the root, the choice of the root segment is very important. Physical placement or pointers are used to store parent-child and twin relationships.

IMS is a hierarchical model database management system from IBM. It uses the data sublanguage **DL/1**. An IMS system may consist of several **physical databases** and **logical databases**. A physical database is actually stored in the form described in the **physical**

DBD, either by sequential placement of segments, or by physical pointers. A logical database may be defined on two or more existing physical databases by choosing segments from them; it is implemented by means of pointers. There are restrictions on which segments may be chosen for logical databases. To create a logical database, the DBA must write a **logical DBD**, giving the structure of the logical database. In addition, the corresponding physical DBDs must be modified to reflect the existence of logical parents and logical children. A **PCB** is used to define the external view of a program or user. It consists of a list of **sensitive segments** and, possibly, **sensitive fields**, chosen from either a physical or logical DBD, and **PROCOPTs**, or permitted operations for the user or program.

The DL/1 DML commands include the **GET, ISRT, DLET,** and **REPL.** The GET has several forms: **GU, GN, GNP, GHU, GHN,** and **GHNP.** These may require an **SSA**, giving segment names with optional conditions along a hierarchical path to the targeted segment. **Command codes D, F,** and **V** permit a limited amount of "backing up" within a tree occurrence.

IMS runs under **MVS**, with **SAM, VSAM,** or **ISAM/OSAM** as the access method. The corresponding IMS storage structures and IMS "access methods" are **HSAM, HISAM, HDAM,** and **HIDAM**. The IMS access method is specified in the DBD.

IMS databases can be spread across different data sets by defining **secondary data set groups. Secondary indexes** allow us to access records on the basis of a value other than the sequence field of the root.

10.13 *Exercises*

1. Consider the tree shown in Figure 10.18 and answer the following questions based on that tree diagram.

   (a) Is the tree balanced?
   (b) Is it binary?
   (c) What is its height?
   (d) Name the nodes along the hierarchical path to node *M*.
   (e) Give the ancestors of node *L*.
   (f) List all the leaves of this tree.
   (g) List the siblings, if any, of node *G*.
   (h) Draw a diagram of one subtree.
   (i) List the descendants of node *C*.
   (j) List the nodes in preorder traversal.

2. Consider the following simplified DBDs for an IMS database:

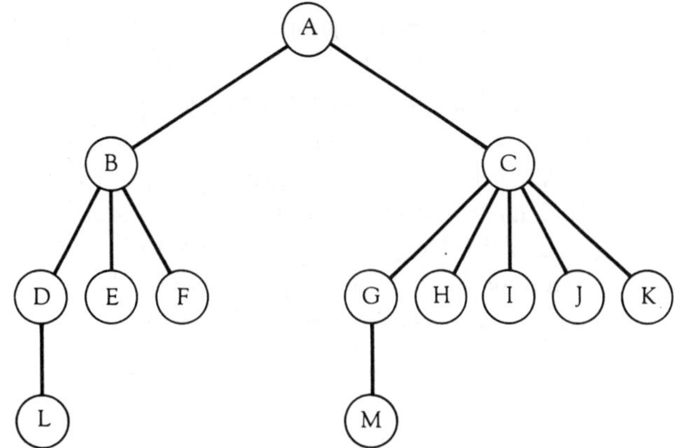

Figure 10.18

```
DBD     NAME=LOCATION,ACCESS=...
DATASET ...
SEGM    NAME=CITY,BYTES=50,PARENT=0
FIELD   NAME=(CITYNAME,SEQ,U),BYTES=20,START=1,TYPE=C
FIELD   NAME=CITYDATA,BYTES=30,START=21,TYPE=C
SEGM    NAME=PERSON,BYTES=36,PARENT=CITY
FIELD   NAME=(EMPID,SEQ,U),BYTES=6,START=1,TYPE=C
FIELD   NAME=EMPNAME,BYTES=30,START=7,TYPE=C
SEGM    NAME=STORE,BYTES=50,PARENT=CITY
FIELD   NAME=(STORENAM,SEQ,U),BYTES=20,START=1,TYPE=C
FIELD   NAME=STOREADD,BYTES=30,START=21,TYPE=C
SEGM    NAME=PART,BYTES=36,PARENT=STORE
FIELD   NAME=(PARTNO,SEQ,U),BYTES=15,START=9,TYPE=C
FIELD   NAME=PARTNAME,BYTES=15,START=9,TYPE=C
FIELD   NAME=QTYSTORD,BYTES=6,START=25,TYPE=P
SEGM    NAME=PARTUSED,BYTES=18,PARENT=(PART,(TASK,MANAGE))
FIELD   NAME=(DATESENT,SEQ,M),BYTES=6,START=1,TYPE=P
FIELD   NAME=QTYSENT,BYTES=6,START=7,TYPE=P
FIELD   NAME=ORDERNO,BYTES=6,START=13,TYPE=P

DBD     NAME=MANAGE,ACCESS=...
DATASET ...
SEGM    NAME=PROJECT,BYTES=35,PARENT=0
FIELD   NAME=(PROJNO,SEQ,U),BYTES=10,START=1,TYPE=C
FIELD   NAME=PROJMGR,BYTES=15,START=11,TYPE=C
FIELD   NAME=STARTDAT,BYTES=6,START=26,TYPE=C
FIELD   NAME=BUDGET,BYTES=4,START=32,TYPE=P
SEGM    NAME=TASK,BYTES=45,PARENT=PROJECT
LCHILD  NAME=(PARTUSED,LOCATION)
FIELD   NAME=(TASKNO,SEQ,U),BYTES=15,START=1,TYPE=C
FIELD   NAME=TASKNAME,BYTES=30,START=16,TYPE=C

DBD     NAME=CITIES,ACCESS=LOGICAL
DATASET LOGICAL
SEGM    NAME=PROJ,SOURCE=(PROJECT,MANAGE)
SEGM    NAME=TASK,SOURCE=(TASK,MANAGE),PARENT=PROJ
SEGM    NAME=PARTS,SOURCE=(PARTUSED,LOCATION),PARENT=TASK
```

Answer the following questions based on the DBD:

(a) Draw tree diagram(s) for the physical structure(s) given.
(b) Draw a diagram for any logical structure that appears.
(c) Why do we have the entry START=21 on the fifth line?
(d) What is the meaning of (...SEQ,U) and (...SEQ,M) on some of the lines?
(e) Explain the special position of PARTUSED.

Directions for Exercises 3–7: Consider the hierarchical structure shown in Figure 10.19. The segments have the following fields:

SEGMENT	FIELDS
HOSPITAL	HOSPNAME, HOSPADD, HOSPTYPE
DEPT	DEPTNAME, DEPTTEL, SUPV
DOCTOR	DRNAME, DRLICNO, DRTEL
STAFF	EMPNAME, EMPNO, JOBTITLE
FACIL	ROOMNO, RMTYPE, SQRFEET
PATIENT	PATNAME, SOCSECNO, BIRTHDAT, INSURNO, ROOMNO
TEST	TESTTYPE, TESTDATE, RESULTS
SURGERY	PROCED, DATE, TIME, OPERROOM

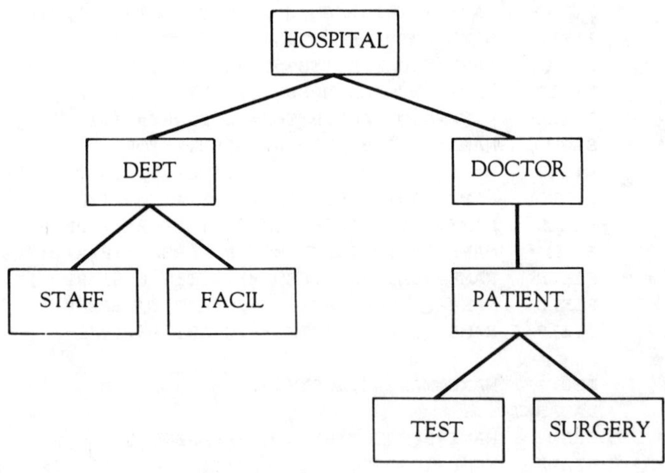

Figure 10.19

3. Write a DBD for an IMS database for this structure.

4. Write a PCB for a program that does not need access to DEPT or any of its dependents, and that does not need to know the BIRTHDAT of the PATIENT segment.

5. Assume that we want to create a logical database in which DEPT and its dependents do not appear, and in which PATIENT is the logical child of a segment called INSURCO, which appears in a physical DBD called INSURDBD. INSURCO contains information about insurance companies.

(a) Show what changes, if any, need to be made to the DBD you wrote for Exercise 3 and the DBD for INSURDBD. Make up fields for INSURCO.
(b) Assuming that INSURCO is the root of the other physical tree, write a logical DBD which includes the INSURCO, PATIENT, TEST, and SURGERY segments, with INSURCO the root, PATIENT its child, and TEST and SURGERY children of PATIENT.

6. Assuming that a user has a PCB which includes the entire physical structure as shown in Figure 10.19, with no hidden fields and no logical relationships, write DL/1 commands to do the following.

(a) Get a list of all doctors assigned to Metropolitan Hospital.
(b) Find all patients of Dr. Jones of City Hospital, with all operations performed on each one.
(c) Get records of all staff members who have the job title "Duty Nurse," regardless of hospital.
(d) Find all the facilities belonging to the Radiology Department of Mercy Hospital.
(e) Change the test results of the patch test performed on Mary Smith from negative to positive.
(f) Add a new doctor record, making up data as needed.
(g) Delete a patient record, making up data as needed.
(h) Find the patient who had an appendectomy performed by Dr. Jones at City Hospital at 8 A.M. September 10, 1990 in operating room 2.
(i) Using any programming language compatible with DL/1, write a procedure to find the total number of square feet belonging to the Cardiology Department at Mercy Hospital.
(j) Using any programming language compatible with DL/1, write a procedure to count the number of caesarian sections performed at Metropolitan Hospital last year.

7. Draw a diagram of an occurrence of the structure shown in Figure 10.19. Make up some data to place in the segments.

8. For the occurrence in Exercise 7, draw a flat representation, as shown in Figure 10.4.

9. For the occurrence in Exercise 7, draw a representation using hierarchical pointers, as shown in Figure 10.15.

10. For the occurrence in Exercise 7, draw a representation using child-and-twin pointers, as shown in Figure 10.15.

10.14 *Bibliography*

Bradley, J. *File and Data Base Techniques*. New York: Holt, Rinehart and Winston, 1982.

Gillenson, M. *Database Step-by-Step*. New York: John Wiley & Sons, 1985.

Silberschatz, A. and Z. Kedem. "Consistency in Hierarchical Database Systems," Journal of the ACM 27:1 (January, 1980) pp. 72-80.

Tsichritzis, D. and F. Lochovsky. *Data Base Management Systems*. New York: Academic Press, 1977.

Walsh, M. *Information Management Systems/Virtual Storage*. Reston, VA: Reston, 1979.

SAMPLE PROJECT: CREATING AND MANIPULATING AN IMS DATABASE FOR CLERICALTEMPS

The first task for this part of the Sample Project is to represent the E-R diagram by means of tree structure diagrams. Generally speaking, we change each entity into a segment type, each attribute of an entity into a field of a segment, and each relationship into a parent-child relationship. We then combine the results into one or more tree structures.

We now apply these steps to our ClericalTemps example.

Step 10.1

Represent one-to-many relationships as parent-child. For the WORKER-JOB relationship, represented on the E-R diagram as ASSIGNMENT, there are descriptive attributes RATERNAME, RATINGDATE, and EMPRATING. We choose to migrate these to JOB, adding them as attributes of the JOB segment. Figure 10.20 shows the one-to-many relationships.

Steps 10.2 and 10.3

Represent entity set pairs with a many-to-many relationship as described in Section 10.11. There are no entity set pairs with a many-to-many relationship in this example.

Step 10.4

Represent ternary relationships. There are no ternary relationships in this example.

Step 10.5

Represent entity sets that participate in more than one relationship by multiple trees, if necessary. WORKER and JOB both participate in two relations. We have already repeated these entity sets in trees.

Step 10.6

Choose a representation for generalization, if needed. There is no generalization or specialization in this example.

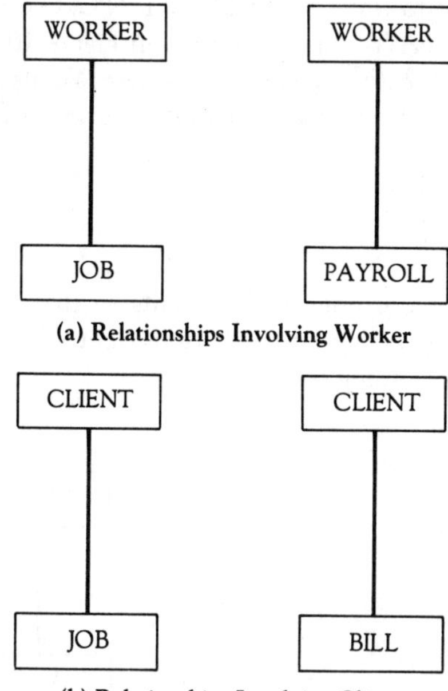

(a) Relationships Involving Worker

(b) Relationships Involving Client

Figure 10.20

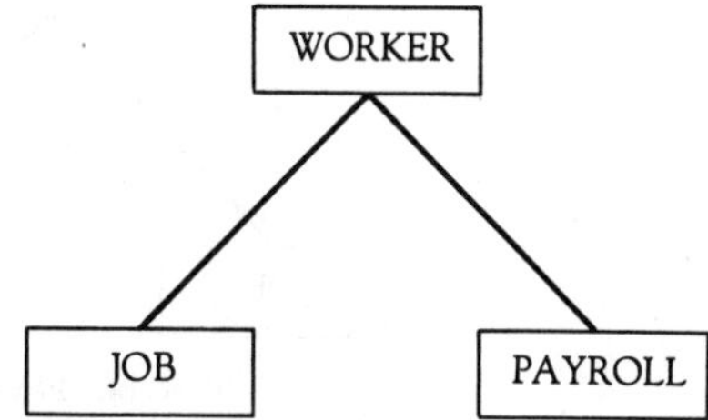

(a) Representing Relationships Involving Worker as Trees

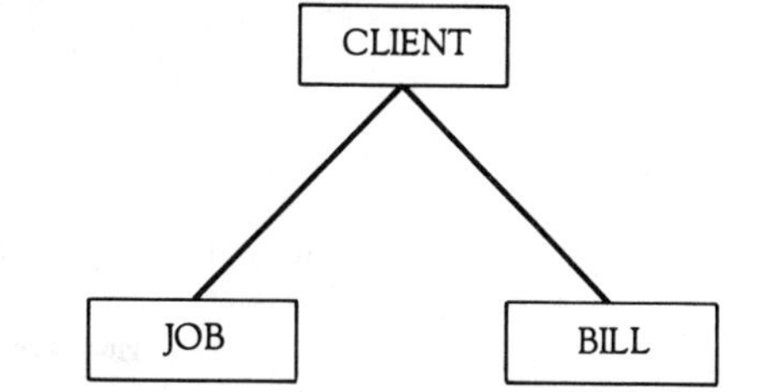

(b) Representing Relationships Involving Client as Trees

Figure 10.21

Step 10.7

Combine into one or more trees. See Figure 10.21. Since JOB appears on both trees, we can eliminate duplication of data by choosing one physical and one logical parent. We will choose to leave JOB with CLIENT. Therefore, the first physical tree becomes the WORKER-PAYROLL tree shown in Figure 10.22(a). The second physical tree, shown in Figure 10.22(b), remains the same. We also need a logical tree, as shown in Figure 10.22(c). Our complete structure is shown in Figure 10.23.

Step 10.8

In each tree, arrange the segments so that the most active ones are on the top left and the least active on the bottom right. There seems to be no need to rearrange our segments according to activity.

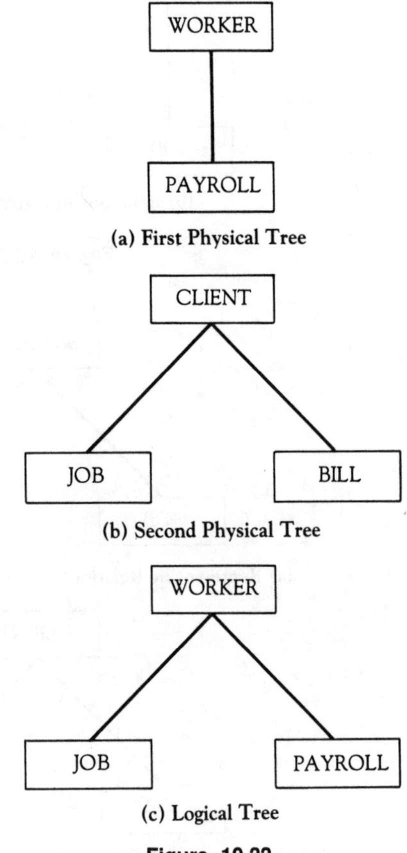

Figure 10.22

Step 10.9

For each physical and logical tree, write a complete DBD, making decisions about IMS access methods and pointer types, if needed.

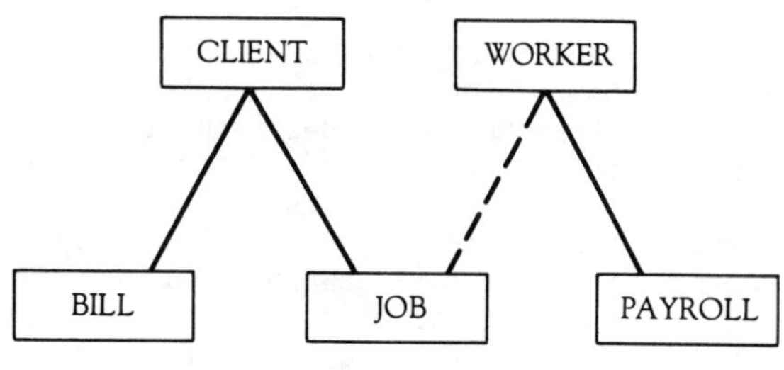

Figure 10.23

```
DBD       NAME=CLIDBD,ACCESS=HDAM...
DATASET   (...details of physical device storage...)
SEGM      NAME=CLIENT,BYTES=114,PARENT=0
FIELD     NAME=(CLID,SEQ,U),BYTES=5,START=1,TYPE=C
FIELD     NAME=CLNAME,BYTES=25,START=6,TYPE=C
FIELD     NAME=CLADD,BYTES=40,START=31,TYPE=C
FIELD     NAME=CLPHONE,BYTES=10,START=71,TYPE=C
FIELD     NAME=CONTACT,BYTES=20,START=81,TYPE=C
FIELD     NAME=BILLYTD,BYTES=7,START=101,TYPE=P
FIELD     NAME=PAYYTD,BYTES=7,START=108,TYPE=P
SEGM      NAME=JOB,BYTES=146,PARENT=(CLIENT,(WORKER,WORKDBD))
FIELD     NAME=(JOB#,SEQ,U),BYTES=8,START=1,TYPE=C
FIELD     NAME=JOBTITLE,BYTES=15,START=9,TYPE=C
FIELD     NAME=STARTDAT,BYTES=6,START=24,TYPE=C
FIELD     NAME=EXPENDDT,BYTES=6,START=30,TYPE=C
FIELD     NAME=DLYRATE,BYTES=4,START=36,TYPE=P
FIELD     NAME=DLYHRS,BYTES=9,START=40,TYPE=C
FIELD     NAME=REPTTONM,BYTES=20,START=49,TYPE=C
FIELD     NAME=REPTTOAD,BYTES=40,START=69,TYPE=C
FIELD     NAME=REPTTOPH,BYTES=10,START=109,TYPE=C
FIELD     NAME=STATUS,BYTES=1,START=119,TYPE=C
FIELD     NAME=RATRNAME,BYTES=20,START=120,TYPE=C
FIELD     NAME=RATNGDAT,BYTES=6,START=140,TYPE=C
FIELD     NAME=EMPRAT,BYTES=1,START=146,TYPE=C
SEGM      NAME=BILL,BYTES=24,PARENT=JOB
FIELD     NAME=(INV#,SEQ,U),BYTES=6,START=1,TYPE=C
FIELD     NAME=BILLDATE,BYTES=6,START=7,TYPE=P
FIELD     NAME=OLDBAL,BYTES=4,START=13,TYPE=P
FIELD     NAME=TOTCHRGS,BYTES=4,START=17,TYPE=P
FIELD     NAME=TOTPAID,BYTES=4,START=21,TYPE=P

DBD       NAME=WORKDBD,ACCESS=HDAM...
DATASET   (...details of physical device storage...)
SEGM      NAME=WORKER,BYTES=121,PARENT=0
LCHILD    NAME=(JOB,CLIBDB)...
FIELD     NAME=(EMPID,SEQ,U),BYTES=5,START=1,TYPE=C
FIELD     NAME=EMPNAME,BYTES=20,START=6,TYPE=C
FIELD     NAME=SSN,BYTES=9,START=26,TYPE=C
FIELD     NAME=EMPADD,BYTES=40,START=35,TYPE=C
FIELD     NAME=EMPHONE,BYTES=10,START=75,TYPE=C
FIELD     NAME=DOB,BYTES=6,START=85,TYPE=C
FIELD     NAME=SEX,BYTES=1,START=91,TYPE=C
FIELD     NAME=DATEHIRD,BYTES=6,START=92,TYPE=C
FIELD     NAME=LASTWORK,BYTES=6,START=98,TYPE=C
```

```
FIELD     NAME=AVRATING,BYTES=2,START=104,TYPE=P
FIELD     NAME=WORDPROC,BYTES=5,START=106,TYPE=C
FIELD     NAME=TYPING,BYTES=2,START=111,TYPE=P
FIELD     NAME=FILING,BYTES=1,START=113,TYPE=C
FIELD     NAME=BOOKKEEP,BYTES=1,START=114,TYPE=C
FIELD     NAME=STENO,BYTES=1,START=115,TYPE=C
FIELD     NAME=AVAIL,BYTES=6,START=116,TYPE=C
SEGM      NAME=PAYROLL,BYTES=57,PARENT=WORKER
FIELD     NAME=(CHECK#,SEQ,U),BYTES=3,START=1,TYPE=P
FIELD     NAME=PAYDATE,BYTES=6,START=4,TYPE=C
FIELD     NAME=GROSS,BYTES=4,START=10,TYPE=P
FIELD     NAME=FED,BYTES=4,START=14,TYPE=P
FIELD     NAME=FICA,BYTES=3,START=18,TYPE=P
FIELD     NAME=STATE,BYTES=3,START=21,TYPE=P
FIELD     NAME=LOCAL,BYTES=3,START=24,TYPE=P
FIELD     NAME=NET,BYTES=4,START=27,TYPE=P
FIELD     NAME=GROSSYTD,BYTES=5,START=31,TYPE=P
FIELD     NAME=NETYTD,BYTES=5,START=36,TYPE=P
FIELD     NAME=FEDYTD,BYTES=5,START=41,TYPE=P
FIELD     NAME=FICAYTD,BYTES=4,START=46,TYPE=P
FIELD     NAME=STATEYTD,BYTES=4,START=50,TYPE=P
FIELD     NAME=LOCYTD,BYTES=4,START=54,TYPE=P

DBD       NAME=LOGLWORK,ACCESS=LOGICAL
DATASET   LOGICAL
SEGM      NAME=WORKER,SOURCE=(WORKER,WORKDBD)
SEGM      NAME=JOB,SOURCE=(JOB,CLIDBD),PARENT=WORKER
SEGM      NAME=PAY,SOURCE=(PAYROLL,WORKDBD),PARENT=WORKER
```

Step 10.10

Decide whether any secondary indexes are needed. If so, describe how you would create them and how they would affect the logical structure of the database, by drawing diagrams similar to those found in Figure 10.17. We might wish to create an index to access WORKER on the EMPNAME. This would provide access to a root, on the basis of the value of a field other than the sequence field. It would be necessary to write a new DBD for the index database that we have to create. It would have the following structure:

```
DBD    NAME=EMPNMDBD,ACCESS=INDEX
SEGM   NAME=EMPNMNDX,BYTES=20
FIELD  NAME=EMPNAME,BYTES=20,START=1
LCHILD NAME=(WORKER,WORKDBD),INDEX=XEMPNAME
```

We also need to modify the WORKER segment by adding the following after the FIELD line for EMPNAME:

```
LCHILD  NAME=(EMPNMNDX,EMPNMDBD),POINTER=INDEX
XDFIELD NAME=XEMPNAME,SRCH=EMPNAME
```

Any user who accesses the database using this index should have the following added to his or her PCB:

```
PROCSEQ=EMPNAMDBD
```

Step 10.11

Decide whether any secondary data set groups are needed. If so, identify which segments are in which data sets. Because of the small number of segments in our databases, we will not create any secondary data sets.

Step 10.12

Choose one of the DBDs and write a PCB for a user or department that you identify. We will use the following PCB:

```
PCB     TYPE=BD,DBDNAME=CLIDBD,KEYLEN=13
SENSEG NAME=CLIENT,PROCOPT=G
SENSEG NAME=JOB,PARENT=CLIENT,PROCOPT=(G,I,R,D)
SENSEG NAME=BILL,PARENT=CLIENT,PROCOPT=(G,I,R,D)
```

This PCB could be used by the billing department to record client payments. It could also be used to retrieve information about clients, or to retrieve, insert, delete, or update information about jobs and payments.

Step 10.13

Using the PCB, write **DL/1 statements** that will process five nonroutine requests for information. For each, write the request in English, followed by the corresponding DL/1.

1. Get the name of the contact person at ABC Corporation.

```
GU    CLIENT(CLNAME='ABC')
```

Once the segment is in the I/O area, we can use a language such as PL/1 to print the desired information:

```
PUT LIST (CONTACT);
```

2. Get full details of all jobs at ABC Corporation that started on December 1, 1989.

```
GU    CLIENT(CLNAME='ABC')

do while (STATUS=0);

      GNP   JOB(STARTDAT='891201');

      /* Now print the details, using PL/1 */

      PUT LIST (JOB#, JOBTITLE, STARTDAT, EXPENDAT, DLYRATE,
      DLYHRS, REPTTONM, REPTTOAD, REPTTOPH, STATUS);

end;
```

3. Record a payment of $350.00 for client C1001, billing date August 31, 1989. Since the billing has been done, the billing record already exists. We are simply updating the AMTPAID field.

```
GHU  CLIENT(CLID='C1001')
     BILL(BILLDATE='890831')

/*  Change the amount paid in the I/O area     */

     AMTPAID=350.00;

/*  Now replace the segment in the database     */

     REPL;
```

4. Find the client who requested a worker for job number J10040.

```
GHU  CLIENT*D
     JOB(JOB#='J10040');
```

5. Find the names and addresses of all clients who request word processing workers.

```
GU     CLIENT*D
       JOB(JOBTITLE='Wordproc');

do while (STATUS=0);

       PUT LIST (CLNAME, CLADD);

       GN CLIENT*D
          JOB(JOBTITLE='Wordproc');

end;
```

Student Project: Creating an IMS Database

For the student project you have chosen, use steps 10.1 to 10.13 as shown in the Sample Project to design, create, and manipulate an IMS database from the E-R diagram you created at the end of Chapter 5.

CHAPTER

11

Other Semantic Models

11 Chapter Objectives

In this chapter you will learn

- why semantic models are needed
- the structure of RM/T, the extended relational model
- the structures and representation of the binary model
- the features and representation of the semantic binary model
- the basic concepts of the semantic database model, SDM
- the features of the functional model
- the common characteristics of object-oriented models
- how an object-oriented model can be represented
- the features of the semantic association model, SAM*

11.1 The Need for Semantic Models

The earliest database systems were extensions of file management systems. Their developers focused on the optimal physical placement of data to provide efficient and predictable performance. The relational model was the first to provide data independence by separating the conceptual or logical level from the physical model. However, the traditional relational model does not allow the designer to express all relationships that can exist in the real-world enterprise, nor to distinguish among the various types of relationships. It is not sufficiently expressive to handle data that does not map well to tables. Semantic models have been developed to provide more semantic content or "meaning" than the relational model. They focus on the external and conceptual levels, as opposed to the record-based network and hierarchical models, which focused on the physical level, and the relational model, which focus on both the conceptual and physical levels. They provide a higher level of abstraction that allows the designer to express data relationships that mirror real-world relationships.

We have already seen an example of one semantic model, the entity-relationship model. We considered an enhanced version of that model that included the abstractions of generalization and aggregation. We used the E-R model as a design tool for our projects, and changed to the record-based models for implementation. In the past, semantic models were used primarily for external and conceptual design in this way. However, some of these models have implementations that provide a physical model as well.

Although semantic models differ considerably in their content, there are some commonalities. A semantic model should provide some method of representing objects or entities, the attributes of the objects, and the various types of relationships among them. A semantic model usually has some method of constructing complex types from simple types, and of producing derived types from types already represented in the schema. We expect to find some forms of abstraction such as generalization and aggregation. Recall that generalization represents an "ISA" relationship between subtypes and a higher-level type, while aggregation represents an "is a part of" relationship between lower-level component objects and a higher-level object. Additional forms of abstraction may include classification and association. In classification we identify an "is an instance of" relationship in which we consider a class of objects to be an instance of a higher-level object class. For example, we might consider the Student class to be an instance of the Person class. In association we consider the "is a member of" relationship between members of a set to be a higher-level set object. The benefits of the semantic richness of these models include

1. increased data independence due to greater separation of logical and physical models.
2. the ability to view the schema at different levels of abstraction, considering various portions of the model independently and at different levels of detail.
3. a decrease in "semantic overloading" found in the record-based models, which require that the same constructs be used to represent fundamentally different types of objects and relationships. Semantic models generally allow the designer to use different constructs to differentiate among several types of relationships.

11.2 *The Extended Relational Model, RM/T*

We begin with **RM/T,** the **extended relational model,** because it is an extension of the familiar relational model. It was developed by Codd and Date using the same formal methods as the relational model. As in the basic relational model, both entities and relationships are represented as **relations** or tables. Table columns represent attributes. The extended model incorporates semantic information by categorizing entities and their corresponding relations, by including a form of abstraction, and by providing general integrity constraints.

The term **entity** is undefined, but it corresponds to our notion of an entity as an object that can be distinguished from other objects in the real world. Entities are grouped into entity sets, called **entity types** in RM/T. Entities are categorized into three **classes: kernel entities**, which are the real-world objects that exist in their own right and that we keep information about, **characteristic entities**, which describe or "characterize" other entities, and **associative entities**, which represent relationships between other entities. Figure 11.1 summarizes the three entity classes. An entity in any one of these classes has **properties** or attributes. One of an entity's properties might be a **designative property**, which identifies a different but related entity. For example, a student is an entity with properties ID, name, major, and credits. Although major is a property of the student entity, it identifies a related entity, department. Note that we are assuming that the department name is the same as the major name. The department, in turn, is an entity with its own properties such as name, chairperson, office, and so on. There is a relationship between the student entity and the department entity which is shown by the major property of the student entity.

Entity Class	Description	Example
Kernel	exists independently of other entities	Student
Characteristic	describes another entity	Educational-Background as an entity related to Faculty
Associative	shows relationship between other entities	Enroll, which shows a relationship between Student and Class

Figure 11.1 The Three RM/T Entity Classes

Any entity, regardless of its class, can belong to different entity types or entity sets simultaneously. These sets may be subsets or supersets of each other. An **entity type hierarchy** is a graphical representation showing entity types that are **subtypes** or **supertypes** of one another. For example, every undergraduate is a student, and undergraduates are assigned class years, as the type hierarchy in Figure 11.2 shows. Thus Student is a supertype of Undergraduate, Junior is a subtype of Undergraduate, and Undergraduate is a subtype of Student.

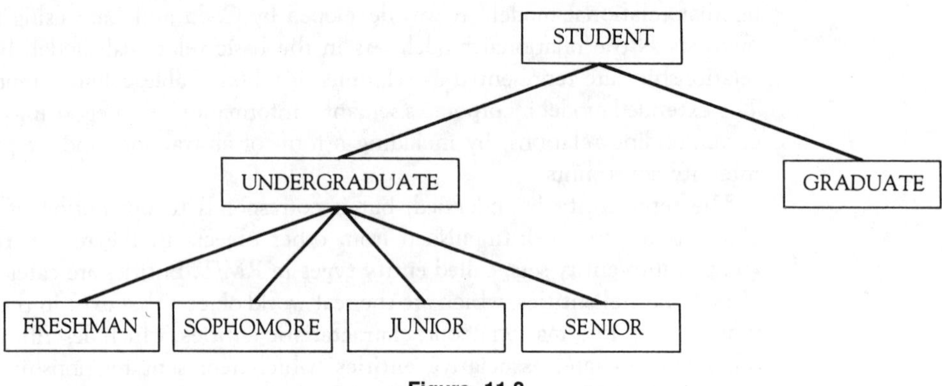

Figure 11.2

An interesting feature of RM/T is that the system assigns its own unique keys or identifiers, called **surrogates,** to entities. These are used internally in place of user-given primary keys. Thus an entity has a unique internal key which is assigned by the system when a user first enters data about that entity and never changes, regardless of modifications to the data. The surrogate is totally unique and will never be changed or used for another entity, even if the present entity data is updated or removed.

Each entity type has a corresponding **E-relation**, a table that contains the surrogates for each entity of that type already in the database. Figure 11.3 shows E-relations for the entity types Student, Department, and Class. Since the actual value of the surrogate is unprintable and not available to the user, we merely refer to it by saying "Surrogate for...." Similarly, each property of an entity is listed in a **P-relation**, which is a table listing the surrogate for each entity and one or more of its property values. There may be one or several P-relations for each E-relation, depending on how the designer chooses to group properties. Figure 11.4 shows sample P-relations for the Student entity type. Note that we could have placed all the property columns in a single table, or split them up into several tables. Each table must have the surrogate column, however. The categorization scheme allows additional constraints to be expressed directly as **integrity rules** for the various entity types and surrogates.

A system catalog for RM/T would contain entries for relations, attributes, and domains, as well as a set of **graph relations** which are tables listing the relationships between relations. There are five such relations: the **property graph relation,** the **characteristic graph relation**, the **association graph relation**, the **designation graph relation**, and the **subtype graph relation**. These tables list the relations of the named type with whatever other relation(s) they are associated. In addition to the basic relational operations defined by Codd for the relational model, some new operations have been created by Codd and Date for the extended model. Although there is no commercial product that supports RM/T, Date and Codd's work contains some implementation details for the model itself, including a hypothetical syntax for creating entity types, expressing the relationships between entity types, and performing the extended relational operations.

STUDENT	Surrogate for
	S1001
	S1002
	S1005
	S1010
	S1013
	S1015
	S1020

CLASS	Surrogate for
	ART103A
	CSC201A
	CSC203A
	HST205A
	MTH101B
	MTH103C

DEPARTMENT	Surrogate for
	Art
	CSC
	History
	Math

Figure 11.3 E-relations for STUDENT, CLASS, DEPARTMENT

STUDENT-NO	Surrogate for	STUID
	S1001	S1001
	S1002	S1002
	S1005	S1005
	S1010	S1010
	S1013	S1013
	S1015	S1015
	S1020	S1020

STUDENT-INFO	Surrogate for	STUNAME	MAJOR	CREDITS
	S1001	Smith,Tom	History	90
	S1002	Chin,David	Math	36
	S1005	Lee,Perry	History	3
	S1010	Burns,Edward	Art	63
	S1013	McCarthy,Owen	Math	9
	S1015	Jones,Mary	Math	42
	S1020	Rivera,Jane	CSC	15

Figure 11.4 P-relations for Student

11.3 *The Binary Model*

The binary model, introduced in 1974 by Abrial, was the first widely publicized semantic model. Several other researchers have proposed various forms of a binary model that uses very simple constructs. Instead of choosing among a large number of constructs, the binary model begins with a minimal set of constructs and builds upon them. The basic constructs are **entity sets** and **binary relations**. The binary model eliminates the distinctions between entities and attributes, and calls both **entities**. Binary relationships between the entities become **facts**. The entire design consists of entity sets connected by facts. Graphically, the entity sets can be represented by circles and the facts by edges or lines connecting the circles. Applying this model to our previous example, STUID is an entity associated with the entity MAJOR. Figure 11.5(a) shows the circles representing the two entity sets, STUID and MAJOR, and the directed line labeled MAJORS-IN shows the fact that a student can have a major or majors. An arrow from MAJOR to STUID would mean that a major can have students enrolled in it. Figure 11.5(b) illustrates both entity sets, STUID and MAJOR, mutually connected by the facts MAJORS-IN and HAS-MAJORS. If we apply this conceptual-level model to actual instances, or **objects**, in the database itself, we can use the same type of diagram to show which objects in the two sets are related. Figure 11.5(c) shows, by the line marked MAJORS-IN starting at S1002, the fact that S1002 has a major in Math. The three lines marked HAS-MAJORS starting at Math and going to S1002, S1013, and S1015 show that Math has these three student majors enrolled in it.

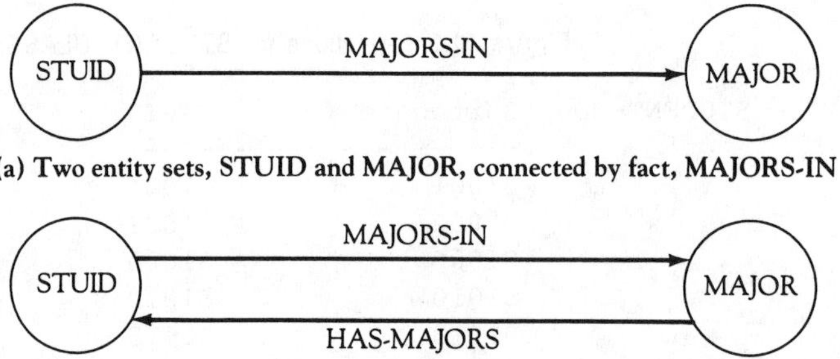

(a) Two entity sets, STUID and MAJOR, connected by fact, MAJORS-IN

(b) Two entity sets, STUID and MAJOR, connected by two facts, MAJORS-IN and HAS-MAJORS

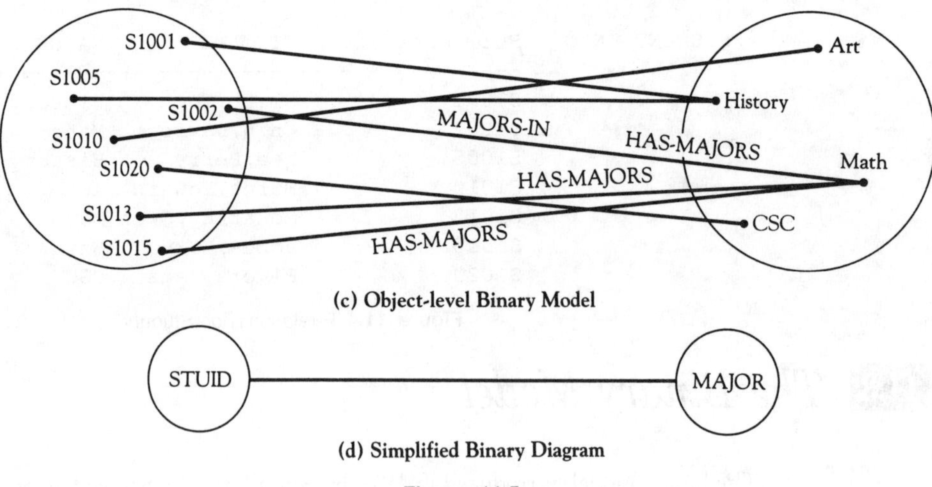

(c) Object-level Binary Model

(d) Simplified Binary Diagram

Figure 11.5

We named the facts in the previous example to allow a clearer discussion of the associations we were interested in. If the meaning of the fact is obvious, we do not need to name it, and merely indicate its existence by drawing a line. If there are associations in both directions, as in this example, we do not need the arrowheads to show direction and can use a single line for both associations. Using both of these simplifications, Figure 11.5(d) means exactly the same as Figure 11.5(b).

In addition to STUID and MAJOR, other entity sets needed for the example about students and courses are STUNAME, CREDITS, COURSE#, CTITLE, FACID, SCHEDULE, ROOM, and GRADE. Figure 11.6(a) shows all the entities and facts that are associated with STUID, and Figure 11.6(b) shows all the entities and facts that are associated with COURSE#. However, we still need to insert GRADE, which is associated with both COURSE# and STUID simultaneously. If we were to connect these three entities as shown in Figure 11.6(c), we would be unable to determine which grade a student received in a particular course. To illustrate, we have chosen only two students who are enrolled in two courses each. The four actual records are as follows:

```
STUID  COURSE#  GRADE
S1002  ART103A  A
S1002  MTH103C  B
S1010  ART103A  B
S1010  MTH103C  A
```

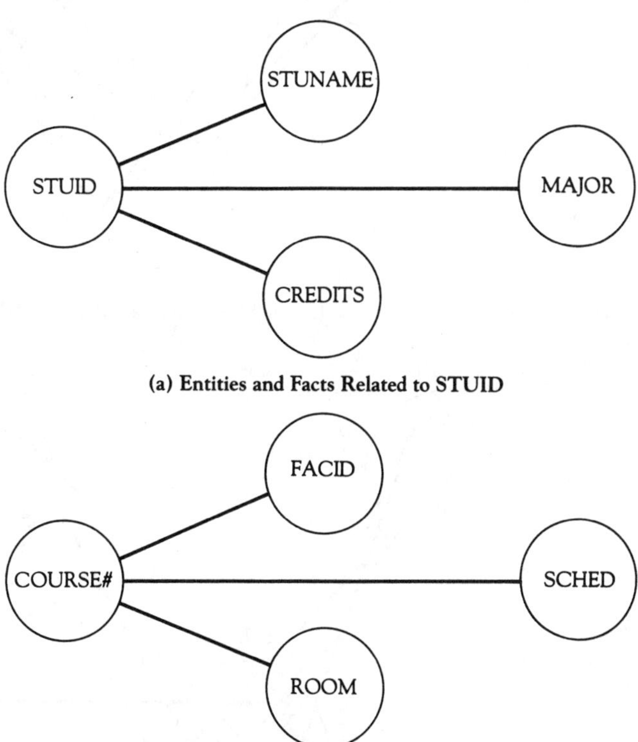

(a) Entities and Facts Related to STUID

(b) Entities and Facts Related to COURSE#

Figure 11.6 (a) and (b)

However, the graph in Figure 11.6(c) could be interpreted to include the following spurious records:

```
S1002  ART103A  B
S1002  MTH103C  A
S1010  ART103C  A
S1010  MTH103C  B
```

To correct this ambiguity, we need another entity set to represent the enrollment of each student in each course. We call this entity set ENROLL and have an entity instance in that set for each interaction, each student enrolled in a particular course. Figure 11.6(d) shows this alternative. Now GRADE is associated with the relationship between STUID and COURSE# rather than with either one individually, and it is clear that the first set of records are the actual ones. The spurious records no longer appear.

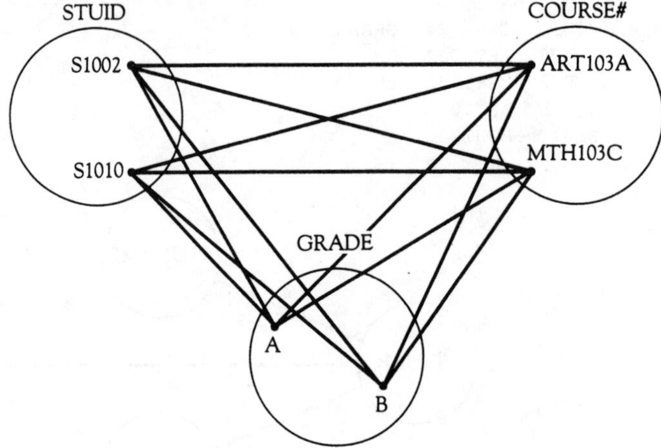

(c) Amibiguous Representation of GRADE

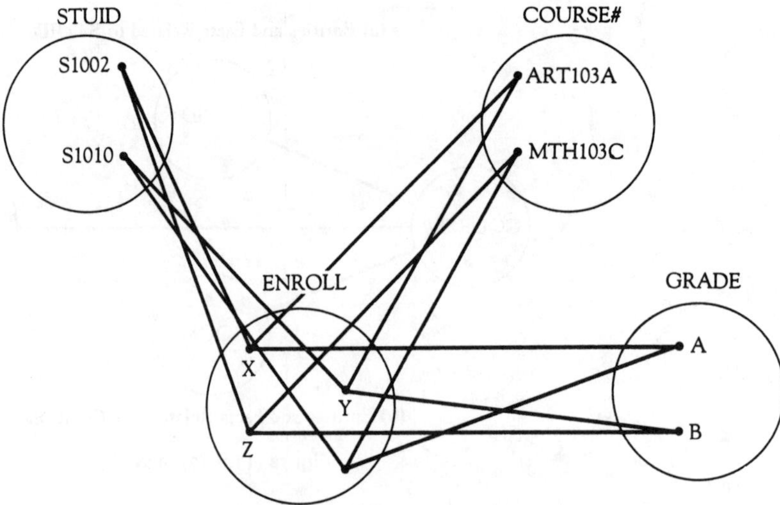

(d) Using an Entity Set for Student-Course Interaction

Figure 11.6 (c) and (d)

11.4 *The Semantic Binary Model*

There are several models that use the word "semantic" in their names. One of them, sometimes called the **semantic binary model,** is described by Rishe. It extends the notion of entities but uses the word **object** instead. An object is an item of interest in the real world. Objects are divided into two classes: **concrete objects** and **abstract objects.** A concrete object or **value** is something that can be printed, such as a name or an amount. An abstract object is a real-world object that cannot be represented directly by a printable value. For example, a student, a course, or a department cannot be represented as such in the computer. A **category** is a grouping of objects, roughly like a mathematical set. It can be defined as a real-world concept which is a property of objects. The concept describes a set of objects that possess the property at any given time. Unlike a set, then, the category does not change over time. The meaning of the category remains the same, while the set of objects having the defining property changes. Examples of categories are Student, Course, Employee, Administrator, and Department. Clearly, the set of students changes as new students are admitted and others are graduated, but the concept of Student remains the same. A category is called a **concrete category** if all of its objects are concrete and an **abstract category** if all of its objects are abstract. An object may belong to several categories simultaneously. For example, an Administrator is also an Employee. Two categories are **disjoint** if they can never have a common member. For example, Student and Course are disjoint. A category is a **subcategory** of another if its set of objects is always a subset of the set of objects in the second category. For example, Administrator is a subcategory of Employee. A category is **finite** if its set of objects at any given time cannot be infinite. For example, the Student category is finite because, at any time, there are a finite number of students in the university.

Objects in the real world can be connected by **relationships.** A **binary relation** is a real-world concept which is a binary property of objects. It is the meaning of the relationship between two objects. At any given time, the relation describes a set of pairs of objects that are related. For example, IS-ENROLLED-IN relates students to courses. The set of pairs that satisfy the relation are pairs of students and the courses they are enrolled in at that time. We could show that a particular student, `s`, is enrolled in a particular course, `c`, by writing

```
s IS-ENROLLED-IN c
```

Domain and range are defined as in mathematics. The model classifies binary relations in various ways. One such classification is **total binary relation**, which means that for every object x in the domain of the relation there is some object y such that x is related to y. The model also discusses **nonbinary relationships**, which are relationships among more than two objects.

In this model, an **instantaneous database** is defined as all the information represented in the database at any given instant. An instantaneous database can be formally represented as a set of unary and binary **facts** or statements. A **unary fact** is a statement that a specified abstract object belongs to a specified category. A **binary fact** is a statement that two objects are related. A **semantic binary model** is a data structure that generates all the instantaneous databases, while a **semantic binary schema** is a description of the databases. It lists all the categories and binary relations in the real world that the database represents.

Schemas are represented graphically, using the following conventions:

- A category is shown by writing the name of the category inside a rectangle.
- Relations from an abstract category to concrete categories are listed inside the rectangle that represents the domain, as

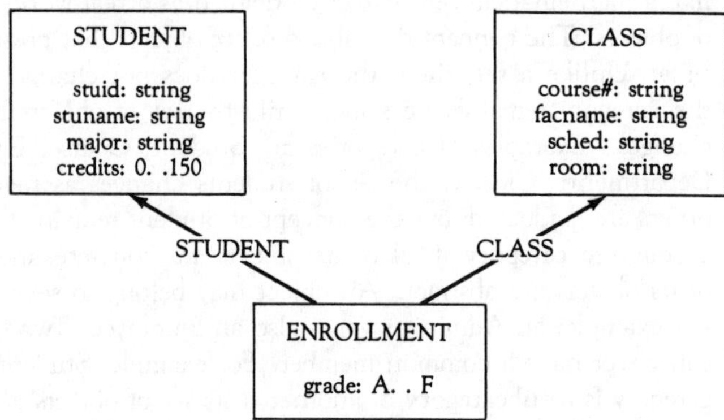

(a) Semantic Binary Schema for Student and Class Data

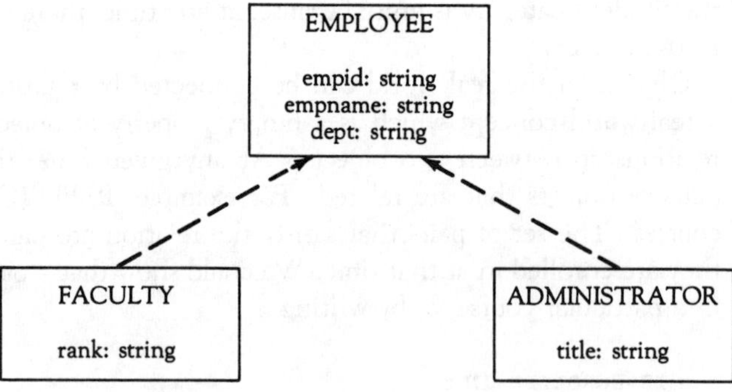

(b) Example of Subcategories in Semantic Binary Model

Figure 11.7

- A relation between two abstract categories is shown by an arrow from the rectangle representing the domain to the rectangle representing the range. The arrow is labeled with the name of the relation.
- A dashed arrow is used to connect a subcategory to its supercategory.
- Categories are considered disjoint, unless otherwise specified, except that categories with a common subcategory or categories that are subcategories of a common supercategory are not disjoint.

Figure 11.7(a) shows a semantic binary schema for the student and course data. Figure 11.7(b) shows a subcategory example, with Administrator and Faculty as subcategories of Employee.

11.5 *The Semantic Database Model, SDM*

The semantic database model (**SDM**) developed by Hammer and McLeod differs from the models described in previous sections in that it provides a large initial set of constructs. It allows the designer multiple perspectives on the same data. It uses the principle of **relativism**, requiring that the database support, on the schema level, different interpretations of the same data. Thus, an item may be considered as an entity in one context and an attribute in another. The model allows descriptions of entities, collections of entities, associations between entities, and structural interconnections among the entity collections. It emphasizes **classification** of entities, so that the database consists of entities organized into classes or types.

For each class, the designer uses a schema that identifies a class **name**, class **members** (which may be categorized as concrete objects, events, higher-level entities like categorizations or aggregations, or names), an optional class **description**, **attributes**, and specification of whether the class is a **base** class (one defined independently of other classes) or **nonbase** class (one defined in terms of other classes, by an interclass connection). Interclass connections may be **subclass** (generalization) or **group** (association). A subclass is defined by a predicate on the members of a class. Depending on the predicate, subclasses may be categorized as **attribute-defined**, defined by **set operations** on existing classes, serving as the **range** of an attribute, or **user-defined**. Grouping or association allows the designer to identify classes that consist of groups of objects. The groups may be identified by specifying constraints (called **expression-defined** grouping class), by listing the classes included (called **enumerated** grouping class), or by aggregation of user-controlled subclasses (called **user-controllable** grouping class). Multiple interclass connections of nonbase classes are not permitted.

Each class has a set of attributes, each of which has several features. These include an attribute **name**, a **value** taken from its **value class** or domain, a specification of its **applicability** (which indicates whether it is a member attribute or a class attribute), and an optional attribute **description**. An attribute's specifications may also tell whether it is **single-valued** or **multivalued**, whether it is permitted to have **null values**, whether it is **updatable**, whether its values must be **exhaustive** (an onto mapping to the value class), and whether it is related to other attributes or refers to other objects in the schema. If an attribute is multivalued, we may also specify whether it is required to be **nonoverlapping**, having no common values for different entities. Hammer and McLeod provide a complete syntax for an SDM data definition language.

11.6 *The Functional Model*

The functional model was introduced by Kerschberg and Pacheco and later developed by Shipman. It uses the concept of the **entity** but it does not distinguish between entities and attributes. Relationships between entities are expressed as **functions** or mappings between entity sets, much like facts in the binary model. In this way, the properties of an entity can be expressed as the result of applying the function to the entity identifier (i.e., the primary key). For the Student entity set the entity identifier is STUID. Using the binary model diagram from Figure 11.5(c), if we apply the function MAJORS-IN to student identifiers, STUID, we will get the major(s) associated with that student. We write this function as

```
MAJORS-IN(STUID)
```

For example,

```
MAJORS-IN(S1001) = History
```

We can also express the inverse of this function as

```
STUID where MAJORS-IN(STUID) = History
```

This gives two values, S1001 and S1005. We would get the same results if we were to apply the HAS-MAJORS function to the Major entity set, or

```
HAS-MAJORS(History) = S1001 AND S1005
```

Notice that this means a function can return several values. This, of course, violates the mathematical definition of a function, but the term is used differently in database theory. If we wish to obtain data that depends on the association between entities, we can do so by using pairs of identifiers as the function argument. For example, to find the grade of a particular student for a particular course, we could simply write

```
GRADE(STUID, COURSE#)
```

Unfortunately, this makes it appear as if the function exists for all combinations of these two identifiers. If we want to show that we are restricting the function to only students enrolled in a particular course, meaning only those combinations that actually exist, we write

```
GRADE(STUID(COURSE#), COURSE#)
```

In 1981, Shipman created the modeling language DAPLEX for the functional model. This language includes declarations of entities and functions. For example, to declare the function MAJORS-IN, we need the identifiers of the two entity sets that are related by the function, namely STUID, and MAJOR, which we declare by

```
DECLARE STUID( ) → ENTITY
DECLARE MAJOR( ) → ENTITY
```

Notice that we do not use an argument for the function in declaring entities. Now we declare the MAJORS-IN function using the entity STUID as the argument and MAJOR as the return:

```
DECLARE MAJORS-IN(STUID) → MAJOR
```

We can also define nested functions as functions of functions and we can declare the inverses of previously defined functions.

11.7 *Object-Oriented Models*

An object-oriented model begins with the notion of physical entities that exist in the real world, and defines an **object** as a collection of properties that describe an entity. Therefore, an object is a representation of an entity. Objects have **names**, which are the same as the names of the entities represented. The collection of properties chosen for an object must be sufficient to describe the entity, that is, it must include those properties that users need to know. In the real world there are **entity classes**, which are sets of entities, and **entity instances**, which are occurrences of entities. Similarly, there are object classes and object instances, which represent particular objects.

Object-oriented programming languages such as SMALLTALK also use the concept of objects. However, those objects exist only while the program is executing. An object-oriented database contains **persistent objects** that exist permanently in the database, but behave in much the same way as objects in programs. Like the programming languages, object-oriented data models use **data abstraction** and **encapsulation**. Both the structure of an object and the allowable operations, called **methods**, for that object are defined. Objects are organized into **classes**. A class is actually an abstract data type that defines both the structure of the objects in it and the set of methods that exist for those objects. An object has an **implementation** that is private and an **interface** that is public and can be seen by users and other objects. The implementation can be changed without changing the interface. The object responds to **messages**, requests for the object to return a value or to change its state. A message names one or more objects and a method to be performed on them. Messages are implemented by the methods. The code for the methods may be generic, capable of operating on objects of different structures. In addition, the same operator may have different effects on different objects. For example, the message "Multiply by 5" sent to a matrix will result in a different operation than the same message sent to an integer.

Classes are arranged in a **class hierarchy**. There is a built-in method for defining new classes. Every new class that is created must be a subclass of some existing class. If there is no appropriate superclass for a new class, it is identified as a subclass of a general system class. Subclasses can inherit structures and methods from superclasses, but inheritance can be overridden. For any class, there is a built-in method for creating new object instances. Objects can also be grouped into more complex objects. Each object instance should have a unique, system-generated **object identifier** that is independent of its attribute values. The object identifier is similar to the surrogate in the RM/T model.

Kroenke and Dolan have described a method for representing objects called an **object diagram**. It consists of a rectangle with the name of the object written underneath and the names of its properties written inside. Objects can be composed of other objects, so some of the properties listed may themselves be objects. In that case, the property name is written in capital letters inside its own rectangle. If the property is permitted to have multiple values, the letters MV appear as a subscript after the property name. The **domain** of a property is the set of its allowable values. For properties that are not themselves objects, the domain has a **physical description**, which gives data type, length, and constraints, and a **semantic description**, which tells what the property means or represents. If the property is itself an object, the domain is a set of object instances. It may be the entire set of instances or just a subset. A **view** is the portion of an object that a particular user or application can see. Figure 11.8(a) shows an object diagram for the student and class data.

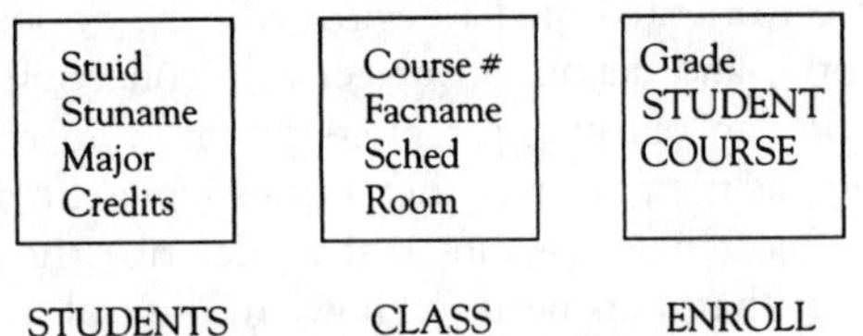

Figure 11.8(a) Object Diagram for Student and Class Data

While object diagrams give a graphical description of object structures and relationships, object **specifications** present the same information textually. Kroenke and Dolan have also described a syntax for object specifications. The specifications consist of **object definitions**, a list of all objects with their properties and the property domains, and **domain definitions**, an alphabetical list of all domains which specifies format, length, any domain constraints, and a semantic description. Their syntax is used in Figure 11.8(b) for the Student and Class example.

There are five classifications of objects according to their structure:

- **Simple objects** have only single-valued properties that are not themselves objects.
- **Composite objects** contain at least one property that is multivalued, but none that are themselves objects. The multivalued property is called a **composite group**.
- **Compound objects** contain at least one property that is itself an object.
- **Association objects** are independent objects that establish a relationship between other objects. Often, they appear as object properties of the objects they connect, and they themselves have keys and nonobject properties.
- **Aggregation objects** are higher-level objects that represent entity groups rather than instances. They contain group properties that apply to all instances of some lower-level object class. The lower-level class **inherits** the properties of the associated aggregation object.

11.8 The Semantic Association Model, SAM*

The semantic association model (SAM*) was developed by Su to support statistical databases, computer-aided design and manufacturing (CAD/CAM) data, and other

```
Object Definitions:

CLASS OBJECT

Course#;  Course-Numbers
Facname;  Faculty-names
Sched;  Class-schedules
Room;  Classrooms

STUDENT OBJECT

Stuid;  Student-ids
Stuname;  Student-names
Major;  Student-majors
Credits;  Student-credits

ENROLL OBJECT

Grade;  Letter-grades
STUDENT;  STUDENT object;  SUBSET[Stuid,Stuname]
CLASS;  CLASS object;  SUBSET[Course#]

Domain Definitions:

Classrooms
     Text 4, mask BNNN
          where B is building code, NNN is room number
     Unique room number for classrooms

Class-schedules
     Text 7
     Days and hour of class meeting

Course-numbers
     Text 7, mask
          Dept-code Text 3
          Number NNN
          Section Text 1
     Unique course number for a course offering

Faculty-names
     Text 15
     Last name of faculty member

Letter-grades
     Text 1
          must be in {A,B,C,D,F,I}
     Alphabetical grade given to student in a course
```

Figure 11.8(b) Object Specifications for Student and Class Data

```
Student-credits
     Numeric 3
          must be in range 0-150
     Number of credits student has completed

Student-ids
     Text 5;  Mask SNNNN
     Unique student number

Student-majors
     Text 15
     Name of major department declared by student

Student-names
     Text 25;  Mask
          Last-name Text 15
          First-name Text 10
     Names of enrolled students
```

Figure 11.8(b) *continued*

commercial applications. It can be considered an object-oriented model. It includes a variety of data types to represent the constructs and relationships needed in these environments. The model consists of network or graph representation of **atomic concepts** and structured objects derived from them. Atomic concepts may be integer, real, string, or Boolean types. Built-in structured types include ordered and unordered sets, vectors, matrices, time, time series, text, and generalized relations (**G-relations**). Operations on these types are also predefined. A G-relation is similar to a non-first-normal-form relation. It is a relation with attributes that may themselves be any atomic or structured data type, including other relations.

SAM* has seven types of **associations** or built-in relationships that can be used for building the network. They are

- **membership**, which allows the designer to list the members of a type.
- **aggregation**, which has its usual meaning of joining together component types into a higher-level type, as in combining attributes to form a relation.
- **interaction**, which is also a type of aggregation in which low-level or concrete concepts are associated to form higher-level or more abstract concepts. Interaction associations permit us to specify cardinality and referential integrity constraints.
- **generalization**, which is an extension of the usual generalization abstraction used to express ISA relationships. The extension allows constraints such as mutual exclusion or intersection of subtypes, set equality, or set-subset relationships.
- **composition**, which allows us to express an "is a part of" abstraction by using a vector of sets.
- **cross-product**, which is a grouping of types that consists of the Cartesian product of the instances of those types.
- **summarization**, which is used to specify attributes for statistics derived from operations such as cross-product and composition associations.

Implementations of SAM* have shown that it is an effective model for the complex data required in statistical and manufacturing applications.

11.9 *Chapter Summary*

Semantic models were developed to provide tools to express real-world relationships more naturally than record-based models. They usually include constructs to represent objects, attributes, and various types of relationships, methods of constructing complex types and derived elements, and some form of abstraction. They increase data independence, allow different levels of abstraction, and decrease semantic overloading.

Codd and Date's **extended relational model**, RM/T, identifies three classes of entities: **kernel, characteristic**, and **associative**. Every entity has **properties,** one of which may be a **designative property** that identifies a related entity. An **entity type hierarchy** shows entity types that are supertypes or subtypes of one another. Each entity has an internal identifier called a **surrogate.** Each entity type has a corresponding **E-relation**, containing the surrogate for each entity instance of that type. A **P-relation** lists the surrogate for each entity and one or more of its property values. Constraints are expressed as **integrity rules**. An RM/T system catalog has entries for relations, attributes, domains, and a set of **graph relations**, listing the relationships between relations. The graph relations are **property**, **characteristic, association, designation, relation**, and **subtype** graph relations.

The **binary model** does not distinguish between entities and attributes, calling both entities. **Facts** are relationships between entities. The conceptual-level design consists of entity sets, represented as circles, connected by facts, or edges. Actual instances, or **objects**, can be shown on the same type of diagram.

In the **semantic binary model** objects may be printable **concrete objects** or real-world, unprintable **abstract objects.** A **category**, a group of objects having a certain property, may also be concrete or abstract. Two categories may be **disjoint** or one may be a **subcategory** of the other. A category may be **finite.** Objects are connected by **relationships**, which may be **binary.** An **instantaneous database** can be represented formally as a set of unary or binary **facts**. A **semantic binary model** is a data structure that generates all the instantaneous databases, and a **semantic binary schema** is a description of the databases. Schemas can be represented graphically.

The semantic database model, SDM, provides a large set of constructs. Emphasis is on **classification** of entities. Interclass connections may be **subtype** or **group**. Subtypes may be **attribute-defined,** defined by **set operations**, the **range** of an attribute, or **user-defined**.

The **functional model** represents relationships between entities as **functions** or mapping between entity sets. The language DAPLEX was created to represent the functional model. It allows declarations of entities and functions, including functions of functions and inverses of functions.

The **object-oriented model** uses **persistent** objects to represent entities. **Data abstraction** and **encapsulation** are used. The **methods** for an object are the allowable operations on it. An object has a private **implementation** and a public **interface**. An object responds to **messages**, requests to return a value or change its state. A message names one or more objects and a method. Methods may use generic code, or the same message may result in different operations on different objects. An **object diagram** is a graphical representation of an object, while an **object specification** is a textual description of an object consisting of object definitions and domain definitions. Objects are classified as **simple, composite, compound, association,** or **aggregation** objects.

The semantic association model, SAM*, is an object-oriented model designed to support statistical and CAD/CAM applications. It uses a graph representation of **atomic concepts** and **structured objects.** There are several built-in structured types and operations, including **G-relations,** which are relations with attributes that may be atomic or structured types. Seven types of built-in **associations** are **membership, aggregation, interaction, generalization, composition, cross-product,** and **summarization.**

11.10 *Exercises*

1. Consider the usual relational schema for the university example:
   STUDENT(STUID, STUNAME, MAJOR, CREDITS)
   FACULTY(FACID, FACNAME, DEPT, RANK)
   CLASS(COURSE#, FACID, SCHED, ROOM)
   ENROLL(COURSE#, STUID, GRADE)

   (a) Give two examples of relationships that are not expressed by this schema.
   (b) Give two examples of constraints that are not expressed by this schema.

2. Consider how the university example fits into the extended relational model.

   (a) Identify kernel, characteristic, and/or associative entities.
   (b) Identify any designative properties.
   (c) Give an example of an entity type hierarchy for the university example other than the one given in Section 11.2.
   (d) Give a set of P-relations for the university example.
   (e) Explain whether the extended model allows you to express the constraints you identified in Exercise 1.

3. Draw a binary model diagram for Faculty and Class data in the university example.

4. Consider the semantic binary model applied to the university example.

   (a) Draw a graphical representation of the schema for the Faculty and Class data.
   (b) Draw a graphical representation of a subcategory other than the one presented in Section 11.4 for the semantic binary model.

5. Consider the functional model of the university example.

(a) Identify and write out functions that would give the properties of the Faculty entity set.
(b) For the Class entity set, assume you have already declared TAUGHT-BY as a function on COURSE# that returns FACID, and TEACHES as a function on FACID that returns COURSE#. Using the tables from Figure 8.2, find the following values:
   (i) TAUGHT-BY(ART103A)
   (ii) COURSE# where TAUGHT-BY(COURSE#) = F105
   (iii) TEACHES(F105)

6. Assume you have an object-oriented database containing an object I which is an integer and an object M which is a matrix.

(a) Assume I has value −4 and M is the 4 X 4 identity matrix, which means that M has 4 rows and 4 columns, with 1s along the main diagonal and 0s elsewhere. What would be the expected result of each of the following messages to I and M?
   (i) "Multiply yourself by 5"
   (ii) "Square yourself"
   (iii) "What is your multiplicative inverse?"
   (iv) "What is your additive inverse?"
(b) For each of the operations in the messages in part (a), briefly describe the receiving object's method.
(c) Identify three other methods for I.
(d) Identify three other methods for M.
(e) Identify one method that involves both I and M.

11.11 *Bibliography*

Abrial, J. R. "Data Semantics," in Klimbie and Koffemen (Ed.), *Data Base Management*. Amsterdam: North-Holland, 1974, pp. 1–59.

Afsarmanesh, H. and D. McLeod. "A Framework for Semantic Database Models," in Ariav and Clifford (Ed.), *New Directions for Database Systems*. Norwood, NJ: Ablex, 1986, pp. 149–167.

Alagic, S. *Object-Oriented Database Programming*. New York: Springer-Verlag, 1989.

Andrews, T. and C. Harris. "Combining Language and Database Advances in an Object-Oriented Development Environment," Proceedings of the ACM Conference on Object-Oriented Programming Systems, Languages, and Applications (1987).

Banerjee, J., W. Kim, H. Kim, and J. Korth. "Semantics and Implementation of Schema Evolution in Object-Oriented Databases," Proceedings of the ACM SIGMOD Conference on Management of Data (1987).

Baroody, J. Jr., and D. DeWitt. "An Object-Oriented Approach to Database System Implementation," ACM Transactions on Database Systems **6**:4 (December, 1981) pp. 576–601.

Clifford, J. and G. Ariav. "Temporal Data Management: Models and Systems," in Ariav and Clifford (Ed.), *New Directions for Database Systems*. Norwood, NJ: Ablex, 1986, pp. 168–185.

Date, C. *An Introduction to Database Systems Volume II* (3rd ed). Reading, MA: Addison-Wesley, 1984.

Dittrich, K. and U. Dayal (Ed.). Proceedings of the International Workshop on Object-Oriented Database Systems. IEEE, 1986.

Elmasri, R. and S. Navathe. "Data Model Integration Using the Structural Model," Proceedings of the ACM SIGMOD Conference on Management of Data (1979) pp. 191–202.

Fishman, D. et. al. "IRIS: An Object-Oriented DBMS," ACM Transactions on Office Information Systems **4**:2 (April, 1986).

Goldberg, A. and D. Robson. *Smalltalk-80: The Language and Its Implementation*. Reading, MA: Addison-Wesley, 1983.

Hammer, M. and D. McLeod "Database Description with SDM: A Semantic Data Model," ACM Transactions on Database Systems **6**:3 (September, 1981) pp. 351–386.

Hull, R. and R. King "Semantic Database Modeling: Survey, Applications, and Research Issues," ACM Computing Surveys **19**:3 (September, 1987) pp. 201–260.

Kerschberg, L. and J. Pacheco. "A Functional Data Base Model," Tech. Rep. Pontificia Univ. Catolica do Rio de Janeiro (1976).

Kroenke, D. and K. Dolan. *Database Processing*. Chicago: Science Research Associates, 1988.

Maier, D., J. Stein, A. Otis, and A. Purdy. "Development of an Object-oriented DBMS," Proceedings of the ACM Conference on Object-Oriented Programming Systems, Languages, and Applications (1986) pp. 472–482.

Navathe, S. "Toward Making the ER Approach Object-Oriented," Proceedings of the International Conference on Entity-Relationship Approach (1988).

Peckham, J. and F. Maryanski "Semantic Data Models," ACM Computing Surveys **20**:3 (September, 1988) pp. 153–189.

Rishe, N. *Database Design Fundamentals*. Englewood Cliffs, NJ: Prentice-Hall, 1988.

Shipman, D. "The Functional Data Model and the Data Language DAPLEX," ACM Transactions on Database Systems **6**:1 (March, 1981) pp. 140–173.

Su, S. "SAM*: A Semantic Association Model for Corporate and Scientific Statistical Databases," *Inf. Sci.* **29** (1983) pp. 151–199.

Su, S. "Modeling Integrated Manufacturing Data with SAM*," IEEE Computer Magazine **10**:1 (January, 1986) pp. 34–49.

Tsichritzis, D. and F. Lochovsky. *Data Models*. Englewood Cliffs, NJ: Prentice-Hall, 1982.

PART IV

IMPLEMENTATION ISSUES

CHAPTER

12

Concurrency Control and Recovery

12 Chapter Objectives

In this chapter you will learn

- the meaning of database recovery
- the meaning of concurrency control
- the characteristics of a transaction
- some causes of database failure
- the nature and purpose of the database transaction log
- why and how checkpoints are performed
- why concurrency control is needed
- the meaning of serializability
- why and how locking is done
- the meaning of deadlock
- how deadlock is detected and broken
- how the two-phase locking protocol works
- what levels of locking may be used
- how timestamping is used for serializability
- how optimistic concurrency control techniques operate

12.1 *Transaction Management*

Regardless of the care with which the database is designed and created, it can easily be damaged or destroyed unless proper concurrency controls and recovery techniques are in place. Database **recovery** means the process of restoring the database to a correct state in the event of a failure. **Concurrency control** is the ability to manage simultaneous processes involving the database without having them interfere with one another. Both are needed to protect the database from data contamination or data loss.

The notion of **transaction** is central to an understanding of both recovery and concurrency control. A transaction can be thought of as a **logical unit of work** on the database. It may be an entire program, a portion of a program, or a single command. It may involve any number of operations on the database. Recall the university database, using the following relational scheme:

```
STUDENT (STUID, STUNAME, MAJOR, CREDITS)
FACULTY (FACID, FACNAME, DEPT, RANK)
CLASS (COURSE#, FACID, SCHED, ROOM)
ENROLL (COURSE#, STUID, GRADE)
```

A simple transaction against this database might be to update the number of credits in a STUDENT record, given the STUID. This task involves locating the block containing the appropriate STUDENT record on disk, bringing the block into the buffer, rewriting the value of the CREDITS field in the record in the buffer, and finally writing the updated block out to disk. Figure 12.1 summarizes the steps in this transaction. A more complicated transaction would be to change the STUID assigned to a particular student. Obviously, we need to locate the appropriate STUDENT record, bring its block into the buffer, update the STUID in the buffer, and write the update to disk as before, but we also need to find all the ENROLL records having the old STUID and update them. If these updates are not made, we will have an **inconsistent state** of the database, a state in which the data is contradictory. A transaction should always bring the database from one consistent state to another. While the transaction is in progress, it is permissible to have a temporary inconsistent state. For example, during the STUID update, there will be some moment when one occurrence of the STUID contains the new value and another still contains the old one. However, at the end of the transaction, all occurrences will agree. A transaction is the entire series of steps necessary to accomplish a logical unit of work, to bring the database to a new consistent state. The transaction is an **atomic process**, a single "all or none" unit. We cannot allow only part of a transaction to execute—either the entire set of steps must be done or none can be done, because a partial transaction would leave the database in an inconsistent state.

There are two ways a transaction can end or **terminate**. If it executes to completion successfully, the transaction is said to be **committed**, and the database is brought to a new consistent state. The other possibility is that the transaction cannot execute successfully. In this case, the transaction is **aborted**. If a transaction is aborted, it is essential that the database be restored to the consistent state it was in before the transaction started. Such a transaction is **undone** or **rolled back**. A committed transaction cannot be aborted. If we decide that the committed transaction was a mistake, we must perform another

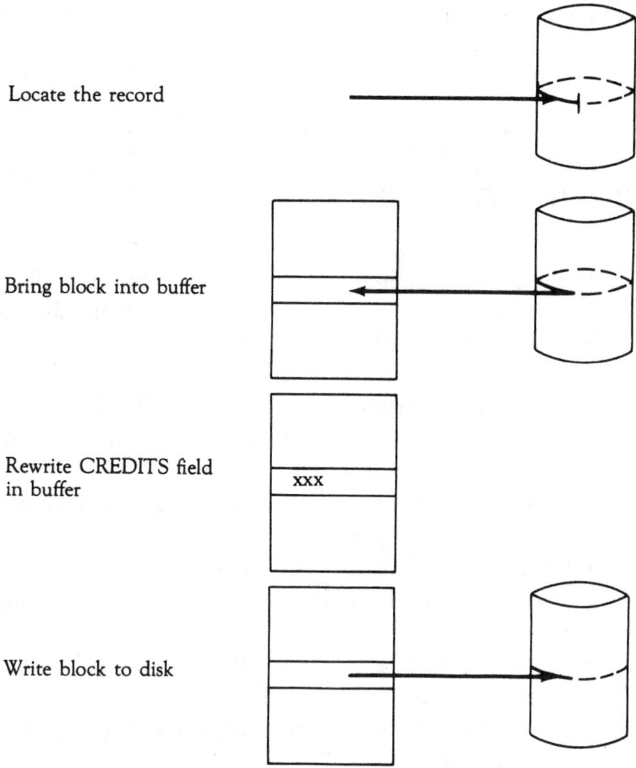

Figure 12.1 Steps in a Simple Transaction

transaction to reverse its effects. However, an aborted transaction that has been rolled back can be restarted at a future time and, depending on the cause of the failure, may successfully execute and commit at that time.

It is usually the responsibility of the programmer to identify the beginning and end of each transaction. The words BEGIN TRANSACTION, END TRANSACTION, COMMIT, and ROLLBACK are available in some DMLs to delimit transactions. If these delimiters are not used, the entire program is usually regarded as a single transaction, with the system automatically performing a COMMIT when the program terminates correctly and a ROLLBACK when it does not. Whenever an explicit or implicit COMMIT or ROLLBACK is reached, at the end of one transaction but before the beginning of another, the system reaches a **synchronization point**. At such a synchpoint, updates are either committed or rolled back, the database is in a consistent state, cursors (which are "position pointers" used by a system to keep its place in a file and are "opened" or activated when the system first accesses the file) are closed, and any locks held for the transaction are released.

Updates made to buffer blocks are not automatically written to disk at each synchpoint. Therefore, there may be a delay between the commit and the actual disk writing. If there is a system failure during this delay, the system must be able to ensure that these updates reach the disk copy of the database. Transactions that have been committed must not committed must be rolled back. Therefore, the transaction is the unit used for recovery.

12.2 *Need for Recovery*

There are many different types of failures that can affect database processing. Some failures affect main memory only, while others involve disk storage or backup storage devices. Among the causes of failure are

- Natural **physical disasters** such as fires, floods, earthquakes, or power outages.
- **Sabotage** or intentional contamination or destruction of data, hardware, or software facilities.
- **Carelessness** or unintentional destruction or contamination of data or facilities by operators or users.
- **Disk malfunctions** such as head crashes, defective disks, or unreadable tracks.
- **System crashes** due to hardware malfunction, resulting in loss of main and cache memory.
- **System software errors** that result in abnormal termination or destruction of the database management system.
- **Applications software errors** such as logical errors in the program that is accessing the database.

Regardless of the cause of the failure, we need to study the possible effects so that we can protect or limit the damage to the database. The principal effects that concern us are the loss of main memory, including database buffers, and the loss of the disk copy of the database. Fortunately, there are techniques that can minimize these effects.

12.3 *Recovery Techniques*

Recovery after any failure consists of restoring the database to a correct state. If a system failure occurs and the database buffers are lost, the disk copy of the database is undamaged. However, the system cannot determine the state of any transaction that was executing at the time of failure, so these active transactions must be rolled back. In addition, transactions that were committed but not yet written to disk are lost, so they must be redone. To keep track of database transactions, the system maintains a special file called a **log** that contains information about all updates to the database. The log may contain the following data:

- **Transaction records**, giving the transaction name and some information about it. For example, there is a record of the form <T starts> showing the start of

a transaction, a record of the form <T,X,c> for each write operation showing the transaction name, the field name, and the new value, a record of the form <T commits> showing the end of the committed transaction, or a record of the form <T aborts> showing that a transaction has aborted.
- **Checkpoint records**, which we will describe shortly.

Figure 12.2 illustrates a program segment and the corresponding log transaction entries.

```
program T
.
.
.
     read (X);
     X := X + 10;
     write (X);
     read (Y);
     Y := 2 * Y;
     write (Y);
end
```

Figure 12.2 (a) The Program Segment

```
(Assume at the start that X and Y both have value 100.)
<T starts>
<T,X,110>
<T,Y,200>
<T commits>
```

Figure 12.2 (b) The Log Entries

Figure 12.2 A Program Segment and its Log Entries

We can use the log to protect against system failures in the following way:

- When a transaction starts, write a record of the form <T starts> to the log.
- When any write operation is performed, do not actually write the update to the database buffers or the database itself. Instead, write a log record of the form <T,X,c>.
- When a transaction is about to commit, write a log record of the form <T commits>, write all the log records for the transaction to disk, and then commit the transaction. Use the log records to perform the actual updates to the database.
- If the transaction aborts, simply ignore the log records for the transaction and do not perform the writes.

This technique is known as an **incremental log with deferred updates.** Note that we write the log records to disk before the transaction is actually committed, so that if a system failure occurs while the actual database updates are in progress, the log records will survive and the updates can be applied later.

In the event of a system failure, we examine the log to identify the transactions that were in progress at the time of failure. Any transaction with log records <T starts> and <T commits> should be **redone**. The **redo** procedure will perform all the writes to the database, using the write log records for the transactions. Recall that all of these have the form <T,X,c>, which means the procedure will write the value *c* to the data item *X*. If this writing has been done already, prior to the failure, the write will have no effect on the data item, so there is no damage done if we write unnecessarily. However, this method guarantees that we will update any data item that was not properly updated prior to the failure. For any transactions with log records <S starts> and <S aborts>, we do nothing, since no actual writing was done to the database, so these transactions do not have to be undone. In the event that a second system crash occurs during recovery, the log records are used again the second time the system is restored. Because of the form of the write log records, it does not matter how many times we redo the writes.

One difficulty with this scheme is that when a failure occurs, we may not know how far back in the log to search and we may wind up redoing transactions that have been safely written to the database. To put some limit on the log searching we need to do, we can use a technique called a **checkpoint**. Checkpoints are scheduled at predetermined intervals and involve the following operations:

- Writing the modified blocks in the database buffers out to disk.
- Writing all log records now in main memory out to disk.
- Writing a checkpoint record to the log. This record contains the names of all transactions that are active at the time of the checkpoint.

Having checkpoints allows us to limit the log search. When a failure occurs, we check the log to find the last transaction that started before the last checkpoint. If transactions are performed serially, any earlier transaction would have committed previously and have been written to the database at the checkpoint. Therefore, we need only redo the one that was active at the checkpoint and any subsequent transactions for which both start and commit records appear in the log. If transactions are performed concurrently, the scheme is only slightly more complicated. Recall that the checkpoint record contains the names of all transactions that were active at checkpoint time. Therefore, we redo all those transactions and all subsequent ones.

A slightly different recovery technique uses an **incremental log with immediate updates.** In this scheme, updates are applied to the database buffers as they occur and written to the database itself when convenient. However, a log record is written first. The scheme for successful transactions is as follows:

- When a transaction starts, write a record of the form <T starts> to the log.
- When a write operation is performed, write a log record containing the name of the transaction, the field name, the old value, and the new value of the field. This has the form <T,X,a,b>.
- Once the log record is written, write the update to the database buffers.
- When convenient, write the updates to the database itself.
- When the transaction commits, write a record of the form <T commits> to the log.

If a transaction aborts, the log can be used to undo it, since it contains all the old values for the updated fields. Because a transaction may have performed several changes to an item, the writes are undone in reverse order. Regardless of whether the transaction's writes have been applied to the database itself, writing the old values guarantees that the database will be restored to its state prior to the start of the transaction.

If the system fails, recovery involves using the log to undo or redo transactions. For any transaction, *T*, for which both <T starts> and <T commits> records appear in the log, we redo by using the log records to write the new values of updated fields. Note that if the new values have already been written to the database, these writes, though unnecessary, will have no effect. However, any write that did not actually reach the database will now be performed. For any transaction, *S*, for which the log contains an <S starts> record, but not an <S commits> record, we will need to undo that transaction. This time the log records are used to write the old values of the affected fields and thus restore the database to its state prior to the transaction's start.

12.4 *Need for Concurrency Control*

One of the major objectives in developing a database is to create an information resource that can be shared by many users. Often, the users need to access data simultaneously. If all users are only reading data, there is no way that they can interfere with one another and there is no need for concurrency control. However, when two users try to make updates simultaneously, or one updates while another reads, there may be conflicts.

Multiprogramming means having two or more programs or transactions processing at the same time. For example, many systems have I/O control systems that can handle I/O operations independently, while the main processor performs other operations. Such systems can allow two or more transactions to execute simultaneously. The system begins executing the first transaction until it reaches an input or output operation. While the I/O is being performed, the main processor, which would otherwise be idle during I/O, switches over to the second transaction and performs whatever operations it can on the second one. Control then returns to the first transaction and its operations are performed until it again reaches an I/O operation. In this way, operations of the two transactions are **interleaved**, with some from one transaction performed, then some from the other, and so on, until all operations for both transactions are completed. Even though both transactions may be perfectly correct in themselves, the interleaving of operations may produce an incorrect outcome. Three examples of potential problems caused by concurrency are **the lost update problem, the uncommitted update problem,** and **the problem of inconsistent analysis.** We will use **schedules,** which are graphical depictions of the execution sequences of transactions, to show the chronological order in which operations are performed.

The Lost Update Problem

Suppose that Jack and Jill have a joint savings account with a balance of $1000. Jill gets paid and decides to deposit $100 to the account, using a branch office near her job. Meanwhile, Jack finds that he needs some spending money and decides to withdraw $50 from the joint account, using a different branch office. If these transactions were executed **serially**, one after the other with no interleaving of operations, the final balance would be $1050 regardless of which was performed first. However, if they are performed concurrently, the final balance may be incorrect. Figure 12.3 is a schedule for a concurrent execution that results in a final balance of $1100. The schedule shows sequential units of time as *t*1, *t*2, and so on, to show the chronological order of operations. The value that a transaction reads for a variable is the one it uses for calculations. Therefore, at time *t*5, Jill's transaction still uses the value it read for BAL, not the new value, which it has not read. When a transaction calculates a new value for a variable, that value is not stored in the variable until a write statement appears. According to the schedule, Jack's update is lost. If Jill had completed first, her update might have been lost, resulting in a final balance of $950.

TIME	Jack's Transaction	Jill's Transaction	BAL
t1	read BAL	...	1000
t2	...	read BAL	1000
t3	BAL := BAL - 50	...	1000
t4	write BAL	...	950
t5	...	BAL := BAL + 100	950
t6	...	write BAL	1100

Figure 12.3 The Lost Update Problem

The Uncommitted Update Problem

The uncommitted update problem occurs with concurrent transactions when the first transaction is permitted to modify a value which is then read by the second transaction, and the first transaction subsequently rolls back its update. Figure 12.4 shows a schedule containing an example of an uncommitted update that causes an error. Here, transaction INTEREST calculates the interest for a savings account, using a rate of 5 percent, while transaction DEPOSIT deposits $1000 to the account, but is rolled back. The starting balance in the account is $1000. If DEPOSIT actually updates the value of the balance to $2000 before INTEREST reads the balance, the amount that INTEREST will store is $2100. However, DEPOSIT is rolled back, which means that the database state should show no effect due to DEPOSIT. The reason for the rollback is unimportant, but it may be that the transaction itself was an error, perhaps crediting the wrong account, or it may be the result of a system crash. Whatever the reason, the interest was calculated on the incorrect balance. When the rollback is performed, the final balance will be incorrect. The value might be $1100, if the rollback algorithm for undoing DEPOSIT is to subtract the amount of the deposit from the current value of BAL, or it might be $1000, if the rollback algorithm is to replace the balance by its value at the time the DEPOSIT transaction started. In the first case, we get twice as much interest as we should, and in the second, we get no interest. The second is actually another version of the lost update problem.

The Problem of Inconsistent Analysis

The problem of inconsistent analysis occurs when a transaction reads several values but a second transaction updates some of them during the execution of the first. Suppose

TIME	DEPOSIT Transaction	INTEREST Transaction	BAL
t1	read BAL	...	1000
t2	BAL := BAL + 1000	...	1000
t3	write BAL	...	2000
t4	...	read BAL	2000
t5	...	BAL := BAL * 1.05	2000
t6	...	write BAL	2100
t7	ROLLBACK	...	?

Figure 12.4 The Uncommitted Update Problem

that we are summing the interest due on all savings accounts, but allowing deposits, withdrawals, and transfers to be performed during this transaction. Figure 12.5 contains a schedule that shows how an incorrect result could be produced. SUMINT finds the sum of the interest due on all accounts. Notice that this transaction does not update the accounts. Its only purpose is to find out how much is due, and crediting the accounts is done separately. Meanwhile, transaction TRANSFER transfers $1000 from account A to account E. The TRANSFER transaction executes correctly and commits. However, it interferes with the SUMINT transaction, which calculates interest on the same $1000 twice, once while it is in account A and again when it reaches account E.

Time	SUMINT	TRANSFER
t1	TOTINT := 0;	...
t2	read BAL_A (Assume 5000)	...
t3	INT := BAL_A * .05	...
t4	TOTINT := TOTINT + INT	...
t5	read BAL_B	...
t6	INT := BAL_B *.05	...
t7	TOTINT := TOTINT + INT	...
t8	...	read BAL_A (Assume 5000)
t9	...	BAL_A := BAL_A -1000
t10	...	write BAL_A (4000)
t11	read BAL_C	...
t12	INT := BAL_C *.05	...
t13	TOTINT := TOTINT + INT	...
t14	...	read BAL_E (Assume 5000)
t15	...	BAL_E := BAL_E + 1000
t16	...	write BAL_E (6000)
t17	read BAL_D	...
t18	INT := BAL_D *.05	...
t19	TOTINT := TOTINT + INT	...
t20	read BAL_E (6000)	...
t21	INT := BAL_E *.05	...
t22	TOTINT := TOTINT + INT	...

Figure 12.5 The Inconsistent Analysis Problem

12.5 *Serializability*

Serial execution of transactions means transactions are performed one after another, without any interleaving of operations. If *A* and *B* are two transactions, there are two possible serial executions: All of transaction *A* is completed first and then all of transaction *B* is done, or all of *B* is completed and then all of *A* is done. In serial execution, there is no interference between transactions, since only one is executing at any given time. If the transactions shown in Figures 12.3 had been executed serially, regardless of whether the deposit or the withdrawal transaction was executed first, the result would have been the same. If the transactions in Figure 12.4 had been done serially, either the DEPOSIT transaction would have been rolled back before the INTEREST transaction started, or the INTEREST would have completed before the DEPOSIT started, so again they would not have interfered with each other. In Figure 12.5, if the TRANSFER transaction had been postponed until the SUMINT transaction completed, or if the TRANSFER had completed before the SUMINT started, the result would have been correct. However, there is no guarantee that the results of all serial executions of a given set of transactions will be identical. In banking, for example, it matters whether interest is calculated for an account before a large deposit is made or after.

The three problems that we described resulted from the concurrency and left the database in an inconsistent state. No serial execution would allow these problems to arise. In most cases, users do not care in what order their transactions are executed as long as no user is made to wait too long. Regardless of which serial schedule is chosen, a serial execution will never leave the database in an inconsistent state, so every serial execution is considered to be correct, even though different results may be produced. Our goal is to find ways to allow transactions to execute concurrently while making sure that they do not interfere with one another, and produce a database state that could be produced by a truly serial execution.

If a set of transactions executes concurrently, we say that the schedule is correct if it produces the same results as some serial execution. Such a schedule is called **serializable.** It is essential to guarantee serializability of concurrent transactions in order to ensure database correctness. In serializability, the following factors are important:

1. If two transactions are only reading a variable, they do not conflict and order is not important.
2. If two transactions operate on (either reading or writing) completely separate variables, they do not conflict and order is not important.
3. If one transaction writes to a variable and another either reads or writes to the same variable, the order of execution is important.

A serializable execution of transactions orders any conflicting operations in the same way as some serial execution, so that the results of the concurrent execution are the same as the results of at least one of the possible serial executions. A facility called a **scheduler** is used to allow operations to be executed immediately, delayed, or rejected. If a transaction's operation is rejected, that transaction is aborted, but it may, of course, be restarted after the conflicting transaction completes. Serializability can be achieved in several ways, but most systems use either locking or timestamping, the two techniques that will be described here. In general, the DBMS has a concurrency control subsystem that is "part of the package" and not directly controllable by either the users or the DBA.

12.6 *Locking*

Locking is more commonly used than timestamping to ensure serializability of concurrent transactions. A transaction "locks" a database object to prevent another transaction from modifying the object. Objects of various sizes, ranging from the entire database down to a data item, may be locked. The size of the object determines the fineness or **granularity** of the lock. The actual lock might be implemented by inserting a flag in the field, record, page, or file to indicate that portion of the database is locked, by keeping a list of locked parts of the database, or other means. Often, there are two categories of locks: **shared** and **exclusive.** If a transaction has a shared lock on an item, it can read the item but not update it. Thus many transactions may have shared locks on the same item at the same time. If a transaction has an exclusive lock on an item, it can both read and update the item. To prevent interference with other transactions, only the requesting transaction can hold an exclusive lock on an item at any given time. Figure 12.6 illustrates a **lock compatibility matrix** that shows which type of lock requests can be granted simultaneously. If transaction 1 holds the type of lock indicated on the left, and transaction 2 requests the lock type indicated on the top of the column, the matrix shows whether the lock request can be granted. As you can see, a shared lock request can be granted if the first transaction holds a shared lock. All other lock requests will be denied.

Transaction 1 Holds	Transaction 2 requests Shared	Exclusive
Shared	Yes	No
Exclusive	No	No

Figure 12.6 Lock Compatibility Matrix

If a system uses locks, any transaction that needs to access a data item must first lock the item, requesting a shared lock for read only access or an exclusive lock for both read and write access. If the item is not already locked by another transaction, the lock will be granted. If the item is currently locked, the system determines whether the request is compatible with the existing lock. If a shared lock is requested on an item that has a shared lock on it, the request will be granted; otherwise, the transaction will have to **wait** until the existing lock is released. A transaction's locks are automatically released when the transaction terminates. In addition, a transaction can explicitly release locks that it holds prior to termination.

12.7 *Deadlock*

The set of items that a transaction reads is called its **read set**, and the set of items that a transaction writes is called its **write set**. In database processing, it is often difficult to identify the read set and write set of a transaction before executing the transaction. Often, records are accessed because of their relationship to other records. Usually, it is impossible to tell in advance exactly which records will be related.

Since we cannot always specify in advance which items need to be locked by a transaction, we make lock requests during the execution of the transaction. These requests can result in a situation called **deadlock**, which occurs when two transactions are each waiting for locks held by the other to be released. Figure 12.7 shows two transactions, *S* and *T*, which are deadlocked because each is waiting for the other to release a lock on an item it holds. At time *t*1, transaction *S* requests and obtains an exclusive lock on item *X*, and at time *t*2, transaction *T* obtains an exclusive lock on item *Y*. Then at *t*3, *S* requests item *Y*. Since *T* holds a lock on *Y*, transaction *S* waits. Meanwhile, at *t*4, *T* requests a lock on item *X*, which is held by transaction *S*. Neither transaction can complete because each is waiting for a lock it cannot obtain until the other completes. Deadlocks involving several transactions can also occur. For example, Figure 12.8 shows four transactions, *Q*, *R*, *S*, and *T* that are deadlocked because *Q* is waiting for a data item locked by *R*, *R* is waiting for a data item locked by *S*, *S* is waiting for a data item locked by *T*, and *T* is waiting for a data item locked by *Q*. Once deadlock occurs, the applications involved cannot resolve the problem. Instead, the system has to recognize that deadlock exists and break the deadlock in some way.

```
Time     Transaction S        Transaction T

t1       Xlock X              ...
t2       ...                  Xlock Y
t3       Request Y            ...
t4       wait                 Request X
t5       wait                 wait
t6       wait                 wait
t7       wait                 wait
...      ...                  ...
```

Figure 12.7 Deadlock with Two Transactions

Time	Trans Q	Trans R	Trans S	Trans T
t1	Xlock Q1	...	...	...
t2	...	Xlock R1	...	...
t3	...	...	Xlock S1	...
t4	...	...	...	Xlock T1
t5	request R1	...	...	...
t6	wait	request S1	...	...
t7	wait	wait	request T1	...
t8	wait	wait	wait	request Q1
t9	wait	wait	wait	wait
...	...	...	...	...

Figure 12.8 Deadlock with Four Transactions

There are two general techniques for handling deadlock: **deadlock prevention**, in which the system looks ahead to see if a transaction would cause a deadlock and never allows deadlock to occur, and **deadlock detection and recovery**, which allows deadlock to occur but once it has, spots and breaks the deadlock. Since it is easier to test for deadlock and break it when it occurs than to prevent it, many systems use the detection and recovery method. Deadlock detection schemes use a **resource request graph** or **wait-for graph** to show which transactions are waiting for resources locked by other transactions. In such a graph, each node is a transaction. An edge indicates that one transaction is waiting for another to release a lock. For example, Figure 12.9(a) shows two transactions, *U* and *V*, with the directed edge from *U* to *V* showing that *U* is waiting for a data item locked by *V*. The wait-for graph is maintained by the system. As new transactions start, new nodes are added to the graph. When a transaction makes a request for a locked resource, an edge is added to the graph. If the resource is unlocked and obtained by the transaction, the edge is erased. In deadlock, the graph will contain a **cycle**, a path that begins with a particular node, goes to at least one other node, and ends up back at the starting node. Figure 12.9(b) shows a wait-for graph in which transactions *S* and *T* are deadlocked, because there is a cycle starting with *S*, going to *T*, and then going back to *S*. This cycle has length 2, because it contains 2 edges or directed paths, *S* to *T*, and *T* to *S*. (Of course, there is also a cycle starting at *T*.) Figure 12.9(c) shows a wait-for graph with a cycle of length 4. This pictures transactions *Q*, *R*, *S*, and *T* previously discussed and shown in Figure 12.8.

The system detects deadlock by periodically checking its wait-for graph for cycles. Note that it must check for cycles of any length, since a cycle may involve many transactions. Once a cycle is detected, the system must resolve the deadlock. It does so by choosing one of the transactions in the cycle as the **victim**, a transaction that will be made to fail and will be undone so that the other transactions can proceed. The victim is arbitrarily chosen by the system. For example, if we chose transaction S shown in Figure 12.9(c), then *R* would obtain its requested data items and could complete and release its locks, so that *Q* could also complete, and finally, *T* could obtain its data items. Then transaction *S*, the victim, could be restarted and could obtain its locks at a later time.

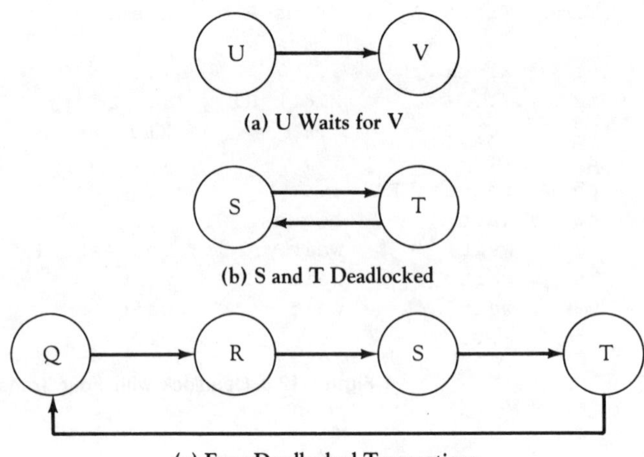

Figure 12.9 Wait-for Graphs

12.8 *Two-Phase Locking*

One locking scheme that ensures serializability is the **two-phase locking protocol**. According to the rules of this protocol, every transaction can go through two phases: first a **growing phase** in which it acquires all the locks needed for the transaction, and then a **shrinking phase** in which it releases its locks. There is no requirement that all locks be obtained simultaneously. Normally, the transaction acquires some locks, does some processing, and goes on to acquire additional locks as needed. However, it never releases any lock until it has reached a stage where no new locks will be needed. The rules are

1. A transaction must acquire a lock on an item before operating on the item. The lock may be exclusive or shared, depending on the type of access needed.
2. Once the transaction releases a single lock, it can never acquire any new locks.

The protocol described above is the strict two-phase locking protocol, which is the most widely used concurrency control mechanism.

The two-phase locking protocol can be refined slightly to maximize concurrency. In this version of two-phase locking, a transaction may at first request shared locks that will allow other transactions concurrent read access to the items. Then when the transaction is ready to do an update, it requests that the shared lock be **upgraded**, or converted into an exclusive lock. Upgrading can take place only during the growing phase, and may require that the transaction wait until another transaction releases a shared lock on the item. Once an item has been updated, its lock can be **downgraded**, converted from an exclusive to a shared mode. Downgrading can take place only during the shrinking phase.

While the two-phase protocol guarantees serializability, it can cause deadlock, since transactions can wait for locks on data items. If two transactions wait for locks on items held by the other, deadlock will occur, and the deadlock detection and recovery scheme described in Section 12.7 will be needed.

12.9 Levels of Locking

Locks can be applied to a single data item, a single record, a file, a group of files, or the entire database. For example, you may recall from Chapter 9 that the IDMS schema allowed us to designate exclusive or shared locks on the database, area, file, record, or data item level. Few systems actually implement data item-level locks because of the overhead involved. Some lock pages at a time. We could express the fineness or **granularity** of locks by a hierarchical structure in which each node represents data objects of different sizes, as shown in Figure 12.10. Here the root node represents the entire database, the level 1 nodes areas, the level 2 nodes files, the level 3 nodes records, and the leaves data items. Whenever a node is locked, all its descendants are also locked. For example, locking file A1 of Figure 12.10 locks records A11, A12, and A13 as well as all their data items. If a second transaction requests an incompatible lock on the same node, the system clearly knows that the lock cannot be granted. For example, a request for an exclusive lock on file A1 will be denied. If the second transaction requests an incompatible lock on any of the descendants of the locked node, the system should check the hierarchical path from the root to the requested node to see if any of its ancestors are locked before deciding whether to grant the lock. Thus if the request is for an exclusive lock on record A11, the system should check its parent, file A1, its grandparent, Area A, and the database itself to see if any of them are locked. When it finds that file A1 is already locked, it denies the request.

What happens if a transaction requests a lock on a node when a descendant of the node is already locked? For example, if a lock is requested on Area A, the system would have to check every file in the area, every record in those files and every data item in those records to see if any of them are locked. To reduce the searching involved in locating locks on descendants, the system can use another type of lock called an **intention** lock. When any node is locked, an intention lock is placed on all the ancestors of the node. Thus if some descendant of Area A (e.g., file A1) is locked, and a request is made for a lock on Area A, the presence of an intention lock on Area A would indicate that some descendant of that node is already locked. Intention locks may use either exclusive or shared mode. To ensure serializability with locking levels, a two-phase protocol is used, meaning no lock can be granted once any node has been unlocked, no node may be locked until its parent is locked by an intention lock, and no node may be unlocked until all its descendants are unlocked. The effect of these rules is to apply locking from the root down, using intention locks until the node requiring an actual shared or exclusive lock is reached, and to release locks from leaves up. However, deadlock is still possible, and must be detected and resolved using the methods discussed previously.

12.10 Timestamping

An alternative concurrency-control mechanism that eliminates the deadlock problem is **timestamping**. In this scheme, no locks are used, so no deadlocks can occur. A

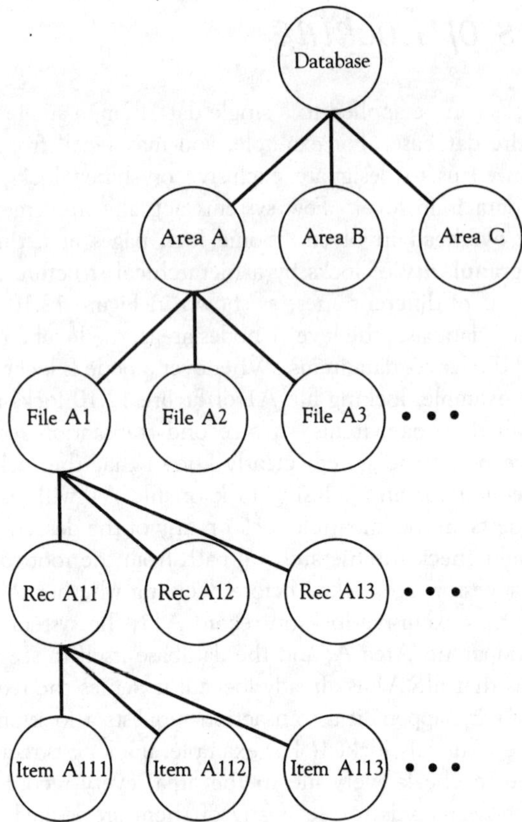

Figure 12.10 Levels of Locking

timestamp for a transaction is a unique identifier that indicates the relative starting time of the transaction. It could be the reading on the internal clock at the time the transaction started, or it could be the value of a logical counter that is incremented every time a new transaction starts. In either case, the timestamp value of each transaction is unique and indicates how "old" the transaction is. The effect of timestamping is to assign a serial order to the transactions. The protocol then makes sure that the order is met, by not permitting any reads or writes that would violate the order. In addition to transaction timestamps, there are timestamps for data items. Each data item contains a Read-Timestamp, giving the timestamp of the last transaction to read the item, and a Write-Timestamp, giving the timestamp of the last transaction to write (update) the item.

Two problems can arise with timestamping:

1. A transaction asks to read an item that has already been updated by a younger (later) transaction.
2. A transaction asks to write an item whose value has already been read or written by a younger transaction.

The first problem can be eliminated by keeping multiple versions of the same data item, each having a content field, a Write-Timestamp of the transaction that did the last write that created the value of the content field and a Read-Timestamp of the transaction that did the last read of that value. When a read is requested by a transaction, the value that is returned is the value of the content field associated with the latest Write-Timestamp that is less than or equal to the timestamp of the current transaction. For example, in Figure 12.11(a) transaction 10 requests a data item that has already been updated by transaction 11. However, an old version of the data item exists, with a content value of 100 and a Write-Timestamp of 9. Since this is the last Write-Timestamp less than or equal to the transaction's timestamp (10), we use that version for transaction 10. The Read-Timestamp of that version is then changed to 10. The effect of this process is to ensure that the two transactions read data items as if they were actually executed serially.

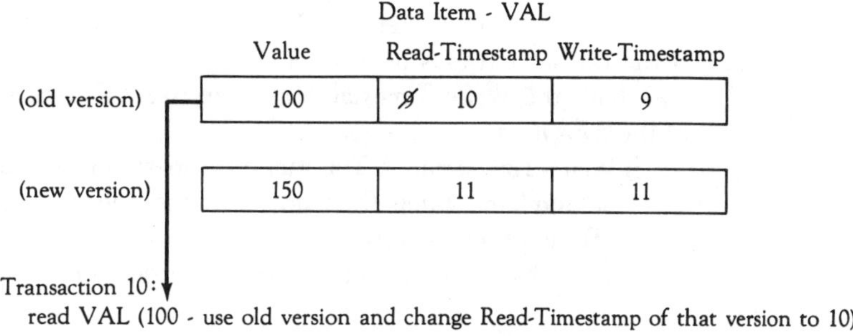

(a) Transaction Reads an Item Already Updated by Younger Transaction

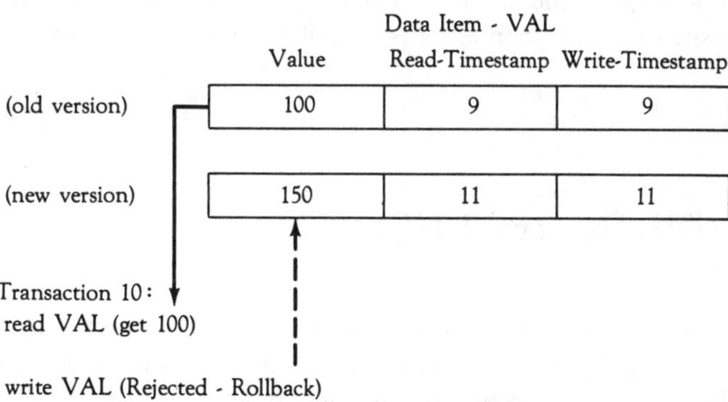

(b) Transaction Tries to Write an Item Already Updated by Younger Transaction

Figure 12.11 Timestamping Examples

The second problem occurs when a transaction is late in doing a write, and a younger transaction has already read the old value or written a new one. In this case the only solution is to roll back the current transaction and restart it using a later timestamp. Figure 12.11(b) illustrates what happens when transaction 10 tries to write an item that has already been updated by transaction 11. In this case, transaction 10 is rolled back. To ensure that no transaction reads values that may be undone by rollback, actual database updates are postponed until a transaction is committed. Thus rollback simply involves not doing the transaction's writes to the database.

The following rules summarize this protocol. We always test the timestamp of the transaction, which we will call **Transaction-Timestamp**, against the **Write-Timestamp** and/or **Read-Timestamp** which identify the transaction(s) that last wrote or read the data item:

1. If the transaction asks to **read** a data item, compare its **Transaction-Timestamp** with the **Write-Timestamp** of the **current version** of the data item.
   If **Write-Timestamp** < **Transaction-Timestamp** then proceed using the current data value and replace **Read-Timestamp** with **Transaction-Timestamp**
   else locate the version whose **Write-Timestamp** is the largest one less than or equal to **Transaction-Timestamp**, use that data value for the current transaction, and replace **Read-Timestamp** with **Transaction-Timestamp**.
2. If the transaction asks to **write** a data item, compare its **Transaction-Timestamp** with both the **Write-Timestamp** and the **Read-Timestamp** of the **current version** of the data item.
   If **Write-Timestamp** < **Transaction-Timestamp** and **Read-Timestamp** < **Transaction-Timestamp** then do the write and replace **Write-Timestamp** with **Transaction-Timestamp**
   else roll back the current transaction, assign a new timestamp, and restart.

This scheme guarantees that transactions will be serializable and the results will be equivalent to a serial execution schedule in which the transactions are executed in chronological order by the timestamps. That is, the results will be as if all of transaction 1 were executed, then all of transaction 2, and so on, with no interleaving.

12.11 *Optimistic Techniques*

In many environments, conflicts between transactions are relatively rare, and the extra processing required to apply locking schemes is unnecessary for most of the transactions. There is a class of techniques that eliminates this overhead. **Optimistic techniques**, also called **validation techniques**, work under the assumption that conflict will normally not occur. They allow transactions to proceed as if there were no concurrency problems, but just before a transaction commits, a check is performed to determine whether conflict has occurred. If there is a conflict, the transaction must be rolled back. Since the assumption is that conflict rarely occurs, rollback will be rare. The occasional rollback is the price to be paid for eliminating locks. These techniques allow more concurrency than traditional schemes, since no locking is done.

In optimistic schemes, a transaction goes through two or three phases in order, depending on whether it is a read-only or an updating transaction:

1. A **read phase**, which extends from the start of the transaction until just before it commits. During this phase, the transaction reads the values of all variables it needs and stores them in local variables. If the transaction does any writes, they are done to a local copy of the data, not to the database itself.
2. A **validation phase**, which follows the read phase. During this time, the transaction tests to determine whether there is any interference. For a read-only transaction, this consists of checking to see that there was no error caused by another transaction that was active when the data values were read. If no error occurred, the transaction is committed. If interference occurred, the transaction is aborted and restarted. For a transaction that does updates, validation consists of determining whether the current transaction will leave the database in a consistent state, with serializability maintained. If not, the transaction is aborted. If the update transaction passes the validation test, it goes on to a third phase.
3. A **write phase**, which follows the successful validation phase for update transactions. During this phase, the updates made to the local copy are applied to the database itself.

The validation phase is accomplished by examining the reads and writes of transactions that may cause interference. Each transaction is assigned a timestamp at the end of its read phase. In addition, its starting time, which is the time it started its execution, and its finishing time, which is the time it finished (including its write phase, if any) are recorded. To pass the validation test, **one** of the following must be true:

1. All transactions with earlier timestamps must have finished (including their writes) before the current transaction started.

OR

2. If the current transaction starts before an earlier one finishes, then

   (a) the items written by the earlier transaction are not the ones read by the current transaction, **and**

   (b) the earlier transaction completes its write phase before the current transaction enters its validation phase.

Rule 2(a) guarantees that the writes of the earlier transaction are not read by the current transaction, while rule 2(b) guarantees that the writes are done serially.

Although optimistic techniques are very efficient when there are few conflicts, they can result in rollback of individual transactions. Note that the rollback involves only a local copy of the data, so there are no cascading rollbacks, since the writes have not actually reached the database. However, if the aborted transaction is a long one, valuable processing time will be lost, since the transaction must be restarted. If rollback occurs often, it is an indication that the optimistic method is a poor choice for concurrency control in that particular environment.

12.12 Chapter Summary

Database **recovery** is the process of restoring the database to a correct state after a failure. **Concurrency control** is the ability to allow simultaneous use of the database without having users interfere with one another. Both protect the database.

A **transaction** is a logical unit of work that takes the database from one consistent state to another. Transactions can terminate successfully and **commit** or unsuccessfully and be **aborted**. Aborted transactions must be undone or **rolled back**. When transactions are done serially, a **synchronization point** occurs when a transaction ends, but before another begins. The transaction is the unit of recovery. Causes of failure are physical disasters, sabotage, carelessness, disk malfunctions, system crashes, system software errors, applications software errors, and others. They can result in the loss of main memory and/or the disk copy of the database. Recovery techniques minimize these effects.

To facilitate recovery, the system keeps a **log** containing **transaction records** that identify the start of transactions, give information about write operations, and identify the end of transactions. Using an **incremental log with deferred updates**, writes are done initially to the log only, and the log records are used to perform actual updates to the database. If the system fails, it examines the log to determine which transactions it needs to **redo**, but there is no need to **undo** any writes. At a **checkpoint**, all modified buffer blocks, all log records, and a checkpoint record identifying all active transactions are written to disk. If a failure occurs, the checkpoint records identify which transactions need to be redone. Using an **incremental log with immediate updates** an update may be made to the database itself at any time after a log record is written. The log can be used to undo as well as to redo transactions in the event of failure.

Concurrency control is needed when transactions are permitted to process simultaneously. Without it, problems of **lost update, uncommitted update**, and **inconsistent analysis** can arise. Serial execution means executing one transaction at a time, with no interleaving of operations. A **schedule** shows the timing of the operations of transactions. A schedule is **serializable** if it produces the same results as a serial schedule.

Two methods that guarantee serializability are **locking** and **timestamping**. Locks may be **exclusive** or **shared**. A **lock compatibility matrix** shows which type of locks can be granted simultaneously. Because transactions can wait for locks, **deadlock**, a situation in which two or more transactions wait for locks being held by one another, can occur. **Deadlock detection schemes** use a **wait-for** graph to identify deadlock. A **cycle** indicates deadlock. It is resolved by choosing a **victim**, a transaction that will be made to fail.

In **two-phase locking,** a transaction acquires all its locks before releasing any. A variation allows transactions to **upgrade** shared locks to exclusive locks just before a write during the growing phase. In the shrinking phase, a transaction may **downgrade** an exclusive lock to a shared lock.

A tree may be used to represent the granularity of locks in a system that allows locking of different-sized objects. When an item is locked, all its descendants are also locked. When a new transaction requests a lock, it is easy to check all the ancestors of the object to see whether they are already locked. To show whether any of the node's descendants are locked, an intention lock is placed on all the ancestors of any node being locked. Serializability is ensured by using a two-phase locking protocol.

In a **timestamping** protocol, each transaction is given a timestamp that gives the relative order of the transaction, and each data item has a **Read-Timestamp** and a **Write-Timestamp**. Problems arise when a transaction tries to read or write an item already updated by a younger transaction. The protocol takes care of these problems by keeping multiple versions of the same data item, and by rolling back transactions that cannot execute correctly.

Optimistic techniques can be used when conflicts are rare. Each transaction starts with a **read phase**, during which it reads all variables it needs, stores them as local variables, and writes to the local copy only. It then moves to a **validation phase**, during which the system determines whether there was any interference. If not, it moves on to a **write phase** and applies the updates to the database. If there was interference, the transaction is aborted instead of moving to the write phase.

12.13 *Exercises*

1. Assume a system having an incremental log with immediate updates has the following log entries, ending with a system crash:

```
<R starts>
<R,X,1,5>
<R,Y,-1,0>
<R commits>
<S starts>
<S,Z,8,12>
<checkpoint record>
<S,X,5,10>
<T starts>
<T,Y,0,15>
<S commits>
--------system crash--------
```

   (a) Which transactions, if any, need to be redone?
   (b) Which transactions, if any, need to be undone?
   (c) Which transactions, if any, are not affected by the crash?

2. Now assume the system uses an incremental log with deferred updates.
   (a) Rewrite the log entries for the transactions in Exercise 1 for this logging method.
   (b) Which transactions, if any, need to redone after the failure?
   (c) Which transactions, if any, need to be undone?
   (d) Which transactions, if any, are not affected by the crash?

3. (a) Suppose that the log in Exercise 1 contained the entry <S aborts> in place of the entry <S commits>. If the system crash occurred before the rollback took place, what changes, if any, would you make in the recovery process?

(b) If the system uses an incremental log with deferred updates and S aborted just prior to failure, what changes, if any, would you make in the recovery process of Exercise 2?

4. Assume the following transactions are to be performed:

```
Transaction S:
read(A);
A:=A+10;
write(A);
read(B);
B:=B-5;
write(B);
Transaction T:
read(A);
A:=A+5;
write(A);
```

(a) If the initial value of A is 100 and the initial value of B is 50, what are their final values if we perform the transactions serially, using order S,T?
(b) What are the final values of A and B is the order of execution is T,S?

5. Change the assignment statement in transaction T in Exercise 4 to A:=A$*$2. Assume the initial values for A and B are still 100 and 50, respectively.
(a) What are the final values of A and B using order S,T?
(b) What are the final values of A and B using order T,S?

6. (a) Write a schedule for an execution of transactions S and T of Exercise 4 that illustrates the lost update problem.
(b) Write a schedule for an execution of S and T that illustrates the uncommitted update problem.
(c) Write a transaction, V, that calculates a running sum by adding data items A and B from transaction S at different times. Write a schedule for S and V that demonstrates the problem of inconsistent analysis.

7. Extend the lock compatibility matrix shown in Figure 12.6 to include a request by transaction 2 for lock upgrading during the growing phase of a two-phase protocol. Under what circumstances will an upgrade be granted? When will a lock downgrade be granted?

8. Extend the lock compatibility matrix shown in Figure 12.6 to include both shared and exclusive intention locks.

9. Apply the two-phase locking protocol to the schedules shown in Figures 12.3, 12.4, and 12.5 by adding statements such as "request Xlock BAL" or "grant Slock SUM". Will the protocol allow the execution of those schedules?

10. Apply the timestamping protocol to the schedules shown in Figures 12.3, 12.4, and

12.5 by issuing timestamps as needed. Will the protocol allow the execution of those schedules?

11. Apply the two-phase locking protocol to the serial schedules of Exercise 4. Will the protocol allow the execution of those schedules?

12. Apply the timestamping protocol to the schedules of Exercise 4. Will the protocol allow the execution of those schedules?

13. Apply the two-phase locking protocol to the schedules you devised in Exercise 6. Will the protocol allow the execution of those schedules?

14. Apply the timestamping protocol to the schedules you devised in Exercise 6. Will the protocol allow the execution of those schedules?

12.14 *Bibliography*

Badal, D. S. "The Analysis of the Effects of Concurrency Control on Distributed Database System Performance," Proceedings of the International Conference on Very Large Data Bases (1980), pp. 376–383.

Bayer, R., K. Elhardt, H. Heller, and A. Reiser. "Distributed Concurrency Control in Database Systems," Proceedings of the International Conference on Very Large Data Bases (1980) pp. 275–284.

Bernstein, P., V. Hadzilacos, and N. Goodman. *Concurrency Control and Recovery in Database Systems*. Reading, MA: Addison-Wesley, 1988.

Cardenas, A. *Data Base Management Systems*. Boston: Allyn & Bacon, 1985.

Chandy, K., J. Browne, C. Dissly, and W. Uhrig. "Analytic Models for Rollback and Recovery Strategies in Database Systems," IEEE Transactions on Software Engineering **SE-1**:1 (March, 1975) pp. 9–36.

Date, C. *An Introduction to Database Systems*. Reading, MA: Addison-Wesley, 1986.

Garcia-Molina, H. and J. Kent. "An Experimental Evaluation of Crash Recovery Algorithms," Proceedings of the Fourth ACM Symposium on Principles of Database Systems (1985) pp. 113–121.

Gray, J. "Notes on Data Base Operating Systems," in Bayer, Graham, and Seegmuller (Ed.), *Operating Systems: An Advanced Course*. Berlin: Springer-Verlag, 1978, pp. 393–481.

Gray, J. "The Transaction Concept: Virtues and Limitations," Proceedings of the International Conference on Very Large Data Bases (1981) pp. 144–154.

Gray, J., R. Lorie, and G. Putzulo. "Granularity of Locks and Degrees of Consistency in a Shared Data Base," Proceedings of the International Conference on Very Large Data Bases (1975) pp. 428–451.

Gray, J., P. McJones, and M. Blasgen. "The Recovery Manager of the System R Database Manager," ACM Computing Surveys **13**:2 (June, 1981) pp. 223–242.

Kedem, Z. and A. Silberschatz. "Controlling Concurrency Using Locking Protocols," Proceedings Twentieth Annual IEEE Symposium on Foundations of Computer Science (1979) pp. 275–285.

Kedem, Z. and A. Silberschatz. "Non-two Phase Locking Protocols with Shared and Exclusive Locks," Proceedings of the International Conference on Very Large Data Bases (1980) pp. 309–320.

Kedem, Z. and A. Silberschatz. "Locking Protocols: From Exclusive to Shared Locks," Journal of the ACM **30**:4 (October, 1983) pp. 787–804.

Kung, H. and J. Robinson "Optimistic Concurrency Control," ACM Transactions on Database Systems **6**:2 (June, 1981) pp. 213–226.

Korth, H. "Locking Primitives in a Database System," Journal of the ACM **30**:1 (January, 1983) pp. 55–79.

Korth, H. and A. Silberschatz. *Database System Concepts*. New York: McGraw-Hill, 1986.

Lehman, P. and S. Yao. "Efficient Locking for Concurrent Operations on B-trees," ACM Transactions on Database Systems **6**:4 (December, 1981) pp. 65–670.

Lien, E. and P. Weinberger. "Consistency, Concurrency, and Crash Recovery," Proceedings of the ACM SIGMOD International Conference on Management of Data (1978) pp. 9–14.

Manber, U. and R. Ladner. "Concurrency Control in a Dynamic Search Structure," ACM Transactions on Database Systems **9**:3 (September, 1984) pp. 439–455.

Papadimitriou, C. "The Serializability of Concurrent Database Updates," Journal of the ACM **26**:4 (October, 1979) pp. 631–653.

Papadimitriou, C. *The Theory of Database Concurrency Control*. Rockville, MD: Computer Science Press, 1986.

Papadimitriou, C., P. Bernstein, and J. Rothnie. "Some Computational Problems Related to Database Concurrency Control," Proceedings of the Conference on Theoretical Computer Science (1977) pp. 275–282.

Papidimitriou, C. and P. Kanellakis. "On Concurrency Control by Multiple Versions," ACM Transactions on Database Systems **9**:1 (March, 1974) pp. 89–99.

Ries, D. "The Effect of Concurrency Control on the Performance of a Distributed Database Management System," Proceedings of the Berkeley Workshop on Distributed Data Management and Computer Networks (1979) pp. 75–112.

Ries, D. and M. Stonebraker. "Effects of Locking Granularity in a Database Management System," ACM Transactions on Database Systems **2**:3 (September, 1977) pp. 233–246.

Sagiv, Y. "Concurrent Operations on B-trees with Overtaking," Proceedings of the ACM Symposium on Principles of Database Systems (1985) pp. 28–37.

Schlageter, G. "Optimistic Methods for Concurrency Control in Distributed Database Systems," Proceedings of the International Conference on Very Large Data Bases (1981).

Skeen, D. "Nonblocking Commit Protocols," Proceedings of the ACM SIGMOD International Conference on Management of Data (1981) pp. 133–142.

Ullman, J. *Principles of Database and Knowledge-Base Systems Volume I*. Rockville, MD: Computer Science Press, 1988.

Vasta, J. *Understanding Data Base Management Systems*. Belmont, CA: Wadsworth, 1985.

Verhofstadt, J. "Recovery Techniques for Database Systems," ACM Computing Surveys **10**:2 (June, 1978) pp. 167–195.

Yannakakis, M. "A Theory of Safe Locking Policies in Database Systems," Journal of the ACM **29**:3 (1982) pp. 718–740.

Yannakakis, M. "Serializability by Locking," Journal of the ACM **31**:2 (1984) pp. 227–245.

CHAPTER

13

Security and Integrity

13 Chapter Objectives

In this chapter you will learn

- the meaning of database security
- the relationship between privacy and security
- examples of accidental or deliberate threats to security
- some physical security measures
- the meaning of user authentication
- the meaning of authorization
- the meaning and representation of access control
- how the view functions as a security device
- the purpose of the security log and audit trail
- how and why data encryption is performed
- how security is enforced in some systems–DB2, IDMS/R, IMS
- the meaning of database integrity
- examples of constraints
- how integrity constraints can be expressed and enforced
- how integrity is checked in some systems–DB2, IDMS/R, IMS

13.1 *Database Security*

Database security means protecting the database from unauthorized access, modification, or destruction. Since the database represents an essential corporate resource, security is an important goal. In addition to the need to preserve and protect data for the smooth functioning of the organization, database designers have a responsibility to protect the privacy of individuals about whom data is kept. **Privacy is the right of individuals to have some control over information about themselves.** Many countries have legal statutes designed to protect certain matters of privacy, and every organization that collects and stores information about individuals is legally obliged to adopt policies that conform to local privacy legislation. The database design should reflect the organization's commitment to protection of individual rights by including only those items the organization has a right to know. In addition, privacy must be guarded by protecting stored information that is of a sensitive nature.

Security threats can occur either **accidentally** or **deliberately**. Some examples of accidental security violations are:

- The user may unintentionally request an object or an operation for which he or she should not be authorized, and the request may be granted because of an oversight in authorization procedures or because of an error in the database management system or operating system.
- A person may accidentally be sent a message that should be directed to another user, resulting in unauthorized disclosure of database contents.
- A communications system error may result in connecting a user to a session that belongs to another user with different access privileges.
- Occasionally, the operating system may accidentally overwrite files and destroy part of the database, may fetch the wrong files and then inadvertently send them to the user, or may fail to erase files that should be destroyed.

Deliberate security violations occur when a user intentionally gains unauthorized access and/or performs unauthorized operations on the database. A disgruntled employee who is familiar with the organization's computer system poses a tremendous threat to security. Industrial spies seeking information for competitors also threaten security. There are many ways that deliberate security breaches can be accomplished, including

- Wiretapping of communication lines to intercept messages to and from the database.
- Electronic eavesdropping, to pick up signals from terminals, printers, or other devices within a building.
- Reading display screens and reading or copying printouts left unsupervised by authorized users.
- Impersonating an authorized user or a user with greater access by using his or her sign-on and password.
- Writing systems programs with illegal code to bypass the database management system and its authorization mechanism and access database data directly through the operating system.

- Writing applications programs with code that performs unauthorized operations.
- Deriving information about hidden data by clever querying of the database.
- Removing physical storage devices from the computer room.
- Making physical copies of stored files without going through the database management system, thereby bypassing its security mechanisms.
- Bribing, blackmailing, or otherwise influencing authorized users in order to use them as agents in obtaining information or damaging the database.

13.2 *Physical Security and User Authentication*

Database security is best implemented as part of a broader security control plan. The plan should begin with physical security measures for the building itself, with special precautions for the computer room. Designing a physically secure building is clearly outside the domain of the database designer. However, the DBA or data administrator should be able to suggest measures that would control access to database facilities. Often these begin at the front door, where all employees should be identified visually by guards, by using badges, handprints, sign-ins, or other mechanisms. Additional identification should be required to enter the computer room itself. Physical security measures should be extended to cover any location where off-line data such as backups are stored as well.

Because physical security of individual terminals may be difficult to implement, security control of terminals requires **authentication** of users. Authentication means verifying the identity of the user, checking to ensure that the actual user is who he or she claims to be. It is usually implemented at the operating system level. When the user signs on, he or she enters a user ID, which is checked for validity. The system then has a user profile for that ID, giving information about the user. The profile normally includes a password, which is allegedly known only to the user. Passwords should be kept secret and changed frequently. A simple security precaution is for the system to require that passwords be changed monthly. The system should obviously never display passwords at sign-in time, and the stored profiles should be kept secure, possibly in encrypted form. Although passwords are the most widely used authentication method, they are not very secure, since users sometimes write them down, choose words that are easy to guess, or share them with others. In some organizations, users must insert badges or keys when they log on. In others, voice, fingerprints, or other physical characteristics of the user are examined. Some use an authentication procedure rather than a single password. A procedure might consist of answering a series of questions and would take longer and be more difficult to reproduce than a password. Although authentication is usually done only at the operating system level, it is possible to require it again at the database level. At the very least, this would require that the user produce an additional password to access the database.

13.3 *Authorization*

In addition to authentication, most database management systems designed for multiple users have their own security subsystems. These subsystems provide for user authorization, some method by which users are assigned rights to use database objects. Most multiple-user systems have an **authorization language** which is part of the data sublanguage. The DBA uses the language to specify users' rights by means of **authorization rules**, statements that specify which users have access to what information, and what operations they are permitted to use on what data. The authorization mechanism is designed to protect the database by preventing people from unauthorized reading, updating, or destruction of database contents. These restrictions are added to the security mechanisms provided by the operating system. However, in a surprisingly large number of cases, database security subsystems are minimal or are not fully utilized. Recognizing that data is a valuable corporate resource, the designer should include available security mechanisms as an important factor in evaluating alternative database management systems, and should develop effective security policies utilizing whatever controls are available with the system chosen.

13.4 *Access Control*

Access control is the means by which authorizations are implemented. Access control means making sure that data or other resources are accessed only in authorized ways. In planning access, the DBA might use an **access control matrix** for the database, as shown in Figure 13.1. The column headings represent database objects, which may be the names of tables, views, subschemas, data items, data aggregates, records, files, areas, or other categories, depending on the database model and management system used. The row labels represent individuals, groups of users, or applications. The cell entries specify the type of access permitted. Values of entries will also depend on the particular system used, but the choices usually include READ, WRITE, UPDATE, DELETE, and their combinations. Once the access control matrix is complete, the DBA must use the appropriate authorization language to implement it. The DBA, of course, is permitted to create and change the structure of the database, as well as to use the authorization language to grant data access to others or to revoke access. Some systems allow the DBA to delegate some of this authorization power. In that case, certain users might be permitted to modify existing database structures or to create new structures as well as updating data occurrences. In a multiuser environment, such changes may have consequences for other users. Since the DBA is often the only one who has a comprehensive view of all users' data needs, it is often unwise to grant this authorization. The DBA can sometimes grant users the power to authorize other users to perform operations on the database. However, having many such "authorizers" can be extremely dangerous. Since authorizers may create other authorizers, the situation can get out of hand very quickly, making it difficult for the DBA to revoke authorizations.

SUBJECT	OBJECT					
	CLASS Table	COURSE#	FACID	FACNAME	FAC Table	•••
User U1001	Read	Read	All	All	All	•••
User U1002	Update	Update	Read	Read	Read	•••
User U1003	Read	Read	Write	Update	Read	•••
•••						
•••						
•••						

Figure 13.1 Part of a Database Access Control Matrix

13.5 *Using Views for Access Control*

The view is a widely used method for implementing access control. Each of the record-based models has its own method of specifying external models or views. The view mechanism has a twofold purpose. It is a facility for the user, simplifying and customizing the external model through which the user deals with the database, freeing the user from the complexities of the underlying model. It is also a security device, hiding structures and data that the user should not see. In the relational model, an external model consists of some combination of base tables and relational views. The hierarchical model provides users with a view that is a subset of some physical or logical tree. The network model view is described in the subschema, which allows us to specify the areas, records, and sets to be included, and permits us to exclude, rename, reorder, and regroup data items and other database objects. Each model therefore has some mechanism by which it restricts users to certain portions of the database.

13.6 *Other System Security Tools: Security Logs, Audit Trails, Encryption*

Another important security tool is the **security log**, which is a journal that keeps a record of all attempted security violations. The violation can be simply recorded in the log, or it can trigger an immediate message to the operator or the DBA. Knowing about the existence of the log can be a deterrent in itself. If the DBA suspects that data is being compromised without triggering security log entries, it is possible to set up an **audit trail**. Such an auditing system records all access to the database, keeping information about the user who requested the access, the operation performed, the terminal used, the time of occurrence, the data item, its (old) value, and its new value, if any. The audit trail can therefore uncover the sources of suspicious operations on the database, even if they are performed by authorized users, such as disgruntled employees.

To provide for the possibility of anyone accessing files directly through the operating system or stealing files, data may be stored in the database in encrypted form. Only the database management system can unscramble the data, so that anyone who obtains data by any other means will receive jumbled information. Encryption should also be used whenever data is communicated to other sites, so that wiretappers will also receive scrambled data. Encryption requires a **cipher system**, which consists of the following components:

1. **An encrypting algorithm**, which takes the normal text, called **plaintext**, as input, performs some operations on it, and produces the encrypted text, called **ciphertext**, as output.
2. **An encrypting key**, a value which is part of the input for the encrypting algorithm, and is chosen from a very large set of possible keys.
3. **A decrypting algorithm**, which operates on the ciphertext as input and produces the plaintext as output.
4. **A decryption key**, a value which is part of the input for the decryption algorithm, and is chosen from a very large set of possible keys.

There are two schemes that are widely used for encryption. The first is the **Data Encryption Standard (DES)** devised by the National Bureau of Standards, and the second is **public-key encryption.** In the DES scheme, the algorithm itself is public, while the key is private. The decryption key is the same as the encryption key, and the decryption algorithm is the inverse of the encryption algorithm. Because the algorithm is a standard, it is possible to put a hardware implementation on a single chip, so that encryption and decryption are very fast and cheap compared to a software implementation of the algorithm. However, the key must be kept secure or the encryption is worthless, since anyone with the key has access to the data. The DES algorithm uses a 64-bit key on 64-bit blocks of plaintext, producing 64-bit blocks of ciphertext. Within a block, characters are substituted and rearranged according to the value of the key. Figure 13.2 gives an overview of the DES process. A major problem with the DES system is that the security depends on the secrecy of the key. However, it is necessary to distribute the key to receivers of encrypted messages. If telecommunications lines are used, transmitting the key in plaintext would allow wiretappers easy access to encrypted messages. Often, more secure lines are used for key distribution, or keys are distributed by mail or messenger.

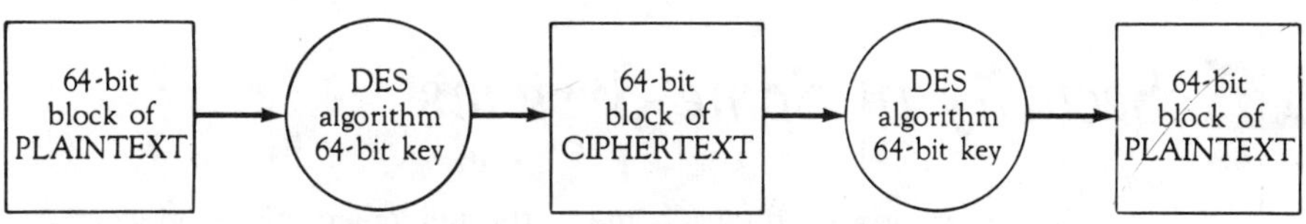

Figure 13.2 Overview of Encryption Using DES

The public-key encryption system uses pairs of prime numbers. For each user, a pair of large prime numbers is chosen as the user's **private key**, and the product of the pair becomes the **public key** of that user. Public keys are shared freely, so that anyone wishing to send a message to a user can find his or her public key easily. The public key is then used as input to an encryption algorithm, which produces the ciphertext for that user. When the user receives an encrypted message, he or she must produce the prime factors of the public key. Since there is no quick or easy method of finding the prime factors of a large number, it is extremely difficult for an intruder to find these factors. However, an intruder who is determined to break the key can do so, provided that he or she is willing to commit substantial resources to the task. Public keys have been broken using parallel processing to search for the prime factors in a reasonable amount of time. Figure 13.3 provides an overview of public-key encryption. This method is only as secure as the private key, so that users must be given their private keys in some secure fashion, and must protect the private keys against disclosure.

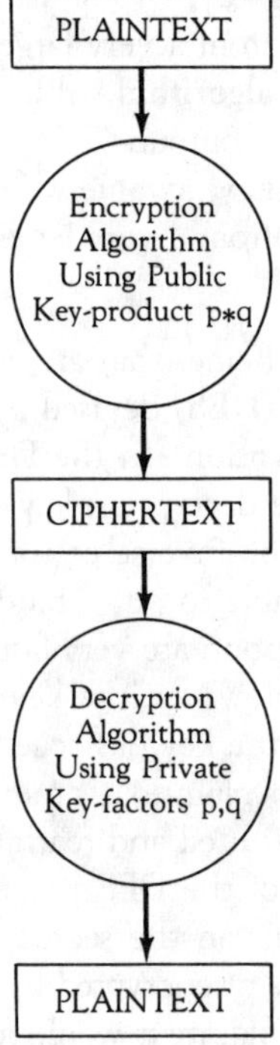

Figure 13.3 Public-Key Encryption Process

13.7 *Security in Some Systems*

In this section we discuss some of the implementations of access control found in representative systems.

13.7.1 *DB2 Access Control*

DB2 provides security primarily through the two mechanisms of the view and the authorization language. Since DB2 runs under MVS, it depends on the operating system to perform user authentication. No further authentication is performed when the user invokes DB2, but the user ID must be known to DB2.

The DB2 view allows the DBA to hide selected rows or columns of existing tables, and allows data to be materialized from one or more base tables. By specifying restrictions in the WHERE line of the SELECT statement used to create views, the view can be made **value-dependent.** Figure 13.4(a) gives an example of a view created from the STUDENT table by including only data about students whose major is 'CSC'. **Value-independent** views are created by specifying columns of base tables and omitting the WHERE line of the SELECT statement. Figure 13.4 (b) gives an example of a view of the STUDENT table showing only columns STUID, STUNAME, and MAJOR.

```
CREATE VIEW CSCMAJ
AS  SELECT STUID, STUNAME, CREDITS
    FROM STUDENT
    WHERE MAJOR = 'CSC';
```

Figure 13.4(a) Value-Dependent View

```
CREATE VIEW VIEW SUBSTU
AS    SELECT STUID, STUNAME, MAJOR
      FROM STUDENT;
```

Figure 13.4(b) Value-Independent View

Figure 13.4 DB2 Views as Access Control Mechanisms

Although the view can specify what items a user is permitted to see, the authorization system is used to specify the type of access permitted. It is also used to provide access to base tables. When DB2 is first installed, the user ID of one administrator, who should be the DBA, is made known to DB2 as part of the installation procedure. This user is then given the **SYSADM** privilege, allowing him or her to perform all legal operations during the lifetime of the system. A person with SYSADM privileges may in turn grant authorizations to others, including even the SYSADM privileges, but may revoke authorizations also. However, the original SYSADM privilege given at the time of installation can never be revoked; it remains attached to the user ID provided at installation time.

Authorization is granted by means of the statement

```
GRANT <privilege-list> [ ON <object-type object-name>] TO <user-list>
[WITH GRANT OPTION];
```

For example, the command

```
GRANT SELECT, UPDATE, INSERT, DELETE ON TABLE STUDENT TO U1002;
```

allows the user with ID U1002 to perform the four specified operations on the STUDENT table.

The privilege list for tables may include SELECT, UPDATE, INSERT, DELETE, ALTER, and INDEX. For views, all of these except ALTER and INDEX are permitted, provided that they are legal. If a user is to be given all permitted privileges for an object, the phrase ALL PRIVILEGES may be used in place of a list. If the object type is a table, the keyword TABLE is not needed.

Other privileges are EXECUTE (for application plans), CREATETAB (for databases), USE (for tablespaces), and CREATEDBC, a system privilege that allows users to create new databases. A user who creates objects is automatically granted authorization on those objects. If the WITH GRANT OPTION appears, the user is given power to grant the same options to other users. In this way, additional authorizers are created. Examples of authorizations are:

```
GRANT EXECUTE ON PLAN REGISTER TO U1005;
```

This permits user U1005 to execute the application program called REGISTER.

```
GRANT USE OF TABLESPACE SPACEA TO U1010;
```

This command allows user U1010 to store tables that he or she creates in tablespace SPACEA.

```
GRANT CREATETAB ON DATABASE STUDB TO U1015, U1020 WITH GRANT OPTION;
```

This allows users U1015 and U1020 to create tables for database STUDB, and permits them to pass this privilege along to others.

```
GRANT CREATEDBC TO U1025;
```

This allows user U1025 to create new databases.

Anyone who is an authorizer can revoke the privileges that he or she has authorized. This is done with a REVOKE statement, which has the form

```
REVOKE <privilege-list> [ON <object-type object-list>] FROM <user-list>;
```

The following statement removes the UPDATE privilege for the FACULTY table from user U1030:

```
REVOKE UPDATE ON TABLE FACULTY FROM U1030;
```

The ability of users with the grant option to authorize other users can lead to the development of an authorization graph which is a tree or a network structure. Figure 13.5 shows such an authorization graph. Here, the DBA, who originally had the SYSADM privilege, gave privileges WITH GRANT OPTION to users U101, U102, and U103. U101 passed along privileges to U201 and U202. U102 also passed a privilege to U202,

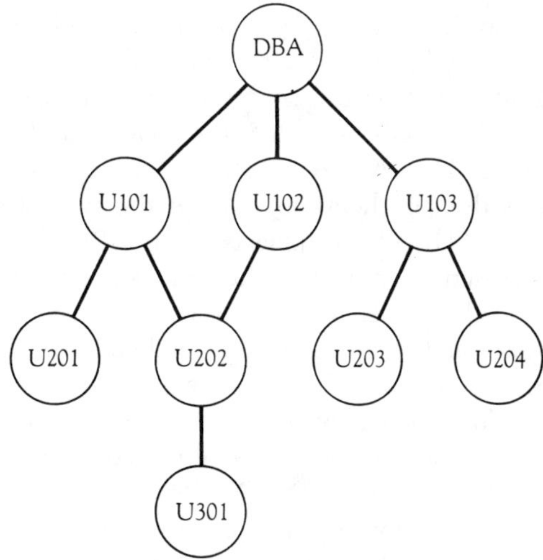

Figure 13.5 An Authorization Graph for DB2

with the grant option, and U202 passed a privilege to U301. U103 authorized U203 and U204.

If a person has grant option for a certain privilege and the privilege is later revoked, all users who received authorization from that person have privileges received from that person revoked as well. In this way, revocations **cascade** or trigger other revocations. However, if a user obtained the same privilege from two authorizers, one of whom has authorization revoked, the user still retains the privilege from the other authorizer. Thus, if the DBA revoked the authorization of user U101 in Figure 13.5, U201 would lose all privileges, but U202 would retain whatever privileges were received from U102. Since U202 has the grant option, user U101 could regain privileges from U202. In this way, unscrupulous users could conspire to retain privileges despite attempts by the DBA to revoke them. For this reason, the person with SYSADM privileges should be very careful about passing the WITH GRANT OPTION to others.

Although DB2 provides the extensive security features described here, the entire set of mechanisms is optional and can be disabled when DB2 is installed. Only in rare cases should this be done, however.

13.7.2 *IDMS/R Security*

The core of IDMS/R includes an integrated data dictionary (IDD) as well as the IDMS/R engine. The IDD contains external views (subschemas), the schema, and security information that is checked whenever an operation is performed against the database. Like DB2's, the security features of IDMS/R are optional. They must be specifically invoked to be effective.

In the schema, the SCHEMA NAME statement allows the DBA to list the IDs of users who are permitted to access the schema itself, and the type of operations they can perform on the schema. Optional privacy locks can be assigned to various levels, such as areas, records, sets, or data items. The locks may require passwords or procedures. Any DML command can trigger a security procedure as well.

An IDMS/R subschema lists the areas, records, and sets to be included in the view. The SUBSCHEMA NAME section can list the IDs of all users who are permitted to access the subschema itself, with the type of operations they can perform on the subschema. The various objects described in the subschema can each have their own access restrictions. For areas, these include restrictions on the way the READY command can be used. A user of the subschema can be given permission to open the area for retrieval or update in a protected mode or not. However, there is no security check to authenticate the user of the subschema, so anyone who is able to produce the subschema name could theoretically obtain access. For records, the subschema can specify which of the DML commands the user is permitted to write. For sets, the subschema can specify whether the user can use the CONNECT and DISCONNECT commands as well as the DML commands for record access through a set.

Unless the DBA provides otherwise, any user can access the database through a program by using any legal subschema. To restrict such access, the DBA has to use **program registration**, a data dictionary listing of all applications programs permitted to access the database and the names of the subschemas each can use. However, an unscrupulous user who knows the name of a program could still run the registered program. To prevent this, the program itself should include an authorization section, in which it checks the database for user authorizations and compares the ID of the user to the list of authorized users.

13.7.3 *IMS Security*

IMS provides extensive security measures for authenticating users who attempt to access IMS transactions. These include verifying the sign-on to be sure that the user is authorized to access IMS, checking the user's authorization to execute the transaction, requesting additional passwords for specific transactions or commands, and permitting certain processes to be requested only from specific terminals. When the transaction accesses the database, it must go through the appropriate program communication block (PCB). The PCB gives a list of segments and fields to which the program is sensitive, thereby preventing access to all unnamed objects. The PCB also lists the processing options, PROCOPTS, for the program. To enforce these security measures, IMS provides a **security log**, which records information about attempted security violations.

13.8 *Integrity Constraints*

Database integrity refers to the correctness and consistency of stored data. It can be considered another form of database protection. While it is related to security, it has broader implications. Security involves protecting the data from unauthorized operations, while integrity is concerned with the quality of the data itself. Integrity is usually expressed in terms of **constraints** which are **consistency rules that the database is not permitted to violate.** The major objective of concurrency control, discussed in Chapter 12, is to ensure that the database is in a consistent state after transactions are performed concurrently. However, there are many other situations in which consistency must be checked.

We have already seen some examples of integrity constraints in previous chapters. We review those and add others in the following list of constraints:

1. **Entity integrity** is a constraint on primary key values that states that no attribute of a primary key value may be null.
2. **Referential integrity** is a constraint on foreign key values that states that if a foreign key exists in a relation, then either the foreign key value must match the primary key value of some tuple in its home relation or the foreign key value must be completely null.
3. **Functional dependency** is a constraint between the determinant and the attributes it determines, which states that for each value of the determinant, there is only one value for each of the attributes it determines.
4. **Multivalued dependencies** can occur among three sets of attributes, *A*, *B*, and C. According to this constraint, *A* multidetermines *B* if and only if the set of *B* values associated with each *A* value is independent of the C values.
5. **Join dependency** means that a relation can be reconstructed by taking the join of its projections.
6. A **domain constraint** restricts the possible values for a data item to a specific set called its domain.
7. **The cardinality of a relationship** is a constraint on the number of entities that can be related.
8. **The set retention class** in the network model is a constraint that limits deletion of records.
9. **The existence dependency** of a child on the parent in the hierarchical model is a constraint that limits both insertion and deletion of segments.
10. **General constraints** are restrictions that are expressible only as arbitrary predicates about the data. An example for the university database is that no class may be scheduled for room H221 after 2 P.M.

Most database management systems are lacking in their ability to express constraints. At best, they permit us to identify keys or other fields that must have unique or nonnull values, and they may allow us to partially specify domains. However, the designers of SQL proposed a strong mechanism for expressing constraints called an **assertion.** An assertion is a statement containing a predicate about the database. It has the general form

```
ASSERT <assertion-name>: <predicate>
```

If we wish to express a constraint on a single relation the form would be

```
ASSERT <assertion-name> ON <relation-name> <predicate>
```

For example, to be sure a grade is a valid one, we could specify

```
ASSERT GRADE-CONSTRAINT ON ENROLL
GRADE IN {A,B,C,D,F,I}
```

To express a referential constraint we might use a form such as the one in the following example:

```
ASSERT FACULTY-CONSTRAINT ON CLASS
CLASS.FACID IN (SELECT FACID FROM FACULTY)
```

If such assertions are made after the database has been created, the system must first test to see if there are any violations of them in the present extension. From then on, integrity could be preserved by testing for integrity violations only when the database is updated. The easiest way to implement this is by creating relation integrity rule **triggers**, which are statements that identify the conditions that should set off the trigger and the response to the trigger. For example, to specify that a class record should be rejected if the faculty ID is not a valid one we might write

```
BEFORE INSERTING CLASS
CLASS.FACID IN (SELECT FACID FROM FACULTY)
ELSE REJECT
```

13.9 *Integrity Checking Methods Used in Some Systems: DB2, IMS, IDMS/R*

Although the SQL proposals contained many suggestions for implementing integrity constraints, they were not included in the early versions of DB2. While the present version does not allow general constraints, it does allow the designer to identify both primary and foreign keys in the CREATE TABLE command, as explained in Chapter 8. When we insert or update a record, DB2 checks the primary key data values for the record to ensure that none are null and that the value specified for the key is not already present in the table. When we insert or update a value for a foreign key in a dependent table, the system checks to ensure that it is either wholly or partially null, or that it matches a value of the primary key in the home table. If we try to update a value for a primary key in a home relation that has matching foreign key values in a dependent table, the system will reject the update.

When we identify a foreign key, we have the option of using an ON DELETE clause to specify a deletion rule that determines what happens to the dependent table when we delete a record from the home relation. For example, we might write the following foreign key specification for the ENROLL table:

```
FOREIGN KEY (STUID) REFERENCES STUDENT
ON DELETE CASCADE;
```

In this case, we choose to have deletions from the STUDENT table "cascade" to the ENROLL table, which means that when a student's record is deleted, all enrollment records having matching STUID value will also be deleted. If we choose ON DELETE SET NULL, a deletion in the home relation results in having the matching foreign key values in the dependent table set to null. The ON DELETE RESTRICT specification will not allow us to delete any record in the home relation if there is a matching foreign key value in the dependent relation.

IMS also provides some limited integrity support. The domain is incompletely specified by assigning a data type and length to each field. The sequence field can be forced to be unique, unless the M specification is used in the DBD. The one-to-many nature of the parent-child relationship enforces a cardinality constraint between segments. Referential integrity is automatically enforced because a child segment must have an associated parent segment. The form of the DL/1 DML statements, which require an SSA for inserting, replacing, or deleting, further enforces integrity. IMS also allows triggered procedures in the form of "exit routines," which are procedures that can be called when segments are inserted or updated.

IDMS/R also supports limited specification of domains by allowing a data type for each data item. The DUPLICATES ARE NOT ALLOWED option permits us to enforce uniqueness for keys. The insertion and retention classes allow existence constraints of various types to be expressed. Unfortunately, one of the integrity features found in the DBTG model, the CHECK option, which allowed general constraints to be expressed, was dropped from IDMS/R.

13.10 *Chapter Summary*

Database **security** means protecting the database from unauthorized access, modification, or destruction. **Privacy** is the right of individuals to control information about themselves, and is guaranteed by statute in many countries. Individual privacy can be protected by database security. Security violations can be accidental or deliberate, and can be accomplished in a variety of ways. A security control plan begins with physical security measures for the building and the computer room. Security control of terminals involves user **authentication**, verifying the identity of users. The operating system normally has some means of establishing a user's identity, using user profiles, user IDs, passwords, authentication procedures, badges, keys, or physical characteristics of the user. Additional authentication can be required to access the database.

Most database management systems designed for multiple users have a security subsystem. These subsystems provide for **authorization,** by which users are assigned rights to use database objects. Most have an **authorization language** that allows the DBA to write **authorization rules** specifying which users have what type of access to database objects. **Access control** covers the mechanisms for implementing authorizations. An **access control matrix** identifies what types of operations users are permitted to perform on database objects. The DBA can sometimes delegate authorization powers to others.

Views can be used as a simple method for implementing access control. A **security log** is a journal for storing records of attempted security violations. An **audit trail** records all access to the database, keeping information about the requestor, the operation performed, the terminal used, the time, data items, and values involved. **Encryption** uses a **cipher system** that consists of an **encryption algorithm**, an **encrypting key**, a **decrypting algorithm**, and a **decryption key**. Two schemes that are widely used for encryption are the **Data Encryption Standard** and **public-key encryption.**

DB2 uses the view mechanism and an authorization language to provide security. The GRANT statement is used for authorization, and the REVOKE statement is used to retract authorization. In IDMS/R the Integrated Data Dictionary contains information about the schema, subschemas (views), privacy locks, and **program registration**. IMS security includes extensive authentication checking. The program communication block (PCB) specifies the external view and permitted operations. A **security log** is available for recording attempted security violations of IMS databases.

Integrity refers to the correctness and consistency of stored data, and can be considered another means of protecting the database. Integrity is expressed as **constraints** or consistency rules. Some integrity constraints are entity integrity, referential integrity, functional dependency, multivalued dependencies, join dependencies, domain constraints, cardinality of relationships, set retention classes, existence dependencies, and general constraints. One mechanism that could be used to express constraints is the **assertion**, a statement containing a predicate about the database. The integrity subsystems of most database management systems are quite limited.

13.11 Exercises

1. For each of the following, write SQL statements to create views where needed and to grant the indicated privileges for the University database:

```
STUDENT(STUID, STUNAME, MAJOR, CREDITS)
FACULTY(FACID, FACNAME, DEPT, RANK)
CLASS(COURSE#, FACID, SCHED, ROOM)
ENROLL(COURSE#, STUID, GRADE).
```

   (a) Give permission to read the tables STUDENT and CLASS to user 201, a clerk in the dean's office. The user may also read ENROLL, but without the GRADE attribute.
   (b) Give permission to read and modify the tables FACULTY and CLASS to user 151, an assistant dean. This user may authorize other users to read and modify CLASS, but not FACULTY.
   (c) Give permission to user 150, the registrar, to read and modify STUDENT, CLASS, and ENROLL, and to grant other users these rights, with authorization privileges.
   (d) User 300 is an academic advisor who is a faculty member with FACID F300. Give this user permission to read all CLASS records. For those students majoring in his or her department allow the user to read STUDENT records and to modify ENROLL records.

(e) Revoke the authorization privileges of the assistant dean, but reinstate his or her own reading and modification privileges.

(f) Using an authorization graph, show how a clerk who had received authorization from the assistant dean could conspire with another clerk to keep privileges, even when the assistant dean's authorization privileges are revoked.

2. Users are sometimes granted permission to access statistical information such as sums, counts, or averages but not information about individuals. Special precautions must be taken when users are permitted access to statistical data to ensure that they are not able to deduce data about individuals. For example, assume FACULTY has an additional attribute, SALARY, but a user is restricted to asking questions about total salaries and average salaries, not individual salaries.

   (a) Write a legal SQL query that will allow the user to find the salary of the only faculty member who is an instructor in the Art Department.

   (b) Assume the system will refuse to answer queries for which only one record satisfies the predicate, as in part (a). Write a legal set of queries that would allow the user to deduce the salary of the art instructor.

   (c) To prevent users from deducing information about individuals the system may restrict queries by requiring that the number of records satisfying the predicate must be at least five and that the number of records satisfying a pair of queries simultaneously cannot exceed three. Would these restrictions make your query for (a) and (b) illegal? If so, is there another legal set of queries that will allow you to deduce the salary of the art instructor?

3. Consider the following schema for a DB2 database:

```
WORKER (EMPID, EMPNAME, EMPMGR, DEPT, BIRTHDATE, HIREDATE, SALARY)
PROJECT (PROJ#, PROJNAME, PROJMGR, BUDGET, STARTDATE, EXPECTED_DURATION)
ASSIGN (PROJ#, EMPID, HOURS_ASSIGNED, RATING)
```

   (a) Identify any foreign keys in the above schema.

   (b) For each foreign key, choose a deletion rule, RESTRICT, CASCADE, or SET NULL, and justify your choice.

   (c) Write the CREATE TABLE commands to create this database, specifying primary and foreign keys completely.

   (d) Identify any other constraints that have not been expressed in the CREATE TABLE commands. For each, identify the type of constraint, using the categories listed in Section 13.8.

4. Assume the data about workers and projects described in Exercise 3 is to be placed into a network model. We have two sets, WORKER-ASSIGN and PROJECT-ASSIGN, with ASSIGN an intersection record acting as the member type in both sets.

   (a) Choose a suitable set insertion class and set retention class for each of these set types and justify your choice.

(b) Identify any constraints that are not expressed by set insertion and set retention classes, and explain how the constraint can be expressed in the network model or IDMS/R, if it is possible to express it.

13.12 *Bibliography*

Atre, S. *Data Base: Structured Techniques for Design, Performance, and Management*. New York: John Wiley & Sons, 1980.

Brathwaite, K. *Data Administration*. New York: John Wiley & Sons, 1985.

Date, C. *An Introduction to Database Systems*. Reading, MA: Addison-Wesley, 1986.

Date, C. *A Guide to INGRES*. Reading, MA: Addison-Wesley, 1987.

Denning, P. *Cryptography and Data Security*. Reading, MA: Addison-Wesley, 1982.

Eswaran, K., J. Gray, R. Lorie, and I. Traiger. "The Notions of Consistency and Predicate Locks in a Database System," Communications of the ACM **19**:11 (November, 1976) pp. 624-633.

Fagin, R. "On An Authorization Mechanism," ACM Transactions on Database Systems **3**:3 (September, 1978) pp. 310-319.

Fernandez, E., R. Summers, and C. Wood. *Database Security and Integrity*. Reading, MA: Addison-Wesley, 1981.

Griffiths, P. and B. Wade. "An Authorization Mechanism for a Relational Database System," ACM Transactions on Database Systems **1**:3 (September, 1976) pp. 242-255.

Korth, H. and A. Silberschatz. *Database System Concepts*. New York: McGraw-Hill, 1986.

Litton, G. *Introduction to Database Management: A Practical Approach*. Dubuque, IA: Wm. C. Brown, 1987.

Rivest, R., A. Shamir, and L. Adelman. "On Digital Signatures and Public Key Cryptosystems," Communications of the ACM **21**:2 (February, 1978) pp. 120-126.

Ullman, J. *Principles of Database and Knowledge-Base Systems Volume I*. Rockville, MD: Computer Science Press, 1988.

Wiederhold, G. *File Organization for Database Design*. New York: McGraw-Hill, 1987.

CHAPTER

14

Query Optimization

14 Chapter Objectives

In this chapter you will learn

- how a query is interpreted
- how a query tree represents relational algebra expressions
- why SELECT operations should be performed early
- how conjunctive conditions can be executed efficiently
- when PROJECT operations should be performed
- some rules for equivalence of algebraic operations
- heuristics for query optimization
- factors that determine the cost of a query
- how to estimate the cost of various methods of performing SELECT operations
- how to estimate the cost of various methods of performing JOIN operations
- methods of processing other operations

14.1 Interpretation and Optimization of Queries

In Chapter 8 we saw that some SQL queries could be expressed in different ways. For example, in a SELECT statement involving two or more tables, we could sometimes choose between a join and a subquery. Similarly, in Chapter 6 we considered different sequences of relational algebra commands that turned out to be equivalent. We noted in passing that certain formulations of these queries were more efficient than others. In this chapter we examine relative efficiency more closely and discuss some techniques for improving the efficiency of queries.

When a relational database management system receives a high-level query in a language such as SQL, it first checks the query syntax to ensure that the language is used correctly. The syntactically correct query is then validated, checked to verify that the attributes, tables, or views referred to are actual database objects. The query then has to be translated into some form that the system can use. For example, although a query may be expressed in SQL externally, the system must transform it into a lower-level internal representation that it can actually use for processing. Relational algebra may be used for this internal representation because its operations are easily transformed into system operations. Relational calculus may be used in place of relational algebra. The system then examines the internal representation and uses its knowledge of relational algebra operations to determine whether the operations could be rearranged or changed to produce an equivalent, but more efficient, representation. Once the internal representation is as efficient as possible, the system can use its knowledge of table size, indexes, order of tuples, and distribution of values to determine exactly how the query will be processed. In doing so, it estimates the "cost" of alternative execution plans and chooses the plan with the least estimated cost. To estimate cost, it considers the number and type of disk accesses required, the amount of internal and external memory needed, the processing time required, and communication costs, if any. The execution plan is then coded and executed at the appropriate time. Figure 14.1 summarizes this process for an SQL query. Although optimization of this type is time consuming, the potential savings in execution time and size of intermediate results can be tremendous, so it is worthwhile to spend the time optimizing before the query is executed.

Unlike relational database management systems, network and hierarchical systems traditionally leave optimization to the programmer. These systems have preestablished access paths, which the programmer must be aware of in order to "navigate" successfully in the database. Therefore these systems usually do not include query optimization facilities.

14.2 Algebraic Techniques for Query Transformation

Recall the university database, whose schema is

```
STUDENT(STUID, STUNAME, MAJOR, CREDITS)
FACULTY (FACID, FACNAME, DEPT, RANK)
CLASS (COURSE#, FACID, SCHED, ROOM)
ENROLL (COURSE#, STUID, GRADE)
```

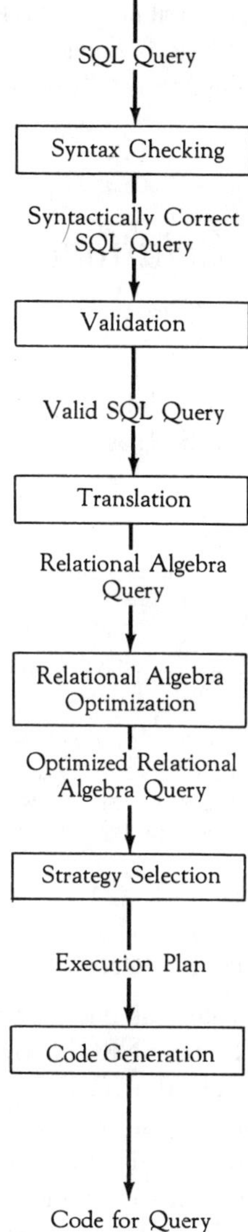

Figure 14.1

We will use this schema to illustrate manipulation of relational algebra queries.

A technique that is often used to represent relational algebra expressions is a **query tree** or a parse tree for an expression. Such a tree is a graphical representation of the operations and operands in a relational algebra expression. Relations are represented by leaf nodes, and unary or binary operations are represented by internal, nonleaf nodes of the tree. In executing a query tree, an internal node can be executed when its operands are available. The node is then replaced by the result of the operation it represents. The root node is the last to be executed, and it is replaced by the result of the entire tree. If relational calculus is used instead, the query tree is replaced by a **query graph** or **connection hypergraph**. The graph has nodes to represent each constant that appears in a query and each attribute in a relation, allowing repeats for attributes that appear in more than one relation. Edges connecting attribute nodes represent join conditions among tuple variables. Edges connecting constant nodes to attribute nodes represent selection conditions.

14.2.1 *The Initial Relational Algebra Expression and Query Tree*

The query "Find the schedules and rooms of all courses taken by any mathematics major" could be expressed in SQL as

```
SELECT  SCHED, ROOM
FROM    CLASS, ENROLL, STUDENT
WHERE   MAJOR = 'Math' AND CLASS.COURSE# = ENROLL.COURSE# AND
        ENROLL.STUID = STUDENT.STUID;
```

One relational algebra translation for this SQL query is

```
JOIN STUDENT, ENROLL GIVING TEMP1
JOIN TEMP1, CLASS GIVING TEMP2
SELECT TEMP2 WHERE MAJOR = 'Math' GIVING TEMP3
PROJECT TEMP3 OVER SCHED, ROOM
```

or symbolically:

$$\pi_{\text{SCHED,ROOM}}(\sigma_{\text{MAJOR='Math'}}((\text{STUDENT} \mid\times\mid \text{ENROLL}) \mid\times\mid \text{CLASS}))$$

If we were to execute this query as written, we would begin by forming the natural join of STUDENT and ENROLL over their common column, STUID. Since this is a key for STUDENT, the number of tuples in the join is simply the cardinality of ENROLL, since there will be exactly one match in STUDENT for each STUID in ENROLL. Now we join this result with CLASS, again producing an intermediate table containing one tuple for each tuple in ENROLL, since we are joining over COURSE#, the key of CLASS. The intermediate table has attributes STUID, STUNAME, MAJOR, CREDITS, COURSE#, GRADE, FACID, SCHED, and ROOM. We then perform a selection on the intermediate table, choosing only those rows where the value of MAJOR is 'Math'. Finally, we project over two columns, SCHED and ROOM, eliminating duplicates, if any. The query tree corresponding to this expression is shown in Figure 14.2(a).

14.2.2 *Performing SELECT Operations Early*

If we assume that STUDENT has 10,000 records, CLASS has 2500 records, and ENROLL has 50,000 records, the execution just described would involve producing an

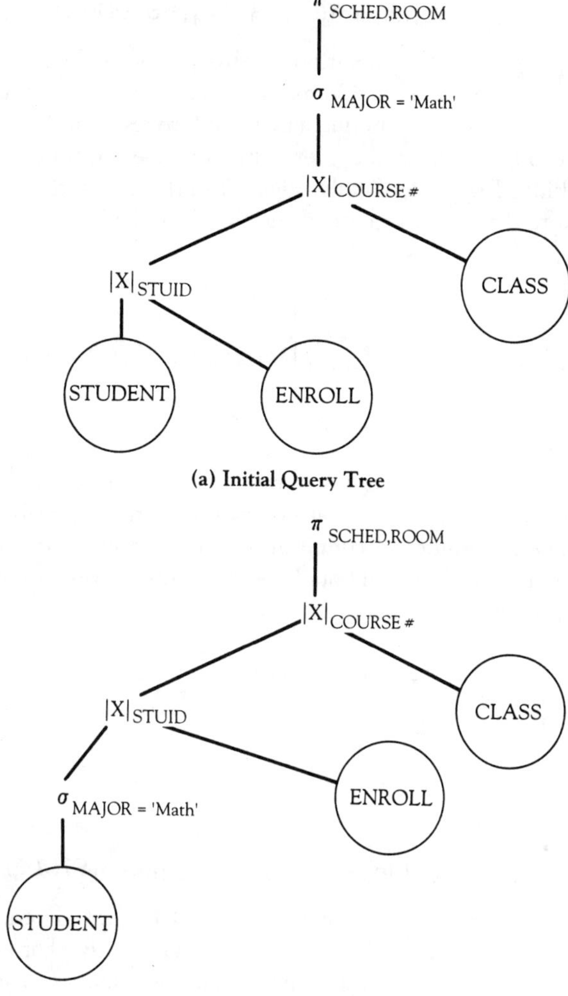

(a) Initial Query Tree

(b) Revised Query Tree

Figure 14.2

intermediate table with 50,000 fairly long records, of which only a small number, those with MAJOR = 'Math', are chosen in the next operation. We could easily reduce the size of the intermediate table by performing the SELECT operation earlier and considering only those students whose major is mathematics. We could rewrite the query as

```
SELECT STUDENT WHERE MAJOR = 'Math' GIVING T1
JOIN T1, ENROLL GIVING T2
JOIN T2, CLASS GIVING T3
PROJECT T3 OVER SCHED, ROOM
```

or symbolically,

$$\pi_{SCHED,ROOM}(((\sigma_{MAJOR='Math'}(STUDENT)) \,|\times|\, ENROLL) \,|\times|\, CLASS)$$

By reordering the operations in this way, we reduce the size of the intermediate table. If we assume there are 400 mathematics majors, each taking about five courses, we would expect only 2000 intermediate records to result from the join, a significant reduction from the 50,000 expected earlier. This example illustrates the savings possible by performing SELECT operations early. Figure 14.2(b) shows the query tree for the revised expression. Note that we have pushed the SELECT down close to a leaf of the tree.

14.2.3 *Evaluating Conjunctive Conditions*

If the query involved an additional selection criterion, such as finding the schedules and rooms of courses taken by those math majors who have more than 100 credits, we would want to apply that criterion as early as possible as well. In that case we would have a **conjunctive condition**, so called because it involves a conjunction or "and" of conditions. We could apply both selection criteria directly to the STUDENT relation before doing the first join:

```
SELECT STUDENT WHERE MAJOR = 'Math' AND CREDITS>100 GIVING T1
JOIN T1, ENROLL GIVING T2
JOIN T2, CLASS GIVING T3
PROJECT T3 OVER SCHED, ROOM
```

or symbolically,

$$\pi_{SCHED,ROOM}(((\sigma_{MAJOR='Math'\&CREDITS>100}(STUDENT)) \,|\times|\, ENROLL) \,|\times|\, CLASS)$$

This reduces the size of the join still further. Even if the second selection criterion refers to another table, it is best to do it early. For example, if we had been asked to find the schedules and rooms for all mathematics majors who have received a grade of F, we would be unable to apply the conjunction condition

```
MAJOR = 'Math' AND GRADE ='F'
```

to the STUDENT table, since the GRADE appears on the ENROLL table. We could form the join first and then apply the conjunctive condition and evaluate the rest of the query as follows:

```
JOIN STUDENT, ENROLL GIVING T1
SELECT T1 WHERE MAJOR = 'Math' AND GRADE ='F' GIVING T2
JOIN T2, CLASS GIVING T3
PROJECT T3 OVER SCHED, ROOM
```

which is

$$\pi_{SCHED,ROOM}((\sigma_{MAJOR='Math'\&GRADE='F'}(STUDENT \,|\times|\, ENROLL)) \,|\times|\, CLASS)$$

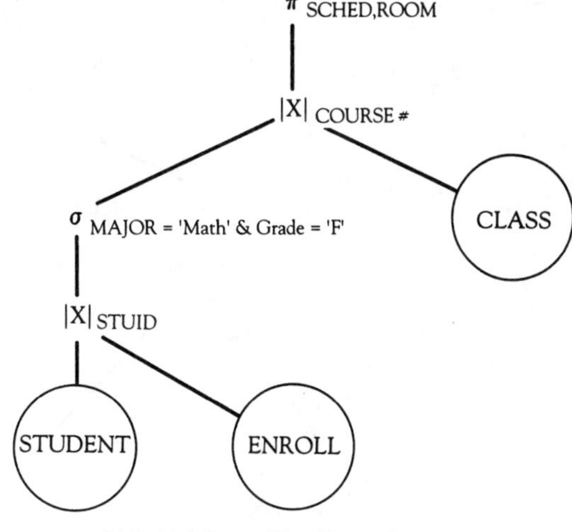

(a) Initial Query Tree Using Conjunction

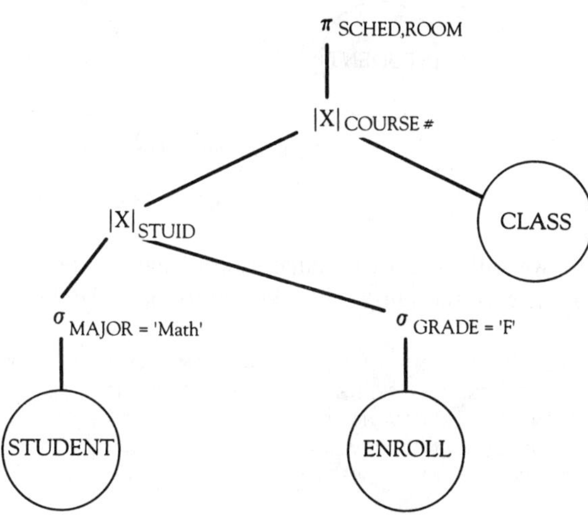

(b) Improved Query Tree Using Conjunction

Figure 14.3

Figure 14.3(a) shows the query tree for this expression. Unfortunately, this brings us back to an intermediate table size of 50,000 records.

We could break up the selection criteria as follows:

```
JOIN STUDENT,ENROLL GIVING T1
SELECT T1 WHERE GRADE = 'F' GIVING T2
SELECT T2 WHERE MAJOR = 'Math' GIVING T3
```

This can be written symbolically as

$$\sigma_{MAJOR='Math'}(\sigma_{GRADE='F'}(STUDENT \mid\times\mid ENROLL))$$

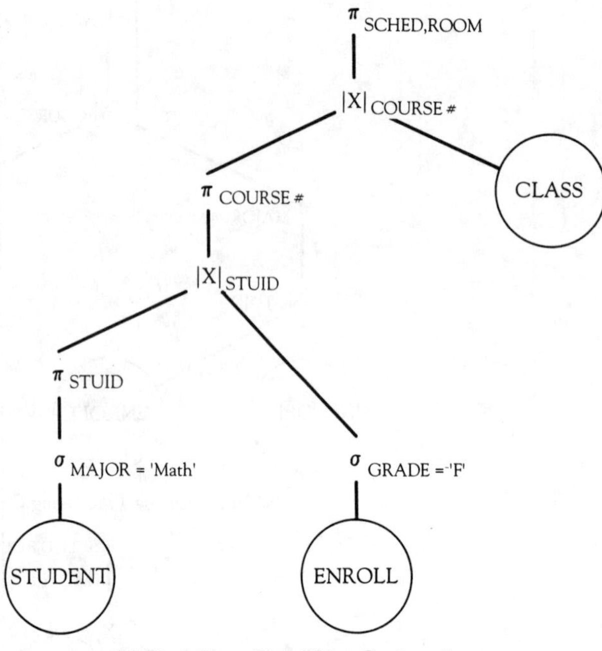

(c) Final Query Tree Using Conjunction

Figure 14.3 *(continued)*

Here we still have a very large intermediate table. However, if we apply both selections to their corresponding tables before the join we get a better form:

```
SELECT STUDENT WHERE MAJOR = 'Math' GIVING T1
SELECT ENROLL WHERE GRADE = 'F' GIVING T2
JOIN T1, T2 GIVING T3
JOIN T3, CLASS GIVING T4
PROJECT T4 OVER SCHED, ROOM
```

or symbolically,

$$\pi_{SCHED,ROOM}(((\sigma_{MAJOR='Math'}(STUDENT))\ |\times|\ (\sigma_{GRADE='F'}(ENROLL)))\ |\times|\ CLASS)$$

Figure 14.3(b) gives the query tree for this version. It is much more efficient than earlier versions, since it reduces the chosen tuples of both the STUDENT table and the ENROLL table before doing the join, keeping joined tuples to a minimum.

14.2.4 *Performing PROJECT Early*

We noted earlier that our intermediate table resulting from the two joins consisted of very long records. Regardless of when the selections or joins were performed, the intermediate table always had all of the attributes from the three original tables. We could use projection to reduce the size of the tuples in the intermediate tables. In doing so, we must be careful not to drop any attributes that will be needed later. Taking as our query "Find the schedule and room of all courses taken by math majors who have an F in any course," we could add projections to reduce the size of intermediate tables:

```
SELECT STUDENT WHERE MAJOR = 'Math' GIVING T1
PROJECT T1 OVER STUID GIVING T2
SELECT ENROLL WHERE GRADE = 'F' GIVING T3
JOIN T2,T3 GIVING T4
PROJECT T4 OVER COURSE# GIVING T5
JOIN T5, CLASS GIVING T6
PROJECT T6 OVER SCHED, ROOM
```

or symbolically,

$$\pi_{SCHED,ROOM}((\pi_{COURSE\#}((\pi_{STUID}(\sigma_{MAJOR='MATH'}(STUDENT))) \mid\times\mid (\sigma_{GRADE='F'}(ENROLL)))) \mid\times\mid CLASS)$$

The query tree for this expression is shown in Figure 14.3(c). Whether it is worthwhile performing all the projections depends on the amount of space saved and the costs involved in processing a projection. In any case, if we decide to do projections, we should do them early, before joins when possible.

14.2.5 *Properties of the Natural Join*

The natural join is associative. If R, S, and T are relations, then

$$(R \mid\times\mid S) \mid\times\mid T \equiv R \mid\times\mid (S \mid\times\mid T)$$

In the example shown in Figure 14.2, we found

$$(STUDENT \mid\times\mid ENROLL) \mid\times\mid CLASS$$

By associativity, we could have processed this as

$$STUDENT \mid\times\mid (ENROLL \mid\times\mid CLASS)$$

Thus we could have found the join of ENROLL and CLASS and formed a large intermediate table which we would have joined with the tuples of STUDENT for which the MAJOR has value 'Math'. This would have been less efficient than the method we chose. However, there may be instances in which associativity can be used to reduce the size of results.

The natural join is also commutative, if we ignore column order. If R and S are relations, then

$$R \mid\times\mid S \text{ is equivalent to } S \mid\times\mid R$$

Therefore, $ENROLL \mid\times\mid CLASS \equiv CLASS \mid\times\mid ENROLL$. Using both commutativity and associativity, we could have executed our query as

$$(STUDENT \mid\times\mid CLASS) \mid\times\mid ENROLL$$

This would have been an inefficient choice, since STUDENT and CLASS have no common attributes, so their natural join becomes their product. If we had 10,000 STUDENT records and 2500 CLASS records, as we assumed earlier, the intermediate table would have 25,000,000 records. There is obviously no advantage in rearranging the joins for this example. However, if we had started with this expression, we could have used the properties of the natural join to develop the more efficient form seen earlier in Figure 14.3.

14.2.6 *Equivalence of Algebraic Operations*

Our examples showed some of the ways that relational algebra expressions could be transformed into equivalent ones that were more efficient. We consider two relations to be equivalent if they have the same attributes, even though the attribute order may be different, and if the values associated with those attributes are identical for corresponding tuples of the two relations. The following list presents some laws governing operations in relational algebra, where R, S, and T represent relations or expressions involving relations. It is possible to prove all of the rules listed here, although we will not present the proofs.

1. **Joins and products are commutative.** The commutative law holds for all types of joins and products. Recall we used theta, θ, to stand for any condition for a join. Then we have

$$R \times S \equiv S \times R \quad \text{and}$$
$$R \,|\times|_{\theta}\, S \equiv S \,|\times|_{\theta}\, R \quad \text{and}$$
$$R \,|\times|\, S \equiv S \,|\times|\, R$$

2. **Joins and products are associative.** Natural joins, theta joins, and products are all associative. We have

$$(R \times S) \times T \equiv R \times (S \times T)$$
$$(R \,|\times|_{\theta}\, S) \,|\times|_{\theta}\, T \equiv R \,|\times|_{\theta}\, (S \,|\times|_{\theta}\, T)$$
$$(R \,|\times|\, S) \,|\times|\, T \equiv R \,|\times|\, (S \,|\times|\, T)$$

3. **Select is commutative.** If p and q are selection conditions, then

$$\sigma_p(\sigma_q(R)) \equiv \sigma_q(\sigma_p(R))$$

4. **Conjunctive selects can cascade into individual selects.** If we have a series of select conditions connected by "and," we can break up the conjunction into a sequence of individual selects

$$\sigma_{p\&q\&\cdots\&z}(R) \equiv \sigma_p(\sigma_q(\cdots(\sigma_z(R))\cdots))$$

Obviously, we can use the equivalence in the other direction to combine cascading selects into a conjunctive select, when convenient.

5. **Projects can cascade.** If **list1**, **list2**, ... ,**listn** are lists of attribute names such that each of the **list2**, ... ,**listn** contains **list1**, then

$$\pi_{\text{list1}}(\pi_{\text{list2}}(\cdots\pi_{\text{listn}}(R)\cdots)) \equiv \pi_{\text{list1}}(R)$$

This means that only the last project has to be executed.

6. **Select and project may commute.** If the selection condition involves only the attributes in the projection list, **projlist**, then select and project commute:

$$\pi_{\text{projlist}}(\sigma_{p}(R)) \equiv \sigma_{p}(\pi_{\text{projlist}}(R))$$

7. **Select and join (or product) may commute.** If the selection condition involves only attributes of one of the tables being joined, then select and join (or product) commute. If we assume that the predicate p involves only attributes of R, then the following holds:

$$\sigma_{p}(R \mid\times\mid S) \equiv (\sigma_{p}(R)) \mid\times\mid S$$

Here, the natural join can be replaced by a theta join or a product.

8. **Select may distribute over join (or product).** If the selection condition is a conjunctive condition having the form p **and** q, where p involves only the attributes of relation R and q involves only the attributes of relation S, then the select distributes over the join:

$$\sigma_{p\&q}(R \mid\times\mid S) \equiv (\sigma_{p}(R)) \mid\times\mid (\sigma_{q}(S))$$

Again, the natural join can be replaced by a theta join or product.

9. **Project may distribute over product (or join).** If the projection list, **projlist**, can be split into separate lists, **list1** and **list2**, so that list1 contains only attributes of R and list2 contains only attributes of S, then

$$\pi_{\text{projlist}}(R \times S) \equiv (\pi_{\text{list1}}(R)) \times (\pi_{\text{list2}}(S))$$

For a theta join, the distributive law holds if the join condition involves only attributes of **projlist**. If it involves additional attributes, they must first be added to the projection list on the left. Then they are placed with either **list1** or **list2** on the right, depending on which relation or relational expression they are associated with. After the join is performed, a final projection onto the original projection list must be done.

10. **Set operations of union and intersection are commutative.**

$$R \cup S \equiv S \cup R$$

$$R \cap S \equiv S \cap R$$

However, set difference is not commutative.

11. **Set operations of union and intersection are individually associative.**

$$(R \cup S) \cup T \equiv R \cup (S \cup T)$$

$$(R \cap S) \cap T \equiv R \cap (S \cap T)$$

Although union and intersection are associative when used individually, they cannot be mixed in an expression. Set difference is not associative.

12. **Select distributes over set union, set intersection, and set difference.**

$$\sigma_p(R \cup S) \equiv \sigma_p(R) \cup \sigma_p(S)$$

$$\sigma_p(R \cap S) \equiv \sigma_p(R) \cap \sigma_p(S)$$

$$\sigma_p(R - S) \equiv \sigma_p(R) - \sigma_p(S)$$

13. **Project distributes over set union, set intersection, and set difference.**

$$\pi_{\text{projlist}}(R \cup S) \equiv (\pi_{\text{projlist}}(R)) \cup (\pi_{\text{projlist}}(S))$$

$$\pi_{\text{projlist}}(R \cap S) \equiv (\pi_{\text{projlist}}(R)) \cap (\pi_{\text{projlist}}(S))$$

$$\pi_{\text{projlist}}(R - S) \equiv (\pi_{\text{projlist}}(R)) - (\pi_{\text{projlist}}(S))$$

14. **Project is idempotent, which means that repeating it produces the same result.**

$$\pi_{\text{projlist}}(\pi_{\text{projlist}}(R)) \equiv \pi_{\text{projlist}}(R)$$

Also, if the set of attributes $\{A1, A2, \ldots, An\}$ is a subset of the set of attributes $\{B1, B2, \ldots, Bm\}$ then

$$\pi_{A1,A2,\ldots,An}(R) \equiv \pi_{A1,A2,\ldots,An}(\pi_{B1,B2,\ldots,Bm}(R))$$

15. **Select is idempotent.**

$$\sigma_p(\sigma_p(R)) \equiv \sigma_p(R)$$

Also, if p is a predicate and $p = q \;\&\; r$, then

$$\sigma_p(R) \equiv \sigma_q(\sigma_r(R))$$

This list of transformations is not exhaustive, but it is sufficient to illustrate possible substitutions that the query optimizer could consider for given algebraic expressions.

14.2.7 *Heuristics for Query Optimization*

Heuristics are "rules of thumb" that can be used to help solve problems. They are not always guaranteed to work in a particular situation, but they are techniques that we can try out to see if they produce a good result. We now examine some heuristics that have been developed for optimizing relational algebra expressions. A cardinal rule is to try to reduce the size of intermediate results by doing selects and projects as early as possible, and to execute first those selects and projects that reduce the table sizes as much as possible. The heuristics are:

1. Do selection as early as possible. If appropriate, use cascading of selects, commutativity of selects with projects and products, and distributivity of select over set union, set intersection, and set difference to move the selection as far down the query tree as possible.

2. Do projection early. If appropriate, use cascading of projects, distributivity of projection over product and set union, intersection, and difference, and commutativity of selection and projection to move the projection as far down the query tree as possible. Examine all projections to see if some are unnecessary.
3. If a product appears as an argument for a selection, where the selection involves attributes of the tables in the product, transform the product into a join. If the selection involves attributes of only one of the tables in the product, apply the selection to that table first.
4. If there is a sequence of selections and/or projections, use commutativity or cascading to combine them into one selection, one projection, or a selection followed by a projection and apply them simultaneously to each tuple as it is retrieved. If a join or product is to be followed by a sequence of selections or projections, apply them to each tuple of the join or product as soon as it is constructed.
5. Use associativity of join, product, union, and intersection to rearrange relations in the query tree so that the selection operation that will produce the smallest table will be executed first.
6. If a subexpression appears more than once in the query tree, and the result it produces is not too large, compute it once and save it. This is especially useful when querying on views, since the same subexpression must be used to construct the view each time.

These heuristics can be incorporated into an algorithm that a query optimizer could use to produce the optimized relational algebra query, as shown for the university example query in Figure 14.3(c). In fact, we used these rules to optimize the query. The next step is for the strategy selector to choose an execution plan.

14.3 *Processing Techniques and Cost Estimation*

To develop an execution plan, the strategy selector must consider the various ways each of the operations in the query tree could be executed. It "prices" each method by considering the costs of the processes involved.

14.3.1 *Cost Factors*

The cost of executing a query is determined by the access cost to files, the processing costs once data is in main memory, the cost of writing and storing any intermediate results, the communication costs if the system is distributed, and the cost of writing the final results to storage. In calculating these costs, the system must use statistics stored in the data dictionary and knowledge about the size, structure and access methods of each file.

A table may be stored in **packed** form, in which blocks contain only tuples from that table, or in **unpacked** form, in which tuples from the table are interspersed with tuples from other tables. If the storage form is packed, we could estimate the number of blocks needed to hold the table if we knew the tuple size, number of tuples, and capacity of the blocks.

For our university example, if we store the STUDENT relation in packed form in blocks of 512 bytes, and each of the 10,000 student records is 50 bytes long, then 10 records fit per block, ignoring any overhead for block headers, and so on. We need 10,000/10 or 1000 blocks to hold this file in packed form. If the storage form is unpacked, it is more difficult to calculate the number of blocks needed. In the worst case, we assume every tuple of the relation is in a different block.

The access cost is the number of blocks that must be brought into main memory for reading or that must be written out to secondary storage for writing. The values associated with access cost are

- $t(R)$, the number of tuples in the relation R.
- $b(R)$, the number of blocks needed to store the relation R, if R is stored in packed form.
- $bf(R)$, the number of tuples of R per block, also called the blocking factor of R.

If R is packed, then $b(R) = t(R)/bf(R)$.

The tuples in the blocks containing R may be arranged in some order, often by increasing value of a primary key, but sometimes by the value of a secondary key. Alternatively, they may be in random order, or hashed on the value of a primary key. The access method used determines the storage structure. The file may be accessed by an index on the primary key, secondary indexes on non-primary-key attributes, or a hashing function. For each table, we may have one **clustered** index, so that tuples with the same value of the index appear in the same block. Other indexes will then be **nonclustered**. An index may be **dense**, having an entry for each tuple of the relation, or **nondense**. The index may use a multilevel structure such as a B+ tree or not. The purpose of the index is to speed access to the data file, but we must first access the index itself, so the additional overhead of accessing the index must be considered in the access cost. However, it is usually slight compared to the cost of accessing the data records. When using indexes, we will use **l(index-name),** the number of levels in a multilevel index or the average number of index accesses needed to find an entry. The purpose of an index is to tell us which records of the file have a particular value for an attribute. For cost estimation, we often need an estimate of the number of such records. The data dictionary may store the statistic

$$n(A, R), \text{ the number of distinct values of attribute } A \text{ in relation } R.$$

From this statistic, we can approximate the number of tuples that have a particular value for A. If we assume that the values of A are uniformly distributed in R, then the number of tuples expected to have a particular value, c, for A, which we will call the **selection size** or $s(A = c, R)$, is

$$s(A = c, R) = t(R)/n(A, R)$$

If the attribute, A, is a primary key, each tuple will have a unique value for that attribute, so $n(A, R) = t(R)$ and the selection size is 1.

To illustrate the use of the formula, suppose that we try to estimate the number of students in the university with a major of mathematics. We know there are 10,000 students, so t(STUDENT) = 10,000. Let us assume there are 25 possible major subjects, so n(MAJOR, STUDENT) = 25. Then we can estimate the number of math majors as

```
s(MAJOR='Math',STUDENT) = t(STUDENT)/n(MAJOR,STUDENT) = 10,000/25
= 400
```

Notice that we have to assume that majors are uniformly distributed—that the number of students choosing each major is about equal.

14.3.2 *Cost of Processing Selects*

We use these factors to estimate the cost of various techniques for performing a selection. Our choice depends to a great extent on whether the file has an index and, if so, what type of index exists.

Using a Hash Key to Retrieve a Single Record

If A is a hash key, then we apply the hashing algorithm to calculate the target address for the record. If there is no overflow, the expected number of accesses is 1. If there is overflow, we can get an estimate of the average number of accesses required to reach a record, depending on the amount of overflow and the overflow handling method used.

Selection Using Equality on a Primary Key Using an Index

To see how we can estimate cost in this case, consider the simple selection

$$\sigma_{\text{STUID}='\text{S1001}'}(\text{STUDENT})$$

Since STUID is the primary key, if we have an index on STUID, we retrieve whatever index blocks are needed and go directly to the record from the index. The cost is therefore **l(index-name) + 1**.

Selection Using Equality on a Clustering Index on a Secondary Key Attribute

If our selection has the form

$$\sigma_{\text{A}=\text{c}}(R)$$

and we have a clustering index on attribute A, which is not the primary key, we use the selection size for the indexed field divided by the blocking factor to estimate the number of blocks we have to retrieve. Note that we assume the tuples of R having value $A = c$ reside on contiguous blocks, so this calculation simply estimates the number of blocks needed to store these tuples. We add that to the number of index accesses needed. The cost is then

$$\text{l(index} - \text{name)} + (s(A = c, R))/bf(R)$$

For example, if we have a clustering index on MAJOR in the STUDENT file, then to select students with a major of mathematics, we would assume that the 400 records expected to have this value for MAJOR would be stored on contiguous blocks and the index would point to the first block. Then we could simply retrieve the following blocks to find all 400 records.

Selection Using Equality on a Nonclustering Index on a Secondary Key Attribute

For the predicate $A = c$ with nonclustering index on secondary key A, the number of tuples that satisfy the condition is the selection size of the index, $s(A = c, R)$, and we must assume that the tuples are on different blocks. The cost is the number of index accesses plus the number of blocks for the tuples that satisfy the condition, or

$$\text{l(index} - \text{name)} + s(A = c, R)$$

If we had an index for MAJOR in STUDENT but it was not a clustering index, we would find records having a MAJOR value of 'Math' by reading the index node for 'Math' and going from there to each tuple it points to.

Selection Using Inequality on a Primary Key with File in Order by Primary Key

If the selection condition is $A < c$, $A <= c$, $A > c$, or $A >= c$, where A is the primary key and the file is in order by A, we can use the index to locate the record $A = c$. Then we access all the records before (or after) this one. If we assume that roughly half the records satisfy the inequality, these records will be packed in the blocks before (or after) the block containing the record with $A = c$. The number of accesses is

$$\text{l(index} - \text{name)} + b(R)/2$$

We could use this technique to find all STUDENT records with STUID less than a specific value, say S5005, where the STUDENT file is in order by STUID. Note that the assumption that half the records satisfy the condition can be incorrect for an individual case, but it is the best we can do. The estimate will be too large sometimes and too small at other times, but is correct on the average.

Selection Using Inequality on a Secondary Index Stored as a B+ tree

If the selection condition is $A < c$, $A <= c$, $A > c$, or $A >= c$, where A is not the primary key, and there is a B+ tree index for A, we can use the leaf nodes of the B+ tree to access records in order by the value of A. Recall that the leaf nodes of a B+ tree have horizontal pointers to allow sequential access on the value of the indexed attribute. We assume that approximately half the records satisfy the inequality, so that about half of the leaf nodes of the index have to be accessed, and these lead, in turn, to half the tuples, which may be on separate blocks. We also use the index to find the node for $A = c$ initially. The cost is, therefore,

$$\text{l(index-name)} + \text{(number of leaf blocks in index)}/2 + t(R)/2$$

We could use this technique to find all STUDENT records with value of CREDITS greater than some constant, say 30, provided that we have a B+ tree index on CREDITS.

Selection Using a Binary Search on an Ordered File with No Index

If the predicate has the form $A = c$, where A is a key with unique values and records are arranged in order by A, a binary search may be used to access the record with A value of c. Using the cost of the binary search, the cost of this method under these conditions is approximately $\log_2 b(R)$.

If A is not a key attribute, there may be several records with A value of c, and the estimate must be adjusted to consider the selection size, $s(A = c, R)$ divided by the number of records per block. In that case, we get an estimate of

$$\log_2 b(R) + s(A = c, R)/bf(R)$$

Selection Using a Linear Search on an Unordered File with No Index

Here, every tuple of the relation must be retrieved to see whether it satisfies the predicate. Since we assume that we are dealing with a packed file, we need to retrieve all the blocks of the file, so the cost of this method is $b(R)$, the number of blocks in R. This is the "worst-case" method.

Conjunctive Selection with a Composite Index

If the predicate is a conjunction and a composite index exists for the attributes in the predicate, this case reduces to one of the previous cases, depending on whether the attributes represent a composite key, whether the file is ordered by the composite, and whether the index is clustered or a B+ tree.

Conjunctive Selection Without a Composite Index

If one of the conditions involves an attribute that is a primary key or hash key, is used for ordering records in the file, or has a B+ tree index or a clustering index, we use the appropriate method from those described previously to retrieve records that satisfy that part of the predicate. Once we retrieve the records, we check to see if they satisfy the rest of the conditions. If no attribute can be used for efficient retrieval, we use the linear search method and check all the conditions simultaneously for each tuple.

14.3.3 *Processing Joins*

An important cost factor to consider in processing joins is the size of the result. If R and S are relations of size $t(R)$ and $t(S)$ respectively, then to calculate the size of their join, we need to estimate the number of tuples of R that will match tuples of S on the corresponding attributes. Two special cases exist. If the tables have no common attributes the join becomes a product, and the number of tuples in the result is $t(R) * t(S)$.

If the set of common attributes is a key for one of the relations, the number of tuples in the join can be no larger than the number of tuples in the other relation, since each of these can match no more than one of the key values. For example, if the common attributes are a key for R, then the size of the join is less than or equal to $t(S)$.

The difficult case is the general one in which the common attributes do not form a key and the relations have some matches. We must first estimate the number of matches. Let us assume that there is one common attribute, A, and that its values are uniformly distributed in both relations. For a particular value, c, of A in R, we would expect the number of tuples in S having a matching value of c for A to be the selection size of A in S, or $s(A = c, S)$. We saw earlier that an estimate of the selection size is the number of tuples in S divided by the number of different values for A in S, or $t(S)/n(A, S)$. This gives us the number of matches in S for a particular tuple in R. However, since there are $t(R)$ tuples in R, each of which may have this number of matches, the total expected number of matches in the join is

$$t(R \,|\times|\, S) = (t(R) * t(S))/n(A, S)$$

If we had started by considering tuples in S and looked for matches in R, we would have derived a slightly different formula

$$(t(S) * t(R))/n(A, R)$$

Normally, we take the formula that gives the smaller result.

Now we consider different methods of performing a join. The choice depends on the size of the files, whether the files are sorted on the join attribute, and whether indexes exist for the join attributes.

Nested Loops Using Blocks

If we assume that both R and S are packed relations, having $b(R)$ and $b(S)$ blocks respectively, and we have two buffers, we can bring the first block of R into the first buffer, and then bring each block of S, in turn, into the second buffer. We compare each tuple of the R block with each tuple of the S block before switching in the next S block. When we have finished all the S blocks, we bring the next R block into the first buffer, and go through all the S blocks again. We repeat this process until all of R has been compared with all of S. The algorithm is

```
for each block of R
     for each block of S
           for each tuple in the R block
                for each tuple in the S block
                     if the tuples satisfy the condition then add to join
                end
           end
     end
end
```

The number of accesses to read the data for this process is

$$b(R) + (b(R) * b(S))$$

since each block of R has to be read, and each block of S has to be read once for each block of R. Because the result may be large, we should add to the estimate the cost of writing the result, which is determined by the number of expected matches and the blocking factor for the file that will contain the join, which we call RS. If A is the attribute to be matched in the join, our total cost for reading and writing becomes

$$b(R) + (b(R) * b(S)) + ((t(R) * t(S))/n(A, S))/bf(RS)$$

Combining the last two divisors, we get

$$b(R) + (b(R) * b(S)) + (t(R) * t(S))/(n(A, S) * bf(RS))$$

We could use this method to compute the reading cost for performing the join STUDENT |×| ENROLL. Let us assume for the moment that STUDENT has 10,000 tuples, occupying 1000 blocks, and ENROLL has 50,000 tuples, occupying 5000 blocks. Using STUDENT for the outside loop, our reading cost for this example is b(STUDENT) + (b(STUDENT)$*b$(ENROLL)) or 1000 + (1000$*$5000), which is 5,001,000. Since STUID is a key of STUDENT, we have a special case, and the number of tuples in the product is just t(ENROLL) or 50,000. If we assume that six tuples of the join fit per block, the result fits in 8334 blocks, so our writing cost involves accessing an additional 8334 blocks.

Note that if R and S were not packed relations, we could not use the block-by-block method, and would have to assume each tuple is on a separate block. The result then would have been much larger, namely

$$t(R) + (t(R) * t(S)) + (t(R) * t(S))/(n(A, S) * bf(RS))$$

provided that we could write RS as a packed relation. For STUDENT |×| ENROLL, the reading cost would be

$$t(\text{STUDENT}) + (t(\text{STUDENT}) * t(\text{ENROLL})) \text{ or } 10,000 + (10,000 * 50,000),$$

which is 500,010,000. The writing cost would be the same as for the packed case, 8334.

It is important to note that the size of the file chosen for the outer loop has a significant effect on the cost, since the number of tuples (for the unpacked case) or the number of blocks (for the packed case) in the outer loop file must be added to the product of the sizes of the two files. Therefore, we should pick the smaller file for the outside loop. If we had chosen to use ENROLL for the outer loop, our result for the packed case would have been 5,005,000 and for the unpacked case 500,050,000.

If the buffer can hold more than two blocks, the best strategy is to read into the buffer as many blocks as possible from the file in the outer loop, and save buffer space for only one block from the file in the inner loop. For example, if $b(B)$ is the number of blocks the buffer can hold, then, using R as the file for the outer loop and S as the file for the inner loop, we should read $b(B) - 1$ blocks of R into the buffer at a time, and only 1 block of S. The total number of blocks of R accessed is still $b(R)$, but the total number of S blocks that need to be accessed is reduced to approximately $b(S) * (b(R)/(b(B) - 1))$. The cost of accessing the files then becomes

$$b(R) + b(S) * (b(R)/(b(B) - 1))$$

However, if one of the relations fits in main memory, we should choose that one for the inner loop. For example, suppose that S fits in main memory. Then S has to be read only once, and we should store it in main memory while switching in blocks of R. The cost of reading the two packed files then reduces to

$$b(R) + b(S)$$

Sort-Merge Join

The most efficient join strategy is achieved when both files are sorted on the attribute to be joined. In this case, the join algorithm is a variation on the algorithm for merging two sorted files. When the files are sorted, we would expect that all tuples having a specific value, say c, for the join attribute, A, would be in a single block in each relation. We begin the join by bringing the first block of each relation into the buffer and finding all the records in R with the first value for A, and then all the records in S with that same value. These are then joined and written to the result file. Then we move on to the next value in each of the files, and so on. Each block of each file will be read only once, unless there are some records with the same A value in different blocks, which is unlikely. Therefore, the cost for accessing the two files is just

$$b(R) + b(S)$$

Because this join is so efficient, it may be worthwhile to sort the files before a join. In that case, the cost of sorting, which depends on the sorting method used, would have to be added to the cost of accessing the files. In addition, we should add the cost of writing the results.

Using an Index or Hash Key

If one of the files, S, has an index on the common attribute A, or if A is a hash key for S, then each tuple of R would be retrieved in the usual way, and the index or hashing algorithm used to find all the matching records of S. We could use this to find STUDENT |×| ENROLL if we access each ENROLL record in sequence and then use the index on STUID to find each matching STUDENT record. The cost of this method depends on the type of index. For example, if A is the primary key of S, we have a primary index on S and the access cost is the cost of accessing all the blocks of R plus the cost of reading the index and accessing one record of S for each of the tuples in R:

$$b(R) + (t(R) * (\text{l(indexname)} + 1))$$

If the index is a clustering index with selection size $s(A = c, S)$, we get

$$b(R) + (t(R) * (\text{l(indexname)} + s(A = c, S)/bf(S)))$$

If we have a hash function instead of an index, the cost is

$$b(R) + (t(R) * h)$$

where h is the average number of accesses to get to a block from its hash key value. If the index is a secondary index, we get

$$b(R) + (t(R) * (l(\text{indexname}) + s(A{=}c, S)))$$

In each case, we would then have to add the cost of writing the resulting file.

14.3.4 *Processing Other Operations*

If a projection has a projection list containing a key of the relation, the projection can be performed by taking each tuple of the relation and copying to the results file only the values of the attributes in the projection list. There will be no duplicates, because of the presence of the key. If the projection list consists of nonkey attributes only, we must eliminate duplicates. This can be done by sorting the resulting file so that duplicates will appear next to one another, and then eliminating any tuple that is a duplicate of the previous one until no duplicates remain. To calculate the cost, we find the sum of the cost of accessing all the tuples or blocks of the relation, plus the cost of writing the temporary file, the cost of sorting the temporary file, the cost of accessing the temporary file from secondary storage, and the cost of writing the final results file. Another method is to put the results into a hash file. Each new result is then checked with tuples in the bucket and dropped if it is a duplicate.

The set operations of union, intersection, and difference can be done only on files that are union-compatible, having identical structures. If we sort both files on the same attributes, we can then modify the sort-merge algorithm to do union, placing in the results file any tuple that appears in either of the original files, but dropping duplicates. To do intersection, we use the same basic algorithm, but place in the results file only the tuples that appear in both of the original files. For set difference, $R - S$, we examine each tuple of R and place it in the results file if it has no match in S. In each case, the cost is the sum of the cost of accessing all the tuples of both files, sorting both, and writing the temporary sorted files, accessing the temporary files to do the merge, and writing the final file.

14.4 *Chapter Summary*

Relational database management systems check each query for syntax errors, translate the query into an internal representation, rearrange or change the operations to produce an efficient order of operations, estimate the cost of executing the query using various plans, and choose the most efficient execution plan. A **query tree** can be used to represent relational algebra operations. Using properties such as commutativity, associativity, and distributivity, operations can be rearranged to produce an equivalent but more efficient query tree. Heuristics guide in the selection of properties to apply. Simple rules such as "Do selection early" and "Do projection early" can result in tremendous cost savings. To choose the actual execution plan, the system considers factors such as access cost for files, processing costs, costs of writing and storing intermediate results, communication costs, and the cost of writing final results. The size, structure, and access methods for files must be considered. The system stores statistics such as the number of tuples in each relation, the number of blocks for packed relations, the blocking factor for each file, the number of levels in each index, and the number of distinct values for each attribute. When choosing a plan involving an index, the type of index is very significant. There are several methods of processing selects and joins, and the system uses its statistics to estimate the cost of each method before choosing one. Other operations such as projection and set operations have simpler access plans.

14.5 Exercises

Schema for Exercises 1–5:

STUDENT (STUID, STUNAME, MAJOR, CREDITS)
FACULTY (FACID, FACNAME, DEPT, RANK)
CLASS (COURSE#, FACID, SCHED, ROOM)
ENROLL (COURSE#, STUID, GRADE)

1. Write the query tree for the following relational algebra expression:

```
SELECT CLASS WHERE ROOM = 'A205' GIVING T1
JOIN T1,FACULTY GIVING T2
PROJECT T2 OVER FACNAME,DEPT
```

or symbolically,

$$\pi_{FACNAME,DEPT}((\sigma_{ROOM='A205'}(CLASS))\ |\times|\ FACULTY)$$

2. Consider the following SQL query for the university example:

```
SELECT FACNAME, SCHED, COURSE#
FROM   FACULTY, CLASS, ENROLL, STUDENT
WHERE  STUNAME = 'Burns,Edward' AND CLASS.COURSE# =
       ENROLL.COURSE# AND FACULTY.FACID = CLASS.FACID AND
       STUDENT.STUID = ENROLL.STUID;
```

   (a) Write an inefficient relational algebra expression for this query.
   (b) Using equivalences of relational algebra expressions, rewrite your relational algebra expression in a more efficient form. Explain why the new expression is more efficient.

3. Write an efficient relational algebra expression for the following SQL query:

```
SELECT STUNAME, GRADE, COURSE#
FROM   STUDENT, ENROLL, CLASS, FACULTY
WHERE  FACNAME = 'Tanaka' AND SCHED = 'MTHF12' AND
       CLASS.COURSE# = ENROLL.COURSE# AND FACULTY.FACID =
       CLASS.FACID AND STUDENT.STUID = ENROLL.STUID;
```

Explain why your relational algebra expression is efficient.

4. Consider the query tree shown in Figure 14.4. Using the heuristics given in Section 14.2.7, write two different optimized query trees for this expression.

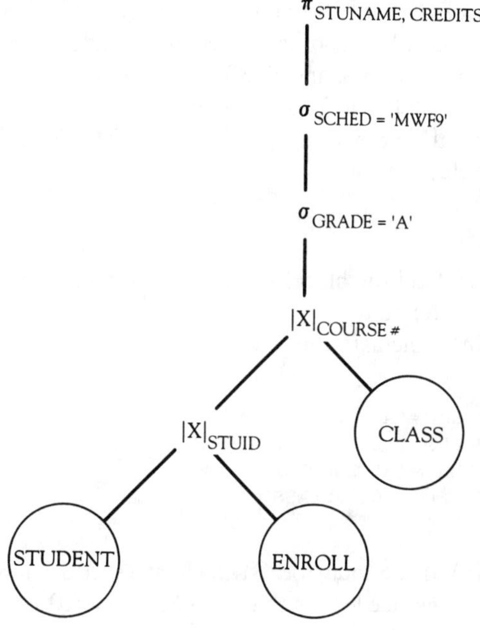

Figure 14.4

5. Write the initial query tree for the following relational algebra expression:

```
JOIN CLASS, ENROLL GIVING T1
JOIN T1, STUDENT GIVING T2
SELECT T2 WHERE FACID = 'F101' GIVING T3
SELECT T3 WHERE MAJOR = 'Art' GIVING T4
PROJECT T4 OVER STUNAME
```

or symbolically,

$$\pi_{STUNAME}(\sigma_{MAJOR='Art'}(\sigma_{FACID='F101'}((CLASS \; |\times| \; ENROLL) \; |\times| \; STUDENT)))$$

Using the heuristics given in Section 14.2.7, optimize the query tree.

Directions for Exercises 6–14: Assume we have the following information about the university database:

- All tables are stored in packed form in blocks of length 1024 bytes.
- STUDENT has 10,000 tuples, each 50 bytes long. It is hashed on STUID, the primary key, and has a secondary index (nonclustering) on STUNAME. There are 8000 values for STUNAME, 25 values for MAJOR, and 150 values for CREDITS.
- FACULTY has 800 tuples of length 120 bytes. It has a clustering index on FACID, the primary key. There is a secondary index using a B+ tree structure on DEPT. FACNAME has 650 values, DEPT has 25 values, and RANK has 4 values.
- CLASS has 2500 tuples with length of 80 bytes. It is hashed on COURSE#, the primary key, and has no secondary indexes. FACID has 700 values here, SCHED has 35 values, and ROOM has 350 values.
- ENROLL has 50,000 tuples with length of 50 bytes. It has a composite index on the primary key, COURSE#,STUID, and no other index. GRADE has 10 values.

6. (a) Find the blocking factor and total number of blocks needed for each of the four relations.
(b) Calculate the following selection sizes:

```
s(MAJOR='Art',STUDENT)
s(RANK='Professor',FACULTY)
s(GRADE='A',ENROLL)
s(ROOM='A205',CLASS)
```

(c) If the index on STUNAME is in the form of a B+ tree, how many levels will be needed for the index? Assume 20 pointers per node.

7. (a) Estimate the size of CLASS |×| ENROLL.
(b) Estimate the size of STUDENT |×| FACULTY, where MAJOR in STUDENT is compared with DEPT in FACULTY.
(c) Estimate the size of FACULTY |×| CLASS.
(d) Estimate the size of FACULTY |×| ENROLL.

8. Find the access cost only (no writing costs) of CLASS |×| ENROLL using nested loops with
(a) CLASS as the outside loop and buffer size of only two blocks.
(b) ENROLL as the outside loop and buffer size of two blocks.
(c) CLASS as the outside loop and buffer size of 10 blocks.
(d) ENROLL as the outside loop and buffer size of 10 blocks.

9. Find the total cost for FACULTY |×| STUDENT using MAJOR and DEPT as the joined fields and assuming that the buffer holds only two blocks, using

(a) Nested loops, where you choose the best placement of relations in inside and outside loops. Include the cost of writing the results.
(b) The secondary index (a B+ tree having two levels) on DEPT. Add the cost of writing the results, as found for part (a).

10. Find the access cost for performing ENROLL |×| STUDENT, using the hash key on STUID. Assume that the average number of accesses to retrieve a STUDENT record given STUID is 2.

11. Give an efficient strategy for each of the following SELECT operations and give the cost of each:
(a) `SELECT STUDENT WHERE STUID = 'S1001'`
(b) `SELECT STUDENT WHERE STUNAME = 'Smith,Tom'`
(c) `SELECT STUDENT WHERE MAJOR = 'Art'`
(d) `SELECT STUDENT WHERE CREDITS >= 100`
(e) `SELECT FACULTY WHERE DEPT = 'History' and RANK = 'Professor'`
(f) `SELECT CLASS WHERE FACID = 'F101'`
(g) `SELECT ENROLL WHERE GRADE = 'A'`

12. Assume we wish to form the three-way join

CLASS |×| ENROLL |×| STUDENT

(a) Estimate the cost of (CLASS |×| ENROLL) |×| STUDENT, using the most efficient strategies for each of the two joins.
(b) Estimate the cost of CLASS |×| (ENROLL |×| STUDENT), using the most efficient strategies for the two joins.
(c) Consider the following method:

```
for each block of ENROLL
     for each tuple in the ENROLL block
          use the value of STUID from the ENROLL tuple as the
                hash key for STUDENT and get the matching STUDENT tuple
          use the value of COURSE# from the ENROLL tuple as the
                hash key for CLASS and get the matching CLASS tuple
           write out the join of the three tuples
     end
end
```

Find the estimated cost of this method. Assume that the average number of accesses for a hash key value is 2.

14.6 Bibliography

Aho, A., Y. Sagiv, and J. Ullman. "Efficient Optimization of a Class of Relational Expressions," ACM Transactions on Database Systems 4:4 (December, 1979) pp. 435-454.

Aho, A., Y. Sagiv, and J. Ullman. "Equivalences Among Relational Expressions," SIAM Journal of Computing **8**:2 (June, 1979) pp.218-246.

Aho, A. and J. Ullman. "Optimal Partial Match Retrieval When Fields are Independently Specified," ACM Transactions on Database Systems **4**:2, (June, 1979) pp. 168-179.

Date, C. *An Introduction to Database Systems*. Reading, MA: Addison-Wesley, 1986.

Elmasri, R. and S. Navathe. *Fundamentals of Database Systems*. Redwood City, CA: Benjamin/Cummings, 1989.

Hall, P. "Optimization of a Single Relational Expression in a Relational Data Base System," IBM Journal of Research and Development **20**:3 (May, 1976) pp. 244-257.

Jarke, M. and J. Koch. "Query Optimization in Database Systems," ACM Computing Surveys **16**:2 (June, 1984) pp. 111-152.

Kim, W, D. Reiner, and D. Batory (Ed.). *Query Processing in Database Systems*. Berlin: Springer-Verlag, 1985.

King, J. "QUIST: A System for Semantic Query Optimization in Relational Databases," Proceedings of the International Conference on Very Large Data Bases (1981) pp. 510-517.

Korth, H. and A. Silberschatz. *Database System Concepts*. New York: McGraw-Hill, 1986.

Rivest, R. "Partial Match Retrieval via the Method of Superimposed Codes," *SIAM Journal of Computing* **5**:1 (1976) pp. 19-50.

Selinger, P. et. al. "Access Path Selection in a Relational Database Management System," Proceedings of the ACM SIGMOD International Conference on Management of Data (1979) pp. 23-34.

Ullman, J. *Principles of Database and Knowledge-Base Systems Volume II*. Rockville, MD: Computer Science Press, 1989.

Wong, E. and K. Youssefi. "Decomposition – A Strategy for Query Processing," ACM Transactions on Database Systems **1**:3 (September, 1976) pp. 223-241.

PART V

SPECIAL TOPICS

CHAPTER

15

Distributed Databases

15 Chapter Objectives

In this chapter you will learn

- the definition of a distributed database system
- the advantages of distribution
- basic data communications concepts for distributed databases
- the factors to be considered in designing a distributed database system
- alternative architectures for a distributed system
- the identity and functions of the components of a distributed database system
- factors in the data placement decision
- data placement alternatives
- how the other distributed database system components are placed
- problems in update synchronization and some solutions
- how the distributed database management system decomposes and processes requests for data
- the structure of some existing distributed database management systems

15.1 *Rationale for Distribution*

A **distributed database system** is one in which multiple database sites are linked by a communications system in such a way that the data at any site is available to users at other sites. Normally, each site or node has a complete data processing system, with its own data administration function, personnel, users, hardware, and software, including a local database, database management system, and communications software. At the very least, a site must have memory and a communications processor. The sites are usually geographically remote and are linked by a telecommunications system (a **long-haul system**), although it is possible to have a distributed system using microcomputers linked by a **local area network** within a single building or small area. Another possibility is that the database system may reside on a single computer and the data itself may be distributed across different devices. Ideally, users need not be aware of the true location of the data they access, and the system appears to be a local database to them. Depending on the needs of the organization, distributed databases can have the following advantages over a single, centralized system:

1. **Local autonomy.** The most important objective of any distributed system is to allow the user to have more direct control over the system that he or she uses. If each site has its own system, more of the basic data processing functions such as systems analysis, applications programming, operations, and data entry can be done locally, resulting in greater local control and user satisfaction than if these functions were performed at a central site, remote from user concerns and issues. At the same time, the designers of a distributed system need to insist on centralized planning and coordination, so that standards can be developed and enforced, and the individual systems will be compatible.
2. **Improved reliability.** A distributed system is more reliable than a centralized one, because processing is done at several sites, so failure of a single node does not halt the entire system. Distributed systems can be designed to continue to function despite failure of a node or a communications link. If a single node fails, users at that site may be unable to use the system, or their requests may be rerouted to another site. Users at other sites are unaffected unless they require data stored only at the failed node or processing that is performed only at the failed node. If a link fails, the node may be isolated, but the rest of the system can continue to operate. In some systems, the node may have other lines that can be used in place of the failed one.
3. **Better data availability.** Distributed database systems often provide for replication of data. If a node fails, or the only link to a node is down, its data is still available, provided that a copy is kept somewhere else in the system.
4. **Increased performance.** As the organizational data processing requirements increase, the existing system may be unable to handle the processing load. In a centralized system, a system upgrade, with accompanying changes in hardware and software, or a change to a new system, with major conversion of software, may be necessary to provide the performance increase required. A distributed system is

basically modular, allowing new processors to be added as needed. Depending on the network **topology**, or physical layout, new sites may be easy to integrate.

5. **Reduced response time.** A distributed system should be so designed that data is stored at the location where it is used most often. This allows faster access to local data than a centralized system serving remote sites. However, in a poorly designed distributed system, the communications system may be heavily used, resulting in greater response time.
6. **Lower communications costs.** If data used locally is stored locally, communications costs will be lower, since the network will not be used for most requests. In a centralized system, the communications network is needed for all remote requests. However, we must consider the additional cost for each copy of the database software, additional storage costs for multiple copies of data items and software, higher hardware costs, and higher operating costs that distribution can entail.

15.2 *Architecture of a Distributed Processing System*

Factors the designer of a distributed database system must consider in choosing an architecture include **data placement**, **type of communications system**, **data models supported**, and **types of applications**. Data placement alternatives are discussed in detail in Section 15.5. They differ in the amount of data replication they permit. Each alternative dictates a different type of system, using different update and request decomposition procedures. If the communications system is slow and expensive to use, as it usually is for long-haul systems, this favors local storage and processing. A fast, inexpensive system like a local area network favors centralized storage and processing. Various data models and accompanying manipulation languages are supported in distributed systems, just as they are in centralized systems. In general, a designer should avoid models that use record-at-a-time retrieval and choose those that allow set level operations, because of the number of messages that are required for programmer-navigated retrieval. This is one reason why the relational model appears to be the one most often used for distributed databases. In considering the types of applications to be performed against the database, the designer needs to estimate the size of the database, the number of transactions, the amount of data transactions require, the complexity of transactions, the number of retrievals relative to the number of updates, and the number of transactions that refer to local data as opposed to remote data. Alternatives include centralized data and processing with local data entry, local snapshot of a centralized database with local data entry and editing, distributed data and processing with all sites linked to central site, distributed data and processing with all sites interconnected but not integrated, and true distributed data and database management function with the distribution being transparent to the user.

A distributed system may be **homogeneous** or **heterogeneous**. In a homogeneous system, all nodes use the same hardware and software for the database system. In a heterogeneous system, nodes may have different hardware and/or software. Since a homogeneous system is much easier to design and manage, a designer would normally choose such a system. Heterogeneous systems usually result when individual sites make their own hardware and software decisions, and communications are added later. The designer then has the task of tying together the disparate systems. In a heterogeneous system, translations are needed to allow the databases to communicate. Since transparency is a major objective, the user at a particular site makes requests in the language of the database management system at that site. The system then has the responsibility of locating the data, which may be at another site that has different hardware and software. The request may even require coordination of data stored at several sites, all using different facilities. If two sites have different hardware but the same database management systems, the translation is not too difficult, consisting mainly of changing codes and word lengths. If they have the same hardware but different software, the translation is difficult, requiring that the data model and data structures of one system be expressed in terms of the models and structures of another. For example, if one database is relational and the other uses the network model, records and sets must be interpreted in table form. In addition, the query languages must be translated. For example, the SELECT..FROM..WHERE must become a FIND and GET. The worst situation involves different hardware and software. This requires translation of data models, data structures, query language, word lengths, and codes.

15.3 *Data Communications Concepts*

Data communications is a complicated and rapidly changing field, but some knowledge of it is needed in order to understand distributed systems. The three basic components of any data communications system are the **source**, the **medium**, and the **sink**. The source is the component where the message originates. It may be a terminal at a site where a user makes a request for a particular data item. The medium is the path through which the message travels. These are the links, lines, channels, or circuits that connect the sites. Usually, these are leased from **common carriers**, companies that are licensed to provide communications services. The sink is the component that accepts the message. The sink may be a terminal or a front-end communications processor at a site that has the data item requested by the user. We will assume that in a distributed database system, nodes may both generate and receive messages, thereby serving as both sources and sinks. Messages may consist of requests for data, stored data in response to requests, or other information, such as acknowledgments of messages.

Some communications system characteristics that must be considered are **path establishment time, network delay, transfer rate**, and **reliability**. Path establishment time is the time it takes to set up a path for a message once a site requests such a path. There may be several physical paths that could be used to send a message from one node to another. It takes time for the system to choose one and complete the protocols necessary to verify that a line is available. Network delay means how long it takes a message to go from source to destination. Normally, this is due primarily to the time it takes to execute communications system software at the nodes. However, in satellite communications, there is some measurable propagation delay introduced by the distance the signals must travel. Transfer rate is the rate at which the actual information content is transferred between nodes. Its upper limit is determined by the **bandwidth** of the communications line, which is the range of frequencies the line can handle. Because of overhead such as message headers, error detection and correction codes, retransmission of incorrect messages, and so on, the actual transfer rate may be much lower than the bandwidth would indicate. Reliability means the assurance that the network will accept a message and deliver it to its destination quickly and correctly. Related concepts are **availability**, which means that there is a path when the user requests one, and **accuracy**, which means that the message received is identical to the one sent.

Communications networks may be categorized in several ways. If we examine the method of choosing a path, or **routing**, we can categorize a network as either **point-to-point** or **broadcast**. In a point-to-point (also called **store-and-forward**) network, each site has a dedicated processor called an **interface message processor**, or **IMP**. The IMPs are connected to one another in pairs, as shown in Figure 15.1(a). When a site sends a message to another site, the IMP at the source stores the message and sends it to another IMP, which also stores it and forwards it to another IMP, where the store-and-forward process is repeated until the message reaches the IMP at the destination site. Note that the IMPs are responsible for choosing the path for the message. This routing function can be done once, at the source, or, more commonly, each IMP dynamically chooses the next "leg" of the path, based on its knowledge of the current state of the network. For example, if a line is down or a node is overloaded with messages, it might choose an alternative path. In a point-to-point system, if a site wishes to send a message to all sites, it must send several separate messages. In a broadcast network, all sites receive all messages, but each message has a prefix that identifies the destination node or nodes, so other nodes will simply ignore it. This is the routing method used with a satellite, as shown in Figure 15.1(b) and with a bus, as shown in Figure 15.1(c).

Another method of categorizing a network is by its **topology**, or layout. Common topologies include the **star**, the **ring** or **loop**, the **fully interconnected**, the **hierarchical**, and the **mixed** or **irregular**. These are shown in Figure 15.2. In evaluating a network design for distributed databases, several factors should be considered. **Modularity** means the ease with which we can add new nodes to the system. When a new site is established, lines must be added to connect it to the network and the communications software must be updated so that messages will be routed to the new node. The star topology is highly modular, while the fully interconnected system is the least modular. **Bottleneck vulnerability** means the likelihood that some nodes will become overloaded. For example, if the star topology is chosen, the central node is likely to be overloaded, since every message goes through it. The network should be so designed that the load can be shifted from an overworked node when a bottleneck occurs. **Fault tolerance** is the ability to continue functioning despite the failure of a node or a line. It should be possible to isolate a failed node and allow the rest of the system to continue functioning, without directing any messages to the failed node. If a line fails, it may be necessary to isolate the node, or if the node has another line, its processing may continue with no messages routed through the failed line. **Routing flexibility** is the number of ways a message can be routed between nodes. Highly flexible routing increases reliability and

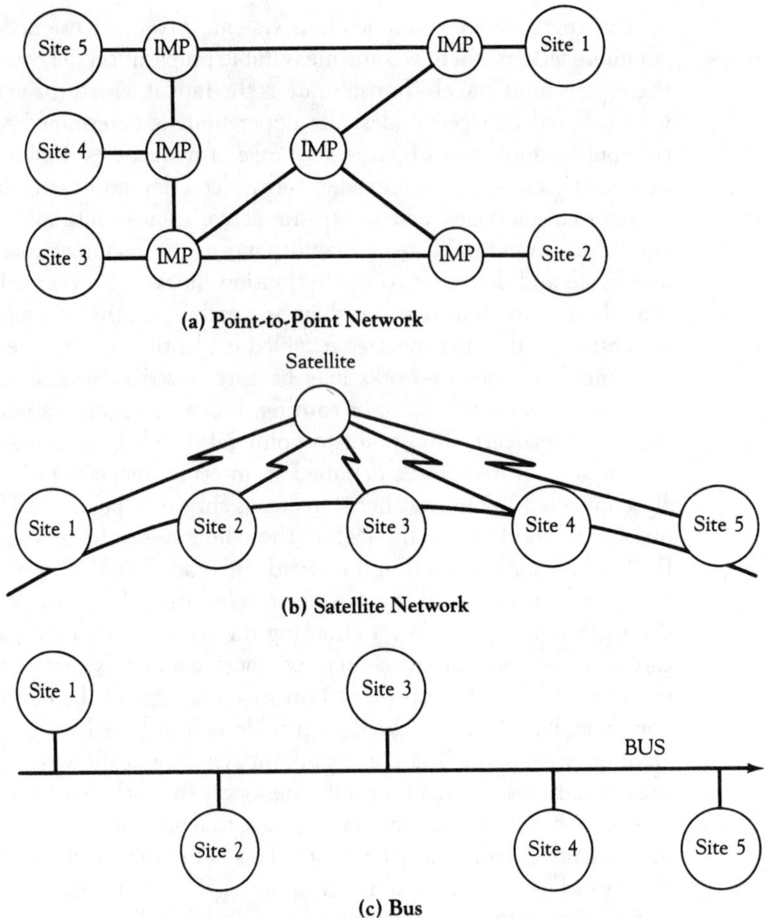

Figure 15.1 Networks Categorized by Routing

fault tolerance. The fully interconnected topology has the greatest routing flexibility. **Complexity** means the number of decisions the communications software must make to send messages. The more complex the network, the more complicated the routing algorithm will be and the more decisions the software will have to make. Complexity is related to routing flexibility, and the fully interconnected system is also the most complex.

Because of the very large number of computer systems in the marketplace, there is an organized attempt to standardize communications network architecture so that systems of different manufacturers will be able to communicate. The **International Standards Organization (ISO)** has proposed a seven-layer model called the **Open Systems Interconnection Reference Model (OSI)**, pictured in Figure 15.3. Each of the layers of the OSI model performs a set of functions and provides support for the layer above. Therefore, there is an interface between adjacent layers of the same system.

Protocols are needed to handle communications between corresponding layers of different systems. Although manufacturers can develop unique interfaces for the layers in

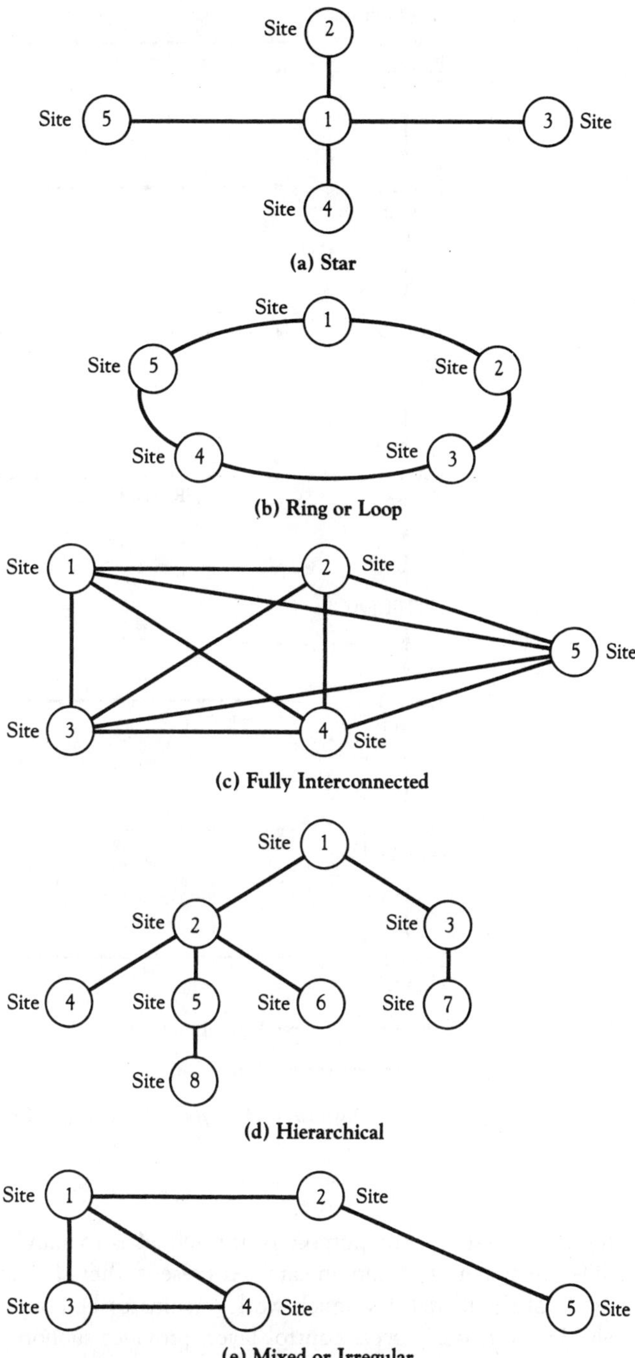

Figure 15.2 Networks Categorized by Topology

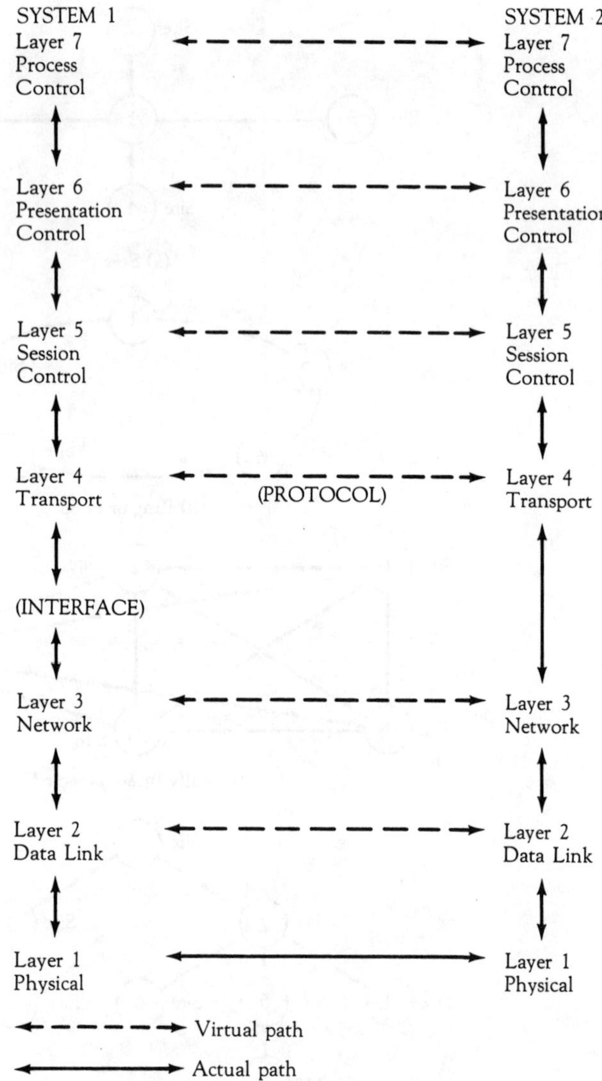

Figure 15.3 Layers of the ISO OSI Model

their own systems, the purpose of the model is to standardize the protocols that allow different systems to communicate. At present, there is some standardization of the lower levels of the model, but much work remains to be done to standardize the higher levels. Layer 7, the process control layer, provides support for applications programs and system software. Functions of this level include file transfer control, operator support, timestamping of messages, and distributed database activities such as pipelining (delivering transactions in sequence), integrity controls, and deadlock prevention or detection. This is the level of support needed for true distributed database management.

15.4 Components of a Distributed Database System

A distributed database system normally has the following software components:

- Data communications component (DC).
- Local database management component (DBMS).
- Global data dictionary (GDD).
- Distributed database management component (DDBMS).

Figure 15.4 illustrates these software components. The data communications component is the software at each node that links it to the network. It is responsible for providing the first five layers of the OSI architecture. This DC component includes a complete description of the network's nodes and lines. For each node, it identifies processing performed, storage capacity, processing power, and its current state. For each link, it identifies nodes it connects, type of link, bandwidth, protocols required, and the present state of the link. The local database management component is a standard database management system, responsible for controlling the local data at each site that has a database. It normally has its own data dictionary for local data. The global data dictionary is a repository of information about the distributed database. It includes a list of all data items with their location and other information about data stored anywhere in the distributed system. The distributed database component is the management system for the global database. It has many functions, including the following:

1. **Provides the user interface. Location transparency** is one of the major objectives of distributed databases. Ideally, the user need not specify the node at which data is located, but acts as if all data is stored locally and accessed by the local DBMS. The local DBMS, however, is unaware of the distribution, so only requests that can be satisfied locally should be sent to the local DBMS. The DDBMS, therefore, intercepts all requests for data.
2. **Locates the data.** After receiving a request for data, the DDBMS consults the global data directory to find the node or nodes where the data is stored. If the request can be filled entirely at the local node, it passes the query on to the local DBMS, which processes it. Otherwise, it must devise and carry out a plan for getting the data.
3. **Processes queries.** Queries may be categorized as **local, remote**, or **compound**. A local request is one that can be filled by the local DBMS. Local requests are simply handed down to the local DBMS, which finds the data and passes it back to the DDBMS, which passes it to the user. (Recall that the local DBMS has no user interface.) A remote request is one that can be filled completely at another node. In this case, the DDBMS passes the request to the DBMS at that node and waits for the response, which it then presents to the user. A compound request is one that requires information from several nodes. To process a compound request, the DDBMS has to decompose the query into several remote and local requests that, together, will provide the information needed. It then directs each query to the appropriate DBMS, which processes it and returns the data to the DDBMS. The DDBMS then coordinates the data received to formulate a response for the user.

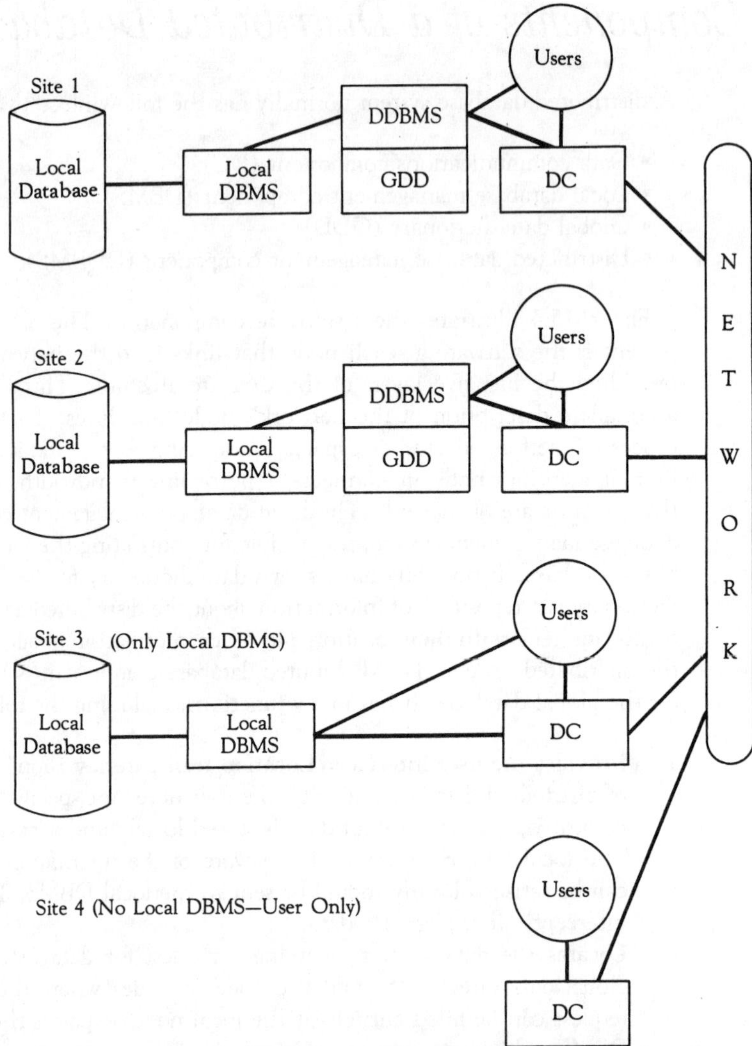

Figure 15.4 Components of a Distributed Database System

4. **Provides network-wide concurrency control and recovery procedures.** Although each local DBMS is responsible for handling update and recovery for its own data, only the DDBMS is aware of systemwide problems. Network-wide recovery procedures are needed because, if a local node fails, although the local DBMS can recover the local database to its condition at the time of failure, only the DDBMS can keep track of and apply changes made while the node was inactive. Network-wide concurrency control is needed to prevent simultaneous users at different sites from interfering with one another.
5. **Provides translation of queries and data in heterogeneous systems.** In heterogeneous systems with different hardware but the same local DBMS, minor translations of codes and word lengths, and slight changes due to differences in implementa-

tion are needed. If the local DBMSs are different, major translation is needed. This includes changing from the query language of one DBMS into that of another and changing data models and data structures. If both hardware and DBMSs are different, both types of translation are needed.

15.5 *Data Placement*

One of the most important decisions that a distributed database designer has to make is data placement. There are four basic alternatives: **centralized, replicated, partitioned,** or **hybrid**, as shown in Figure 15.5. Some of these require additional analysis to "fine tune" the placement of data. In deciding among data placement alternatives, the following factors need to be considered:

ALTERNATIVE:

CRITERION:	CENTRALIZED	REPLICATED	PARTITIONED	HYBRID
LOCALITY OF REFERENCE	lowest	highest	* should be high	* should be high
RELIABILITY	lowest	highest	high for system low for item	*
AVAILABILITY	lowest	highest	high for system low for item	*
STORAGE COSTS	lowest	highest	lowest	* should be average
LOAD DISTRIBUTION	poor	best	good	* should be good
COMMUNICATION COSTS	highest	low, except for updates	* should be low	* should be low

*depends on exact placement decisions made

Figure 15.5 Evaluation of Data Placement Alternatives

1. **Locality of data reference.** The data should be placed at the site where it is used most often. The designer studies the applications to identify the sites where they are performed, and attempts to place the data in such a way that most accesses are local.
2. **Reliability of the data.** By storing multiple copies of the data in geographically remote sites, the designer maximizes the probability that the data will be recoverable in case of physical damage to any site.
3. **Data availability.** As with reliability, storing multiple copies assures users that data

items will be available to them, even if the site from which the items are normally accessed is unavailable due to failure of the node or its only link.

4. **Storage capacities and costs.** Although the cost of data storage is not as high as the cost of data transmission, nodes may have different storage capacities and storage costs. These must be considered in deciding where data should be kept. Storage costs are minimized when a single copy of each data item is kept.
5. **Distribution of processing load.** One of the reasons for choosing a distributed system is to distribute the workload so that processing power will be used most effectively. This objective must be balanced against locality of data reference.
6. **Communications costs.** The designer must consider the cost of using the communications network to retrieve data. Retrieval costs and retrieval time are minimized when each site has its own copy of all the data. However, when the data is updated, the changes must then be sent to all sites. If the data is very volatile, this results in high communications costs for update synchronization.

The four placement alternatives are the following:

1. **Centralized:** This consists of a single database and DBMS stored in one location, with users distributed. There is no need for a DDBMS or global data dictionary, since there is no real distribution of data. Retrieval costs are high, because all users, except those at the central site, use the network for all accesses. Storage costs are low, since only one copy of each item is kept. There is no need for update synchronization, and the standard concurrency control mechanism is sufficient. Reliability is low and availability is poor, because a failure at the central node results in the loss of the entire system. The workload may be distributed, but remote nodes need to access the database to perform applications, so locality of data reference is low. This alternative is not a true distributed database system.
2. **Replicated:** With this alternative, a complete copy of the database is kept at each node. Advantages are maximum locality of reference, reliability, data availability, and processing load distribution. Storage costs are highest in this alternative. Communications costs for retrievals are low, but cost of updates is high, since every site must receive every update. If updates are very infrequent, this alternative is a good one.
3. **Partitioned:** Here, there is only one copy of each data item, but the data is distributed across nodes. To allow this, the database is split into disjoint **fragments** or parts. If the database is a relational one, fragments may be vertical table subsets, formed by projection, or horizontal subsets, formed by selection on global relations. In any **horizontal fragmentation scheme**, each tuple of every relation must be assigned to one or more fragments such that taking the union of the fragments results in the original relation; for the partitioned case, a tuple is assigned to exactly one fragment. In a **vertical fragmentation scheme**, the projections must be lossless, so that the original relations can be reconstructed by taking the join of the fragments. The easiest method of ensuring that projections are lossless is to include the key in each fragment; however, this violates the disjointness condition, since key attributes would then be replicated. The designer may choose to accept key replication, or the system may have a method of adding a tuple ID, a unique identifier

for each tuple, invisible to the user. The system would then include the tuple ID in each vertical fragment of the tuple and would use that identifier to perform joins. Besides vertical and horizontal fragments, there may be **mixed fragments**, obtained by successive applications of select and project operations. This alternative requires careful analysis to ensure that data items are assigned to the appropriate site. See Figure 15.6 for examples of fragmentation.

STUDENT

STUID	STUNAME	MAJOR	CREDITS
S1001	Smith,Tom	History	90
S1010	Burns,Edward	Art	63
S1015	Jones, Mary	Math	42
S1002	Chin,David	Math	36
S1020	Rivera, Jane	CSC	15
S1013	McCarthy, Owen	Math	9

(a) Horizontal Fragment: SELECT STUDENT WHERE MAJOR = 'Math'

STUDENT

STUID	STUNAME	MAJOR	CREDITS
S1001	Smith, Tom	History	90
S1010	Burns,Edward	Art	63
S1015	Jones, Mary	Math	42
S1002	Chin, David	Math	36
S1020	Rivera, Jane	CSC	15
S1013	McCarthy, Owen	Math	9

(b) Vertical Fragment: PROJECT STUDENT OVER (STUID, MAJOR)

STUDENT

STUID	STUNAME	MAJOR	CREDITS
S1001	Smith,Tom	History	90
S1010	Burns,Edward	Art	63
S1015	Jones, Mary	Math	42
S1002	Chin,David	Math	36
S1020	Rivera, Jane	CSC	15
S1013	McCarthy, Owen	Math	9

(c) Mixed Fragment: SELECT STUDENT WHERE MAJOR = 'MATH' GIVING TEMP PROJECT TEMP OVER (STUID,MAJOR)

Figure 15.6 Fragmentation

If data items have been assigned to the site where they are used most often, locality of data reference will be high with this alternative. Since only one copy of each item is stored, data reliability and availability for a specific item are low. However, failure of a node results in the loss of only that node's data, so the system-wide reliability and availability are higher than in the centralized case. Storage costs are low, and communications costs of a well-designed system should be low. The processing load should also be well distributed if the data is properly distributed.

4. **Hybrid:** In this alternative, different portions of the database are distributed differently. For example, those records or files with high locality of reference are partitioned, while those commonly used by all nodes are replicated, if updates are infrequent. Those that are needed by all nodes, but updated so frequently that synchronization would be a problem, are centralized. This alternative is designed to optimize data placement, so all the advantages and none of the disadvantages of the other methods are possible. However, very careful analysis of data and processing is required with this plan.

15.6 Placement of the DDBMS and Other Components

Although we have discussed only data placement so far, in actuality all of the system components must be studied to determine best placement. The data communications component and its network description, the DBMS, the global data dictionary, and the DDBMS could all be placed using any of the four alternatives: centralized, replicated, partitioned, or hybrid.

Placement of the Data Communications Component

Each node in a communications network must have some data communications software and hardware. However, some sites, especially those that do not contain a database, may simply switch messages. There may be sites that do not make routing decisions, but only generate or accept their own messages and forward messages for other nodes along a preassigned path. These do not need the entire network description, nor is their communications software as complicated as that of other nodes. The usual choice for placement of the DC component is replication, because all sites need to communicate, and because updates to the software are rare, so there is no update synchronization problem. Hybrid is an option, particularly if different sites have varying storage and processing capabilities. If that is the choice, certain nodes will have a "fully loaded" DC component, while others will have minimal communications components. Note that the placement of the DC component is, at least theoretically, independent of the placement of the other components.

Placement of the Local Database Management System

After choosing data placement, the designer of a distributed system has to determine where to put the database management system. Any node that has data must have a

DBMS to manage it. It must also have its own database dictionary for local data. In a homogeneous system, all nodes would have the same DBMS, which would be replicated at each node. Of course, the data dictionary entries would be different at each node. If the system were heterogeneous, different DBMSs would appear at different nodes.

Placement of the Global Data Dictionary

The placement of the global data dictionary need not coincide with placement of the database. The global data dictionary could be centralized, regardless of the placement decisions made for data or communications. In that case, all requests would require access to that node to perform query decomposition. It could be replicated at every node, since updates would be made only when the database is reorganized in some way. It could be partitioned, with different data items, schemas, or subschemas appearing at different nodes. This might cause a heavy communications load, since the DDBMS would need to query many nodes to find out where certain items are stored. It could also be hybrid, with some information centralized, some replicated, and some partitioned. If there is sufficient storage space, replicated is the usual choice, since this decreases the communications costs.

Placement of the Distributed Database Management System

Placement of this component normally coincides with placement of the global data dictionary, since it needs to consult the dictionary to locate data. Because updates to the DDBMS are relatively rare, replication is the usual choice, provided that every node has sufficient storage space and processing power.

15.7 Update Synchronization Problem

We have already considered problems of concurrency control in a centralized system (Chapter 12). In a distributed database, these same problems arise, but are compounded by the distribution. In addition, there are concurrency problems that are peculiar to distributed databases. Techniques that provided solutions in the centralized case may be extended to cover the distributed case. Some of the problems that must be solved are the following:

The Lost Update Problem: This situation can occur in a centralized system, and we have already seen both the problem and its solution. Briefly, if two users try to update the same data item at the same time, and there is no concurrency control mechanism, one update may be lost. This problem is even more likely to occur in a distributed system, because of the delays introduced by the communications system.

Single Transaction Consistency Problem: This problem occurs in a centralized system but is more serious in a distributed system. It develops when a single transaction must update several related items. If the transaction is permitted to update some, but not all the items, the state of the database will be inconsistent. In a distributed system, the various items to be updated may appear in different locations. It is essential that all of the updates be performed, regardless of where they appear.

Multiple-Copy Consistency Problem: This problem occurs in distributed systems when there are several copies of the same data item in different locations. We must be sure that each location receives and performs the update. In Chapter 12 we discussed serializability of transactions. Locking was the first method we considered, and we examined the problem of deadlock, the situation in which two transactions each wait for data items being held by the other. We looked at deadlock detection methods, using a wait-for graph. We also examined timestamping as a method for concurrency control. In a distributed system, concurrency problems are compounded because there are usually multiple copies of data items spread across the system, and concurrent transactions can enter from different sites. In fact, if the database is either centralized or partitioned, so that there is only one copy of each item, and all requests are either local (can be filled at local site) or remote (can be filled completely at one other site), the usual mechanisms are sufficient. Problems arise when there are multiple copies of data items or there are compound requests, requests that require access to data at more than one site.

Update synchronization procedures used with distributed databases include **global locking**, **primary copy synchronization**, **majority consensus**, and **multiple protocol synchronization**. The first two guarantee complete consistency for transactions, meaning that no matter where a transaction is entered or processed, it will produce the same results. The last two promise only **convergent consistency**, meaning that if all updates already in the system were performed before any new ones were accepted, the database would become completely consistent. They do permit momentary inconsistency, during the time when an update has been completed at one site but not yet at another. This could cause the same transaction to produce two different results, depending on which site is used for access.

Global Locking

This is, conceptually, the simplest of the four methods. It produces perfect consistency but has high communications costs and poor performance because of the length of time the locks are held. The basic plan is to have each node lock the data item(s) involved, update each copy, and release all locks. Figure 15.7 shows the steps involved in this method. Note that for this small system, 20 messages are needed to complete this procedure, assuming that no problems arise. If some site is unable to lock the data item(s) because another transaction has already caused them to be locked, one of the transactions will have to be rolled back, causing unlock messages for the rollback itself, and that transaction will have to be performed later, requiring all 20 messages once again. Therefore, the actual number of messages may be higher than 20. In addition, further complications could arise if one of the nodes or links has failed. In the case of a line failure, rerouting may be used, and the system could continue as before. If no other line exists, the node is isolated, and the line failure is treated as a node failure. The system can recognize a node failure either by self-reporting of the failed node, or if that is not possible, by a time-out method. In that case, if a node fails to respond to a message within a prespecified time, it is assumed to have failed and recovery procedures are started. It is essential that the time-out be sufficiently long that recovery procedures

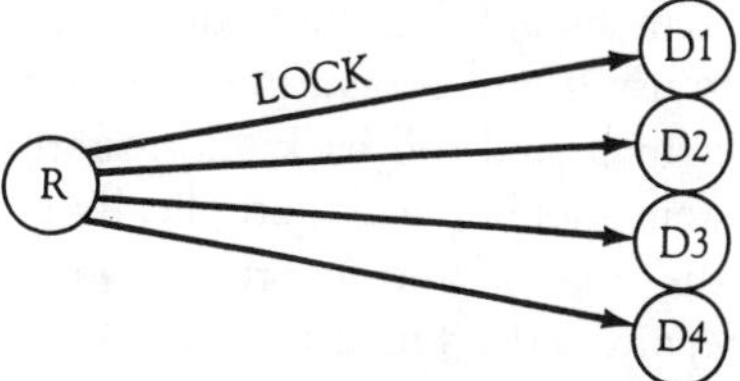

(a) **Step 1: Requesting node sends a lock request to all data nodes**

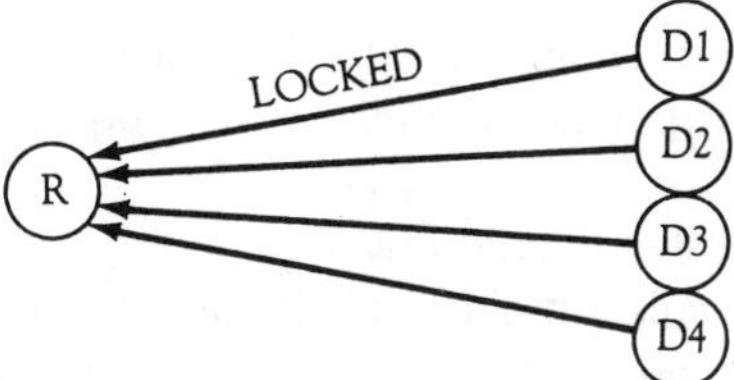

(b) **Step 2: Each data node responds that data is locked:**

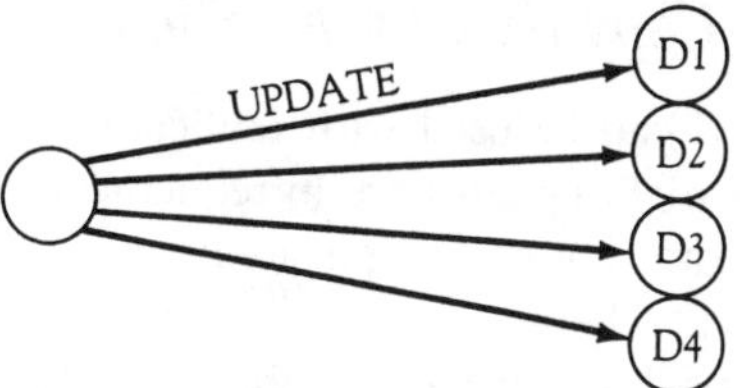

(c) **Step 3: Requesting node issues actual update request**

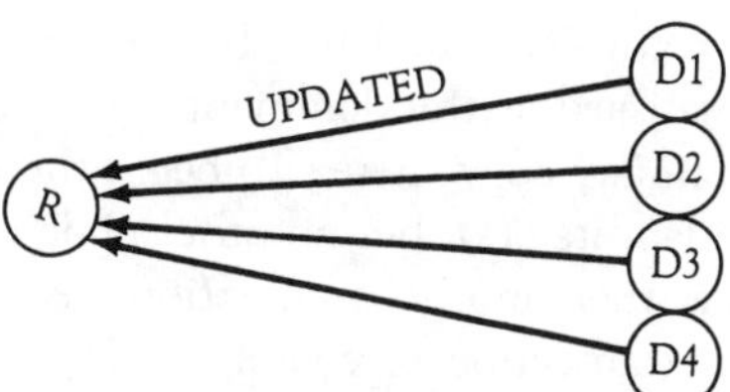

(d) **Step 4: Each data node performs its update and responds when update is complete**

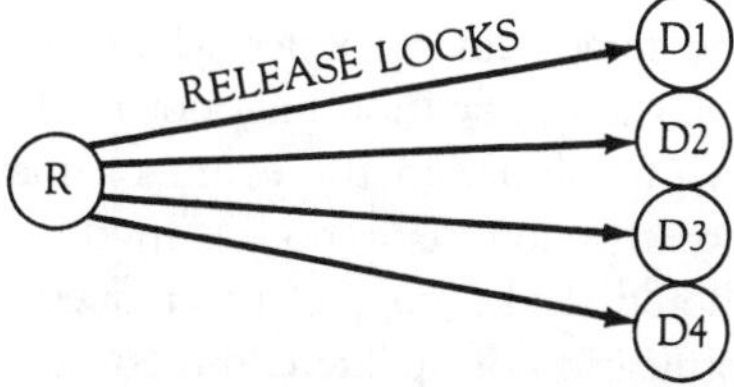

(e) **Step 5: Requesting node sends message to release locks:**

Figure 15.7 Steps in Global Locking

are not triggered unnecessarily. The following steps are used to allow the system to continue following failure of a node:

1. The system should flag the node or line as failed, to prevent any other node from trying to use it and generating a second recovery procedure.
2. The system should roll back and restart any transactions affected by the failure.
3. The system should check periodically to see if the node has recovered, or, alternatively, the node should report when it has been repaired.
4. Once repaired, the failed node must do local recovery, meaning that it rolls back any partial transactions which were active at the time of failure, taking into account any network-wide adjustments made.
5. After local recovery, the failed node must update its copy of the data, so that it matches the current state of the database. The system keeps a log of changes made during the node's failure for this purpose.

There are slight variations of these steps depending on whether the requesting node or a data node fails, the time of failure, and whether communications are parallel (messages broadcast to all nodes simultaneously) or serial (messages sent to one node at a time, with forwarding of messages).

Primary Copy Synchronization

This method can be used with replicated or hybrid data distribution where locality of reference is high, updates are infrequent, and nodes do not always need the very latest version of data. For each replicated data item, one copy is chosen as the **primary copy**, and the node where it is stored is the **dominant node**. Normally, different nodes are dominant for different parts of the data. The network data directory must show which is the primary copy of each data item. When an update is entered at any node, the DDBMS determines where the primary copy is, and sends the update there first, even before doing any local update. It is essential that the entire update transaction be completely satisfied at the dominant node, so all variables to be read or written must have their primary copy there. To begin the update, the dominant node locks its local copy of the data item(s), but no other node does so. If the dominant node is unable to obtain a lock, then another transaction has already locked an item, so the update must wait for that transaction to complete. This ensures serializability for each item. Once the lock has been obtained, the dominant node performs its update and then controls updates of all other copies, usually starting at the node where the request was entered. The user at that node may be notified when the local copy is updated, even though there may be some remote nodes where the new values have not yet been entered. Alternatively, the notification may not be done until all copies have been updated.

To improve reliability in the event of dominant node failure, a backup node could be chosen for the dominant node. In that case, before the dominant node does an update, it should send a copy of the request to its backup. If the dominant node does not send notification of update completion shortly after this message, the backup node uses a time-out to determine whether the dominant node has failed. If a failure occurs, the backup node then acts as the dominant node, notifying all other nodes that it is now dominant, sending a copy of the request to its own backup node, locking data and performing its own update, and supervising the updates at the other nodes. It is also responsible for supplying data needed when the actual dominant node recovers. If nondominant nodes fail, the system continues to function, and the dominant node is responsible for keeping a log of changes made while the node was down, to be used in recovery. This process is actually more complicated than this description suggests, since a node may be dominant for some data items and not for others.

The primary copy approach has lower communications costs and better performance than global locking, since there is less locking. However, it is not useful unless locality of reference is high, updates are infrequent, and nodes do not always need the latest version of data.

Majority Consensus Synchronization

This method uses timestamping instead of locking, and a voting system to determine whether to perform an update. An update can be performed if a majority of nodes votes to accept it. In Chapter 12 we discussed timestamping in a centralized system. We extend the notion for the distributed case by specifying that timestamps will have two parts: The first is the usual timestamp generated by the local clock or logical counter, and the second part is the node identifier. Since the clock or counter is advanced at each node for each transaction, this guarantees that every transaction will have a unique timestamp, although two transaction timestamps may have the same first part. It would be desirable to have some type of global clock, so we could determine which of two transactions entered at different sites was actually first, but it is virtually impossible to fully synchronize all the local clocks involved. Instead, there is usually some scheme to prevent local timestamps from diverging too much. For example, there may be a rule that if a node receives a timestamp with first part, t, greater than its current clock reading, it automatically advances its clock to $t + 1$. This prevents nodes that have frequent transactions from getting too far ahead of less active nodes.

As in the centralized case, every data item is stored with a timestamp, indicating when the item was last modified. The procedure used is the following:

1. Retrieve the variables to be read (called read or base variables) with their timestamps.
2. Determine new values for the variables to be written (called write or object variables).
3. Issue the update request.
4. Perform the synchronization protocol.

With this protocol, a majority of nodes must vote to accept an update in order for it to be performed. Each node that gets the request examines the timestamps of the read variables in its local database and then executes the following **voting procedure:**

- If any local read variable has a timestamp that is later than the transaction's timestamp, it votes to reject the update, because the transaction is using obsolete data. One rejection is sufficient to abort the entire transaction.
- If all local items used as read variables have earlier timestamps than the transaction's, the node looks to see if any were involved as write variables in pending requests that it has already voted on but not yet performed. If none are involved in pending requests, it votes to accept. If the request conflicts with a pending

one, the node examines the priority of each. If the new request has a higher priority than the pending one, it votes to pass, which warns other nodes of a possible conflict. If the pending request has a higher priority than the new one, it does not vote.

Once it decides on its own vote, if a serial communications procedure is being used, the node examines the current state of the request and follows a **request resolution procedure**:

- If the node votes to reject the request, it immediately broadcasts the rejection to all nodes.
- If it votes to accept the update and finds that its acceptance now creates a majority, it broadcasts a message that the request has been accepted.
- If it votes to pass and finds that it is no longer possible for a majority to accept the request, it broadcasts a reject to all nodes.
- Otherwise, it simply transmits the request and cumulative voting results to the next node, where the procedure is repeated.

If the communications procedure is parallel rather than serial, a coordinator node, possibly the site where the update originated, is responsible for administering the request resolution procedure.

5. Perform the update. Regardless of the method of communication, a decision will be reached, and all nodes will be notified. If the update is rejected, all nodes delete the request and reevaluate any requests that were passed or not voted on because of conflicts with the deleted one. If the update is accepted, each node determines whether there is any pending request that conflicts with the accepted update. If so, it votes to reject the pending request, and notifies all other nodes of its rejection. Each node also follows the **update application rule** for accepted updates:

- If the local timestamp on a write variable is earlier than the transaction's timestamp, it updates the write variable.
- If the local timestamp of a write variable is later than the transaction's timestamp, the update is not performed because it is obsolete, since the variable has already been updated by a later transaction.

6. Notify the requesting node the update has been performed. This permits the requesting node to notify the user that the update has been completed. Notification is also used to improve reliability, since failure to notify within a specified time allows the requesting node to use a time-out to determine whether a data node has failed. Similar notification procedures can be used by all nodes in the serial communications case to identify and isolate failed nodes. Since only a majority is needed, the procedure can continue despite failure of a data node. If the requesting node has a backup that receives a copy of each request, the backup node can take over for a failed requesting node, allowing the procedure to continue despite failure of the requesting node as well.

Multiple Protocol Synchronization

This method is used by SDD-1, a distributed system prototype developed by Computer Corporation of America. It also uses timestamps, but avoids much of the overhead found in the previous method by a careful examination of transactions. At design time, the DBA identifies the set of data items to be read (called the **read set**) and the set of data items to be written (called the **write set**) of each transaction, determines which of four protocols will be required, and enters that information in a **transaction class table**. When an update request is entered, the originating node issues a transaction timestamp, using a concatenation of its internal clock reading and node identifier. Each data item has a timestamp which consists of the timestamp of the last transaction that wrote it. The four protocols, P1, P2, P3, and P4, are as follows:

P1: This protocol is the fastest and simplest of the four. It uses only local locks, and does not wait for acknowledgments from other nodes before allowing local users to access updated data. It is used only when data is primarily of local interest or the update is providing a new data item value that is independent of the old value. The following steps are performed by the originating node:

1. It locks the local copy of the transaction's read and write sets.
2. It updates the local copy.
3. It broadcasts the update to all other nodes.
4. It unlocks the local data and notifies the user that the update is complete.

This protocol allows users at remote nodes to have obsolete data temporarily, but that is not a major problem since the data is not of primary interest there or the new value is independent of the old one.

P2: This is used for retrievals when the data is of local interest at some other node, so P1 is not sufficient. In that case, the originating node assigns a transaction timestamp equal to the most recent timestamp in its read set. The following steps are performed by the originating node:

1. It accepts the request and sets the timestamp as described above.
2. It sends the request and its timestamp to all nodes.
3. It waits until all other nodes respond that they will accept the transaction.
4. After receiving acceptances from all other nodes, it performs the local update following the steps of the P1 protocol: lock local read and write sets, perform local update, broadcast the result, unlock and notify user.

A node never rejects a P2 (or P3, to be described later) transaction, although it can delay processing until the update can be performed correctly. While the originating node is waiting for the other nodes to respond, it can perform requests that have earlier timestamps and that do not update the pending transaction's read set. Other nodes respond to requests in the following way:

- If the node is idle, it returns an accept with a timestamp which is either its current clock reading or the one of the transaction, whichever is later.

- If the node is busy, it attempts to process requests in timestamp order. If its queue has requests with timestamps that are earlier than the new one, it performs the earlier ones before accepting the new request. If the new request has a timestamp earlier than any on the queue, it immediately acknowledges the new request and accepts it, so that the originating node can begin its own update. If the new request has an earlier timestamp than the one being processed, the node sends an immediate accept with a timestamp equal to the one currently being processed.

Once an update has been accepted, each node uses the update application rule as in majority consensus–updating data items only if their timestamps are earlier than that of the transaction.

P3: This protocol is used for updates in which the new value of a data item is determined by the present value, so P1 is not sufficient. The originating node assigns a transaction timestamp equal to the current value of its internal clock. Once the timestamp is issued, the steps of the protocol are identical to those of P2.

P4: This is the most complicated protocol and has the most overhead. It is used for transactions that have not been classified at design time. The objective of this protocol is to ensure that unanticipated requests do not interfere with requests using simpler protocols. Basically, when a P4 request is entered, the originating node is responsible for making sure that all current requests are performed before the new one. The node that originates a P4 request advances its timestamp device to an arbitrary future time and assigns this as the timestamp of the transaction. The hope is that the new timestamp will be later than all timestamps currently in the system. If there is any current transaction with a later timestamp, the node that is processing it sends a reject back to the originating node, which again advances its timestamp, attaching a still later one to the P4 request. Once all nodes recognize that the request has the latest timestamp and accept it, the P2/P3 protocol is applied.

15.8 *Request Decomposition*

Even in a centralized database, requests expressed in a high-level language such as SQL have to be decomposed into machine-level operations. However, a distributed environment requires additional request decomposition procedures. As described earlier, database queries can be categorized as local, remote, or compound. In satisfying a compound request, the DDBMS is responsible for breaking down the query into several subqueries, each of which is directed to a specific node for processing. The DDBMS must then collect and coordinate the responses to obtain an overall result. Ideally, the user should not be aware of the distribution of data, and should not need to specify where the data items are located.

Some or all of the following steps must be performed in answering a query:

1. **The DDBMS accepts the request.** Recall that the user interface is the responsibility of the DDBMS rather than the local DBMS at each node. Because the local DBMS is not aware of the distribution, it is unable to handle queries about data items not stored locally.
2. **It checks the validity of the request.** This requires checking that the correct query language syntax is used, and that the data items referred to actually exist. This is external level validity checking, which requires that the DDBMS have access to the user's subschema.
3. **It maps external to conceptual level.** The DDBMS maps the user's data names and views to the corresponding conceptual-level objects.
4. **It checks authorization.** Access control information must be available to the DDBMS, so that it can check whether the user is authorized to perform the operations requested on the data items specified. This checking should be done both at the user's node and at every node where the request is processed. This is conceptual level checking, and requires that the schema be available to the DDBMS.
5. **It determines a request processing strategy.** The DDBMS must consult the global data dictionary to determine the location of the data items requested. If the request is local or remote, it goes on to the next step. If the request is compound, it must break it into subqueries and direct each to a node. There may be several ways of breaking up the query, so the DDBMS normally uses some form of optimization to determine which decomposition to use. Optimization in a centralized system involves several techniques. In a distributed system, the optimization also includes the use of the communications system. An objective of optimization might be minimizing response time, which would dictate decomposing the request in such a manner that parallel processing could be performed at several nodes, especially if the communications system is fast and the processing load is light. Sometimes several nodes perform the same process, and results are obtained from the one that finishes first. If the system is heavily used, other objectives might be more appropriate. These include minimizing total processing time, which consists of the sum of the processing times of the nodes, even though the processing may be simultaneous, and the time used for executing communications software and consolidating the results. In selecting an algorithm, optimization requires that the DDBMS find all the ways of processing the query and then "cost out" each one, by using mathematical formulas that include processing costs, communications costs, and storage costs. Because of the difficulty of finding all possible processing methods, a "hill climbing" method is often used. This consists of finding an initial solution and costing it out, then evaluating a slightly different alternative, choosing the better of the two. The better one then becomes the basis for a comparison with another alternative, and the process continues until no other method can be found or a certain number of iterations fail to produce substantial improvement.
6. **If the system is heterogeneous, it translates each query into the DML of the data node.** In remote or compound requests, the node where the data is located may use a different DBMS from the user's node. Therefore, the DDBMS must provide translation due to hardware and software differences.

7. **It encrypts the request.** Security is improved if every request and every response is encrypted before being passed to the communications system. The receiving node must then decrypt the message before processing.
8. **Depending on the system, the local data communications component may determine the routing.** The requesting node must provide logical identifiers for each node that is to receive a subrequest. The function of translating the logical to a physical identifier and choosing a path requires a network description, which is available to the DC component. Routing may be direct or indirect, requiring that the message pass through intermediate nodes. If indirect, the routing may be determined by the originating node in advance, or may be dynamically determined by the intermediate nodes.
9. **The DC component transmits the message through the communications system.** Since communications between databases are process-to-process communications, the message must pass down through all layers at the source node, be transmitted to the destination, and pass back up through all the layers at the destination node.
10. **The DDBMS decrypts the request.** If the message was encrypted at the source, it must now be decrypted before processing can begin.
11. **The DDBMS performs update synchronization, if needed.** If the request is an update, the DDBMS at the receiving node must go through synchronization procedures, as described in Section 15.7.
12. **The local DBMS at the data node performs logical and physical binding and determines local processing strategy.**
13. **The local DBMS or file manager performs the physical I/O operations.**
14. **If the system is heterogeneous, the DDBMS translates the data.** The requesting node, data node, or some intermediate node may perform any necessary translation.
15. **The DDBMS send the results to the destination node.** Normally, query results are returned to the requesting node, but other nodes might also be specified as destinations. The results might be encrypted before they are returned
16. **It coordinates the results and prepares the response for the user.** The requesting node usually coordinates the entire query decomposition process, and is normally the site where final consolidation of partial results is performed. In addition, the DDBMS at that node consults the user's external model to present data in the form the user expects.
17. **It returns the results to the user.** Since the user interface is provided by the DDBMS, it is responsible for displaying the results.

15.9 *Current Models and Applications*

15.9.1 *SDD-1*

SDD-1, **System for Distributed Databases**, was developed during the late 1970s by the Computer Corporation of America as the first prototype of a distributed database management system. It uses **ARPANET**, a preexisting communications network developed using funds from the Advanced Research Projects Agency of the United States Department of Defense (ARPA). The network was designed to use packet switching to link computer centers at universities and research agencies throughout the United States. The application chosen for the implementation of SDD-1 was naval command and control operations, which require a database to keep track of ships—their classes, characteristics, readiness for combat, and weapons. Because of the nature of this application, reliability was a high priority of the designers, so the system allows for much replication. SDD-1 is implemented on DEC machines using **Datacomputer**, an existing database management system, with its own data manipulation language, Datalanguage. It uses the relational model, allowing both vertical and horizontal fragments to be created and then replicated at many sites. The components of the system are **Data Modules (DMs)**, **Transaction Modules (TMs)**, and a **Reliable Network (RelNet)**. Each site can have one TM and/or up to three DMs. All sites are connected to the RelNet. The DM is the local data manager and functions much as the local DBMS described in this chapter. The TM is the network data manager, performing the functions associated with the DDBMS. The RelNet interconnects the other two components at various sites. Its important features include guaranteed delivery of messages despite failure of nodes, transaction control, monitoring of all sites to determine their status, and a global network clock for synchronization. Figure 15.8 illustrates the architecture of SDD-1. The system provides location, fragmentation, and replication transparency. It uses query optimization based on a "hill climbing" method. Concurrency control is based on timestamping, using the multiple-protocol synchronization techniques described in Section 15.7. The recovery system uses an improved version of the two-phase commit, the **four-phase commit**, a commitment protocol using backups whose purpose is to ensure reliability despite failure of the coordinator node. The system catalog, like any other data, is arbitrarily fragmented and replicated, meaning that a catalog entry may be anywhere in the system. To aid in finding a particular catalog entry, a higher-level catalog, called the **directory locator**, is replicated at every site.

15.9.2 *R**

R* is a prototype distributed database management system under development by IBM. It runs on IBM mainframes using SNA, and is basically an extension of System R, the prototype relational DBMS on which SQL and DB2 are based. All data is stored in the form of relations, with no fragmentation or replication permitted. There is location transparency, so that the programmer need not specify the data site for transactions. A primary objective in the design of R* is **local autonomy**, meaning that each site can manipulate its data independently of other sites (except in the case of the two-phase commit protocol) and each site can control access to its data from other sites.

The SQL language has been extended in R* to allow system-wide naming of objects and movement of objects from site to site. An object in R* has a **printname**, which is the one usually used when the object is referenced externally, and a **system-wide name**, which is a unique identifier consisting of four parts, as follows:

```
<creator ID>@<creator-site>.<object>@<birth-site>
```

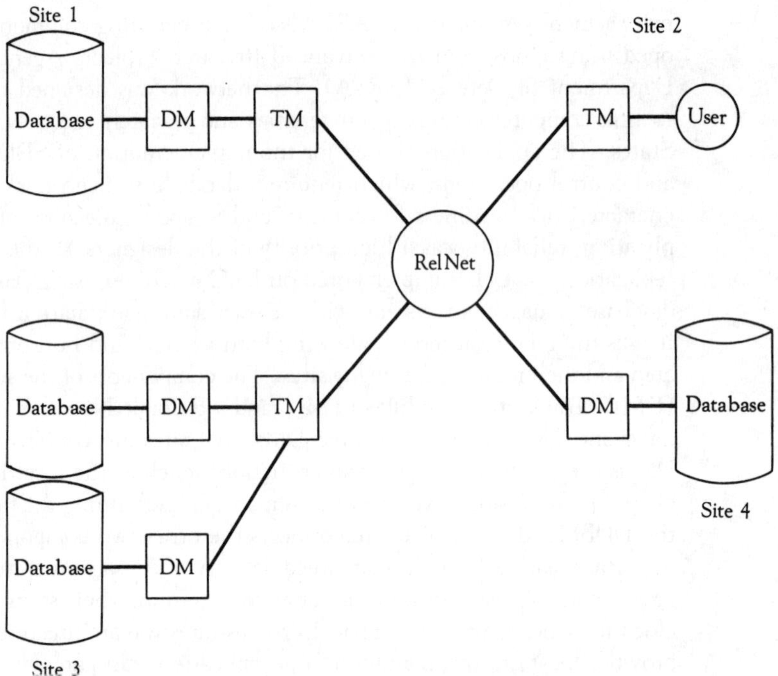

Figure 15.8 The Architecture of SDD-1

The first two parts are automatically assigned by the system when a user creates an object. The third is the name of the object as chosen by its creator. The fourth is the ID of the site where the object is first stored. Note that when the object is moved, its system-wide name will be unchanged. The printname may be the same as the object name, or it may be some synonym. Each site maintains a synonym table that maps user names for objects to their system-wide names. Each site also contains a list of objects for which it is the current site as well as a list of objects for which it is the birth site, along with the ID of the current site for those objects. When a particular object is requested, the node can determine the system-wide name and, if it is not the current site for the object, the location of the birth site, which, in turn can determine the current site.

R* has three major components: a **local DBMS**, a **transaction manager**, and a **data communications system**. The local DBMS is based on System R, the data communications system is SNA, and the transaction manager is the equivalent of the DDBMS. The transaction manager can be invoked by either an application program or a user interface facility. When a request is received, the site where it is entered becomes the **master** and is responsible for parsing, determining system-wide names, catalog lookup, and so on. It then devises a global plan, which may include both a local access module and remote accesses. Each other site, or **apprentice**, is sent its own portion of the access plan, and it in turn performs parsing, catalog lookup, local optimization, binding, and so on, to produce its local access module for finding the required data. Note that even apprentices have complete local autonomy over their own data.

R* uses locking, and a variation of the two-phase commit protocol for concurrency control.

15.9.3 *Distributed INGRES*

Distributed INGRES is a distributed version of INGRES, a relational database management system developed at the University of California at Berkeley. It can run on interconnected DEC PDP-11s, using either a local area network or a long-haul network. It provides location transparency and horizontal, but not vertical, data fragmentation. Fragments may be replicated, with one copy being designated as the primary copy. Updates can be handled in either of two ways. The first, the **performance algorithm**, updates the primary copy and then propagates updates of all other copies. The second, the **reliable algorithm**, updates all copies immediately. Distributed INGRES uses two-phase locking for concurrency control, with deadlock detection and resolution being performed by a single deadlock detector that analyzes all wait-for information. Each transaction is a single statement in QUEL, the DML used by INGRES. The system uses a version of a two-phase commit protocol for recovery.

INGRES/STAR from Relational Technology provides database management for heterogeneous distributed systems. The major system components are the INGRES/STAR Distributed Data Manager, INGRES/NET, and INGRES gateways. The distributed data manager receives SQL queries, decomposes them, and manages the results. It uses a global data dictionary that can be replicated as needed. It controls query optimization, integrity, and concurrency, using a two-phase commit protocol. The communications software, INGRES/NET, provides support for several different protocols. There are gateways to dBase and VAX/VMS files as well as to DB2 and SQL/DS databases.

15.9.4 *Other Distributed Systems*

Many other prototype distributed database management systems have been developed. In addition to SDD-1, the Computer Corporation of America has a prototype called Distributed Data Manager (DDM), a distributed system that uses the functional data model and its language, Daplex, embedded in ADA programs. The same company has developed Multibase, also based on the functional model and Daplex, to link heterogeneous databases. Researchers at Honeywell developed a prototype called Distributed Database Testbed System (DDTS) using a model similar to the Entity-Relationship model to link IDS/II databases. Unity is a protoype relational system developed at Bell Labs. Prime Computers has a prototype using the network model. The French government sponsored a project called Sirius that produced several prototypes, one of which, Sirius-Delta, was implemented. Nixdorf Computer AG has developed a system called VDN which was initiated at the Technical University of Berlin.

Among widely-used database management systems that include distributed capabilities is DB2. The present release allows different DB2 databases to communicate through

CICS, permitting reads from different sites, but updates from only a single site. Oracle Corporation has announced that it will offer distribution in the next release of the Oracle database management system, including distribution transparency, query and update capabilities from different sites, and the two-phase commit protocol. Tandem Corporations Non-Stop SQL, described in Chapter 16, is a functional distributed database system.

15.10 *Chapter Summary*

A **distributed database system** has multiple sites connected by a communications system, so that data at any site is available to users at other sites. The system may be a **long-haul system**, in which sites are geographically far apart, or a **local area network**, in which they are close together. Advantages of distribution may include **local autonomy, improved reliability, better data availability, increased performance, reduced response time**, and **lower communications costs.**

In a data communications system, basic components include the **source, medium,** and **sink**. System characteristics that must be considered are **path establishment time, network delay, transfer rate**, and **reliability. Routing** may be **point-to-point (store-and-forward),** which involves pairwise-connected **IMPs** or **broadcast**, as with a satellite or bus. Possible network topologies include **star, ring (loop), fully interconnected, hierarchical,** and **mixed (irregular).** The design may be evaluated in terms of **modularity, bottleneck vulnerability, fault tolerance, routing flexibility,** and **complexity.**

The designer of a distributed database system must consider the **type of communications system, data models supported, types of applications**, and **data placement alternatives.** Final design can range from **centralized data and processing with local data entry**, to **true distributed data and database management function.** Such a system may be **homogeneous**, where all nodes use the same hardware and software, or **heterogeneous**, where nodes have different hardware or software. Heterogeneous systems require translations of codes and word lengths due to hardware differences, or of data models and data structures due to software differences.

A distributed database system has the following software components: **data communications component, local database management system, global data dictionary,** and **distributed database management system component.** The responsibilities of the distributed database management system include **providing the user interface, locating the data, processing queries, providing network-wide concurrency control and recovery procedures,** and **providing translation in heterogeneous systems. Data placement alternatives** are **centralized, replicated, partitioned,** and **hybrid**. Factors to be considered in making the data placement decision are **locality of reference, reliability of data, availability of data, storage capacities and costs, distribution of processing load,** and **communications costs.** The other components of a distributed database system may be placed using any of the four alternatives.

One of the most difficult tasks of a distributed database management system is **update synchronization.** Problems that can arise include the **lost update problem, single-transaction inconsistency**, and **multiple-copy inconsistency.** Solutions for the distributed case include techniques such as **global locking, primary copy synchronization, majority consensus**, and **multiple protocol synchronization**.

Another important task of the distributed database management system is **request decomposition,** which includes several steps, the most difficult of which is to **determine a request processing strategy** and supervise its execution.

Current distributed database management systems include **SDD-1, R*, Distributed INGRES, INGRES/STAR,** and others.

15.11 *Exercises*

1. Assume a university has three campuses, Downtown, Midtown, and Uptown. Students are associated with one home campus, but may attend classes at all three. Faculty members are not associated with a particular campus, and may teach classes at all three. The same courses may be offered at all locations, but the campus of each course offering (class) is identified. The global schema is

```
STUDENT (STUID, HOME_CAMPUS, STUNAME, MAJOR, CREDITS)
FACULTY (FACID, FACNAME, DEPT, RANK)
CLASS (COURSE#, CAMPUS, CTITLE, FACID, SCHED, ROOM)
ENROLL (STUID, COURSE#, CAMPUS, GRADE)
```

   (a) Choose a data distribution plan for this data and justify your choice, using the criteria described in Section 15.5.

   (b) Write a fragmentation schema, as follows: Decide how the data should be fragmented to fit the distribution plan. Use relational algebra or SQL commands to create the fragments. For each fragment, identify the location(s) where it will be stored.

2. A database is to store information for a real estate agency that uses multiple listings. Properties for sale are visited by an agent (the listing agent) who collects information. Once listed, the property can be sold by any agent in any office (the selling agent). However, once a binder (a declaration of a buyer's intention to purchase and a deposit) is placed on the property, no agent can show the property to another prospective buyer. If no contract follows within a month, or if the buyer retracts the binder, the property becomes available again. Prospective buyers may register with only one agent. When the property is sold, the commission is divided between the listing agent and the selling agent, who may be the same person. Assume the following schema is used:

```
SALES_OFFICE (NAME, ADDRESS, NO_OF_AGENTS, GENERAL-TEL)
AGENT (AGENT_NAME, SALES_OFFICE_NAME, AGENT_TEL)
LISTING (ADDRESS, TYPE, STYLE, SIZE, ASKING_PRICE, DATE_LISTED,
OWNER_NAME, OWNER_TEL, FEATURES)
```

```
PROS_BUYER (NAME, ADDRESS, TEL, TYPE_WANTED, STYLE_WANTED, SIZE_WANTED,
HIGHEST_PRICE, DATE_REGISTERED, AGENT_NAME)
BINDER (BUYER_NAME, LISTING_ADDRESS, AGENT, AMOUNT_BID, DATE_BID, STATUS,
DATE_CANCELLED)
```

For simplicity, assume all names are unique. The attribute FEATURES in LISTING is a description of the property consisting of at most 100 characters.

(a) Choose a data distribution plan for this data and justify your choice, using the criteria described in Section 15.5.

(b) Write a fragmentation schema, as described in Exercise 1(b).

(c) Explain how the following query would be answered: Find the names and addresses of all prospective buyers and their agents for a new listing. It is a residence (i.e., TYPE=RESIDENCE), colonial style, with ten rooms (i.e., SIZE=10), and asking price of $400,000.

15.12 *Bibliography*

Apers, P., A. Hevner, and S. Yao. "Optimization Algorithms for Distributed Queries," IEEE Transactions on Software Engineering, **SE9**:1, (January, 1983), pp. 57-68.

Attar, R., P. Bernstein, and N. Goodman. "Site Initialization, Recovery, and Backup in a Distributed Database System," Proceedings Berkeley Workshop on Distributed Data Management and Computer Networks (1982) pp. 185-202.

Bernstein, P. and N. Goodman. "Timestamp-based Algorithms for Concurrency Control in Distributed Database Systems," Proceedings of the International Conference on Very Large Data Bases (1980) pp. 285-300.

Bernstein, P., D. Shipman, and J. Rothnie, Jr. "Concurrency Control for Distributed Databases (SDD-1)," ACM Transactions on Database Systems **5**:1 (January, 1980) pp. 13-51.

Bernstein, P., N. Goodman, E. Wong, C. Reeve, and J. Rothnie, Jr. "Query Processing in a System for Distributed Databases (SDD-1)," ACM Transactions on Database Systems **6**:4 (December, 1980), pp.52-68.

Bhargava, B. (Ed.). *Concurrency and Reliability in Distributed Systems*, New York: Van Nostrand-Reinhold, 1987.

Bonczek, R., C. Holsapple, and A. Whinston. *Micro Database Management*. Orlando, FL: Academic Press, 1984.

Bray, O. *Distributed Database Management Systems*. Lexington, MA: Lexington Books, 1982.

Ceri, S. and G. Pelagatti. *Distributed Databases: Principles and Systems*. New York: McGraw-Hill, 1984.

Chorafas, D. *DBMS for Distributed Computers and Networks*. New York: Petrocelli, 1983.

Date, C. *An Introduction to Database Systems*. Reading, MA: Addison-Wesley, 1986.

Date, C. *A Guide to INGRES*. Reading, MA: Addison-Wesley, 1987.

Delobel, C. and W. Litwin (Ed.). "Distributed Data Bases" Proceedings of the International Symposium on Distributed Databases. Amsterdam: North-Holland, 1980.

Epstein, R., M. Stonebraker, and E. Wong. "Distributed Query Processing in a Relational Database System," Proceedings of the ACM SIGMOD Conference on Management of Data (1978) pp. 169-180.

Garcia-Molina, H. "Elections in Distributed Computing Systems," IEEE Transactions on Computers **31**:1 (January, 1982) pp 48-59.

Garcia-Molina, H. "Using Semantic Knowledge for Transaction Processing in a Distributed Database," ACM Transactions on Database Systems **8**:2 (June, 1983) pp. 186-213.

Garcia-Molina, H. and J. Kent. "An Experimental Evaluation of Crash Recovery Algorithms," Proceedings of the Fourth ACM Symposium on Principles of Database Systems (1985) pp. 113-121.

Gelenbe, E. and R. Sevcik. "Analysis of Update Synchronization for Multiple Copy Data Bases," Proceedings of the Berkeley Workshop on Distributed Data Management and Computer Networks (1978) pp. 69-90.

Hammer, M. and D. Shipman. "Reliability Mechanisms for SDD-1: A System for Distributed Databases," ACM Transactions on Database Systems **5**:4 (December, 1980) pp. 431-466.

Hevner, A. and S. Yao. "Query Processing in Distributed Database Systems," IEEE Transactions on Software Engineering **5**:3 (May, 1979) pp. 177-187.

Kerschberg, L., P. Ting, and S. Yao. "Query Optimization in Star Computer Networks," ACM Transactions on Database Systems **7**:4 (December, 1982) pp. 678-711.

Korth, H. and A. Silberschatz. *Database System Concepts*. New York: McGraw-Hill, 1986.

Lindsay, B. et. al. "Computation and Communication in R*: A Distributed Database Manager," ACM Transactions on Computer Systems **2**:1 (January, 1984) pp. 24-38.

Lorie, R. "Physical Integrity in a Large Segmented Database," ACM Transactions on Database Systems **2**:1 (March, 1977) pp. 91-104.

Menasce, D. and R. Muntz. "Locking and Deadlock Detection in Distributed Data Bases," IEEE Transactions on Software Engineering **SE-5**:3 (May, 1979) pp. 195-202.

Menasce, D., G. Popek, and R. Muntz. "A Locking Protocol for Resource Coordination in Distributed Databases," ACM Transactions on Database Systems **5**:2 (June, 1980) pp. 103-138.

Minoura, T. and G. Wiederhold. "Resilient Extended True-Copy Token Scheme for a Distributed Database," IEEE Transactions on Software Engineering **8**:3 (May, 1981).

Mohon, C. "Recent and Future Trends in Distributed Database Management," in Ariav, G. and J. Clifford (Ed.). *New Directions for Database Systems*. Norwood, NJ: Ablex, 1986 pp.35-52.

Mohon, C., B. Lindsay, and R. Obermarck. "Transaction Management in the R* Distributed Database Management System," ACM Transactions on Database Systems. **11**:4 (December, 1986) pp. 378-396.

Morgan, H. and K. Levin. "Optimal Program and Data Locations in Computer Networks," Communications of the ACM **20**:5 (May, 1977) pp. 315-322.

Obermarck, R. "Distributed Deadlock Detection Algorithm," ACM Transactions on Database Systems **7**:2 (June, 1982) pp. 187-208.

Reed, D. "Implementing Atomic Actions on Decentralized Data," ACM Transactions on Computer Systems 1:1 (February, 1983) pp. 3-23.

Ries, D. "The Effect of Concurrency Control on the Performance of a Distributed Database Management System," Proceedings of the Berkeley Workshop on Distributed Data Management and Computer Networks (1979) pp. 75-112.

Rothnie, J. et. al. "Introduction to a System for Distributed Databases (SDD-1)," ACM Transactions on Database Systems 5:1 (March, 1980) pp. 1-17.

Rothnie, J. and N. Goodman. "A Survey of Research and Development in Distributed Database Management," Proceedings of the International Conference on Very Large Databases (1977) pp. 48-62.

Schlageter, G. "Optimistic Methods for Concurrency Control in Distributed Database Systems," Proceedings of the International Conference on Very Large Data Bases (1981).

Skeen, D., F. Cristian, and A. El Abbadi. "An Efficient Fault-tolerant Algorithm for Replicated Data Management," Proceedings of the ACM Symposium on Principles of Database Systems (1985) pp. 215-229.

Skeen, D. and M. Stonebraker. "A Formal Model of Crash Recovery in a Distributed System," Proceedings Berkeley Workshop on Distributed Database Systems (1981) pp. 129-142.

Skeen, D. and D. Wright. "Increasing Availability in Partitioned Database Systems," Proceedings of the ACM Symposium on Principles of Database Systems (1984) pp. 290-299.

Thomas, R. "A Majority Consensus Approach to Concurrency Control," ACM Transactions on Database Systems 4:2 (June, 1978) pp. 180-219.

Traiger, I, J. Gray, C. Galtieri, and B. Lindsay. "Transactions and Consistency in Distributed Database Management Systems," ACM Transactions on Database Systems 7:3 (September, 1982) pp. 323-342.

SAMPLE PROJECT: PLANNING THE DISTRIBUTION OF THE RELATIONAL DATABASE FOR CLERICALTEMPS

We will assume that ClericalTemps has expanded to four locations, a main office and three branches. We want to distribute the database among these locations. We use the set of normalized relations developed in Chapter 7 as a global schema and use the steps that follow to plan the distribution of the database. The global schema is

```
WORKER (EMPID, EMPNAME, SSN, EMPADD, EMPPHONE, DOB, SEX, DATEHIRED,
LASTDATEWORKED, AVERRATING, WORDPROC, TYPING, FILING, BOOKKPING, STENO,
AVAILCODE)

CLIENT (CLID, CLNAME, CLADD, CLPHONE, CONTACT, BILLINGYTD,
PAYMENTSYTD)
```

```
JOB (JOB#, CLID, JOBTITLE, STARTDATE, EXPECTENDDATE, DAILYRATE,
DAILYHOURS, REPORTTONAME, REPORTTOADD, REPORTTOPHONE, JOBSTATUS)

PAYROLL (CHECK#, EMPID, PAYDATE, GROSS, FED, FICA, STATE, LOCAL,
GROSSYTD, FEDYTD, FICAYTD, STATEYTD, LOCALYTD)

BILL (INVOICE#, CLID, BILLDATE, OLDBAL, TOTCHARGES, TOTPAID)

ASSIGNMENT (JOB#, EMPID, RATERNAME, RATINGDATE, EMPRATING)
```

Step 15.1:

Write out a set of end-user locations and the applications performed at each.

Applications performed at branch offices:

(1) Maintaining worker records
(2) Maintaining client records
(3) Entering job requests
(4) Matching workers to jobs
(5) Entering worker evaluations
(6) Producing client reports
(7) Producing worker reports
(8) Producing reports of current assignments

Applications performed at main office only:

(9) Producing accounts receivable report
(10) Producing weekly client bill
(11) Entering client payments
(12) Producing weekly payroll report
(13) Producing worker pay stub and paycheck
(14) Producing end-of-year wage and tax statement

Step 15.2:

For each application, decide what data is required.

(1) Maintaining worker records–Worker table
(2) Maintaining client records–Client table
(3) Entering job requests–Job table
(4) Matching workers to jobs–Job table and Worker table
(5) Entering worker evaluations–Assignment table
(6) Producing client reports–Client table
(7) Producing worker reports–Worker, Job, and Assignment tables

(8) Producing current assignments reports–Worker, Client, Job, and Assignment tables
(9) Producing accounts receivable report–Client and Job tables
(10) Producing weekly client bill–Client and Job tables
(11) Entering client payments–Client and Bill tables
(12) Producing weekly payroll report–Worker, Payroll, Job, and Assignment tables
(13) Producing worker pay stub and paycheck–Worker, Payroll, Job, and Assignment tables
(14) Producing end-of-year wage and tax statement–Payroll and Worker tables

Step 15.3:

Using the normalized tables, perform selection and projection operations to create the set of vertical, horizontal, and mixed data fragments needed for each end user and application.

Worker table: Each branch office requires records of workers registered at that branch. If we use a code for the branch as part of the EMPID, a horizontal subset can be chosen by taking only those rows having the appropriate branch code for each location. We call these fragments Worker1, Worker2, and Worker3. The main office also requires the entire Worker table.

Client table: Each branch needs records of clients who place job requests at that branch. A branch code can be introduced in CLID to identify the appropriate branch, and a horizontal fragment can be identified for each branch. The main office requires the entire Client table. The fragments are called Client1, Client2, and Client3.

Job table: Each branch requires records of jobs placed at that branch. The corresponding fragments are called Job1, Job2, and Job3. The main office needs job records for reports. If a job can be filled by a worker from another branch, that branch needs access to the job record.

Payroll table: The main office needs the entire Payroll table.

Bill table: The main office needs the entire Bill table.

Assignment table: Each branch office needs records of assignments for its own jobs and workers. The fragments are called Assign1, Assign2, and Assign3. The main office needs assignment records for reports.

Step 15.4:

For each fragment that is required at more than one user or application location, decide whether the fragment can be replicated, by considering frequency of use and of update.

Worker table: Keep primary copy at the site where the worker is registered. Keep another copy at the main site. The main site copy of worker records from branches can be updated weekly, since it is needed there primarily for weekly payroll processing or annual W2 forms.

Client table: Use the same scheme as for the Worker table. The main office uses its copy primarily for weekly bills and payment records. The main office should send weekly updates of BILLINGYTD and PAYMENTSYTD to branch offices.

Job table: Use the same scheme as for the Worker table. Each branch should send weekly updates to the main site for payroll and billing.

Payroll table: The entire Payroll table should be kept at the main office.

Bill table: The Bill table should be kept at the main office.

Assignment table: The primary copy of assignment records should be kept at the office where the job was entered, and a second copy should be kept at the main office. In the rare event that a worker from a different branch was assigned to the job, another copy should be kept there. Updates should be sent weekly to the main office.

Step 15.5:

Use a matrix to make a table showing a geographical network, listing nodes, applications at each, and data fragments at each.

See Figure 15.9 for the geographical network for ClericalTemps.

Step 15.6:

For each application in the geographical network, determine whether access will be local, remote, or compound. Make up a table showing each site, the number of programs or end users requiring local access, the number requiring remote access, and the number requiring compound access.

All applications shown in the geographical network for ClericalTemps require local access only. In the rare event of matching a worker to a job assignment at another branch, there is remote access. The requesting node sends data about the job to the branch, where the searching process takes place. Data about the worker(s) matched is returned to the requesting node. Worker assignment and evaluation data is returned to the worker's branch.

Step 15.7:

For each of the nonlocal accesses, identify the user or application and the location of the data. Estimate the number of accesses required per day. If it is high, justify your choice of nonlocal storage.

The only nonlocal access is matching a worker to a job at another branch. The number of such accesses is less than one per day.

Step 15.8:

Make any adjustments indicated by your analysis of applications and traffic, and plan a final geographical network.

There is no need to adjust the geographical network shown in Figure 15.9.

Student Project: Planning for Distribution

For the project you have chosen, assume that the processing is to be distributed to at least four locations. Identify the applications that will be performed at each of the locations, and then follow the steps shown in the Sample Project to plan the distribution of your database.

Nodes				
Application	Main	Branch 1	Branch 2	Branch 3
(1)	Worker	Worker1	Worker2	Worker3
(2)	Client	Client1	Client2	Client3
(3)	Job	Job1	Job2	Job3
(4)		Job1 Worker1	Job2 Worker 2	Job3 Worker3
(5)		Assign1	Assign2	Assign3
(6)		Client1	Client2	Client3
(7)		Worker1 Job1 Assign1	Worker2 Job2 Assign2	Worker3 Job3 Assign3
(8)		Worker1 Job1 Client1 Assign1	Worker2 Job2 Client2 Assign2	Worker3 Job3 Client3 Assign3
(9)	Client Job			
(10)	Client Job			
(11)	Client Bill			
(12)	Worker Payroll Job Assignment			
(13)	Worker Payroll Job Assignment			
(14)	Payroll Worker			

Figure 15.9 Geographical Network for ClericalTemps

CHAPTER

16

Database Machines

16 Chapter Objectives

In this chapter you will learn

- why back-end processors are used
- the functions database machines perform
- possible database machine configurations
- how a storage hierarchy may be designed and used
- the advantages of using multiple back-end processors
- advantages and potential disadvantages of database machines
- some examples of current database machines

16.1 *Back-end Processors*

The function of a **back-end processor** or **database machine** is similar to that of a **front-end communications processor**. It is common to use a dedicated front-end processor for communications functions. The front end controls all communications between the user and the host. It handles different transmission speeds, allows various encoding methods, performs error detection and correction, regularly polls terminals for messages, routes messages from the host, and manages the flow of message traffic between the host and terminals. Since the host computer does not need to perform these functions, it is freed to do other tasks. The efficiency of the host is greatly enhanced by this offloading of some of its workload to the front end.

Similarly, a back-end database machine is a dedicated processor that handles all database access. This frees the host for other tasks, improves database performance, and can provide other advantages such as improved data security. Some of the functions that database machines perform are:

- They accept user requests for data and do the usual mapping and interpretation tasks of the DBMS to identify the stored records needed.
- They check user authorization and perform other security checks.
- They identify the physical records needed.
- They choose the path that will be used to access data.
- They provide concurrency control, integrity enforcement, and recovery systems.
- They control the physical storage devices on which the data resides.
- They direct actual data access.
- They prepare retrieved data for users.

A database machine can offer dramatic database performance improvements because it can use hardware specifically designed for database operations. Since the back-end processor is dedicated to database operations, its operating system does not have to provide support for the whole range of functions a general purpose host computer must offer, thereby reducing its overhead. If the only function of the back end is to accept data requests from the host and perform the requested operations on the database, it is possible to microcode many of the operations and to use specialized architecture and storage devices that maximize performance and minimize cost.

Figure 16.1 shows a conventional system having a front end and a general-purpose computer without a back end. Here, the front end is responsible for communications, while the general-purpose computer runs the usual system software, the applications programs, and the DBMS. When database data is needed, the host is responsible for processing the data request and managing the device controllers so that the requested data can be retrieved from disk. When a back end is introduced, as shown in Figure 16.2, the entire DBMS can be moved to the dedicated processor. The database machine accepts requests from the host computer, its DBMS translates the requests into operations to be performed on the database, and its device controllers retrieve the data from storage devices. It then returns the requested data to the host. The host computer itself does not control the devices on which the database resides. This frees the host to do other processing while database operations are being performed. Note that the host may control storage devices for files that are not part of the database. These may be needed for applications that do not access the database.

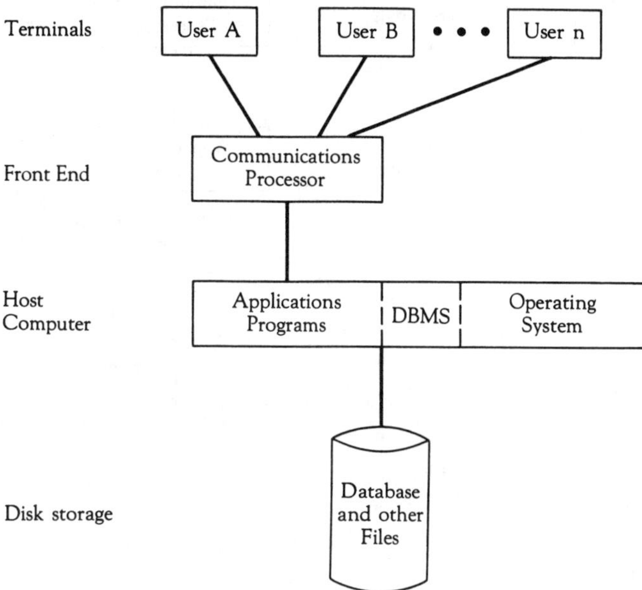

Figure 16.1 Conventional System with Front End but no Back End

Although we have pictured the database machine as containing the entire DBMS, different architectures are possible. Figure 16.3 shows various configurations for database machines, ignoring the front end and nondatabase files.

1. In Figure 16.3(a) we show a **general-purpose computer used as a back end** dedicated to database management. The back end, which may be a minicomputer, acts as a slave for the mainframe host. The slave contains the DBMS and performs all the usual data management functions, including the management of device controllers, except that it does not provide a user interface. The host contains the user interface, but passes any database requests in unprocessed form to the slave.
2. Figure 16.3(b) shows a **special-purpose computer used as a back end**. Here, the back end has been tailored by modifying the operating system and by microcoding some of the DBMS software to speed data searching. Microcoding allows selected operations such as the JOIN to be performed rapidly in the main memory of the back end, using patterns that are determined in advance. The back end is responsible for management of the device controllers and has no user interface.
3. In Figure 16.3(c) we show an **intelligent controller** used to perform selected functions of the DBMS. In this configuration, the host computer contains most of the DBMS, but the intelligent control unit does the low-level data management

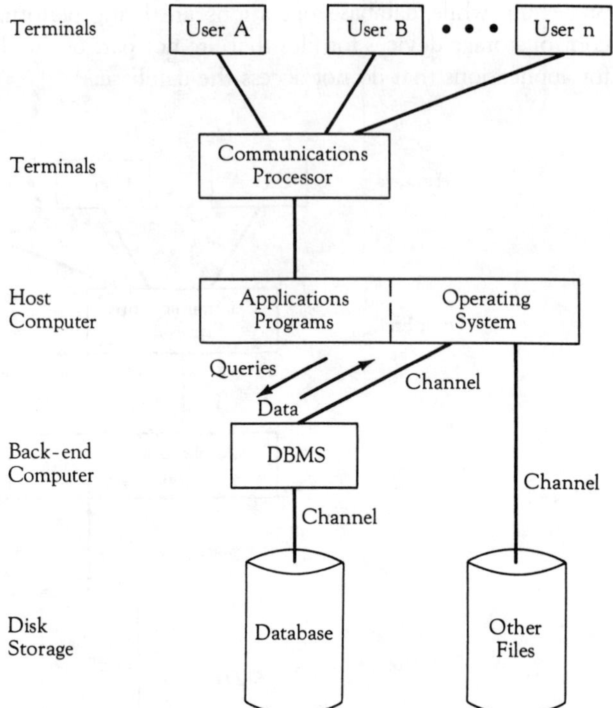

Figure 16.2 System with Front End and Back End

functions. It may do **associative processing** (described in Section 16.2), which handles the logical to physical mapping. The intelligent controller may have several microprocessors that can perform functions such as parallel searching of large storage areas. Having some of the DBMS logic in the controller allows searching on the basis of data content, data qualification and error correction, sorting, and other data processing functions to be done by the control unit. Higher-level DBMS functions still reside in the host computer.

4. Figure 16.3(d) shows a **specialized back-end computer and an intelligent controller**, combining the features of the two previous configurations. Here, the DBMS resides in the back-end computer, which has a specialized operating system and microcoding that allows rapid main-memory data operations. In addition, the intelligent controller uses associative processing and provides logic for searching in the database.
5. Any of the previous configurations could be modified in a network environment so that the back end can serve as a slave to **several hosts**. Figure 16.3(e) shows a system with several general-purpose host computers and a single specialized database computer, which has an intelligent controller. Variations of this configuration would include replacing the specialized database computer by a dedicated general-purpose computer or providing a user interface for the database computer so that it could receive on-line queries from terminal users.

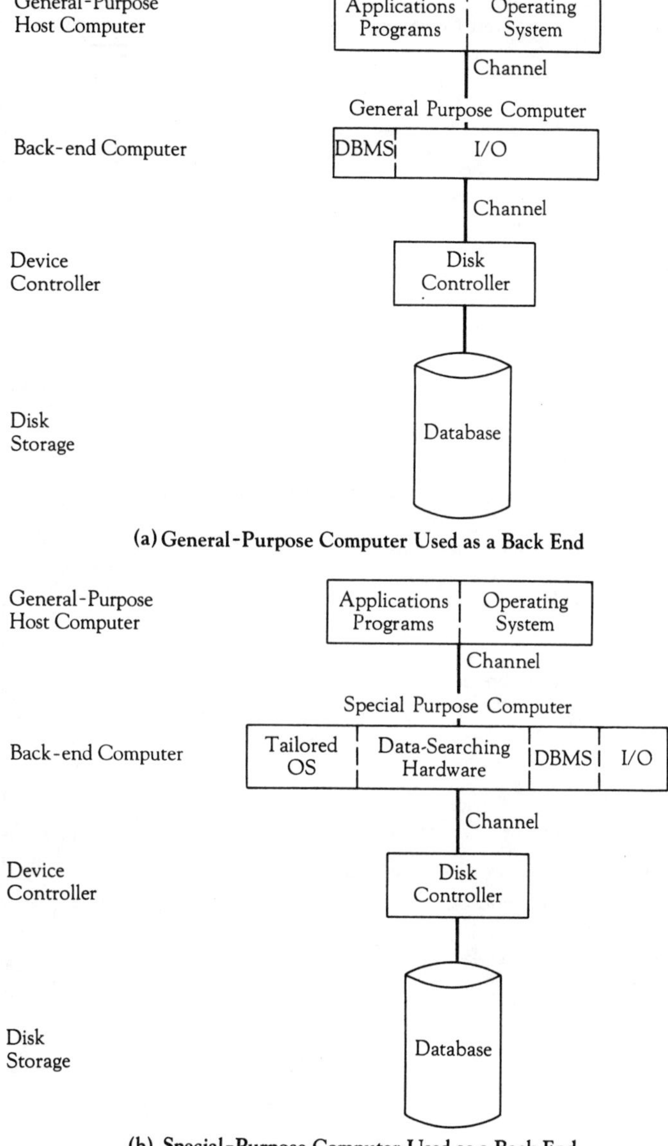

Figure 16.3 Architectures for Database Computers

16.2 *Associative Processors*

An **associative processor** or **content-addressable processor** performs the logical to physical mapping. It is capable of finding data by value rather than by address. We would like to be able to search the database as if there were a fixed read/write head for every

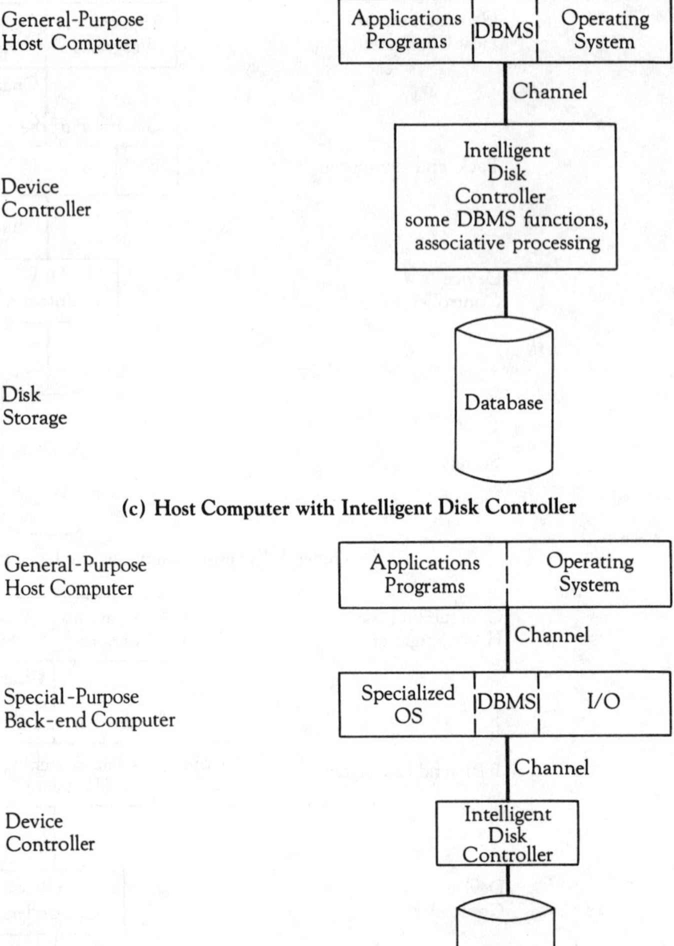

(c) Host Computer with Intelligent Disk Controller

(d) Specialized Back-end Computer and Intelligent Controller

Figure 16.3 *(continued)*

track, and the read/write head had a microprocessor so that it could perform comparison operations right on the track. This would allow us to find records that we want by direct examination of their values rather than by address. One way to implement this is to use **parallel associative storage**, which allows a large storage unit to be searched in parallel. This can use an array of processing elements, with each element operating on a partition of the database. Another implementation uses cache memory, which is referred to in this context as **content-addressable memory**. A third implementation uses **serial associative storage**, in which a storage unit can be searched serially for qualified data, meaning that only those items that meet the search criteria are retrieved.

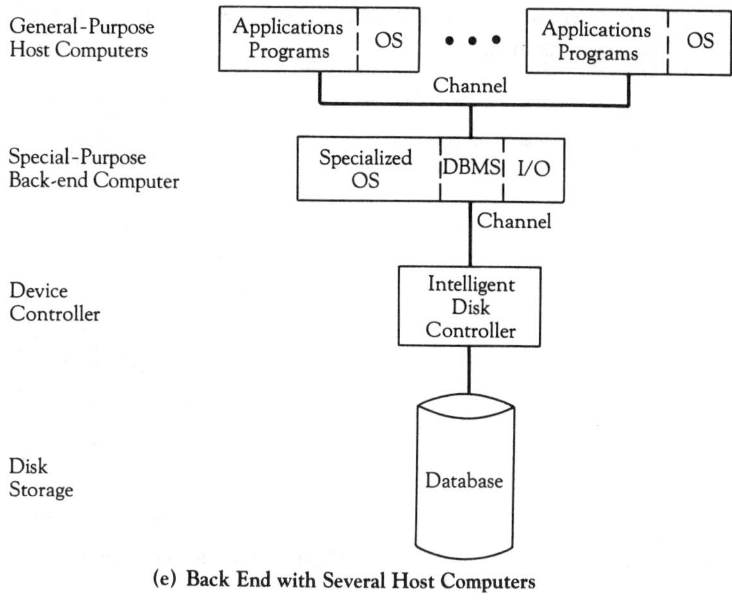

(e) Back End with Several Host Computers

Figure 16.3 *(continued)*

16.3 *Storage Hierarchies*

A **storage hierarchy** consists of several types of storage devices, ranging from very fast and expensive to comparatively slow and cheap. Figure 16.4 shows a general-purpose host computer with a back end that manages a range of storage devices. Fastest access is to the processor cache, a portion of the CPU that holds the records or indexes needed most often. Access to these is almost instantaneous. Slightly slower access is provided to main storage, where records are swapped into and out of buffers as needed. Below this, portions of the database are kept on secondary storage devices. The fastest of these peripheral devices, which may be a fixed-head disk or other fast device, forms the disk cache. This holds pages that are needed frequently. Below this is regular disk storage, which holds pages having average rates of access. At the bottom end is mass storage, which holds records that are needed infrequently. Access times for these records may be a few seconds, because extensive staging is required to retrieve them. In an ideal environment, data **percolates** or moves automatically to faster devices as it is accessed more often. For example, in an airline reservation system, reservation records for flights three months from today may be kept in regular disk storage. As the date nears, they may be moved to a faster device because they will be accessed more often. Once the flight is over, the reservation records will rarely be needed, so they can be moved to mass storage. A database machine may be able to handle this staging automatically, either by periodic moving of records on the basis of rules such as "Reservations for flights within the next 10 days go to disk cache," or on the basis of statistics about record accesses. This creates a self-managing storage hierarchy under the control of the database machine.

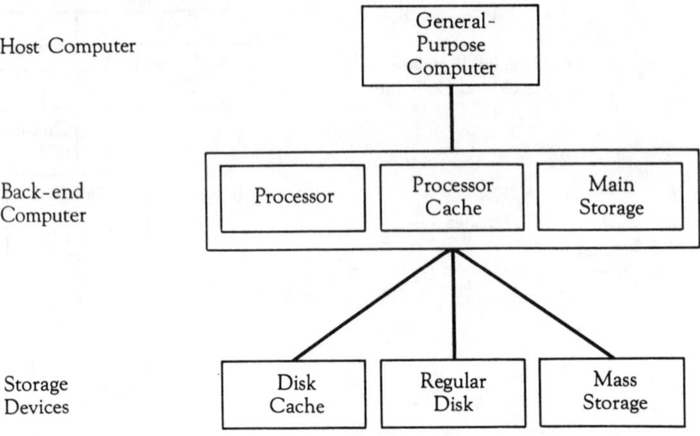

Figure 16.4 Storage Hierarchy

16.4 *Parallel Back Ends*

Figure 16.3(e) showed a configuration in which a single back end served multiple hosts. It is also possible to have multiple back ends serving either a single host or multiple hosts, as shown in Figure 16.5. This architecture introduces redundancy both in the hardware components and in the communication links between the components. This is desirable for environments where reliability is a very high priority. In the single-back-end configuration, failure of the back end itself or of the link to the back end results in the unavailability of the database. When there are multiple back ends, as in Figure 16.5, the built-in redundancy ensures the survivability of the database despite failure of a processor or a communication line. The more processors and the more lines involved, the more reliable the system. Our example shows two host computers which are linked by a programmable switch to three back-end processors. The back-end processors are linked to one another and are able to communicate directly. The back ends serve as backups for one another, so that if one fails there are still two processors that can perform its tasks. A programmable switch connects the processors to database files. We show three separate devices holding the database files. To achieve maximum reliability, we could require that these contain three separate copies of the complete database. We note that any update must then be made to all three copies, because this is essentially a fully replicated distributed database. If the data is fully replicated, each storage device also has two backups, so the data remains available despite one or two device failures. A slightly less reliable system would keep only one copy of each item, but partition the data over the three devices. Processing of the unaffected portions can still continue despite the failure of one device.

The multiple-back-end configuration may appear to be a waste of resources except when failure occurs. However, multiple processors can be used to share the processing

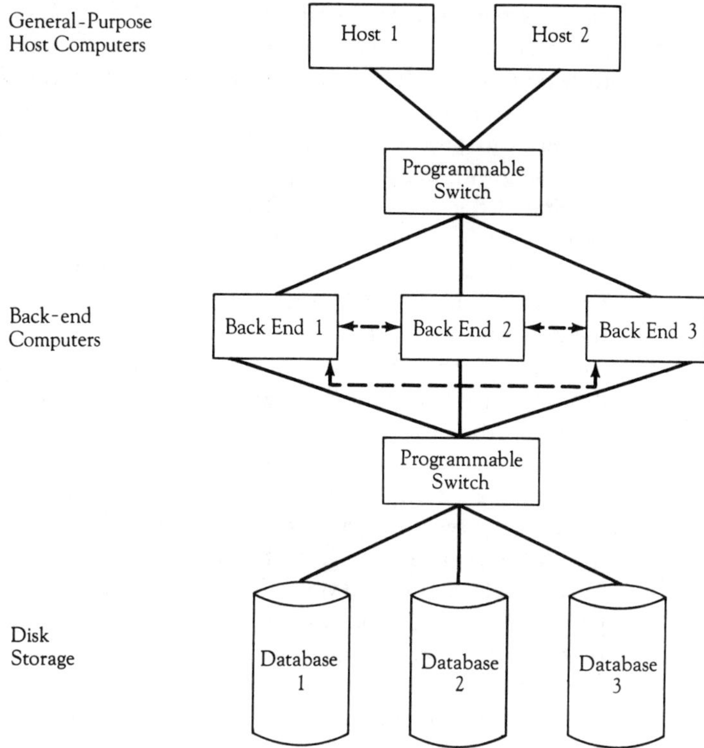

Figure 16.5 Multiple Back Ends

load and provide greater overall processing power. When a database request is made by either of the two hosts, the request is switched to the back end that is idle or has the least amount of work, so that **load balancing** or automatic sharing of work among the three back ends is accomplished. In the event of failure of a back end or of a link to or from a back end, the load is shifted to the two surviving processors. The result is that the user may be unaware of the failure, except that response time will be slower.

16.5 Rationale for Database Machines

Depending on the configuration chosen, database machines can provide the following benefits:

1. **Greater performance at lower cost.** A specialized database computer can provide efficient storage management and superior database performance at a relatively low price. The specialized smaller operating system and the microcoding of operations allow vendors to offer these devices at an attractive price. Since the host computer is performing other operations while database operations are being done, parallel processing is possible, improving overall system performance. In addition, the host

main memory that was occupied by the DBMS is now freed for other uses. This performance boost and freeing of resources may allow an expensive system upgrade to be postponed. The back end itself can be tuned or upgraded without affecting the host, as long as the interface remains the same. This allows vendors of database machines to take advantage of the newest technology for storage and database processing with minimal disruption.

2. **Sharing of the database.** The database machine can act as a back end for several hosts, allowing all users to share the same database. The back end provides the data service and handles concurrency control for all the hosts.
3. **Improved security and integrity.** If the database machine has no user interface, the only access to it is through the host computer requests. Since it controls the database files, there is no way clever programmers can bypass the DBMS and access database files directly through the operating system, as there would be if the DBMS resided in the host computer. This benefit is possible only if the database files do not share devices with files directly under the control of the host. Security may also be more economical if several hosts use the same back end, since the back end provides the security service for all of them. The same is true of integrity, since the back end can do integrity checking for all the hosts.
4. **Greater selection of DBMS's.** If a particular DBMS cannot run on the general-purpose computer, it may run on a database machine that could connect with the host. This allows a designer more options if the selection of DBMSs to run on the host is very limited. In practice, vendors of database machines design their processors to run on only the most popular hosts, so this advantage may be difficult to realize.
5. **Flexibility.** Various configurations of hosts and back ends are possible, allowing the DBA to choose the one that best fits the needs of the organization. Several hosts can be connected to a single database machine, permitting the data resource to be shared. If one or more hosts are connected to several back ends, parallel database operations are possible, and load balancing can result in even greater performance gains. Reliability is also increased by the redundancy introduced.

There are also potential disadvantages of database machines:

1. **There is greater vulnerability.** Introducing a second computer into a configuration increases the likelihood of hardware failure, simply because there is another unit to fail. If there is a single back end that handles all database processing, its failure means that the database is unavailable. This can be overcome if there are multiple back ends or if the host is capable of taking over the database processing while the back end is down.
2. **Potential cost benefits may not be realized.** If the amount of database processing is too small, offloading it from the mainframe may be a mistake. In order for the cost benefits to be realized, nearly half of all processing should be database access. The back end itself may be quite costly, and its usefulness may be limited because of its specialized function, unless the environment is data-intensive.
3. **Additional communications are necessary.** Although a back end may speed up overall query processing, the processing of a particular query may in fact be slower

because there is additional communications overhead between the host and the back end. Requests for data must be sent from the host and responses to queries must come back from the database machine. This adds a new communications layer to the system.

4. **Support is more complex.** Since the database machine and the host may be purchased from different vendors, if a problem occurs, it may be difficult to identify responsibility for fixing it. Because the mainframe vendor may blame the back end and the back-end vendor blame the mainframe, support is more complex.
5. **The database machine can create a bottleneck.** If several hosts are connected to the same back end, it may become overloaded, and the resulting slowing of data into and out of the database machine may slow down all the hosts.
6. **The database machine may become technically obsolete.** If the back end is purchased from an independent vendor, it may be difficult to upgrade when new models of the host computer become available, since the back-end vendor may not have the commitment to product development to keep up with new models of the host. Even when the commitment is there, there will be a lag before the back end can catch up. If the back-end vendor is not responsive to developments in storage and processing technology, the buyer may be stuck with old technology.

16.6 *Examples of Database Machines*

16.6.1 *Britton-Lee IDM*

One of the first commercial database machines was Britton-Lee's **Intelligent Database Machine (IDM)**, announced in 1981. It was an integrated hardware and software system, using a back end especially designed for database management and a DBMS based on INGRES. It supported several mainframes, including the DEC VAX and PDP-11, IBM 370, 4300, and 308X/309X series computers. IDM used its own language, **IDL** (Intelligent Database Language) to create and manipulate the database. IDM provided transaction management, query optimization, cached data, security, concurrency control, backup and recovery, and audit trailing. It had a specially modified operating system for data access, several microprocessors for specific tasks, a database accelerator to speed execution of common processes, disk cache for frequently used pages, and B-tree indexes for any number of columns.

Britton-Lee has since announced several improved versions of its pioneering system. In 1988, the **BL8000 Shared Database System** became available. The BL8000 hardware is a specially designed back-end computer, and the **Integrated Database Manager (IDM)** software is made up of a front-end component that runs on the host computer and a back-end component that runs on the BL8000. Figure 16.6 shows the overall

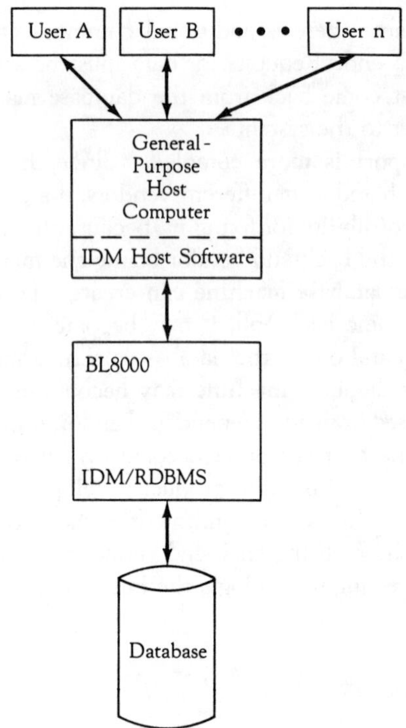

Figure 16.6 System Architecture for Britton-Lee BL8000 Shared Database System

system architecture for the BL8000 Shared Database System. The BL8000 back-end, running the **IDM RDBMS** (Relational Database Management System), provides access to data that can be shared by multiple host computers, including IBM mainframes, IBM PCs, DEC, AT&T, and Sun systems. The base configuration of the BL8000 back-end computer is shown in Figure 16.7 and includes the following components:

1. A **Relational Database Processor**, which is a 32-bit **RISC (Reduced Instruction Set Computer)** processor optimized for database operations. It consists of 256 registers, organized into 16 sets of 16 registers. It uses register switching for most subroutine calls, allowing subroutines to execute many times faster than if registers were saved and restored from memory.
2. A two-megabyte **Procedure Memory,** consisting of fast static RAM chips. This contains all the code of the BL8000 simplified operating system and the database management system (RDBMS) in what is essentially a big cache. It is used by the Relational Database Processor, and is connected to it by the **Procedure Memory Bus**, an 80-megabyte per second bus dedicated to Database Processor/Procedure Memory instruction transfer that provides an access time to the memory banks of 50 nanoseconds.
3. A **Data Memory**, a cache memory consisting of up to sixteen 16-megabyte data memory boards to hold data, tables, and indexes during processing. This RAM is large enough to allow all the data for some applications to remain in main memory

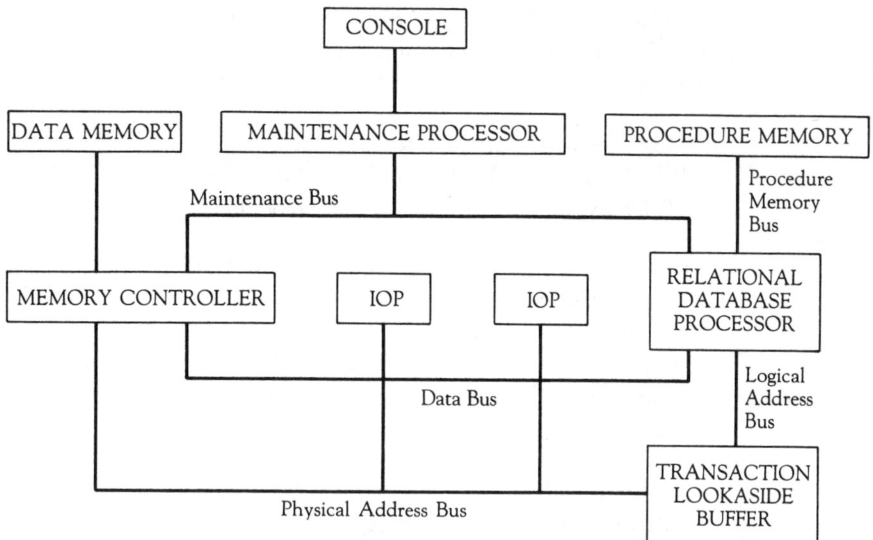

Figure 16.7 Base Configuration of BL8000

during processing, thus speeding up execution. It is entirely separate from Procedure Memory.

4. A **Memory Controller Board** to manage the Data Memory pool. There is a memory protection scheme that allows each process to write only to memory assigned to it. This prevents a lower-level process from modifying data from a higher-level process.
5. A **Maintenance Processor**, which is an AT&T PC6300 Plus dedicated to monitoring the system. Each board in the system has error detection schemes that pass information about errors to the Maintenance Processor by way of a **Maintenance Bus**. The Maintenance Processor then logs the error on hard disk, diagnoses it, and attempts to correct it. A console displays information about system errors and other events. The Maintenance Processor is responsible for loading system software, running diagnostics, logging errors, displaying console output, and reading console input, among other tasks.
6. At least two **I/O Processors (IOPs)**, each of which is a board having a Motorola 68020 chip, two Intel 8032 chips, and a local memory buffer. The IOPs are responsible for all data transfer between the peripherals and the Data Memory, and operate independently of the main processor. Each IOP manages two **Small Computer System Interface (SCSI)** buses.
7. The **Transaction Lookaside Buffer (TLB),** which translates logical addresses provided by the Database Processor into physical addresses used by the Data Memory System.
8. Five specialized buses, including a **Data Bus**, a **Logical Address Bus**, a **Physical Address Bus**, a **Maintenance Bus**, and a **Procedure Memory Bus**.
9. **Disk and memory support**. Each BL8000 can currently access up to 56 spindles, holding about 40 gigabytes of data and up to 256 megabytes of memory addresses, which allows the system to keep frequently used pages in main memory. Britton-Lee claims the architecture can handle up to 150 spindles.

The **Integrated Database Manager (IDM)** software has both front-end software which resides in the host computer and back-end software which runs on the BL8000. The major software components in IDM are the following:

1. **Host-Resident Software** for popular computers and operating systems, including IBM VM/CMS, IBM PC DOS and MS DOS, DEC VAX VMS and UNIX, AT&T 3B family, Apollo, and SUN. IDM supplies:

   - Two query languages, standard **SQL** and **IDL** (Intelligent Data Language), a variant of QUEL developed by Britton-Lee.
   - Support for several **fourth generation language (4GL) tools** from other vendors, including **FOCUS** from IBI, **PC/SQL** Link from Micro Decisionware, **Omnibase** from Signal Technology, Inc., **JAM** from JYACC, and **Freeform** from Dimension Software Systems, Inc.
   - **IDM/Applications Development Facility,** which provides support for applications written in high-level programming languages.
   - **IDM/DBA,** a set of utilities for the DBA.
   - **IDM/Network**, communication software that links the IDM host resident software or 4GL and RDBMS, the back-end relational database management system.

2. **IDM/RDBMS Software for the BL8000**. This is the basic database management system for the BL8000 back end, and it does the following:

   - Supplies the basic data management services.
   - Maintains the data dictionary.
   - Performs the database queries.
   - Manages concurrent use of the database.
   - Supervises backup and recovery operations.
   - Provides utilities for disk maintenance, including disk formatting, mirror copying, dump/load, and database checker routines that are done on-line without database shutdown.
   - Provides a security system beyond the host security subsystem, requiring user identification and validation, and makes its storage devices unavailable except through the RDBMS.
   - Manages process scheduling and resource sharing.
   - Provides performance-monitoring tools for the DBA.
   - Provides transaction control, logging, and automatic recovery.
   - Allows mirrored disks to provide intact images of critical data to protect it from loss.
   - Provides a system called the **SAFE** disk, which replaces journal rollback and can guarantee rapid system restart regardless of the size of the database. The SAFE disk is used to take snapshots of the entire Data Memory periodically, so that it can be reloaded at restart. In addition, a transaction log is kept.
   - Provides read/write locking of shared data, including **Read Through Locks**, a locking technique that maximizes concurrency.

Figure 16.8 shows the software tools available for the BL8000 system.

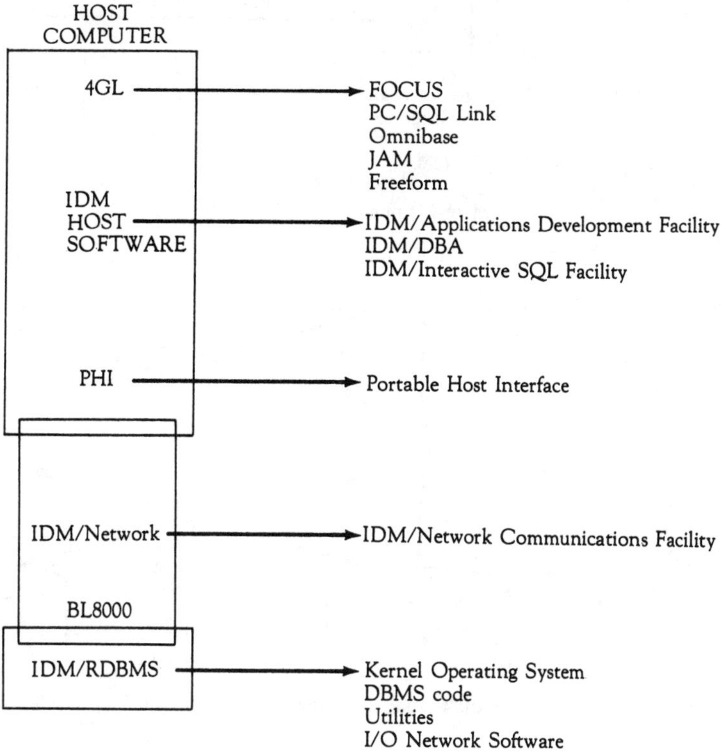

Figure 16.8 Software Tools for BL8000

16.6.2 *Tandem Non-Stop Architecture*

The **Tandem Non-Stop System** was introduced in the early 1980s. It is designed to provide high performance and reliability by duplication of components. The basic hardware consists of between two and 16 processors which communicate with one another by means of an **Inter-Processor Bus**. Each processor module contains a central processing unit, a main memory, an I/O channel, and an Inter-Processor Bus interface. Figure 16.9 shows an overview of the architecture of the Tandem system. In this diagram, each processor can control a disk controller, but only one processor at a time actually controls it. The processors act as backups for each other. Each process or application is assigned to one primary processor and a backup processor, which can take over execution if the primary one fails. This duplication of processing units increases reliability. Reliability is further increased by writing all data to two disks, so that processing can continue even if a disk failure occurs.

The original group of Tandem database products are collectively called **ENCOMPASS**. The group includes

- **ENSCRIBE**, a relational database manager that supports key-sequenced, entry-sequenced, and relative files.

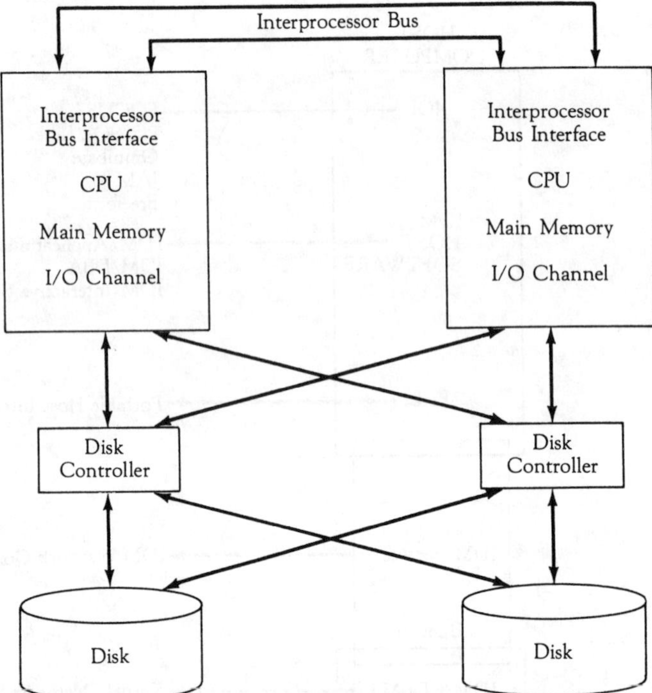

Figure 16.9 Overview of Tandem Non-Stop System Architecture

- **DDL**, a data definition language that allows the DBA to define the database objects. Structures are stored in a data dictionary.
- **ENFORM**, a nonprocedural query language.
- **PATHWAY**, a facility that provides an interface for designing and controlling transactions.
- **TMF**, which manages transactions and recovery.

Using its network software, **EXPAND**, along with ENCOMPASS, Tandem was one of the pioneers in the development of distributed databases.

In 1988, Tandem added **NON-STOP SQL**, a distributed relational database management system. It uses the standard Tandem Non-Stop architecture having up to 16 processors connected by high-speed buses to form a system or a node of a system. Clusters of such nodes can be connected by communications links to provide a modular system. Hardware and software redundancy features such as alternative physical paths to I/O devices, mirrored disks, and pairing of processors are preserved in Non-Stop SQL. Non-Stop SQL runs under the Guardian operating system. It is not compatible with the Encompass products, but it can run on the same system, using the same file system, disk manager, and transaction log. Both SQL and Enscribe statements can appear in the same application program. Non-Stop SQL components include the following:

- **SQLCI (SQL Conversational Interface)**, which provides interactive execution of SQL statements, on-line help for users, diagnostic messages, and a report writer. It is written in **TAL, Tandem Application Language**.

- **Program interfaces** for **COBOL, Pascal,** and **C** programs.
- The **SQL Compiler,** which devises an optimized access plan for each SQL statement.
- The **SQL Executor**, which executes both DML and DDL statements.
- The **Catalog Manager,** which handles all changes to the distributed dictionary, an active integrated data dictionary.
- A set of **utility programs** that allow conversion to and from Enscribe files, generate where-used reports for tables and views, perform file management operations, update database statistics, and perform backup and restore operations.
- **PATHMAKER**, a code generator that may be used for screen generation.
- A **File System** to handle the physical schema.
- A set of **disk processes** to manage disk volumes.
- Access to **TMF**, Tandem's transaction and recovery manager.
- Measurement and tuning tools such as **EXPLAIN**, a facility that shows a query plan, **MEASURE**, a performance monitor, and statistics for all SQL operations.

Non-Stop SQL provides location transparency for distributed database users.

16.6.3 *Teradata DBC/1012*

Model 1 of this system was announced in 1984 as a back end for the IBM 370 mainframe series. A minimal configuration for this system is pictured in Figure 16.10. It has multiple processors, called Access Module Processors, that manage disk storage units each holding up to 500 megabytes. Data is distributed on the storage units in such a way that all are involved in answering a query. The mainframe communicates with the Access Module Processors through a set of Interface Processors. These receive queries from the host and do the translation process before handing the request to the Access Modules. They also prepare and format the response for the host. The entire system is linked by an intelligent network, which routes messages between the Interface Processors and the Access Module Processors and also contains logic to assist in database queries. The system allows designers to add additional microprocessor subsystems as needed.

In 1988 Teradata announced the DBC/1012 Model 3, an Intel 80386-based processor capable of supporting very large databases. It uses parallel CPUs to process SQL queries. It interfaces with a variety of mainframe, minicomputer, workstation, and personal computer systems. The system can be configured with from three to 1024 processors, allowing processor speed to approach three billion instructions per second. Each of the processors has at least four megabytes of dynamic RAM, expandable to eight megabytes. Disk cache is used to boost response time. The new Model 3 is hardware and software compatible with the Intel 80286-based Model 2. The system is highly modular, allowing additional processing modules and storage units to be added as needed. The basic system components are

- **TDP**, Teradata Director Program, host-resident software that manages activity between the host and the back end. If there are multiple hosts, there must be one TDP for each host.

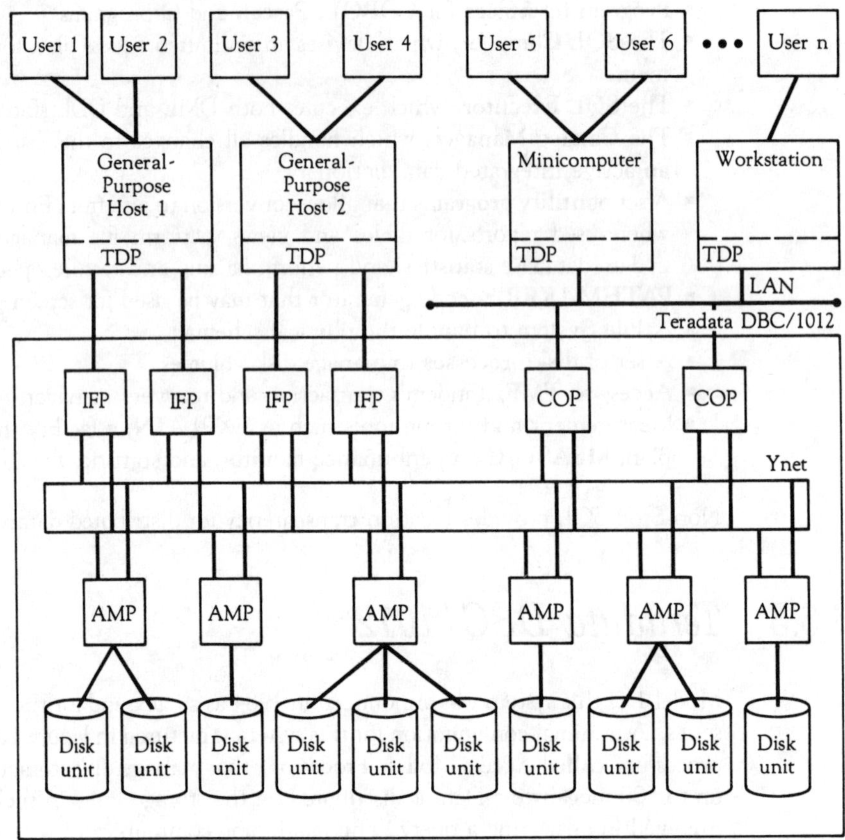

Figure 16.10 Minimal Configuration for Teradata DBC 1012

- **IFPs**, Interface Processors, that receive data requests from mainframes, interpret them, route subrequests, and coordinate responses for users. There must be at least two IFPs per host. Each has a channel interface controller, a processor, and two interfaces to the bus.
- **COPs**, Communication Processors, that receive, interpret, and route data requests from minicomputers, workstations, or personal computers. Each COP has a LAN adapter, a CPU, and two bus interfaces.
- **AMPs**, Access Module Processors, that manipulate the data base. Each AMP manages up to four disk units.
- **Disk storage units**, high-volume Winchester disks on which the database is partitioned for parallel processing. A two-megabyte disk cache is available for each AMP, and primary and secondary copies of important data can be made.
- **Ynet**, an intelligent bus that receives messages from IFPs or COPs, broadcasts work messages to the AMPs, manages communications among AMPs, merges results of subrequests, and sends data back to IFPs or COPs. The system requires

two Ynets that serve as backups for each other. The Ynet can interconnect up to 1024 processors.

Teradata and several third-party vendors also supply a variety of host software packages for use with the system.

16.7 Chapter Summary

Just as a dedicated **front-end communications processor** is used to offload some of the host's workload, a **back-end machine dedicated to database processing** can handle all database access. A database machine accepts user requests, identifies the stored records needed, performs user authorization, checks security, identifies physical records needed, chooses a data access path, controls concurrency, enforces integrity, directs database recovery, controls the physical storage devices, directs actual data access, and prepares retrieved data for users. A dedicated database machine can offer superior performance because it uses a relatively simple operating system, specialized architecture and storage devices, and microcoding of operations.

There are several possible configurations for database machines, using various combinations of general-purpose or special-purpose computers, intelligent controllers, one or more hosts, and one or more back-end computers. Often, **associative processors** are used to handle logical to physical mapping. A database machine may manage a **storage hierarchy** consisting of several types of storage devices over which data is staged or moved as needed to faster or slower devices. Multiple database machines can serve either single or multiple hosts, making the system more reliable. In addition to serving as backups for one another, parallel back-end processors permit **load balancing** or automatic sharing of the workload.

Advantages of database machines are greater performance at lower cost, database sharing, improved security and integrity, greater selection of DBMS software, and configuration flexibility. Some possible disadvantages are greater vulnerability, failure to realize cost benefits, need for additional communications, more complex support, possibility of bottleneck at the back end, and technical obsolescence of the database machine. Some vendors of database machines are **Britton-Lee**, **Tandem**, and **Teradata**.

16.8 Bibliography

Cardenas, A. *Data Base Management Systems*. Boston: Allyn & Bacon, 1985.

Hsiao, D. (Ed.). *Advanced Database Machine Architecture*. Englewood Cliffs, NJ: Prentice-Hall, 1983.

Hsiao, D. "Future Database Machine Architectures," in G. Ariav and J. Clifford (Ed.). *New Directions for Database Systems*. Norwood, NJ: Ablex, 1986 pp. 13–18.

Su, S. *Database Computers*. New York: McGraw-Hill, 1988.

CHAPTER

17

Knowledge-Based Management Systems

17 Chapter Objectives

In this chapter you will learn

- how a knowledge-based system differs from a database
- the components of an expert system
- the types of decision making an expert system supports
- the objectives of a knowledge-based management system
- some alternative architectures for a knowledge-based management system
- the components of a knowledge-based management system
- several methods of representing knowledge
- the focus of some knowledge-based projects

17.1 *Objectives of a Knowledge-Based Management System*

Most traditional databases store a large number of facts about the operations of an organization, the so-called **operational data**. Recall from earlier chapters the distinction between the intension and the extension of a database. The intension is the permanent structure, while the extension is the instantaneous database, with whatever data it contains at a given moment. As data changes or updates are made, different database instances or extensions are created. The extensional database contains **extensional knowledge**, facts about the environment that are verifiable by observation of the real world and are updated by designated users or clerks. Extensional knowledge is used to support **operational decisions**, such as whether inventory of an item has reached its reorder point or whether all of a student's grades this semester are C or better. Access to this data is usually through applications programs or predefined transactions, since on-line query languages are often too difficult and require too much training for nontechnical users. Database management systems have as their major objective the efficient management and protection of data, while allowing simultaneous use of the data resource.

Decision makers often need knowledge that is not stored in the database and not easily derivable from the stored facts by the usual database management system methods. A **knowledge-based system** contains such **intensional knowledge**. Its focus is at a higher level of abstraction, on the level of the database intension. It includes **metadata**, information about the data itself. Other types of intensional knowledge may be supplied by experts in the field. **Derived knowledge** is intensional knowledge produced by painstaking examination of the database instances in an effort to generate some conclusions about the data. Updates of intensional knowledge are comparatively rare, and are performed by experts or by application of logical rules rather than by clerks.

An **expert system** is a system that contains a representation of a body of knowledge about some specific field or application and uses its knowledge to help users solve problems. An expert system has two important components. One is a **knowledge base**, and the other is an **inference engine**, which is the control mechanism of the system. The knowledge in the knowledge base is structured or represented in a manner that makes it machine processable so that inferences can be made from it. The inference engine draws conclusions by examining the stated problem and comparing it with the stored knowledge. The comparison may use **analysis**, breaking down the problem into parts, or **synthesis,** putting together partial solutions to form a complete answer. The mechanisms used may involve **pattern matching, theorem proving**, extensive **searching,** or a **knowledge-representation language compiler** such as a Prolog compiler.

An expert system typically supports **decision making** and **planning** rather than operational activities. It represents a body of knowledge about the environment rather than a set of facts. The knowledge it contains is relatively permanent and refers to sets of objects instead of individual instances. For example, while a database might be able to tell us whether an inventory item has reached its reorder point, an expert system could help us decide what the reorder point should be. Similarly, a database may tell us whether a student has a C in each course this semester, but an expert system could suggest alternative courses of action to be taken if the student's grade in a major course or grade-point average is below a C. A knowledge base can be used to store information about the database intension, explicitly representing the classes of database objects and constraints. It can also store statistical data about the database extension, such as the number of tuples that exist in a relation or the number of tuples that have a certain value for an attribute.

Since the expert system is intended to support decision making, it is important that the user be able to access its information quickly and easily when decisions must be made. Therefore, such systems usually provide some version of **natural language** or **fifth-generation language** so that users can access the information needed without extensive training and without explicitly invoking predefined transactions.

Although expert systems allow us to represent and to process knowledge, they lack the power of a database management system. They store a very limited amount of data, usually small enough to fit in main memory during processing. In addition, they do not provide the usual database management functions of efficient file organization, fast data access, concurrency control, security enforcement, integrity checking, and so on.

A **knowledge-based management system** combines a database management system and an expert system. It provides representation of both data and knowledge, a method of processing the knowledge, and an efficient system for organizing both the database and the knowledge base. It provides support for both operational and planning decisions. The basic objective, then, of a knowledge-based management system is to represent and provide data and knowledge about the data to nontechnical users to support their decision making.

Specific objectives of a knowledge-based management system are:

1. To provide the usual database management system services to both the database and the knowledge base, including efficient organization of large amounts of data, fast data access, concurrency control, integrity rule checking, transaction management, security enforcement, physical and logical independence, and so on.
2. To provide better user interfaces, including using natural language for queries.
3. To use knowledge-based query optimization, including use of integrity rules, database statistics, and meta-knowledge for single queries.
4. To extend optimization to multiple queries by recognizing common subexpressions and remembering query results.
5. To maintain consistency by semantic integrity checking using rule-based or logic-based techniques from artificial intelligence.

17.2 *Architecture of Knowledge-Based Management Systems*

Several alternative architectures exist for knowledge-based management systems. The choice depends on the volume of data and transactions, the presence or absence of a preexisting database, data usage, the volatility of the data, data security requirements, and the data access requirements. Proposed architectures are shown in Figure 17.1 and include

1. **Adding some database features to an expert system.** Most expert systems store a very limited amount of data which fits in main memory during processing. However, they can be enhanced to provide simple database features, such as data manipulation and data access strategies.
2. **Adding some intelligence to a database management system.** With this alternative, an existing database is enhanced by adding some logic to the database language. For example, since relational calculus is basically a logical language, a system using a similar language could be extended to store and process knowledge about itself.
3. **Incorporating a database management system within an expert system.** This solution may be considered when there is a lot of data to be stored. Several research projects have focused on using Prolog to build relational database extensions for expert systems.
4. **Loose coupling of an expert system and a database management system.** This architecture uses an existing database. When the expert system is functioning, it takes a snapshot of the portion of the database it needs and stores it as its own file. The expert system acts as a casual user of the database.
5. **Tight coupling of an expert system and an external database management system.** Here there is a conventional database management system, and the expert system acts as an "intelligent" rather than a casual user of the database. There must be a communication link between the two systems. The expert system treats the database as an extension of its own knowledge base. It generates and directs queries to the database management system and transforms responses into knowledge.

Whatever architecture is chosen, a knowledge-based system should contain a **database** of facts about the subject area, a **database management system** that provides the usual DBMS functions, a **knowledge base** consisting of some representation of information about the subject, a **reasoner** or inference program that applies the rules, and a **user interface** using natural language. Figure 17.2 illustrates these components.

There are at present no true commercial knowledge-based systems that provide all the functions just described. One problem is that there is no general agreement about what an expert system should do. Building a knowledge base requires a tremendous amount of time and talent. When the system is operational, processing overhead is very heavy. Often, users are disappointed to find that the knowledge-based system is very limited in its usefulness or very rigid. At this time, knowledge-based systems are still at the prototype stage, with several important research projects focusing on the representation and manipulation of knowledge about data stored in a database. There are several commercial products that allow users to create expert systems without large databases of factual data and without database management systems. There are usually called **expert system shells**, and are available even for microcomputers. They do not include databases of facts or database management systems, because the knowledge base that is to be supplied by the user is normally small, and performance is not a major issue. Therefore, elegant data organization and management techniques are not needed.

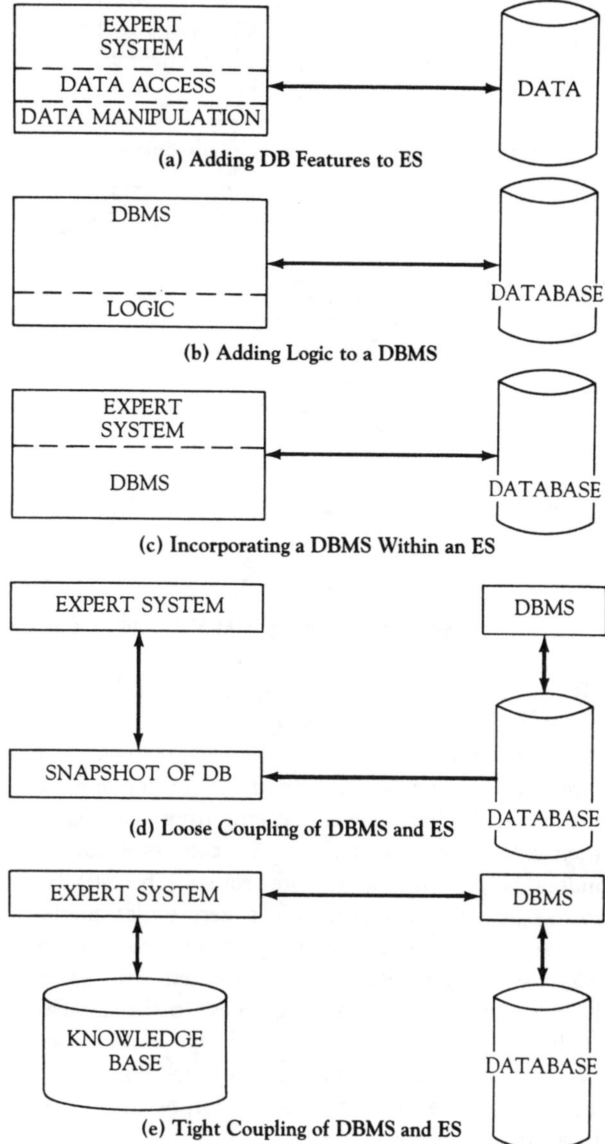

Figure 17.1 Alternative Architectures for Coupling Expert Systems and Database Management Systems

Early research efforts focused on tying together existing database management systems and expert systems. An expert system can serve as either a front end or a back end to a database. As a front end, the expert system acts as a casual user, submitting queries to the database management system. For example, **PC Easy** from Texas Instruments is a simple expert system shell that can interact with Ashton Tate's **dBase** database management system line. Using these two products, users can create a database with

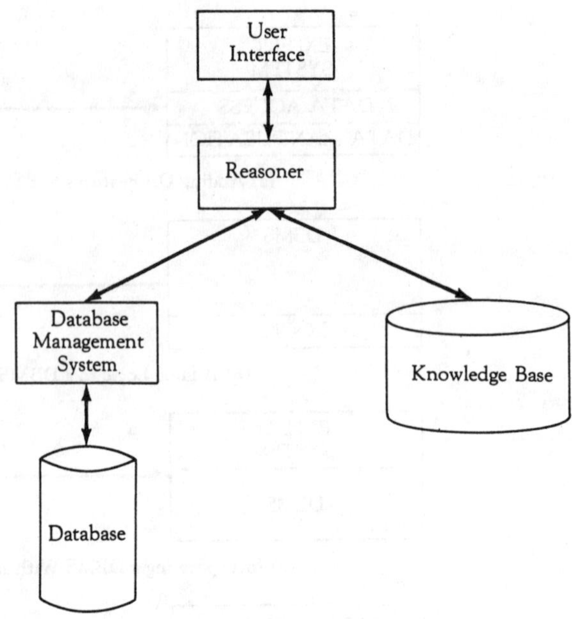

Figure 17.2 Architecture of a Knowledge-Based Management Systems

dBase and a rule-based knowledge base with PC Easy. PC Easy commands can be used to retrieve or modify data in the database. One problem with such a loosely coupled system in which an expert system is simply layered on top of a database is that queries submitted to the database are performed using only the usual DBMS procedures, whereas the knowledge base may contain intensional and statistical information that could make their processing more efficient. A second problem is that each query would be processed individually, even if queries are related. The DBMS, unlike an expert system, is unable to recognize the relationships between similar queries.

Major university research projects are focusing on integrating the database and knowledge base components into a single system. In these projects, the knowledge base is used in processing queries requiring access to the database. Among the major issues being studied are query optimization and representation of knowledge. The problems of applying database management system techniques such as concurrency control, integrity and security checking, and distribution of knowledge to the management of knowledge bases are also being addressed.

17.3 *Methods of Representing Knowledge*

Since a knowledge base must supply information about the meaning and contents of a database, it requires a model that is semantically richer than the traditional database models. Some database models allow us to express some semantic information by permitting us to include various integrity constraints. When integrity constraints can be expressed, they are often treated as bothersome overhead since they must be checked for violations when transactions are performed. They are not used by the database management system in processing queries. A knowledge base must be able to represent knowledge in a direct, machine-processable fashion, so that it can be used to help answer a wider variety of queries more easily than a traditional database management system.

Although "knowledge" is difficult to define, all systems that claim to be knowledge-based must have some means of representing it. They must represent semantic information and must provide support for an inference system. All such representations must use some type of logical representation for knowledge. Common representation modes for knowledge-based systems are **logic-based**, **frame-based**, **procedural**, and **semantic nets.**

17.3.1 *Logic-Based Systems*

A logic-based system uses a form of mathematical logic, usually first-order predicate calculus. You may recall from Chapter 6 that relational calculus is based on the predicate calculus. The knowledge base is made up of predicates which may contain constants, variables, and functions, along with logical connectives and quantifiers. Based on a well-developed mathematical theory, logic provides a widely accepted representation for semantic information and a large body of results about proof theory that allow specification of what is and is not provable for a particular knowledge base.

When a logic-based system is chosen, the underlying database is usually relational. **Prolog** is the language of choice for such systems. In Prolog, the word **term** means a constant or a variable. An **atomic formula** or **unit** consists of a **predicate symbol** and a list of **terms**. An atomic formula has the form $P(t1, t2, \ldots, tn)$, where P is the predicate symbol and the ti are terms or arguments. In Prolog, atomic formulas may include constants, variables, or functions. A **ground unit** is an atomic formula all of whose terms are constants. Given a set of formulas, a **model** is a set of ground units that makes all formulas in the set true. A **minimal model** is one for which no proper subset of itself is a model.

In Prolog-based systems, a formula such as

$$A1 \wedge A2 \wedge \ldots \wedge An \rightarrow B$$

can be interpreted two ways:

1. With the usual **logical** meaning:

   If $A1$ and $A2$ and ... and An are true, then so is B.
2. With a **procedural** interpretation:

   To prove that B is true, first prove that $A1, A2, \ldots, An$ are true.

Prolog, unlike other logical languages, allows both the logical and procedural interpretations. The procedural interpretation will be considered in our discussion of procedural representation. Using the logical interpretation, Prolog can be considered a **declarative language**, one in which the user can express a desired result, without specifying how it should be obtained. Prolog statements such as the implication above are called **rules** and are usually written as **Horn clauses**. Instead of writing the implication

$$A1 \wedge A2 \wedge \cdots \wedge An \rightarrow B$$

we write it as the following Horn clause:

```
B :- A1,A2,...,An.
```

This should be read as "*B* **if** *A*1 and *A*2 and ... and *An*." Note that the commas mean "and" and the period at the end marks the end of the rule. The part on the left of the :– is called the **head** of the rule and the part on the right is called the **body** of the rule. Each of the *Ai* is called a **subgoal**. If we want to assert that *B* is true without conditions, we write

```
B.
```

Standard Prolog notation uses lowercase letters to represent predicates, functions, and constants, and uppercase letters to represent variables. Precise knowledge can be written as unary, binary, or higher-degree predicates. For example,

```
student(X).
```

is a unary predicate which means that *X* is a student. Since we used a variable as an argument, the truth value of the predicate depends on the value of the argument.

A binary predicate might be

```
teaches(X,Y).
```

This means that *Y* teaches *X*, where *Y* is a faculty member and *X* is a course. Another binary predicate is

```
enrolled(X,Z).
```

This means that *Z* is enrolled in *X*. Here, *Z* is a student and *X* is a course.

Simple facts that are stored in the database can be considered as instances of the predicates. They are actually ground units, with values from the database extension serving as constants in the atomic formula. For example,

```
student(S1001).
```

means that S1001 is a student. Similarly,

```
teaches(ART103A, F101).
```

means that F101 teaches ART103A, and

```
enrolled(ART103A,S1001).
```

means that S1001 is enrolled in ART103A.

From these examples, we see a natural correspondence between the Prolog predicates and the relational database, with the database providing an **interpretation** or set of ground units for the logical formulas.

Rules can be expressed by forming Horn clauses involving predicates. For example,

```
teacher-of(S,F) :- teaches(C,F),enrolled(C,S).
```

means that faculty member *F* is a teacher of student *S* if *F* teaches a course *C* and *S* is enrolled in the same course, *C*. Relating this to the database, this means that (*S*,*F*) is a **teacher-of** fact if there exists a course *C* such that (*C*,*F*) is a **teaches** fact and (*C*,*S*) is an **enrolled** fact. This rule can be regarded as representing some knowledge about a derived relationship, **teacher-of**, which corresponds to a **view** in the relational model having attributes STUID and FACID. Using our examples above, we could conclude

```
teacher-of(S1001, F101).
```

By using variables as arguments, predicates can also represent queries. For example,

```
teaches(ART103A,X).
```

means find the faculty member assigned to teach ART103A, while

```
teacher-of(S1001,X).
```

means find the teachers of student S1001. To answer either query, the system must find values for *X* that make the predicate true. The database extension is used in evaluating queries. This means that the system can answer the first query by simply examining the tuples in the CLASS table. However, to answer the second query, it must use the rule for **teaches** given above to interpret the query in terms of the database extension.

Prolog and logical languages in general allow us to express computations that cannot be expressed in conventional data manipulation languages. For example, **recursive** queries involve rules that are defined recursively; that is, they use predicates that are defined in terms of themselves. For example,

```
educates(S,F) :- teacher-of(S,F).
educates(S,F) :- educates(S,X), teacher-of(X,F).
```

is a recursive definition of **educates** which means that *F* educates *S* if either *F* is a **teacher-of** *S* or if there exists some *X* such that *F* is a **teacher-of** *X* and *X* is a **teacher-of** *S*. The predicate **educates** is meant to be true if *F* is a teacher of *S*, or the teacher of a teacher of *S*, or *S*'s teacher's teacher's teacher, and so on. The predicate **educates** is called the **transitive closure** of the **teacher-of** predicate. It defines the set of all people who can be described by using the **teacher-of** predicate repeatedly. Our university example does not store any data that illustrates this relationship, but we can imagine that it could be extended to do so. A conventional DML would be unable to answer a query such as

```
educates(S1001,X).
```

which asks for all the educators of S1001, because it requires recursive operations. We find that we cannot express this simple query in SQL, for example. Besides the transitive closure operator, a more powerful one called the **fixed-point operator** also cannot be expressed in conventional DMLs, but is expressible in Prolog. These examples illustrate the expressive power of Prolog compared to conventional DMLs.

Prolog allows us to express predicates about the extensional database, called **EDB** predicates, that are provable by examining relations in the extension and predicates about the intensional database, called **IDB** predicates, defined by logical rules.

Although logical languages allow us to prove new facts that can be derived from existing facts in the database extension, we have difficulty proving **negative** facts. Going back to the relational model for the university example, suppose that we find no row in the ENROLL table linking student S1001 with course CSC201A. Should we infer that this student is not enrolled in that particular course? Although not usually stated, there is an assumption that information not explicitly represented in the database extension is not true, and we usually assume the converse of the relationship. Therefore, if no row exists showing S1001 enrolled in CSC201A, we assume that S1001 is not enrolled in CSC201A. If we did not make that assumption, we would have to store the complement of each relation, one showing the relationships that do not exist. We would need a table which we might call NONENROLL showing all combinations of STUID and COURSE# that do not occur. Obviously, this would be a large relation, and we would be reluctant to store it. The assumption that if a tuple does not exist in a relation we can infer the converse of that relationship is quite useful in the extensional database. However, when we move to the knowledge base, standard logic does not allow us to conclude that if we cannot prove a fact, its converse must be true. This makes it impossible for us to conclude negative facts using standard logic. For example, suppose that we want to prove

```
~teacher-of(S1001,F105)
```

Examining the extension, we find that there is no course *C* such that

```
teaches(C,F105) ∧ enrolled(C,S1001)
```

is true. This means that there is no logical way to show

```
teacher-of(S1001,F105)
```

using the rule

```
teacher-of(S,F) :- teaches(C,F),enrolled(C,S).
```

However, the lack of such a course is not a logical proof of the negative fact **~teacher-of(S1001,F105)**. There may be enrollment relationships not represented in the current extension, or there may be some other way to prove **teacher-of** besides the rule we have given. Just as it is handy to assume the converse of relationships not explicitly present in an extensional relation, we can sometimes assume a similar rule for the knowledge base. This is called the **closed world assumption**. It states that if an atomic formula with no variables cannot be deduced from the extensional database and the existing rules, you can assume that the formula is not true. This is sometimes called **negation by failure**. Basically, it means that the information stored about a predicate is the only relevant information about it. Because of this, we will not have to store negative knowledge explicitly in the knowledge base. There are, of course, severe restrictions on when we can use the closed world assumption. One is that we must have a finite knowledge base. A second is that we have domain closure, meaning that the only constants that exist are those in the extension and in the rules. Finally, all our rules must be Horn clauses.

Logic-based systems are good for representing knowledge that can be expressed as assertions, but they are less well suited to representing uncertain or incomplete knowledge. It is difficult to model knowledge acquisition or beliefs in such a system. It is also impossible to use any reasoning other than deduction. An example of nondeductive reasoning that has been found to be fruitful in other systems is called **abduction**. It has the form

```
If (A → B) ∧ B, hypothesize A.
```

Clearly, this does not obey the usual rules of logic. However, abduction has been used successfully in some projects.

17.3.2 *Semantic Nets*

Although logic provides a useful method of expressing knowledge and using inference, it does not provide an organizing principle for the knowledge base. The facts appear to be randomly arranged. Semantic networks provide such an organization. Knowledge is expressed as a collection of labeled **nodes** and labeled **arcs** or **edges**. The nodes represent concepts, situations, or objects and the directed arcs represent binary associations between them.

There are several different organizational principles that can be used in semantic nets. Among them are

- **Generalization.** This principle uses the familiar generalization-specialization model which relates a type to a more generic type. A generalization or **ISA** hierarchy links concepts to their subtypes and their supertypes. In a semantic network, generalization is used to link specialized object types to more general ones in such a way that they inherit properties of the generalizations. This simplifies concept description, since many simple concepts in a knowledge base can share a common supertype, whose properties do not need to be repeated in the description of the subtypes. A directed arc connects subtypes to supertype, while an arc in the opposite direction would connect supertypes to their specializations. The arc is interpreted to mean "is a."

- **Aggregation.** This principle provides a different method of organizing, in which parts are linked to a whole. An arc extends from the node representing a part of an object to the node representing the whole of the object. An arc in the opposite direction links objects to their parts and represents decomposition. A common use would be to link attributes to entities. The arc is interpreted to mean "has a."
- **Classification.** This principle is used to connect an occurrence of an object with its type. The occurrence or token represents an entity instance, while the type is an entity set. A classification arc therefore links the token to the type. Its inverse, instantiation, links the type to the token. The arc is interpreted to mean "belongs to."
- **Association.** This is any other organizing principle. If there is a predicate linking two nodes not described by the previous three classifications, we can call it a general association. The arc should then have a label that describes the association. For example, the association between a student and a class might be represented by an arc labeled "TAKES" from the STUDENT node to the CLASS node. The inverse would be represented by the passive form, "IS TAKEN BY", in this case.

Figure 17.3, showing a very incomplete semantic network for a university, illustrates these organizational principles.

In a semantic network, reasoning means traversing the network along the arcs or pattern matching to find a correspondence between the problem and subnets. Since this representation is widely used in other areas of artificial intelligence such as natural-language processing, algorithms and heuristics exist for these processes.

17.3.3 *Frame-Based Systems*

In a **frame-based** system, knowledge is represented as a collection of frames organized in some fashion. Each frame is a complex data structure that represents knowledge about some stereotypical situation or concept. We can think of a frame as a template into which information is fitted. The frame has **slots** for objects that are important in the situation or concept, and can have a variable number of entries per slot. The slots can have associated domains or other constraints on the possible values that can be stored in them. A frame contains information about the situation it represents and data such as how to use the frame, how it relates to other frames in the knowledge base, what the default values for slots are, what procedures are attached to the slot, and so on. The organizing principle may be generalization, with frames representing generalizations or specializations of other frames. In that case, a frame may have an "ISA" relationship to a superior, more generic frame, or a relationship to lower-level, more specialized frames. Figure 17.4 shows an example of a frame representing information about STUDENT. It has slots for procedures to be called when various items are updated, added, or deleted. Frames allow knowledge to be structured, so they can be used to represent more in-

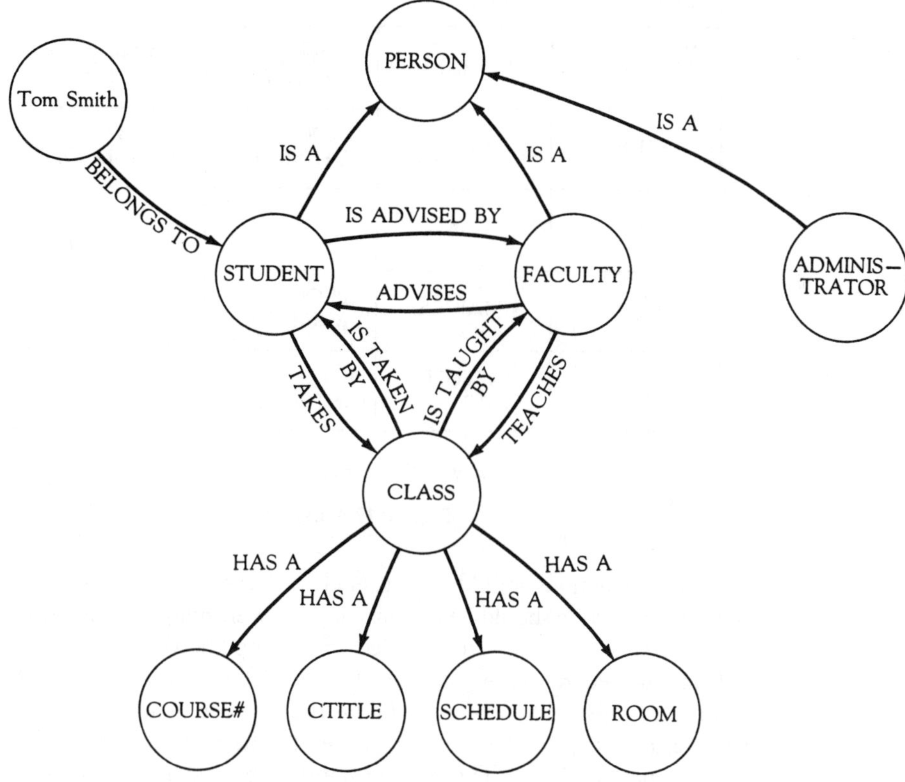

Figure 17.3 Example of a Semantic Network

depth knowledge than rules. They can also provide a hierarchical organization that is not present in logic-based systems.

17.3.4 *Procedural Systems*

In a procedural or rule-based system, knowledge is expressed as a series of logical implications, predicates having the form

```
if <condition> then <action>.
```

A rule-based system is good for representing "shallow" knowledge, where there is not much complexity in the relationship represented by each rule. In such a system, the user is willing to accept the relationship between the condition and the action without further explanation. These rules can be viewed as **triggered** or activated by events that may cause the stated conditions. When an event such as a database update occurs, all rules for the system should theoretically be examined, to determine whether any of them will be triggered by the update. For those rules that place restrictions on values in the database extension, there must be a mechanism that searches rules to determine

FRAME NAME: STUDENT

	DOMAIN	WHEN UPDATED	WHEN ADDED	WHEN DELETED
STUID	S9999	PROC (UPENROLL)	PROC (UNIQUEID)	PROC (DELENROLL)
STUNAME	STRING			
MAJOR	(MAJORS)	PROC (CKMAJOR)	PROC (CKMAJOR)	
CREDITS	INTEGER 0-150	PROC (CNTCOURSES)		

ISA PERSON (superior frame)

Figure 17.4 Example of a Frame

whether any actions should be triggered whenever the database is updated. No update that violates a rule should be permitted. However, rules themselves should be updatable, so that new knowledge can be added or existing knowledge can be revised as needed.

Using procedural representation, the knowledge base is considered to be a collection of **processes** or active agents. Unlike the procedures in programming languages, the knowledge base procedures are not called by the user but are invoked by the inference engine when necessary. The language most often used in this representation is LISP. The PLANNER system is an early and influential implementation of a procedural knowledge base. It uses **pattern-directed procedure invocation**. The knowledge base is considered to be a collection of assertions and theorems (called **daemons**) that protect the database. They are activated whenever the database is updated or searched. When the theorem is activated, it compares the data that is to be updated or retrieved against a **pattern** it has stored. If there is a match, the theorem is executed. PLANNER uses a relatively inefficient method called **backtracking** when a theorem is executed and does not achieve its goal. In that case, its effects are undone and other theorems are tried.

Production rules are often used in pattern-matching systems. Their basic form is

```
if <condition> then <action>
```

The condition or pattern is usually a set of predicates connected by **and,** and the action calls one or more procedures that may modify the knowledge base. From an initial database state, rules are tested until one is found with a pattern that matches the database. Then the action is executed, and the system continues testing other rules. Production rules can represent several types of inference, including

- Situation to appropriate action:

```
if GPA <2.0 then schedule appointment with academic advisor
```

- Premise to conclusion:

```
if student is not enrolled in courses and is not on leave then student
is a dropout
```

- Property inheritance:

```
if major="CSC" then minor="MATH"
```

Production rules are usually provided to the system by an expert rather than derived from the database.

Although for historical reasons LISP is the language most often associated with procedural representations, Prolog could also be used, provided that its statements are given their procedural interpretation, as explained in Section 17.3.1. Thus the Horn clause

```
B :- A1,A2,...,An.
```

should be read as

To prove the head, *B*, first prove all the premises in the body, *A*1, *A*2,...,*An*.

17.4 *Some Sample Systems*

The earliest knowledge-based projects dealing with large volumes of data were undertaken in the 1960s. The **Macsyma** project used LISP to represent knowledge about mathematical techniques for solving physics and mathematics problems. The **Dendral** project, started about the same time, was concerned with analyzing mass spectra to identify chemical compounds. It represented knowledge by data-driven production rules, where the rules were triggered by the presence of data matching the pattern in the premise. A rule-based system using goal-driven rules was first implemented in **Mycin**. It was originally designed to capture and organize the knowledge of specialists in infectious diseases and to provide consultation for doctors treating patients with bacterial infections of the blood. Later, meningitis became its focus. Goal-driven rules begin with a goal such as determining the best treatment for a patient with a specific infection and try to use the rules whose conclusions match the goal. Since the rules are invoked only if their conclusions are appropriate, this method is called **backward chaining** or **goal-directed rule invocation**. The opposite method, **forward chaining** or **data-directed rule invocation**, starts with input data and works with rules by matching their premises. This approach was used in **XCON**, the first commercially developed expert system. It was developed at DEC to configure computer systems. Its forward-chaining method is widely used.

An early frame-based system was **GUS**, a travel planning system. It contained frames for the trip with slots for information such as the traveler and the itinerary.

The itinerary, in turn, would have slots for travel and stay sections. These were further broken down into data for each portion of the trip. The frame-based method is widely used in medical information systems such as **Internist**.

The methods created for these early systems are being extended now by researchers at dozens of universities and commercial software houses who are attempting to apply knowledge-based techniques to a variety of application areas. This integration of expert system and database management system technology is one of the most promising research areas under study.

17.5 *Chapter Summary*

A database contains **extensional knowledge**, and supports operational decisions. A **knowledge base** focuses on a higher level of abstraction, the **intensional knowledge** level, and contains **metadata**, information about data. An **expert system** supports decision making and planning. It consists of a **knowledge base** and an **inference engine** that can draw conclusions from the stored knowledge by analysis or synthesis. Mechanisms used are **pattern matching, theorem proving, searching**, or a **knowledge-representation language** such as Prolog. Access is often through **natural language** or a **fifth-generation language**. A **knowledge-based management system** combines a database management system with an expert system.

A knowledge-based management system should provide the usual database management system services, a natural language user interface, knowledge-based query optimization, optimization for multiple queries, and semantic integrity checking. There are several alternative architectures for knowledge-based systems. Essential components are a **database** of facts, a **database management system**, a **knowledge base** of information, a **reasoner**, and a **user interface**. Early research projects focused on tying together existing systems, but several current projects are focusing on the development of integrated systems. Major problems include representation of knowledge and query optimization. Knowledge may be represented using **logic-based, frame-based, procedural**, or **semantic net** techniques. Some early knowledge-based projects were Macsyma, Dendral, Mycin, XCON, GUS, and Internist.

17.6 *Exercises*

1. According to tradition, Socrates taught Plato, who taught Aristotle, who taught Alexander the Great. Use the notation of Section 17.3.1 to answer the following questions.

(a) Write out all the **teacher-of** facts for this example.
(b) Using the recursive definition of **educates**, write out all the **educates** facts that are derivable from the **teacher-of** facts.
(c) Explain the meaning of each of the following queries and answer each, using the facts found in parts (a) and (b):
   (i) **teacher-of** (Aristotle, X)
   (ii) **teacher-of** (X, Aristotle)
   (iii) **educates** (X, Socrates)
   (iv) **educates** (Plato, X)

2. Make up a relational database extension showing facts about students, subjects, and teachers. One table should show facts about which students study which subjects, and another should show which teachers teach which subjects. Assume each subject is taught by only one teacher.
   (a) Make up three queries involving the facts shown in the table.
   (b) Make another table showing which students like which teachers: Now write a Prolog rule that states that a student likes a subject if he or she likes the teacher of that subject. List the tuples that satisfy this predicate.
   (c) Ignoring the table created in part (b), make a new table showing which students like which subjects. Now write a Prolog rule that states that a student likes a teacher if he or she likes the subject the teacher teaches. List the tuples that satisfy this predicate.
   (d) Using the two tables constructed in parts (b) and (c) write a rule that states that a student enjoys a subject if he or she likes either the subject or the teacher and list the tuples that satisfy this rule.

3. Seven versions of a word processing program have been released: 1.0, 1.1, 2.0, 2.1, 2.2, 3.0, and 3.1. Files in any version can be upgraded to the next version. However, to convert any early version to any later one it is necessary to go through all the intermediate upgrades.
   (a) Let **upgradeable** represent the relationship between a file in each version and one in the next version. Write out all the **upgradeable** facts for this example.
   (b) Write a recursive definition for **convertible**, which shows that any early file can be converted to a file in any later version.
   (c) Write out all the **convertible** facts.
   (d) Write out the following queries:
      (i) To what file versions can files in version 1.1 be upgraded?
      (ii) What file versions can be upgraded to 2.1 files?
      (iii) To what file versions can a file in version 2.0 be converted?
      (iv) What file versions can be converted to version 3.1?

4. Draw a semantic network similar to the one shown in Figure 17.3 for the data in Exercise 1.

5. Draw a frame representation of Employee data for a business organization similar to the one shown in Figure 17.4. Make up attributes and other objects as needed.

17.7 *Bibliography*

Bancilhon, F. and R. Ramakrishnan. "An Amateur's Introduction to Recursive Query-Processing Strategies," ACM SIGMOD International Conference on Management of Data (1986) pp. 16–52.

Bocca, J. "EDUCE: A Marriage of Convenience: Prolog and a Relational Database," Proceedings of the Third International Conference on Logic Programming (1986) Springer-Verlag, pp. 36–45.

Brodie, M. and J. Mylopoulos (Ed.). *On Knowledge Base Management Systems*. New York: Springer-Verlag, 1986.

Brodie, M. and J. Mylopoulos. "Knowledge Bases and Databases: Semantic vs. Computational Theories of Information," in G. Ariav and J. Clifford (Ed.). *New Directions for Database Systems*. Norwood, NJ: Ablex, 1986 pp. 186–218.

Fishman, D. "The DBMS-Expert System Connection," in G. Ariav and J. Clifford (Ed.). *New Directions for Database Systems*. Norwood, NJ: Ablex, 1986 pp. 87–101.

Frost, R. *Introduction to Knowledge Base Systems*. New York: Macmillan, 1986.

Gargarin, G. and E. Gelenbe (Ed.). *New Applications of Data Bases*. London: Academic Press, 1984.

Gallaire, H. and J. Minker (Ed.). *Logic and Databases*. New York: Plenum Press, 1978.

Gallaire, H., J. Minker, and J. Nicholas. "Logic and Databases: A Deductive Approach," ACM Computing Surveys **16**:2 (June, 1984) pp. 154–185.

Gelfond, M., H. Przymusinska., and T. C. Przymusinski. "The Extended Closed World Assumption and its Relationship to Parallel Circumscription," Proceedings of the Fifth ACM Symposium on Principles of Database Systems (1986) pp. 133–139.

Grant, J. *Logical Introduction to Databases*. San Diego: Harcourt Brace Jovanovich, 1987.

Jarke, M., J. Clifford, and Y. Vassiliou. "An Optimizing Prolog Front End to a Relational Query System," ACM SIGMOD International Conference on Management of Data (1984) pp. 296–306.

Kerschberg, L. (Ed.). *Expert Database Systems: Proceedings of the First International Workshop on Expert Database Systems* (1984). Redwood City, CA: Benjamin/Cummings, 1986.

Kerschberg, L. (Ed.). *Expert Database Systems: Proceedings of the First International Conference on Expert Database Systems* (1986). Redwood City, CA: Benjamin/Cummings, 1987.

Kerschberg, L. (Ed). *Expert Database Systems: Proceedings of the Second International Conference on Expert Database Systems* (1988). Redwood City, CA: Benjamin/Cummings, 1989.

Maier, D. "Databases in the Fifth Generation Project: Is Prolog a Database Language?" in G. Ariav and J. Clifford (Ed.). *New Directions for Database Systems*. Norwood, NJ: Ablex, 1986 pp. 18–34.

Maier, D. and D. S. Warren. *Computing with Logic: Logic Programming with Prolog*. Menlo Park,CA: Benjamin/Cummings, 1988.

Minker, J. "On Indefinite Databases and the Closed World Assumption," Proceedings of the Sixth Conference on Automated Deduction, New York: Springer-Verlag, 1982.

Minker, J. *Foundations of Deductive Databases and Logic Programming.* Los Altos: Morgan-Kaufmann, 1988.

Morris, K., J. Ullman, and A. Van Gelder. "Design Overview of the NAIL! System," Proceedings of the Third International Conference on Logic Programming (1986) pp. 554–568.

Rishe, N. *Database Design Fundamentals.* Englewood Cliffs, NJ: Prentice-Hall, 1988.

Sagiv, Y. "Optimizing Datalog Programs," Proceedings of the ACM Symposium on Principles of Database Systems (1987) pp. 349–362.

Ullman, J. *Principles of Database and Knowledge-Base Systems Volume I.* Rockville, MD: Computer Science Press, 1988.

Ullman, J. *Principles of Database and Knowledge-Base Systems Volume II.* Rockville, MD: Computer Science Press, 1989.

Vardi, M. "Querying Logical Databases," Proceedings ACM Symposium on Principles of Database Systems (1985) pp. 57–65.

Wiederhold, G., J. Milton, and D. Sagalowicz. "Applications of Artificial Intelligence in the Knowledge Based Management Systems Project," IEEE Database Engineering Bulletin **6**:4 (December, 1983) pp. 75–82.

Zaniolo, C. "Safety and Compilation of Nonrecursive Horn Clauses," Proceedings of the International Conference on Expert Database Systems (1986) Menlo Park, CA: Benjamin/Cummings pp. 167–178.

INDEX